# HEARING, SOUND, AND THE AUDITORY IN ANCIENT GREECE

# HEARING, SOUND, AND THE AUDITORY IN ANCIENT GREECE

edited by Jill Gordon

INDIANA UNIVERSITY PRESS

This book is a publication of

Indiana University Press
Office of Scholarly Publishing
Herman B Wells Library 350
1320 East 10th Street
Bloomington, Indiana 47405 USA

iupress.org



Manufactured in the United States of America

First printing 2022

Cataloging information is available from the Library of Congress.

ISBN 978-0-253-06281-9 (hdbk.)
ISBN 978-0-253-06282-6 (pbk.)
ISBN 978-0-253-06283-3 (webPDF)

# CONTENTS

## Part III.  Sound Politics



## Part IV.  *Alogos*, Embodiment, and Silence

# ACKNOWLEDGMENTS

vii

MORE SO THAN OTHER ACADEMIC PROJECTS, A VOLUME of essays depends on the work of many and on a community of scholars and others who support their work. I am most grateful to Erin Maidman, my student research assistant, for her meticulous work in the early stages of editing the contributions, setting up the infrastructure for the contributions to be submitted to us, and communicating with the contributors. Thanks also to Colby College for the funding to support Erin's fine work, though my debt to her goes well beyond that.

I want to thank the contributors, as well, for all their work and their responsiveness to queries and requests. The Ancient Philosophy Society has supported my own scholarship, as well as the scholarship of many of the contributors, and I would like to thank the organization personally for fostering such a collegial environment for rigorous and interesting work in ancient philosophy. Every APS meeting is an opportunity to listen and be heard and to engage philosophically with bright, open minds.

Finally, I want to thank Jon for his love and support. It makes so much else possible and beautiful.

# EDITOR'S INTRODUCTION

OUR CULTURE IS A VISUAL ONE, ALMOST OBSESSIVELY so. Sight is the focus of a significant body of philosophical and classical research, whether literally in cognitive, epistemic, and phenomenological studies or in scholarship about sight's symbolic importance to human apprehension of the world. This scholarly attention to sight is perhaps due to our own cultural impulses to turn to the visual.

Among the ancient Greeks, by contrast, we discover finely tuned attention to and valorization of the auditory. They explored the human aural experience deeply, and they deployed the auditory to signify myriad human experiences and natural phenomena. This collected volume presents new research from philosophers and classicists that aims to redirect us to the ways in which sound, listening, voice, and even silence shape and reveal the worldview in these ancient texts. Like all good and provocative philosophical work, the essays also form a bridge across cultural and historical difference to contemporary concerns.

While there was a burst of scholarship in the mid- and late twentieth century focused on the shift from oral to written culture among the Greeks in the classical period, this scholarship primarily focused on the shift toward written texts and the cultural practices, attitudes, and anxieties that accompanied that transition to writing.[1] One might assume that the concerns and artifacts of a culture so rooted in oral communication, oral recitation, and oral performance would necessarily also be rooted in the auditory and finely attuned to aural life, but this scholarship attends to the oral without attending to the aural. Even the groundbreaking and centrally important work by Eric Havelock on this transition from oral to literal culture does not take up hearing or the auditory per se. In distinguishing the "abstract intellectualism" that we think of as philosophy from the oral tradition that preceded it, Havelock describes that previous oral tradition as "a total state of mind which is not our mind and which was not Plato's mind."[2] Havelock's observation is likely true, but the central importance of the aural, even if not the oral, is more continually present in ancient texts. Although Plato's work is placed within this broad cultural transition from oral to written culture, the aural remains a living aspect of Greek life, whether in the quotidian or in the arts. Hearing remains central to the lives of the Greeks for hundreds of years in a way that has lost its vitality in our contemporary, more visually oriented moment.

Jasper Svenbro moves beyond Havelock's work in the direction of the aural, noting that the framing of the issue between oral and literal culture fails to appreciate the full picture of writing among the Greeks. "Greek writing was first and foremost a machine for producing sounds," he says.[3] In a relationship that Svenbro likens to that between *erastês* and *eromenos*, the writer's words subject the reader to them, and the reader becomes a vocal instrument for the writer. Although Svenbro's work does focus on this vocalization and the sound of reading as well as the voice of the reader, its emphasis is not on the experience of an audience or of hearing those sounds.

Scholarly interest in sound studies appears to be increasing in several disciplines, but until recently, the scholarship in ancient philosophy and classics had not turned in this direction—either in the context of ancient theories of perception or cognition, or with respect to the cultural meaning or significance of the auditory in the ancient Greek world—even though there is compelling reason to do so, based both on ancient cultural practices and on the abundance of textual attention to the issue in the ancient world.[4]

The essays in this volume aim to fill the gap left by the dearth of scholarship on the sense of hearing, listening, and the auditory. Ranging historically from archaic Greece to imperial Rome and taking up myth, poetry, tragedy, comedy, dialogue, treatise, and rhetorical speeches, this collection of essays explores a range of issues, opening up new ways to hear these texts and to understand the cultural milieu in which they were written and gained meaning.

I might here provide a precise account of just what hearing, listening, and the auditory refer to, as academic expectations might demand, but that task would, I think, undermine one of the goals of the volume. The volume, taken as a whole, shows that hearing and the auditory are deployed in various and complex ways in Greek texts. One case in point is Michael Naas's essay (though it is only the most explicit example), which shows the complex differences and connection between *phōnē* as sound and *phōnē* as voice. Understanding these semantic subtleties and intricacies is more central to the theme of the volume than arriving at or starting from some singular definition of these terms—likewise when it comes to the question of whether these terms and concepts appear in the ancient texts literally or metaphorically. As with providing singular definitions of hearing, sound, and the auditory, the task of distinguishing these concepts would rather undermine than serve the purposes of the volume. What damage we do to Heraclitus's exhortation to listen to the logos, for example, if we say—either way—that this is meant "merely metaphorically" or "literally." We must literally listen to his words, his logoi; otherwise, we do not get his message or hear the audible jokes, puns, and puzzles in his work—and yet what he exhorts us to listen to ultimately is well beyond something we might do with ears alone, and if we don't "hear" Heraclitus correctly, we have not "heard" him. Several essays present a nuanced (and, in a couple of cases, critical) view of this very dichotomy between the literal and the metaphorical. They thus do a great service by way of probing this distinction and showing where the boundary between them is rather fluid.

I have organized the essays thematically and then historically within those themes, so that the reader can hear resonances and dissonances across various texts and figures in relation to the theme in each part. In part 1, five contributions help lay groundwork by exploring the connections between the sense of hearing and logos, a foundation on which much can be built. The conceptual meanings of *logos* are both complex and varied in the ancient world, from Heraclitus's view of logos as the underlying structure of the cosmos to Aristotle's understanding of logos as what makes humans fitted for the city. Much contemporary scholarly work on logos among the ancients takes logos to be purely expressive, but of course, the logos is heard. We cannot fully appreciate the cultural significance of logos if we limit our understanding of it and focus only on the propositions, logical arguments, rhetorical flourishes, or verbal expression in ancient texts. Words, speeches, arguments, and jokes all make sounds and have hearers, and the hearers and the hearing are every bit as significant as the speakers and what is spoken (or written).

Drew Hyland looks deeply at Heraclitus's repeated use of the metaphor of wakefulness, laying out details of the type of life, or rather the quality of life, that is lived in a wakeful state. Hyland works through our various sensory metaphors for knowing—sight, touch, and hearing—arguing that knowing when cast as metaphorical hearing entails a deeper intimacy and internalization of sound and movement; hearing metaphors of knowing show how we can know that which is moving and flowing and even at odds with itself. And the proper orientation toward the logos is playful. Wakeful living is, Hyland concludes, a particular kind of Heraclitean wisdom comprising playful openness, listening, hearkening, and living, all in accordance with the logos. Michael Shaw plumbs the depths of two elliptical fragments from Empedocles, establishing first that flow and sensate animation are part of the four originary roots and that these ground the effluent theory of sensation. Shaw shows that Empedocles repeatedly thematizes hearing, liquid flow, and plant life in the fragments and that hearing is primary; indeed, Empedocles demands that we *hear* the roots. Ultimately, Shaw argues, sound unites all life, and Empedocles reveals a living universe with the power to hear. Michael Naas begins with the competing claims of Jacques Derrida and Adriana Cavarero that, respectively, Western philosophy is phonocentric and videocentric. At the center of their competing claims is the Greek term *phōnē*, which can mean both "sound" and "voice," and Naas works carefully through Platonic texts to show that the very ambiguity of *phōnē* is productive for Plato: as sound becomes voice—or, to play with the ambiguity, as *phōnē* becomes *phōnē*—it transforms sound and voice into meaningful signifiers useful for the activity of philosophy. Naas concludes by showing how Derrida's and Cavarero's positions are, in the end, more similar than different. Eve Rabinoff looks to Aristotle's *De sensu* and *Metaphysics* to explain how and why hearing, among the senses, contributes the most to intelligence because it conveys logos, and we learn from logos; voice makes the imperceptible perceptible and so addresses the causal question, "Why?" Furthermore, this argument applies equally to practical intelligence and to theoretical intelligence because hearing attunes both human and nonhuman animals to their environments and increases their motivation to action. Turning to *De anima*, Rabinoff examines the sense of touch and its relationship to practical intelligence, arguing that it allows both human and nonhuman animals to manipulate their environment, but its superlative precision in humans makes them the most practically intelligent species. In the final essay of this first section, Sean Alexander Gurd examines the figurative poem the "Egg," by Simias of Rhodes. The literal shape of the poem's words is central in most readings, and hence its visual aspects are taken up in various traditions of how to read it. But Gurd shows even more powerfully how, aside from the visual, the "Egg" is decidedly about sound. It is a "sonorous object," he says, one that self-reflectively explores the relationship between sound and sense. He reveals how the puzzles presented by the poem help situate it in a certain debate about sound and meaning and, moreover, how its very construction says something about that debate.

In part 2, the essays explore connections between hearing and learning, broadly construed, in particular, the role of hearing in the soul and in the transformation of the soul. Jessica Elbert Decker begins with an exploration of Heraclitus's command to listen to the logos, arguing that the logos functions as both a kind of testing and a kind of tuning of the soul. Moreover, Heraclitus's logoi serve as a kind of "reverse lullaby," she argues, waking the slumbering listener through sounds and resonances, aiding in the soul's ability to hear the logos. S. Montgomery Ewegen provides a deep reading of Plato's *Lysis* as a dialogue about listening and about the central role of listening in philosophical activity. The young Lysis proves to be an excellent listener, active and engaged, taking in Socrates's argument that he is ignorant, thus also situating himself ideally for philosophical discourse. To love listening, as Lysis does, is to embrace the emptiness or ignorance that allows reception of the other. The aporetic ending of *Lysis*, Ewegen argues, serves as an exhortation to Lysis (and to us) to embrace that emptiness, embrace his ignorance, and so remain a philosopher. Ryan Drake explores *thorubos*, the Greek term meaning clamor, uproar, hubbub, or commotion. Across several dialogues in Plato's corpus, this sound is associated both with the multitude and with a kind of disorder, its percussive, striking characteristics able to disturb or disrupt the existing order. The noise of the crowd can in some instances prove alluring for young souls, who thus risk bringing that disorder into their souls, disrupting the possibility of self-rule or self-possession. Drake develops a further link in the texts between the multitude and the nonhuman beast—as well as the inarticulate sounds that emanate from them—implying that the human multitude is not quite human. The multitude then has educative limitations, and addressing these limitations, Drake argues, amounts to a soothing of beastly passions. Aside from the multitude, however, there is within each individual soul a parallel danger of *thorubos*: the appetitive desires in the soul behave like disruptive, noisy beasts. Drake concludes by entertaining whether the dialogues indicate that the intellect can overcome the sonic disturbances produced by the appetites in the soul.

In part 3, the essays explore the deep connection between politics and listening. In my own contribution, I look at the explicit and thoroughgoing thematization of hearing in the *Seventh Letter*. Dion and Dionysius are distinguished in terms of their listening habits, and the letter itself exhorts its addressees to listen only to the voice of the letter-writer and encourages them to ignore the voices of slanderers and rumormongers. The so-called digression in the letter is actually a type of hearing test for Dionysius aimed at testing his fitness for philosophy, and the "weakness of logos" referred to in the digression is also a weakness of hearers and hearing and is thus a political weakness as well as an ontological-linguistic weakness. The chapter then considers the politics of listening in the *Seventh Letter*, which entail certain forms of domination, and I speculate on what a more liberated politics of listening might look like and what role the Platonic writings might play as a propaedeutic to better listening in the city. I conclude by arguing that because of the "weakness of logos," Plato's task is inherently paradoxical: Plato calls us to hear what we are not yet able to hear, tyrannizing in order to liberate our sense of hearing. I-Kai Jeng links Aristotle's *Rhetoric* and *Politics*, arguing that both speakers and audience must be good listeners. He begins by showing that Aristotle, contra Plato, believed that rhetoric tended toward truth, the more so the more it was used. Rhetoric is dialogical, according to Aristotle: it depends on the orator's use of reputable opinion as she persuades the audience, but the orator's use of reputable opinion is premised on her prior listening to the audience. The excellent rhetorician is thus necessarily an excellent listener. Jeng then turns to *Politics* 3.11, where Aristotle discusses the role, and the extent of that role, that the multitude should play in the city. In a manner parallel to the dialectic relationship between orator and audience, the virtuous few and the diverse multitude in the city must listen to each other; the views of the former, while virtuous, are incomplete, and they become complete when they listen to the multitude. Jeng turns to the *Nicomachean Ethics* and lays out an original reading of some familiar passages, arguing that Aristotle could be provoking the young to listen and specifically exhorting them to become those active listeners who listen to the multitude. Likewise, he reads a passage in the *Eudemian Ethics* as potentially tempering agonistic politics by urging this same type of listening. Sara Brill situates her work primarily in Aristotle's *Politics* and *De anima*. She first demonstrates that voice is both powerful and vulnerable, and the tyrant exploits this dual quality. By manipulating what is heard and not heard, the tyrant can prohibit frank speaking or parrhesia, he can destroy relationships through slander, and he can create mistrust. At the same time, however, hearing is central to the best city, especially through an education that cultivates sense perception as part of character formation, that is, through *mousikē*. Such an education, she argues, creates community by creating a shared *pathē*. Brill then explores the difficulties inherent in politics when both good regimes and pathological regimes may cultivate this same end—not just shared living (*suzēn*) but shared sensing, *sunaisthēsis*, specifically a hearing together. She offers wariness in the face of this ambiguity of shared perception in two different regimes.

In the final part of the volume, part 4, the authors explore sound and voice quite apart from logos. Rebecca Goldner looks at Sophocles's *Philoctetes* and argues that Philoctetes's sounds of grieving and loss signal a sense of human community. The tragedy introduces themes of speech and meaning throughout, Goldner argues, especially through its three main characters: Philoctetes, whose mournful, inarticulate sounds punctuate the play; Neoptolemus, who is rendered speechless at a particular moment in the play; and the infamously adept speaker and liar, Odysseus, who sets the plot in motion. In addition to whatever meaning is conveyed by spoken dialogue in the play, it introduces its audience to meaning derived from inarticulate sounds and from silences, Goldner shows. Ultimately, Philoctetes's pain and isolation from human community, conveyed through his cries, combined with Neoptolemus's human response to that pain and isolation, constitute successful communication and point us toward a fundamental human connection through sound. Contrary to Aristotle's claim that logos lies at the foundation of the polis, Goldner makes a case that *Philoctetes* shows a deeper foundation, a human connection based on sound, not speech. Kris McLain and Anne-Marie Schultz reconsider the crying of Xanthippe in Socrates's jail cell in light of *Phaedo*'s Pythagorean milieu, arguing that the gender politics within the Pythagorean community can shed light on her role in this dialogue. They look to the traditions of listening among the Pythagorean *akousmatikoi*, and they explore the role of silence in Pythagorean communities. They locate the significance of Xanthippe's cries as well as her silences both in the inner drama of *Phaedo* that takes place in the jail cell, where we see Xanthippe depicted at the beginning and at the end of the drama, and in the outer framing mechanism in which Phaedo relates the story to Echecrates and others with him in Phlius. James Barrett, like Michael Naas, addresses the work of Adriana Cavarero, arguing that the devocalization of logos is linked to the Socratic body, an erotic body from which comes the voice of philosophy. Drawing from a rich array of Greek literature and poetry, Barrett provides a detailed reading of Alcibiades's image of Socrates in the *Symposium* that likens him to the Silenus dolls and to the flute-playing satyr, Marsyas. Tracing a lineage through Aesop, the analogy between Marsyas and Socrates speaks to a beastly ugliness that, in its radical otherness or alterity, bursts the constraints of the conventional. Ugliness produces a marginality from which things can be spoken that otherwise—or from other bodies—cannot be spoken. The aulos or flute to which Socrates's logoi are compared also has its otherness.

Barrett argues that Socrates's strangeness or literally his placelessness, his *atopia*, is linked to the image of the satyr. In satyr play we see the dyadic structure of human/beast and human/divine breaking apart, which sheds light on the *atopia* of Socrates. He crosses boundaries and disturbs familiar categories. Against the devocalization of logos that animates Cavarero's work, Barrett argues that Socrates's embodied vocalization is embodied like no other body; his incomparable body then indicates that his voice sounds like the voice of those who speak in incomparable ways. In the final chapter, Jeremy Bell tackles silence. He traces it genealogically from early Greek texts through imperial Rome, demonstrating that silence has a positive moral valence in the archaic period through classical Greece, but in later Greek culture and carrying forward to the Romans, silence becomes associated with ignorance and deceit or concealment. The earlier period links silence with lēthē, meaning oblivion, forgetfulness, or concealment, and links logos in parallel fashion with memory or *mnemosunē*. Hence, in the earlier period, we memorialize through speech and song what is noble, pious, good, or otherwise worthy of being remembered. But, perhaps more importantly, we sing in order to be sung about, we speak in order to be spoken about. To be silent then is to be lost from memory and to be unsung. Speech in this register then implies a kind of virtue, and silence its opposite. For women in this early period, however, the opposite is the case. Women are thus excluded, Bell argues, not only from effecting action in the world but also from leaving any psychic imprint on the world. Among Roman authors of the first few centuries of the Common Era, we see a shift in valuation of silence, in particular, a silence that is chosen by an agent to demonstrate a kind of superiority or condemnation of others. This transition parallels a shift toward distrust of speech as associated with ethical and intellectual vice. Silence comes to represent sobriety, piety, virtue, and even divinity. The use of speech or logos is increasingly associated with humans' social and political discourse, and so a cleavage develops between human and divine where silence and listening are now seen as avenues to the divine. This value of silence, or at least a circumscribed logos that has no use for prattle or loquaciousness, also attaches to the image of the philosopher. Silence is divine and thus becomes the centerpiece of Roman virtue.

The essays have further resonances among them. Quite aside from the themes that I've used to organize the essays into these four sections—"Listening to the Logoi," "Sound Education," "Sound Politics," and "*Alogos*, Embodiment, and Silence"—there are themes that stretch across and weave through the scholarship. Among them I see fundamental distinctions between human and nonhuman, or even human and beast, that function alongside distinct modes of hearing (Drake, Barrett, and Goldner); the sound of death, dirges, and other related phenomena (Barrett, McLain and Schultz, and Goldner); the type of movement, specific to sound, along a passage or *poros* to reach a hearer, as well as the link between *poros* and aporia, a concept that is central to several Greek texts (Hyland, Shaw, and Ewegen); wholes and parts (Shaw and Gurd); sound as music (Barrett and Gurd); shallower and deeper states of awareness, consciousness, or self-consciousness associated with shallower and deeper states of listening (Hyland, Decker, and Ewegen); the human condition and hearing at the center of both our agency and our limitations (Brill and Goldner); linguistic play concerning homophones, resonances, puns, and the like (Hyland, Decker, Naas, and Gordon); the voice and devocalization in the work of Adriana Cavarero (Naas and Barrett); the role of the multitude in politics and how listening and hearing shape the multitude (Drake and Jeng); and the corresponding role of tyrants and tyranny in politics and the manner in which we can be tyrannized through what we do and do not hear and how we are allowed to hear it (Brill, Gordon, and Bell). No doubt there are other themes and resonances that readers of the volume will hear. The volume is thus broad and deep and filled with connections and entanglements. The depth of analysis in each contributor's chapter powerfully combines with the others to create a symphony that is both complex and harmonious.

One of the reasons that I wanted to put together a volume of essays on hearing, sound, and the auditory in the ancient world was as a gesture of resistance to our hypervisual culture and its emphasis on so much speech without much listening. My hope is that this collection of essays will open up new questions about the ancients' experience of the sound world and will provide new ways to hear these ancient texts. Because I think the best reason to read and study the ancient Greeks is to understand ourselves and our world better—and indeed to live better lives in our world—I also hope that these essays urge readers to think about our own soundscape: to consider what it means to hear and listen, to think about what we hear and how we hear, to understand that what we hear and how we hear it shapes us as individual persons and as humans, to think about our own politics of hearing and how it shapes our communal lives, and to listen to the world and each other, ready for more than just articulate speech.

## Notes

1. Most notably, Eric Havelock's *Preface to Plato* (Cambridge, MA: Belknap Press of Harvard University Press, 1963). As just a few other examples, see also Gilbert Ryle, *Plato's Progress* (Cambridge: Cambridge University Press, 1966); Jackson P. Hershbell, "Reflections on the Orality and Literacy of Plato's Dialogues," in *The Third Way: New Directions in Platonic Studies*, ed. Francisco J. Gonzalez (Lanham, MD: Roman and Littlefield, 1995), 25–40; Elinor West, "Plato's Audiences or How Plato Replies to the Fifth Century Intellectual Mistrust of Letters," in Gonzalez, *Third Way*, 41–60; Joanne Waugh, "Neither Published nor Perished: The Dialogues as Speech, Not Text," in Gonzalez, *Third Way*, 61–79; Thomas Szlezák, *Reading Plato* (New York: Routledge, 1999); Lawrence Hatab, "Writing Knowledge in the Soul: Orality, Literacy, and Plato's Critique of Poetry," *Epoché: A Journal for the History of Philosophy* 11, no. 2 (2007): 319–332.

2. Havelock, *Preface to Plato*, 46.

3. Jasper Svenbro, *Phrasikleia: An Anthropology of Reading in Ancient Greece*, trans. Janel Lloyd (Ithaca, NY: Cornell University Press, 1993), 2.

4. A few notable exceptions include Shane Butler and Sarah Nooter, eds., *Sound and the Ancient Senses* (New York: Routledge, 2019); Sean Gurd, *Dissonance: Auditory Aesthetics in Ancient Greece* (Evanston, IL: Northwestern University Press, 2016); Ömer Aygün, "On Bees and Humans: Phenomenological Explorations of Hearing Sounds, Voices, and Speech in Aristotle," *Epochê: A Journal for the History of Philosophy* 17, no. 2 (2013): 337–350; and Adriana Cavarero, *For More Than One Voice: Toward a Philosophy of Vocal Expression* (Stanford, CA: Stanford University Press, 2005). The recently released volume of work exclusively by classicists, *Voice and Voices in Antiquity: Orality and Literacy in the Ancient World* (London: Brill, 2017), edited by Niall Slater, covers some of the ground that ancient philosophers examined in the 1990s and 2000s about orality and literacy, primarily thinking about the text qua text (for example, narrative voice). It is less thematically focused than this volume on sound and hearing as the Greeks experienced them, and it does not contain explicitly philosophical approaches. In a small but unique volume, *Sonic Intimacy: Voices, Species, Technics (Or How to Listen to the World)* (Stanford, CA: Stanford University Press, 2017), Dominic Pettman takes up voice and listening, though with only passing references to the ancient world, given his primary focus on the current cultural moment. Salomé Voegelin has written two philosophical monographs on sound, *Listening to Noise and Silence: Towards a Philosophy of Sound Art* (London: Bloomsbury, 2010) and *Sonic Possible Worlds: Hearing the Continuum of Sound* (London: Bloomsbury, 2014). Both make original and, one might say, groundbreaking contributions to both analytical (drawing from David Lewis) and phenomenological (drawing from Maurice Merleau-Ponty) studies of sound.

## Bibliography

Aygün, Ömer. "On Bees and Humans: Phenomenological Explorations of Hearing Sounds, Voices, and Speech in Aristotle." *Epochê: A Journal for the History of Philosophy* 17, no. 2 (2013): 337–350.

Butler, Shane, and Sarah Nooter, eds. *Sound and the Ancient Senses.* New York: Routledge, 2019.

Cavarero, Adriana. *For More Than One Voice: Toward a Philosophy of Vocal Expression.* Stanford, CA: Stanford University Press, 2005.

Gonzalez, Francisco J., ed. *The Third Way: New Directions in Platonic Studies.* Lanham, MD: Roman and Littlefield, 1995.

Gurd, Sean. *Dissonance: Auditory Aesthetics in Ancient Greece.* Evanston, IL: Northwestern University Press, 2016.

Hatab, Lawrence. "Writing Knowledge in the Soul: Orality, Literacy, and Plato's Critique of Poetry." *Epoché: A Journal for the History of Philosophy* 11, no. 2 (2007): 319–332.

Havelock, Eric. *Preface to Plato.* Cambridge, MA: Belknap Press of Harvard University Press, 1963.

Hershbell, Jackson P. "Reflections on the Orality and Literacy of Plato's Dialogues." In Gonzalez, *Third Way,* 25–40.

Pettman, Dominic. *Sonic Intimacy: Voices, Species, Technics (Or How to Listen to the World).* Stanford, CA: Stanford University Press, 2017.

Ryle, Gilbert. *Plato's Progress.* Cambridge: Cambridge University Press, 1966.

Slater, Niall. *Voice and Voices in Antiquity: Orality and Literacy in the Ancient World.* Leiden, Neth.: Brill, 2017.

Svenbro, Jasper. *Phrasikleia: An Anthropology of Reading in Ancient Greece.* Translated by Janel Lloyd. Ithaca, NY: Cornell University Press, 1993.

Szlezák, Thomas. *Reading Plato.* New York: Routledge, 1999.

Voegelin, Salomé. *Listening to Noise and Silence: Towards a Philosophy of Sound Art.* London: Bloomsbury, 2010.

———. *Sonic Possible Worlds: Hearing the Continuum of Sound.* London: Bloomsbury, 2014.

Waugh, Joanne. "Neither Published nor Perished: The Dialogues as Speech, Not Text." In Gonzalez, *Third Way,* 61–79.

West, Elinor. "Plato's Audiences or How Plato Replies to the Fifth Century Intellectual Mistrust of Letters." In Gonzalez, *Third Way,* 41–60.

# HEARING, SOUND, AND THE AUDITORY IN ANCIENT GREECE

# PART I

# LISTENING TO THE LOGOI

# 1

## WAKEFUL LIVING, WAKEFUL LISTENING IN HERACLITUS

Drew A. Hyland, Trinity College, Emeritus

IN A COLLECTION OF ESSAYS SUCH AS THIS one, devoted to the theme of the auditory—listening, hearing, speaking—we could hardly avoid considering Heraclitus among the first thinkers relevant to this topic. For one of the many striking things about his thinking is the extent to which he emphasizes the auditory, especially the significance of listening, as his guiding metaphor for the kind of thinking and knowing he proposes. However, as with each of the important philosophical themes that Heraclitus gives us, there is no section or chapter of his work entitled something like "The Importance of Listening." Instead, we must tease out his words on listening from the many other issues in which they are embedded, even as listening itself is embedded among the many issues of our lives.

But this very embeddedness is a source of richness, or so I would like to suggest in this paper. In the case of Heraclitus, one theme in which the issue of listening is again and again embedded is that of wakefulness—a wakefulness that seems to be the necessary context for the very possibility of the listening that Heraclitus has in mind. Accordingly, in this essay I begin with a reflection on the significance of wakefulness in Heraclitus and allow that to lead, as it seems to in his thought, to the question of listening. That allows me in turn to reflect on the profound significance of our choice of metaphors for knowing that Heraclitus's own choice, listening or hearing, exhibits.

# 1. Wakefulness

No fewer than eight of the sayings of Heraclitus employ the theme of wakefulness.[1] I want to risk considering them together here, in the hope of gaining a certain sense of what is at stake for Heraclitus in so often using this theme and how it plays out in his thinking. It is a risk, of course, because if every text demands interpretation—if no text authoritatively interprets itself—then surely Heraclitus's text is exemplary in this regard. We have no literally "authoritative" ordering of his sayings, because Heraclitus leaves us no intended ordering; indeed, it is not even clear that he intended a particular ordering at all. Perhaps he wrote in such a way as to demand of the reader that he or she order the sayings in accordance with his or her own listening to the λόγος. In any case, without even an authoritative ordering of the sayings, and writing in short segments that more resemble aphorisms than arguments, Heraclitus virtually demands of us that we self-consciously interpret his work and that we therefore risk doing violence to it every time we select an order to the sayings we consider (and surely every time we consider only some of them). That said, as preparation for the question of listening, let us risk considering those sayings that put into play the theme of wakefulness, risking the following order.

Four of the sayings introduce what I take to be the guiding force of the image of wakefulness, one often still engaged by us today. That is the image of wakefulness as a higher state of consciousness than sleep and therefore a desirable state for which to strive and to preserve. "Sleep" is the obvious contrast here, and Heraclitus often chastises most of us for living in such a way as to be in effect "asleep while awake." Here are the four basic sayings:

> D-K 1: τοῦ δὲ λόγου τοῦδ᾽ ἐόντος αἰεὶ ἀξύνετοι γίγονται ἄνθρωποι καὶ
> πρόσθεν ἢ ἀκοῦσαι καὶ ἀκούσαντες τὸ πρῶτον. γινομένων γὰρ πάντων
> κατὰ τὸν λόγον τόνδε ἀπείροισιν ἐοίκασι πειρώμενοι καὶ ἐπέων καὶ
> ἔργων τοιουτέων ὁκοίων ἐγὼ διηγεῦμαι κατὰ φύσιν διαιρέων ἕκαστον
> καὶ φράζων ὅκως ἔχει. τοὺς δὲ ἄλλους ἀνθρώπους λανθάνει ὁκόσα
> ἐγερθέντες ποιοῦσιν ὅκωσπερ ὁκόσα εὕδοντες ἐπιλανθάνονται.

> Although this λόγος holds forever, humans fail to comprehend, both before hearing it and after they have heard it. Although all things come to pass in accordance with the λόγος, humans are like the untried when they try such words and works as I set forth, distinguishing each according to its nature, and telling how it is. But other humans are oblivious of what they do when awake, just as they are forgetful of what they do asleep.[2]

D-K 71: μενμῆσθαι δὲ καὶ τοῦ ἐπιλανθανομένου ᾗ ἡ ὁδὸς ἄγει. καὶ ὅτι ᾧ μάλιστα διηνεκῶς ὁμιλοῦσι (λόγῳ τῷ τὰ ὅλα διοικοῦντι) τούτῳ διαφέρονται, καὶ οἷς καθ᾽ ἡμέραν ἐγκυροῦσι, ταῦτα αὐτοῖς ξένα φαίνεται. καὶ ὅτι οὐ δεῖ ὥσπερ καθεύδοντας ποιεῖν καὶ λέγειν.

They forget where the way leads . . . and they are at odds with that with which they most constantly associate. And what they meet with every day seems strange to them, and we should not act and speak like those asleep.

D-K 89: τοῖς ἐγρηγορόσιν ἕνα καὶ κοινὸν κόσμον εἶναι, τῶν δὲ κοιμωμένων ἕκαστον εἰς ἴδιον ἀποστρέφεσθαι.

The cosmos of the waking is one and shared, but those sleeping each turn aside into their private world.

D-K 63: ἐπανίστασθαι καὶ φύλακας γίνεσθαι ἐγερτὶ ζώντων καὶ νεκρῶν.

To rise up and become wakeful guardians of the living and of corpses.

The first saying, D-K 1, is almost universally regarded as the "first" of the Heraclitean sayings, although, strictly, we do not even know this.[3] Regarding wakefulness, it sets the guiding theme well. As he often does, Heraclitus, in stating his case for the λόγος, chastises the majority of humankind for failing to "hear" (and this metaphor for comprehension will become thematic for us presently) what they should hear, even after they have heard it. The final line invokes the image of wakefulness and sleeping. Most of us "live" as if we were in effect "sleeping through life." We "live" with an obliviousness akin to when we are asleep. There is a clear implication here: "mere" living—perhaps we could even say "bare life"—is not a life worth living. Heraclitus implies what Socrates would later make explicit in his defense of his own life: mere life, life that lacks a certain quality, is not a life worth living.[4] The image Heraclitus often invokes for the life worth living, as here, is "wakefulness." And the life too many of us live is akin to a life characterized by the obliviousness of sleeping, even if we are technically awake.

Heraclitus announces in this first saying what will be the primary sign of whether we live wakefully or not: do we or don't we listen to the λόγος, and, as he will soon say, do we *attune* ourselves to the λόγος and so speak and act in attunement with it? D-K 71 says, "We should not act and speak like those asleep." This announces an especially important Heraclitean theme: wakeful living will never be simply a matter of holding the right doctrines or even just speaking the truth. It will always also be a matter of *acting* in accordance with what we have heard. I think this can never be emphasized enough: for Heraclitus, simply hearing the λόγος—as we would say, "knowing" it—is not sufficient. One must also act in accordance with it. Or rather, "knowing" for Heraclitus seems not merely to be an act of mental cognition but must be exhibited in living to be genuine knowledge. This—listening, speaking, and acting in accordance with the logos—will be wakeful living. It will even be what Heraclitus calls "wisdom."

D-K 112 famously says, "To be sophron is the greatest virtue, and wisdom is speaking and acting the truth, hearkening to the nature of things" (σωφρονεῖν ἀρετὴ μεγίστη, καὶ σοφίη ἀληθέα λέγειν καὶ ποιεῖν κατὰ φύσιν ἐπαΐοντας).[5] We might speculate that with what little we have of Heraclitus's predecessors, the Milesian philosophers, "wisdom" was already on the way to being construed largely in terms of what is said. Thales, we are told, said that the arche of all was water, Anaximander said that it was *to apeiron*, and Anaximenes said that it was air. Their "wisdom" was thus in what they said. We are already, it seems, on the way to a conception of wisdom (and so truth) as a property of what is said, as propositional, as entirely cognitive. Heraclitus immediately interrupts that direction, even before it can become hegemonic. Wisdom is a matter of speaking and acting, of speaking and acting the truth, which itself thus is a matter of speaking and acting in a certain way, of paying heed or hearkening to the nature of things (and again, the evocation of the auditory in the word *hearkening* should be heard here). In this, the Platonic Socrates will forever be a Heraclitean. Philosophy for him too is not a body of beliefs, as when we ask, "What's your philosophy?" and expect in response a statement of a set of beliefs about this or that. Philosophy for Socrates as for Heraclitus will always be a matter of living in a certain way—of hearing, speaking, and acting the truth. Perhaps part of the so-called crisis of philosophy in our time is our forgetfulness of this Heraclitean wisdom. Sure that wisdom is a matter of propositions, of knowing and saying what can be verified, we might wonder, are we the sleeping philosophers?

D-K 89, the third saying quoted earlier, announces a crucial consequence of the difference between wakefulness and sleeping: "The cosmos of the waking is one and shared, but those asleep turn aside each into a private world." One characteristic of the wakeful is that theirs is an experience of a cosmos, an ordered whole, which is one and shared (ἕνα καὶ κοινὸν). The sleeping, by contrast, experience a world that is not shared but private for each person and hence not one but manifold, "relative," as we now say. Immediately, we must wonder what it is that is "one and shared" that makes the world of the wakeful a cosmos and from which those who live as asleep are cut off. The answer has already been limned in the first saying above: it is the λόγος that is the unifying force in the world and that makes it, to those sufficiently awake to hear it, a shared world. Clearly, then, much (not to say everything) hinges on the character of the λόγος, to which we must presently turn.

The fourth saying above, again exhibiting the guiding theme of wakefulness, enjoins us to "rise up" (perhaps already a metaphor for wakefulness) and become "wakeful guardians of the living and of corpses." *Guardians* (φύλακας), a word that Plato would soon make famous in the *Republic*, is sometimes translated as "watchers,"[6] but I think that word is too suggestive of passivity, not to mention of the sight metaphor, which Heraclitus employs with striking infrequency. *Guardians* better captures what we have already heard Heraclitus insist, that the mark of wakefulness is not just a certain cognitive ability but acting in a certain way, being wakeful guardians of "the living and corpses." We must ask, what conduct will determine the "wakeful" living that would make us good guardians of the living? And what would it mean to be also good "guardians of corpses," the corpses whom Heraclitus elsewhere directs us to "throw out faster than dung"?[7]

Heraclitus's response to the first question—and perhaps indirectly the second—has already been limned. Guardians, to speak in a Heideggerian mode, are those who preserve and shelter the living, who free them and allow them to be what they are.[8] And what will that mean for Heraclitus? At least this much, or at least to begin with this: to "speak and act the truth, hearkening to the nature of things." Clearly, this hearkening to the nature of things is the very condition for the possibility of our "speaking and acting the truth." And what about corpses? What will it be to "guard" them? Perhaps to shelter and preserve them too, precisely in their difference from the living? Questions abound.

We may get some help—never without questions—from the four other explicit references to wakefulness. But before we turn to them, let us underline what has been said so far: the first four sayings reveal that wakefulness names a certain way of being, a certain attunement or openness to what is shared, the λόγος, as well as a certain responsiveness to what we share, a "speaking and acting the truth, hearkening to the nature of things," captured perceptively in Heraclitus's image of wakeful guardianship. In these sayings, we have already heard the theme of listening as the guiding metaphor invoked for knowing. More must be said about this presently.

The second group of four sayings bearing directly on the theme of wakefulness go as follows:

D-K 26: ἄνθρωπος ἐν εὐφρόνῃ φάος ἅπτεται ἑαυτῷ ἀποσβεσθεὶς ὄψεις, ζῶν δὲ ἅπτεται τεθνεῶτος εὕδων, ἐγρηγορὼς ἅπτεται εὕδοντος.

A man strikes a light for himself in the night, when his sight is quenched. Living, he touches the dead while he is sleeping; waking, he touches the sleeper.

D-K 75: τοὺς καθεύδοντας ἐργάτας καὶ συνεργοὺς τῶν ἐν τῷ κόσμῳ γινομένων.

Those asleep are workers and coworkers in what comes to be in the cosmos.

D-K 21: θάνατός ἐστιν ὁκόσα ἐγερθέντες ὁρέομεν, ὁκόσα δὲ εὕδοντες ὕπνος.

Death is whatever we see when awake; whatever we see while sleeping is sleep.

D-K 88: ταὐτό . . . ζῶν καὶ τεθνηκός καὶ ἐγρηγορὸς καὶ τὸ καθεῦδον καὶ νέον καὶ γηραιόν. τάδε γὰρ μεταπεσόντα ἐκεῖνα ἐστι κἀκεῖνα πάλιν μεταπεσόντα ταῦτα.

The same . . . living and dead, and the waking and sleeping, and young and old. For these transposed are those, and those transposed are these.

Each of these four sayings is meant, even structured grammatically, to astonish. In D-K 26, the first sentence, "A man strikes a light for himself in the night, when his sight is quenched," seems to prepare us for something like, "Just so, in the light of day, he must . . . conduct himself wakefully, or search into himself, or listen to the λόγος," or some such injunction. Instead, utterly counter to our expectation, we read next, "Living, he touches the dead while he is sleeping; waking, he touches the sleeper." The force of the first clause here is immediately puzzling. In one sense, there is something obvious about it: how else but as living might we "touch the dead"? But Heraclitus adds, "while sleeping"! What might it mean that living, we touch the dead, but while sleeping? Charles Kahn's suggestion that Heraclitus is alluding to the dream experience here is certainly plausible.[9] But it might be so in a double sense. In one, perhaps the most obvious sense, we "touch" the dead when dreaming insofar as we can and do, on occasion, dream of the dead. But Heraclitus may also allude here to the notion that in sleep, we "touch" the dead in the sense that we come close to death. Sleeping would thus be a kind of middle or jointure between full living (that is, wakeful living) and death. Asleep, we approach death; hence, those of us who live our lives not wakefully, who "sleep through life," are, as we say, as good as dead. However, this fragment suggests that sleep is not without significance for wakeful living. In sleep, we both dream of the dead and "broach" death ourselves. We get from sleep perhaps our first intimation of the relation between life and death.

But then, what to make of the last clause, "waking, he touches the sleeper"? Only in wakefulness do we "touch" the sleeper in the sense that only when awake (that is, when living wakefully) can we know the difference between wakefulness, sleeping, and death. It is only while awake that we recognize the significance of sleeping and the difference between sleeping and waking. Heraclitus did not write this saying while asleep. We note that Heraclitus is replacing the traditional dichotomy of life and death with a triad: wakeful living, sleeping, and death. But what is the difference among them?

The next two sayings, D-K 75 and 21, seem less to clarify than to deepen the mystery. D-K 75 reads, counterintuitively, "Those asleep are workers and coworkers in what comes to be in the cosmos."[10] What? Would it not be the wakeful, those living wakefully, listening in attunement with the λόγος, who are the workers and coworkers in what comes to be? Not quite! So also are those asleep! We all participate in the happening of the world in accordance with the λόγος, whether we wish it or not, whether we acknowledge it or not, whether we are aware of it or not. Wakeful living, or sleeping through life for that matter, do not change the fact that we are part of the happening of things. Stated differently, sleeping is not nothing, nor is "sleeping" through life. Both are part of the flow of things, part of the endless series of confrontations and oppositions that make the λόγος. Wakefulness might, however, change how we participate in that happening. But then the mystery deepens: how, if at all, does wakefulness change things?

The next saying, D-K 21, again is astonishing: "Death is whatever we see when awake; whatever we see while sleeping is sleep." The second clause is perhaps less surprising than the first: whatever we see while sleeping is sleep? Of course! What we "see" while sleeping could only, it would seem, be dreams. And dreams, Heraclitus here implies, are inseparable from sleep. So indeed, all we see while asleep is sleep, even our dreams. It is the first clause that is so puzzling here. Would we not expect that "whatever we see when awake" is . . . life? But Heraclitus says, "Death is whatever we see when awake." If so, what then is the difference between life and death?

The same! D-K 88 tells us with stunning abruptness, "The same . . . living and dead, and the waking and sleeping, and young and old. For these transposed are those, and those transposed are these." How can these be "the same" if Heraclitus urges us to be wakeful guardians of the happening of things and not live our lives as those asleep?[11] Only, I suggest, if, with Martin Heidegger, we appreciate that "same" does not mean "identical" and especially that it does not mean "no difference." They can be "the same" in the sense that they are part of an "everliving" cycle of opposites turning into one another—life turns into death, out of death comes life (e.g., the death of a human body [and its burial] gives life to whatever organisms develop from the corpse), wakefulness becomes sleep and sleep wakefulness, the young become old, and the old, again through the cycle of death/life, become something "young." Yes, they are "the same." But within that everliving cycle, and in particular within the cycle of wakefulness and sleep, there can be what amounts to an enormous difference for the kind of life we live. Hence, Heraclitus can at once urge us, as participants in the cycle, to strive for wakefulness while acknowledging that in the cosmic order of things, the cycle will continue. As he says with such stunning economy, "These transposed are those, and those transposed are these." Or, as Heraclitus puts a similar point in another saying and in another register, "For the god, all things are beautiful and good and just, but men have taken some things as unjust, others as just."[12] Thus, from the standpoint of the everliving order of things, waking and sleeping, life and death, are the same. But for us, living out our moment in that everliving order, they can be very different indeed.

## 2. Wakeful Listening

What, yet again, will it mean to be "wakeful guardians," to live wakefully? In a surprising choice of metaphor for understanding and knowing, Heraclitus tells us that wakefulness will entail first and foremost a certain "listening," listening to the λόγος, and, as always, speaking and acting in accordance with it. Let us first reflect on this choice of metaphor for comprehension—reflect, that is, on the significance of the Greek (and our) metaphors for understanding.

Like the Greeks, we tend to employ three sense metaphors for understanding and knowing: sight, touch, and hearing (I am guessing that this is also the order of predominance for us). We say often, "Do you see what I mean?" or almost as often, "Do you grasp my meaning?" or again sometimes, "Do you hear what I'm saying; does that sound right to you?" In the vast majority of cases, we take these different metaphors as more or less synonymous, and rarely do we consider the very different nuances in play in each of the sense-metaphors. We might meditate on this obliviousness, this lack of wakefulness and failure to be good guardians, as part of the decline in the richness of our language. But I believe there is good evidence that the Greeks in general, and Heraclitus in particular, were much more self-conscious about their choice of these metaphors, much more attuned—to employ a hearing metaphor loved by Heraclitus—to the different nuances of each metaphor. Let us briefly consider some of those nuances.

I begin with the sight metaphor, probably the predominant metaphor for understanding with both the Greeks and us. "I see what you mean," we say when we think we understand, and we praise the result of this "seeing" as an "insight," literally a "seeing into." Note first that to see something, it must have a certain amount of stability, motionlessness. If something is moving at a high speed, it becomes increasingly difficult to see it.[13] The sight metaphor, that is, is most appropriate when we assume that the objects of our understanding are stable, in the best cases even permanent and unchangeable. It is little wonder then, for example, that the sight metaphor is Plato's preferred metaphor for his "forms," the primary words for which, εἶδος and ἰδέα, are derived from words for "seeing." Arguably the most famous example in all of philosophical literature of the sight metaphor for knowing is the "Cave Analogy" of *Republic* book 7. There, "knowing" is all about "seeing" the right objects. Insofar as the forms are permanent and changeless, the appropriate metaphor for knowing them would indeed be seeing them. A second important feature of the sight metaphor, especially by contrast to the other two, is distance. To see something, the observer must preserve a certain distance from that thing (if I bring something right up against my eyes, I can no longer see it), and with that distance goes a certain presumption of independence between object and seer. When I "see" something (at least in the everyday sense), it preserves a certain independence from me.

My "seeing" it does not change it—it stays as it is when I see it. In general, then, the sight metaphor is perhaps the most appropriate metaphor to use when we want to claim that our knowledge is "objective," a more or less pure "vision" of stable objects.

Things are very different with the metaphor for touch, which historically has usually taken the form of "grasping," as in "I grasp your meaning." In grasping, the distance in the sight metaphor is obliterated. To grasp something implies a degree of control. To grasp something thus can imply that I have it in my power. In early modernity, as the notion that "knowledge is power" became predominant, it is hardly surprising that the grasping metaphor for knowing also rose to prominence.[14] It should be added, however, that more recently some philosophers (and particularly some feminist philosophers) have decisively transformed the metaphor of touch from the notion of power and control to the much more intimate sense of the caress.[15]

To "hear" something entails some very different nuances. For one, whereas in seeing and touching, the object seen or touched stops at the surface of our bodies (the object seen or touched does not enter our bodies), in hearing, the sound actually enters our bodies and is experienced as such.[16] There is therefore something much more intimate about the hearing metaphor. The sound that we hear is literally "internalized" more fully than with sight and touch; the knowledge embodied in the hearing metaphor becomes part of who we are. Perhaps even more important for Heraclitus, the "object" that we hear, the sound, is itself in motion. Unlike the objects of sight and touch, sound is continually, constantly moving. The symphony flows, the notes disappear as I hear them, and this is no less true of the words in the sentences we utter. Hearing, that is, is the metaphor for understanding that reminds us that things need not be stable for us to have intellectual access to them, that something constantly moving can nonetheless be intelligible to us—if we listen in the right way.

Can it be surprising, then, that Heraclitus would choose as his predominant metaphor for understanding that of hearing and listening? οὐκ ἐμοῦ ἀλλὰ τοῦ λόγου ἀκούσαντας ὁμολογεῖν σοφὸν ἓν πάντα εἶναι ("Listening not to me but to the λόγος, it is wise to agree that one [is] all"), says D-K 50. To be sure, Heraclitus occasionally appeals to metaphors of sight, but much the predominant metaphor for him is listening/hearing, and I suggest that given the experience of the world he articulates, it is entirely appropriate—and probably self-consciously chosen—that he would do so. To cite just a few of the many other sayings that engage the metaphor for hearing, what nearly everyone agrees is the first of Heraclitus's sayings (as we have seen), which presumably opens his text, begins, τοῦ δὲ λόγου τοῦδ' ἐόντος αἰεὶ ἀξύνετοι γίνονται ἄνθρωποι καὶ πρόσθεν ἢ ἀκοῦσαι καὶ ἀκούσαντες τὸ πρῶτον ("Of the λόγος which is forever, people are uncomprehending, both before they have heard it and when they have heard it"). D-K 19 reads, ἀκοῦσαι οὐκ ἐπιστάμενοι οὐδ' εἰπεῖν·("[People] do not know how to listen or how to speak"). D-K 34 reads, ἀξύνετοι ἀκούσαντες κωφοῖσιν ἐοίκασι φάτις αὐτοῖσι μαρτυρεῖ παρεόντας ἀπεῖναι ("Not comprehending, they hear like the deaf. The saying is their witness: absent while present"). And speaking of the divine, in D-K 92, Heraclitus says, Σίβυλλα δὲ μαινομένω στόματι ἀγέλαστα καὶ ἀκαλλώπιστα καὶ ἀμύριστα φθεγγομένη ἐτῶν ἐξικνεῖται τῇ φωνῇ διὰ τὸν θεόν ("The Sibyl, with raving mouth, utters things mirthless and unadorned and unperfumed, and her voice carries through a thousand years, because of the god").

Why might Heraclitus privilege the somewhat less typical metaphor of hearing? First of all, he speaks again and again, both with reference to the soul and especially with reference to the cosmos, of the λόγος, and it must be remembered that in Heraclitus's still largely oral culture, *λόγος* meant first and primarily spoken λόγος. As fragment 50 (quoted above) well attests, the λόγος is first and fundamentally that which we must listen to. Even further, we must recall that the λόγος of the soul is not something permanent and stable (which might make the sight metaphor more appropriate) but increases itself, like the ongoing flow of music or the flow of our speech:[17] "The soul has a λόγος, which increases itself" (ψυχῆς ἐστι λόγος ἑαυτὸν αὔξων). And the larger λόγος of the cosmos, the λόγος that is the ever-flowing yet ordered harmony of oppositions and struggles that constitutes the happening of things, as ever changing and flowing, is best comprehended as heard. As my own language in trying to understand Heraclitus has tried to intone, the proper way of understanding for us is not to stand still or try to "halt" the λόγος but to get into an attunement with the happening of things and move along in accord with its flow. To harmonize with this sense of the way the world is, Heraclitus would seem to have privileged just the right metaphor, unusual as it may be. To understand the world is to listen to the λόγος, hearkening (ἐπαΐοντας), as Heraclitus tells us, to the nature of things. And as we have seen, "hearkening," wakeful listening, entails not at all a passive taking in but an open attunement to what is heard and a responding to what is heard. Again, as D-K 112 intones, "wisdom is speaking and acting the truth, hearkening to the nature of things." As wakeful guardians of the living and the dead, we must begin by being good listeners.

And we listen first and foremost to the λόγος. What does it tell us? It tells us that the ordered happening of things, the cosmos, is a dynamic coursing whose most fundamental character is opposition, a never-ending or, better, everliving play of forces that, above all, we must understand as staying in opposition. Eva Brann makes this point convincingly in her recent book on Heraclitus.[18] The λόγος is the contention of opposites and emphatically *not* a "reconciliation" of opposites. It is a "harmony" not of consonance but of dissonance. The first well-known misunderstanding of this point may well have been that of Eryximachus in the speech that Plato gives him in the *Symposium*, where the good doctor, with his own healing art clearly in mind, can only understand Heraclitus as advocating a reconciliation of these opposites, surely not a preservation of the contention.[19] But Heraclitus's point is that the "harmony" of the λόγος resides precisely in the everliving character of the opposition. This everliving opposition happens in manifold ways, from the cosmological to the human and interpersonal. Among the many sayings that express this at the cosmological level, let me cite the following four:

D-K 8: τὸ ἀντίξουν συμφέρον καὶ ἐκ τῶν διαφερόντων καλλίστην ἁρμονίαν καὶ πάντα κατ᾽ ἔριν γίνεσθαι.

What opposes unites, and from what is at variance comes the most beautiful attunement, and all things come to be through conflict.

D-K 51: οὐ ξυνιᾶσιν ὅκως διαφερόμενον ἑωυτῷ ὁμολογέει. παλίντροπος ἁρμονίη ὅκωσπερ τόξου καὶ λύρης.

They do not understand how being at variance it agrees with itself; it is an attunement turning back on itself, like that of the bow and the lyre.

D-K 67: ὁ θεὸς ἡμέρη εὐφρόνη, χειμὼν θέρος, πόλεμος εἰρήνη, κόρος λιμός. ἀλλοιοῦται δὲ ὅκωσπερ ὁκόταν συμμιγῇ θυώμασιν ὀνομάζεται καθ᾽ ἡδονὴν ἑκάστου.

The god: day night, winter summer, war peace, satiety hunger. It alters, as when mingled with perfumes, it gets named according to the pleasure of each one.

D-K 10: συλλάψιες; ὅλα καὶ οὐχ ὅλα, συμφερόμενον διαφερόμενον, συνᾷδον διᾷδον, ἐκ πάντων ἓν καὶ ἐξ ἑνὸς πάντα.

Graspings together: wholes and not wholes, convergent divergent, consonant dissonant, out of all things one, out of one all.[20]

In one register, these all say "the same." The happening of the world, the meaning in the world, arises out of opposition. Or better, it arises *in* the opposition. This is of course compatible with Heraclitus's regular insistence on the constant flow of things, on the flux of everliving fire as the fundamental element, on the flow of the λόγος as it "increases itself." He is not saying that every once in a while the flux and flow of the world stops and we have a period of harmony—a kind of prefiguration of the Empedoclean epoch of total love. No, the harmony occurs *within* the opposition and is constituted by that constant flux of opposing forces. Hearkening to the λόγος will then mean acknowledging that the world and what meaning we find in it is constituted by opposition, and living out that acknowledgment. Out of variance comes the most beautiful attunement.

At the level of the human, the λόγος tells us in D-K 110 that "it is not better for humans to get all that they want. It is disease that makes health sweet and good, hunger satiety, weariness rest" (ἀνθρώποις γίνεσθαι ὁκόσα θέλουσιν οὐκ ἄμεινον. νοῦσος ὑγιείην ἐποίησεν ἡδὺ καὶ ἀγαθόν, λιμὸς κόρον, κάματος ἀνάπαυσιν). More forcefully still, D-K 80 states, "One must realize that struggle [πόλεμον] is shared and conflict [ἔριν] is justice, and that all things come to be in accordance with conflict [ἔριν]" (εἰδέ χρὴ τὸν πόλεμον ἐόντα ξυνὸν καὶ δίκην ἔριν καὶ γινόμενα πάντα κατ᾽ ἔριν καὶ χρεώμενα). Finally and most famously, D-K 53 reads, "Struggle [πόλεμος] is father of all and king of all; some it has shown forth as gods, others humans; some it has made slaves, others free" (πόλεμος πάντων μὲν πατήρ ἐστι, πάντων δὲ βασιλεύς, καὶ τοὺς μὲν θεοὺς ἔδειξε τοὺς δὲ ἀνθρώπους, τοὺς μὲν δούλους ἐποίησε τοὺς δὲ ἐλευθέρους). In each of these, it is important to hear that the conflict, the struggle, *is* the λόγος. It is the play of oppositions among humans that grants the meaning, the λόγος, to our lives. To engage an example that I dwell on later, it is not unlike an athletic contest, where the game is just the struggle among the players or the teams. From the standpoint of, say, an onlooker, the game may be beautiful, even magnificent. But the game itself is the struggle among the players, some of whom will have to suffer the disappointment of losing: "For the god, all things are beautiful and good and just, but men have taken some things as unjust, others as just"[21] (ὡς τῷ μὲν θεῷ καλὰ πάντα καὶ ἀγαθὰ καὶ δίκαια, ἄνθρωποι δὲ ἃ μὲν ἄδικα ὑπειλήφασιν ἃ δὲ δίκαια). The "one" game is the struggle of "many," ἓν πάντα. Wakeful living will be to hearken to this and to play one's life accordingly: "Listening not to me but to the λόγος, it is wise to agree, ἓν πάντα."[22]

# 3. Wakeful Playing

But still, what will that orientation toward the happening of things look like in the event, this hearkening to the λόγος and living accordingly? Heraclitus gives us a rich clue in his famous saying listed as D-K 52: it will be a mode of living that imitates the αἰών, "lifetime" or "life itself." It will be a life that *plays*: αἰὼν παῖς ἐστι παίζων, πεσσεύων. παιδὸς ἡ βασιληίη ("Lifetime is a child playing, moving pieces in a game. Kingship belongs to the child"). And what will this look like? I have translated *αἰὼν* as "lifetime" or even "life itself." The word is clearly related etymologically to the Ionic *αἰεί* and so to *ἀεί*, "always," "forever." So it refers not so much to an individual life as to "life itself." The happening of what we can, with this saying, call the *play* of oppositions in the world and in human lives, which gives the world and our lives what meanings they have, is "a child playing," and we should live accordingly, living playfully. But again, what will this mean?

This is not the Heidegger Circle, and so I will not take time to dwell on this point at length, but it must be said that Heidegger's insistence that Heraclitus's *polemos*, the struggle and opposition of the happening of things, cannot mean merely or even primarily "war."[23] That reading would be entirely incompatible with the strong emphasis that Heraclitus places here and elsewhere on the playful character of the happening of the world. War, to be sure, is struggle, opposition in the extreme. But as the extreme case, it is precisely the breakdown of the playfulness on which Heraclitus insists, the failure to listen to the true character of the contentious logos that is yet a harmony. Indeed, before long, Plato would have his strange character in the *Laws* tell us that the real opposite of play is neither work nor seriousness but war.[24]

However, it must be appreciated that the play to which Heraclitus here refers is not what we sometimes call "idle" child's play. It is not the purposeless and frivolous "playing around," as when a child bangs together his or her parents' pots and pans or when someone doodles with a pencil. No, it is a child playing *a rule-governed game*. This makes all the difference in the meaning of the metaphor. Take almost any rule-governed game that you choose. At any given moment, to play that game is to obey the rules of that game. But there is virtually no rule-governed game whose rules do not change over time. (My brother is on the NCAA basketball "rules committee," which examines the rules of that game every year to see what changes might make it better, safer, or more exciting.) Even so, even as the rules may constantly evolve, to play that game at any given time is to obey the rules of the game as they (temporarily) stand. And of course, to do so, one must keep up with, or stay attuned to, the rules as they evolve. One must hearken to the ever-changing λόγος of the game and play accordingly.

What will it mean to play this way? To be frivolous? To play carelessly, not caring much how well one plays? Not at all! As almost every athlete has experienced, in the very midst of recognizing that the game is "only" a game, that in the world-historical course of things it will mean next to nothing, they are utterly serious and committed. They throw their whole being into the very game whose outcome, they know, will have next to no effect on the world. That delicate and precarious balance of recognizing the utter contingency of what one is doing, yet throwing one's heart and soul into the activity, is the essence of what it means to play.

The "game changers" in the rules of a particular game typically are those in charge of the rules, who stipulate what changes there will be, and to which the players must then respond. No such committee exists when it comes to αἰὸν, to life itself. The openness to what is happening and our responsiveness to it—that is, our hearkening to the λόγος and our "speaking and acting" in accordance with it—will therefore be at once more challenging and more precarious. But that is who we are, wakeful guardians, ones who must be at once open to hearing the λόγος and responsive to it, playing along with the contentious flowing of the λόγος.

## 4. Wakeful Living

σωφρονεῖν ἀρετὴ μεγίστη, καὶ σοφίη ἀληθέα λέγειν καὶ ποιεῖν κατὰ φύσιν ἐπαΐοντας ("To be sophron is the greatest virtue, and wisdom is speaking and acting the truth, hearkening to the nature of things").[25] Why, long before σωφρωσύνη would become anything like "moderation," "temperance," or "self-control"—the typical later translations of the Greek virtue—why before that would Heraclitus join it with wisdom in this most provocative of all his sayings, where he transforms for those of us who would hear him the very nature of "wisdom," making it not just a certain cognitive achievement but a certain sort of living as well; why would he also, in that same sentence, join wisdom with that other virtue? And why, even further, would he say *sōphronein* first before *sophiē*, call *sōphronein* "the greatest virtue," and make it an active verb rather than a noun joined with that other noun, *wisdom*? To be sophron, to act in a sophron-like way—would that perhaps be the greatest virtue precisely because it is the mode of action in accordance with what wisdom is, the mode of action that is "speaking and acting the truth, hearkening to the nature of things"? Could it be the wakeful living that, listening to the λόγος, speaks and acts in accordance with that λόγος, playing along with and in accordance with the happening of things? If so, it would seem that it could not be located in the procrustean metaphysical distinction between activity and passivity. Would to listen, think, and act in a sophron way thus be active as opposed to passive? Passive as opposed to active? Would it alternate between each? Or would it not rather already undercut that distinction and think in a different register from such a distinction? In being wakeful guardians, in listening to and playing along in accordance with the λόγος, in the responsive openness for which such a living would call, would not being sophron then be a first beginning to what a later thinker, thinking in a deeply Heraclitean spirit, would name *Gelassenheit*? For those who have ears, let us hear!

## Notes

1. Diels-Kranz (D-K) numbers: 1, 21, 26, 63, 71, 75, 88, and 89. I find the usual way of referring to Heraclitus's texts as "fragments" to be quite misleading. Each saying can stand by itself. What *may* be fragmentary is the text as a whole—that is, we may not have the entirety of Heraclitus's corpus.

2. All translations are my own, although I am usually guided by those of Charles Kahn in *The Art and Thought of Heraclitus* (Cambridge: Cambridge University Press, 1979). Although I have not followed Kahn's unusual ordering of Heraclitus's sayings, in working through this paper I have come to appreciate even more both the challenge of his task and the thoughtfulness of his ordering.

3. Even Kahn, in his quite original ordering, puts it first. Kahn, *Art and Thought*, 29. The D-K ordering, of course, attempts to be interpretively as neutral as possible, since it follows only the alphabetical order of the later sources from which each saying is derived. This hardly escapes interpretation, since it gives the inevitable impression that there is no λόγος to this discourse on λόγος.

4. Plato, *Apology* 38a: "The unexamined life is not worth living for a human being."

5. ἐπαΐοντας, which I here translate as "hearkening to," should be heard as privileging the sense of hearing. "Paying heed to" is a more common translation, but it does not quite preserve the strong auditory invocation.

6. As in Kahn, *Art and Thought*, 79.

7. D-K 96.

8. They will thus be forerunners of the "preservers" in Martin Heidegger, *The Origins of the Work of Art*, trans. Albert Hofstadter (New York: Harper and Row, 1971), 15–87.

9. Kahn, *Art and Thought*, 214–215.

10. Kahn, quite plausibly, suggests that since the source for this saying, Marcus Aurelius, is quoting from memory, the saying might not be accurate, and he suggests, again plausibly, that perhaps not much can be made of this saying.

11. Kahn's discussion of this saying is as usual very helpful, particularly in his relating of this saying to the many cosmological sayings that attest to how one thing turns into its opposite and thus survives as its opposite. Kahn, *Art and Thought*, 220–227.

12. D-K 102.

13. To make this clear to students, I sometimes hold a pencil still in my hand, ask them if they can "see" it, then begin to shake it around as fast as I can, and ask them if they can still "see" it as well.

14. However, Stanley Rosen argued long ago that the grasping metaphor first began to emerge strongly in Aristotle. See his "Thought and Touch: A Note on Aristotle's *De Anima*," chap. 7 in *The Quarrel between Philosophy and Poetry* (New York: Routledge, 1988).

15. See especially Luce Irigaray, *An Ethics of Sexual Difference*, trans. Carolyn Burke and Gillian C. Gill (Ithaca, NY: Cornell University Press, 1993), especially the chapter "The Fecundity of the Caress." This momentous transformation is surely worth its own study. It should be acknowledged that Sartre, in his famous phenomenology of the caress in *Being and Nothingness*, sees the caress as by no means lessening the element of control, even though it may be less manifestly violent.

16. See Victor Zuckerkandl, *Sound and Symbol*, trans. Willard Trask and Norbert Guterman (New York: Pantheon Books, 1956), for an excellent discussion of this.

17. D-K 115. Or, to cite another famous Heraclitean metaphor, like the flow of a river: "As they step into the same rivers, other and still other waters flow upon them" (D-K 12; see also D-K 91).

18. Eva Brann, *The Logos of Heraclitus* (Philadelphia: Paul Dry Books, 2011), especially chap. 3.

19. Plato, *Symposium* 187a–b. Brann is excellent on this; see Brann, *Logos of Heraclitus*, 72. Eryximachus, we could say, is "softer" than Heraclitus.

20. For others, see D-K 61, 84a, 91, 102, and 126.

21. D-K 102.

22. D-K 50.

23. For an excellent account of Heidegger's reading of Heraclitus's *polemos*, see Gregory Fried, *Heidegger's Polemos: From Being to Politics* (New Haven, CT: Yale University Press, 2000), especially chap. 1.

24. Plato, *Laws* 803c–d.

25. D-K 112.

# Bibliography

Brann, Eva. *The Logos of Heraclitus*. Philadelphia: Paul Dry Books, 2011.

Fried, Gregory. *Heidegger's Polemos: From Being to Politics*. New Haven, CT: Yale University Press, 2000.

Heidegger, Martin. *The Origins of the Work of Art*. Translated by Albert Hofstadter. New York: Harper and Row, 1971.

Irigaray, Luce. *An Ethics of Sexual Difference*. Translated by Carolyn Burke and Gillian C. Gill. Ithaca, NY: Cornell University Press, 1993.

Kahn, Charles. *The Art and Thought of Heraclitus*. Cambridge: Cambridge University Press, 1979.

Rosen, Stanley. "Thought and Touch: A Note on Aristotle's *De Anima*." Chap. 7 in *The Quarrel between Philosophy and Poetry*. New York: Routledge, 1988.

Zuckerkandl, Victor. *Sound and Symbol*. Translated by Willard Trask and Norbert Guterman. New York: Pantheon Books, 1956.

DREW A. HYLAND is Charles A. Dana Professor of Philosophy Emeritus at Trinity College, Hartford, Connecticut. He has written books on ancient Greek philosophy, continental philosophy, and philosophy of sport.

# 2

## SOUND, WATER, AND THE UNITY OF LIFE IN EMPEDOCLES

Michael M. Shaw, Utah Valley University

> **How both tall trees and fish in the sea**
> (πῶς καὶ δένδρεα μακρὰ καὶ εἰνάλιοι καμασῆνες)
>
> —Empedocles B72

## 1. Introduction

A brief analysis in Theophrastus's *De sensu* preserves three words of Empedocles's theory of hearing through the enigmatic fragment B99: "Hearing is like a 'bell (κώδωνα)' with equal sounds, which he calls a 'fleshy branch (σάρκινον ὄζον)'" (A86 and B99).[1] Κώδωνα and σάρκινον ὄζον reveal much in their brevity. The "bell" provides a technological analogy that contrasts with the lantern of fragment B84, used by Empedocles to explain vision. Reading the "fleshy branch" as a telescoped metaphor captures the extent to which he not only attributes properties of plants to animals but more surprisingly attributes properties of animals to plants. These poetic images structure a hierarchy of life that ascribes hearing and other sensations to all living things, including "a bush" (B117) and "tall trees" (B72). Additionally, Pseudo-Aristotle's *On Plants* notes that Empedocles furnishes plants with desire, pleasure, and pain.[2] With sensation and desire belonging to vegetative life, sight alone distinguishes animals from plants and initiates in them the powers of locomotion and sexual reproduction. Vision, a specialized kind of sensation that excludes all plant life, therefore cannot represent an all-encompassing account of perception.

Empedocles's "fleshy branch" circumscribes a basic cluster of sensations infused within every mortal organism that includes touch, taste, smell, and hearing. As a more widely distributed sensation, hearing better captures the unity of life in Empedoclean thought than the limiting conception of vision, which is unique to animal life. An analysis of sound and hearing shows that, unlike Aristotle, Empedocles attributes sensation, desire, and meaningful experience to everything that grows and dies on the earth. While touch, smell, and even taste (along with desire and pleasure) may in some way also be attributed to all mortal creatures by Empedocles,[3] hearing holds a special place. Of the bundle of powers that begins with plants and infiltrates all living things, hearing is the most thoroughly public sense. Along with sight and locomotion, hearing allows for defense and copulation. When elevated to voice, it initiates more complex social organization, and by becoming speech it can produce wisdom and understanding. In stark contrast to Plato and Aristotle, Empedocles's starting point for knowledge is not sight but hearing.

By describing the inner workings of an animal ear as a "fleshy branch," Empedocles connects the power of hearing to plant life. While bushes and trees have neither flesh nor ears, they do possess branches. The metaphor of "fleshy branch" attributes some aspect of the hearing process to plants just as it attributes a plantlike structure to the ears of animals. This paper shows how plant life, as the simplest and most primordial sort of mortal life for Empedocles, includes a rudimentary capacity for hearing, along with pleasure, pain, desire, smell, taste, and touch. These powers form an essential constellation of abilities that belong to all perishable creatures, not only to animal life.

Unlike the Aristotelian view, which excludes plants from all sensation, pleasure, and pain and distinguishes plants from animals by the capacities for sensation, desire, and locomotion, Empedocles alternatively employs the capacities for sight, voice, and speech to differentiate between orders of living creatures. This scheme maintains four levels of perishable organisms: (1) plants, which contain the basic cluster of abilities including sensation, pleasure, pain, and desire; (2) mute but seeing fish, which are the first level of life to participate in sexual reproduction and local movement; (3) land animals, which have voice, ears, developed limbs, and more elaborate socialization; and (4) humans, who have all of these powers nested within them and add speech and understanding.

Empedocles's most unusual description of fish as καμασῆνες, which could be translated as "wagging vine poles," combined with the epithets of "prolific [πολυσπερής]" and "mute [ἄμουσος]," link plants and fish together as the two simplest forms of organized and perishable life. He thus maintains a hierarchy very different from Aristotle's, insofar as he prioritizes hearing over sight since higher-order creatures are distinguished from fish first by voice and then by speech. While vision separates the two simplest forms of life from each other, hearing is accentuated in terms of knowledge and understanding. Both Plato and Aristotle emphasize the special relationship of sight to producing understanding in humans—Plato through the analogy of the sun in *Republic* 6 and Aristotle through the praise of vision in the opening paragraph of *Metaphysics* 1.1.[4] Empedocles, then, provides the framework for an alternative epistemology to this tradition that grounds knowledge more forcefully in sound and speech than in vision.

This paper first elucidates distinct Platonic and Aristotelian interpretations of Empedocles, developing Plato's genealogy of flow as described in the *Theaetetus* in contrast to Aristotle's materialistic account of his predecessors in *Metaphysics*. Both philosophers explain how the divine status of the roots in Empedoclean thought should be contextualized in relation to early Greek philosophy, when poets and philosophers battled over the core material forces of the cosmos and their relationship to the gods. This history of contention culminates in Empedocles's conception of four coeval, living roots (ῥιζώματα), together with love and strife. Maintaining the Platonic account over the Aristotelian, ῥιζώματα are seen to describe four different senses of flow or flux rather than four distinct material elements that can be combined and neatly separated from each other.

With the flowing and animate character of the roots established, the argument turns to the prevalence and priority of hearing in the fragments, especially those considered by Diels and other editors to come earliest in the poem. Empedocles often uses verbs indicative of flowing liquid to describe sound, voice, and speech, supporting the interpretation that sound travels via fluid rather than atomistic effluences. His treatment shows that as hearing begins in sound and culminates in speech, it provides the origin and end of human understanding.[5]

The investigation then moves to how the ontological foundation of the roots grounds Empedocles's theory of sensation, consisting of various streams of ἀπορροαί flowing through a fluid plenum into unique and discreet passageways. Developing his account of sight and hearing shows that mixture of the roots is a condition for the possibility of sensation. In a theory of Empedoclean predominance, each sense is also associated with one root singularly capable of destructively overwhelming that sense. His technological analogies of the lantern and bell elucidate two distinct forms of sensation. The advanced lantern describes the most unique and complex organ that distinguishes animal existence, while the basic bell better captures the experiential foundation of all life. Water, the most obviously flowing root, becomes the paradigm for understanding all of the roots according to the Platonic interpretation followed here, just as hearing is the most significant sensation for the sake of understanding the union of and connection between all mortal life. This coprioritization of water and hearing suggests a deeper connection between the two. This is further reinforced by the essential relationship of both fish and plants to water, supporting an Empedoclean theory of sensory predominance in which sound is communicated primarily through water just as light is transmitted through fire.

The paper concludes by taking up this essential group of sensations into the foundation of a hierarchy that emphasizes the unity of all living things. Aristotle's discussion of flavor in *De sensu* reveals that Empedocles maintains close affinity between water and plants. The fragments also connect plants and fish as the two most basic forms of organic life, both of which lack voice and hold an irreducible relationship to water. These bonds between sound and water, hearing and plants, and water and plants form an Empedoclean syllogism disclosing a hierarchy of life very different from Aristotle's. The latter elevates animal life as "more honorable [τιμιώτερα]" than that of plants by binding sensation intrinsically to desire and locomotion.[6] Empedocles's theory of sensation is grounded first in hearing instead of vision, emphasizing effluences of flowing streams rather than particles suggestive of atomism and promoting water over fire as the basic root from which to understand the others.[7]

## 2. The Platonic Interpretation

The fifth century BCE Sicilian philosopher and poet from Acragas is renowned for his theory of sensation, perhaps best known from Plato's *Meno*. There, Socrates asks Meno if he and Gorgias "both say that there are certain effluences [ἀπορροάς] of existing things, as Empedocles held . . . And passages [πόρους] into which and through which the effluences [αἱ ἀπορροαί] pass" (*Meno* 76c). This marks one of only two passages among authentic

Platonic works that mention Empedocles by name. The second is at *Theaetetus* 152e, where Socrates includes Empedocles with Heraclitus, Protagoras, and the majority of the wise as followers of Homer and the doctrine that like Oceanus, everything flows. Taken together, these passages constitute a Platonic interpretation of Empedocles that asserts effluences of all four roots and that their mixtures always flow like rivers as continuous, liquid streams.[8]

James Eric Butler demonstrates that the key terms from the *Meno*, ἡ ἀπορροή and ὁ πόρος, are best understood as fluid streams. Both W. K. C. Guthrie and M. R. Wright point out that πόρος means "a ford" in Homer, with Guthrie noting that "there is no gap in the water of the river until a body makes its way through."[9] Thus, ὁ πόρος designates a means of passing a river, a ford; it is a way through something and, most originally in Homer, a way to pass through water. Ἡ ἀπορροή, effluence or effluvium, means a flowing off, a stream, or an emanation.[10] Based on a large body of testimony and fragment B89, "of all things that have come to be there are effluences [ἀπορροαί]," these effluences are the likely source of all sensation, nutrition, and experience for Empedocles. Upon developing an account of color grounded in effluences, the *Meno*'s Socrates concludes that this "enables you to tell what sound [φωνήν] and smell [ὀσμὴν] are, and numerous other things of this kind [καὶ ἄλλα πολλὰ τῶν τοιούτων]" (*Meno* 76d–e). Although Plato's Socrates here upholds sight as the model sense, dismissing the others as following obviously from this primary instance, this may result from the Platonic preference for sight as a model for knowledge.

The influence of Protagoras on Theaetetus is as profound as that of Gorgias on Meno. In both eponymous dialogues, Plato suggests that all four of them owe much to Empedocles, the likely teacher of Gorgias. While Socrates's analysis focuses on Protagoras and Heraclitus, Theaetetus's definition that "knowledge is simply perception" (*Theaetetus* 151e) is held to be Empedocles's own view.[11] Socrates attributes this definition to a host of thinkers, and first to Homer: "Let us take it as a fact that all the wise men of the past, with the exception of Parmenides, stand together. Let us take it that we find on this side of Protagoras and Heraclitus and Empedocles; and also the masters of the two kinds of poetry, Epicharmus in comedy and Homer in tragedy. For when Homer talked about 'Ocean, begetter of gods, and Tethys their mother,' he made all things the offspring of flux [ῥοῆς] and motion" (152e). By naming Empedocles, Socrates includes the Acragantine in the followers of flux who constitute a philosophical army "led by Homer as general" (153a, Loeb) that battles against Parmenides alone in championing flux and flow as the source of all things, thereby maintaining that all being is in motion rather than at rest. Taken with the definition of color in the *Meno*, these passages—both focused on the relationship between knowledge and sensation—represent a Platonic interpretation of Empedocles's theory of perception as consisting of myriad effluences flowing like streams and currents through an effectively liquid plenum.[12]

Socrates rests his case on a citation from *Iliad* 14 regarding Oceanus and Tethys, two ancient water deities belonging to the generation of the titans in Hesiod. This Homeric passage holds a unique significance in the Platonic-Aristotelian tradition, quoted here, recalled later by Theodorus as "the tribe of Homer" at 179e, also quoted by Socrates at *Cratylus* 402b to support the view that all things are streams, and then cited by Aristotle in *Metaphysics* A in the context of Thales and the origins of materialism. Not only Heraclitus, so famously portrayed through this river analogy, but also Empedocles is implicated by this interpretation.[13] Homer's army spans Thales to Empedocles, includes philosophers and poets, and connects forces as divergent as water, fire, Zeus, and motion.

An etymological understanding of ἀπορροή and πόρος suggests a genealogy of flux culminating in Empedocles's four roots, best understood as four diverse ways of flowing. A πόρος (a ford or unapparent passageway) and an ἀπορροή (an effluence or flowing away from) correspond to suggest a system of multifarious discrete and coherent streams (ῥεύματα) emanating from all things and into all things, some of them occasionally fording into ports of sensory organs. Instead of atoms and void, Empedocles repeatedly asserts an entirely full universe, such as in B13, "Nothing void in the totality: whence then would anything else come to be?" and B14, "There is no place in the totality that is empty or overflowing." The key terms ἡ ἀπορροή and ὁ πόρος better suit an interpretation of Empedocles grounded in fluid dynamics than one tending toward atomism.[14] Continuous streams of effluences ford the plenum of the cosmos, and when a certain effluence flows into an appropriate pore, sensation occurs. Unlike particles fitting into holes of appropriate shapes and sizes, in the Platonic interpretation, ἀπορροαί are streams fording various channels, crisscrossing other streams, and flowing into caverns, crags, channels, and ports, as they work their way through a plenum and into sensory organs.

Aristotle completely neglects the Platonic focus on flow in *Metaphysics* A.3's analysis of Thales. He cites the same passage from *Iliad* 14 quoted by both Socrates and Theodorus in the *Theaetetus*, "for they made ocean and Tethys the parents of creation" (983b29–33). Aristotle takes from this that Thales "says the principle is water" (983b20).[15] His analysis of Thales from 983b20 to 984a4 includes a discussion of the Homeric citation but makes no reference to flow, flux, or streams. This clarifies the primary divergence between the Platonic and Aristotelian interpretations of their predecessors: where the former advocates a genealogy of flow, the latter prefers a genealogy of materialism.

According to Plato, this theory of effluences represents one of the great achievements of the four-hundred-year struggle of this tradition. This stands in stark contrast to the more influential Aristotelian interpretation of Empedocles, which situates effluences within a rudimentary Democritean atomism in *On Generation and Corruption*.[16] Despite their divergence, however, both Plato and Aristotle prioritize vision in their interpretations: in the *Meno*, Socrates dismisses the other senses as following from the account of sight; Aristotle, who gives the most robust treatment of Empedocles on sight among the five senses, develops his view by considering how effluences fit into pores in vision.[17] The Platonic genealogy of flow accommodates Empedocles's cosmological plenum more authentically than Aristotelian materialism, which leads to confusion with atomism and ultimately to the demand for void to account for the theory of sensation through pores. While Plato may lead us astray because of his preferential treatment of sight, his genealogy of flow better captures the foundation of Empedocles's thought than Aristotle's genealogy of matter as elements.

## 3. Hear First

Empedocles emerges as leading the army of flow with his account of the roots as four equal and coeternal divinities. Unlike in Hesiod, they are not born first but exist perpetually, and the cosmic cycle occurs only as a product of their mixture through love and strife. Water, earth, fire, and aither do not make the gods; for Empedocles, they are the gods. He does not combine, as Aristotle suggests, different conceptions of matter—the liquid water of Thales with the misty air of Anaximenes with the burning fire of Heraclitus, contributing a solid conception of earth either on his own or from the poetic tradition including Xenophanes.[18] The influence of the era does weigh heavily on him insofar as Empedocles conceives not of flowing water and static earth but of four different senses of flow, each with its own nature (φύσις), character (ἦθος), and domain (τιμῆς).[19] These are not four different material elements that can be neatly combined and separated from each other but four different ways of flowing, or four different kinds of currents streaming and communicating through a totality composed of only the mixture of these four interconnected roots.

The theory of pores develops from the idea of streams and fording rivers. Understanding the roots as four distinct conceptions of flowing streams within a plenum interacting as currents in a system reminiscent of fluid dynamics, instead of anything resembling atomism or particles, facilitates an interpretation of pores and effluences etymologically consistent with Empedocles's language. His account of sensation, grounded in effluences and pores, involves the uninterrupted continuity of these streams. Water most clearly captures this flow characteristic of all the roots. Before exploring the possible connection between the root of water, the transmission of sound, and the sense of hearing, I must develop the unique significance of hearing in Empedocles's extant fragments.

Fragment B6 identifies four roots (ῥιζώματα) as coequal, irreducible ruling sources. Empedocles only names four Olympian deities, but they are widely agreed to signify what Aristotle calls the four elements.[20] Exactly how they map onto each other is a source of controversy, except the relationship between Nestis and water because Empedocles provides more detail with her epithet than any of the others:

> The four roots of all things hear first [τέσσαρα γὰρ πάντων ῥιζώματα πρῶτον ἄκουε]:
> shining Zeus, life-giving Hera, Aidoneus [Ζεὺς ἀργὴς Ἥρη τε φερέσβιος ἠδ᾽ Ἀιδωνεύς],
> and Nestis, who by her tears moistens the mortal spring [Νῆστίς θ᾽, ἡ δακρύοις τέγγει κρούνωμα βρότειον]. (B6)

The four ῥιζώματα, "root clumps" or "root systems," of all things each serve as a "foundation" and "living source of increase and growth" as well as a "basic nature." Everything consists of only these four sources being perpetually mixed and separated by the powers of love and strife according to precise and complex ratios. Zeus, Hera, Aidoneus, and Nestis represent fire, aither, earth, and water. Hera's aither gives life, and Zeus's fire shines for sight.[21]

Before identifying the divine avatars of the roots, Empedocles demands not that we know or see them but that we "hear first [πρῶτον ἄκουε]." This most clearly indicates that we should first hear (ἄκουε) the four ῥιζώματα given their primacy as principles in Empedocles. However, it also suggests that the first thing we should do is hear. Butler notes that Nestis receives the longest and clearest epithet, which he attributes to her significance as the most obviously flowing of the roots.[22] Poetically, this suggests a connection between hearing at the beginning and water at the end of the fragment, asserting some degree of primacy to and perhaps also a relationship between sound and water.

Empedocles demands not only that we hear the four roots first but also that hearing itself is first. B6 is, however, notoriously unclear on what he is saying and what we are hearing, with the exception of Nestis's relationship to water. No matter how each divinity maps onto the roots, Empedocles may conceive of them all as flowing streams, as Plato insists in the *Theaetetus*. Attention to the interrelationship between flow and hearing will draw out the common characteristic of flow shared by all the roots.

Empedocles's use of "tears [δακρύα]," "moisten [τέγγει]," and "spring [κρούνωμα]" definitively identifies Nestis with the root of water. However, these terms also call to mind the mixture of water and earth. *Τέγγειν* means to moisten or soften and would describe the mixing of earth and water to make clay. Κρούνωμα, or springs, are water streaming from the earth (and have a direct relation to Tethys). Δακρύα, tears, of course, are notoriously salty.[23] All three cases indicate that water, in its mortal state (βρότειος), is always mixed with or flowing from the earth. As such, water will be of more or less pure degrees, allowing for different mixtures of mostly water to intermingle with each other as sustained, self-identical streams within a larger watery or airy milieu. Earth in Empedocles is said to flow, and the mixture of water and earth is necessary for flavor in Empedocles's account of taste as preserved by Aristotle.[24]

Interpreting the first line of fragment B6 as relating not only to the priority of the roots but also to the importance of hearing for Empedocles suggests a possible priority to hearing in some sense, although Empedocles highly values each of the senses in their own right.[25] Because of the full line of detail, B6 also suggests a similar prioritization of water. The clarity and detail of the description of Nestis indicate a heightened significance placed on water, indicating a relationship first between sound and water and further between water, sound, and the other roots, especially earth, considering Nestis's three mixtures of water and earth. The four ῥιζώματα, living sources of growth, also constitute a metaphor taken from vegetative life. The four gods, the most fundamental and divine sources, are like plants in their most intrinsic operations; and plants, then, are like gods.

The Empedoclean prioritization of hearing is supported by fragments beyond B6, as all of the fragments considered by Diels to be among the first six emphasize the priority of hearing, which, while different from sound, requires sound. B1 apparently opened Empedocles's *On Nature* with a greeting to his friend from Acragas: "Pausanias, son of prudent Anchites, *hearken* [σὺ δὲ κλῦθι]." The imperative κλῦθι means "give ear to or to hear."[26] *You hear me*; hearken; listen to me. The verb emphasizes the connection between hearing and knowing. Empedocles first demands to be heard in order to be understood. Unlike Plato's analogy of the sun in *Republic* 6 or the opening of Aristotle's *Metaphysics* 1, the starting point to knowledge in Empedocles is hearing, not sight.

Fragment B2 speaks of the inadequate knowledge of the majority who are persuaded by only their limited experience: everyone "claims to have found the whole [τὸ δ' ὅλον]. Thus, these things are neither beheld [ἐπιδερκτά] by men, nor heard [ἐπακουστά], nor comprehended by mind [νόωι περιληπτά]" (lines 7–8). Empedocles lists three failures of human beings: ἐπιδερκτὰ, from ἐπιδερκόμαι, "to look upon, behold"; ἐπακουστά, from ἐπακούω, "to listen to or hearken to; to hear" (LSJ, s.v.); and νόωι περιληπτά, to be comprehended by mind. Each of these corresponds to a true form of beholding or seeing, hearing or hearkening, and understanding. Hearing, too, is a way to know.[27]

Perhaps no fragment emphasizes the importance of speech and hearing more than B3, lines 1–8 (emphasis mine):

> But you gods, turn away from my *tongue* their madness,
> And from *holy mouths channel a pure fountain.*
> [ἐκ δ'ὁσίων στομάτων καθαρὴν ὀχετεύσατε πηγήν]
> And you, *Muse* [Μοῦσα], white-armed memorious maiden,
> I implore: what things are fit for creatures of day *to hear*,
> Send, driving your compliant chariot from the house of Reverence.
> Do not be forced to pluck the blossoms of illustrious honor
> From mortals, by boldly *saying* more than is holy,
> And then to sit on the heights of wisdom.

The fragment begins with Empedocles's own tongue and holy mouths, seeking a divine muse for truth instead of the madness of humanity. In the first instance, this fragment, placed third by Diels, second by Wright, and fourth by Graham, conceives of speech as a pure fountain or stream flowing from holy mouths. Most notably, speech, conveyed by sound and hearing in line 4, is understood directly as a flowing stream. Empedocles emphasizes hearing the pure stream or fountain flowing from the holy mouths of the muse to mortal creatures, as opposed to the madness infiltrating Empedocles's own tongue. Sound flows like water.

Empedocles's demand to "channel a pure fountain [καθαρὴν ὀχετεύσατε πηγήν]" holds metaphorical reverberations from its etymological origins. Ὀχετεύσατε (from ὀχετεύω) first appears in Empedocles and Herodotus and means "to channel, as a stream in a ditch." This verb derives from ὀχετηγός (itself etymologically from ὀχετ + ἀγῶ), used by Homer in *Iliad* 21.257 during Achilles's battle with the river Xanthus.[28] The flowing river makes a mighty roar and chases Achilles. Homer develops a simile to capture this moment:

> And on his [Achilles's] chest the bronze rang terribly while he swerved from beneath the flood and fled ever onward, and the river followed after, flowing [ῥέων] with a mighty roar [ὀρυμαγδῷ]. As a man who guides its flow [ὀχετηγὸς] leads from a dusky spring a stream of water [ὕδατι ῥόον] among his plants and garden plots, a mattock in his hands, and clears away the dams from the channel, and as it flows all the pebbles beneath are swept along, and it glides swiftly onward with murmuring sound down a sloping place and outstrips even him who guides it, just so did the flood of the river ever overtake Achilles, fleet of foot though he was; for the gods are mightier than men. (21.254–264)

The passage highlights the sound of the conflict, the bronze of Achilles's armor clanging terribly and the river roaring mightily. The sound of bronze (such as a bell) and the sound of water appear loudest in Homer, who here develops a simile of irrigation. As farmers lead the flow of a river to their crops, so does the river alter its course in chasing after Achilles. Empedocles, using the same basic term for irrigation, develops his own telescoped metaphor: as one diverts a stream from a river to a farm, so does one channel the true divine speech of the muses from among the infinite chatter of the multitude into one's ear.

Πηγή means "running water" in Homer and is always plural.[29] To channel a pure stream (καθαρὴν ὀχετεύσατε πηγήν) means to find a single stream, an effluence of sound transformed into speech, and divert it from out of the totality of language into one's own ears, as if irrigating a field. The flowing character of this pure stream is represented by the meter and thus flowing music of Empedocles's poetry. That language, sound, and hearing are described in terms of such a vivid metaphor of water and passageways is more than a mere analogy for Empedocles. The theory of effluences is perfectly captured by the image of irrigating fields with ditches drawn off from a larger source of flowing water. Similarly, effluvia traveling as sound into ears are easily understood through this metaphor. Empedocles's persistent use of aquatic imagery such as water, streams, irrigation ditches, and fountains again confirms Socrates's interpretation of the flowing river Oceanus in the *Theaetetus*: flowing water as the source of all things.

Fragment B3 describes hearing in terms of an Oceanic stream. Like B1 and B2, it emphasizes beginning from hearing and adds from the flowing language of the muse (Μοῦσα) in order to learn wisdom. Like Homer, Empedocles finds that gods are stronger than mortals, and the pure stream carries only what the divine muse thinks fit for mortal ears. Rather than learn everything through divine speech, which seems too powerful for mortals, humans must move from the liquid language of the muse, following its directive, to the equal authority of the other senses, as the concluding lines of B3 demand:

> But come, behold [ἄθρει] each thing by every means it is clear,
> Not holding any *view* more reliable than *hearing*,
> Nor resounding *hearing* beyond the clarifications of *tongue*;
> Nor from any of the other things, by which there is a *passageway* to
> understanding [πόρος ἐστὶ νοῆσαι],
> Withhold trust, but understand each thing in the way it is clear.
> (Translation modified; emphasis mine)

Empedocles places "view" and "hearing" on equal footing,[30] and both rival language, the clarifications of the tongue. Hearing, vision, and language all offer something of their own to wisdom. Speech and the tongue designate a different sense for Empedocles than sound and hearing, although both are conveyed through the ear in humans. Not only hearing but "other things" offer "a passageway to understanding [πόρος ἐστὶ νοῆσαι]" beyond the truths of vision and speech, likely smell, taste, and touch. With this rare use of πόρος, Empedocles indicates that every sense offers pores to understanding, through which effluences ostensibly can pass. Plato seems to pick up on precisely the generalization of "any of the other things" in the *Meno* when Socrates insists that smell, hearing, and the other senses are like sight. B3, however, emphasizes that all the senses should be understood in terms of pores and flow and does not ground this conception in vision.

Other fragments draw attention to the flowing character of the roots—for example, B115, lines 8–11, "Sea *spews* him onto the surface of the earth, and earth to the *rays* of the shining sun, who casts him into the *whirls* of aither"; B21, lines 3–6, "Sun, shining to sight and everywhere hot, immortal things which are *soaked in heat* and blazing beam, *and rain, dark* and chilling in everything, and *from earth flow* out intertwined and solid things"; and B39, "If the depths of earth and plentiful aither are unbounded, as the *words* coming vainly through the tongue of the mouths of many are *poured out*, of those who have seen little of the totality" (emphasis mine). These passages from B3, B21, B39, and B115 capture Empedocles's basic theory of sensation. Like Theaetetus, he believes that knowledge, understanding, and wisdom are all sensation. They emerge from the proper attunement to each sense through its unique πόρος. We can say from B3 that sight, sound, and language all have distinct pores and effluvia and that there are others as well. While this fragment begins with the holy speech of the muses, B1, B2, and B6 proclaim the heightened significance of hearing as the starting point of knowledge for Empedocles. From these four fragments, Empedocles finds hearing and sound to be (1) understood in terms of water and flowing streams, (2) the starting point of understanding, and (3) the first model for pores and effluences.

Fragments B4 and B5 also develop the theme of hearing, language, and sound with little mention of sight:

> Moreover, base men very much distrust authorities;
> but as the assurance of our *muse* [μούσης] bids,
> know, analyzing the *speech* [λόγοιο] in your heart. (B4; emphasis mine)

The theme of the muse and her musical, metrical language returns as the only true authority in B4. *Μοῦσα* means music as well as muse, and for Empedocles the muses will hold essential relationships to linguistic meter and melody as well as speech and sound. The linguistic, musical, and vocal authority holds the highest rank for Empedocles.

As is often the case with Empedocles, B5 uses an unusual word for the context: "Shelter in your mute wits [Στεγάσσι φρενὸς ἔλλοπος εἴσω]," which, according to Plutarch, Empedocles apparently insists of Pausanias.[31] Again, a traditionally early fragment appeals to sound, this time to its absence, in imploring Pausanias, "in Pythagorean fashion," not to reveal his teachings.[32] *Στεγάσσις* means "to shelter in an (often waterproof) covering." The genitive of *ἔλλοψ*, *ἔλλοπος* means "mute, of fish," and is originally found in Hesiod (LSJ, s.v.). It is likely that a Greek of Empedocles's world would have a difficult time hearing *ἔλλοπος* and not recalling fish. Empedocles commands Pausanias to take cover from the endless flowing chatter in his own silence just as fish navigate through water in silence.

With his use of ἔλλοψ, Empedocles not only demands silence of his disciple but recalls an important feature of fish in early Greek biology: they lack all voice but can hear. This is exactly what is demanded of Pausanias, to hear without exercising speech. While this demands that Pausanias act like a fish, it also develops the characteristics of fish when compared with other fragments. Fish hold an important place in Empedoclean thought as a stage both in biological development and in the cycle of reincarnation. Ultimately, mute fish will demonstrate at least three things for Empedocles: (1) that sound travels through water, (2) that it is possible to hear without having voice, and (3) that voice and speech are capacities that belong to animals after hearing and sight have been acquired.[33] Some of these characteristics will turn out to be shared with plants, which seem one step lower than fish on the Empedoclean scale, as they lack eyes and vision as well as voice. Their foundational relationship to the four roots and their often-emphasized close relationship to water and fish may indicate that mute plants, too, hear through water and that ultimately all hearing occurs as effluences of linguistic streams traveling through a plenum, with some relationship to water. Should appropriate effluences encounter an ear, hearing will be much improved.

By demanding to hear the four roots first, B6 reveals the primacy of the roots as the sources of all things. These four ῥιζώματα, or root clumps such as would belong to a massive tree, are the foundations and ever-present basic natures of mortal creatures; yet they also serve as living sources of growth that interact with the powers of love and strife. When examined alongside the other traditionally early Empedoclean fragments, the additional prioritization of hearing emerges. B1–B5 all reinforce the significance of hearing and the relationship between sensation and flow. By understanding his arche as roots, Empedocles champions the foundational character of plant life. By insisting that we hear them, he advocates the primacy of sound. Through the extensive description of Nestis in B6 and the use of liquid metaphors in the other traditionally early fragments, he indicates the priority of water. As developed below, sound, water, and plant life form a primordial triumvirate for Empedocles.

## 4. Sensation and the Four Roots

Hearing provides the common foundation to organized life and speech the most specialized tool for revealing the truth of the cosmos. All sensation occurs through effluences, for which the flow characteristic of water provides the basic account. All sensation also occurs, somehow, always by the self-perception of each root, in hylozoic fashion.[34] B109 comprises the most commonly quoted lines from all of Empedocles and describes these roots as being the sources of sensation. When it is first quoted in extant literature by Aristotle in *De anima* A.2, he too emphasizes the living nature of the ῥιζώματα. He writes, "Empedocles declares that it is formed out of all his elements [στοιχείων], *each of them also being soul* [εἶναι δὲ καὶ ἕκαστον ψυχὴ τούτων]; his words are" (404b11–12; emphasis mine):

> By earth we behold [ὀπώπαμεν] earth, by water water,
> by aither divine [δῖον] aither, but by fire blinding [ἀίδηλον] fire
> by affection affection, strife by dreadful [λυγρῶι] strife. (B109)

While Aristotle quotes Empedocles directly, his interpretation clouds the exact meaning of the fragment. *Ψυχή* appears once in the extant fragments, likely signifying the life of a mortal creature rather than a soul in a Platonic or Aristotelian sense.[35] Aristotle also anachronistically calls the roots "elements" (στοιχείων). However, he does notice that it is not precisely that the roots make up soul but that each of the roots is itself also soul. Sensation is so obviously associated with soul for Aristotle that he can't help but assume each root is soul, because each root perceives.

B109 distributes a single verb, ὀπώπαμεν,[36] across the four roots, love, and strife. All sensation occurs by the roots perceiving themselves. According to the theory of effluences, the roots that make up the living thing perceive the roots that make up the world through the connection of effluvia and pores. Empedocles attributes three adjectives directly to one of the six primary realities, but only one clearly relates directly to perception: *blinding* fire (πῦρ ἀίδηλον) emphasizes a unique connection between fire and vision. However, this connection is grounded in the destructive force of pure fire by itself, which does not cause vision but destroys it. The adjective ἀίδηλον, "making unseen, annihilating, destructive," strangely identifies the supposed cause of sight with the destruction of sight. Like staring directly into the sun, to behold pure fire would be blinding. This adjective, ultimately derived from ὁράω through an alpha privative, stands in stark opposition to the initial and thoroughly distributed verb ὀπώπαμεν.[37]

How does one behold, or see, with that which on its own destroys sight? For Empedocles, the roots, in their immortal purity, exceed the capacity for mortal comprehension or perception. Mortals, as mixed, can behold the roots only in mixed form. The pure ontological source is too powerful and must be mixed with other roots to be perceived at all. As blinding, fire by itself actually inhibits sight. Empedocles thus uses the sun as a metaphor for fire: the purest fire we can see is the most blinding light, the power of the sun. As Plato points out in *Republic* 6, excessive darkness and excessive brightness both destroy the power of sight. Aristotle extends this to hearing: "And as hearing apprehends both sound and silence, of which one is audible and the other is inaudible, and also over loud sound as sight does what is bright" (*De anima* 422a20).[38]

The oppositional use of ἀίδηλον and ὀπώπαμεν shows that fire by itself is blinding, so it must be mixed with the other roots to temper its overwhelming nature and become visible. In the same way, a direct relationship between sound and water would demand that water perceived without mixture would produce overwhelming, deafening sound that would be destructive of hearing, such as the blaring of bronze or the roaring of a river in Homer. Sensation requires mixture to temper the overwhelming power of these archaic sources in their ontological purity. Without mixture, there can be no sensation. At a limit moment in his cosmic cycle, when the roots as ontological realities exist in their pure and unmixed forms, ontic beings do not exist at all. Only by withdrawing from its purity into mixture does fire becomes less blinding and more visible and the other roots less overwhelming and more sensible.

In *De sensu* chapter 5, Aristotle discusses humans and animals being overwhelmed and destroyed by smells such as charcoal and sulfur (444b28–445a5), showing that the same power of blinding light belongs to destructive smells. In chapter 2 during a discussion of Empedocles in which he quotes the extensive fragment B84, Aristotle aligns each sense with one of his own four elements, perhaps in some way revising Empedocles's theory: "Evidently the following is the only method by which we can allot and adapt each of the sense organs to one of the elements" (438b17–19). He connects the eye and sight with water, hearing and sound with air, smell with fire, and touch and taste ("a form of touch") with earth (438b19–439a2). Empedocles does link a sense to a predominant root, but only according to its ἀίδηλον, or destructive, nature. The sun does not overwhelm hearing but only sight. The impossible roar of a mighty flowing river does not overwhelm smell but, on the hypothesis pursued here, only hearing. Insofar as a root is singularly capable of destroying a sense, it may be said to predominate that sense.

Theophrastus notes that for Empedocles the best capacity for sensation belongs to the best mixtures, the most evenly tempered mixtures of the four roots in which the destructive force of the source is both perfectly neutralized and maximally perceptible: "Those who have the elements in equal or nearly equal mixture and do not have them too far apart or again too small or excessive in measure are the most intelligent and have the most accurate sense perceptions."[39] Mortal creatures, having been mixed into compounds ontologically different from the purity of their essence as the four roots, sense the mixtures outside themselves through mixtures within themselves. The better the mixture, the better each sense is able to overcome the destructive power of a root in its purity and behold it.

Keeping in mind the destructive force of each root in its purity, fragments B84 and B99 both describe sensation according to an analogy based on human technology. As B99 compares hearing to a bell, B84 describes vision through an analogy between a lamp and the eye:

> As when someone contemplating a trip readies a lamp,
> a beam of shining fire for a winter night,
> attaching a screen to block winds from all directions,
> which scatter the breath of gusty winds,
> but light leaps out, insofar as it is more tenuous [ὅσον ταναώτερον ἦεν],
> and it shines over the threshold with untiring rays;
> just so primal fire [ὠγύγιον πῦρ] confined in membranes
> [and] fine tissues is hidden in a circular pupil,
> with the membranes sheltering it from the circulation of deep water,
> while it emits fire insofar as that is more tenuous [ὅσον ταναώτερον ἦεν].
> (B84)

As a lamp holds fire within a central area protected from the wind by a circular screen on a cold night, so is primal fire (ὠγύγιον, or ogygian, πῦρ) contained within the membranes of a circular pupil composed of deep water.[40] A subtle ring composition surrounds the core of this analogy. Empedocles notes in line 5 that the light leaps out of the lantern "insofar as it is more tenuous" while being protected from the winds by a screen and in line 10 that the eye emits fire "insofar as that is more tenuous," while the primal fire in the pupil is protected from the deep water of the eye by membranes. In both cases, the identical Greek phrase ὅσον ταναώτερον ἦεν brackets the analogy. Within this ring, the analogy has four components: first, the screen of a lantern as the membrane of an eye; second, gusty wind blowing out a fire as water circulating in an eyeball drowning out fire; third, the stretched-out fire of a lantern as the stretched-out primal fire within a pupil; and fourth, the screen protecting fire from wind in a lamp as the membrane protects fire from water in an eye.

The screen permits light to get out without wind getting in, as the membrane permits fire to get out without water getting in. In both cases, the fire emits effluvia from out of the source through the protective cover into the world. Perception must involve continuous streams of effluences that actually connect the perceiver to the source of the perception. The repeated ταναώτερον, "more tenuous"—really "more flowing, outstretched, and thin"—fire extends into a hostile environment and is protected from destruction by that environment by some sort of membrane or screen. The fire is more tenuous, more outstretched and thin, than the protective cover and is able to flow through it to connect the perceiving roots in the mortal creature with the perceptible roots in the world.

For Empedocles, then, sight involves effluences flowing both out of and into the eye. Aristotle's confusion clarifies Empedocles's view: "At times, then, he explains vision in this way, but at other times he accounts for it by emanations [ταῖς ἀπορροίααις] from objects seen" (438a4–5).[41] One explanation involves the light of the primal fire issuing from the eye as light issues from a lamp. The other involves effluences emanating from things seen. Aristotle fails to consider that this interrelationship would be best understood as streams flowing from things joining with streams flowing from eyes.

Theophrastus adds details to Aristotle's interpretation: "Empedocles says the same thing about all the senses, and claims that sensation results from things fitting into the pores (τοὺς πόρους τοὺς) of each sense."[42] Theophrastus first extends the account to all the senses and then develops the view that some pores fit together with specific effluences. The effluences related to sight do not fit into those related to smell or hearing, and so on. He references the lantern analogy: "[Empedocles] says fire is inside, and outside it [water], earth, and air, though which what is fine passes just as the light of a lantern. There are alternating pores for fire and water, of which we perceive white by those for fire, black by those for water, for each fits in the corresponding pore. And colors are conveyed to the sight through effluences (τὴν ἀπορροήν)."[43] This passage conveys two related aspects of Empedocles's theory of vision: first, the eye itself is composed of all the roots, fire and water as well as "earth and air"; second, vision sees all of the roots as effluences of color.

For Theophrastus, Empedocles clearly holds white to be the color of fire and black that of water here as well as in A69a. Fragments B21, B94, and B111 confirm the connection between water and black color for Empedocles. Additionally, in A92 Aëtius confirms the association between black and water and white and fire, and he adds that red is the color of earth and yellow of air (or, more likely, aither). This testimony suggests a four-color theory of primary colors grounded in the four roots.[44] Through effluences emanating from the strangely "ogygian" primal fire deep within the eye joining with effluences emanating toward the eye from things in the world, vision sees all of the roots through effluences of color. Theophrastus details how eyes can be hard or soft and have more or less water and more or less internal fire, how these different compositions of eyes see better or worse in various conditions, and how the construction of pores and effluences account for these differences. The best eye has the best blend: "It is best for the organ to be blended, and the best blend is a composition of equal parts of both (ἀμφοῖν) elements. And this is his account of sight."[45] While a perfect blend of fire and water is required for the best sight, earth and aither must also be involved in the constitution of the eye and the colors it sees.

Empedocles's theory of vision demonstrates that (1) mixture is required for sensation, (2) sight involves a very specialized and unusual primal fire in the eye itself that allows for the perception of colors, and (3) depending on their mixtures and constitutions, some eyes see better than others in different conditions. The first point clarifies that while sensation is by each root of itself, this never occurs in ontological purity. The second shows that sight and the capacity to perceive effluences of color involve a relationship to fire that the other senses lack. Without an eye and its primal fire, vision would be impossible for Empedocles. The third point illustrates a gradation of sensation in which more perfect eyes see better and less perfect eyes see poorly.

Empedocles's account of respiration in fragment B100 suggests that this gradation extends beyond better and worse organs. The word ῥινῶν in line 4 could mean either "skin" or "nose." Following Charles Kahn's conception of "studied ambiguity," M. R. Wright persuasively argues that "Empedocles supposed that primitive animal types breathe in and out through pores in the skin (and perhaps there is an implication that plants 'breathe' through their leaf surfaces), but in the higher animal types there are two particularly large 'holes' in the surface—the nostrils—which are primary examples of pore-breathing."[46] Breathing for Empedocles can occur through the organ of the nose with its nostrils or directly through microscopic pores in animal skin or plant leaves. The organ perfects the sense, so animals with the best mixtures of the roots in their nostrils will smell most perfectly. Plants and animals without nostrils breath through pores but do not have the same facility with smell, explaining how "in this way everything has a share of breath and smell" (B102). Aristotle agrees that "lungless" animals breathe and notes that the view was held by Democritus and others.[47]

## 5. Branch and Bell

The unique relationship between fire, sight, and eyes allows for better and worse eyes. For breathing and smell, however, the relationship to fire does not hold. Here, Empedocles extends the power of sensation beyond the specialized organ to the basic makeup of the living thing itself. One cannot see without eyes but can breathe and smell without a nose. Aristotle notes that fish smell underwater at *De sensu* 443a1–5. In Empedocles's theory of hearing, these points should be kept in mind. First, the relationship between fire and sight distinguishes vision from the other senses. Second, the ear improves the ability to hear sound well but it is not requisite for hearing.[48]

Empedocles captures the more intricate nature of vision through the simile of the lantern. This complex wonder of human technology improves on the more basic torch or fire, controlling the light with a sophisticated artifact. The simpler bell, while also a product of human technology, represents a more common artifact that captures a broader swath of organic diversity. Where the sophisticated lantern represents the distinction between plants and animals, the basic bell of fragment B99 captures both their dissimilarity manifested through the organ of the ear and their similarity insofar as both are perishable creatures imbued with the power to hear.[49] That is, Empedocles uses the more complicated technology of the lantern as an analogy for the more distinctive power of sight in animals. The more basic technology of the bell captures the prevalence of hearing throughout all forms of mortal life, including the most basic.

Aristotle oddly does not even mention Empedocles in his account of sound in *De anima* 2.8, and even more unusually, the discussion of sound in *De sensu*, promised in chapter 3 at 439a10–12, never occurs.[50] We cannot know why Aristotle neglects the treatment of sound and Empedocles's contribution to auditory theory. However, the Stagirite's focus on respiration, vision, and Empedocles's contributions to the understanding of both may have created a false picture for posterity. The extensive fragments B84 (on the lantern and sight) preserved in Aristotle's *De sensu* and B100 (on the clepsydra and respiration) preserved in Aristotle's *On Youth, Old Age, Life, Death, and Respiration* more likely provide an indication of Aristotle's interest rather than Empedocles's overall view. It is not that Empedocles prioritizes sight, breath, and smell over hearing but that Aristotle and his influence on posterity may give the false impression that this is the case.

Theophrastus, however, briefly reconstructs Empedocles's account of hearing, preserving incomplete but significant details of his view in spite of Aristotle's neglect: "Hearing comes about from sounds inside. For when [air] is set in motion by the voice, it echoes inside. Hearing is like a 'bell' with equal sounds (κώδωνα τῶν ἴσων), which he calls a 'fleshy branch' (σάρκινον ὄζον). Air in motion strikes against the solid parts and makes an echo."[51] Theophrastus relates much in this brief passage. Because hearing comes from "sounds inside," we know that Empedocles's σάρκινον ὄζον refers to the inner ear rather than the outer part of the ear, or the pinna. Σάρκινος, an adjective meaning "of the flesh or made of flesh" (LSJ, s.v.), is combined with ὄζος, a noun meaning bough, branch, or twig (LSJ, s.v.).[52] Quite literally, the metaphor describes "a branch made out of flesh." The analogy with plants is completely lost by Diels's proposed emendation of "fleshy bone (ὀστοῦν)" for "fleshy branch," which results not from textual corruption but from interpretive frustration.[53]

The bell inside the ear also has "equal sounds," which distinguishes it from the more irregular sounds of an actual bell or trumpet. This bell, hanging inside the ear and ringing with equal sounds, is what Empedocles calls a "fleshy branch." Aëtius preserves additional information in testimony A93 that supports this interpretation: "Empedocles says hearing comes about from the impact of air on cartilage, which he says hangs inside the ear like a bell swinging and clanging."[54] As swinging and clanging, the bell must hang inside the ear beyond immediate view, as we never observe this activity.

The bell and fleshy branch describe the inner structure of the ear according to metaphors derived from human technology and plant life. The technological bell suggests the perfection of hearing through equal sounds, which much like human technology improves on the natural condition. The more simplistic design of the bell than the lamp, together with the comparison to plant life, suggests that simpler forms of hearing exist, much like the distinction between respiration and smell through nostrils and through pores in the skin.

The fleshy branch as the inside of the ear suggests an analogy between pores in the ear and the circulatory system on the one hand and the vascular system of plants on the other. While plants lack the fleshy branch that produces equal sounds, their vegetative branches could maintain a relationship to hearing. This would most likely occur via water traveling through their roots and stems, an internal system of pores to deliver effluences. Lacking cartilage, plants would not have the equal sounds of the bell, but they would hear by the water distributed throughout their bodies.

Theophrastus's discussion contains textual corruption, where "air" is inserted. While this insertion may be likely, it would only be on an Aristotelian misinterpretation that confuses aither, air, and water in Empedocles.[55] Air is best understood as a modification of water, as moist but more diffuse, perhaps mixed with aither or fire rather than earth. Overall, the account is difficult to confidently develop from the testimony. It seems that watery air inside the ear provides a medium for effluences of sound to resound coherently as voice and speech. Based on the necessity of mixture for sensation, it seems that water would likely play an analogous role to fire in sight. The water in the ear makes hearing mixtures of the roots as effluences of sound possible.

The metaphor with tree and plant life suggests that as plants carry water through their roots and stems, so do effluences of water travel into the ear and resound in the body. Most importantly, relating the power of hearing to the anatomy of plant life indicates that plants also have the power of hearing. With evidence that plants smell, breathe, and feel pleasure and pain, it should not be surprising that plants would taste or hear for Empedocles. Aristotle's criticism of Empedocles in his analysis of flavor reveals a connection between plants, water, and taste. Never one-sided, Empedocles's consistent use of metaphor and analogy develops connections between two things. If hearing in animals holds a relationship to plant life, then plant life likely holds some relationship to hearing.

In his discussion of metaphor and analogy in *Poetics* chapter 21, Aristotle relies heavily on the work of Empedocles.[56] A telescoped metaphor is formed by transferring properties between disparate things: "Thus a cup is in relation to Dionysus what a shield is to Ares. The cup accordingly will be described as the 'shield of Dionysus' and the shield as 'the cup of Ares'" (1457b20–22). Similarly, "as old age is to life, so is evening to day. One will accordingly describe evening as the 'old age of the day'—or by the Empedoclean equivalent; and old age as the 'evening' or 'sunset of life'"

(1457b22–24). Sunset is the end of the day, and old age is the end of life. Both are beautiful, fleeting, and the limit of a set period. This pattern repeats itself throughout Empedocles, but the case at issue is most clear. As flesh is to animal, so branch is to plant. To describe the inner ear as a fleshy branch is to assert that both plants and animals have internal systems that carry effluences, that sound travels through such effluences, and that as animals hear through such a system, so do plants. Not only does the ear resemble vegetative life; vegetative life also possesses the relevant capacity of animal life.

## 6. Water and Plants

Aristotle's account of nutrition and flavor in relation to plants in *De sensu* proceeds by heavy criticism of Empedocles. This analysis reveals that unlike Aristotle, Empedocles holds a close relationship between water and nutrition. For Empedocles, plants receive nutrition through water they draw from the ground, but according to Aristotle, "the falsity of that [position] held by Empedocles is only too evident . . . their qualities are not due to their drawing anything from the water in the ground, but to a change which they undergo within the pericarp itself" (441a10–15). Aristotle criticizes Empedocles on two fronts. First, "water contains in itself the various kinds of savour, though in amounts so small as to be imperceptible, which is the doctrine of Empedocles" (441a4). Second, "on this theory they would enter water not because it is cold, but because it is wet" (477b30).[57] While Aristotle rejects both hypotheses, he confirms that Empedocles maintains an essential relationship between plants and water. Mixed effluences of roots, predominated to some extent by earth, travel through a watery plenum to nourish plant life and constitute the flavor of plants with respect to animal taste.

This lays a foundation for a theory of plant taste as one where effluences of flavor are carried through plant vascular systems. Aristotle believes that plants receive nutrition from the dry earth, and water serves mainly a cooling function in their metabolism. For Empedocles, plants need the wetness of the water to carry effluences of taste for the sake of their nutrition. Other evidence from testimonia confirms that water carries various effluences to plants through their roots, branches, and leaves. In A70, Aëtius relates,

> Empedocles says trees were the first living things to grow up from the earth. . . . Fruits are the surplus of water and fire in plants. And those having a shortage of moisture when it dries out in the summer shed their leaves, while those having more moisture keep their leaves, like

the bay, the olive, and the palm. Differences in flavors result [from] different compositions and plants' drawing nourishment from different materials in the soil, as in the case of the grapevine. What makes wine good is not the different varieties of vines, but the different compositions of the soil that nourishes them.[58]

Empedocles maintains a critical relationship between plants and water beyond only the effluences of taste intimated by Aristotle. Aëtius conveys that trees are the primordial type of life on the earth. Fruit involves excess water, and plants that have sufficient water do not shed their leaves. The contents of the earth are transmitted into plants through water to produce grapes and wine. All of this confirms that water carries various effluent mixtures throughout plants to cause both flavor and taste, as well as nourishment. Without mouth, tongue, nose, or nostrils, there is evidence that plants nevertheless experience rudimentary sensations associated with those organs.[59]

The "fleshy branch" fragment, as an Empedoclean telescoped metaphor, more clearly and directly attributes the sense of hearing to plants than the more accepted evidence for taste and smell. Smell, taste, and hearing share similar methods of organization into effluences: a flowing effluence with predominance of earth leads to taste, of aither leads to smell, and of water leads to hearing. As all sensation requires mixture, these effluences are distinguished from sight only by the lack of the primal fire within the eye. Thus, effluences of fire do not extend out of the organism without an eye, so the apprehension of color through vision requires an additional layer besides taste, smell, and hearing. Vision, then, becomes the distinguishing sense, a special case, and the opposite of what Socrates says at *Meno* 76d about using it as a model for the other senses. Vision requires the unusual outflow of the primal fire in the eye, while the other senses do not.

Because fire and light are only directly involved in sight, and because only it can destructively overwhelm sight, fire predominates sight. Plutarch preserves a line of Empedocles in a discussion of hearing at night in the dark: "Of night, solitary, blind-eyed" (B49). Without fire, there can be no sight, but there is still sound; and water, as black in color, can still transmit sound without light: "And you shall produce from black rain timely drought" (B111.6) and "rain, dark and chilling in everything" (B21.5). Only in sight do the more thinly stretched-out effluences of fire transmit color through what we call air, but for Empedocles air was a plenum perhaps composed of aither and water.

Evidence supports the notion that smell and taste occur without sense organs but are improved by sense organs. B99 adds hearing to this cluster of basic sensations that belong to every living thing and can permeate an organism through surface pores (such as breath and smell) or root and vascular systems (such as nutrition and taste). Because the inner ear constitutes the fleshy branch and bell swinging and clanging, it is more likely that plants hear through the transmission of water effluences through their branches than through pores in their leaves.

The "bell" and "lantern" support different conceptions of effluences. Aristotle admits confusion on whether light emanating from the eye causes vision, complaining that "at times, then, he [Empedocles] explains vision in this way, but at other times he accounts for it by emanations from objects seen" (*Sense* 438a4–5). Empedocles does advocate two theories of sensation: a general theory of effluences (ἀπορροαί) and a specialized notion of vision that includes the outflow from a primal fire in the eye likened to light issuing from a lantern. The bell of the ear, in contrast, provides an internal echo chamber that equalizes sounds emanating into the ear from outside. Sight requires a component not included in hearing, making its analysis dependent on an understanding of sound. In this way, hearing is more primary than sight for Empedocles: the account of the latter depends on that of the former. Furthermore, all things that see must also first be able to hear; in Aristotle's language, sight for Empedocles is nested within hearing and the other senses.

Where sight requires light and holds an essential relationship to fire, a handful of clues in Empedocles suggest a similar relationship between sound and water. First, B99's attribution of hearing to plants reinforces other evidence that plants sense and desire. Aristotle's *De sensu* demonstrates that Empedocles maintains a close relationship between plants and water. Empedocles also emphasizes connections between vegetative life and fish that further implicate hearing with water. Water, then, permeates the most basic kinds of life. Additionally, hearing occupies a primary position in Empedocles's fragments as the starting point of learning and understanding in sound and their culmination in speech. Finally, sound and water are united through liquid and flowing metaphors of Empedocles's language. More than any other root, water shares a primordial bond with sound.

## 7. Fish and the Unity of Life

Empedocles's account of breathing in B100 demonstrates that smell and breath can occur more perfectly with a nose and nostrils or less perfectly through pores spread invisibly throughout the skin of animals and bodies of plants. By referring to the ear as a σάρκινον ὄζον, Empedocles shows that the ear, as an organ of hearing, improves on the basic transmission of sound through pores. He thus includes hearing within a fundamental cluster of sensations belonging to all mortal creatures. Plants touch, taste, smell, and hear; fish include sight, other animals voice, and humans speech. This hierarchy of life both includes vegetation as an important component in the cycle of reincarnation and argues that all living things incorporate every sense into their being except sight. Empedocles thus insists of humans, "Upon him, through sight, comes also longing for copulation" (B64).[60] He argues that plants emerge when the world is young, have both sexes within them, and reproduce asexually. Animal life, which begins with sight, also initiates the life of sexual reproduction.[61]

The third word of a fragment preserved from Empedocles by Theophrastus on hearing provides additional support for this interpretation. The "bell" of the ear distinguishes animal hearing from plant hearing, allowing for a regulated perception of sound in creatures with ears akin to the regulated vision of the world provided by eyes. Plant hearing could not allow for communication but only a raw experience of sound through effluences traveling through their pores. Animal sense organs, then, focus and perfect what can be otherwise experienced more purely but imperfectly through the internal organic systems of plants in the case of taste, smell, and hearing.

Through his understanding of sound and hearing, Empedocles develops a hierarchy of life that both unites and distinguishes all living creatures. The connection of all life through reincarnation is well known through fragments such as B117: "For ere now I have been a boy, a girl; a bush, a fowl, and a fish [ἰχθύς] traveling in the sea." This involves not only analogous features between various forms of animal and plant life, as B82 intimates—"hair, leaves, thick feathers of fowls; and scales on stout limbs are all the same"—but also a common cluster of sensuous experience fundamental to all perishable creatures. This includes touch, smell, taste, and hearing but excludes sight, voice, and language.[62]

With sight comes the capacity for sexual reproduction, first manifested in mute fish. With voice seem to come more developed limbs and social existence on land and air. With speech come knowledge and the crafts. Empedocles believes that plants have both sexes within them and were the first perishable creatures to be generated when the world was young, as both Aëtius and Pseudo-Aristotle's *On Plants* confirm.[63] B62 describes the shadowy origins of "men and much-lamenting women" as "shoots [ὄρπηκας]" brought up "at night." Shoots, ὄρπηκας, is primarily used of saplings, and as Wright points out, "with this word Empedocles relates human life to plant life."[64] These shoots, not necessarily trees but at least resembling them, are "forms which did not yet manifest any pleasant figure of limbs / nor voice, nor organ of speech native to humans" (B62; translation modified). In the simplest times and for the most basic creatures, there are but limited functional limbs (at least not arms and legs), no voice, and no speech. These are characteristics shared by fish and plants.

B79 emphasizes the connection between trees and fish, reptiles, and birds: "Thus tall trees first lay olive eggs." Trees lay their olives without vision and sexual reproduction. Fish lay their eggs with vision and sexual reproduction. Birds and reptiles lay their eggs with vision, voice, and developed limbs. Plutarch notes the unusual word that Empedocles uses for *fish* in both B72 and B74:

Leading the uncultured race of prolific fish [φῦλον ἄμουσον ἄγουσα πολυσπερέων καμασήνων]. (B74)

How both tall trees and fish in the sea [πῶς καὶ δένδρεα μακρὰ καὶ εἰνάλιοι καμασῆνες]. (B72)

Plutarch preserved B72 in wondering about Empedocles's strange use of καμασῆνες (with καμασήνων also used in B74), a word he appears to have coined or invented. The etymology is quite difficult, but Pierre Chantraine's *Dictionnaire Étymologique de la Langue Grecque* states, "A connection with κάμαξ is plausible," as well as citing possible Slavic and Russian origins.[65] Empedocles does not often use foreign words, yet he regularly employs Homeric terms for various and sometimes unexpected purposes. *Κάμαξ* means "vine-pole, vine-prop" (LSJ, s.v.), and at *Iliad* 18.563 one of the many wonders set on the shield of Achilles, encircled by flowing Oceanus, is a prolific vineyard in which "the vines were set up throughout on silver poles [κάμαξι]." Σαίνω, aorist ἔσηνα, means "to wag the tail, fawn," and appears at Hesiod, *Theogony* 77, and Homer, *Odyssey* 10.219 and 17.302 (LSJ, s.v.). An etymological derivation from κάμαξ + σηνα, which could contract to καμασῆνα and then καμασῆνες for the exclusively plural word, would mean literally from Homeric and Hesiodic usages "a wagging vine-pole," thereby emphasizing the close biological connection between fish and plants. Fish are essentially plants with eyes and ears. They can see and hear better through their organs, so they sexually reproduce and locomote. Instead of a fish needing a pole, as a vine needs a pole on which to grow and move, fish provide their own mobility-poles through their skeletons.

B74 attributes two adjectives to the genitive plural καμασήνων, ἄμουσον and πολυσπερέων. Ἄμουσος here means "without song" when applied to fish by Empedocles, and it also means "without the muses," "without taste or refinement," or, when attributed to sounds, "unmusical or discordant" (LSJ, s.v.). The genitive plural of πολυσπερής, πολυσπερέων means "widespread, spread over the earth" and appears at *Iliad* 2.804, *Odyssey* 11.365, and *Theogony* 365. LSJ attributes the meaning "fruitful" to the instance in B74. At *Theogony* 365, πολυσπερέες describes the three thousand daughters of Oceanus dispersed throughout the earth and sea. At *Iliad* 2.804, using πολυσπερέων, the identical form used by Empedocles, Iris tells Hector to let each leader rally his troops out of Troy, as there is such a *prolific* variety of languages among them. The Greek army dwarfs the prolific soldiers of the Trojans, however; as Iris warns, "Never yet have I seen [ὄπωπα] an army like this in quality and size; for like leaves or sands do they come over the plain" (*Iliad* 2.799–801). More πολυσπερείς than the Trojan allies, the Greek army resembles the prolific, ubiquitous nature of leaves or sand. Plants and trees, then, would be the most prolific form of life for Homer.

As prolific and voiceless, Empedoclean fish resemble Empedoclean plant life. Without voice, they likely hear less perfectly than is required to make out precise forms of communication among members of a species, so that the sound would be unmusical and discordant. Aristotle notes that fish smell and hear in water at *De sensu* 444b8–9 and are voiceless at *De anima* 2.8, 420b10, and 421a5. Plant hearing, altogether without ears and resembling breathing through pores rather than nostrils, would prove even more discordant. Because of the inner working of the ear resembling a fleshy branch, plant smelling likely occurs through pores in the leaves transmitted through effluences of predominantly aither, while plant hearing occurs through stems and branches transmitted through effluences of predominantly water.

The partial fragment B72, "How both tall trees and fish in the sea," points to these similarities among plants and fish as the two most basic forms of perishable life in Empedocles's cosmos. Both lack developed and widely functional limbs, both smell, both are exceptionally prolific, both are mute, and both hear. Fish, with eyes and a mobile, self-directed vine-pole, also engage in locomotion and the longing for copulation. While for Empedocles locomotion is tied to sight and sexual reproduction, in contrast to Aristotle it is not coextensive with sensation in general. Sound and hearing provide the most common form of sensation, clustered together with smell, taste, and touch. They also afford the first pathway to complex organic community when combined with voice and ultimately to human knowledge when developed into speech.[66]

When Empedocles demands that his disciple Pausanias take shelter in his mute wits (στεγάσοι φρενὸς ἔλλοπος εἴσω), he interweaves the themes into a complicated mosaic.[67] Pausanias must observe Pythagorean silence and like a fish remain mute among the flowing oceans and rivers of languages, opinions, and truths. He must take cover, shelter, from the effluences flowing all around and into him as a fish can live and breathe in water. This also raises the biological point, emphasized in B74, that mute fish hear in the water. Plants, too, hold an essential relationship to water for Empedocles by receiving nutrition and likely taste through their vascular system. By describing the ear as a "fleshy branch," he attributes the power of hearing to this most unlikely candidate, further connecting fish and plants as mute, prolific, tied to water, and able to hear. They also both reproduce through analogous fruit and eggs but lack the more organized and specialized lifestyle of land animals and birds. Fish, however, are wagging plants, self-moving vine-poles that engage in sexual reproduction because of vision. By conceiving of fish as wagging plants, Empedocles shows that fish reproduce sexually because of sight but that all other sensations are held in common with plants, including hearing.

## 8. Conclusion

Favoring the core of the Platonic interpretation over the Aristotelian draws attention to the relationship between effluences and flow, which when applied to a plenum require a model grounded in an archaic sense of fluid dynamics. Empedocles envisions this in terms of fording rivers, irrigating fields, and navigating ships into ports, so that more or less solid or diffuse effluences intermingle throughout the whole and occasionally result in sensation. The importance of the metaphor of flow taken from water to describe the basic motions of all the roots and their effluences is shown first through the full line dedicated exclusively to Nestis in B6. The primacy of hearing in this fragment and elsewhere, as well as the proliferation of liquid and flowing language to describe sound, speech, and the roots themselves, grounds water, sound, and language as most fundamental to Empedocles's thought. Sight, developed with the technological analogy of a lantern, indicates a more specialized form of sensation in which fire predominates but is tempered through mixture with the other roots. The "fleshy branch" metaphor reveals an interconnected knot of sensations that belong to all mortal living things, and another technological analogy, the "bell," reveals that the ear can perfect hearing sound into the more measured capacity to hear voice and ultimately language.

Plants are clearly included in the cycle of reincarnation, and Empedocles often draws analogies between various kinds of life. "Thus tall trees first lay olive eggs" (B79) compares the bearing of olives to the sexual reproduction of animals with eyes and the corresponding division of sexes. Water-nourished fish hear but lack voice. So too with plants. Eyes and locomotion distinguish plant and animal life for Empedocles, not more basic sensation and desire. Understood through an Empedoclean poetics, the metaphor of the "fleshy branch" cannot be read as one-way—that is, the analogy always extends in both directions. When scales are related to bark, olives to eggs, or egg whites to milk, something is attributed from the former to the latter and the latter to the former. The fleshy branch is not an exception to this law. The plantlike properties of the ear also imply that auditory properties belong to plants. When interpreted with other evidence in the fragments, the incomplete "how both tall trees and fish in the sea" says a great deal. It emphasizes how both are nourished through water; are prolific; lay eggs or olives; have scales or bark, leaves or skin, roots or mouth; live without voice; and hear.

Water, naturally black in color for Empedocles, transmits sound in complete absence of light through water in deep caves or on the darkest of nights. Requiring neither fire nor light, black water predominates in sound. Thus does Empedocles emphasize the importance of hearing at night. By describing hearing language as channeling a fountain, Empedocles reveals that effluences of sound too flow like streams. Unlike streams of fire, streams of liquid sound require no color or light for their transmission. Flowing through the Empedoclean plenum, mixed more or less with the other roots, watery effluences of sound unite all life from plant to person.

## Notes

1. Daniel W. Graham, *The Texts of Early Greek Philosophy, Parts I and II* (New York: Cambridge University Press, 2010), 400–401. Translations of Empedocles and other pre-Socratics are from Graham, *Texts*, cited by Diels-Kranz number.

2. Graham, *Texts*, 389, 407. Pseudo-Aristotle, *On Plants*, in Aristotle, *The Complete Works of Aristotle*, ed. Jonathan Barnes (Princeton, NJ: Princeton University Press, 1984): "Now Anaxagoras and Empedocles say that [plants] are influenced by desire; they also assert that they have sensation and sadness and pleasure" (815a24–26). While this text, back-translated from Arabic to Latin, was not written by Aristotle, in the first book Empedocles is mentioned six times (815a20; 815b16 [possess intelligence]; 817a2 [sexes in plants]; 817a11; 817a35–6, "And Empedocles is right when he said the tall trees do not bear their young"; and 817b35, "Empedocles was right when he said plants had their birth when the world was yet small and its perfection not attained") and Anaxagoras four (815a16, 815b15 [also Democritus], 816b26 [plants have respiration], and 817a25). See John Burnet, *Early Greek Philosophy*, 4th ed. (New York: Meridian Books, 1968), 241–242. The author is familiar with their work and confidently attributes the thesis about plants to both of them. See also Graham, *Texts*, 385, A70, where Aëtius confirms that plants are the first creatures to be born, draws connections between plants and animals, links plant nutrition with water, and indicates that soil has to do with taste.

3. Empedoclean roots likely have hylozoic properties, so that in some way the roots themselves experience, live, and ground the sensations of mortal plants and animals composed of them. See section 4 of this chapter.

4. Republic 6, 507c–509b, in Plato, *Complete Works*, ed. John M. Cooper (Indianapolis: Hackett, 1997); Aristotle, *Metaphysics* 1.1, 980a20–27, in *Complete Works*.

5. In B3.9–13, Empedocles praises all of the senses for their unique contributions to knowledge, so the question regards primacy rather than contribution. See John Sallis, *The Figure of Nature: On Greek Origins* (Bloomington: Indiana University Press, 2016), 44.

6. Aristotle, *On Sense and Sensibilia*, in *Complete Works*, 477a16–19: "Animals higher in the scale of creation [τὰ τιμιώτερα τῶν ζῴων] have more heat; for they must at the same time have a higher form [τιμιωτέρας] of soul; for they have a higher nature than that of fishes [τιμιώτερα γὰρ τὰ τοιαῦτα τῆς φύσεως τῆς τῶν ἰχθύων]." See also Aristotle, *De anima*, in *Complete Works*, 413a21–413b10: "The first characteristic of animal life is sensation" (413b3); and Aristotle, *De sensu*, in *Complete Works*, 436b110–20: "Every animal *qua* animal must have sensation," and "those senses which act through external media, such as smell, hearing and vision, belong to such animals as are capable of locomotion" (436b18–20). For Aristotle, animals begin at taste and touch, but locomotion requires smell.

7. Aristotle, *Metaphysics*, in *Complete Works*, 985a31–b3: "He was the first to speak of four material elements; yet he does not *use* four, but treats them as two only; he treats fire by itself, and its opposites—earth, air, and water—as one kind of thing. We may learn this by study of his verses."

8. Plato, *Meno* and *Theaetetus*, in *Complete Works*. See also *Cratylus* 402b for an additional reference to Oceanus in *Iliad* 14 and the spurious mid-fourth-century BCE *Sisyphus* 389a for an additional reference to Empedocles.

9. W. K. C. Guthrie, *A History of Greek Philosophy*, vol. 2 (New York: Cambridge University Press, 1980), 234n3; M. R. Wright, *Empedocles: The Extant Fragments* (Indianapolis: Hackett, 1995), 230.

10. James Eric Butler, "Effluvia: Empedocles Studies," *Epoché* 9, no. 2 (2005): 215–231; see 216 and 228 on the etymology of ἀπορροή and πόρος. See Sallis, *Figure*, especially 72–73, 90–98, and 112–121 on flow in the *Theaetetus* and 42–57 on the four roots in Empedocles as natural sources of becoming and growth. Wright, *Empedocles*, 230; Homer, *Iliad I and II*, trans. A. T. Murray, rev. William F. Wyatt (Cambridge, MA: Harvard University Press, 1999), 2.59, 14.433. See Henry George Liddell and Robert Scott, *A Greek-English Lexicon*, 9th

ed., rev. Sir Henry Stuart Jones (New York: Oxford University Press, 1996), s.v. for πόρος as a passageway, pathway, through or over water, and as "the paths of the sea" in Homer, *Odyssey I*, trans. A. T. Murray, rev. George Dimock (Cambridge, MA: Harvard University Press, 1998), 12.259. LSJ, s.v., on the later verb ἀπορρέω, meaning "to flow or run off, stream forth," which does not appear before the fifth century BCE. See Empedocles B3, B21, and B39 for extant instances of πόρος.

11.  For example, B108, "Inasmuch as they become different, it was ever present to them to think different thoughts," and B107, "For from these all things being joined together are compounded, and by these they think and experience pleasure and pain" (translation modified). On the relationship to Gorgias, see Diogenes Laertius, *Lives of Eminent Philosophers*, vol. 2, trans. R. D. Hicks (Cambridge, MA: Harvard University Press, 1995), 373; *Meno* 71c on Gorgias and Meno; and *Meno* 76c on Empedocles, Gorgias, and Meno.

12.  With Parmenides, Plato also includes Melissus at *Theaetetus* 180e and 183e, and Xenophanes at Plato, *Sophist*, in *Complete Works*, 242d. On the plenum in Empedocles, see Sallis, *Figure*, 47–48, 128; Burnet, *Early Greek Philosophy*, 227; Guthrie, *History*, 2:139. The translation "led by Homer as general" (153a) is from the Loeb edition: Plato, *Theaetetus and Sophist*, trans. Harold North Fowler (Cambridge, MA: Harvard University Press, 1996). Plato reemphasizes the extent to which the philosophers of flux emerge out of the Homeric treatment of water through Theodorus at *Theaetetus* 180d: "[The ancients] used poetical forms which concealed from the majority of men their real meaning, namely, that Ocean and Tethys, the origin of all things, are actually flowing streams [ῥεύματα] and nothing stands still."

13.  This connection with Homer originates with Hippias of Elis's *Synagoge* "Collection." See, for example, Jaap Mansfeld, *Studies in the Historiography of Greek Philosophy* (Assen/Maastricht: Van Gorcum, 1990), 84–96; Andreas Patzer, *Der Sophist Hippias als Philosophiehistoriker* (Freiburg: Karl Alber, 1986). Plato offers a complicated mosaic of warring philosophical schools beginning with Thales. From 173c–175e, Socrates distinguishes between a practical person and a philosopher, with Thales named at 174a and his investigation of astronomy developed into the paradigm of the philosophical type at 175d–e. This situates Thales as the earliest philosopher, not grounded precisely on an emphasis on water but rather because of his emphasis on flow. Socrates and Theodorus "consider and test this moving Being" (179d) maintained by Protagoras, Heraclitus, and Empedocles because it lies at the foundation of the view "that knowledge and perception are the same thing" (179d). Theodorus aligns the Protagorean and Heraclitean doctrines and follows Socrates in tracing both back to Homer: "You know, Socrates, these Heraclitean doctrines (or, as you say, Homeric or still more ancient)" (179e). They set out to consider the views of the Heracliteans and Parmenideans, the one upholding a moving being, the others a One that stands still (180e). See Sallis, *Figure*, 67–68, on Thales in the *Theaetetus*. Oceanus also appears on the shield of Achilles in *Iliad* 18 and at 21.194–197. See Guthrie, *History*, 1:60.

14.  See Butler, "Effluvia," 215–216, 225–228; he notes the conflict between fluid mechanics in a plenum and atomism on 227. Aristotle considers motion without void in Plato's *Timaeus* in *On Youth, Old Age, Life and Death, and Respiration*, in *Complete Works*, 472b6–24; Aristotle's quotation of Empedocles B100 on respiration occurs at 473b8.

15.  Aristotle (*Metaphysics*, 983b20–984a4) notes that Thales held that the earth rests on water, that nutriment is moist, that heat comes from the moist, that seeds are moist, and that water is the principle of the moist.

16.  Concerning Empedocles and atomism, see Aristotle, *On Generation and Corruption*, in *Complete Works*, 325b5; Friedrich Nietzsche, *The Pre-Platonic Philosophers*, trans. Greg

Whitlock (Chicago: University of Illinois Press, 1995), 117–118; Burnet, *Early Greek Philosophy*, 234; Guthrie, *History*, 2:149–152, 149n1. Empedocles, an approximate contemporary of Anaxagoras, was said to be old during Democritus's youth (Burnet, 331). On Leucippus, also likely born at least a generation after Empedocles, see Burnet, 332: "It is therefore more probable that Leukippos derived it [the doctrine of pores] from Empedocles. Nor is it at all probable that Anaxagoras knew anything of the theory of Leukippos. It is true that he denied the existence of the void; but it does not follow that anyone had already maintained that doctrine in the atomist sense."

17. Aristotle, *De sensu* 473b10–438a8, 440a15–20, 434b1–2. The discussion of vision in *On Sense and Sensibilia* preserves all of the extensive fragment B84.

18. The impact of Xenophanes perhaps leads directly to his theory of sensation. Xenophanes writes, "All of him sees, all thinks, all hears [ἀκούει]" (B24/F24, 110–111). With an unlimited universe and a monotheistic nonanthropomorphic god that is identified with the whole, Xenophanes develops a pre-Parmenidean physics with Milesian roots, grounded in the material principles of earth and water. However much Xenophanes identifies god with earth and water, to that extent earth and water themselves would see and hear. On Empedocles and Xenophanes, see Graham, *Texts*, 119 (text 53); André Laks and Glenn W. Most, *Early Greek Philosophy: Western Greek Thinkers, Part 2* (Cambridge, MA: Harvard University Press, 2016), 339. On earth and water, see Graham, *Texts*, "All things which come to be and grow are from earth and water" (B29); "For we all come to be from earth and water" (B33); and texts 46, 47,48, 49, and 50. For Xenophanes, air is a modification of water, as are wind and cloud, and the mixture of water and earth make up everything else: "Sea is the source of water and the source of wind. . . . the great wide sea is the sire of clouds and winds and rivers" (B30).

19. See Hesiod, *Works and Days*, in *Theogony, Works and Days, Shield*, trans. Apostolos N. Athanassakis (Baltimore: Johns Hopkins University Press, 2004), lines 115–120, on creation *in cognito*, which contrasts with the perpetual being of Homer's Oceanus and Empedocles' roots. For φύσις, ἦθος, τιμῆς, see Empedocles B17.28, τιμῆς δ' ἄλλης ἄλλο μέδει, πάρα δ' ἦθος ἑκάσσωι, and B110.4–5, "For these will grow [αὔξει] / In each character [ἦθος], according to its own nature [ὅπη φύσις ἐστὶν ἑκάστωι]."

20. See, for example, Graham, *Texts*, 423; Wright, *Empedocles*, 165–166; Burnet, *Early Greek Philosophy*, 229; Guthrie, *History*, 2:144–146; Nietzsche, *Pre-Platonic Philosophers*, 116–117; G. S. Kirk, J. E. R. Raven, and M. Schofield, *The Presocratic Philosophers*, 2nd ed. (New York: Cambridge University Press, 1983), 286.

21. On aither as a root rather than air, as well as on the four roots controversy, see Peter Kingsley, "Empedocles and His Interpreters: The Four Element Doxography," *Phronesis* 39, no. 3 (1994): 235–254; Michael M. Shaw, "Aither and the Four Roots in Empedocles," *Research in Phenomenology* 44 (2014): 170–193. On ῥιζώματα, see LSJ, s.v.; Wright, *Empedocles*, 164–165. See Sallis, *Figure*, 52, on στοιχεῖον as anachronistic.

22. Butler, "Effluvia," 218–219.

23. LSJ, s.v.

24. Empedocles B21.6; Aristotle, *De sensu* 441a10–20.

25. See, for example, B3.8–14.

26. Imperative of κλύω, meaning "to hear, perceive or know; to give ear to, attend to." The imperative generally indicates "to hear or listen to" (LSJ, s.v.).

27. Plutarch takes lines 7–8 as a reference to Xenophanes B34, indicating that human beings cannot know the complete truth. Yet the language also echoes Xenophanes B24: "All

of him sees, all thinks, all hears [οὖλος ὁρᾶι, οὖλος δὲ νοεῖ, οὖλος δέ τ' ἀκούει]." On this point, Empedocles does have a critique of Xenophanes: rather than distributing sight and hearing throughout god, he develops an enhanced role for the sensory organ. See Wright, *Empedocles*, 155; Graham, *Texts*, 127: "Now the plain truth no man has seen nor will any / know concerning the gods and what I have said concerning all things" (Xenophanes B34.1–2).

28. LSJ, s.v.; see Butler, "Effluvia," 217, 220–221 for the same verb in Empedocles B35.

29. LSJ, s.v. Sophocles uses πηγή as "source," as Oedipus wishes he could stab out the fount of hearing like he did that of seeing. In an Empedoclean account, the eye can be destroyed basically by extinguishing the fire within the organ. There is no fire in the ear, and the fount of hearing can therefore not be extinguished in the same way.

30. Plato notes the similarity between sight and antistrophe at *Republic* 530d, and Aristotle notes the connection between hearing and intelligence at *De sensu* 437a4–17.

31. Graham, *Texts*, 341. On ἔλλοπος, see also B117; Wright, *Empedocles*, 275, 293.

32. Graham, *Texts*, 341.

33. These points are developed in section 7 of this chapter.

34. See Guthrie, *History*, 2:143, on the hylozoic character of Empedocles's roots.

35. Fragment B138, "Having drawn off life [ψυχὴν] with bronze"; see Wright, *Empedocles*, 288.

36. Perfect first plural, meaning "behold, perceive, observe, see (an object)" when transitive (LSJ, s.v. "ὁράω").

37. LSJ 36 and 817: ἀίδηλον is derived as an alpha privative from ϝιδεῖν; see H. W. Smythe, *Greek Grammar* (Cambridge, MA: Harvard University Press, 1984), 145–146, secs. 431 and 431D on the original digamma in εἶδον, ὁράω. Ὀπώπαμεν is the perfect first plural of ὁράω, meaning "behold, perceive, observe, see (an object)" when transitive (LSJ, s.v.).

38. See B21.3, B22.2, and B115.10–11 on the sun in Empedocles. Aristotle notes the destructive olfactory power of sulfur and bitumen at *De sensu* 445a1.

39. Theophrastus, *De sensu* 1.11, in Graham, *Texts*, 402. Also, "those who have a moderate blend in some organs are gifted in that thing. Thus some are good speakers, some good craftsmen, because the latter have a good blend in their hands, the former in their tongue, and similarly with other abilities" (Graham, *Texts*, 402).

40. Ὠγύγιος, or *ogygian*, means "primeval, original; of or from Ogyges, mythical ancient king of Attica" (LSJ, s.v.). See John I. Beare, *Greek Theories of Elementary Cognition from Alcmaeon to Aristotle* (Oxford: Clarendon, 1906), 18, on the primal fire in the eye; see A. A. Long, "Thinking and Sense-Perception in Empedocles: Mysticism or Materialism?," *Classical Quarterly* 16, no. 2 (1966): 256–276, especially 262–264 on B84. See *Odyssey* 1.101: Ogygia Island, in the center of the sea and home of Calypso, is where Odysseus is marooned (Homer, *The Odyssey*, trans. Robert Fagles [New York: Penguin Books, 1997], 534; LSJ, s.v. "Ὠγυγία").

41. Aristotle writes, "If the eye were actually fire, as Empedocles says, and as is stated in the *Timaeus*, and if vision occurred when light issues from the eye as from a lantern, why should not vision be equally possible in the dark" (*De sensu*, in *Complete Works*, 437b11–14); and, "Empedocles seems sometimes to imagine that one sees because light issues from the eye" (437b24–26). Aristotle returns to the lamp simile: "It is a fact that when in war men have been struck on the temple so as to sever the channels [τοὺς πόρους τοὺς] from the eye, darkness has seemed to fall on them as if a lamp has failed, because the transparent substance, called the pupil, has been cut off, like a lamp screen" (438b13–16).

42. Graham, *Texts*, 401.

43. Graham, 401.

44. On the black color of water, see Empedocles B21.5, "And rain, dark and chilling in everything"; B94, "And black color arises from the shadow on the bottom of the river and likewise is seen in hollow caverns"; and B111.2, "And you shall produce from black rain timely drought." Aristotle's criticism of perceiving color through effluences at *De sensu* 440a15–20 is likely directed against Empedocles (at least in part) and provides further evidence of his view: "To say with the ancients that colors are due to emanations, and that the visibility of object is due to such a cause is absurd. For they must, in any case, explain sense-perception through touch." Aristotle often refers to Empedocles's theory of emanations as explaining all sensation through touch via the contact of effluences with pores. For example, see 442a29, 443b1, and 440a15. This also shows further indebtedness to Xenophanes, in critiquing his three-color theory of primaries (B32: "purple and scarlet and green"). See also Plato, *Republic* 617a, on the color of stars as yellow, red, and white (no black). Beare (*Greek Theories*, 22) suggests possible confusion with Democritus's theory of color, proposing that Empedocles maintains only white and black as primary.

45. Graham, *Texts*, 401.

46. Wright, *Empedocles*, 246.

47. "That creatures that do not breathe have the olfactory sense is evident" (*De sensu* 444b7); see also *On Youth*, in *Complete Works*, 470b28.

48. Beare comments that by describing the ear as a κώδωνα Empedocles conceives it "as having a determining power over the *quality* of the sensation to be produced by the ἀπόρροιαι" (*Greek Theories*, 24n2). According to Theophrastus, Democritus held that air "enters the whole body equally, but especially and most of all it enters the ears" (Graham, *Texts*, 585).

49. Long notes the connection between the two analogies in "Thinking and Sense-Perception," 265.

50. W. S. Hett, "Introduction to *On Sense and Sensible Objects*," in Aristotle, *On the Soul, Parva Naturalia, On Breath*, trans. W. S. Hett (Cambridge, MA: Harvard University Press, 1957), 207: "Sound is dismissed" and "never mentioned except incidentally."

51. Graham, *Texts*, 400–401, A86, B99.

52. Σάρκινον derives from the noun σάρξ, which usually means "flesh" or "animal flesh" but also means "fleshy pulp of fruit," but probably the first such use is by Theophrastus (LSJ, s.v.). The emphasis on the *inner* ear almost certainly indicates dissection. See also Long, "Thinking and Sense-Perception," 265, 265n3; Beare, *Greek Theories*, 95–97.

53. See Beare, *Greek Theories*, 96. Beare's influential text uses the translation "fleshy bone" as well.

54. Graham, *Texts*, 403.

55. See Shaw, "Aither," 170–182, 180n4; Burnet, *Early Greek Philosophy*, 228–229; Guthrie, *History*, 2:145–146, 187, on the confusion of water, air, and aither. To some extent, Aristotle sides with Empedocles over Alcmaeon of Croton in *De anima* 2.8, in *Complete Works*, arguing that hearing does not occur because of void inside the ear but rather because of air inside the ear. Aristotle defines sound as "an impact of two solids against one another and against the air. The latter condition is satisfied when the air impinged upon does not retreat before the blow, i.e. is not dissipated by it" (419b20–22). Air, understood by most as empty space, causes hearing (419b33–35): "Only when its dissipation is prevented

is its movement sound. The air in the ear is built into a chamber just to prevent this dissipating movement, in order that the animal may accurately apprehend all varieties of the movements of the air outside" (420a8–11). And "what we hear with is a chamber which contains a bounded mass of air" (420a18–19). See Beare, *Greek Theories*, 11–13, 93–94, on Alcmaeon.

56. Aristotle defines *metaphor* as follows in *Poetics*, in *Complete Works*: "Metaphor consists in giving the thing a name that belongs to something else; the transference being either from genus to species, or from species to genus, or from species to species, or on grounds of analogy" (1457b7–9). B138 is an example at 1457b14: "Drawing the life with the bronze."

57. Aristotle, *On Respiration*, in *On the Soul*.

58. Graham, *Texts*, 385.

59. Aristotle notes that fish smell and hear in water at *De sensu* 444b8–9 and that they are voiceless at *De anima* 420b10 and 421a5.

60. For the context of B64, see Brad Inwood, *The Poem of Empedocles: A Text and Translation with an Introduction* (Toronto: University of Toronto Press, 2001), 125.

61. Plants: touch, smell, taste, hearing. Fish: touch, smell, taste, hearing, sight. Animals: touch, smell, taste, hearing, sight, voice. Humans: touch, smell, taste, hearing, sight, voice, speech. See Wright, *Empedocles*, 296, on B99 as highlighting this relationship between plants and animals, and 290–292 on the hierarchy of lives; see 264 on plants and animals breathing through leaves and skin.

62. Aristotle, *De sensu*, in *Complete Works*, 442a29: "Democritus and most of the natural philosophers who treat of sense-perception proceed quite irrationally, for they represent all objects of sense as objects of touch."

63. Graham, *Texts*, 385.

64. Wright, *Empedocles*, 216.

65. Pierre Chantraine, *Dictionnaire Étymologique de la Langue Grecque* (Paris: Klincksieck, 1968), 489: "Fish poorly identified, see Thompson *Fishes*, s.v. In accordance with the relation between ἠλακατήν and ἠλακάτη, one might posit κάμασος, with a suffix like that of πέτασος, κόμπασος, etc. Outside of Greek one might compare with Frisk Lithuanian *šãmas*, Latvian *sams*, Russian fish name *som* for *silure* [= catfish, apparently]. A connection with κάμαξ is plausible. See Strömberg *Fischnamen* 36" (translated into English by Daniel W. Graham). LSJ, s.v., merely relates, "καμασῆνες, ων, οἱ, fish, Emp. 72, 74."

66. See Aristotle, *De sensu* 446b23–27 on sound, smell, and sight as communal sensations.

67. The corrupted fragment B117 attributes ἔλλοπος directly to fish according to Wright (*Empedocles*, 276) but not Graham (*Texts*, 406–407).

# Bibliography

Aristotle. *The Complete Works of Aristotle*. Edited by Jonathan Barnes. Princeton, NJ: Princeton University Press, 1984.

———. *On the Soul, Parva Naturalia, On Breath*. Translated by W. S. Hett. Cambridge: Harvard University Press, 1957.

Beare, John I. *Greek Theories of Elementary Cognition from Alcmaeon to Aristotle*. Oxford: Clarendon, 1906.

Burnet, John. *Early Greek Philosophy.* 4th ed. New York: Meridian Books, 1968.

Butler, James Eric. "Effluvia: Empedocles Studies." *Epoché* 9, no. 2 (2005): 215–231.

Chantraine, Pierre. *Dictionnaire Étymologique de la Langue Grecque.* Paris: Klincksieck, 1968.

Diogenes Laertius. *Lives of Eminent Philosophers.* Vol. 2. Translated by R. D. Hicks. Cambridge, MA: Harvard University Press, 1995.

Graham, Daniel W. *The Texts of Early Greek Philosophy, Parts I and II.* New York: Cambridge University Press, 2010.

Guthrie, W. K. C. *A History of Greek Philosophy.* Vols 1 and 2. New York: Cambridge University Press, 1980.

Hesiod. *Theogony, Works and Days, Shield.* Translated by Apostolos N. Athanassakis. Baltimore: Johns Hopkins University Press, 2004.

Hett, W. S. "Introduction to *On Sense and Sensible Objects.*" In Aristotle, *On the Soul, Parva Naturalia, On Breath*, vii–xiii.

Homer. *Iliad I and II.* Translated by A. T. Murray. Revised by William F. Wyatt. Cambridge, MA: Harvard University Press, 1999.

———. *The Odyssey.* Translated by Robert Fagles. Introduction and Notes by Bernard Knox. New York: Penguin Books, 1997.

———. *Odyssey I.* Translated by A. T. Murray. Revised by George Dimock. Cambridge, MA: Harvard University Press, 1998.

Inwood, Brad. *The Poem of Empedocles: A Text and Translation with an Introduction.* Toronto: University of Toronto Press, 2001.

Kingsley, Peter. "Empedocles and His Interpreters: The Four-Element Doxography." *Phronesis* 39, no. 3 (1994): 235–254.

Kirk, G. S., J. E. R. Raven, and M. Schofield. *The Presocratic Philosophers.* 2nd ed. New York: Cambridge University Press, 1983.

Laks, André and Glenn W. Most. *Early Greek Philosophy: Western Greek Thinkers, Part 2.* Cambridge, MA: Harvard University Press, 2016.

Liddell, Henry George, and Robert Scott. *A Greek-English Lexicon.* 9th ed. Revised by Sir Henry Stuart Jones. New York: Oxford University Press, 1996.

Long, A. A. "Thinking and Sense-Perception in Empedocles: Mysticism or Materialism?" *Classical Quarterly* 16, no. 2 (1966): 256–276.

Mansfeld, Jaap. *Studies in the Historiography of Greek Philosophy.* Assen/Maastricht: Van Gorcum, 1990.

Nietzsche, Friedrich. *The Pre-Platonic Philosophers.* Translated by Greg Whitlock. Chicago: University of Illinois Press, 1995.

Patzer, Andreas. *Der Sophist Hippias als Philosophiehistoriker.* Freiburg: Karl Alber, 1986.

Plato. *Complete Works.* Edited by John M. Cooper. Indianapolis: Hackett, 1997.

———. *Theaetetus and Sophist.* Translated by Harold North Fowler. Cambridge, MA: Harvard University Press, 1996.

Pseudo-Aristotle. *On Plants.* In Aristotle, *The Complete Works of Aristotle*, 1251–1271.

Sallis, John. *The Figure of Nature: On Greek Origins.* Bloomington: Indiana University Press, 2016.

Shaw, Michael M. "Aither and the Four Roots in Empedocles." *Research in Phenomenology* 44 (2014): 170–193.

Smythe, H. W. *Greek Grammar*. Cambridge, MA: Harvard University Press, 1984.
Wright, M. R. *Empedocles: The Extant Fragments*. Indianapolis: Hackett, 1995.

MICHAEL M. SHAW is Professor of Philosophy and Classical Studies Coordinator at Utah Valley University. His research focuses on Empedocles, Anaxagoras, and Aristotle.

# 3

## INDOOR VOICES

### *Adriana Cavarero and Jacques Derrida on the Devocalization of Logos in Plato*

Michael Naas, DePaul University


## 1. For More Than One *Phōnē*

*Phōnē*: it is a simple enough Greek word, just two syllables, each with a single Greek consonant and vowel, and it is at the root of many English words we know or at least think we know well, beginning with *phoneme* and *phonetics* but then also, in the last two centuries, *phonograph, gramophone, stereophone, telephone*, and so on. At the origin, then, of all these names for technologies designed to record sounds and voices for the future or to transmit them over great distances, we know or at least think we know what *phono-* means and, as a result, what *phōnē* must have meant for the ancient Greeks. At its greatest level of generality, it would seem to have meant "sound," sound of any kind, anything that might be heard or received by a human or animal ear, but then also, more specifically, "voice," and the human voice first and foremost.

As it happens, this same *phōnē* has been at the center of several important debates in contemporary philosophy about the very nature of Western philosophy and especially its origins in the ancient Greeks. In his 1967 work *Of Grammatology*, for example, Jacques Derrida claimed that Western philosophy is essentially phonocentric in its privileging of speech—live speech—over writing, a privileging that has been fundamental in shaping the way philosophy has understood everything from the relationship between being and becoming or reality and appearance to the difference (and then the hierarchy) between soul and body, men and women, humans and animals, and so on. More recently, Adriana Cavarero has taken issue with this characterization of Western thought, arguing that Western philosophy has been essentially videocentric in its privileging of meaning over speech—of the eye over the ear—a privileging that was made possible through the exclusion of that same *phōnē* that Derrida claimed to be so central to Western philosophy.[1] And to make matters even more complicated, Cavarero has argued that this videocentrism has its origins in the very same texts and thinkers where Derrida locates the beginnings of phonocentrism—namely, the Greeks and, in particular, Plato.

The aim of this essay is to try to clarify—to disambiguate, as it were—the various meanings and nuances of this word *phōnē* in Plato's thought or writing in order to provide a few suggestions about how to resolve the debate over this supposed phonocentrism of Western philosophy. I thus look at Plato's use of the word *phōnē* throughout the dialogues so as then to focus more closely on a couple of key passages from the *Philebus* where Plato seems to be working with a fundamental ambiguity in the Greek word *phōnē* as sound and/or voice. This ambiguity is crucial, I argue, to determining the relationship or the opposition in Plato between order and disorder, meaning and sensibility, the limited and the unlimited, the human and the animal, the soul and the body, and so on. I thus hope to show how an analysis of *phōnē* in Plato has implications that go far beyond merely the linguistic, inflecting the entire matrix or architecture not just of Plato's dialogues but of Western metaphysics more generally.

## 2. Disambiguating *Phōnē*

What, then, is *phōnē* in Plato? What is a *phōnē* or what are *phōnai* in the dialogues? Let me begin with what is perhaps the best known—but probably most exceptional—of all of Plato's uses of the word: Socrates's claim in the *Apology* that his daimonion came to him over the course of his life in the form of a *phōnē*—that is, in the form of a voice to dissuade him from doing what he was about to do. He says in the *Apology*, "I have had this from my childhood; it is a sort of voice [*phōnē*] that comes to me, and when it comes it always holds me back from what I am thinking of doing" (*Apology* 31d). Though we are not told exactly what this voice, this *phōnē*, says or how it says it, we do know that Socrates hears it as meaningful, as expressing warning or caution, disapproval of some kind. Socrates attests to something similar in *Phaedrus*: "My good friend, when I was about to cross the stream, the spirit [daimonion] and the sign [*sēmeion*] that usually comes to me came—it always holds me back from something I am about to do—and I thought I heard a voice [*phōnē*] from it which forbade my going away before clearing my conscious, as if I had committed some sin against deity" (*Phaedrus* 242c). Once again, what Socrates hears (or feigns to have heard—it makes little difference for the sake of the present argument) is not just sound but voice—meaningful sound in the form of a voice telling him not to do what he was thinking of doing. Socrates understands at once the message and the source of the message, at once the voice of his daimonion and his daimonion as voice. A *phōnē* is thus not only heard but also understood, recognized in itself and with respect to its origin or its cause. In the *Symposium*, Apollodorus recounts how those present at Agathon's house "heard the voice [*phōnē*] of Alcibiades" as he was entering (*Symposium* 212d); in other words, they heard not just a voice making identifiable sounds but a voice that could itself be identified.[2]

Hence, *phōnē* can mean voice—a particular voice, a particular human voice, like Alcibiades's—but also human speech or language more generally. Protagoras speaks in his fable recounting the development of human beings of the way in which man was "enabled by his skill to articulate speech and words [*phōnēn kai onomatai*], and to invent dwellings, clothes, sandals, beds, and the foods that are of the earth" (*Protagoras* 322a). *Phōnē* here seems to mean not just voice but a general capacity for speech or an art of speech that enabled humankind—and only humankind—to develop other arts. Elsewhere, *phōnē* seems to mean not language as a whole but a particular language—the Greek *phōnē*, for example—as opposed to a foreign language or tongue, a barbarian *phōnē* (*Cratylus* 409e; *Eighth Letter* 353e; *Protagoras* 341c, 346d; *Laws* 777b). It can also mean a dialect or way of speaking in a particular language—for example, the "modern language [*hē . . . nea phōnē*]" of the Greeks as opposed to their "ancient" language ([*hē palaia phōnē*) (*Cratylus* 418b, 421d), modern pronunciation as opposed to the "Attic dialect [*tēi Attikēi phōnēi*]" or the "old Attic pronunciation [*tēn palaian phōnēn*]" (*Cratylus* 398d).[3]

As human language or as a human voice—and in all the cases thus far (with the sole exception of the daimonion), it is a human voice we are talking about—*phōnē* is what human beings use to communicate with one another, the means by which they communicate both meaning (the content of what they are saying) and something about themselves (their origin or identity, audible in their language, voice, dialect, or accent). It is hardly surprising, then, that *phōnē* would be understood elsewhere as the counterpart or accompaniment of gesture, particularly bodily gesture imitated on the stage. In the *Republic*, for example, Socrates contrasts pure narration or diegesis, the narration of people's actions and words, with "imitation in voices and gestures [*mimēseōs phōnais te kai schēmasin*]" (*Republic* 397a–b; see also *Gorgias* 474e; *Laws* 654c; *Cratylus* 423b). It is right here, however, that *phōnē* begins to take on meanings that exceed the human. In the *Laws*, for instance, the Athenian says that gestures and sounds, *phōnai*, are shared by both humans and animals: "Every young creature [*to neon*]," he says, "is incapable of keeping either its body [*sōmasi*] or its tongue [*phōnais*] quiet, and is always striving to move and to cry, leaping and skipping and delighting in dances and games, and uttering, also, noises [*phōnas*] of every description" (*Laws* 653d). Animals too thus seem to have *phōnai*; they too are capable of producing or of uttering *phōnai*. In this case, *phōnē* seems to mean not "voice"—meaningful voice—but "sound" or even "noise."

In *For More Than One Voice*, Cavarero draws our attention to this somewhat surprising flexibility in the word *phōnē*. She there speaks of "the strange poverty of the Greek philosophical language—which indicates both 'sound' and 'voice' with the single term *phōnē*" (*MO* 178). It is indeed a strange "poverty," but we will see shortly the way in which Plato not only compensates for this poverty but turns it to his advantage, transforming it into a genuine resource for his thought, trading on this ambiguity in order to distinguish between two different valences or meanings of *phōnē*—one related to the human and everything associated with it and one related to the animal.

It is important to note that in the passage from the *Laws* just cited, *phōnai* are attributed not to humans and animals in general but to all "young creatures"—at once human and nonhuman. All young creatures, it is said, make sounds, have *phōnai*, but it seems that only some of these creatures—only humans—will go on to develop a *phōnē* in the more restricted sense of the term—that is, as voice. Though the same word, *phōnē*, is used to characterize the sounds of both animals and humans, those sounds can and must be further delimited, distinguished to prevent the conflation of the two. Hence, the Athenian speaks in the same passage of "animal sounds [*phōnēs thēriōdous*]" that human beings would do well not to imitate (*Laws* 669e), animal sounds, animal *phōnai*, that should not be imitated not because of what they say or mean but because of their more or less pure vocality—that is, because of their lack of meaning. Indeed, the Athenian argues that the Muses would never themselves combine and so would never condone poets combining "in a single piece the cries of beasts and men [*thērion phōnas kai anthrōpōn*], the clash of instruments, and noises [*psophous*] of all kinds" (*Laws* 669c).[4] He is thus warning against the combination or conflation of human voices (*phōnai*) with human and animal sounds (*phōnai*), and these voices and sounds with other kinds of noises (*psophoi*)—noises so different from or so discordant with these voices and sounds that a wholly other word, *psophoi*, is called for. We see Plato here reckoning with the fact that, in the Greek of his time, the same word *phōnē* was commonly applied to both humans and animals, just as Cavarero notes. Plato must thus distinguish between two valences of *phōnē*, one oriented toward meaning, toward a semantic content, toward the human voice, and the other toward the sensible, toward the animal, toward sound as the material element of voice. Animals make sounds—unordered sounds, as we will see in a moment—but those sounds never rise to the level of voice in the human sense. Were two terms, *voice* and *sound*, available to Plato, one could well imagine him distinguishing human from animal on the basis of the two terms. But without such a pre-given distinction, Plato must resort to other strategies for attuning his reader or his listener to the subtle and yet essential difference between *phōnē* and *phōnē*.

But there is yet another complication, yet another aspect of the "strange poverty" Cavarero finds in the word *phōnē*. In the *Republic*, the term *phōnē* is used to describe not just the voices of humans or the sounds of animals but the "sounds of instruments." The term appears yet again in the context of a discourse on imitation, on the things a speaker should and should not imitate. Socrates there says that "the more debased" a speaker is,

> the less will he shrink from imitating anything and everything. He will think nothing unworthy of himself, so that he will attempt, seriously and in the presence of many, to imitate all things . . . claps of thunder, and the noise of wind and hail and axles and pulleys, and the notes of trumpets and flutes and pan-pipes, and the sounds of all instruments [*pantōn organōn phōnas*], and the cries [*phthongous*] of dogs, sheep, and birds; and so his style will depend wholly on imitation in voice and gesture [*mimēseōs phōnais te kai schēmasin*], or will contain but a little of pure narration. (*Republic* 397a–b)

Plato's suspicion of this kind of imitation is clear. The human voice is debased when it seeks to imitate the sounds of animals, instruments, or natural sounds—that is, nonhuman sounds that might evoke some emotion in the listener but convey no genuine meaning. What must be censured is the human voice lowering itself to the level of mere sound, imitating various sounds that might be recognized as the sounds of certain nonhuman things but that lack the kinds of uniquely human sounds that convey some further meaning.

But this reference to the *phōnai* of instruments can be understood in yet another way. In the *Timaeus*, it is said that both speech (logos) and music (*mousikē*) make use of *phōnē*, the first using the human voice to produce meaningful discourse and the second using sound to produce harmony: "Concerning sound [*phōnēs*] also and hearing, . . . they were bestowed by the Gods with the same object and for the same reasons; for it was for these same purposes that speech [logos] was ordained, and it makes the greatest contribution thereto; music too, in so far as it uses audible sound [*phōnēi*], was bestowed for the sake of harmony" (*Timaeus* 47c). Whereas Plato in the *Laws* tried to distinguish human *phōnai* from animal *phōnai*, he here compares the use of *phōnē* in speech, in logos, to the use of *phōnē* in music.[5] What licenses this comparison, it seems, is the ordering of sounds in both, the fact that sounds are arranged in both speech and music in an ordered sequence. In the case of speech, elementary sounds—letters (*stoicheia* or *grammata*)—are combined and ordered into syllables, syllables that are then combined into words, and words (nouns and verbs) into phrases, all with the aim of producing meaningful discourse. In music, elementary sounds, often called *phthongoi* or notes, are combined to produce harmony.[6] In the *Theaetetus*, Socrates makes this parallel or analogy even more explicit: "In learning, you were merely constantly trying to distinguish between the letters [*stoicheia*] both by sight and by hearing, keeping each of them distinct from the rest, that you might not be disturbed by their sequence when they were spoken or written. . . . And in the music school was not perfect attainment the ability to follow each note [*phthongōi*] and tell which string produced it; and everyone would agree that notes are the elements [*stoicheia*] of music?" (*Theaetetus* 206a; see also *Republic* 400a; *Laws* 812d). *Phthongoi*, notes, are thus the basic elements (*stoicheia*) of music in the same way that *grammata*, letters, are the basic elements (*stoicheia*) of speaking or writing. Learning to speak and to write involves learning what syllables and words can be combined, and the same can be said for music "in connection with high and low sounds [*phthongous*]" (*Sophist* 253a–b).[7]

It thus appears that *phōnē*, in the case of both speech and music, is oriented by a relation to order. It is oriented toward meaning and harmony, toward ordered sequences of elements, and away from sound as sound, away from the voice as embodied sound. What is essential is thus the meaning of a sentence in the case of speech, especially one that can be either affirmed or denied, and the order and harmony of sounds in the case of music, while what is inessential in both is the unordered nature of these sounds as sounds. By itself and qualified in no other way, then, *phōnē* can be understood as the material vehicle or medium for meaning or for harmony. In the *Phaedo*, Socrates says that while voice, *phōnē*, could be cited as a cause or as the medium or means for talking, it must not be confused with its end or its essence, which is the exchange not of sound or of voice but of sense or meaning. That is why Socrates mocks those who would cite "voice [*phōnas*] and air and hearing and countless other things of the sort as causes for our talking with each other" (*Phaedo* 98d). Voice might be the material cause of talking but certainly not its formal or its final cause.

There is thus an audible aspect of a *phōnē*, that which can be perceived or heard. But what makes a *phōnē* a *phōnē* in the fullest sense of the term seems to be the meaning to which that sound gives access—that is, not the meaning in or of the sound, which can always be that of some nonhuman entity (the indication of an animal, an instrument, or some natural phenomenon), but the meaning above and beyond the sound itself. In the *Theaetetus* again, Socrates, trying to get Theaetetus to recognize that perception is not the same thing as knowledge, recalls that we can fail to understand the language of foreigners and yet still hear the sounds they produce or the voices with which they utter them. In other words, "before having learned the language of foreigners [*tōn barbarōn . . . phōnēn*]," we can nonetheless say that in written language "we both see and know the form and color" of the letters and "in the spoken language we both hear and at the same time know the higher and lower notes" (*Theaetetus*163b). It is thus a certain knowledge beyond color and sound, a certain access to what is called in the *Critias* the dianoia behind sound or voice, that allows us to understand any one language and to translate it into another: "Since Solon was planning to make use of the story for his own poetry, he had found, on investigating the meaning [*dunamin*] of the names, that those Egyptians who had first written them down had translated [*metenēnochotas*] them into their own tongue [*phōnēn*]. So he himself in turn recovered the original sense [*dianoian*] of each name, and rendering it into our tongue [*phōnēn*], wrote it down so" (*Critias* 113a–b).

*Phōnē* is thus indeed both voice and sound, as Cavarero says, though it always edges, as she also shows, toward human voice and thus toward meaningful speech rather than sound—in short, toward the human rather than the animal. That is why Cavarero argues that "the Greek philosophers—who were bothered by a *phōnē* that was shared by animals and men—took care to emphasize that in man this *phōnē* is a *phōnē sēmantikē*, a 'signifying voice,' while the animal's is not" (*MO* 32). In the course of her reading of Aristotle's *Poetics*, she can thus write this of the *phōnē sēmantikē*: "Although the phonetic elements—namely, the letters and syllables—that compose the nouns and verbs are insignificant [*asēmoi*], the verbs and nouns that result from this composition are finally *phōnē sēmantikē*. As a composition of nouns and verbs, therefore, *phōnē sēmantikē* is logos" (*MO* 54). While this phrase, *phōnē sēmantikē*, comes from Aristotle's *Poetics* and is to be found nowhere as such in Plato, Cavarero claims that "a similar theory" can be found in Plato in a passage from the *Philebus* where Plato is not just using the term *phōnē* but seeking to describe or define it. It is a passage where, as we will now see, Plato's strategy for disambiguating the very ambiguous *phōnē* he inherited is on full display.

## 3. *Phōnē* as One and Indefinite: *Philebus* 17b

Having seen the fundamental ambiguity in the Greek *phōnē* and the way in which it is inflected in Plato toward voice rather than sound, we are ready to read one of the more enigmatic but also more interesting uses of the term in Plato. It occurs near the beginning of the *Philebus* as Socrates, attempting to understand the nature of pleasure as indefinite or infinitely varied, gives the example of *phōnē*. Here is the passage in Greek, followed by five different English translations:

Phōnē *men hēmin esti pou mia dia tou stomatos iousa, kai apeiros au plēthei, pantōn te kai hekastou.*

Fowler: "*Sound*, which passes out through the mouth of each and all of us, is one, and yet again it is infinite in number."[8]

Hackforth: "The *sound* that proceeds through our mouths, yours and mine and everybody's, is one, isn't it, and also an unlimited variety?"[9]

Gosling: "*Vocal sound* is, you will agree, a single thing that comes out of our mouths, of indeterminate variety, whether you consider an individual or the population at large."[10]

Frede: "The *sound* that comes out of the mouth is one for each and every one of us, but then it is also unlimited in number."[11]

Jowett: "The *sound* which passes through the lips whether of an individual or of all men is one and yet infinite."[12]

The English translations are near unanimous in their translation of *phōnē* by *sound* or *vocal sound*. I say *near* unanimous because there is at least one discordant voice, one translator, Seth Benardete, who translates *phōnē* by the other word we have seen English translations of Plato use—the one toward which, as I have argued, Plato quite consistently orients this term: "Although there is no doubt that our *voice*, the voice of each and every one of us, which proceeds through the mouth, is one and, in turn, unlimited in multitude."[13]

There thus appear to be two schools of thought—and thus of translation—one major, one minor.[14] Since we are talking about the sound that comes out of a clearly human mouth, it makes sense to translate *phōnē*, as Benardete does, by *voice*, the human voice. But insofar as what is coming out of this human mouth is not yet divided into meaningful, ordered sequences but is instead seen or heard as one, as a single stream, or else as an indefinite, infinite many, it makes sense to speak, as the majority of the English translations do, of sound. As for Cavarero, she comes down on the side of Benardete. Just after the passage cited above where she is commenting on the *phōnē sēmantikē* of Aristotle, she writes, "A similar theory can be found in Plato's texts, which go even further in emphasizing this anonymous character of the *phōnē*. As Socrates says in the *Philebus*, 'The *voice* [*phōnē*] that comes out of my mouth is one and infinite [*apeiros*] and multiple: it is the voice of everyone and each one'" (*MO* 54). Hence, Cavarero, like Benardete, translates *phōnē* here not as *sound* but as *voice*, though her explanation of the passage uses both *sound* and *voice*:

Considered in general, the voice is "one"—that is, appertains to a single category, namely, a category of sounds emitted by the mouth of each and every one. It appertains, in short, to the human capacity for phonation. Although this phonation is presented as variegated, it nevertheless also presents itself as indeterminate [*apeiron*]. And this indeterminacy applies not only to the strict sense of the term *phōnē* as the human voice, but also to the broader sense of *phōnē* as acoustically perceptible sound in general. Socrates in fact notes that the problem raised here also concerns the art of music. (*MO* 54)

According to this passage from the *Philebus*, the voice or sound that comes out of the human mouth, human *phōnē*, is at once one and an indefinite many, at once a single stream without difference or articulation and an infinitely varied or infinitely differentiated many with no identifiable differences or articulations. In either case, communication or dialogue as the exchange of identifiable, meaningful sounds—sounds ordered by or as voice—appears impossible. Plato thus seems to be drawing our attention to the very place where *phōnē* is turned into *phōnē*—that is, where sound is transformed into voice, where sound as sound is turned into logos or meaningful discourse. The ambiguity in *phōnē* that we have been following cannot but challenge both the translator and the interpreter of this curious passage, for reading *phōnē* as either sound or voice will have serious implications for the way we understand everything from sound and meaning to the unordered and the ordered, the animal and the human, the child and the adult, and so on. It is thus no wonder that translations would differ at this crucial juncture.

To demonstrate the lack of meaning in *phōnē* as either one or indefinite, it will be useful to look briefly at the term that here modifies *phōnē*—namely, *apeiros*, a word that is just as flexible as *phōnē*. For just as Plato trades on the fact that *phōnē* can mean, as we have seen, both "sound" and "voice," so he takes advantage of the fact that the adjective *apeiros* can mean two very distinct things depending on the use that is being made of it and which of its two roots is being evoked. While context usually makes it clear which of the two is intended in any given passage, there are one or two places—including the *Philebus*—where Plato himself actually takes advantage of these differing meanings to shed a mutually illuminating light on them.

In the first of its two meanings, then, *apeiros, -on*, would come from *peira, peiraō, peiraomai*, meaning "to try" or "to attempt," "to experience" or "to have experience of something"—words at the origin of our words *empirical, empiricism*, and so on. *Apeiros* would combine this root with the alpha-privative to qualify someone who is *in*experienced, *in*expert, *un*versed, and so on. In the *Theaetetus*, we see Socrates complimenting Theaetetus on not being inexperienced in the kind of argument that Socrates is trying to conduct: "You follow me, I take it, Theaetetus, for I think you not new [*ouk apeiros*, not inexperienced] at such things" (*Theaetetus* 155c). When it comes to philosophical conversation or dialectic, being *apeiros*, inexperienced, is clearly undesirable. The sentiment is echoed in the *Symposium* when Alcibiades says, in his encomium of Socrates, that those who have never heard Socrates, that is, those who are "inexpert [or inexperienced] and thoughtless [*apeiros kai anoētos*] might laugh his speeches to scorn," filled as they are with "pack-asses, smiths, cobblers, tanners" and the like (*Symposium* 221e; see also *Hippias Major* 289e). In other words, to know Socrates is to love him, but to know him one must become experienced in his way of speaking. Those who remain inexperienced or *apeiros* with regard to Socrates thus end up unjustly and inappropriately laughing at him and his way of speaking.

To be *apeiros*, under this first root, thus suggests not having experience when experience would be beneficial—for example, being unskilled or uneducated in a certain skill or craft that would be useful to know (see *Protagoras* 328a), being uneducated or uninformed about letters or books (*Apology* 26d), being inexperienced or unaccustomed to living in a particular state of law (*Laws* 752b), or being unaccustomed, *apeiros*, to "manly toils" but accustomed, *empeiros*, to "a delicate and unmanly mode of life" (*Phaedrus* 239c). The term *apeiros* is thus applied almost always as a criticism or censure; it is almost always a negative evaluation.[15] In the *Gorgias*, Socrates goes so far as to say that experience is what allows us to lead our lives with art, while inexperience gives us over to chance: "There are many arts amongst mankind that have been discovered experimentally, as the result of experiences [*ek tōn empeirōn empeirōs*], for experience [*empeiria*] conducts the course of our life according to art [*kata technēn*], but inexperience according to chance [*apeiria de kata tuchēn*]. Of these several and various men partake in various ways, and the best men of the best. Gorgias here is one of these, and he is a partner in the finest art of all" (*Gorgias* 448c). While genuine knowledge is always best for Plato, experience is second best and always far better than being *apeiros* or without inexperience, especially since, as we will see, being inexperienced is not completely unrelated to thinking the indefinite or thinking in an indefinite way.

The second meaning of *apeiros* would come from the same alpha-privative combined now with another root—namely, *peras* or *peiras*, which means "limit," "end," or "boundary." What is *apeiros* would thus be what is limitless, interminable, unlimited, boundless, infinite, innumerable. In the passage from the *Philebus* that we have been looking at, it is clearly this meaning that is meant. Sound/voice is at once one and *apeiros*, which is to say unlimited, boundless, indefinite. Without any further description or determination, this could sound like a neutral designation or even something positive. But Plato's use of the term in other dialogues leaves little room for doubt about the generally negative sense of this meaning as well. For just as there are two distinct meanings to *apeiros*, based on two different roots, so there are two different valences—both negative—to this second meaning of the word: an ontological valence but also, before that, an ethical valence. As to the latter, the Athenian of the *Laws* speaks of how wealth can breed in those with a bad nature or upbringing "countless lustings after its insatiable and endless acquisition [*tēs aplēstou kai apeirou ktēseōs*]" (*Laws* 870a). That is why laws must be established, to keep "impious men" from doing things that end up "increasing infinitely [*eis apeiron*] their own iniquity" (*Laws* 910). We see a similar use of the term in the *Republic*, as Socrates speaks of those who "abandon themselves to the unlimited [*apeiron*] acquisition of wealth, disregarding the limit [*horon*] set by our necessary wants" (*Republic* 373d). The philosopher, as Socrates later says, is someone who is able to resist this limitlessness, a man who "will not let himself be dazzled by the felicitations of the multitude and pile up the mass of his wealth without measure [*apeiron*], involving himself in measureless [*aperanta*] ills" (*Republic* 591d). To be *apeiros* in this more ethical sense is to have unbridled or unlimited desire, to be tempted by the uncountable multitude, to lust after unlimited wealth.

When we thus combine this systematic disapproval of those who are *apeiros* in this more ethical sense with the fact that the other meaning of *apeiros* as inexperienced or untried is also almost always negative, we have good reason to suspect that Plato's more ontological use of the term in *Philebus* and elsewhere might come with similarly negative shadings and implications. In fact, in at least two places in the dialogues, Plato himself not only brings the two meanings of *apeiros* into contact with one another but lets the one play off of or resonate with the other in just this way. In the first of these, from the *Timaeus*, the question at hand is whether the universe, the *kosmos*, should be considered one or many. Timaeus there says:

> Now in reasoning about all these things, a man might question whether he ought to affirm the existence of an infinite diversity [*apeirous*] of universes [*kosmous*] or a limited number [*peras*]; and if he questioned aright he would conclude that the doctrine of an infinite diversity [*apeirous*] is that of a man unversed [*ontōs apeirou tinos einai*] in matters wherein he ought to be versed [*empeiron*]; but the question whether they ought really to be described as one Universe or five is one which

might with more reason give us pause. Now our view declares the universe to be essentially one, in accordance with the probable account [*eikota logon*]. (*Timaeus* 55c)

Timaeus's reasoning here about the number of universes is telling. He argues that probability is on the side of there being just one; it is most likely that there is only one. But it is not unreasonable, he suggests, that there are many universes, for example, five—a small, determinate number. What is then excluded from serious consideration is the possibility of there being an infinite or unlimited number. As Timaeus argues, only an inexperienced or unversed thinker, an *apeiros* thinker, would think that there is an *apeiros* number of universes—that is, an unlimited or unreckonable number. Only the thinker unversed in such speculation would think that the universe or, perhaps, the pluriverse, the multiverse, is in fact infinite in number.

A passage from the dialogue from which we set out, the *Philebus*, plays on these two meanings in a similar way. Socrates there says, "The infinite number [*to apeiron*] of individuals and the infinite number in each of them makes you in every instance indefinite in thought [*apeiron . . . tou phronein*, inexperienced in thought] and of no account [*ouk enlogimon*] and not to be considered among [*oud' en arithmon*, counted among] the wise, so long as you have never fixed your eye upon any definite number [*arithmon*] in anything" (*Philebus* 17e). It is hard to imagine a more playful Plato or a more inventive one, exploiting the multiple (but not infinite) meanings of this homophone *apeiros* to make his point: the indefinite number of individuals and the indefinite number in each of those individuals is liable to make one an indefinite or an inexperienced thinker—that is, a thinker who is not to be counted among the wise. So long as a thinker has not found, determined, or counted a definite number in these things, he will forever remain a thinker of no account.

In both of these passages, the negativity attached to *apeiros* in the first sense seems to rub off, as it were, on the second sense. Indeed, it is difficult to find in Plato any unequivocally positive references to what is *apeiros* as either inexperienced or unlimited. Nowhere do we find a positive reference to, say, the seemingly infinite, awe-inspiring, or wonder-provoking number of stars in the sky. In fact, the only time we hear talk about the sun and moon and stars in conjunction with *apeiros* is when, in the *Laws*, the Athenian uses the adverb *apeirōs* to criticize those who are inexperienced about number, about counting, and about the circuits of the sun, moon, and stars (see

*Laws* 818c). The point there is that being ignorant or inexperienced about number makes one unsuited to be a ruler, a supervisor, or, it is implied, a philosopher. Being inexperienced (*apeiros*) about numbers—so inexperienced that one knows nothing of the determinate numbers between one and the infinite (*to apeiron*)—makes one ill-suited to be a ruler or philosopher or even, in the end, a human being in the highest and fullest sense of the term.

There is one final use of the term *apeiros* in Plato that deserves mention here. It occurs in the *Statesman* as the Stranger, in his myth of the two ages, is recounting the moment right near the end of the Age of Zeus when the entire universe risks being destroyed, its unity and all the unities within it undone, dissolved into the "boundless sea of diversity," the infinite sea of difference. The Stranger there says that God, seeing the "dire trouble [*aporias*]" of the universe, fearing that "it might founder in the tempest of confusion and sink in the boundless sea of diversity [*eis ton tēs anomoiotētos apeiron onta ponton duēi*]," took back up his position of helmsman and thereby restored order to the universe (*Statesman* 273d). Once again, the unlimited—the boundless sea of difference or unlikeness— is no friend of the universe. It is what undoes all individual identities in the universe and the universe itself as an identifiable whole. It is, as it were, the opposite of the one, the enemy of the one cosmos or universe.

We would thus do well to keep all this in mind when we read in the *Philebus* that sound—like pleasure—is or can be considered to be either one or indefinite. Indeed, Plato's reason for recalling the infiniteness or indefiniteness of *phōnē* is to help us understand the infiniteness or indefiniteness of pleasure, which is the explicit theme of the dialogue. As Socrates recalls later in the dialogue, they had agreed that "pleasure was itself infinite [*apeiros*], and belonged to the class which, in and by itself, has not and never will have either beginning or middle or end" (*Philebus* 31a; see also 23c, 24b, 24e, 25d, 32a, 41d). From the outset, the implication is that while *phōnē* certainly can be considered simply as one or as infinite, it ought not be, for we will learn little about it so long as we continue to consider it in just this way. In this more ontological sense, then, *apeiros* marks the far end of a spectrum or scale that runs from one to a definite and countable many to myriads—a word with which *apeiros* is sometimes paired (see *Sophist* 251b; *Epinomis* 987a)—to the absolutely infinite, indefinite, or uncountable. Only the inexperienced thinker, a thinker unversed in dialects, will persist in saying that something like *phōnē* is either one or infinite and not then go on to find a finite number of forms or beings between these two extremes.

Plato's point throughout the *Philebus* seems to be that whenever we begin with the one or with some unity, we "must not turn immediately to infinity [*apeirou*] but to some definite number [*arithmon*]" between them (*Philebus* 18a). In other words, says Socrates, "we must not apply the idea of the infinite to plurality until we have a view of its whole number between infinity and one [*metaxu tou apeirou te kai tou henos*]" (*Philebus* 16d). We must not jump, as it were, from the one to the infinite without first finding some plurality or definite many within the whole. Then and only then can we "let each unit of everything pass on unhindered into infinity [*eis to apeiron*]" (*Philebus* 16e; see also 18e).[16]

That is precisely the lesson that immediately follows Socrates's evocation of *phōnē* at *Philebus* 17b. Socrates proceeds to tell the story of how some "god or godlike man," the one the Egyptians call Theuth—the same Theuth who, in the *Phaedrus*, is credited with having invented writing (see *Phaedrus* 274c–e)—observed both "that sound was infinite [*phōnēn apeiron*]" and yet also "that the vowel sounds in that infinity [*ta phōnē entaentōi apeirōi*] were not one, but many, and again that there were other elements which were not vowels [*phōnēs*] but did have a sonant quality [*phōnēs men ou, phthongou de metechonta tinos*], and that these also had a definite number [*arithmon*]" (*Philebus* 18b–c). Hence, Theuth began with the one, with this single stream of sound, but then went on to distinguish various kinds of letters "until he knew the number of them and gave to each and all the name of letters [*stoicheion*]" (*Philebus* 18c). Finally, "perceiving that none of us could learn any one of them alone by itself without learning them all, and considering that this was a common bond [*desmon*] which made them in a way all one, he assigned to them all a single science and called it grammar [*grammatikēn*]" (*Philebus* 18c–d).

When we combine this important passage from the *Philebus* with others from the *Cratylus*, *Sophist*, and *Theaetetus*, we get a pretty good picture of how meaning comes about for Plato. Among the infinite variety of sounds within the human voice, a finite number of these—namely, letters, *grammata*—can be determined. These letters—the fundamental elements, the *stoicheia*, of language, which are themselves nonsignifying—can then be divided into various categories: vowels (*phōnēenta*), consonants (*aphōna*) or mutes (*aphthonga*), and so on.[17] The art of grammar will then allow one to determine which letters can be joined to form syllables, which syllables can be combined to form words—at once nouns and verbs, which are defined in the *Sophist* as "two kinds of vocal indications of being [*tōn tēi phōnēi peri tēn ousian dēlōmatōn*]" (*Sophist* 261e)—and then which words can be combined to form statements or logoi (that is, claims, statements, propositions, or assertions), the true aim, it would seem, of the *phōnē sēmantikē* (see *Sophist* 253b, 262a; *Cratylus* 383a, 389d). *Phōnē* is thus indeed at once one and indefinite, at once a single stream or an endless sea of differences, but the art of grammar allows us to find a determinate number of letters, in addition to the laws of their combination, between these two extremes.

Between sound and voice, then—between the one and the indefinite, on the one hand, and a definite many, on the other—*phōnē* is what facilitates this transformation of nonsignifying elements into meaningful logos. It is not surprising, therefore, that translations of *Philebus* 17b differ in the way we have seen or that Cavarero puts so much emphasis on this passage. *Phōnē* can be considered either one or infinite, either a single sound or an indefinite number, before being broken up into a definite number—that is, before being understood (or heard) as voice. It is when the one or the indefinite becomes a countable many that *phōnē* as sound finally becomes *phōnē* as voice. It is the ambiguity inherent in the Greek *phōnē* that makes this possible, an ambiguity that allows Plato to turn that "poverty" of Greek philosophical language into a genuine "resource" for philosophy.

It is hardly insignificant that the ambiguity of *phōnē* is here concentrated or located in the mouth, specifically the human mouth (the *stoma*), as if the human were the only animal to have a mouth—in addition to a voice—in the highest or fullest sense of the term. In the *Timaeus*, it is said that the mouth is the place where food is, as it were, converted or transformed into logos, the place where nutrition enters and words exit, where what is necessary is transformed into what is good: "And those who fashioned the features of our mouth [*stomatos*] fashioned it with teeth and tongue and lips, even as it is fashioned now, for ends both necessary [*anankaiōn*] and most good [*aristōn*], contriving it as an entrance [*eisodon*] with a view to necessary ends, and as an outlet [*exodon*] with a view to the ends most good. For all that enters in and supplies food to the body is necessary; while the stream of speech [*logōn*] which flows out and ministers to intelligence [*phronēsi*] is of all streams the fairest and most good" (*Timaeus* 75d–e). The mouth is the place where the necessary is converted into the good, where nourishment for the body is turned into intelligence that exits the soul. Food comes in, and sound comes out, sound that, ideally, has been ordered and organized as a voice that attempts to convey as clearly and as closely as possible the wordless, soundless announcements of the soul itself.[18] As the

Stranger famously asserts in the *Sophist*, "Thought [dianoia] and speech [logos] are the same; only the former, which is a silent inner conversation [*dialogos aneu phōnēs*, dialogue without voice or without sound] of the soul with itself, has been given the special name of thought [dianoia]" (*Sophist* 263e).[19] Dianoia, thought, would thus be speech or dialogue without voice or sound, while logos, which is said to be the "same" as dianoia, would be "the stream that flows from the soul in vocal utterance through the mouth [*to . . . rheuma dia tou stomatos ion meta phthongou*]" (*Sophist* 263e).[20] The mouth is, then, the place where *phōnē* as sound, as a stream of sound, gets converted into *phōnē* as voice, the place where a stream of meaningless sounds becomes a stream of meaningful logos in sound. That is why Plato's logocentrism is also always a phonocentrism.

## 4. "Extraneous Voices"

In *For More Than One Voice*, Cavarero argues that Western philosophy, beginning with the Greeks, has essentially ignored or excluded the voice, concentrating instead on thought or on universal meaning as what comes before or exceeds the always singular voice. According to Cavarero, Western metaphysics is essentially the story of "how logos lost its voice," the story of the "devocalization of logos," beginning in Plato and Aristotle (*MO* 33). It is the story of the loss of voice and the substitution of a universalizing thought or semantics for that voice. We would thus find in Plato the beginnings of "the metaphysical dream that stands ready to sacrifice the vocality of speech in order not to have to worry about the existence of others" (*MO* 46), an existence that is made most manifest and compelling through the voice.

The foregoing analysis of *phōnē* in Plato has done nothing but confirm these claims of Cavarero. When Cavarero argues, for example, that it is "symptomatic that, in the classical era, the Greek word *phōnē* is applied to both human and animal sound, as well as to any other audible sound" (*MO* 19), we know that this is a symptom of something that metaphysics will attempt to reject or exclude, a "prephilosophical thread," as Cavarero calls it, from Greek culture and religion that ties the voice to breath in such a way as to root voice in the body and, by extension, in the animal or the animal part of man. Greek philosophy, beginning with Plato, would have taken its distance from this prephilosophical past by disambiguating the *phōnē*, distinguishing sound from voice, the animal from the human, and so on.

Though logos as speech or language would seem to imply voice and thus speakers, philosophy, beginning with Plato, would have done everything it could to avoid these implications, using "precise strategies" that prevent it from "getting caught up in the very question of the voice" (*MO* 9)—strategies such as disambiguating the word *phōnē* or else exploiting the ambiguity of *apeiros* to distinguish undifferentiated or infinitely differentiated sound from the precise, limited articulations of human voice. We have seen how Plato was thus able to turn what Cavarero calls "the strange poverty of the Greek philosophical language—which indicates both 'sound' and 'voice' with the single term *phōnē*" (*MO* 178)—into a genuine resource for philosophy. What seemed like an obstacle to philosophy, a poverty in philosophical language, a "prephilosophical thread" that confused sound and voice, the animal and the human, became a genuine philosophical resource for distinguishing sound from voice, the animal from the human. One is reminded of Socrates/Diotima's tale about Eros in the *Symposium* where Penia, or poverty, proves herself more resourceful than Poros, or resource, himself. The ambiguity that surrounds *phōnē* is thus used by Plato not to question or undo the oppositions and hierarchies that his philosophy establishes (human and animal, voice and sound, meaning and expression, and so on) but to confirm and consolidate them—all in an attempt, as Cavarero argues, to denigrate or exclude the vocal.

One can thus understand why Cavarero would take issue with what Derrida has characterized as Western philosophy's phonocentrism. Western philosophy from Plato on has centered on the exclusion of voice rather than its privileging, as the term *phonocentrism* would seem to suggest. And yet Derrida's argument in "Plato's Pharmacy" and elsewhere regarding the nature of this phonocentrism is much closer to Cavarero's than Cavarero believes. Though it is impossible here to address in full Cavarero's detailed reading and critique of Derrida in the appendix to *For More Than One Voice*, which is ambivalently titled "Dedicated to Derrida" (*MO* 213–241), allow me to make just a couple of comments to try to bring Derrida and Cavarero closer together on this theme of *phōnē*.

Derrida uses the term *phonocentrism* to indicate the Western philosophical tradition's emphasis on *phōnē* not as sound but as voice—that is, its privileging of voice in relation to meaning, of a voice (as opposed to both sound and, interestingly, writing) that attempts to make itself as transparent as possible, which is to say, as silent as possible, in order to give access to meaning itself.[21] It is on this condition that the *Sophist* is able to say, as we saw above, that "thought [dianoia] and speech [logos] are the same," though the former can be defined as "a silent inner conversation of the soul with itself"—that is, as a dialogue without voice or without sound inside the soul (*Sophist* 263e). And it is on this same condition that, in the *Phaedrus*, true speech (that is, "the living and breathing word of him who knows, of which the written word may justly be called the image") can be called "writing in the soul"—an inner writing, as it were, without sound and without image (*Phaedrus* 276a). Hence, Derrida's critique of philosophy's phonocentrism is a critique of the very same exclusion that concerns Cavarero: the exclusion of an elemental, signifying voice, or else a differential, signifying writing, in favor of a phonetic voice that aims always for a transparent presentation of meaning through voice. Phonocentrism is thus nothing other than the neutralization of the differential, material aspect of language in both writing and speech. Hence, Derrida's reading of Western philosophy's denigration of writing in favor of speech does not entail the claim that philosophy has favored *phōnē* understood as sound. On the contrary, this kind of *phōnē* is precisely what must be neutralized to allow one to hear that soundless voice of a soul that would come before both speech and writing. Insofar as Plato posits writing in the restricted sense of the term as extraneous to voice and subordinate to it, voice is, by the very same logic, extraneous to thought understood as "writing in the soul" and subordinate to thought as "a silent inner conversation of the soul with itself." Whether Derrida would agree with Cavarero that this neutralization of *phōnē* signals philosophy's videocentrism is not clear, but he would almost certainly agree that in Plato we find an attempt to neutralize the differential structure of both writing and speech to give access to a silent conversation within the soul that is able to approach the "visible" forms (the *eidē*) themselves. It is this neutralization of both writing and speech that thus promises to give rise to a sort of "indoor voice"—to risk a term used by parents and teachers today to educate young children on how to set limits to their voices—an "indoor voice" that would exceed both writing and speech in perfect conformity with what Cavarero has called the "devocalization of logos."

The phonocentrism that Derrida criticizes revolves around a *phōnē* that, as the foregoing analysis has tried to show, is oriented toward meaning rather than sound, the human rather than the animal—in short, toward logos and ultimately toward dianoia as the soul's silent conversation with itself. That is why Derrida often spoke not just of phonocentrism but of phonologocentrism, indicating the way in which a particular kind of *phōnē*, one that makes itself—or seems to make itself—as transparent as possible, lends itself to logos as meaning.

Let me simply conclude, then, by returning to one final use of the word *phōnē* in Plato. It is to be found in the *Protagoras* as Socrates is trying to get Protagoras to engage in direct dialogue rather than discuss the words of poets who are not there to explain or defend their words. In short, Socrates is trying to get Protagoras to use his own voice to explain his own views rather than use the "extraneous voices" of poets. Socrates says,

> Let us talk no more of poems and verses, but consider the points on which I questioned you at first, Protagoras . . . For it seems to me that arguing about poetry is comparable to the wine-parties of common market-folk. These people, owing to their inability to carry on a familiar conversation over their wine by means of their own voices and discussion [*dia tēs heautōn phōnēs . . . kai tōn logōn*]—such is their lack of education—put a premium on flute-girls by hiring the extraneous voice [*allotrian phōnēn*] of the flute at a high price, and carry on their intercourse by means of its utterance [*phōnēs*]. But where the party consists of thorough gentlemen who have had a proper education, you will see neither flute-girls nor dancing-girls nor harp-girls, but only the company contenting themselves with their own conversations [*dia tēs hautōn phōnēs*], and none of these fooleries and frolics—each speaking and listening decently in his turn, even though they may drink a great deal of wine. And so a gathering like this of ours, when it includes such men as most of us claim to be, requires no extraneous voices [*allotrias phōnēs*], not even of the poets, whom one cannot question on the sense of what they say. . . . No, this sort of meeting is avoided by men of culture, who prefer to converse directly with each other, and to use their own way of speech [*en tois heautōn logois*] in putting one another by turns to the test. (*Protagoras* 347c–348a)[22]

Socrates thus encourages Protagoras to use his own voice, his own unique voice, rather than rely on the voices of others. But both Cavarero and Derrida would no doubt read Socrates's critique of these "extraneous voices" of the poets as indicative of Plato's view that the voice itself is extraneous, extraneous or supplementary to the meaning that is conveyed by that voice. On this point Cavarero and Derrida would be, I think, in agreement and would speak with a single voice—a single voice that is, on both of their accounts, always more than one.

# Notes

1. Adriana Cavarero, *For More Than One Voice*, trans. Paul A. Kottman (Stanford, CA: Stanford University Press, 2005); hereafter cited parenthetically in the text and abbreviated as *MO*.

2. We see something similar in the *Protagoras* as Socrates, "recognizing the voice [*phōnēn gnous*]" of Hippocrates at the door of his house, goes out to greet him (*Protagoras* 310b). Except where otherwise noted, I have used the Loeb Classical Library's translations for all Plato dialogues.

3. In the *Apology*, Socrates compares his lack of familiarity with the language of the law courts to just such a foreign tongue or foreign dialect (*phōnē*) (see *Apology* 17d). Hence, *phōnē* can be used to describe a particular dialect or accent within a particular language (see *Laws* 642c; *Phaedo* 62a; *Protagoras* 341b), even a particular expression (*Theaetetus* 183b) or way of speaking within a particular language—speaking with a voice of lamentation, for example (see *Laws* 960a), or speaking quickly (see *Statesman* 306c), with a deep voice (*Protagoras* 316a), or loudly (see *Protagoras* 310b; *Laws* 934d), or, as Socrates says in the *Republic* with regard to poets or the actors they hire, speaking with "loud, persuasive voices [*phōnai*]" that "draw the polities toward tyrannies or democracies" (*Republic* 568c; see also *Laws* 817c; *Gorgias* 502b–503a), a use of the term that suggests the potential dangers, the political dangers, of the voice. A *phōnē* can also be the voice with which one sings (see *Lysis* 204d; *Phaedrus* 259d; *Laws* 666d).

4. In the *Fifth Letter*, it is said that each form of government, each polity, like an animal, has its own *phōnē*, its own kind of language (*Fifth Letter* 321d–e).

5. For Plato's critique of wind instruments, and particularly the flute, see *MO* 69: "Besides the fact that they swell the cheeks and deform the face, they require breath and thus impede the flutist from speaking. In other words, the flute lets itself, dangerously, represent the *phōnē* in the double sense of the term: voice and sound."

6. Cavarero writes, "Whether through singing or through playing an instrument, music makes some order out of the vast sea of sound because it distinguishes acute tones from grave tones and defines the intervals between them. Both the musical doctrine of harmony and the order of alphabetic script deal with an analysis of sounds in order to distinguish them from one another through opposition and difference. These are, in other words, two analogous ways of ordering the infinite multiplicity of sonorous emissions" (*MO* 54).

7. Closely related to *phōnē*, and sometimes more or less synonymous with it (see *Sophist* 263e; *Protagoras* 356c), is *phthongos*, often translated as "vocal utterance." Whereas *phōnē* more often than not seems to suggest the voice or speech in general, *phthongos* is usually more specific, more like a sound or note, the particular sound of a voice (see *Menexenus* 235b) or particular sounds within a voice. *Phthongos* is thus often used in the plural, as in quick, slow, shrill, or deep *phthongoi* (see *Timaeus* 80a), *phthongoi* in harmony with one another (see *Phaedo* 86c–d; *Republic* 530e–531a), or, according to a repeated analogy, *phthongoi* that can be as beautiful or pleasing as sights (see *Hippias Major* 298a; *Philebus* 51b; *Republic* 476b). In the *Republic*, the vocal utterances—the cries or sounds—of brave men are also called *phthongoi*. Less than genuine speech, less than a *phōnē sēmantikē*, these *phthongoi* are nonetheless capable of conveying character or virtue, which is why they are sometimes worthy of being imitated (see *Republic* 399a).

8. Plato, *Philebus*, trans. Harold N. Fowler (Cambridge, MA: Harvard University Press, 1975).

9. Plato, *Philebus*, trans. R. Hackforth, in *The Collected Dialogues of Plato*, ed. Edith Hamilton and Huntington Cairns (Princeton, NJ: Princeton University Press, 1980), 1093.

10. Plato, *Philebus*, trans. J. C. B. Gosling (Oxford: Clarendon, 1975).

11. Plato, *Philebus*, trans. Dorothea Frede, in *The Complete Works*, ed. John M. Cooper (Indianapolis: Hackett, 1997).

12. Plato, *The Dialogues of Plato*, vol. 4, trans. Benjamin Jowett (Oxford: Clarendon, 1931).

13. Seth Benardete, trans., *The Tragedy and Comedy of Life: Plato's "Philebus"* (Chicago: University of Chicago Press, 1991).

14. There is the same ambiguity, the same division and difference of opinion, in French translations: "Il y a, j'imagine, unité de *son* émis par la bouche; et, en revanche, émis par la bouche de tous les individus et de chaque individu, le *son vocal* est quantitativement infini." Plato, *Oeuvres complètes*, trans. Léon Robin (Paris: Gallimard, 1950). "La *voix* qui sort de notre bouche est une et en même temps infinie en nombre pour tous et pour chacun." Plato, *Sophiste, Politique, Philèbe, Timée, Critias*, trans. Émile Chambry (Paris: Garnier Frères, Flammarion, 1969).

15. This sometimes means having experience of things that would ultimately be bad or dangerous to one's health or well-being. The idea seems to be that without such experience one becomes even more vulnerable to those bad or dangerous things. Only the very young, therefore, those who are still too vulnerable, too uneducated, or too inexperienced to protect themselves against evil influences, should remain completely unexposed to—inexperienced in—such "evil natures" (*Republic* 409a).

16. Socrates says just before this, "The ancients, who were better than we and lived nearer the gods, handed down the tradition that all the things which are ever said to exist are sprung from the one and the many and have inherent in them the finite [*peras*] and the infinite [*apeirian*]" (*Philebus* 16c; see also *Parmenides* 158d).

17. In addition to *Philebus* 18b–c, see *Theaetetus* 203b; *Sophist* 253a; *Cratylus* 393d, 424c.

18. In the *Laws*, the Athenian argues that the goal of legislation would be for the youth to affirm the laws in unison, without dissent, as if they were speaking, he says, with a single mouth, a single *stoma*, a single *phōnē* or voice. Hence, the law will prescribe that the youth not inquire into the rightness or wrongness of laws but that "all shall declare in unison, with one mouth and one voice [*miai . . . phōnēi kai ex henos stomatos pantas symphōnein*], that all are rightly established by divine enactment" (*Laws* 634e; see also *Laws* 890d; *Euthydemus* 293a). The goal of legislation is for everyone—and particularly the young—to utter the same laws and the same things about the laws, affirming those laws with a single, meaningful voice spoken out of a single mouth. It is as if the goal of the state is to have its citizens approximate the harmony of the Sirens described at the end of the *Republic*, the unity of individual voices—eight in all—contributing to a single harmony: "And the spindle turned on the knees of Necessity, and up above on each of the rims of the circles a Siren stood, borne around in its revolution and uttering one sound [*phōnēn mian*], one note [*hena tonon*], and from all the eight there was the concord of a single harmony" (*Republic* 617b).

19. As the *Timaeus* confirms, the announcement or the logos of soul is "without speech or sound [*aneu phthongoi kai ēchēs*]" (*Timaeus* 37b).

20. In the *Theaetetus*, we are given a definition of *logos* as "making one's own thought clear through speech by means of verbs and nouns [*dianoian emphanē poiein dia phōnēs meta rhēmatōn te kai onomatōn*], imaging the opinion in the stream that flows through the lips [*eis tēn dia tou stomatos rhoēn*], as a mirror or water" (*Theaetetus* 206d).

21.  Interestingly, the word *phonocentrism* appears nowhere in the essay in which Derrida takes up most fully the so-called priority of speech over writing in Plato—namely, "Plato's Pharmacy" (in *Dissemination*, trans. Barbara Johnson [Chicago: University of Chicago Press, 1981], 61–171). Moreover, the word *phōnē*, which is used in the *Phaedrus* to describe the "voice" of Socrates's *daimonion*, as we saw, appears nowhere in the famous critique of writing that attracts so much of Derrida's attention.

22.  We see something similar at the beginning of the *Symposium* when the flute-girl is sent away, leaving the guests—all male—to entertain themselves through conversation, through logoi, without any other sounds or extraneous voices to accompany them (*Symposium* 176e).

## Bibliography

Benardete, Seth, trans. *The Tragedy and Comedy of Life: Plato's "Philebus."* Chicago: University of Chicago Press, 1991.

Cavarero, Adriana. *For More Than One Voice.* Translated by Paul A. Kottman. Stanford, CA: Stanford University Press, 2005.

Derrida, Jacques. "Plato's Pharmacy." In *Dissemination*, translated by Barbara Johnson, 61–171. Chicago: University of Chicago Press, 1981.

Plato. *The Dialogues of Plato.* Vol. 4. Translated by Benjamin Jowett. Oxford: Clarendon, 1931.

———. *Oeuvres complètes.* Translated by Léon Robin. Paris: Gallimard, 1950.

———. *Philebus.* Translated by Harold N. Fowler. Cambridge, MA: Harvard University Press, 1975.

———. *Philebus.* Translated by Dorothea Frede. In *The Complete Works*, edited by John M. Cooper, 398–456. Indianapolis: Hackett, 1997.

———. *Philebus.* Translated by J. C. B. Gosling. Oxford: Clarendon, 1975.

———. *Philebus.* Translated by R. Hackforth. In *The Collected Dialogues of Plato*, edited by Edith Hamilton and Huntington Cairns, 1086–1150. Princeton, NJ: Princeton University Press, 1980.

———. *Sophiste, Politique, Philèbe, Timée, Critias.* Translated by Émile Chambry. Paris: Garnier Frères, Flammarion, 1969.

MICHAEL NAAS is Professor of Philosophy at DePaul University in Chicago. He is author of *Plato and the Invention of Life* and coeditor with Jeremy Bell of *Plato's Animals: Gadflies, Horses, Swans, and Other Philosophical Beasts* (Indiana University Press, 2015).

# 4

# HEARING, TOUCH, AND PRACTICAL INTELLIGENCE IN ARISTOTLE'S PHILOSOPHY

Eve Rabinoff

Colloquially and philosophically, sight is a common sensory metaphor for knowledge, perhaps most memorably articulated in Plato's simile of the sun in *Republic* 6. Aristotle seems to take this metaphor seriously, declaring, in the famous opening passage of his *Metaphysics*, that human beings love the sense of sight because "most of all the senses, [it] makes us know and brings to light many differences between things" (*Metaphysics* 1.1 980a26–27, McKeon). It is surprising, then, to find that elsewhere Aristotle eschews sight's contribution to knowledge in favor of hearing's contribution. In *De sensu* we read (I've highlighted the central claim),

> But those senses which act through external media, such as smell, hearing, and vision, belong to such animals as are capable of locomotion. To all those which possess them they are a means of preservation, in order that they may be aware of their food before they pursue it, and may avoid what is inferior or destructive, while in those that have intelligence (*phronēsis*), also these senses exist for the sake of well-being; for they inform us of many differences, from which arises understanding (*phronēsis*), both of the objects of thought (*noēta*) and of the affairs of practical life (*prakta*).
>
> Of these faculties, for the mere necessities of life and in itself, sight is the more important, but for the mind (*nous*) and indirectly

hearing is the more important. For the faculty of sight informs us of many differences of all kinds, because all bodies have a share of color, so that it is chiefly by this medium that we perceive the common sensibles. (By these I mean shape, magnitude, movement, and number.) *But hearing only conveys differences of sound* (psophos)*, and to a few animals differences of voice* (phonē)*. Indirectly, hearing makes the largest contribution to intelligence* (phronēsis)*. For discourse (lo-gos), which is the cause of learning, is so because it is audible; but it is audible not in itself but indirectly, because it is composed of words, and each word is a symbol* (sumbolon)*.* Consequently, of those who have been deprived of one sense or other from birth, the blind are more intelligent than the deaf and the dumb. (*De sensu* 1.436b18–437a16, Hett)

In contrast to the more famous *Metaphysics* passage, here Aristotle determines that sight is, by its nature, useful not for making us know but for the necessities of life. Instead, hearing is, incidentally, most useful when it comes to intelligence, for it is the medium of logos, the cause of learning. Indeed, even in that famous first chapter of the *Metaphysics*, Aristotle identifies hearing as a necessary condition for animal learning: "By nature animals are born with the faculty of sensation, and from sensation memory is produced in some of them, though not in others. And therefore the former are more intelligent and apt at learning that those which cannot remember; those which are incapable of hearing sounds (*psophos*) are intelligent (*phronimos*) though they cannot be taught (*aneu tou manthanein*), e.g. the bee, and any other race of animals that may be like it; and those which besides memory have this sense of hearing can be taught" (*Metaphysics* 1.1 980a27–b25, McKeon). Adding to the puzzle is a strange passage in *De Anima*, where neither sight nor hearing but touch is the sense that bears on intelligence. We read, "[Touch] is the sense which is most precise in humans. For in the other senses humans are surpassed by many other animals, whereas in the case of touch humans differ from others in being by a long measure more precise. Humans are, accordingly (*dio*), the most intelligent (*phronimōtaton*) of animals. As an indication of this: in the human race, natural aptitude (*euphuēs*) depends upon this sensory faculty but not upon any other. For whereas those with hard flesh have no natural aptitude for thought (*dianoia*), those with delicate flesh do" (421a19–26, Shields). Humans are the most intelligent species of animal because we have the most precise sense of touch. This is a surprising claim, for the sense of touch seems to have the least to do with intelligence: unlike hearing, it is an inarticulate sense, and unlike sight, it does not reveal many differences of all kinds.

These passages raise three sets of questions that correspond to three sections below. The *De sensu* passage asserts that hearing makes the largest contribution to intelligence because it conveys logos, which is the cause of learning. If logos is the cause of learning, why is it especially audible as opposed to, say, visible, as in written texts? What makes hearing, in particular, suitable to the conveyance of logos, rather than sight? I address these questions in section 1. I argue that hearing is the most suitable for conveying logos because speech is expressive and, furthermore, that hearing is necessary for learning because, in being expressive, voice makes perceptible the imperceptible and can therefore convey the why and not merely the that.

The passage in *De sensu* also suggests that hearing contributes both to theoretical intelligence and to practical intelligence. The distance senses contribute to understanding (*phronēsis*) both the intelligible (*noēta*), the objects of theoretical intelligence, and the practical (*prakta*) (437a2–3), the concern of practical intelligence, and hearing contributes the most to *phronēsis* (437a11–12). This, with the *Metaphysics* claim concerning animal learning, raises another question: in what respect does hearing contribute to practical intelligence, in both humans and other animals? I address this question in section 2. I argue that the sense of hearing gives the animal increased initiative to take action and that it enlarges the animal's attunement to its environment and to its aims.

The *De Anima* passage claims that the accuracy of the sense of touch is the foundation for our species' intelligence. In what sense? What is it about the sense of touch that prepares us well for thinking? Why should this be so? I address these questions briefly in section 3. I argue that touch is the sense primarily involved in successfully manipulating one's environment and, by extension, in acting. The precision of the human species' sense of touch indicates that this is the most practically intelligent species of animal.

## 1. Hearing Logos

### *Hearing, Sound, and Voice*

Aristotle's discussion of hearing in *De anima* 2.8 begins, in accord with his method, by delineating the audible: sound (*psophos*). He begins by distinguishing between what does and what does not have sound: sponges and wool and the like do not have sound, whereas things that are solid and smooth, like bronze, do have sound (419b6–9, 13–15), because sound is produced by means of an impact between two solid objects setting a "block" of air in motion (419b18–25). This unified air (419b34–420a2) reaches the ear, which contains unmoving air within it to perceive the variations in the motion of the sounded air (420a9–11).[1]

In drawing this distinction between what does and what does not have sound, Aristotle demarcates what is, properly speaking, a *sound* from other, derivatively audible, phenomena.[2] Consider the case of the sponge, which does not sound: when you drop a wet sponge on the counter, it makes a thud (even a dry sponge would make a small plop). This is an audible phenomenon that is not, according to Aristotle, a sound—it is perhaps a *noise* but not a sound.[3] Aristotle does not articulate the principle on which he draws this distinction. What he does say, however, suggests that sound (and not noise) is determinate: sound is produced by the impact of one solid object with another solid, smooth object such that the air is moved in a single and continuous way, so that the ear can "accurately perceive" it (420a10). To exaggerate a bit, a sponge dropping on the counter does not produce a sound because there is no one thing to hear; it is an indeterminate noise instead. Noises are derivatively audible—we hear indeterminate and indistinct things only because we hear sound. In other words, it is because we are attuned to hearing sounds that we also hear noises; a world devoid of sound would be a world of white noise, which we listen to precisely when we do not want to hear anything at all.

Aristotle also distinguishes sound from voice: voice is a certain sound of one who is ensouled (420b5–6), produced by those animals that breathe and have a trachea (420b22–31). But not all sounds that animals make are voice; "rather, it is necessary for what does the striking to be ensouled and to proceed with a definite imagination (*meta phantasias tinos*), since it is certainly the case that voice is a definite significant sound (*sēmantikos tis psophos*)" (420b31–33, Shields). This rules out sounds such as coughs, sneezes, tsks, burps, applause, and so on—these sounds are not voiced.

This distinction parallels the distinction between sound and noise. Just as noises are marked off from sound because they are indefinite, so vocal phenomena like coughs are marked off from voice because these, too, are indefinite, though in a different respect. Voiced sounds are significant and "proceed with a definite imagination"; animals have hearing "so that something may be signified (*sēmainein*) to" the animal (*De anima* 3.13 435b24). This implies that voiced sounds communicate and that they communicate something definite. In the most basic sense, voiced sounds communicate pleasure and pain (*Politics* 1.2 1253a10–14), but even in the animal world they can be much more sophisticated than that. They may communicate danger, call to mate, celebrate a victory in a fight (see *History of Animals* 4.9), or simply sing (e.g., *History of Animals* 8.11). By contrast, a cough communicates nothing; at best, it is a sign of illness. A cough, we might say, is an indefinite voice, just as a noise is an indefinite sound. Yet a cough is not the same sort of sound as a ringing bell, for the cough is a sound made by an ensouled creature; unlike a bell, a cough signals the presence of a person (ahem, ahem). It is, however, derivatively voiced—it is because we are attuned to hearing voices that we also hear other sounds as of ensouled creatures; a world without voices would be a world without coughs, too.

These distinctions show that sound in general is determinate (as compared to indeterminate noises) and that voice in particular is a sound that communicates something determinate (as compared to other sounds that living creatures make). Furthermore, it is first of all the ability to hear what is definite that illuminates the indefinite sounds. This is perhaps the reason that Aristotle is comfortable saying, sometimes, the bees do not hear (e.g., *Metaphysics* 980b23–24), despite their buzzing communication with one another: to actually hear noise depends on the ability to hear sound.[4]

Cows' lows, birds' calls, cats' meows—all of these sounds communicate pleasure and pain, impending danger, desire to mate, a challenge to fight. However, they do so largely inarticulately; only human beings articulate their voice in speech: "Speech (*dialektos*) is the articulation of voice by means of the tongue. Now vowel sounds are produced by the voice and the larynx; consonantal sounds by the tongue and the lips; and of these speech consists" (*History of Animals* 4.9 535a30–b1, Peck). There are other animals, such as birds, that articulate their voice by means of the tongue (*History of Animals* 4.9 536a20–23; cf. 536b11–12), but, lacking consonants and vowels, they do not speak. Speech belongs to human beings alone (536b1–2), and only human beings use voice to convey logos (*Generation of Animals* 5.7 786b19–22).

We have here an initial answer to the question of the connection between hearing and logos. Hearing is especially suited to the conveyance of logos because logos is voiced in speech, and speech is audible. It is, however, only an initial answer. This does not explain why logos is audible. Furthermore, Aristotle suggests not only that logos can be expressed vocally but that it is primarily so expressed. This is suggested by Aristotle's (odious) contention, in our *De sensu* passage, that "of those who have been deprived of one sense or other from birth, the blind are more intelligent than the deaf and the dumb": the intelligence made possible by the sense of hearing, Aristotle seems to think, cannot simply be replaced or made up for by another sense. Aristotle makes this priority of the vocal, and hence of hearing, explicit in the opening of *De interpretatione*: "Now the voiced (*ta en tē phōnē*) are symbols (*sumbola*) of affections (*pathēmata*) in the soul, and written marks symbols of the voiced" (16a3–4, Ackrill, modified). The written word, Aristotle asserts, is a symbol of the spoken; speech is prior to the writing. To explain why Aristotle asserts the priority of the spoken word, let us return to the *De sensu* passage with which we began.

## Expressive Voice, Expressive Speech

Let us cite the *De sensu* passage again:

> But those senses which act through external media, such as smell, hearing, and vision, belong to such animals as are capable of locomotion. To all those which possess them they are a means of preservation, in order that they may be aware of their food before they pursue it, and may avoid what is inferior or destructive, while in those that have intelligence (*phronēsis*), also these senses exist for the sake of well-being; for they inform us of many differences, from which arises understanding (*phronēsis*), both of the objects of thought (*noēta*) and of the affairs of practical life (*prakta*).
>
> Of these faculties, for the mere necessities of life and in itself, sight is the more important, but for the mind (*nous*) and indirectly hearing is the more important. For the faculty of sight informs us of many differences of all kinds, because all bodies have a share of color, so that it is chiefly by this medium that we perceive the common sensibles. (By these I mean shape, magnitude, movement, and number.) But hearing only conveys differences of sound (*psophos*), and to a few animals differences of voice (*phonē*). Indirectly, hearing makes the largest contribution to intelligence (*phronēsis*). For discourse (*logos*), which is the cause of learning, is so because it is audible; but it is audible not in itself but indirectly, because it is composed of words, and each word is a symbol (*sumbolon*). Consequently, of those who have been deprived of one sense or other from birth, the blind are more intelligent than the deaf and the dumb. (*De sensu* 1.436b18–437a16, Hett)

Sight is primarily and by its nature useful for the necessities of life because "all bodies have a share of color, so that it is chiefly by this medium that we perceive the common sensibles." When it comes to the practical task of self-preservation—figuring out where to go, what to eat, where to live, what to avoid—sight is most useful because it gives us a preview of the bodies, the physical objects, that we will engage with in providing for ourselves. Self-preservation is a concrete, bodily pursuit—ingesting food, fighting predators, building abodes. Because all bodies have color, all bodies are visible in their motion, number, magnitude, and shape, and therefore we can see them before we need to touch them—that is, eat, build with, or fight them. This makes sight and its distinctions useful for the necessities of life. By contrast, "hearing only conveys differences of sound, and to a few animals differences of voice." Hearing does not convey the full physicality of the world we engage with in our practical pursuits. We do not hear the size of the tree we need to build our houses; we do not hear how fast an enemy is approaching. Compared with sight and its "many differences of all kinds," hearing is ill-suited to aid us in the project of self-preservation.

However, it is precisely what renders hearing ill-suited to provide for necessity that renders it suited to make "the largest contribution to intelligence (*phronēsis*)." Sight is best suited to convey bodily differences, which implies that sight is best suited to convey what is present. Hearing, by contrast, conveys what is invisible, absent, or imperceptible, by means of voice and speech. Voice expresses something; the visible simply presents itself. This implies that sight is limited to conveying the that, whereas hearing can convey the why.

Aristotle is clear that voice is a sign of pleasure and pain and that speech reveals the advantageous and the disadvantageous, the just and the unjust (which is why humankind alone has the power of speech; *Politics* 1.2 1253a10–22). In signifying pleasure and pain, voice makes perceptible to other animals an individual creature's pleasure and pain, which is otherwise imperceptible to the hearer; voice may also signify anticipated (absent) pleasure or pain in cries of warning or challenges to fight. Speech similarly is a sign of *pathēmata*, impressions, in the soul (*De interpretatione* 16a3–7), which are themselves likenesses (*homoiōmata*) of the realities (*pragmata*) that produce the impressions (*De interpretatione* 16a6–8).[5] Unlike voice, however, speech is articulate: voice operates in cries, but speech operates in words and sentences. Because of this articulation, speech is capable of complex signification: speech may assert the truth of something or deny it, it may express hope or prayer, or it may describe a sunset, formulate a scientific theory, define a concept, or ask for explanation. Unlike mere voice, speech can articulate the what, the why, and the how of things. Speech can exceed description of events and make perceptible what is constitutively imperceptible—causes, definitions, theory.[6] These things—definitions, causes, as such—will never become visible. We do not see "animal with *logos*" or the proof of the Pythagorean theorem, though these may have visual representations.

Voice thus conveys, perceptually, what is invisible, absent, or imperceptible. The visible may represent what is absent but does not directly convey it, as voice does. Aristotle's discussion of images and likenesses in *De memoria* illustrates the distinction I have in mind. In *De memoria*, Aristotle asks, "How can one remember something which is not present, since it is only the affection that is present, and the fact (*pragmatos*) is not?" (450a25–27). He answers the question a page later, saying,

> How, then, does he remember what is not present? This would imply that one can also see and hear what is not present. But surely in a sense this can and does occur. Just as the picture painted on the panel is at once a picture (*zōon*) and a portrait (*eikōn*), and though one and the same, is both, yet the essence of the two is not the same, and it is possible to think of it both as a picture and as a portrait, so in the same way we must regard (*hupolabein*) the image (*phantasma*) within us both as an object of contemplation in itself and as an image of something else. In so far as we consider it in itself, it is an object of contemplation or an image, but in so far as we consider it in relation to something else, e.g. as a likeness (*eikōn*), it is also an aid to memory. Hence when the stimulus of it is operative, if the soul perceives it as independent, it appears as a thought, or an image; but if it is considered in relation to something else, it is as though one contemplated a figure in a picture as a portrait. (450b18–30, Hett, modified)[7]

Aristotle's explanation relies on the observation that there are different perceptual attitudes available to take toward a given perceptual object, image (*phantasma*), or object of contemplation (*noēma*): the object may be taken up (*hupolambanein*) independently and considered in itself, or it may be taken up in relation to something else.[8] If it is perceived in the former mode, it is simply an object of contemplation or perception, or an image; if the latter, it is a likeness that refers to what it is a likeness of. So, for example, when one is presented with a painting, say, Kehinde Wiley's portrait of Barack Obama, one can see the painting a couple of different ways. One can see the paint and the color, or an image of a person; otherwise, one can see the person Obama, who is out in the world somewhere. If the former, one is perceiving what is present, the painting qua painting; if the latter, one is, in a sense, perceiving what is absent, the person Obama. Similarly, when I see a birch tree, that may be all there is to it, or I may take it as a reminder of the birch tree in the yard of my childhood home; when I hear a melody, I may enjoy it simply as such, or I may take it as a reminder of the last time I heard that song.[9]

Voice admits of a similar flexibility. When I hear a recording of Humphrey Bogart speaking, I may simply hear that voice, or I may hear it in relation to my favorite Bogart film and remember a past experience watching *The Big Sleep*. However, there is an aspect of voice that elides the taking-as-a-likeness attitude: even when considered in itself and not in relation to another, voice signifies something absent. Aristotle characterizes voice as a significant sound (*sēmantikos psophos*) produced by an ensouled creature with a certain imagination (*phantasia*) (*De anima* 2.9 420b31–33).[10] He characterizes the kind of hearing that is necessary for animal learning (presumably by voice) as that which can perceive differences in signs (*History of Animals* 9.1 608a17–21); animals have hearing "so that something may be signified (*sēmainein*) to" the animal (*De anima* 3.13 435b24, Shields). Though the idea that voice is a sign seems to suggest that voice is significant due to its association with something else—as the portrait of Obama signifies the person Obama—this cannot be the case. For if voice signified in this way, it would undermine Aristotle's distinction between sound and voice: voice would simply be a sound like any other sound, which can be taken to indicate or remind one of something else. The sound of a bell ringing may be taken up in relation to dinnertime and, by repeated association, become a sign of dinner. If the significance of voice derived from such association, from being taken up in relation to something else, it would simply be a sound. Just as a bell ringing may be taken as an indication that food is on its way, so a cry of pain is a sound that may be taken to indicate pain. But Aristotle does not treat voice this way—the sound of a bell ringing is not voice, though they both have melody, register, and articulation (*De anima* 2.8 420b7–9).

Because voice is distinguished from sound by virtue of being significant, and because any sound can acquire significance—become a sign of something else—by virtue of associations and memory (as in the case of Pavlov's dogs), Aristotle must mean that voice signifies without association. The notion of "expression" offers an alternate model of signification. The light of day, for example, signifies that the sun is out, but not by being associated with the sun; rather, the light is the expression of the sun's presence. Similarly, a wail is a cry that signifies grief not by being associated with the experience but because the wail is the expression of the experience. In other words, when one hears a wail, it is the grief that one hears—one does not hear a sound that one then relates to one's own experience of grief. One need not have experienced grief oneself to grasp the meaning of the cry. The wail is, in a way, the vocal part of the grief, not an external indication of it. Voice signifies by expression, not by association.

Voice expresses what is absent; the visible represents what is absent. This may be explained by differences in the mechanisms of hearing and sight. What is directly conveyed by sight is the presence of bodies—sight is primarily of color, and "color lies at the limit of the body" (*De sensu* 3 439a31–32, Hett). Sight is of color, and color conveys the body of which it is the color. Sound, however, is the effect of one object striking another—as Aristotle remarks, "Actual sound always occurs as the sound of something, in relation to something, and in something; for what produces it is an impact" (*De anima* 2.8 419b9–11, Shields). Sound does not convey the body (bodies) that produces it, as color does; hearing is not of the body that produces sound in the way that sight is of the colored body. What we see is a red ball, but what we hear is simply a clang or a ping; we do not directly hear the pots or the tins that make these sounds. In this respect, and unlike color, sound is untethered from its source object. Voice is a sound—what we hear when we hear a voice is its pitch, tone, modulation, duration, roughness or smoothness, articulation, and so on, not the air and the trachea that produce it.

This structural feature of sound allows it to float free of the present circumstances, which makes it suitable to express things absent and imperceptible. This is most obvious in the case of speech: we can make predictions about future events, we can discuss fictional characters, and we can reminisce over things past. But it is also observable in voice. Voice is initiated and produced by the animal to signify something to another (*De anima* 3.13 435b24) in accord with a certain *phantasia* (*De anima* 2.8 420b32). *Phantasia*, imagination, is the psychic faculty responsible for producing mental images (*phantasmata*) (*De anima* 3.3 428a1–2) derived from perceptions (*De anima*

3.3 429a4–5).[11] *Phantasia* presents images of desired objects to be pursued (*De motu animalium* 7 701a32–33), and it is responsible for memory (*De memoria* 1 451a14–17). *Phantasia* presents perceptual objects, either when they are not currently present (*De anima* 3.3 428a6–8) or concurrently with perception (as in the case of indistinct perceptions; *De anima* 3.3 428a12–15). When an animal uses its voice with a certain *phantasia*, it may signify either some present state of affairs or some remembered or desired state of affairs. The animal may signify the pain or pleasure it is presently experiencing, or it may voice a warning of an expected pain, and so on.[12]

Voice expresses, while the visible represents, what is absent. If this is so, it indeed follows that speech is prior to the written word, for the expressive ability of written language derives from the spoken. In *Generation of Animals* 5, Aristotle remarks that human beings "alone among the animals use the voice for rational speech (*logos*), of which voice is the material" (786b21, Peck) and, in *History of Animals* 4.9, that "human beings have the same voice the world over, but different varieties of speech" (536b19–20, Peck). Voice is the material of speech, common to all human beings despite differences in language. This suggests that voice lends its original expressiveness to speech. Indeed, without sharing a language, two people can vocally express joy, sorrow, fear, anguish, and so on.

Though speech borrows voice's expressivity, speech also transcends voice. In other words, speech is not simply a more complex use of voice, articulated, as it is, into vowels and consonants (*History of Animals* 4.9 535a31–b1). For Aristotle identifies articulated voice in animals with tongues of the appropriate kind (*History of Animals* 4.9 536a2–4, 536a20–22, 536b11–13)—but this is not speech, which only humankind possesses. What is voiced, even articulately by animals, is not named (cf. *De interpretatione* 2 16a28–29). To express grief in a wail is not to name the experience "grief." Furthermore, whereas voice is significant sound, the basic elements of speech—consonants, vowels, and the syllables they combine to produce—are meaningless: "A sentence (*logos*) is a significant spoken sound (*phōnē sēmantikē*) some part of which is significant in separation—as an expression, not as an affirmation. I mean that 'animal,' for instance, signifies something, but not that it is or is not (though it will be an affirmation or negation if something is added); the single syllables of 'animal,' on the other hand, signify nothing. Nor is the 'ice' in 'mice' significant; here it is simply a spoken sound (*phōnē*)" (*De interpretatione* 4 16b26–32, Ackrill). The significance of names, verbs, and the sentences they combine to form emerges out of insignificant sounds. Or, more precisely, the significance of speech emerges out of insignificant voiced sounds—syllables are not unvoiced sounds like snapping fingers or ringing bells. The syllable *ba*, for example, expresses nothing, yet it is an articulated use of voice. Speech, then, does not simply make more precise, by means of articulation, the expressiveness of voice, for if this were so, *ba* would be significant.

Voice expresses and speech names—grief can be vocally expressed in a wail and also named as "grief." The name is "a spoken sound (*phōnē*) significant by convention" (*De interpretatione* 16a19, Ackrill). Unlike the wail, whose sound (the tenor, timbre, pitch, modulation, etc.) naturally expresses the experience of grief, the sound "grief" has no such natural connection— the syllables of the word are meaningless on their own. The conventionality of language yields the result that words, being composed of meaningless components, abstract from the experience being named. Unlike a wail, which is a direct expression of the pain of grief—the vocal component of grief—the word *grief*, because of the meaninglessness of its components, expresses the pain of grief abstractly, as a reality anyone might experience, or no one. This makes it so that language can express not only the experience but the reality of the experience—language releases the expression of grief from the experience of it. Grief can be named, discussed, analyzed, and identified in the absence of the experience of it. The temporality of speech thus differs from the temporality of voice: voice expresses something urgent, something practically relevant to the circumstance; speech expresses abstractly, whether or not the circumstances require it. Language, therefore, is also suited to the expression of timelessly true realities—the realities of metaphysics, definitions, and explanatory theories. Language expresses logoi.

Let us return once more to our *De sensu* passage: "Indirectly, hearing makes the largest contribution to intelligence (*phronēsis*). For discourse (*logos*), which is the cause of learning, is so because it is audible; but it is audible not in itself but indirectly, because it is composed of words, and each word is a symbol (*sumbolon*)" (437a11–15). We may now see why this is the case: speech borrows the innate expressiveness of voice, which derives from its being untethered from the physicality of its source. Voice is not of the trachea and air that produce it, the way that sight is of the colored body. However, speech, due to its use of words that are built out of meaningless syllables and are therefore only conventionally significant, expresses reality abstractly. That is, speech expresses reality in the form of concepts; it expresses thoughts. Because of this, it is capable of expressing logoi.

Logos is the cause of learning because it is incidentally audible. In one respect, it is clear why this is so. In the *Metaphysics*, Aristotle distinguishes between one who knows, the artisan, and one who is practically capable but lacks knowledge, the experienced person, on the basis that the former and not the latter knows the cause (981a24–30). Speech expresses the logos that explains why things are so, and thus speech is the cause of learning. Furthermore, "it is a sign of the man who knows and of the man who does not know, that the former can teach, and therefore we think art more truly knowledge than experience is; for artists can teach, and men of experience cannot" (981b7–10). The one who knows can teach—can explain the reason why, vocally. Hearing therefore contributes greatly to theoretical knowledge.

Recall that the *De sensu* passage suggested that hearing contributes both to theoretical and to practical intelligence. The reason that hearing contributes to practical intelligence remains a question. This is illustrated by Aristotle's distinction between the artisan and the person of experience: the person of experience is capable—and perhaps even more capable than the artisan—of succeeding at her tasks, which suggests that she has practical intelligence, at least in some form. Yet she does not know the cause, nor is she able to teach. Aristotle similarly observes the limitation of logoi to effectively instruct a person about ethics: one may learn the correct account of the good but nonetheless act poorly, making poor decisions (*Nicomachean Ethics* 2.4 1105b9–18, cf. 7.3). I turn now to why and how hearing contributes to practical intelligence.

## 2. Hearing and Practical Intelligence

The question of why and how hearing contributes to practical intelligence, despite the limitation of logos to produce successful action, takes two forms. On the one hand, it is a question of what hearing contributes to *human* practical intelligence. How does hearing speech contribute to human *phronēsis*, if not by offering explanations of why things are so? What other function does speech have that bears on practical intelligence? On the other hand, Aristotle implies that animals that can hear are more intelligent (*phronimoteroi*) than animals that cannot, and only those animals that can hear can learn. How does hearing contribute to animal intelligence? Animals do not have speech, nor can they understand the reasons why. What, then, does an animal with hearing learn? To prepare to answer these questions, I first discuss practical intelligence, as it appears in humans and in other animals. (I refer to human practical intelligence as practical wisdom to make the distinction clear.) Afterward, I argue that hearing contributes to practical intelligence in two ways: it enlarges the animal's (human or otherwise) attunement to its environment, and it allows the animal increased initiative in its activity.

## Practical Wisdom

Aristotle often describes animals as *phronimos* (e.g., *Parts of Animals* 2.2 648a10; *History of Animals* 7.5 611a16, 8.10 614b18) and sometimes as having *phronēsis* (e.g., *De anima* 3.3 427b10; *Generation of Animals* 3.2 753a12; *History of Animals* 8.1 608a15). Clearly, animals express practical intelligence in their behaviors: they communicate with one another, care for their young, hunt prey, elude predators, build nests, gather food, store acorns, and so on. They succeed, in other words, in complex behaviors that accomplish their aims and through which they express their natures. For example, Aristotle describes as intelligent animals that heal themselves of an ailment by finding and eating a medicinal plant. Wild goats that have been shot with an arrow seek out dittany, which is believed to expel arrows; hounds relieve themselves of a particular pain by eating a particular grass that makes them vomit; and the panther that has been poisoned by panther-bane seeks out human dung, which helps it (*History of Animals* 8.6 612a1–8).

Clearly, animals display intelligence in their ability to engage in complex behaviors that accomplish their practical aims. Equally clearly, to Aristotle at least, animals other than humans lack the capacity, *nous*, that houses our practical intelligence and our ability to reason—animals lack the practical rationality that enables humans to deliberate, to recollect, to understand principles and causes, to plan, to choose, and to speak. Instead, animal practical intelligence resembles human practical wisdom by analogy (*History of Animals* 7.1 588a28–31): the purpose that rational thought serves in us is served by an analogous capacity, *phantasia*, in other animals (*De anima* 3.10 433a9–10; *De motu animalium* 6 700b18–21), just as feathers on birds and scales on fish are analogous to one another (*Parts of Animals* 1.4 644a21–22) or a human's bone is analogous to a fish's spine (*Parts of Animals* 1.4 644b11–13). Yet, "intellect (*nous*)—at any rate what is called intellect in the sense of intelligence (*phronēsis*)—does not appear to belong similarly to all animals, nor even to all humans" (*De anima* 1.2 404b5–6, Shields, modified). Practical intelligence in other animals, though not identical to it, is analogously similar to human practical wisdom.

To uncover this similarity and to see what kind of intelligence animals possess, I use Aristotle's account of practical wisdom as a key and a foil. Practical wisdom is, in the first place, an intellectual virtue—it is one of the virtues that belong to the strictly and actively rational part of the soul. The work of the intellectual virtues is to attain the truth (*Nicomachean Ethics* 1139b12), and the truth that practical wisdom attains is a practical truth (*Nicomachean Ethics* 1140b20–21, cf. 1139a21–31)—the person of practical wisdom realizes the human good in action (*Nicomachean Ethics* 1140b4–6, 1141b12–14). Practical wisdom is thus both an intellectual accomplishment and a practical accomplishment: the practically wise person is both able to understand and hold on to the conception of the human good and able to translate this understanding into action. Whatever the intelligence of practical wisdom is, it is manifest in both thought and action.

And this makes sense given the way that Aristotle understands animal movement, the structure of which is common to both human and nonhuman animals. The animal (human or otherwise) always moves for the sake of something, and this serves as the origin of its action (*De motu animalium* 6 700b15; *De anima* 3.9 432b15–16). For the animal to act for the sake of something, say, food, that food must appear to the animal, appear to the animal as good, and, furthermore, appear to be something that can be procured—that is, that can be realized in action (*prakton*) (*De motu animalium* 6 700b25–29; *De anima* 3.10 433a27–30). But the appearance of a realizable good is not sufficient by itself to move the animal—the animal must, perhaps more fundamentally, also desire the realizable good. Thus, it is the object of desire that initiates animal motion (*De motu animalium* 6 700b23–24; *De anima* 3.10 433a27–30), but the desired object as presented by imagination (*phantasia*) or practical thinking (*De motu animalium* 11 703b18, 7 33–36). In other words, the animal's cognitive faculties (perceptual in the case of other animals, rational and perceptual in the case of humans) construe an object as good, as desirable, and as achievable.

Construing an object as good, desirable, and achievable already requires some intelligence, for, on any of these vectors, the animal could get it wrong. For example, when my cat chases a laser, he construes the laser as something he can catch, and he is wrong about this. Similarly, when my cat tries to break open his bag of food to have his fill, he is construing an excessive amount of food as good and desirable; he is wrong about this too (at least insofar as his health is concerned). Intelligently accomplishing its aim requires that the animal correctly construe its object. This is even more forcefully the case with human animals, for we must construe both the aim and the object of desire well. Our cognitive faculties must not only construe this particular object of desire correctly but also construe the general aim of our desires well. That is, not only must this piece of cake be perceived as sweet, desirable, and in our reach, but we must also have a sense of what is good in general for us and fit that desirable piece of cake into our overall aims of, say, health and enjoyment. As Aristotle remarks in *Nicomachean Ethics* 3.4, "The serious person is distinguished perhaps most of all by his seeing what is true in each case, just as if he were a rule and measure of them. But in the case of the man, a deception appears to occur on account of the pleasure involved, for what is not good appears to them as good" (1113a32–b1, Bartlett and Collins).

Human action shares the basic structure of motion with other animals: we, too, act for the sake of something desired that appears to us as good, desirable, and possible to realize in action. Our action, however, has the further characteristic of being rational. Aristotle characterizes this succinctly in *De anima*'s discussion of animal motion: "Hence, as was said, while perceptual imagination belongs to other animals, deliberative imagination belongs to rational animals (since whether one is to do this or that is already the work of reasoning—and it is necessary that measuring take place by one thing, inasmuch as one pursues what is greater and can, consequently, make one out of many images)" (*De anima* 3.11 434a5–10, Shields). The power of reason enables us to hold open more than one possible course of action and also to compare and decide between them ("whether one is to do this or that is already the work of reasoning"). Human action is decided on, not merely desired. This introduces a difference in the structure of human activity as compared to the movement of other animals: human action takes the form of responding to—deciding—a question. Aristotle emphasizes this by way of contrast in *De motu animalium*:

> But as sometimes happens when we ask dialectical questions, so here thinking (*dianoia*) does not stop and consider at all the second of the two premises, the obvious one. For example, if taking walks is good for a man, it does not waste time considering that he is a man. Hence

> whatever we do without reasoning, we do quickly. For whenever a
> creature is actually using perception or *phantasia* or thought (*nous*)
> towards the thing-for-the-sake-of-which, he does at once what he de-
> sires. For the activity of the desire *takes the place of questioning or
> thinking* (noēsis). "I have to drink," says appetite. "Here's drink," says
> perception or *phantasia* or thought. At once he drinks. This, then, is
> the way that animals are impelled to move and act. (701a25–34, Nuss-
> baum, slightly modified; emphasis mine.)

In some cases of human action, desire supersedes the deliberation about
what to do; it "takes the place of questioning or thinking." After a long walk
on a hot day, if one sees a drinking fountain, one will not need to consider
another course of action—whether it is good to drink or whether one is a
thirsty human being—rather, desire does the deciding work of questioning
and thinking. However, this is a special case of human motion; more typically *human* activity results from thinking about and deciding a question
about how to act and what to do.

The process of deciding the question of action takes the form of deliberation. Aristotle introduces the practically wise person as one who is good
at deliberating about what is good for herself, with respect to living well
in general (*Nicomachean Ethics* 1140a25–28). Good deliberation, he argues,
is distinct from opinion (*doxa*), for "correctness of opinion is truth; at the
same time too, everything of which there is an opinion is already determined" (1142b11–12, Bartlett and Collins). By contrast, "good deliberation is
correctness of thinking, for thinking is not yet an assertion: opinion is not
an investigation into something but is already a specific assertion, whereas
he who deliberates—whether he deliberates well or even deliberates badly—
is investigating something and calculating" (1142b12–15, Bartlett and Collins). Deliberation is a process of thinking that leads to a decision and to
action, a determination of what to do or how to do it. It is an investigation,
seeking to answer a question. We only deliberate about "matters that are for
the most part so, where it is unclear how they will turn out and in which
something is undetermined" (*Nicomachean Ethics* 3.3 1112b8–9, Bartlett
and Collins), among the things that we can affect through action.

This seems to be what it means to say that human beings act rationally:
we have the ability to hold open and consider different courses of action,
and we have the ability to produce an account or argument (logos, 1142b12)
that decides which course of action to take. A rational action, however, may

or may not also be intelligent. The akratic, for example, acts rationally but not intelligently; she acts in accordance with a certain logos, though driven by appetite to pursue an ignoble goal (*Nicomachean Ethics* 7.3 1147a35–b3).

This distinction between rational and intelligent action is reflected in Aristotle's distinction between good deliberation (deliberating well and with respect to a good aim) and successful deliberation or successful action (achieving one's aim, even if that aim is bad). Good deliberation requires more than producing an argument, a logos, for a certain course of action. Successful deliberation may not be good, for one might successfully determine how to achieve a contemptible goal. Nor is success at accomplishing a worthy goal necessarily a mark of good deliberation: one may attain a worthy goal but through faulty means, or one may simply take too long in deliberating (1142b16–28). To act rationally, then, is not to act intelligently. Instead, good deliberation is "correctness of thinking" (1142b12–13), which requires that the deliberator both aim at something truly good and correctly reason out how to realize that good, and all in a timely manner (1142b16–28).

This distinction between good deliberation and successful deliberation, on the one hand, and good deliberation and successful action, on the other, highlights two features necessary for practical rationality to be practical wisdom. First, practical wisdom requires the correct understanding of what is good, of the aim of action. This is necessary if deliberation is to be good deliberation (as opposed to merely correct deliberation), and the practically wise person is manifestly one who is a good deliberator both concerning particular goals and about the human good in general (*Nicomachean Ethics* 6.5 1140a25–28; cf. 6.9 1142b29–33). The practically wise person is good at deliberating because practical wisdom is the true conviction of the aim of action (*Nicomachean Ethics* 6.9 1142b33); it is that state of the soul by which what is truly good appears so and appears as that for the sake of which one acts (6.5 1140b7–21). This, then, is one feature of practical wisdom: grasping what is truly good in the realm of action and grasping it as the principle of action. Second, the practically wise person also deliberates correctly concerning this principle of action and acts upon the conclusion of this deliberation. The practically wise person grasps the aim of action and correctly identifies the means to accomplishing this aim.

Furthermore, because practical wisdom is an intellectual virtue concerned with action, the practically wise person must be familiar with and well attuned to the particulars that action concerns (1141b14–16). In *Nicomachean*

*Ethics* 3.3, Aristotle delineates the boundaries between which deliberation happens. We do not deliberate about ends, in the sense that the doctor does not deliberate about whether to heal someone (1112b11–15). Neither do we deliberate about particulars, such as whether a loaf of bread is well made, because we have a perception of this (1112b33–1113a2). Instead, we deliberate about how and through what means the ends will come about (1112b15–16), and, having reached a conclusion, we choose and enact that conclusion. Indeed, "these ultimate particulars are the principles of that for the sake of which one acts: the universals arise from the particulars. Of these, then, one must have a perception, and this perception is intellect" (1143b4–5, Bartlett and Collins). This, then, yields another feature of the practical intelligence of rational animals: the ability to notice and accurately perceive the particulars by means of which one acts.

These three features of practical wisdom—grasping the right aim of action, good deliberation, and attunement to particulars—are, in a certain sense, elements of one and the same dynamic. To act well, one must have the right aim in mind: that for the sake of which one acts must appear to the actor and appear good, desirable, and achievable in action (just as is the case for animal movement generally). For us human beings, the appearance of the aim of action takes two forms: a general aim, such as "be generous," and the specification of that general aim in a particular course of action. In neither case is the aim or its appearance guaranteed or natural, nor is it guaranteed that the two will be in harmony. Thus, one might be mistaken about what in general to aim for, or one may be right about the general aim but oblivious to its specific manifestation. Good deliberation consists in correctness about the goal and correctness about the particulars: if one deliberates correctly toward the realization of a bad aim, such deliberation is not good; conversely, if one deliberates incorrectly toward the realization of the right aim, the deliberation is bad. Instead, good deliberation is "the correctness that accords with what is beneficial and aims at what one ought, in the right manner, and at the right time" (1142b27–28, Bartlett and Collins).

### Practical Intelligence

Practical wisdom, we've seen, consists in grasping the human good, both in general and in particular circumstances, as the aim of action; in reasoning correctly about how to realize the human good in action (that is, identifying the right means); and in being appropriately sensitive to the particulars within which the action is realized. Let us see, now, whether and how these features are manifest in animal practical intelligence. Recall that Aristotle describes certain animals' ability to treat their own ailments by means of ingesting a medicinal herb as intelligent. Such behavior is complex, involving a desire to be rid of the pain, an understanding that eating this plant will relieve the pain, a recognition that this is the sort of pain to be healed in this manner, the ability to look for the plant (which presumably requires familiarity with where the plant grows), the ability to recognize the plant, and the desire to eat it, despite its unpleasantness (cf. *History of Animals* 8.5 611b20–23). Already we can see how this behavior is analogous to practically wise behavior: it is undertaken for the sake of a good (relief from pain and self-preservation), which appears to the animal as desirable and capable of being accomplished; it identifies the correct means of realizing the aim (the medicinal plant); and it requires sensitivity and appropriate attunement to the particulars of the environment (the right plant and where to find the plant).

More specifically, in *De motu animalium*, Aristotle outlines the explanatory structure of animal motion by comparison with a syllogism. In a theoretical syllogism, thinking of two premises together yields the thought of the conclusion (7 701a10–11). Similarly, in animal motion, two premises yield a conclusion, but in this case the conclusion is an action (701a11–12), and the kinds of premises that yield action are the premises of the good and the possible (701a24–25). Desire is always for something good or apparently good (700b25–29); this serves as the first premise. A means of realizing this good is identified; this is the second premise, and it is the way that the desired object is construed as practically realizable. The conclusion that follows from desiring something and recognizing the means of realizing it is the action. Two of Aristotle's illustrations of this accord with this form: "I should make something good; a house is something good. At once he makes a house" (701a16–17, Nussbaum). Here, the desired object is "something good." But this is impossible to realize, because it is unspecific. So, the second premise, "a house is something good," represents the desired object construed as something possible to achieve. The illustration that follows this one provides more detail: "I need a covering; a cloak is a covering. I need a cloak. What I need, I have to make; I need a cloak. I have to make a cloak. And the conclusion, the 'I have to make a cloak,' is an action. And he acts from a starting point. If there is to be a cloak, there must necessarily be this first, and if this, this. And this he does at once" (701a17–22, Nussbaum). The original object of desire, a covering, is unspecific, as in the first illustration. Hence, to be construed as something that can be accomplished, it must be specified: a cloak is a covering. Then the general means of realizing this specified aim are identified: I have to make what I need, which means I have to make a cloak. Aristotle regards this as the starting point (*archē*) of the action, from which the means are determined more and more specifically, until the immediate action to take is apparent.

The cases under consideration, wherein the animal heals itself by means of eating a medicinal plant, conform to this structure. The animal desires something good (painlessness) and specific (to be rid of *this* pain), and it identifies the means to achieve that desire (eating the medicinal plant). The conclusion "I need to eat the medicinal plant" is an action. It is telling that Aristotle includes deliberating about the means of making a cloak in the action. This suggests, on the one hand, that human deliberation is a component of the action and that, on the other hand, nonhuman animals "deliberate" in deed rather than thought. As Aristotle says, "Every deliberation is an investigation (*zētēsis*)" (*Nicomachean Ethics* 1112b23, Bartlett and Collins); similarly, the wild goats in Crete seek out (*zētein*) medicinal herbs when shot with arrows, to expel them (*History of Animals* 8.6 612a1–4), and panthers look for (*zētein*) human dung to neutralize the effects of panther-bane (612a6–7).[13]

Aristotle's account of animal motion explains all animal motion, both the intelligent and the unintelligent. We must then explain what is intelligent about such intelligent behavior. In a general way, such behavior is intelligent insofar as it is an instance of the animal's ability to successfully navigate its environment and to pursue and successfully accomplish its aims. It is practically intelligent in its understanding of what is necessary to accomplish its aims and in its understanding of how to shape its circumstances so that what is necessary is also available and possible. (Another instance of animal intelligence that Aristotle relates is that of the swallow, who creates a kind of mortar for her nest out of mud and sticks, and, when there isn't enough mud, she creates more by wetting herself and rolling around in the dust! [*History of Animals* 8.7 612b18–27]) By contrast, unintelligent animals cannot navigate their environments or accomplish their aims. As Aristotle describes it, a sheep "wanders into deserted places towards nothing, and often in wintry weather it goes out from indoors, and when caught in the snow they are unwilling to go away unless the shepherd moves them, but are left behind and perish unless the shepherds bring males, and then they follow" (*History of Animals* 8.3 610b24–27, Balme). This is an animal that does not understand what is good for it, let alone how to accomplish it or what the circumstances demand. Its action is markedly unsuccessful and therefore also unintelligent.

### Hearing and Practical Intelligence

Practical intelligence, in both humans and other animals, consists in grasping the good as a realizable aim, through discovery of the right means, and enacting it with appropriate sensitivity to one's surroundings. Let us now return to what hearing contributes to practical intelligence in humans and other animals.

Voice and speech are communicative. An animal voices its pain or pleasure to another, and the other hears the pain that the animal is experiencing. Or an animal may warn another of an impending pain, a threat—an animal may voice what may become another's experience. The ability to hear voice thus situates the animal in a social context by providing a sense of the existence of perspectives and experiences other than one's own.[14] Voice expresses, in a way, an animal's internal life (its pleasures and pains) so that other animals can become cognizant of it. In communicating its pleasures and pains, an animal is communicating what appears good or bad to it. Pleasure is, after all, an apparent good (*Nicomachean Ethics* 3.4 1113a33–b2; *De motu animalium* 6 700b28–29). Speech may be used to do so as well, in discourses about ethics as well as in articulations of preferences and the like. The communicative feature of voice and speech thus broadens an animal's attunement to the good and to the aims of action. Cranes, for example, have a leader who forgoes sleep in order to act as a lookout, "and whenever he perceives something, he signals with a cry" (*History of Animals* 8.10 618b21–26, Balme). Similarly, discussing the virtues, say, draws them to one's attention as a factor in living and acting well.

The ability to hear voice and speech also increases the animal's attunement to its surroundings. I'll begin with an illustration. In a yoga class, one might adopt the poses by imitating what one sees the instructor doing. However, as anyone who has practiced yoga can attest, this does not work very well. As soon as the instructor describes where to place one's weight, for example, or which muscle should be carrying the pose, or how one's neck ought to be aligned, the entire posture changes—even if outwardly it looks the same. This experience may, I believe, be generalized to most cases of instruction: hearing how one ought to do something draws one's attention to things otherwise unnoticed. And hearing is suitable for this, because its objects, voice and speech, are communicative. When an animal gives a cry of warning, it alerts others' attention to an incoming danger; in general, voice and speech may convey things outside the hearer's own experience or perspective, which serves to attune one to those kinds of things in the future.

Furthermore, voice and hearing have a transitive quality: in *Generation of Animals* 5.2 we read, "This, too, is why we are able to understand (*mathēsis*) what is said and to repeat what is heard, for whatever the character of the movement was which entered through the sense-organ, the character of the movement caused by means of the voice is the same in its turn—they might be two impressions from one and the same die. So, if you have heard a thing, you can utter it" (781a26–30, Peck). Once instruction is given, one can repeat it—to oneself or others—and continue to draw attention to the unnoticed. This increased attunement or sensitivity to one's surroundings thus helps ensure that one's deliberation, or seeking of means, is done successfully—nothing is left out.

Voice (and hearing) also give the animal greater initiative in conducting its life, for it enables the animal to express something in a way that does not implicate it in the circumstances it is talking about. For example, a bird may signal with a cry of warning the presence of a predator. This is an expression of an anticipated pain but an inactive one. The bird need not flee the predator (perhaps it is hidden or out of reach) or challenge it. By contrast, a bodily expression of such things does implicate the animal in the action. An animal may express aggressiveness through its bodily posture, and doing so is itself an act of aggression. Or an animal may cower in fear at the sight of the aggressor; doing so is itself to capitulate to the danger. To give voice to such things enables the animal to take preparatory action, to avoid the danger or to outsmart the predator. Voice and hearing thus better enable the animal to "deliberate," to seek out means to achieving its goals.

All in all, then, hearing contributes to practical wisdom in expanding the grasp of the good, by virtue of being open to the perspectives of others and participating in the well-being of a community. Thus, the leader crane puts aside sleep as the good it ought to pursue, for the sake of protecting the group while they sleep. Similarly, the human community speaks about and discusses justice and injustice, the relationship between pleasure and the good, the nature of friendship, and so on. Hearing also contributes to practical intelligence by enlarging the animal's attunement to its environment, by virtue of alerting it to otherwise unnoticed features of its situation. Finally, hearing enables the animal to better deliberate, for the ability to communicate increases the animal's initiative, making it better able to act in pursuit of aims rather than react to the urgency of circumstances. Similarly, human beings deliberate best in concert with one another, at least in matters of great importance (*Nicomachean Ethics* 3.3 1112b10–11).

## 3. Touch

Let us turn now to Aristotle's puzzling comment about the relationship of touch to practical intelligence. Recall that Aristotle remarks that human beings are the most intelligent animals due to the precision of our sense of touch and that those with delicate flesh are naturally suited to thinking (*De anima* 421a19–26). Hearing makes the largest contribution to intelligence because it expresses logoi; by contrast, it is the precision of the human species' sense of touch that marks us out as the most intelligent of the animals. This is a sharp contrast: whereas hearing contributes to intelligence because of its ability to express a certain kind of content, touch is related to intelligence because of the precision of the sense itself. In other words, the fact that dogs can hear a greater range of sounds than human beings has no bearing on the relative intelligence of the two species, but the fact that human touch is more discriminating than that of dogs does bear on our species' greater intelligence (or such is Aristotle's claim).

One other feature of Aristotle's discussion of the sense of touch bears on the interpretation of its relationship to our species' intelligence. When Aristotle claims that the precision of the sense of touch is related to human intelligence, he draws a contrast with our least precise sense, the sense of smell. He explains that the sense of smell is imprecise in human beings, "for humans smell things weakly and do not perceive any object of smell without its being painful or pleasant, because the sensory organ is imprecise" (*De anima* 421a10–12). Similarly, "it is likely that hard-eyed animals perceive colours in this way, and that the variations among colours are not especially clear for them, excepting those which do and do not inspire fear. So too is the human race when it comes to smell" (421a10–15). When a sense is especially imprecise, it perceives its objects only with pleasure or pain, as something to pursue or avoid (*De anima* 431a9–14). By contrast, a more precise sense, such as sight, "makes us know and brings to light many differences between things" (*Metaphysics* 1.1 980a26–27, McKeon). Aristotle is not denying that the objects of a precise sense may be pleasant or painful. Indeed, his discussion of the painfully destructive extremes of the various sensory objects precludes this (*De anima* 431a10, with 435b5–14). Instead, the point is that the only relevant distinction revealed by our imprecise sense of smell is a scent's pleasantness or painfulness. If a scent is neither pleasant nor painful, it goes unnoticed, unsensed. In the case of a precise sense, however, other distinctions, in addition to the painfulness or pleasantness of a sensation, are perceived. So, for example, when touching a piece of cloth, I will perceive an irregularity in the weave, even though such an irregularity is neither pleasant nor painful.

The contrast between precise and imprecise senses suggests that an imprecise sense leads directly to action, flight or pursuit, by indicating immediate threats and benefits (the scent of toxic chemicals or cookies, for example), whereas a precise sense indicates many things, which may or may not be relevant to taking immediate action. In other words, scents, for a human being, are overridden by their pleasantness or painfulness, whereas tactile objects, though some are pleasant and others painful, are not always prominently so.

This feature of touch's precision, that it discerns distinctions other than the pleasantness or painfulness of its objects, offers a clue about the relationship between touch and intelligence. The imprecise mode of sensing would seem to prevent inquiry or deliberation: a noxious scent immediately repulses me, and I exit the room, instinctually and without thinking. By contrast, I may grope around in the dark for my glasses (a kind of "inquiry" in action) without being overly attracted to or repulsed by the things I touch along the way. This relative freedom from the temptations of pleasure and the repulsions of pain make it possible to manipulate the environment—to build houses, make clothes, and so on. To manipulate the bricks of the house, for example, the feel of the bricks ought to be neither so pleasant as to elicit continued touch nor so painful as to prevent moving the bricks around. Moreover, because the tactile sense of the brick is relatively neutral, neither pleasant nor painful, it is possible to inspect it, to consider its qualities as suitable (or not) for building, and so on. In short, intense pleasure and pain get in the way of successful manipulation of one's environment, for they merely yield pursuit or avoidance, not a sustained engagement. Similarly, in order to deliberate and to act well, one cannot be overly swayed by the temptations of the pleasant and the repulsion of the painful. As is commonly said, pleasure clouds one's judgment.

Aristotle's claim, however, is not only that the sense of touch is suited to practical thinking but that "in the human race, natural aptitude (*euphuēs*) depends upon this sensory faculty but not upon any other. For whereas those with hard flesh have no natural aptitude for thought (*dianoia*), those with delicate flesh do" (421a23–26, Shields). This is a strong claim. Being naturally suited to thinking and to practical intelligence depends on touch alone. This can perhaps be explained if we keep in mind that practical intelligence is bound up with action: to be practically intelligent is to be able to find the medicine that will expel the arrow or to build the nest. At a basic level, practical intelligence is the ability to successfully manipulate one's environment—that is, to engage tactilely with the tools and materials one needs to accomplish one's aims. Not only, then, does the precision of the sense of touch enable successful manipulation of the environment by distinguishing properties beyond pleasure or pain belonging to the tactile objects, but touch is precisely the site of enactment of such successful manipulation of the environment.

## 4. Conclusion

Hearing contributes to intelligence because sound and voice are the means to convey the imperceptible—the absent or the conceptual. Hearing contributes to practical intelligence by expanding the animal's attunement to the world and by providing greater initiative in action. And the precision of the sense of touch relates to the human being's intelligence because of its ability to perceive distinctions that are not overridden by pleasure and pain, thus providing for a kind of active deliberation and successful manipulation of one's environment. Despite the immediacy of the sense of touch, the precision of this sense in humans shares with the sense of hearing a degree of abstraction and freedom from the given demands of pleasure and pain. In such freedom, the space for deliberation and understanding is opened up.

### Notes

1. See Mark Johnstone, "Aristotle on Sounds," *British Journal for the History of Philosophy* 21, no. 5 (2013): 631–648, for a detailed investigation of the mechanism of sound, especially pp. 2–10 concerning the motion of the air.

2. See *De anima* 2.10 422a20–31. Here Aristotle distinguishes two senses in which something may be imperceptible, using sight as an illustration. First, something may

be completely invisible, in the sense that it is constitutively impossible to see it. In fact, Aristotle frequently uses the invisibility of voice to illustrate this kind of impossibility (e.g., *Metaphysics* 11.9 1066a36–b5; *Physics* 3.4 204a2–4, 3.5 204a12–13). Second, something may be invisible "when something happens to lack or have only slightly what it naturally has" (Shields). Aristotle here switches to the sense of taste to illustrate this sense: something may be said to be untasteable if it has a very weak flavor or if it is destructive of the sense. For example, we might call a bland meal tasteless, or extremely spicy or hot food that destroys our taste buds we might call tasteless. I take it that the noise of, say, a sponge dropping on the counter is inaudible in this second sense.

3. See Ömer Aygün, *The Middle Included: Logos in Aristotle* (Evanston, IL: Northwestern University Press, 2017), 146–155, for an illuminating discussion of this distinction.

4. See Aygün, 146–155, for an articulation of this problem and an insightful resolution.

5. Steven DiMattei, "Rereading Aristotle's *De interpretatione* 16a3–8: Verbal Propositions as Symbols of the Process of Reasoning," *Ancient Philosophy* 26, no. 1 (2006): 1–21, offers a close reading of these important lines wherein he emphasizes the "'symbolic' rapport between verbal propositions (*ta en te phone*) and their mental judgments (*pathemata*), and the actual facts (*pragmata)* they represent" (3).

6. Of course, voice may convey something present and visible to all. The point here is that it is better suited than the visible to convey what is *not* present or visible.

7. In this passage, Aristotle is explaining how we can remember what is not present, which means that his main aim is to explain how an internal image in the psyche can bring to mind something absent and past. However, as he indicates early in the passage, his explanation extends to acts of perception, too: "This would imply that one can also see and hear what is not present. But surely in a sense this can and does occur." It is thus relevant here.

8. See S. Everson, *Aristotle on Perception* (Oxford: Clarendon, 1997), chap. 5, 193–221, for an analysis of this distinction.

9. I set aside the disputed issue of incidental perception. See chap. 1, sec. 2, in my *Perception in Aristotle's Ethics* (Evanston, IL: Northwestern University Press, 2018), for discussion.

10. Aristotle uses the term *sēmantikos* primarily in the context of voice, speech, and language. According to a TLG search, *sēmantikos* appears twenty-two times in the Aristotelian corpus. Eight of these instances are in *De interpretatione*, eight in *Poetics*, and one in the *De anima* passage we've been discussing. Thesaurus Linguae Graecae Digital Library, ed. Maria C. Pantelia, University of California, Irvine, accessed June 17, 2018, http://stephanus.tlg.uci.edu.

11. See Victor Caston, "Why Aristotle Needs Imagination," *Phronesis* 41, no. 1 (1996): 20–55, for a compelling interpretation of *phantasia* and its importance for understanding intentionality. See Caleb Cohoe, "When and Why Understanding Needs *Phantasmata*: A Moderate Interpretation of Aristotle's De memoria and De anima on the Role of Images in Intellectual Activities," *Phronēsis* 61, no. 3 (2016): 337–372, for a response and an alternate interpretation.

12. Voice is not the only perceptual object that is expressive. As Aristotle draws a distinction between sound and voice, he might just as readily have drawn a distinction between, say, the (visible) posture of a plant and the posture of an ensouled creature that proceeds in accord with a certain *phantasia*. For example, a cat's posture with an arched back, flattened ears, and teeth bared signifies aggression—this cat is ready to fight. The

posture of a Venus flytrap, like a sound, may acquire such signification by association with the aggressive posture of animals, but it does not express aggression the way a cat's posture may. What is distinctive about the expressiveness of voice is that it is uniquely suited to expressing what is absent and imperceptible. Visible, bodily expressions can only express in the present. A tearful face does indeed signify an otherwise imperceptible (to the viewer) experience of sorrow, but it does not express an absent sorrow (a future or past sorrow), nor does it express the cause of the sorrow.

13. Similar intelligence is shown in strategies employed in luring prey and fighting predators (612a12–20), defense and protection (611a22–b17), nest-building (*History of Animals* 8.7 612b18–27), and caring for offspring (*History of Animals* 8.612b27–31; *History of Animals* 8.5 611a15–22; *Generation of Animals* 3.2 753a 7–14).

14. Hearing makes possible living together, as Aristotle indicates in a passage from the *Politics*: a sign that humankind is a naturally political animal is her possession of speech.

# Bibliography

## *Translations*

Ackrill, J. L. *Aristotle: Categories and De interpretatione.* 1963. Reprint, Oxford: Oxford University Press, 2002.

Balme, D. M. *Aristotle: History of Animals, Books VII–X.* Cambridge, MA: Harvard University Press, 1991.

Bartlett, Robert C., and Susan D. Collins. *Aristotle's Nicomachean Ethics.* Chicago: University of Chicago Press, 2011.

Hett, W. S. *Aristotle: On the Soul, Parva Naturalia, On Breath.* Cambridge, MA: Harvard University Press, 1957.

McKeon, Richard. *The Basic Works of Aristotle.* New York: Random House, 1941.

Nussbaum, Martha. *Aristotle's De motu animalium.* Princeton, NJ: Princeton University Press, 1978.

Peck, A. L. *Aristotle: Generation of Animals.* 1942. Reprint, Cambridge, MA: Harvard University Press, 2000).

———. *Aristotle: History of Animals, Books IV–VI.* Cambridge, MA: Harvard University Press, 1970.

Peck, A. L., and E. S. Forster. *Aristotle: Parts of Animals, Movement of Animals, Progression of Animals.* Revised ed. Cambridge, MA: Harvard University Press, 1961.

Shields, Christopher. *Aristotle: De anima.* Oxford: Oxford University Press, 2016.

## *Literature*

Aygün, Ömer. *The Middle Included: Logos in Aristotle.* Evanston, IL: Northwestern University Press, 2017.

Caston, Victor. "Why Aristotle Needs Imagination." *Phronesis* 41, no. 1 (1996): 20–55.

Cohoe, Caleb. "When and Why Understanding Needs *Phantasmata*: A Moderate Interpretation of Aristotle's De memoria and De anima on the Role of Images in Intellectual Activities." *Phronēsis* 61, no. 3 (2016): 337–372.

DiMattei, Steven. "Rereading Aristotle's *De interpretatione* 16a3–8: Verbal Propositions as Symbols of the Process of Reasoning." *Ancient Philosophy* 26, no. 1 (2006): 1–21.

Everson, S. *Aristotle on Perception*. Oxford: Clarendon, 1997.

Johnstone, Mark. "Aristotle on Sounds." *British Journal for the History of Philosophy* 21, no. 5 (2013): 631–648.

Rabinoff, Eve. *Perception in Aristotle's Ethics*. Evanston, IL: Northwestern University Press, 2018.

Thesaurus Linguae Graecae Digital Library. Edited by Maria C. Pantelia. University of California, Irvine. Accessed June 17, 2018. http://stephanus.tlg.uci.edu.

EVE RABINOFF is author of *Perception in Aristotle's Ethics*. She now works in the nonprofit sector.

# 5

## LISTENING TO THE "EGG"

Sean Alexander Gurd, University of Texas at Austin

We murder to dissect.

—William Wordsworth

### 1.

THE THING CALLED THE "EGG" IS TO BE found in the fifteenth book of the Palatine anthology, a tenth-century collection of shorter Greek poems that includes sizable amounts of material from important Hellenistic poetry collections. Made by Simias of Rhodes (usually thought to have lived at the end of the fourth century BCE, at the very beginning of the "Hellenistic" age),[1] this "Egg" also turns up once or twice in fifteenth- and sixteenth-century manuscript codices containing Theocritus's poetry.[2] Almost always it appears in the context of other "figure poems," works that are created according to unusual formal constraints: they have identifiable metrical structures, but they also appear on the page with an identifiable or at least unusual shape—there are "Wings," "Altars," and a "Syrinx" (or "Pan-pipe") in addition to the "Egg." In both the earlier Palatine version and the later Theocritean texts, the "Egg" is written out in something resembling ovoid form. Early modern editors knew the later Theocritean codices first—not until the seventeenth century was the much earlier Palatine anthology published.[3] As it happens, these later Theocritean copies of the "Egg" are hopelessly garbled from a linguistic point of view—so garbled, in fact, that one copyist gave up in despair, remarking that "there are many mistakes in it; it is set forth here as it was in the exemplar."[4] These codices contain an "Egg" that was, in the words of its most recent commentator, "merely a picture drawn with letters that could not speak."[5] It had shape and sound but no meaning.

The discovery of the Palatine anthology by Claude de Saumaise in 1619 made it clear that the noisome form of the Theocritean manuscripts' "Egg" was the result of a scrambled transmission. The anthology's text made a little more sense, and Saumaise printed a reasonably legible text (fig. 5.1), partly with its help and partly *ingenii fiducia*.[6] A great deal more *ingenium* has been expended since then; Jan Kwapisz's recent edition prints a nearly two-page apparatus with the text, and practically every word has been contested one way or another. Here is that most recent text, laid out to reflect the shape of the manuscripts (Kwapisz himself arranges the text differently—see below):

Κωτίλας

τῇ τόδ' ἄτριον νέον

πρόφρων δὲ θυμῷ δέξο, δὴ γὰρ ἁγνᾶς

τὸ μὲν θεῶν ἐριβόας Ἑρμᾶς ἔκιξε κᾶρυξ

ἄνωγε δ' ἐκ μέτρου μονοβάμονος μέγαν πάροιθ' ἀέξειν

θοῶς δ' ὕπερθεν ὠκυ λέχριον φέρων νεῦμα ποδῶν σποράδην πίφαυσκεν

θοαῖς ἴσ' αἰόλαις νεβροῖς κῶλ' ἀλλάσσων, ὀρσιπόδων ἐλάφων τέκεσσι

πᾶσαι κραιπνοῖς ὑπὲρ ἄκρων ἱέμεναι ποσὶ λόφων κατ' ἀρθμίας ἴχνος τιθήνας

καί τις ὠμόθυμος ἀμφίπαλτον αἶψ' αὐδὰν θὴρ ἐν κόλποις δεξάμενος θαλαμᾶν μυχοιτάτῳ

κᾷτ' ὦκα βοᾶς ἀκοὰν μεθέπων ὅγ' ἄφαρ λάσιον νιφοβόλων ἀν' ὀρέων ἔσσυται ἄγκος.

ταῖς δὴ δαίμων κλυτὸς ἴσα θοοῖσι (πέδον) ποσὶν δονέων ποσὶ πολύπλοκα μεθίει μέτρα μολπᾶς.

ῥίμφα πετρόκοιτον ἐκλιπὼν ὄρουσ' εὐνὰν ματρὸς πλαγκτὸν μαιόμενος βαλιᾶς ἑλεῖν τέκος

βλαχαὶ δ' οἰῶν πολυβότων ἀν' ὀρέων νομὸν ἔβαν τανυσφύρων τ' (εἰς) ἄντρα Νυμφᾶν

ταὶ δ' ἀμβρότῳ πόθῳ φίλας ματρὸς ῥώοντ' αἶψα μεθ' ἱμερόεντα μαζόν,

ἴχνει θενὼν γὰρ (θεὸς) παναίολον Πιερίδων ὁμόδουπον αὐδάν,

ἀριθμὸν εἰς ἄκραν δεκάδ' ἰχνίων κοσμῶν νέμων τε ῥυθμόν,

φῦλ' ἐς βροτῶν ὑπὸ φίλας ἑλὼν πτεροῖσι ματρός,

λίγειά μιν κάμ' ἀμφὶ ματρὸς ὠδίς

Δωρίας ἀηδόνος

Ματέρος

Because the poem is called "Egg" and because it seems to call *itself* an egg, commentators have objected to the shape of the poem; it doesn't really look like an egg, if we're being honest. Kwapisz calls it "quite unsatisfactory" as a species of visual poetry.[7] Various solutions to the apparent

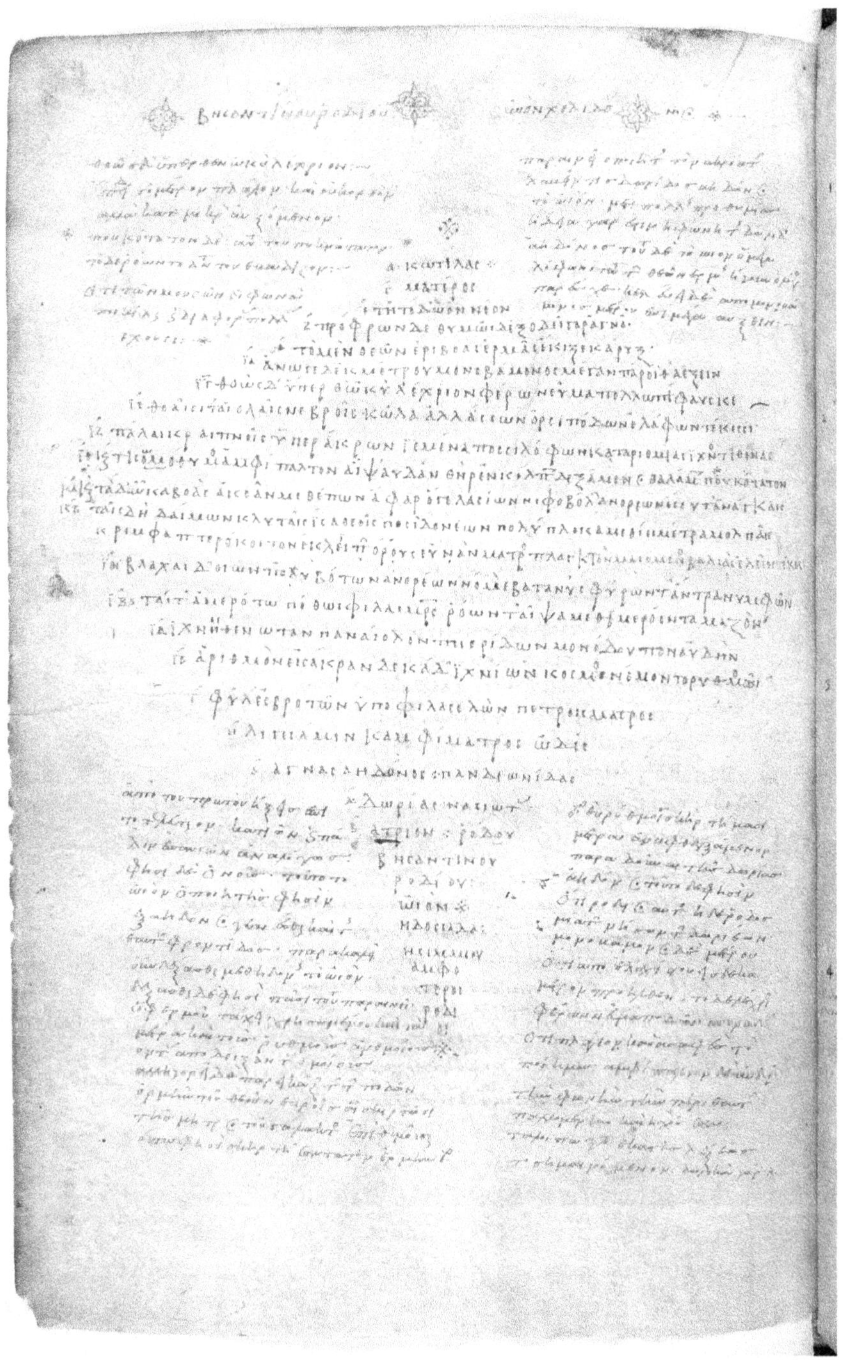

Fig. 5.1. The "Egg" as it appears in the Palantine Anthology (Paris, Bibliothèque National, Supplément grec 384, f. 30v. Reproduction courtesy of the BnF).

inexactitude of the shape have been invented and disparaged over the last century or so; one popular hypothesis is that the poem was written to be inscribed on an ostrich egg, so that the "ovoid" form would be apparent only in its substrate, not in its words.[8] A second interpretation, introduced by Félix Buffière and reasserted by P. LeGrand, was to imagine the lines written in a spiral, beginning in the center and working out. This would—or at least could—produce an egg-like shape.[9]

I have not yet attempted to translate the "Egg," because it is not yet clear how to read it. Extraordinary levels of imaginative power would be required to understand this text if you were to read from left to right and top to bottom, and eventually even the most aggressive exegete would have to give up, I suspect, in despair. But we are told by the late-antique metrical writer Hephaestion that the "Egg" is an *antithetikon*—that is, a poem in which the lines are to be read in alternating order, first the first line, then the last, then the second line, then the second last, and so on. Hephaestion says that such compositions are rare but that the "Egg" of Simias of Rhodes is an example.[10] Hephaestion's indication of the rationale for the "Egg's" appearance in the manuscripts (and early editions) also gives a reading order, and a number of editors, including Hermann Fraenkel and Kwapisz, have preferred to print the text in a way that represents this reading order, an arrangement that gives a series of ever-growing couplets, leading to a triangular or wedge-like shape. In this version, the first number is the reading-order number; the second is the line number if the piece were laid out antithetically, in "egg" shape:

1/1    Κω‛τίλας

2/20   ματέρος

3/2    τῇ τόδ᾽ ἄτριον νέον

4/19   Δωρίας ἀηδόνος·

5/3    πρόφρων δὲ θυμῷ δέξο, δὴ γὰρ ἁγνᾶς

6/18   λίγειά μιν κάμ᾽ ἀμφὶ ματρὸς ὠδίς·

7/4    τὸ μὲν θεῶν ἐριβόας Ἑρμᾶς ἔκιξε κᾶρυξ

8/17   φῦλ᾽ ἐς βροτῶν ὑπὸ φίλας ἑλὼν πτεροῖσι ματρός,

9/5    ἄνωγε δ᾽ ἐκ μέτρου μονοβάμονος μέγαν πάροιθ᾽ ἀέξειν

10/16  ἀριθμὸν εἰς ἄκραν δεκάδ᾽ ἰχνίων κοσμῶν νέμων τε ῥυθμόν,

11/6   θοῶς δ᾽ ὕπερθεν ὠκυ λέχριον φέρων νεῦμα ποδῶν σποράδην πίφαυσκεν

12/15  ἴχνει θενὼν γὰρ (θεὸς) παναίολον Πιερίδων ὁμόδουπον αὐδάν,

13/7  θοαῖς ἴσ' αἰόλαις νεβροῖς κῶλ' ἀλλάσσων, ὀρσιπόδων ἐλάφων
      τέκεσσι·
14/14 ταὶ δ' ἀμβρότῳ πόθῳ φίλας ματρὸς ῥώοντ' αἶψα μεθ' ἱμερόεντα
      μαζόν,
15/8  πᾶσαι κραιπνοῖς ὑπὲρ ἄκρων ἱέμεναι ποσὶ λόφων κατ' ἀρθμίας
      ἴχνος τιθήνας·
16/13 βλαχαὶ δ' οἰῶν πολυβότων ἀν' ὀρέων νομὸν ἔβαν τανυσφύρων τ'
      (εἰς) ἄντρα Νυμφᾶν·
17/9  καί τις ὠμόθυμος ἀμφίπαλτον αἶψ' αὐδὰν θὴρ ἐν κόλποις
      δεξάμενος θαλαμᾶν μυχοιτάτῳ
18/12 ῥίμφα πετρόκοιτον ἐκλιπὼν ὄρουσ' εὐνὰν ματρὸς πλαγκτὸν
      μαιόμενος βαλιᾶς ἑλεῖν τέκος·
19/10 κᾆτ' ὦκα βοᾶς ἀκοὰν μεθέπων ὅγ' ἄφαρ λάσιον νιφοβόλων ἀν'
      ὀρέων ἔσσυται ἄγκος.
20/11 ταῖς δὴ δαίμων κλυτὸς ἴσα θοοῖσι (πέδον) ποσὶν δονέων ποσὶ
      πολύπλοκα μεθίει μέτρα
      μολπᾶς.

Take this new warp of its chattering mother, the Dorian nightingale:
receive it benevolently in your breast, for there was a shrill labor-
pang of a pure mother over it. Wide-shouting Hermes, herald of the
gods, took it from beneath the wings of its mother and carried it to
the tribe of mortals, and after ordering and distributing the rhythm
he instructed that what was earlier a lone-walking foot should grow
to a full decade of steps. And bearing a swift, slantwise nod of his
feet, striking the earth with his foot, he quickly made known everywhere the all-flashing, thudding-together shout of the Muses, alternating limbs like quick, dappled fawns, children of the fast-footed
deer; fawns who, out of ambrosial desire for their mother, dart fast
after her lovely teat, all-surging with rapid feet over the high ridges
after the trace of the nurse with whom they would be united. And
the bleating of those sheep goes through the pastures of the generous mountains and into the caves of the slender-ankled Nymphs; and
some flesh-loving beast, receiving their echoing cry in the innermost
folds of his bed chamber, drives swiftly forward, leaving his rocky
resting place in a rage to take the children of a dappled mother, and
then fast following the sound of their cries he hastens through the

overgrown dell of the snow-clad mountains. Like unto these fawns did the glorious god, agitating the plain with his swift feet, send forth the many-woven meters of the song.

This text, the most recent, happens also to be printed by an editor who doubts that the "Egg" is really about its shape at all. Indeed, Kwapisz imagines that its original inscriptional form may have been without line breaks entirely:

Κωτίλας ματέρος τῆ τόδ' ἄτριον νέον Δωρίας ἀηδόνος· πρόφρων δὲ θυμῷ δέξο, δὴ γὰρ ἀγνᾶς λίγειά μιν κάμ' ἀμφὶ ματρὸς ὠδίς· τὸ μὲν θεῶν ἐριβόας Ἑρμᾶς ἔκιξε κᾶρυξ φῦλ' ἐς βροτῶν ὑπὸ φίλας ἑλὼν πτεροῖσι ματρός, ἄνωγε δ' ἐκ μέτρου μονοβάμονος μέγαν πάροιθ' ἀέξειν ἀριθμὸν εἰς ἄκραν δεκάδ' ἰχνίων κοσμῶν νέμων τε ῥυθμόν, θοῶς δ' ὕπερθεν ὠκυ λέχριον φέρων νεῦμα ποδῶν σποράδην πίφαυσκεν ἴχνει θενὼν γὰρ (θεὸς) παναίολον Πιερίδων ὁμόδουπον αὐδάν, θοαῖς ἴσ' αἰόλαις νεβροῖς κῶλ' ἀλλάσσων, ὀρσιπόδων ἐλάφων τέκεσσι· ταὶ δ' ἀμβρότῳ πόθῳ φίλας ματρὸς ῥώοντ' αἶψα μεθ' ἱμερόεντα μαζόν, πᾶσαι κραιπνοῖς ὑπὲρ ἄκρων ἱέμεναι ποσὶ λόφων κατ' ἀρθμίας ἴχνος τιθήνας· βλαχαὶ δ' οἰῶν πολυβότων ἀν' ὀρέων νομὸν ἔβαν τανυσφύρων τ' (εἰς) ἄντρα Νυμφᾶν· καί τις ὠμόθυμος ἀμφίπαλτον αἶψ' αὐδὰν θὴρ ἐν κόλποις δεξάμενος θαλαμᾶν μυχοιτάτῳ ῥίμφα πετρόκοιτον ἐκλιπὼν ὄρουσ' εὐνὰν ματρὸς πλαγκτὸν μαιόμενος βαλιᾶς ἑλεῖν τέκος· κᾷτ' ὦκα βοᾶς ἀκοὰν μεθέπων ὅγ' ἄφαρ λάσιον νιφοβόλων ἀν' ὀρέων ἔσσυται ἄγκος. ταῖς δὴ δαίμων κλυτὸς ἶσα θοοῖσι (πέδον) ποσὶν δονέων ποσὶ πολύπλοκα μεθίει μέτρα μολπᾶς.

This is how Timotheus's *Persians* is written out in our oldest example of lyric text, from about the same time.[11] The theory and editorial practice that led to the representing of lyric song in verses was an invention of the late classical or early Alexandrian period, a little later than the "Egg" is thought to have been composed,[12] and Kwapisz suggests that an important part of the "Egg's" conception is that it conceals, within the generic presentation of lyric without line breaks, an innovative and highly sophisticated approach to metrical composition: "The reader would have had to figure out the colometry by him or herself, led by internal suggestions (lines 9–10)— the poem would have been, then, a sort of metrical riddle."[13]

Given its paradosis and critical reception, it begins to appear that *poem* is barely the right word for whatever the "Egg" is. In its graphical form and unstable text, even in the fluctuating and difficult way it makes sense, the "Egg" seems more like a living thing, a virtual object whose written and printed instantiations do little more than express readers' ideas of it. We moderns tend to think of a poem as a verbal artifact, something artfully made from words. But the *fact* part of *artifact* seems inaccurate here: here we have a thing in words that has not been made (*facta*) but that is in the process of making itself via the mediate agency of its befuddled readers. So close is the interaction between its form and its interpretations that *egg* might not be the right word for it either—so called by Hephaestion in his work on metrics, it contained the line τῇ τός ᾠὸν νέον (take this new egg) in the manuscripts and the early printed editions, but texts since Fraenkel's 1915 edition print τῇ τόδ' ἄτριον νέον (take this new warp). The word *egg* has disappeared, along with the ovoid form. Is the word *poem* at all accurate for something of such fluidity and complexity?

And yet, and at the same time, *poem* appears to be exactly the right word. It was around Simias's lifetime that a distinction began to emerge between *poiētēs*, *poiēma*, and *poiēsis*. This distinction is traditionally ascribed to Neoptolemus of Parium, though it has cognates in other writers and roots in Aristotle, and we may safely use his definitions as guideposts here. *Poiētēs* designated the possessor of the craft, a soul with a *hexis poiētikē*, to use Aristotle's terminology. *Poiēsis* designated the semantic or signifying aspect of the poem (its status, as Aristotle would have put it, of being an imitation); while the *poiēma* or "poem" designated the sensual appearance resulting from the specifics of a text's combination of words, including its sound and its rhythm.[14] And we will see that whatever its shape on the page, the "Egg" is a sonorous object, a text about sound and a text structured in sound. But it is also a curiously intractable object, one that encourages us to listen carefully but also dramatizes (pessimistically, one might say) the relationship between sound and meaning—the closer we get to the sound of the egg, the more we lose it.

**2.**

The "Egg" draws attention to sound from the first word (I read Kwapisz's text). Κωτίλας, "chattering," is widely associated with birds, particularly with swallows or (as here) nightingales; combined with ἀήδονος in 4/19, it signals that the "Egg" will have a metapoetic theme (the scholiasts thought the "Dorian nightingale" was Simias himself).[15] Sound-words return in

6/18, where "shrill" (λίγεια) labor-pangs of the nightingale attend its birth. A pun might associate these birth-pangs (ὠδίς) with song (ὠδή). Hermes, who appears in the next line, is ἐριβόας, "wide-shouting" (7/4). Hermes's fostering of the egg leads to an "all-flashing, thudding-together shout of the Muse" (12/15). The cries of the fawns awaken the "flesh-eating beast" in 16/13 and are his target in 17/9 and 18/10. In constantly drawing attention to sound, the "Egg" encourages that we listen to it.

Indeed, its "meaning," taken on its own, is unclear and hard to follow, a kind of dreamlike series of metaphors and similes that hold together, if they do hold together, only by following a figurative logic in which the very sound of the poem is analogized through a series of metapoetic images. Consider the "new warp" of 3/12, and note that the rhythmic structure of the "Egg" itself is described as "much woven" (πολυπλοκά) in 20/11. Weaving had important musical significance, so we may understand a self-reflexive logic at work here; the poem may be describing its own texture ("texture" is also a metaphor drawn from weaving).[16] Or consider Hermes's presence. Why is he stealing eggs—or is it delicately woven clothes—from beneath the wings of watchful mothers? The scholiast's solution, that he is "the most large-voiced of the gods" (μεγαλοφωνότατος τῶν θεῶν), seems like a stretch to me, though Hermes is hardly a silent god.[17] But Hermes is also a thief and the inventor of the lyre—features linked in his Homeric hymn. Could they be combined here, with the god at once stealing and "inventing" a new poetic form? And Hermes is also a trickster (again a characteristic strongly in evidence in his hymn) and a messenger god, and the "Egg" is nothing if it is not a remarkable demonstration of literary wile, constantly asking about whether or how its message might get through and provoking hyperaware reflection about the process of interpretation (or *hermeneutics*). Certainly, his subsequent actions are entirely connected with the development and growth of the poem; he sets off a dance of the Muses distinctly reminiscent of the opening of Hesiod's *Theogony*, particularly in the thudding of feet.[18] The subsequent transition to deer is more obscure. It is clearly a metaphor for the sound of the dance—but why deer? According to Julián Méndez Dosuna, the source of the simile is Sappho, who also seems to have used it to describe swiftly dancing legs.[19] That "swiftness," which recurs throughout the "Egg," may also be metapoetic; I return to it below. The "feet" (11/6) of the dance step, and by extension those of the young deer, almost certainly refer to the rhythm of the poem—"feet" is a securely attested technical term for rhythm by the fourth century.[20] Adjectives associated with musical aesthetics proliferate in the final couplets: παναίολον (12/15), αἰόλαις (13/7), ἱμερόεντα (14/14), and πολυπλοκά (20/11). And, of course, there is the crucial couplet (8–9/5–16) in which Hermes bids the "Egg" to grow "from a single-walking foot" to a full "decade." This, as we will see, is a riddling reference to the piece's rhythmic construction—a fact alluded to as well in the last line, where the song is said to have "many-woven meters."

Since "Hermes bade that from what was earlier a walking-alone foot it should grow / to a full decade of steps after ordering and distributing the rhythm," modern scholars have understood that the lines of the poem grow somehow from a "monometer" or a single foot to a decameter or a series of ten feet. That has influenced the length and order of the lines (compare Kwapisz's text with Saumaise's—the latter has two "monometers" at beginning and end; Kwapisz has only one) and is a good example of how readers' theories of form and content are intimately connected in the textual tradition. The scholiast's source, or whoever first identified these lines as containing a metrical statement, must have seen (or heard) a poem in which the lines *did* grow from one to ten feet. (They do not obviously do so in any of the surviving manuscript texts.) Kwapisz gives the following metrical analysis:

```
1–2    – ◡ –
3–4    – ◡ – | ◡ – ◡ –
5–6    ◡ – ◡ – | × – ◡ – | ◡ – –
7–8    × – ◡ – | ◡ ◡ ◡ – | × – ◡ – | ◡ – –
9–10   ◡ – ◡ – | ◡ – ◡ ◡ | – ◡ – | × – ◡ – | ◡ – –
11–12  ◡ – ◡ – | – ◡ – | ◡ – ◡ – | – ◡ ◡ – | ◡ ◡ – | ◡ – –
13–14  × – ◡ – | ◡ – ◡ – | – – | – – | – ◡ ◡ – | ◡ ◡ – | ◡ ◡ – | ◡ – –
15–16  – – | – – | ◡ ◡ ◡ – | ◡ ◡ ◡ – | ◡ ◡ ◡ – | ◡ – ◡ – | – – | ◡ – –
17–18  – ◡ – | ◡ – ◡ – | ◡ – ◡ – | – – | – – | – – | – ◡ ◡ – | ◡ ◡ – | ◡ – ◡ –
19–20  – – | ◡ ◡ – | ◡ ◡ – | ◡ ◡ – | ◡ ◡ – | ◡ ◡ – | ◡ ◡ ◡ – | ◡ ◡ ◡ – | – ◡ ◡ | – –
```

Kwapisz concludes that Simias thinks in terms of "the small *metron*, which always remains the basic structural element."[21] We note that the "central" twelve lines (central, that is, if the poem is laid out antithetically, as it is in the manuscripts) end with a bacchius; the dominant rhythmic feel is iambic, but there is no line without a cretic or similar form mixed in. If the feet were divided into temporal units according to the conventional method of treating one short syllable as equal to two long syllables, and each foot was divided into two parts more or less at the middle, and then the internal ratios reduced, we would see that Simias works only with feet whose internal time structures are 1:1 or 2:3 ("hemiolas"—the cretic and bacchius):

    ˘ – ˘ –   3:3 = 1:1
    – –       2:2 = 1:1
    ˘ ˘ –     2:2 = 1:1
    ˘ – –     3:2
    – ˘ –     3:2

Whether or not this is an arbitrary set of observations will have to wait for a few pages.

If Kwapisz is correct and the text was initially written without any line breaks at all, that would be true also of the metrical structure, which would initially occur like this:

    – ˘ – – ˘ – – ˘ – ˘ – ˘ – – ˘ – ˘ – ˘ – ˘ – ˘ – – – – ˘ – ˘ – – ˘ – ˘ – ˘ – ˘ – – ˘
    – ˘ – ˘ ˘ ˘ – – – ˘ – ˘ – – – – ˘ – ˘ ˘ ˘ – ˘ – ˘ – ˘ – – – ˘ – ˘ – ˘ – ˘ ˘ – ˘ – ˘ –
    ˘ – ˘ – – ˘ – ˘ – ˘ – ˘ ˘ – ˘ – – – ˘ – ˘ – – ˘ – ˘ – – ˘ – ˘ – ˘ – – ˘ ˘ – ˘ ˘ ˘ – ˘
    – – ˘ – ˘ – – ˘ – ˘ – ˘ – ˘ ˘ – ˘ ˘ – ˘ – – ˘ – ˘ – ˘ – ˘ – – – – ˘ – ˘ ˘ – ˘ ˘ ˘ – ˘
    ˘ – ˘ – – – ˘ – ˘ – ˘ – – – – – ˘ ˘ – ˘ ˘ – ˘ ˘ – ˘ – – – – – ˘ ˘ ˘ – ˘ ˘ – ˘ ˘ ˘ – ˘
    ˘ ˘ – ˘ – ˘ – – – ˘ – – – – – – ˘ ˘ – ˘ ˘ ˘ – ˘ ˘ ˘ – ˘ ˘ – ˘ – ˘ – – – ˘ – – – ˘ – –
    ˘ – ˘ – ˘ – – – – – – – – ˘ ˘ – ˘ ˘ – ˘ – ˘ – ˘ – – ˘ – ˘ – ˘ – ˘ – ˘ – ˘ – – – – – – ˘
    ˘ – ˘ ˘ – ˘ – ˘ – – – ˘ ˘ – ˘ ˘ – ˘ ˘ – ˘ ˘ – ˘ ˘ – ˘ ˘ – ˘ ˘ ˘ – ˘ ˘ ˘ – – ˘ ˘ – – ˘
    ˘ – ˘ ˘ – ˘ ˘ – ˘ ˘ – ˘ ˘ – ˘ ˘ ˘ – ˘ ˘ ˘ – – ˘ ˘ – –

The words of the text might prompt a reader to suspect that the "Egg" must be scanned, that there was a rhythm of some kind to be sought out and appreciated. Such a reader might have been helped by the ˘– – pattern, which ends a good many of the central verses and creates a conventional lyric clausula with the iambs it follows.[22] But the first and last couplets would have depended on the reader having figured out the metrical schema of the poem; they would then be able to search for monads and decades of feet in these sections of the text.[23]

I cannot doubt that the "Egg" is intimately concerned with its own rhythm. And we can, provisionally at least, say that its rhythm is a matter of its sound; this is a claim that is encouraged by the text itself, with its frequent references to sound and music. But there are reasons to wonder if "rhythm" really is identical to "sound," and while I make this equation in the early parts of the essay, my drift is to increasingly problematize it. Indeed, I think the "Egg" does something far more profound than just propose a riddle whose solution is itself, the method of whose solution is to discern a link between its sounds and its meaning. When we read it in the context of contemporary discussions, particularly as these concerned rhythm and meter, we find the "Egg" asking about the possibilities and the dangers inherent in any attempt to link sound and sense; indeed, it may imply that such questions are unanswerable.

**3.**

Let us imagine that Kwapisz is right: that in its first textual form, the "Egg" was neither a series of ever-lengthening couplets nor laid out in the shape of an egg but simply a block of text, presented without any clear indication of where one verse ended and the next began. It is quite safe to imagine this, since if the "Egg" was ever read or recited out loud, it was presented in such a way—verse endings are graphical conventions that make visually clear what is supposed to be audible on its own terms. Nothing like the "Egg," it is safe to assume, had ever been heard, at least by a Greek ear, in the later fourth or early fifth century. How would a reader or listener have understood what they were encountering?

When modern scholars attempt to analyze the meter of a poem, we do so with a theoretical armature grounded in almost a millennium of ancient theory, combined with some nineteenth-century innovations and some twentieth-century linguistics.[24] Those in the fourth century BCE relied on a different though not unrelated set of ideas and questions. To appreciate how Simias or an early reader might have approached the "Egg" as a rhythmic construction, it seems worthwhile to set out some of the details of their rhythmic awareness, as this could have been informed by philosophy and literary theory.

The "Egg" relies, as we have seen, on the idea that one could measure the length of a verse by the number of metra it contained—it is to grow from "one to ten" (9–10/5–16). The idea that a line of verse could have a specific and countable number of measures was not innovative in Simias's day. We find the first recorded indication of such an awareness in Herodotus, who occasionally introduces a passage of verse, an inscription, or an oracle by describing its meter: he refers to a subsequent metrical citation as "in a hexameter" or "in trimeters."[25] Such expressions always introduce a verse, but not all verse citations are so introduced. Perhaps he mentions the meter to report the result of an analysis, and we are to understand that Herodotus thinks it is somehow new information that a given passage is in hexameters or trimeters; or perhaps he presents the designation as received knowledge. He might also have done it to help readers—his texts probably didn't break verses into lines in his written text, and so he might have wanted to flag verse sections as verse by designating their rhythmic form (this hypothesis is challenged by the fact that his practice is inconsistent). In the first case, we might be speaking of a newish intellectual tool that Herodotus thought readers might find interesting; in the second case, we would be speaking of a widespread awareness that Herodotus exploits to deal with a relatively new communications technology (written prose). If it's true that even Ionian stichic forms like the iambic trimeter and the dactylic hexameter were originally formed around longer cola, then the interpretation of the epic line as six dactyls would have been a theoretical imposition on an older, perhaps more intuitive practice.[26] Nor is it beyond the range of possibility that the later sixth or early fifth century BCE should have seen such theoretical innovation; this was the time of the new dithyramb and of tragedy and comedy at Athens, just a little after the metrical innovations of Stesichorus in the west.

I find it intriguing, too, that Herodotus specifies the number of metra but not the kind of metra in each case—he refers to hexameters and trimeters, not dactylic hexameters and iambic trimeters. This could be because everybody just knew trimeters were iambs and hexameters were dactyls; but it could also be because (as we will see shortly) all metra were felt as a strong and a weak signal grouped together—in this regard, dactyls and iambs were formally identical. Herodotus or his readers may simply not have been interested in the fact that the metra in each line were different. But we are a long way into the realms of speculation here.

Metrical terminology is again presented as newfangled and sophisticated in Aristophanes's *Clouds*, first performed in the 420s BCE and rewritten sometime after that, but never performed again.[27] Here the farmer Strepsiades is proposing to study with "Socrates" in his *Bouleuterion* but struggling to get his head around some of the concepts:

Σω. ἄγε δή, τί βούλει πρῶτα νυνὶ μανθάνειν
ὧν οὐκ ἐδιδάχθης πώποτ' οὐδέν; εἰπέ μοι.
πότερα περὶ μέτρων ἢ περὶ ἐπῶν ἢ ῥυθμῶν;
Στ. περὶ τῶν μέτρων ἔγωγ'· ἔναγχος γάρ ποτε

ὑπ᾿ ἀλφιταμοιβοῦ παρεκόπην διχοινίκῳ.
Σω. οὐ τοῦτ᾿ ἐρωτῶ σ᾿, ἀλλ᾿ ὅτι κάλλιστον μέτρον
ἡγεῖ· πότερα τὸ τρίμετρον ἢ τὸ τετράμετρον;
Στ. ἐγὼ μὲν οὐδὲν πρότερον ἡμιέκτεω.
Σω. οὐδὲν λέγεις, ὤνθρωπε.
Στ. περίδου νυν ἐμοί,
εἰ μὴ τετράμετρόν ἐστιν ἡμιέκτεων.
Σω. ἐς κόρακας· ὡς ἄγροικος εἶ καὶ δυσμαθής.²⁸

Socrates: Come then, what do you want to learn first, of the things you've never learned before? Tell me. Do you want to learn about measure ["meters"], or about words, or about rhythms?
Strepsiades: About measures; for just now I was swindled out of three pints by a grain dealer.
Socrates: No, not that kind of measure. What do you think is the most beautiful? The trimeter or the tetrameter?
Strepsiades: Definitely the half-sixth.
Socrates: That doesn't mean anything, man.
Strepsiades: Blow me down if a tetrameter doesn't come out of a half-sixth.
Socrates: Bloody hell. You're an idiot.

That "Socrates" is dealing with these ideas in the *Bouleuterion* suggests that in the second half of the fifth century metrical analysis could still be characterized as cutting edge, the province of upstart intellectuals who are perhaps ridiculously disconnected from actual musical practice. While the earliest works of music theory came from the pens of what today would be called arts practitioners—Lasus of Hermione (who redesigned the music for the dithyrambic competitions in Athens under the Pisistratids) composed the earliest known theoretical work, *On Harmony,* and Sophocles's *On the Chorus* must have included some discussion of rhythm and its expression in dance (or vice versa)—the second half of the fifth century shows a series of figures whose primary activity was not music engaging in musical matters. We know of works "on rhythm and meter" by the polymath and professional teacher Hippias of Elis,²⁹ as well as by the Athenian materialist philosopher Democritus.³⁰ The Pythagoreanizing Tarentine cosmologist Philolaus wrote on rhythm, too,³¹ as did the shadowy figure Damon, about whom we seem to know less and less as the years progress.³² The rise of interest in metrics, rhythm, and other aspects of music among intellectuals who were not primarily musicians set the stage for what I think was a decisive fourth-century development: music theory became an aspect of the system of knowledge called "philosophy." It is above all on theories developed there, and not by musicians or poets of the previous centuries, that Simias ultimately relies.

Greek singers had long identified their songs with dance forms.[33] This tendency continues when we begin to see signs of philosophers identifying different measures, or "feet." Simultaneously, two other themes emerge: feet are analyzed in terms of the relative lengths of their parts, and different meters are associated with distinctive characters or ἤθη. Exactly what these ἤθη were was a matter of disagreement, but the word ἦθος would be consistently linked, one way or another, with metrical structures. This matters because even as the technical description of feet in terms of their numerical structures took hold, the meaning of these feet was felt to reside in their ἤθη. Ἤθη could be experienced by anyone regardless of their technical training or their ability to do metrical analysis. Indeed, two trends developed simultaneously in the early philosophy of rhythm: a numerological track, highly abstract and assumed to be available only to advanced theorists, and an ethical track, which treats rhythm in terms of its character and assumes universal application.

Plato gives us our first glimpse of this complex of themes, in a well-known section of *Republic* 3 during which Socrates is discussing what musical forms should be admitted into a just city. Socrates asserts that he and his interlocutors should not investigate complex (ποικίλους) or variegated (παντοδαπάς) steps (βάσεις) but rather should consider what rhythms belong to a composed (κοσμίου) and courageous (ἀνδρείου) life. Here, in what amounts to the hypothesis for Socrates's subsequent brief discussions, he broaches the themes both of the nature of feet and of their ethical importance. Deferring to Glaucon's supposed expertise in musical matters, Socrates elicits from his conversational partner the observation that there are three forms (εἴδη) from which the steps (βάσεις) are woven (πλέκονται). Note the weaving metaphor; Simias uses it to describe the "many-woven meters" (πολυπλοκὰ μέτρα) of the "Egg." Glaucon is unable to connect the different metrical forms with "what life each imitates," so Socrates suggests that they follow Damon, who made some arguments about the political significance of certain musical forms.[34] With Damon as a guide, Socrates suggests that certain steps are appropriate to illiberality, hubris, madness, and other ills, while others are appropriate to the opposite, presumably liberality, prudence, and sanity.

Socrates also unfolds a numerical analysis, signaling approval of a rhythm with "equal up and down" (ἄνω καὶ κάτω). This appears to refer to feet in which the duration of the first half (ἄνω) is equal to the duration of the second half (κάτω; think about the movement of a dancing foot, which might rise into the air for two beats, then touch down for two more). Dactyls (– ◡ ◡), spondees (– –), anapests (◡ ◡ –), and the like belong in this category. The next part of Socrates's claim is harder to understand; but it seems to refer to iambs and trochees, in which "up" and "down" are in a ratio of 1:2 and 2:1. Socrates is theorizing metrical feet simultaneously as dance steps and as mathematical entities, defined by the ratio (λόγος) between the two parts of a characteristic movement.

Damon's role in elaborating theories like this, once held to be securely established, is now much more doubtful thanks to the work of Robert Wallace.[35] But I think it is likely that another figure is lying in the background here as well, and ultimately this figure may be more important within the broader picture of Plato's work: the late fifth-century Tarantine Philolaus. A significant Pythagorean musicologist, Philolaus interpreted the musical concords as ratios, projecting the latter into the structure of the cosmos.[36] He also wrote on rhythm and meter, though we know very little about his doctrine. A Pythagorean-connected mathematical musicologist who theorized musical scales in terms of the numerical ratios defining concords can be expected, I think, to have thought about rhythm in an equally mathematical mode. The one concrete report we do have about Philolaus's rhythmic work is that it articulated theories about how and why the soul was connected to its body.[37] That suggests that Philolaus connected the numerical structure of meter with the soul's embodied form and points toward a second reason for identifying "ethical" meanings in rhythm: its numbers were homologous with the numbers in souls that expressed it. This is an idea Plato was sympathetic to, at least judging from what we find in the *Timaeus*. The *Republic*, too, trades on the idea that the soul is or should be in harmony (συμφωνία).[38]

In Aristotle's *Rhetoric*, we find the same interest in the numerical relations between parts of a foot combined with the description of its character or ἦθος. Rhythm is, he says, a way of counting the form of speech (ὁ δὲ τοῦ σχήματος τῆς λέξεως ἀριθμὸς ῥυθμός ἐστιν).[39] His advocacy of rhythm in prose expresses themes that are wired deeply into the circuitry of Aristotelian "hylomorphism," the doctrine that what is has both form and matter (as well as a maker and a purpose). The "formal cause," as he put it, provided limits or boundaries to a thing's material cause; without it, matter was both unlimited and unknowable. Aristotle is clearly working with this schema in his discussion of prose rhythm; he asserts that unrhythmic prose is indefinite (τὸ δὲ ἄρρυθμον ἀπέραντον), and as a result "unknowable" (ἄγνωστον τὸ ἄπειρον).[40] Rhythm, we might say, provides speech with a form and a kind of commensurability for the ear and mind, making it easier to assimilate.

For Aristotle, rhythm also has meaning, inasmuch as each of the metrical feet refers, through its character, to specific previously existing speech genres that themselves may be intuitively known by an orator's audience. Developing ideas we have already glimpsed in Plato, Aristotle asserts that different rhythms have different characters: the "heroic" (ἡρῷος) is "august but not lacking in a harmony typical of speech" (σεμνῆς ἀλλ' οὐ λεκτικῆς ἁρμονίας δεόμενης), the iambic is closest to the common speech, the trochaic is the lewdest or most comic (κορδακικώτερος), and the paian has yet to have its character well defined, though rhetoricians have used it since Thrasymachus.[41] These rhythms can also be distinguished numerically: the heroic is a unity (1:1), the iamb and trochee are in the ratio of 1:2 or 2:1, and the paian is a hemiola (3:2). Aristotle does not say so, but his analysis presumes the same division of the foot into "up" and "down" that we have seen in Plato and will see again in Aristoxenus. A number of details are new. First, the paian (3:2) recommends itself, we are told, because it is a "mean" between 1:1 and 2:1. Second, Aristotle's rhythmic characters are remarkably bland; while the heroic is "serious" and the trochaic is lewd, the iamb and paian are merely distinct. Because the iamb is proximal to common speech, it associates the rhythm with a certain "type" ("normal" people), but it is also devoid of any explicit moral assessment. (In the *Poetics*, however, Aristotle is more explicit: he asserts that tragedy, whose origin he claims was in improvisation and satyr play, naturally began to use the iambic trimeter as its emotions became grander and more serious, leaving behind tetrameter as more appropriate for a comic mode.[42]) The paian, in turn, is distinguished but not described. We are a long way from the specificity with which he treats the ἤθη of the musical modes in the *Politics*, which is in direct dialogue with the ethical theory retailed in Plato and lines musical expression up with states of soul.[43] Here the rhythms are associated with little more than performance genres: the heroic is solemn because it is the rhythm of the epic, a genre Aristotle treats alongside tragedy in the *Poetics*; the trochaic is lewd because it is most commonly met with in comedy; and the iamb is defined as belonging to the common speech (i.e., it is associated with the speech genre of "regular talk").[44] The willingness to avoid explicit moral statements about rhythmic form would become a significant theme, and perhaps also a matter for some debate, in the work of some of his students.

Aristotle's proposal that arrhythmic prose was relatively hard to cognize was repeated by Aristoxenus, a first-generation student of the Stagirite who made his most significant (and most well-known) contributions in the philosophical interpretation of music. Traces of his doctrine on rhythm, likely encapsulated in a work called the *Elements of Rhythm*, have survived in a number of substantial secondhand reports; there is also an extensive papyrus fragment that contains ideas that, if they are not his, are quite similar.[45] Aristoxenus's position was strictly Aristotelian: rhythm imposed form on an audible substrate, or a "thing to be rhythmed";[46] without rhythm, this musical substrate was, like matter, hard to know. Aristides Quintilianus, possibly working from an Aristoxenian source, said that unrhythmed melodies were hard to grasp.[47]

What is an "unrhythmed melody"? Not one that did not take place in time but one whose durations did not meet certain specific criteria: if the durations were not ordered so as to satisfy these stipulations, the expression was unrhythmic. Criterion one was that the two parts of a foot, the "up" and the "down," must be commensurate with each other—that is, their lengths must be measurable with the same unit of measurement (otherwise, the foot is called "irrational" and arrhythmic). Aristoxenus specifies that he does not mean "commensurable" in a "purely numerical" sense. It's unclear what this means. One possibility is that he is waving off the fact that it is always possible to subdivide any pair of durations into some tiny unit that goes evenly into both. Rather, he seems to treat the minimal unit as the length of the short syllable. A foot will satisfy the "commensurability criterion" when both "up" and "down" are measurable as some whole number of shorts. Criterion two was that the two parts of a foot must be in one of only three ratios: unity (1:1), duple (2:1 or 1:2), or hemiolic (2:3 or 3:2). He calls these "dactylic," "iambic," and "paionic";[48] confusingly, the iambic metron, which has an up of ◡ – and a down of the same, turns out to be "dactylic" because of the ratio of its parts. These are almost the same categories used by Aristotle and alluded to in the *Republic*. But Aristoxenus is far more interested in the way these rhythms combine than were earlier authors. His theory is less easy to reconstruct, but it is clear that a major principle governing how feet could be combined in the production of a musical rhythm was appropriateness (τὸ οἰκεῖον) and whether or not the combination preserved the ἦθος of a piece.[49]

Aristoxenus's rhythmic writings have not survived in anything even remotely resembling intact form, and far more is missing than has survived. But a more wide-angled look at his entire corpus supports the idea that he refused all but the most tenuous connection between musical structure and ethical or social states. Aristoxenus was explicit on this point, though he was writing about scales and tunings rather than rhythms: it is possible, he says, to measure the distance between notes in a scale (for example, one might observe that the first four notes in a modern major scale are two, two, and one semitones apart from each other). But Aristoxenus also asserts that this approach ignores the fact that when we listen to a musical performance, we do not measure the intervals. Instead, he says, our ear just feels the character (ἦθος) of the piece's tuning. These characters are not moral or political but musically immanent—the chromatic genus, for example, has a "chromatic ἦθος."[50] This is in stark contrast to the claims of Plato, who associated the Lydian mode with unmanly lamentation and the Dorian with courage and action; even Aristotle, though more diffident on this front, associated musical structures with definite states of soul and worried about their educational consequences.[51] The peripatetic philosopher Heraclides of Pontus shows a very strong tendency to associate musical material with moral and even ethnic character: he denied that any tuning that was not associated with an old Greek ethnos was truly a *harmonia*. Of these true harmonies, there were three: the Dorian, associated especially with austere and warlike Lacedaimonia; the Aeolian, associated with the splendid and haughty Aeolian Islands; and the Iastian, associated with the Ionians of Miletus.[52] Such tendencies had interdisciplinary support. In addition to Plato, who associated music, moral or psychological conditions, and political structures,[53] Heraclides could have looked to Hippocrates, who derived elements of ethnic character (ἦθος) from environmental contexts,[54] or even to Aeschines and Demosthenes, who cast aspersions on each other's virtue on the basis of the sounds that came out of their mouths.[55] There was a widespread tendency, in other words, to link character with some other factor—music, environment, voice, and so on. Aristoxenus accepts the terminology but restricts it by treating music as an autonomous area of performance and perception to be discussed only on its own terms.[56] Rhythms or scales have ἦθος, but he is unwilling to associate this with any moral character or function—the character of a tuning or a rhythm is no more than its "feeling," the sort of thing one would perceive without counting or scanning, and he thinks it amounts to overreach to claim that these "feelings" have any kind of moral or political consequences. Indeed, we find him complaining about auditors who expect him to pass judgment on which modes help and which modes harm souls; he says they have ignored his qualification that he will do so "only in so far as it is possible for modes to have such an effect."[57]

The disagreement between figures like Heraclides and Aristoxenus over whether there was a link between musical ἦθος and moral or political character had fateful consequences for the course of Hellenistic theorizing about poetry and sound, and I think it is crucial for understanding the context of the "Egg." But before plunging into that topic, it may be worth articulating how the metrical consciousness of the fourth century interfaces with the way the "Egg" is built—and with the way it might have been "solved" by a reader. Again assuming Kwapisz's text and metrical analysis, we observe that the "Egg" is constructed of the following feet:

3:2 (a) – ◡ – (or ◡ ◡ ◡ –) (b) ◡ – – (allowing substitutions in both longs)
1:1 (c) – – (or ◡ ◡ –)
1:1 (d) ◡ – ◡ – (or – – ◡ –)[58]

The "Egg" immediately juxtaposes feet of the 2:3 and 1:1 variety. Consider the first four verses in succession:

– ◡ –

– ◡ –

– ◡ – | ◡ – ◡ –

– ◡ – | ◡ – ◡ –

The first two lines are 2:3 feet; the third and fourth are made from a 2:3 foot followed by a 1:1 foot. Someone who had read fourth-century metrical theory would have thought of these as qualitatively different rhythms. Someone who had read Aristoxenus might have asked whether they were appropriately placed together.

In 5–6/3–18, the hemiolic idea is deployed only at the end of the line, where it could be interpreted as a catalectic iambic metron, a characteristic gesture of closure:[59]

◡ – ◡ – | × – ◡ – | ◡ – –

(Run into the previous line, which ended ◡ – ◡ –, the first part of this couplet could well have fooled a reader into feeling it as a catalectic iambic tetrameter.) The next five couplets retain this hemiolic "tag"; hemiolic ideas are also dispersed among the "dactylic" iambic metra in such a way that the construction of the first six couplets could be characterized as dominated by the interplay of single and hemiolic rhythms. A successful reading would depend on detecting this and lucidly expressing the flow of words in order to emphasize the run of metrical feet.

In line 11/6, the playful alternation of iambic (i.e., "unities") and paionic (i.e., "hemiolic") ideas is interrupted, first by a choriamb (– ˘ ˘ –) and then by an anapest (˘ ˘ –). Together, these might be interpreted as – ˘ ˘ – ˘ ˘ –, one of the basic units of Pindaric "dactylo-epitritic" rhythm. But the metrical scheme demands that it be interpreted as two feet—otherwise we would not have the requisite number of six feet in this line (remember that the text described itself as gradually increasing from one to ten feet). Both of these feet are "dactylic," in Aristoxenus's sense, since both evince a relationship of unity between the up and the down; but the anapest is two short syllables shorter than the choriamb. Since they are the same type as the iambic meter but two-thirds the length, they might be said to quicken the rhythm (as long as a reader is scanning and thinking rhythmically); now up and down alternate more rapidly. These "shorter" feet begin to proliferate in what follows; they occur three times out of seven in the seventh couplet, four times out of nine in the ninth couplet, and eight times out of ten in the tenth couplet. That the impression of speed could be the right one here is suggested by a curious lexical detail: line 11/6, the first to include an anapest, begins with θοῶς, "quickly," and then, two words later, adds ὠκύ (which means "the same," more or less). It's as though the "Egg" were alerting us to the uptick in tempo with its imagery; and this is an impression that only gets stronger with the subsequent proliferation of "fast" words: θοαῖς and ὀρσιπόδων (neither, perversely, coinciding with quick feet in 13/7), αἶψα (14/14), κραίπνοις (15/8), αἶψα (17/9), ῥίμφα (18/12), ὦκα (19/10), and θοοῦσι (20/11).

If indeed, as Kwapisz suggests, the "Egg" was originally presented without any graphical indication of line ends, just as a run of words, prose-like, on the page, readers may well have "felt" the rhythm before they scanned it. That something rhythmically interesting was going on might have been particularly palpable at those points where things change a little bit and a 1:1 foot is followed by a 3:2 foot, or the 1:1 feet become two-thirds shorter. This feeling, perhaps initially quite indistinct, could have become more acute when the words refer to decades of feet and "much-woven meters"; that could prompt a more assiduous hunt for rhythmic signals leading eventually, perhaps, to a complete scansion.

Clearly, however, things didn't go perfectly according to plan, at least not if the modern texts are right: readers did engage actively in the "Egg," but their engagement didn't result in a complete scansion. Rather, it led to the production of garbled, miscopied texts, laid out on the basis of a false idea that the poem was an *antithetikon* meant to look like an egg.

**4.**

The "Egg" describes its own metrical construction not just by referring directly to the number of metra in the longest line but also in more figurative, less direct, and more doubtful ways. Take the poem's speed words, for example: for the most part, they describe the speed of fawns' feet. Why am I not overreading when I suggest that they refer also to the rhythm of the text? Is it appropriate to think of spondees and anapests as "youthful," "playful," "gamboling meters" (recall that Aristotle called the dactyl "serious")? Such questions seem unavoidable not just because a certain amount of skepticism is always useful in exegesis but because exactly such questions seem to have found their way to the heart of literary-theoretical debates in the Hellenistic period. Most of this debate comes after Simias, as it happens, but it is rooted in fourth-century discussions of music and rhythm, and an imaginative historian might be prompted to imagine that Simias's work could have egged the debate on.

The relations of sound and sense in poetry were a subject of significant debate among Hellenistic poetic theorists, especially in the area of what has come to be called "euphonist" theory. We know this body of theory primarily from Philodemus's *On Poems*, though echoes of it can be heard in Dionysius of Halicarnassus, Longinus, and elsewhere.[60] *On Poems* engages with Crates of Malos, who seems to have written a lengthy critical summary of euphonist theory. The issue, in essence, was to what degree a composition was defined by its sound (*poiēma*) or whether the poem's meaning (*poiēsis*) was also important. The most radical of the euphonists, figures such as Pausimachus, denied that the signified meaning of a poem was relevant to the appreciation of that poem—only the specific sonic arrangement mattered.[61] Pausimachus also claimed that good poetry, being defined exclusively by the synthesis of sounds, was perfectly capable of representing bad people—ἤθη are part of the ποιήσις, the representation, and not part of the ποιήμα, the sonic and distinctive part.[62] This was debated. Another theorist by the name of Andromenides seems to have argued that there was ἦθος both in the representation and in the ἐποποιΐα, which refers, it seems, to issues relating to word choice including rhythm and sound. Crates, for his part, appears to have argued that the lexical texture was important but that it was assisted by the use of ἦθος in the representation.[63] Consequently, one should judge "not the meaning, but not without the meaning."[64] The most radical of the euphonists seem to owe a lot, as Richard Janko saw, to Aristoxenus.[65] Although Pausimachus associated ἦθος only with representation, his assertion that the ear could recognize a good poem on the basis of its sound alone is similar to Aristoxenus's claim that the ear just recognized the ἦθος of tunings, as well as his unwillingness to associate tunings and rhythms with moral character. In contrast, positions like that of Crates and Andromenides related form and content much more closely. These debates began, it seems, early in the third century BCE, perhaps provoked by philosophers of Aristoxenus's vintage. I think the "Egg" can be shown to be relevant to these debates. Pausimachus would assert that one discerned something like the "Egg" as a poem only inasmuch as it evinced a series of pulses, up and down, and also perhaps a fluctuating tempo as different feet are heard; he would have added that it was constituted by and in this perceptive activity, positively excluding the relevance of its meaning. But what if the poem were about itself? It isn't clear how or whether the "Egg's" meaning could be associated with any other composition or dissociated from the rhythm in which it is expressed. Indeed, if the poem was originally inscribed without line breaks, its meaning would have played a central role in guiding a reader to listen for the feet. Given these considerations, it would appear that the radical euphonist position is inadequate here: one should not deny the relevance of the meaning to the rhythm, at least not in the case of the "Egg."

Unfortunately, things are not so simple. Fourth-century theorists—foremost Aristotle and Aristoxenus—argued that sound and sense could be coordinated by evaluating their appropriateness to each other; when they were appropriate, an ἦθος was the aesthetic (i.e., perceptible) consequence.[66] Here, to be sure, we are dealing with intangibles, and I am unable to support my next observation with any securely traceable ancient source. But as an intellectual technology, ἦθος seems built, at least in part, to handle such intangibles: if a music theorist or a metrician can identify structures with great precision, nontheorists can only experience the "feeling" of a piece, a metaphorical or epiphenomenal screen covering over the more technical components hidden below the threshold of perception. Of course, the "Egg" is incomprehensible without technical knowledge, but that very fact makes it possible for us to ask about the relationship between the "objectivities" of meter and rhythm and the "subjectivities" of tone and feel.

On one reading, the "Egg" is a remarkably melancholy (not to say pessimistic) meditation on the loss brought about by technical insight, as though to "solve" the text's riddle (i.e., to achieve awareness of its metrical structure) were also to kill it. At about the middle of the poem's journey, Simias introduces a metaphor for the meter, one that also leads, I think, to a metaphor for the reader's progress: the feet of the poem are like the feet of fawns gamboling in the mountains after their mother. The uproar of their vibrant play awakens a "flesh-eating beast," who sets out to kill one for a meal. We've already seen that the reference to fawns may be a reference to dance and hence to rhythm; I'm willing to bet, with Raymond A. Prier, that the hunting beast is a metaphor for a reader on the track, as it were, of a proper analysis of the poem.[67] Forms of δέχομαι occur twice in the "Egg": once in offering it to the reader (5/3) and once in describing the beast hearing the sounds in his lair (17/9). Reader and hunter alike have to use their ears to get what they want. Thus, the sounds of the deer (the sounds of the poem) arouse a beast (a reader), who sets out to hunt a fawn (to analyze the meter). Little difficulty there, except for the affective overtones of the whole thing—for "solving" the poem is equated with killing a fawn, as though knowledge of the poem's secret somehow destroyed the poem. The issue is less about the ethics of eating venison than about the fact that after one has killed and eaten a deer, it's gone—similarly, at least by the logic of the metaphor at work here, the poem would vanish once one had "understood" it.

Nor is the beginning of the poem any more optimistic, for this "Egg" was stolen from its mother, the "chattering nightingale," by Hermes. I suggested that Hermes is present here in part because of his role as the inventor of the lyre, another musical innovation associated with a theft. Of course, the lyre started as a tortoise who had the misfortune to cross the young god's path; the result was its death and transformation into a musical instrument. Hermes has done something only slightly less terrible here: he has stolen something from a mother. That mother, the nightingale, could easily be read as a metaphor for the lyric tradition, in which it had long functioned as a metapoetic figure for singers. As I suggested in section 3, the measurement of poetic meter in terms of metra or feet was not a "natural" or "organic" part of the lyric tradition but an innovation, perhaps dating to the early fifth century, and was associated above all with theorists rather than musicians. The "Egg," self-consciously built out of these theoretical entities, is thus in some sense a foster child torn from its lyric origins.

And for a reader who equally self-consciously goes looking for a metrical structure corresponding to the "Egg's" self-description, the fully scanned object that results is itself torn from its nest in perception, less a sonorous object than an effect of meaning, an artifact produced by following the directions embedded in the representation. Here it is not sound but sense that has priority. After all, there is a difference between the sound of a poem and its meter: meters are intellectual objects, ideal patterns that are highly abstract and quite distinct from the auditory realia of speech. Indeed, any metrical schematization which assumes the equivalence of two short syllables to one long syllable, or the equivalence of two "identical" feet in two different places in a text, ignores what for want of a better term we can call the *actual* sonorous contours of the utterance. Both temporal and metrical equivalence are abstractions, conventional but ideal concepts drawn from but definitely not identical to the aural/oral phenomena. As A. M. Devine and Laurence D. Stephens put it in *The Prosody of Greek Speech*, "The poet and his audience do not assess metricality on the basis of the actual durations they hear in each utterance, for the relatively trivial reason that every utterance, like every snowflake, is in fact unique. . . . The categories of language to which metre is sensitive must clearly be more general and more abstract than the precisely quantified phonetic measurements of nonce utterances, if metre is to be able to function as a system shared by an entire speech community."[68] When or if we "solve" the "Egg" by attending to its sounds (as the "Egg" seems to direct us to do), we also learn to stop listening to it. If, as I have suggested, ἦθος is an affective content that can be perceived without awareness of the more technical elements that determine it, the "Egg" seems to agree. The feeling of the poem's sound and the results of its metrical analysis are mutually exclusive: one either feels or understands, but not both. This is a pessimistic view of theory, to say the least. But it is also, more crucially, an outright refusal, in the end, of the sustainability of any theory of poetry grounded in sound—for meter is not sound but an ideal construction, a projection of sense. This would reject not only the radical euphonist position of Pausimachus, who denied the relevance of meaning to poetry, but even the more moderate position of a critic such as Crates, who argued that we judged both the sound and the sense. The line of thinking prompted by the "Egg's" allegory of reading is that only meaning matters; even the sound, here, is a function, as it were, of the sense.

This returns me, in a way, to my initial observation about the "Egg": it both is and is not a poem. It is a poem, inasmuch as its sound lies at the forefront of attention, part of the triggering process that contributes to the riddle's solution. But it also is not a poem, inasmuch as the solution involves a move away from sound and feeling to an awareness of structure. That the consequences of this "awareness" of structure have not been excellent for the "Egg" is clear from the disasters sustained in its textual tradition; at the very least, some attempt or attempts to "understand" it were central to that long process of disintegration. All we can do after such a fall is try to pick up the pieces.

## Notes

1. Hermann Fraenkel, *De Simia Rhodio* (Göttingen: Officina Academica Dieterichiana, 1915), 10–11.

2. I rely on the text and apparatus of Jan Kwapisz, *The Greek Figure Poems*, vol. 19 of *Hellenistica Groningana* (Leuven: Peeters, 2013).

3. Claude de Saumaise, *Duarum inscriptionum veterum Herodis Attici Rhetoris et Regillae coniugis honori positarum explicatio: Eiusdem Ad Dosiadae Aras, Simmiae Rhodii Ouum, Alas, Securim Theocriti fistulam notae* (Hieronymum Drouart, 1619).

4. Πολλὰ δὲ ἐν αὐτῷ ἡμάρτηται· ἀλλ᾿ ὡς ἐν τῷ ἀντιγράφῳ ἦν, οὕτω καὶ κεῖται. Kwapisz, *Greek Figure Poems*, 50, citing MS Z (Laurentianus Ashburhamiensis, 1174); he refers the reader to Silvia Strodel, *Zur Überlieferung und zum Verständnis der hellenistischen Technopaignien.Studien zur klassischen Philologie, 0172–1798*, vol. 132 (New York: Peter Lang, 2002), 15.

5. Kwapisz, *Greek Figure Poems*, 50.

6. Saumaise, *Duarum inscriptionum veterum*, 159.

7. Kwapisz, *Greek Figure Poems*, 19. In fact, there is debate among editors over whether or not the shape really is that of an egg. Félix Buffière (*Anthologie Grecque: Première partie—Anthologie Palatine. T. 12* [Paris: Les Belles Lettres, 1970], 141) says it is perfectly egg-shaped; P. Legrand (*Bucoliques Grecs* [Paris: Société d'édition "Les Belles lettres," 1925], 223) says it is not.

8. Alan Cameron, *Callimachus and His Critics* (Princeton, NJ: Princeton University Press, 1995), 36a.77; Raymond A. Prier, "And Who Is the Woof? Response, Ecphrasis and the 'Egg' of Simmias," *Quaderni Urbinati di Cultura Classica* 46, no. 1 (1994): 79–92; Romero Guichard, "Simias' Pattern Poems: The Margins of the Canon," in *Beyond the Canon*, ed. M. Annette Harder, Remco F. Regtuit, and Gerrigje Catharina Wakker (Leuven: Peeters, 2006), 89–90.

9. Buffière, *Anthologie Grecque*; LeGrand, *Bucoliques Grecs*, 225.

10. Hephaestion, *De poematis* 68; cf. *Introductio metrica* 62 (Max Consbruch, *Hephaestionis Enchiridion: Bibliotheca scriptorum Graecorum et Romanorum Teubneriana* [Leipzig: Teubner, 1906]).

11. The papyrus is housed in the Staatliches Museum with the catalogue number P. Berol 9875. An image and bibliography can be conveniently viewed at https://berlpap.smb .museum/02776/.

12. Traditionally, Aristophanes of Byzantium is thought to have begun the colometric representation of lyric verses. Rudolf Pfeiffer, *History of Classical Scholarship: From the Beginnings to the End of the Hellenistic Age* (Oxford: Clarendon, 1968), 87–88.

13. Kwapisz, *Greek Figure Poems*, 37.

14. Philodemus, *On Poems* 5, col. 15.1–17 (in Cecilia Mangoni, *Philodemus: Il quinto libro della poetica (PHerc. 1425 e 1538)—La Scuola di Epicuro*, vol. 14 [Naples: Bibliopolis, 1993]). Compare Elizabeth Asmis, "Neoptolemus and the Classification of Poetry," *Classical Philology* 87 (1992): 206–231; James I. Porter, "Content and Form in Philodemus: The History of an Evasion," in *Philodemus and Poetry*, ed. Dirk D. Obbink (Oxford: Oxford University Press, 1995), 97–147, especially 104–105.

15. See, e.g., Bacchylides 3.98; Aara Suksi, "The Poet at Colonus: Nightingales in Sophocles," *Mnemosyne* 54 (2001): 646–658.

16. See Aristides Quintilianus, *De musica* 1.12; Cleonides, *Isagoge* 14; Bacchius 48–49; Martianus Capella 8.

17. See Kwapisz, *Greek Figure Poems*, 119.

18. Hesiod, *Theogony* 39–43, with my remarks in Sean Gurd, *Dissonance: Ancient Greek Auditory Aesthetics* (New York: Fordham University Press, 2016), 34–35.

19. See Michael Gronewald and Robert W. Daniel, "Ein neuer Sappho-Papyrus," *Zeitschrift für Papyrologie und Epigraphik* 147 (2004): 1–8; Michael Gronewald and Robert W. Daniel, "Nachtrag zum neuen Sappho-Papyrus," *Zeitschrift für Papyrologie und Epigraphik* 149 (2004): 1–4. "Simias' and Theocritus' deer are the literary offspring of Sappho's fawns," says Julián Méndez Dosuna, "The Literary Progeny of Sappho's Fawns: Simias' 'Egg' (AP 15.27.13–20) and Theocritus 30.18," *Mnemosyne* 61 (2008): 193.

20. Plato, *Republic* 399e–400a; Aristoxenus, *Elementa rhythmica* 2 passim.

21. Kwapisz, *Greek Figure Poems*, 41.

22. The Bacchius can also be interpreted as a catalectic iamb. See Paul Maas, *Greek Metre* (Oxford: Clarendon, 1962), 43.

23. Who was such a reader, and what was the result of such an analysis? A number of possibilities present themselves. It might have been a private reader, some literary friend of Simias, for example, who received this text (or a collection of them) and in the privacy of their study began to puzzle out the weird object they had been sent. The reader might have been *ananagnōstēs*, someone (usually enslaved) who was trained to read texts aloud for their owner. In these cases, the metrical analysis that the "Egg" seems to ask for would lead to a voicing, to a making-heard of the graphical signals on the papyrus. But it might also have been a listener, one who merely reclined as the reader gave voice to the text; and such a listener would have had to hear the patterns presented aurally.

24. My metrical toolbox relies on Maas, *Greek Metre*; M. L. West, *Introduction to Greek Metre* (New York: Oxford University Press, 1987); A. M. Devine and Laurence D. Stephens, *The Prosody of Greek Speech* (New York: Oxford University Press, 1994); Bruno Gentili and Liana Lomiento, *Metrics and Rhythmics: History of Poetic Forms in Ancient Greece* (Pisa: F. Serra, 2008).

25. Herodotus 1.47, 1.64, 1.174, 5.60, 5.61, 7.220, cf. 1.13.

26. See West, *Introduction to Greek Metre*, 19–20.

27. K. J. Dover, ed., *Aristophanes' Clouds* (Oxford: Clarendon, 1968), lxxx–xcviii.

28. Aristophanes, *Clouds* 636–646.

29. Diels-Kranz (D-K) 86 A2, A11.

30. D-K 68 A46.

31. D-K 44 A22.

32. Plato, *Republic* 3.400A; see Robert W. Wallace, *Reconstructing Damon: Music, Wisdom Teaching, and Politics in Perikles' Athens*, 1st ed. (Oxford: Oxford University Press, 2015), for an excellent and skeptical treatment of the sources on Damon.

33. See William Mullen, *Choreia: Pindar and Dance* (Princeton, NJ: Princeton University Press, 1982); A. P. David, *The Dance of the Muses: Choral Theory and Ancient Greek Poetics* (Oxford: Oxford University Press, 2006); James H. Collins, "Dancing the Virtues, Becoming Virtuous: Procedural Memory and Ethical Presence," *Ramus* 42 (2013): 183–206; Naomi A. Weiss, *The Music of Tragedy: Performance and Imagination in Euripidean Theater*, Joan Palevsky Imprint in Classical Literature (Oakland: University of California Press, 2018).

34. Plato, *Republic* 399ff.

35. Wallace, *Reconstructing Damon*.

36. D-K 44 B.

37. D-K 44 A22.

38. See, e.g., Plato, *Republic* 4.430.

39. *Rhetoric* 1408b.28–30.

40. *Rhetoric* 1408b.21ff.

41. *Rhetoric* 1408b.30–36. At *Poetics* 1459a.30ff, he says that the hexameter is the most static and serious, while the trimeter and trochaic are "kinetic," the first being appropriate for action and the second for dance.

42. *Poetics* 1449a.21ff.

43. *Politics* 1340a.14–1340b.7.

44. This association between the character of a meter and its typical performance genre may have an analogue in Aristoxenus's treatment of musical character. See Sean Gurd, *The Origins of Music Theory in the Age of Plato* (London: Bloomsbury, 2019), chap. 5.

45. Lionel Pearson, *Aristoxenus, Elementa rhythmica: The Fragment of Book II and the Additional Evidence for Aristoxenean Rhythmic Theory* (Oxford: Clarendon, 1990) contains the best texts, though his interpretation is unconvincing. See the important work of L. Calvié, "Le fragment rythmique du P.Oxy. 9 + 2687 attribué à Aristoxène de Tarente," *Revue de philologie, de littérature et d'histoire anciennes* 88 (2014): 7–54, and my remarks in Gurd, *Origins of Music Theory*, 128–134.

46. *Elementa rhythmica* 2.3 and passim.

47. Aristides Quintilianus, *De musica* 1.13 (31.10–13, Winnington-Ingram).

48. *Elementa Harmonica* 2.30, Pearson.

49. See *Oxyrhynchus Papyrus* 4.6.21, with "Plutarch," *De musica* 1143c (also Aristoxenian in origin).

50. *Elementa Harmonica* 2.48.15–49.1.

51. *Politics* 130a.14–1340b.19.

52. Fragment 163; Fritz Wehrli, *Die Schule des Aristoteles* (Basel: B. Schwabe, 1944).

53. Plato, *Republic* 4.424c.6.

54. *Airs Waters Places* 4.23, 24. See Frédérique Woerther, *L'éthos Aristotélicien: Genèse d'une notion rhétorique*, Textes et traditions 14 (Paris: Vrin, 2007), 74–78. On ethos in general, see also Warren D. Anderson, *Ethos and Education in Greek Music. The Evidence of Poetry and Philosophy* (Cambridge, MA: Harvard University Press, 1966).

55.  Nancy Worman, *The Cast of Character: Style in Greek Literature* (Austin: University of Texas Press, 2002).

56.  See Andrew Barker, *The Science of Harmonics in Classical Greece* (Cambridge: Cambridge University Press, 2007), 136–262.

57.  *Elementa Harmonica* 2.31.

58.  Although the iamb on its own is a "duple" foot (1:2), the iambic metron (c), as we have seen, is a "dactylic" or "unity" (1:1). The substitution of a long syllable in the place of a short one, which occurs at 7–8/4–17 and 13–14/7–14, is a problem here—it might have been corrected in performance once a reader had discerned the unusual metrical structure of the whole.

59.  Maas, *Greek Metre*, 43.

60.  On euphonism, see in particular Asmis, "Neoptolemus and Poetry"; Elizabeth Asmis, "Crates on Poetic Criticism," *Phoenix* 46 (1992): 138–169; David L. Blank, "Diogenes of Babylon and Thekritikoi in Philodemus: A Preliminary Suggestion," *Cronache ercolanesi: Bollettino del Centro internazionale per lo studio dei papiri ercolanesi* 24 (1994): 55–62; Porter, "Content and Form."

61.  See Richard Janko, ed., *Philodemus: On Poems, I*, in *Philodemus: Aesthetic Works*, vol. 1 (New York: Oxford University Press, 2000), 165–189.

62.  Janko, 67.1.

63.  Janko, 132.21.

64.  Janko, 123.

65.  Janko, 173.

66.  See Gurd, *Origins of Music Theory*, 146–153.

67.  Prier, "Who Is the Woof," 90.

68.  Devine and Stephens, *Prosody of Greek Speech*, 45.

# Bibliography

Anderson, Warren D. *Ethos and Education in Greek Music. The Evidence of Poetry and Philosophy.* Cambridge, MA: Harvard University Press, 1966.

Asmis, Elizabeth. "Crates on Poetic Criticism." *Phoenix* 46 (1992): 138–169.

———. "Neoptolemus and the Classification of Poetry." *Classical Philology* 87 (1992): 206–231.

Barker, Andrew. *The Science of Harmonics in Classical Greece.* Cambridge: Cambridge University Press, 2007.

Blank, David L. "Diogenes of Babylon and the Kritikoi in Philodemus: A Preliminary Suggestion." *Cronache ercolanesi: Bollettino del Centro internazionale per lo studio dei papiri ercolanesi* 24 (1994): 55–62.

Buffière, Félix. *Anthologie Grecque: Première partie—Anthologie Palatine. T. 12.* Paris: Les Belles Lettres, 1970.

Calvié, L. "Le fragment rythmique du P.Oxy. 9 + 2687 attribué à Aristoxène de Tarente." *Revue de philologie, de littérature et d'histoire anciennes* 88 (2014): 7–54.

Cameron, Alan. *Callimachus and His Critics.* Princeton, NJ: Princeton University Press, 1995.

Collins, James H. "Dancing the Virtues, Becoming Virtuous: Procedural Memory and Ethical Presence." *Ramus* 42 (2013): 183–206.

Consbruch, Max. *Hephaestionis Enchiridion: Bibliotheca scriptorum Graecorum et Romanorum Teubneriana.* Leipzig: Teubner, 1906.

David, A. P. *The Dance of the Muses: Choral Theory and Ancient Greek Poetics*. Oxford: Oxford University Press, 2006.

Devine, A. M., and Laurence D. Stephens. *The Prosody of Greek Speech*. New York: Oxford University Press, 1994.

Dosuna, Julián Méndez. "The Literary Progeny of Sappho's Fawns: Simias' 'Egg' (AP 15.27.13–20) and Theocritus 30.18." *Mnemosyne* 61 (2008): 192–206.

Dover, K. J., ed. *Aristophanes' Clouds*. Oxford: Clarendon, 1968.

Fraenkel, Hermann. *De Simia Rhodio*. Göttingen: Officina Academica Dieterichiana, 1915.

Gentili, Bruno, and Liana Lomiento. *Metrics and Rhythmics: History of Poetic Forms in Ancient Greece*. Pisa: F. Serra, 2008.

Gronewald, Michael, and Robert W. Daniel. "Nachtrag zum neuen Sappho-Papyrus." *Zeitschrift für Papyrologie und Epigraphik* 149 (2004): 1–4.

———. "Ein neuer Sappho-Papyrus." *Zeitschrift für Papyrologie und Epigraphik* 147 (2004): 1–8.

Guichard, Romero. "Simias' Pattern Poems: The Margins of the Canon." In *Beyond the Canon*, edited by M. Annette Harder, Remco F. Regtuit, and Gerrigje Catharina Wakker, 83–103. Leuven: Peeters, 2006.

Gurd, Sean. *Dissonance: Ancient Greek Auditory Aesthetics*. New York: Fordham University Press, 2016.

———. *The Origins of Music Theory in the Age of Plato*. London: Bloomsbury, 2019.

Janko, Richard, ed. *Philodemus: On Poems, I*. In *Philodemus: Aesthetic Works*, vol. 1. New York: Oxford University Press, 2000.

Kwapisz, Jan. *The Greek Figure Poems*. Vol. 19 of *Hellenistica Groningana*. Leuven: Peeters, 2013.

Legrand, P. *Bucoliques Grecs*. Paris: Société d'édition "Les Belles lettres," 1925.

Maas, Paul. *Greek Metre*. Oxford: Clarendon, 1962.

Mangoni, Cecilia. *Philodemus: Il quinto libro della poetica (PHerc. 1425 e 1538)—La Scuola di Epicuro*. Vol. 14. Naples: Bibliopolis, 1993.

Mullen, William. *Choreia: Pindar and Dance*. Princeton, NJ: Princeton University Press, 1982.

Pearson, Lionel. *Aristoxenus, Elementa rhythmica: The Fragment of Book II and the Additional Evidence for Aristoxenean Rhythmic Theory*. Oxford: Clarendon, 1990.

Pfeiffer, Rudolf. *History of Classical Scholarship: From the Beginnings to the End of the Hellenistic Age*. Oxford: Clarendon, 1968.

Porter, James I. "Content and Form in Philodemus: The History of an Evasion." In *Philodemus and Poetry*, edited by Dirk D. Obbink, 97–147. Oxford: Oxford University Press, 1995.

Prier, Raymond A. "And Who Is the Woof? Response, Ecphrasis and the 'Egg' of Simmias." *Quaderni Urbinati di Cultura Classica* 46, no. 1 (1994): 79–92.

Saumaise, Claude de. *Duarum inscriptionum veterum Herodis Attici Rhetoris et Regillae coniugis honori positarum explicatio: Eiusdem Ad Dosiadae Aras, Simmiae Rhodii Ouum, Alas, Securim Theocriti fistulam notae*. Hieronymum Drouart, 1619.

Strodel, Silvia. *Zur Überlieferung und zum Verständnis der hellenistischen Technopaignien.Studien zur klassischen Philologie, 0172–1798*. Vol. 132. New York: Peter Lang, 2002.

Suksi, Aara. "The Poet at Colonus: Nightingales in Sophocles." *Mnemosyne* 54 (2001): 646–658.

Wallace, Robert W. *Reconstructing Damon: Music, Wisdom Teaching, and Politics in Perikles'
Athens.* 1st ed. Oxford: Oxford University Press, 2015.
Wehrli, Fritz. *Die Schule des Aristoteles.* Basel: B. Schwabe, 1944.
Weiss, Naomi A. *The Music of Tragedy: Performance and Imagination in Euripidean Theater.*
Joan Palevsky Imprint in Classical Literature. Oakland: University of California Press,
2018.
West, M. L. *Introduction to Greek Metre.* New York: Oxford University Press, 1987.
Woerther, Frédérique. *L'éthos Aristotélicien: Genèse d'une notion rhétorique.* Textes et
traditions 14. Paris: Vrin, 2007.
Worman, Nancy. *The Cast of Character: Style in Greek Literature.* Austin: University of Texas
Press, 2002.

SEAN ALEXANDER GURD is Professor of Classics at the University of Texas
at Austin. He is author of *Iphigenias at Aulis: Textual Multiplicity, Radical
Philology, Work in Progress: Literary Revision as Social Performance in Ancient
Rome, Dissonance: Auditory Aesthetics in Ancient Greece,* and *The Origins of
Music Theory in the Age of Plato.*

# PART II
# SOUND EDUCATION

# 6

## LIKE THOSE WHO ARE UNTESTED

### *Heraclitus's Logos as Tuning Instrument for* Psuche

Jessica Elbert Decker, California State University, San Marcos

Although this *logos* is forever (*aiei*) human beings are forever uncomprehending (*axunetoi*), both before hearing it and once they have heard. Although all things come to pass in accordance with this *logos*, human beings are like those without experience (*apeiroi*) when they try such words and works as I set forth distinguishing each according to (its) nature (*kata phusin*) and telling how it is. But other human beings are oblivious of what they do awake just as what they do asleep escapes them.

—Heraclitus, D-K 1

THIS ANALYSIS AIMS TO EXPLORE THE PUZZLES ABOUT hearing the logos that are raised in D-K 1's introduction to Heraclitus's teaching and to emphasize the manner in which Heraclitus's logos (the arrangement of words that make up the fragments) is not a static teaching or doctrine; instead, the fragments are an instrument for active engagement with the student. In D-K 1, Heraclitus calls uncomprehending human beings *apeiron*, without experience, or untested, despite the ever presence of logos. Using the imagery and language that Heraclitus offers in his fragments, particularly the language and themes constellated by the puzzle of "hearing the *logos*" presented in D-K 1, this analysis demonstrates that Heraclitus's logos can be understood as a tuning instrument for *psuche*—a means of "testing" that crucially involves hearing—and that this experience, the process of engaging with the fragments, is the true content of his teaching and leads to self-knowledge.

In Heraclitus's programmatic first fragment, he introduces his teaching by diagnosing a specific problem: the human failure to understand the logos "both before hearing it and once they have heard." [1] In this first line of D-K 1, Heraclitus has already raised a host of ambiguities and philosophical puzzles; for this analysis, I focus on three of these puzzles. First and perhaps most pressing, what does Heraclitus mean by *logos*? He seems to be referring to his own words, his account, while at the same time suggesting something more by calling logos eternal (*aiei*) and saying that everything happens in accordance with it. The next puzzle that arises in the first line of D-K 1 is Heraclitus's strange insistence that human beings fail to grasp logos "both *before* hearing it and once they have heard." If Heraclitus simply means his own account, then it would seem somewhat unfair to fault human beings for failing to understand before they had heard; however, if Heraclitus means both his own logos (the fragments) and some other, more mysterious logos that is at once eternal and ubiquitous, then his strange statement implies that his logos (his account) is somehow the same as this other, eternal logos. [2]

The final puzzle I consider in this densely packed and challenging first line of D-K 1 is Heraclitus's use of the model of hearing, which is consistent throughout the fragments as the primary means of human access to logos. [3] Since the logos is something that can be heard (and I explore the nuances of this), Heraclitus suggests in his use of the term *logos* that he does mean to refer to language and speech—although there is something more at work here. If *logos* refers only to his words and account, then hearing the logos is unproblematic, but if *logos* refers to his words and some eternal (*aiei*) thing through which everything happens, then what does it mean to hear logos?

This analysis proceeds by first examining D-K 1 as a programmatic introduction to Heraclitus's teaching and method and emphasizing the priority of hearing as a model for access to logos through reading other fragments that contain musical or sonic language alongside D-K 1's methodological outline. This model of hearing orients my exploration of logos and its relation to speech, addressing the question, How does listening to the logos allow one to be wise and "speak in agreement" (*homologein*) with logos, as D-K 50 instructs? [4] After all these wheels have been set in motion, attention is paid to Heraclitus's innovative use of the term *psuche*. In Homer, this word seemed to refer simply to breath or to the shades of the dead in the underworld; Heraclitus imbues this term with more nuanced meanings. [5] *Psuche*, for Heraclitus, is a process more than it is a noun or object; we might be tempted to say that *psuche*, for Heraclitus, is the thinking and perceiving subject, but that can be said only with the caveat that it is a moving subject, the subject as a continuous process of change and growth. In the only two fragments dealing explicitly with the activity of *psuche*, Heraclitus tells us two crucial things: *psuche* has a logos that is so deep as to be limitless (D-K 45), and *psuche* has a logos that is self-increasing (D-K 115).[6] It is especially significant that both of these fragments that explicitly name *psuche* also name the logos that belongs to *psuche*, making these concepts deeply coindicated in Heraclitus's teaching. These descriptions of the activity of *psuche* are instrumental in demonstrating the manner in which Heraclitus's logos is designed as a means of tuning *psuche*.

## 1. The Challenge: Testing and Tuning in D-K 1

In D-K 1, Heraclitus offers a dense and challenging introduction to his teaching. The first line of D-K 1 says, "Although this *logos* is forever human beings are forever uncomprehending both before hearing it and once they have heard." As Charles Kahn has pointed out, Heraclitus is adopting the traditional preamble of prose authors of his time in identifying his logos, which we expect to be his teaching, and then subverting any direct or clear understanding of it.[7] What we expect to hear is a scientific account, in the tradition of his contemporaries, but what we get instead is a densely obscure and paradoxical text. As Kahn explains, "Whereas the general tendency of Ionian prose is towards directness and clarity of expression, the distinctive trait of Heraclitus' own style is more than Delphic delight in paradox, enigma, and equivocation."[8] By adopting the traditional form of a programmatic introduction to his teaching, Heraclitus creates the expectation that the logos he mentions is his teaching, but he frustrates that expectation by simultaneously telling us that this logos is eternal and everything happens in accordance with it. Instead of offering a clear account of his scientific findings, as many Milesian thinkers evidently did, Heraclitus instead suggests that we will not understand his teaching even after hearing it. In other words, the introduction to his teaching is not a clear doorway into his philosophical ideas but instead a challenging obstacle with no apparent way past it. The problem is not simple incomprehension, which could presumably be rectified by learning some account; Heraclitus suggests that what human beings fail to hear is not merely his own words but this other, eternal logos that his words somehow embody or perform.[9]

Further clues to these puzzles abound in Heraclitus's precise use of language in this first fragment; he uses the word *axunetoi*, translated as "uncomprehending," and says that human beings are *apeiroi*, or "without experience." These two alpha-privative words suggest their opposites, in traditional Heraclitean style, as any term in a pair of opposites is haunted by its complement in Heraclitus's text. The term *axunetoi* is far more precise than its English translation "uncomprehending"; it literally says something closer to "not together with" (*a-syn*) or, to use some sonic and musical language, "out of sync." So Heraclitus does not merely say that human beings fail to understand; he identifies the precise manner in which they do not comprehend—they are out of sync with logos, somehow "not together with" logos; they are alienated or disassociated from logos despite its eternal character and ubiquity.

Throughout the fragments, Heraclitus consistently uses the term *xunon* to suggest unity, and D-K 34 repeats the term *axunetoi* in the same context as D-K 1, saying, "*Axunetoi* they hear like the deaf. The saying is their witness: absent while present."[10] This *axunetoi* state of human beings is twofold in the manner suggested by D-K 1 and D-K 34: human beings cannot hear the logos, but this inability also means that they are unable to properly speak. D-K 19 says this plainly: "Not knowing how to listen, neither can they speak." If human beings are to learn to speak properly, their failure to hear the logos (which is a direct result of their *axunetoi* state) must be remedied. D-K 50 offers a model of this antidote: "Listening not to me but to *logos* it is wise to speak in agreement [*homologein*] that all things are one." To approach this remedy, however, the problem raised by Heraclitus's dubbing of human beings as *apeiroi*, or lacking experience, must be further explored.

These two negated terms, *axunetoi* and *apeiroi*, signal that the better state for human beings would be their opposites: humans who are "in sync" with logos could possess the requisite experience. The lack of experience suggested by *apeiroi* is complex, however, since Heraclitus has described logos as both eternal and ubiquitous. How can human beings remain *apeiroi* despite this pervasive and ever-present logos? D-K 17 addresses this problem of inexperience: "Most human beings do not think things in the way they encounter them nor do they recognize their own experience, but imagine for themselves." Though the logos is ever present, the problem with human perception is one of recognition—a theme repeated throughout Heraclitus's fragments.[11] The sound and hearing metaphors that occur throughout Heraclitus's fragments offer some insight into this problem, if we consider the out-of-sync state of human beings without experience: they cannot hear logos because they are not properly attuned to it. Heraclitus offers an example of this need for proper attunement in D-K 107 when he says, "Eyes and ears are poor witnesses for human beings if they have barbarian souls." The implication is that people who do not speak the language hear only sounds and not words or meaning; non-Greek foreigners are barbarians because they speak only "bar bar bar"—to the untrained ear, they speak nonsense. However, once the language is learned, what is heard takes on a different character; it takes on meaning and nuance, and patterns emerge.

The human beings with "barbarian souls" lack experience of the language, so they are incapable of recognizing the patterns of words and syntax. Learning Heraclitus's logos is like learning a language, as the student becomes more familiar with the tendencies of the sounds and words throughout the fragments, especially in their resonance with one another. Following the metaphors of sound and hearing raised by Heraclitus, this process of learning can be understood as akin to tuning an instrument so that the student can, through practice and repetition, learn to hear and speak attuned to logos, with new resonances always increasing the symphony as the logos that belongs to *psuche* increases (as D-K 115 suggests) through the experience of change and difference. Experience is the vehicle for this increase and the necessary condition for any understanding.

Heraclitus's intricately crafted logos offers the student a means of engaging in the continuous process of self-testing, a way of tuning *psuche* and gaining experience, especially self-knowledge. The word Heraclitus uses to name human beings as without experience, *apeiroi*, also has other dimensions of meaning; it means "untested" or "untried," as D-K 1 picks up by saying that human beings seem *apeiroi* "when they *try* such words and works as I set forth." In Homer's *Odyssey*, when the hero, Odysseus, returns to his home in disguise, he tests or "makes trial" of Eumaeus with his speech to see where the swineherd's heart and loyalties truly lie.[12] This trial or testing of the swineherd is emblematic of the kind of testing that Heraclitus's teaching offers; it is a means of seeing into one's own patterns of thinking and perceiving, of testing one's self. This aspect of Heraclitus's method is remarkably similar to Socrates's practice of elenchus, both as a means of testing the student and as a path to self-knowledge. The emphasis on self-knowledge is essential to Heraclitus's conception of wisdom; as D-K 101 says, "I went in search of myself," or D-K 112, "It belongs to all human beings to know themselves and think soundly."

Heraclitus's fragments do not only address individual experience, such as the activity of *psuche*; they seem to be suggesting an order to the *kosmos* itself. D-K 1 says that everything happens in accordance with logos, and in more blatantly cosmic fragments such as D-K 30, *kosmos* is named as "everliving fire kindled in measures and in measures extinguished." So how does this self-experience and, hopefully, the self-knowledge gained from this experience allow for the possibility of understanding the *kosmos*? This is where Heraclitus's strange use of logos registers in its other form, not merely the account or Heraclitus's words but something through which all things happen, something that is eternal (*aiei*). If everything happens in accordance with logos, then our perception and thinking are not excluded from this principle; in fact, even the human incomprehension must happen in accordance with logos. Before the student can tune her psyche to the eternal logos, it must first be tuned to itself, just as a lyre player sounds the strings against one another to hear their resonance. Only then, when the instrument (psyche) is tuned to itself, can it be tuned to something outside, such as logos or other players of the lyre. This metaphor of psyche "tuning to itself" describes the process of self-understanding that Heraclitus's teaching offers.

Understanding logos in this structuring sense, Heraclitus's method of emphasizing self-knowledge as a necessary condition for any knowledge of the world may be akin to Plato's method in *Republic*, in which we must understand justice in the soul to be analogous to justice in the city.[13] In both of these models, Heraclitus and Plato seem to suggest symmetry between microcosm and macrocosm; as Heraclitus says in D-K 124, "*Kosmos* is a heap of random sweepings." It doesn't matter which bits are taken at random; if logos is ubiquitous and eternal, then even the random sweepings will faithfully attest to this order.[14] Gaining self-knowledge, then, is not merely knowledge of the self but is a path toward understanding the patternings of *kosmos*, since *psuche* and *kosmos* are both patterned by logos.

In this way, Heraclitus is exploiting the ambiguity of logos to refer to language and speech in their broadest form, as a thing that grows and changes (just as languages and all other living things do), and it does so according to regular patterns that can be discerned with practice and attention. But to say that logos simply means language is not quite right, because that would exclude our visual perceptions and other senses, which are essential to our experience. Heraclitus holds direct experience in the highest regard; as D-K 55 says, "Whatever comes from sight, hearing, learning from experience: this I prefer." In contrast, Heraclitus's D-K 40 accuses Hesiod, Pythagoras, Xenophanes, and Hecataeus of *polymathie*, claiming that it "does not teach understanding."[15] If direct experience is Heraclitus's way, then this allows him to claim that his words and works will be capable of "distinguish[ing] each according to (its) nature and telling how it is," the description of his method offered in D-K 1.[16] The wisdom Heraclitus offers is not doctrine or *polymathie* but a way of understanding through direct experience that we might now refer to as "subjectivity."[17] The ability to hear logos, when human beings are "in sync" with it, allows for direct experience that can in turn offer wisdom where *polymathie* fails to bear fruit. Furthermore, if logos can be said to describe patternings (keeping this description broad enough to allow for multiple registers of meaning), then the ability to speak *kata phusin*, or according to nature, depends on this direct experience of hearing logos.

## 2. Sonic Language: The Key Device of Resonance in Heraclitus

What precisely is meant by "hearing *logos*" remains somewhat mysterious, however, and is explored through an analysis of Heraclitus's consistent use of musical and sonic language throughout the fragments. In the ancient Greek world, especially in the oral culture that preceded Heraclitus, poetry and music were inextricable from one another. This fact is easy to overlook, when our contemporary culture tends to see these as separate aesthetic genres, though they certainly overlap in content and method. Heraclitus does not write in traditional poetic form, but he does not write in traditional prose either; his text is deeply poetic in its use of devices such as repetition, plays on words, rhymes, assonance, consonance, homonyms, and resonance between fragments. In discussing the medium of Heraclitus's text, Kevin Robb has insightfully described it as "a special form of poeticized speech which has been rhythmed in ways which will be seductive to the ear and to the memory."[18]

Mnemonic devices such as rhyme and cadence work, like music, as aids to the memory, and the final line of Heraclitus's D-K 1 makes it very clear that memory is key to his teaching. After telling us that human beings remain uncomprehending even after hearing the (eternal) logos, and without experience when they try to understand his logos, Heraclitus concludes his programmatic first fragment with "But other human beings are oblivious (*lanthanoi*) of what they do awake just as what they do asleep escapes (*epilanthanantoi*) them." This last line of D-K 1 is the hidden way into Heraclitus's teaching; what human beings lack is memory—they are so utterly lost in forgetting that waking and sleeping are indistinguishable.[19] Heraclitus's logos, in this way, is the precise opposite of a lullaby, a kind of symphony that slowly grows until it is loud enough to awaken the sleeper.

While logos is never represented explicitly as music in Heraclitus, there are numerous instances of musical or sonic language. The most obvious cases are the lyre of D-K 51 and the *harmonie* of D-K 54 and D-K 51.[20] Heraclitus's use of the term *harmonie* has multiple resonances: *harmonie* means joining or fastening together, such as the caulking together of the planks of a ship.[21] Whether making music or ships, *harmonie* requires that there be at least two things to be joined, voices or planks. In this way, *harmonie* is an image of multiplicity that joins together into unity. Heraclitus's fragments perform this *harmonie*, or fastening together, through a device that Kahn has named *resonance*.[22] Resonance, as Kahn points out, manifests in many different ways throughout the fragments. The repetition of a single word is the most obvious case, but cognate words, repetition of themes and images, and closely connected terms (such as *conflict* and *strife*) recur throughout Heraclitus's text. The effect of this resonance is to "link together *all* the major themes of Heraclitus' discourse into a single network of connected thoughts, thus articulating his general claim that 'all things are one.'"[23] Resonance, like a fluid glue, is the *harmonie* or fastening together of all the fragments into one teaching, and the activity of fastening together requires both hearing and memory. The student learns to hear this "invisible harmony" that is "better than the visible one" (D-K 54) through her own experience of working through the fragments.

In explaining all the nuances of meaning in the ancient Greek word *harmonie*, Kahn remarks that "another figurative use is for the tuning of a musical instrument, the 'fitting together' of different strings to produce the desired scale or key."[24] *Harmonie* as tuning is very significant because it is a kind of testing: the strings are tested against or alongside one another. Heraclitus's fragsments do precisely this: when the student learns to sound each fragment, she begins to hear resonances with all the other fragments and recognize the manner in which they speak the same. The goal is expressed in D-K 50: "Listening not to me but to *logos* it is wise to speak in agreement (*homologein*) that all things are one." Heraclitus offers a model of this "speaking same" in his many and diverse fragments, as they all resonate with one another to create one sound.

However, the paradox of this arrangement must not be forgotten, as the fragments speak the same while simultaneously speaking difference—they are not identical but diverse and differing, which makes their *harmonie* all the more astonishing. In D-K 1, Heraclitus hints at this crucial point by saying that his method is "to distinguish (*diaireon*) each according to (its) nature (*kata phusin*)." Heraclitus does not begin with unity; he begins with the careful division, as words cognate with *diaireon* imply (particularly in Plato's method), of each thing *kata phusin*, according to (its) nature.[25] Each thing must be separated out from all other things to distinguish it, but knowing the part is not knowing the whole. This may sound contrary, as I argued earlier that each part in fact expresses the whole through resonance, and random sweepings would point to the entire cosmic scheme, but this is precisely the kind of reversal (like the *tropai* of D-K 31a) that Heraclitus sets up. Like an Escher drawing, it keeps turning backward on itself (*palintropos*, as in D-K 51's bow and lyre), leaving no ground for the laying down of doctrines, but in motion like the famed river. There is fitting together, *harmonie*, but there is no *harmonie* without conflict and strife, which is a major theme in Heraclitus's frequent use of opposing pairs. Musically, a harmony is only such through its movement and divergence from the melody.

With these musical devices in mind, examination of Heraclitus's use of the term *harmonie* can begin, hearing D-K 54 and D-K 51 sing together in resonance:

D-K 54: The unapparent (*aphanes*) *harmonie* is better than the apparent (*phaneres*) one.

D-K 51: They do not comprehend how a thing agrees (*homologeei*) at variance (*diapheromenon*) with itself; it is a backwards-stretched (*palintropos*) *harmonie* like that of the bow or the lyre.

D-K 54 implies that whatever *harmonie* means, it is happening in a double manner—in a visible, apparent, or obvious (*phaneres*) way and also in a subtler, invisible, unapparent, or hidden way (*aphanes*).[26] Heraclitus uses language to demonstrate this double *harmonie*, this backward-stretched nature; his method is to perform these movements within the fragments in a way that can be heard. Many of his fragments contain complementary and/or oppositional pairs, such as "unapparent" and "apparent" in D-K 54, but D-K 51 makes it clear that he does not mean only that things differ from one another; he is making a much more radical claim: each thing differs from itself.

If we distinguish something from other things (for example, by giving it a name), we imbue that thing with identity, which is a kind of unity—a thing is itself and no other thing; it is identical only with itself. But to imbue the thing with this identity and unity, we distinguish it from all the other things—and this is an act of our thinking and language, a conception that is not necessarily true of the world itself. For example, we name the thing "bow," but the thing remains self-differing, and the name does not entirely capture the thing; a tension remains because things are constantly in motion. The bow and the lyre invoke an image of tension, as the backward-stretching tension of the string(s) is what makes the instrument work; a lyre without tension will not play, just as a bowstring without tension cannot shoot an arrow. The apparent harmony may be understood as the identity we ascribe to an object, like the bow, in giving it a name and recognizing it as a distinct thing. The unapparent harmony is recognizing that it fails to remain still and contained by its name or our conception of it, recognizing that it is continually undergoing a process of change and self-differing; in fact, this process of self-differing (what we usually think of as growth, when we describe living things) *is* the identity.[27]

There are several fragments that address this problem of naming in Heraclitus, too many to recount in detail here, but D-K 48 is particularly relevant to this analysis: "The name of the bow (*bios*) is life, its work is death."[28] The word *bios* was written without the accent in Heraclitus's time, so the name of the bow is a pure homonym with *bios* as life. Heraclitus exploits the manner in which a homonym can "speak the same" (*homologein*) while revealing the unapparent harmony—the difference that persists within the unity of the thing. It is also significant to note that the name of the bow is here the apparent *harmonie*, while the work of the bow requires experience to understand—this is the unapparent *harmonie*. In D-K 1, Heraclitus foreshadows these two registers by referring to his "words and *works*" instead of simply indicating his words. In hearing the name *bow*, we are acquainted only with the apparent *harmonie*, the word for the bow. In learning to hear the manner in which the name signals this self-differing, the student is gaining experience ("hearing the *logos*") in that she is recognizing the paradoxical, backward-stretched nature that Heraclitus continually emphasizes. The "barbarian souls" of D-K 107 may hear the name—in other words, they can hear the sound of the word *bios*—but they do not grasp its meaning in a deeper sense. Their hearing is empty; they "hear like the deaf, absent while present," as D-K 34 suggests.

In the extant fragments, D-K 10 is perhaps one of the clearest structural models of Heraclitus's paradoxical unity-in-multiplicity theme. It reminds the student of the backward-stretched image of the bow and the lyre by repeating *diapheromenon* (as in D-K 51), and it subtly invokes hearing and harmony with the pair *synaidon/diaidon*. All these voices singing together while simultaneously singing apart produce a symphony, which is the true nature of Heraclitus's composition:

> D-K 10: *Syllapsies*: whole and not wholes drawn together (*sympheromenon*) drawn apart (*diapheromenon*) singing together (*synaidon*) singing apart (*diaidon*) from all things one and from one thing all.

The most perplexing element of D-K 10 is the opening sound: *syllapsies*. *Syllapsies* means taking together and conjunction, and its usage is often related to sounds, such as in the word *syllable*; but it also means grasping, seizing, or apprehending.[29] Kahn translates it as "graspings," though it is ambiguous as to who or what is grasping and what they might be grasping. As Philip Wheelwright has pointed out, the distinction between subject and object is not always clear in ancient Greek grammar, and Heraclitus exploits this ambiguity frequently. The structure of the fragment is a common one in Heraclitus: a term is presented as an implied unity and then followed by oppositional or complementary pairs; this happens explicitly in D-K 67 (*Theos*) and in similar form in D-K 30 (*kosmos*) and D-K 31a (*tropai* of fire). Kahn's discussion of *syllapsies* suggests a robust meaning that hearkens to the ambiguity and abstraction presented in this word; the oppositional or complementary words that follow are not concrete, like day and night, but conceptions, pointing to our process of thinking and perceiving (*phronesis*).[30] Thus, the agency involved in these "graspings" is likely to be the processes of *phronesis* in human beings.

*Syllapsies* is cognate with *katalepsetai*, which means "to seize or apprehend"; this word appears in both D-K 28 and D-K 66. Applying the device of resonance, these other two cases of *katalepsetai* may help illuminate Heraclitus's use of *syllapsies* in D-K 10:

D-K 28b: Justice will *katalepsetai* those who invent lies and those who swear to them.

D-K 66: Fire coming on will judge (*krinei*) and *katalepsetai* all things.

In D-K 28b, the agent is Justice, and the object of seizure is inventors and swearers of lies—this is significant because it explicitly invokes speech. D-K 66 is similar because the agent, here named as fire, will not only seize or apprehend all things but will judge them (*krinei*). Justice in D-K 28b and fire in D-K 66 are both cast as cosmic forces, and their agency seems to be law: just as all things happen in accordance with logos, for example, "all things" will be judged and seized by fire. These formulations imply necessity, and their inevitability can be compared to that of physical patterns, such as the *tropai* of fire in D-K 31a or the kindling/extinguishing of *kosmos* as ever-living fire in D-K 30. This reading is supported by D-K 94, which once again names Justice as keeper of physical laws and measures (*metra*): "The sun will not transgress his measures. If he does, the Furies, ministers of Justice, will find him out." Reading this constellation of fragments together, we can conclude that *katalepsetai* is associated with justice and with cosmic (or natural, in the sense of *kata phusin*) law.

Returning to the *syllapsies* of D-K 10, its importance as cognate of *katalepsetai* begins to reveal itself: these "graspings," which are associated with the processes of *phronesis*, happen in accordance with justice, or cosmic/natural law. Just as the incomprehension (*axunetoi*) of human beings in D-K 1 must happen in accordance with logos, since Heraclitus is very clear that everything happens in accordance with logos, these graspings must also happen according to law. D-K 10 suggests that though these graspings seem to fail at capturing the whole truth, they nevertheless are part of a larger process of learning to comprehend or learning to hear logos.

This conclusion is supported by D-K 67, which has the same structure as D-K 10, beginning with an implied unity (*theos*) and then listing opposition pairs—but D-K 67 offers a different clue to understanding these similarly structured fragments:

D-K 67: *Theos*: day and night winter and summer war and peace satiety and hunger. It alters, as when mingled with perfumes, it gets named according to the pleasure of each one.

*Theos* names divinity, but not any god or goddess in particular; it is a general or abstract name for divinity. The list of opposing pairs that follows could be understood as the "many" that comprises the unity *theos*, just as the list of opposing pairs in D-K 10 refers to the "graspings." In D-K 67, however, Heraclitus gives us another clue as to the relationship between the first term named and the list of paired terms that follows: he says "it alters" (presumably referring to *theos*, but the "it" is left ambiguous) and "gets named according to the pleasure (*hedone*) of each one." *Theos* does not remain the same; it continually alters or changes, and yet, despite this constant change, the names that human beings use to identify *theos* break the unity down into opposing conceptual pairs. As in D-K 48's bow, whose name is life and work is death, the name fails to capture the thing named. D-K 32 is emblematic of this philosophical claim: "The wise is one alone unwilling and willing to be called by the name *Zēnos*." The god named in D-K 32 is Zeus, but Heraclitus strategically uses the archaic form *Zēnos* to play on the word for life (*zēn*) and indicate motion.[31] The name is appropriate (hence "willing"), but the name fails to capture the multiplicity and motion of what it names (hence "unwilling").

The *syllapsies* of D-K 10, if we follow the logic of its twin in structure (D-K 67), implies that these graspings, like the ineffective names of D-K 67, fail to capture the things named. The manner in which these graspings fail is further illuminated: the processes of *phronesis*, particularly in the use of language and naming, seize or arrest (*katalepsetai*) things in motion, essentially freezing them and attempting to make them stay in place. As Kahn points out, before Aristotle, "the only sense attested for *syllepsis* is the bodily notion of 'seizing, laying hold of, arresting, apprehending.'"[32] Human beings have no choice but to use language, but the manner in which we understand our experience through language can result in this arbitrary "freezing" of a moving world into static concepts and things. "It alters," but our concepts, names, and categories reflect a completely different model of the world; we imagine a world that stays still, a world in which we can make statements that are clearly either true or false. Heraclitus's insistence on the intractable paradox of the world radically challenges this paradigm. The model of music underscored in this reading emphasizes the movement of Heraclitus's teaching and the manner in which language can be in motion, as in a sung *harmonie* or the consonant and dissonant notes of the lyre.

The processes of our *phronesis*, as they arrest or seize moving things in order to conceptualize them, are responsible for the *axunetoi* state of human beings. *Anthropoi* are cut off or alienated from logos not through some malicious power but because of the habitual processes of human thinking and perception, especially our inability to see the unity in what we perceive as opposite. To hear logos and experience a *xunon* (shared) state rather than an *axunetoi* (uncomprehending) one, Heraclitus offers us his logos—the fragments—as a means of first recognizing our out-of-sync state and then of remedying it through a continuous process of "testing." This testing results in the experience necessary to hear the logos, rather than remaining "barbarian souls" who do not understand the language. To understand this process of testing as self-knowledge, some attention must be paid to Heraclitus's innovative use of the term *psuche* in the fragments. As we shall see, the model of music and the metaphor of "tuning *psuche*" are appropriate because music is a perfect model of movement and measure— just as the *kosmos* is continually in motion, never pure flux because of its measure (as in D-K 30's everliving fire), *psuche* and its processes of *phronesis* must adapt to this motion.

## 3. Heraclitus's Logos as a Tuning Instrument for *Psuche*

The state of human beings described in D-K 1 presents, in nuclear form, the primary problem that Heraclitus designs his teaching to remedy: *anthropoi* are fundamentally forgetful, incapable of hearing logos (even after they have heard), incapable of comprehension (*axunetoi*) of logos, and lacking experience *(apieron)* despite the ever presence of logos. This *axunetoi* state is described throughout the fragments, particularly in Heraclitus's claim that most human beings live in a "private world" despite the shared or *xunon* logos. This private world is like an echo chamber where the subject can hear only herself, disassociated from the shared and eternal logos. D-K 2 states this most directly, though the theme recurs in diverse forms throughout the fragments: "Although this *logos* is shared (*xunos*) most human beings live as though their thinking (*phronēsin*) were a private (*idion*) possession." In this final section, I explore how Heraclitus's logos can be understood as a tuning instrument for *psuche*. D-K 2 sets up the problem that *psuche* faces in the private world, unable to hear the eternal logos, and specifies that the problem lies in our *phronēsis*, our thinking and perception. As we have seen, *logos* means "language and speech" (though Heraclitus expands the meaning of *logos* in challenging ways), so our thinking and our use of language are deeply implicated in this problem of the private world. D-K 89 repeats this theme: "The world of the waking is one and shared (*koinos*) but the sleeping turn aside each to his own private world (*idion kosmos*)." This fragment is likely to be a paraphrase, because Plutarch uses *koinos* for Heraclitus's consistent *xunos*, but the themes of waking/sleeping and the disassociated *idion* world of human beings are certainly genuine Heraclitean claims. Reading D-K 2 and D-K 89 in resonance with D-K 1, we can conclude that the disassociated or out-of-sync (*axunetoi*) state of human beings is synonymous with the private order or *idion kosmos* described here.

The challenge of D-K 1 sets up a seemingly impossible obstacle in saying that human beings remain uncomprehending even after they have heard and are incapable of "trying" or testing such words and works as Heraclitus sets forth. To hear logos and all its resonances, human beings need to find a way of becoming aware of this *idion kosmos*, of changing the out-of-sync (*axunetoi*) state into a shared (*xynos*) one. As we learned in exploring the last line of D-K 1, memory is key to this process since human beings are so deeply permeated by forgetting as to be incapable of distinguishing waking from sleeping. Heraclitus's fragments provide a means of learning how to see the patterns that our thinking follows (our "private order") so that we might gain self-understanding through awareness of these habits and patterns of thinking.

Heraclitus describes the process of becoming aware of the *idion kosmos* in the language of *psuche*; in our contemporary terms, we could say that this is a psychological process. The images of waking and sleeping, introduced in D-K 1 and echoed throughout the fragments, offer a model of what his teaching is designed to do: essentially, it is a way of waking up a sleeper. This model is expressed most directly (though perhaps also most enigmatically) in D-K 26: "A man kindles (*haptetai*) his own light in the night when his sight is extinguished. Living he touches (*haptetai*) the dead in his sleep; having awakened, he sets fire to (*haptetai*) the sleeper." Heraclitus's repetition of the term *haptetai* in this fragment is significant for two reasons: first, the sustained and dense repetition can be read as emphasis, and second, the repetition plays on the multiplicity of meaning conjured by the term *haptetai*. The primary meaning of the term, used in this way in the fragment, is to "kindle" or "set fire to" something. This reading makes sense because of Heraclitus's obvious emphasis on fire as an emblematic symbol of both Justice (reading D-K 28b and D-K 66 in resonance) and the order and patterns of logos, as the *kosmos* is described as everliving fire kindled and extinguished in measure (D-K 30). But there are multiple resonances of meaning happening in this repetition: cognate with *haptetai* are a whole string of verb forms of the *hap-* variety that, in Homer, mean "to fasten" or "bind to."[33] Other forms and usages listed in the lexicon include "to join," "to grasp," "to fasten upon or attack," "to lay hands on," "to touch," "to grasp with the senses," and "to perceive."[34] Heraclitus's use of *haptetai* invokes (at least) two key themes in his teaching that I have been exploring: "fastening" or "binding to" hearkens back to the *harmonie* of D-K 51 and D-K 54, and "grasping" or "laying hands on" recalls the *syllapsies* of D-K 10 and its cognate *katalepsetai* in D-K 28b and D-K 66.

D-K 26 places *haptetai* between several pairs of opposites—day/night, light/dark, life/death, and waking/sleeping—supporting the reading of the term as not only "kindling" but also fastening or binding, joining the opposites together. The obvious meaning of "kindles his own light" is the lighting of lamps when darkness falls, but it also refers to the dream state where the sleeper is disassociated from the world but still has a kind of private experience. The regularity of these processes is stressed by the repetition of *haptetai*—Heraclitus suggests a symmetry of measure between these processes of day/night, waking/sleeping, and life/death. The larger processes of the *kosmos* (day/night) are reflected in the processes of individual living things (waking/sleeping and life/death). Kahn points out that Heraclitus's syntax in the first line is puzzling because it is not the man's eyes that are extinguished but the man himself (*aposbestheis opseis*). This indicates that Heraclitus is not only describing human sight in D-K 26; he means all the human processes of thinking and perception (*phronesis*) as well as the final extinguishing of death, and these processes belong to *psuche*.[35] As Kahn says, reading D-K 26, "The description of our psychic experience in terms of quenching and kindling suggests that the soul must have its own mode of exemplifying the cycle of everliving fire, its own mode of survival and revival where life and death will somehow alternate like sleeping and waking."[36] Kahn's suggestion implies that not only can the soul wake itself up from sleep, but, through an analogous process, it could bring itself back to life after death. Heraclitus's insistence that "day and night are one" (D-K 57), "immortals mortal, mortals immortal" (D-K 62), and "the beginning and the end are shared in the circumference of a circle" (D-K 103) seems to suggest a cyclic conception of this movement between opposites.

If that state of sleeping and dream is, for Heraclitus, an image of the *axunetoi* state of human beings, cut off or disassociated from logos in such a radical way that they fail to hear it, some investigation of what is happening in this state of sleep is essential. In the final line of D-K 1, Heraclitus says that human beings are "oblivious (*lanthanoi*) of what they do (*poiein*) awake just as what they do (*poiein*) asleep escapes (*epilanthanontai*) them." This is usually understood as a grim metaphor where human beings are sleepwalking through their lives, not recognizing their own experience (as D-K 17 says). While this is certainly true, another aspect of this line emerges if we take seriously Heraclitus's mention of his "words and *works*" in D-K 1 and pay attention to actions as well as words: what do human beings "do"—the verb is *poiein*—while they are asleep? The word that Heraclitus uses here is much denser in meaning than the English word *do* makes clear; it is also "to make" or "to create," such as in the crafting of poetry or art. The final line of D-K 1 could be read as "human beings are oblivious of what they make while they are awake, just as what they create asleep escapes them." While *poiein* can mean everyday making or doing, Heraclitus uses the same verb in D-K 30 where the *kosmos* is everliving fire that "no man nor god has made (*epoiesen*)"; so while the term can refer to trivial makings and doings, it can also be used to describe more spectacular makings, such as the creation of a *kosmos*. In the case of the oblivious human beings of D-K 1, what they create is an *idion kosmos*, a private order akin to the world of dream.

This creating or making is the activity of *psuche*, and for Heraclitus, the activity of *psuche* is deeply involved in language, as both D-K 45 and D-K 115 describe the activities of a logos that belongs to *psuche*. The logos of *psuche* refers to the order that *psuche* creates, especially the order of language that structures our thinking and understanding.

> D-K 115: To *psuche* belongs a *logos* that increases itself.

> D-K 45: You will not find out the limits (*peirata*) of *psuche* by going even if you travel over every way, so deep (*bathus*) is its *logos*.

Robb has pointed out that D-K 45 echoes a Homeric line, specifically when Circe is aiding Odysseus in his journey to the underworld to speak with the dead: "She made the boundaries (*peirata*), which are of Okeanos deep-running (*bathurroou*)."[37] Robb argues that Heraclitus strategically invokes this Homeric line through cadence and sound and, furthermore, that "the Homeric images unmistakably imply that the Heraclitean task is what we would call psychological, one of exploring or testing or using *psuche* as on a prescribed route or in a proper exercise. For Heraclitus, this activity of the *psuche* is primarily an exercise in cognition and in the correct use of language."[38] Just as Odysseus is traveling to the limits of the world to cross the boundary into the underworld, *psuche* explores its own limits by "traveling over every way"—gaining experience and self-knowledge. If *psuche* is implicated in measured processes such as kindling and extinguishing, as Kahn argued in his reading of D-K 26, then this activity of *psuche* would be continuous, perhaps endless through the mechanisms of repetition and difference ("You will not find out the limits of *psyche* by going"; D-K 45).

D-K 115 brings another dimension to this understanding of *psuche*: the logos of *psuche* tends to "increase itself" or grow. The problem of D-K 1 remains, however, as it seems that *psuche* can grow its own private world and persist in its *axunetoi* state, unable to hear logos. As D-K 17 says, "Most human beings do not think things in the way they encounter them, nor do they recognize their own experience, but imagine for themselves (*heoutoisi dokeousi*)." Any growth of the private world gets the sleeper nowhere, as she is no closer to hearing logos or understanding her own experience in her disassociated state. So how might the sleeper be awakened so that she might hear logos and gain the requisite experience that would allow her to speak in agreement (*homologein*) and recognize unity?

Heraclitus's logos (his fragments) can be understood as a reverse lullaby, a way of slowly waking the sleeper through sound and hearing. The barbarian souls of D-K 107 do not understand the language, so they hear only noise; just so, a sleeper can sleep through all kinds of sounds if they do not have any particular significance—she can tune them out, so to speak. However, certain patterned sounds are sure to catch her attention and, possibly, if they are persistent and regular enough, wake her. Heraclitus's logos uses the device of resonance, along with all its repetitions, as a means of creating this regular, persistent, and meaningful sound—it is like a subtle knocking. Even a dreamer will recognize the sound patterns of someone knocking on their chamber door, and this is Heraclitus's subtle key to outgrowing (as D-K 115 suggests) the *idion kosmos*. Sound and hearing are the best means available for waking a sleeper, since her other senses are not active in the state of sleep—sounds can seep into a dream in a way that other sense experiences cannot.

To hear these resonances and their measures, it is essential to read Heraclitus's fragments in the ancient Greek, as they were composed. As an example of this cadence and "knocking" that I have described here, hear the syntax of the cosmic fragment D-K 30: "*Kosmos* the same for all no man nor god has made (*epoiesen*) but it ever was and ever will be (*aei kai estin kai estai*) fire everliving, kindled (*haptomenon*) in measures (*metra*) and in measures (*metra*) extinguished." While the Greek word *metra* does not connote musical measures as in the English term *measure*, it is impossible to create music (or poetry) without rhythm or meter. Heraclitus's use of poetic techniques throughout the fragments implies that this element of meter is significant, although he does not write in formal epic or lyric form. The movement that Heraclitus demonstrates in D-K 30 is an oscillation, as fire is kindled and then extinguished. But the key apprehension here is that Heraclitus does not just tell us about these measures; the text performs this oscillation in the syntax of the words: the *oute* (*oute tis theon oute anthropon*), the *kai* (*aei kai estin kai estai*) and the *metra* (*haptomenon metra kai haposbennumenon metra*) all demonstrate this alternation within the text itself.[39] To return to the musical analogy, Heraclitus is, in D-K 30, playing a rhythm as a demonstration of how to play the strings together in a harmonious and ordered way.

Heraclitus's logos creates a kind of gymnasium for the memory, where *psuche* can practice its growth or "increase" through recognizing the associations generated through the key device of resonance—the sounds of the fragments take on shape; they pattern like a language. The process of "increase" named in D-K 115 happens through this activity of *psuche*, as it "travels over every way" and gains experience. In Heraclitus's teaching, *psuche* learns to hear logos by first hearing the resonance between fragments (the subtle knocking of repetition), and the sound only grows as the student focuses her attention on all of the other fragments in order to hear, through resonance, how they "speak the same" (*homologein*). This kind of growth is exponential, since the fragments are so dense (or perhaps *bathus*, deep) and they resonate with one another in multiple registers.[40]

Listening and hearing are essential receptive activities of *psuche*. To hear the eternal logos, *kata phusin*, the student must be able to distinguish her own sounds from all the others—indeed, to first become aware that she is creating (*poiein*) her own order. Upon awakening, hearing the persistent knocking that Heraclitus sets up in his logos through resonance, the student recognizes that she has been casting her own patterns, like a person waking from a dream. D-K 17 says this plainly: "Most human beings do not think things in the way they encounter them, nor do they recognize their own experience, but imagine for themselves (*heoutoisi dokeousi*)." When these imaginings become visible, the student is able to recognize her own experience and how it congeals into her opinions; the final phrase of D-K 17 can also be translated as "believe their own opinions" or "seem to themselves," as words cognate with *dokein* imply opinion, seeming, or imagining. The activity of the student in engaging with Heraclitus's fragments and their resonance essentially holds up a mirror to her processes of thinking, especially habits of thinking, so that they become visible and audible.

Heraclitus's teaching emphasizes and prioritizes change and difference. The idiosyncratic (playing on *idion kosmos*) thinking and perception of the student is necessary—Heraclitus does not suggest that it can or should be eliminated. Instead, his teaching is designed to allow the student to gain self-awareness of her subjectivity. The problem with human *phronēsis* is not that it is subjective but that it tends to create static names and concepts despite the unceasing movement of the *kosmos*. Human thinking is out of sync with reality because it freezes (arrests or apprehends, as *katalepsetai* implies) the experience of the moving *kosmos* into fixed and immobile names, concepts, and categories. Heraclitus's teaching performs the motions of the *kosmos*—for example, the unity among seemingly discrete parts (expressed through the resonance between fragments) and the oscillation between opposites that is so frequently emphasized in the fragments. Human beings fail to hear logos because they are out of sync in this manner—their processes of *phronesis*, the structures of human thinking and language, remain immobile and are therefore incapable of hearing the movement of logos. The language and imagery of music that I have highlighted throughout Heraclitus's teaching express, through analogy, this kind of movement. Heraclitus's teaching is designed to adapt human processes of thinking (*phronesis*) in such a way that they can move along with the moving *kosmos* instead of freezing or arresting those movements to construct a private understanding.

Returning to the initial puzzles raised by D-K 1, what does it mean to hear logos, and how is Heraclitus's logos (his fragments) somehow the same as the eternal logos that "all things happen in accordance" with? Heraclitus's fragments create a moving order (*kosmos*) in the medium of language, and resonance is the key device through which his fragments accomplish this movement. Because resonance must be heard, "hearing *logos*" refers to the recognition of this order. Like the barbarian souls of D-K 107 learning a new language, the student is able to slowly become aware of patterns and order in Heraclitus's logos. This experience—which D-K 1 suggests is crucial—is simultaneously a process of self-understanding that can lead the student to hear her own patterns of thinking so that she might recognize these habits in order to leave them behind.[41] In the state of disassociation suggested by *axunetoi* (out of sync) in D-K 1 and D-K 34, these habits and processes of thinking are invisible to human beings; they are so deeply ingrained in human experience that they are hidden from our awareness. Heraclitus's logos creates a kind of miniature moving *kosmos*, and he models its movements on those of the larger *kosmos*—this symmetry is what makes Heraclitus's logos somehow the same as the eternal logos. In this way, Heraclitus's logos is an instrument for *psuche* to learn how to hear the patternings of logos and attune itself to those movements, for *psuche* to recognize those movements and to think, perceive, and even dance along with them.

## Notes

1. Heraclitus, D-K 1. Translations throughout this paper are often my own arrangements but are informed by Philip Wheelwright, *Heraclitus* (Princeton, NJ: Princeton University Press, 1959); T. M. Robinson, *Heraclitus: Fragments, a Text and Translation* (Toronto: University of Toronto Press, 1987); Daniel Graham, *Explaining the Cosmos: The Ionian Tradition of Scientific Philosophy* (Princeton, NJ: Princeton University Press, 2006); and frequently follow Charles Kahn, *The Art and Thought of Heraclitus* (Cambridge: Cambridge University Press, 1979).

2. I use the ambiguous and vague phrase "somehow the same" deliberately, because it is imperative to avoid projecting anachronistic notions of "representation" or "imitation" onto the thought of Heraclitus; as we will see in examining his method, the relationship between his logos (his words and teaching) and the eternal logos is paradoxical and complex. See, for example, J. P. Vernant, "Birth of Images," in *Mortals and Immortals: Collected Essays*, ed. Froma I. Zeitlin (Princeton, NJ: Princeton University Press, 1991), 164–185, for an account of mimesis in archaic thought and the radical shift in meaning that occurs in the work of Plato. See also Peter Struck, *The Birth of the Symbol* (Princeton, NJ: Princeton University Press, 2004), for a discussion of early enigmatic texts (Heraclitus's text is an example of this kind of text) and the rejection of these in favor of very different models of representation that come to be standardized through the influence of Aristotle's *Poetics* and *Rhetoric*, where clarity and metaphor become prized as ideals.

3. The constellation of fragments that directly address the issues of listening, hearing, and speaking are D-K 1, D-K 34, D-K 50, and D-K 19.

4. D-K 50: "Listening not to me but to *logos* it is wise to speak in agreement (*homologein*) all things are one."

5. H. G. Liddel and R. Scott, *Greek-English Lexicon with a Revised Supplement* (Oxford: Oxford University Press, 1996).

6. D-K 45: "You will not discover the limits of *psuche* by going even if you travel over every way so deep is its *logos*." D-K 115: "To *psuche* belongs a *logos* that increases itself."

7. Kahn (*Art and Thought*, 97) provides examples of texts that begin with this formula, self-reference of the account, and concludes, "We know that when Heraclitus begins his proem with a reference to his own *logos* he is following a literary tradition well established among early prose authors."

8. Kahn, 97.

9. Heraclitus's placement of the word *aiei*, translated here as "forever," creates syntactic ambiguity since it may refer to either the logos or the human incomprehension of it; many translations repeat the word to retain its double reference. See Kahn's discussion of this ambiguity (*Art and Thought*, 93–94, 97).

10. Heraclitus uses the term *xunon* in D-K 114, D-K 2, D-K 80, D-K 103, and probably D-K 89, where Plutarch arguably inserts *koinos* for Heraclitus's Ionian *xunon*.

11. The theme of recognition (*ginoskein* and cognates) occurs in D-K 108, D-K 17, D-K 57, D-K 106, D-K 56, and D-K 86 and explicitly and implicitly in many other fragments, making it one of the best examples of resonance in Heraclitus's text. These words are associated with knowing, but in the text of Heraclitus, the emphasis is on recognition, having acquaintance with, familiarity, rather than "knowing" in the intellectual sense.

12. In the Loeb edition, A. T. Murray translates *peiretizon* as "making trial." *Odyssey* 14, 459–460; 15, 304–305.

13. Plato, *Republic* 2, 368c–d.

14. The presence of DNA in all the cells of living bodies is an interesting demonstration of this kind of pervasive order.

15. In D-K 129, Pythagoras is accused of *polymathie* and, perhaps worse, *kakotechnie* or "ill skill," as Eva Brann cleverly translates (*The Logos of Heraclitus* [Philadelphia: Paul Dry Books, 2011], 29). *Polymathie* is evidently Heraclitus's own coinage. *Kakotechnie* is a distressing term. Kahn cleverly translates it as "artful knavery"; Robinson has "disreputable craftsmanship." Translating it as "evil technology" carries stronger connotations than the Greek as well as anachronistic ones, but it is tempting, given Heraclitus's implied critique via satire and subversion of the traditional Milesian teachings of his era. See Kahn's discussion of D-K 1 as mimicry with a twist, aimed at programmatic Milesian scientific accounts of the time (*Art and Thought*, 96–98).

16. The final line of D-K 1 is discussed below.

17. Heraclitus's use of *idios* in contrast to *xunon* suggests "idiosyncratic" perception and experience. While "subjectivity" is certainly not a concept that he has at his disposal, his descriptions of the situated and relational character of perception imply subjective experience (see D-K 61, where seawater is nourishing to fish but deadly to men; D-K 9, where "asses prefer garbage to gold"; D-K 102, "For god all things are fair and good and just, but men have taken some things as unjust, others as just"; D-K 79, "A man is found foolish by a god as a child by a man"; etc.).

18. Kevin Robb, "Preliterate Ages and the Linguistic Art of Heraclitus," in *Language and Thought in Early Greek Philosophy*, ed. Kevin Robb (La Salle, IL: Hegeler Institute, 1983), 183. Eric Havelock also emphasizes the significance of mnemonic device in Heraclitus ("The Linguistic Task of the Presocratics Part One: Ionian Science in Search of an Abstract Vocabulary," in *Language and Thought in Early Greek Philosophy*, ed. Kevin Robb [La Salle, IL: Hegeler Institute, 1983], 7–82).

19. This repetition of terms cognate with *lēthē* (forgetting) in the final line of D-K 1 makes the appearance of *alēthea* in D-K 112 an interesting set of opposites—for Heraclitus, *alēthea* as truth suggests the register of memory, *a-lēthea*.

20. *Harmonie* is also, and more commonly in Heraclitus's time, used to describe the fitting together of planks in shipbuilding; see also D-K 10's *sunadon*, "singing together," and *diadon*, "singing apart."

21. Liddel and Scott, *Lexicon*, 244.

22. Kahn, *Art and Thought*, 89–91.

23. Kahn, 90.

24. Kahn, 196.

25. In Plato's *Sophist* and *Statesman*, the method of division is most prominent, but because it is crucial to the dialectical method, it organizes many of the dialogues.

26. In fact, D-K 123 suggests that *physis* has the character of *kryptesthai*—hiddenness or "encryption" is a constitutive dimension of the processes of *physis*. See Emanuela Bianchi, "Nature Trouble: Ancient *Physis* and Queer Performativity," in *Antiquities beyond Humanism*, ed. Emanuela Bianchi, Sara Brill, and Brooke Holmes (Oxford: Oxford University Press, 2019), 211–238, for an insightful discussion of this hidden character of *physis*.

27. D-K 12's "same river" with "other and other waters" and D-K 125's *kykeon* that "separates if it is not stirred" are other explicit examples of this dynamic identity.

28. Heraclitus explicitly addresses the problem of naming in D-K 48 (the bow), D-K 32 (Zeus), D-K 67 (*Theos*), and D-K 23 (Justice); in each of these cases, the name fails to capture the thing named. This aspect of Heraclitus's teaching is clearly under discussion in Plato's *Cratylus*, though the identification of Heraclitus's position as "flux" is problematic, as it misses the paradox of sameness/difference by prioritizing difference and erasing unity.

29. Liddel and Scott, *Lexicon*, 1673.

30. Kahn, *Art and Thought*, 281–286.

31. This fragment has at least sixteen different possible constructions, as Serge Mouraviev has demonstrated ("The Hidden Patterns of the Logos: Poetic Form and Philosophical Content in Heraclitus," in *The Philosophy of Logos*, vol. 1, ed. K. I. Boudouris [Athens: International Center for Greek Philosophy and Culture, 1996], 149–168); the terms *one*, *wise*, and *alone* can be moved around in the fragment, creating multiple plausible grammatical arrangements. In this way, the fragment performs the motion invoked by the play on *Zenos* and the word for life.

32. Kahn, *Art and Thought*, 281.

33. Liddel and Scott, *Lexicon*, 231. Interestingly, the example cited in the lexicon comes from *Odyssey* 21.408 and is said of a lyre string, but the context of the scene is Odysseus stringing his bow before the doomed suitors: "So spoke the suitors, but resourceful Odysseus, as soon as he had lifted the great bow and scanned it on every side—just as when a man well-skilled in the lyre and in song easily stretches the string about a new peg, making fast at either end the twisted sheep-gut—so without effort did Odysseus string the great bow." *Odyssey* 21.404–409.

34. Liddel and Scott, *Lexicon*, 231.

35. Heraclitus's use of the poetic *euphrone* for night allows for sound play with *phronesis*.

36. Kahn, *Art and Thought*, 214.

37. *Odyssey* 11.13, cited in Robb, "Preliterate Ages," 336.

38. Robb, 336.

39. See Jessica Elbert Decker, "Everliving Fire: The Synaptic Motion of Life in Heraclitus," *Epoche: A Journal for the History of Philosophy* 19, no. 2 (2015): 173–180, for a detailed discussion of these oscillations of fire.

40. The density of the fragments is very significant; Kahn names the two primary devices of Heraclitus's method as resonance and "linguistic density" (*Art and Thought*, 89), where one word or image contains multiple resonances and associations.

41. D-K 56 expresses this method of recognizing habits in order to leave them behind, as Homer was fooled by the fishing boys catching lice who say, "What we see and catch we leave behind, what we neither see nor catch we carry away with us." See Roman Dilcher's detailed reading of D-K 56 in "How Not to Conceive Heraclitean Harmony," in *Doctrine and Doxography: Studies on Heraclitus and Pythagoras*, ed. David Sider and Dirk Obbink (Berlin: De Gruyter, 2013), 263–280.

# Bibliography

Bianchi, Emanuela. "Nature Trouble: Ancient *Physis* and Queer Performativity." In *Antiquities beyond Humanism*, edited by Emanuela Bianchi, Sara Brill, and Brooke Holmes, 211–238. Oxford: Oxford University Press, 2019.

Brann, Eva. *The Logos of Heraclitus*. Philadelphia: Paul Dry Books, 2011.

Decker, Jessica Elbert. "Everliving Fire: The Synaptic Motion of Life in Heraclitus." *Epoche: A Journal for the History of Philosophy* 19, no. 2 (2015): 173–180.

Dilcher, Roman. "How Not to Conceive Heraclitean Harmony." In *Doctrine and Doxography: Studies on Heraclitus and Pythagoras*, edited by David Sider and Dirk Obbink, 263–280. Berlin: De Gruyter, 2013.

Graham, Daniel. *Explaining the Cosmos: The Ionian Tradition of Scientific Philosophy*. Princeton, NJ: Princeton University Press, 2006.

Havelock, Eric. "The Linguistic Task of the Presocratics Part One: Ionian Science in Search of an Abstract Vocabulary." In *Language and Thought in Early Greek Philosophy*, edited by Kevin Robb, 7–82. La Salle, IL: Hegeler Institute, 1983.

Homer. *Odyssey*. Loeb Classical Library Edition. Translated by A. T. Murray. Revised by George E. Dimock. Cambridge, MA: Harvard University Press, 1995.

Kahn, Charles. *The Art and Thought of Heraclitus*. Cambridge: Cambridge University Press, 1979.

Liddel, H. G., and R. Scott. *Greek-English Lexicon with a Revised Supplement*. Oxford: Oxford University Press, 1996.

Mouraviev, Serge. "The Hidden Patterns of the Logos: Poetic Form and Philosophical Content in Heraclitus." In *The Philosophy of Logos*, vol. 1, edited by K. I. Boudouris, 149–168. Athens: International Center for Greek Philosophy and Culture, 1996.

Plato. *Cratylus*. Translated by H. N. Fowler for Loeb Classical Library. Boston: Harvard University Press, 1926.

———. *Republic*. Translated by G. M. A. Grube. Indianapolis: Hackett, 1992.

Robb, Kevin. "Preliterate Ages and the Linguistic Art of Heraclitus." In *Language and Thought in Early Greek Philosophy*, edited by Kevin Robb, 153–206. La Salle, IL: Hegeler Institute, 1983.

Robinson, T. M. *Heraclitus: Fragments, a Text and Translation*. Toronto: University of Toronto Press, 1987.

Struck, Peter. *The Birth of the Symbol*. Princeton, NJ: Princeton University Press, 2004.

Vernant, J. P. "Birth of Images." In *Mortals and Immortals: Collected Essays*, edited by Froma I. Zeitlin, 164–185. Princeton, NJ: Princeton University Press, 1991.

Wheelwright, Philip. *Heraclitus*. Princeton, NJ: Princeton University Press, 1959.

JESSICA ELBERT DECKER is Associate Professor of Philosophy at California State University at San Marcos and has published numerous articles on pre-Socratic philosophy and feminist interpretations of ancient texts. She is coeditor, with Dylan Winchock, of *Borderlands and Liminal Subjects: Transgressing the Limit in Philosophy and Literature*.

# 7

# PHILOSOPHICAL LISTENING IN PLATO'S *LYSIS*

S. Montgomery Ewegen, Trinity College

> The lovers of learning know that when philosophy gets hold of their soul, it is imprisoned in and clinging to the body, and that it is forced to examine other things through it as through a cage and not by itself, and that it wallows in every kind of ignorance. Philosophy sees that the worst feature of this imprisonment is that it is due to desires, so that the prisoner himself is contributing to his own incarceration most of all. As I say, the lovers of learning know that philosophy gets hold of their soul when it is in that state, then gently encourages it and tries to free it by showing them that investigation through the eyes is full of deceit, *as is that through the ears* and the other senses.
>
> —Socrates, in Plato, *Phaedo* 82d–83a

PLATO'S *LYSIS* BEGINS WITH SOCRATES SPEAKING: "I WAS making my way from the Academy straight[1] to the Lyceum, by the road outside the town wall—just under the wall, in fact; and when I reached the little gate that leads to the spring of Panops, I chanced there upon Hippothales, son of Hieronymus, and Ctesippus of Paeania, and some other youths with them, standing in a group together" (*Lysis* 203a). To whom is Socrates speaking? He is speaking to *us*.[2] There is no other character named at the beginning of the *Lysis* as being present; there is no set of ears present at that beginning to hear Socrates's words other than our own. Unlike the *Symposium*, for example, where the character Apollodorus tells his story to an unnamed group of people (*Symposium* 172a), the *Lysis* presents Socrates speaking directly to the reader and in this respect is closer to the *Republic* or *Char-mides* in form. To the extent that Socrates is speaking directly to the reader, without mediation through any other character, the *Lysis* demands of us a heightened act of listening—it is as though we ourselves are the characters to whom Socrates directs his λόγοι, characters who therefore ought to make an effort to attend to his words assiduously.[3]

As is the case with every so-called Platonic dialogue, understanding the *Lysis* depends on the reader's ability to attend to the text, to discern clearly the meaning of what is said in the dialogue. This requires attending not only to what is said in the text by the various characters—or, in the case of the *Lysis*, by Socrates, who as the narrator is the only character who actually speaks—but also to what the text itself says, to what the words themselves, beyond the questions or statements of the characters, make manifest. Above all, it depends on the extent to which one is able to empty one's own head of all preconceptions regarding Plato and so-called Platonic philosophy and allow the text, to the extent possible, to present itself in its own voice. As the auditor to whom Socrates is speaking, everything depends on one's ability to listen attentively to what the text says and to think critically about it.

In what follows, I argue that when one listens to the *Lysis*, one hears a story about listening itself—that is, about how one ought to listen to Socratic λόγοι and about the effects that such listening has on those who undertake it. As will be seen, the *Lysis* is above all a story about the possibility and impossibility of genuine listening—genuine attending to—and the sort of philosophical awakening that is possible when one does so. It is, finally, a story about the inability to sustain such genuine listening and the concomitant tendency toward impoverished listening that characterizes the human condition.

## 1. "In One Ear . . ."

The very first word that one hears when one listens to the *Lysis*—that is, the very first word of the text itself—is ἐπορευόμην, a conjugation of the verb πορεύω, "to go or pass through a πόρος" (a "passage," "duct," or "opening"). The verb πορεύω refers to the act of moving through a passage, of undertaking a movement from one place to another along a pathway or road. Very often, the word entails the additional sense of ferrying or carrying across, of crossing from one place to another in such a way as to bear something in such a crossing (such as a ship carrying cargo across the sea). From its very beginning, then, the text of the *Lysis* is concerned with the phenomenon of passage and, more importantly, conveyance.[4]

Dramatically speaking, the passage in question is that of Socrates from the Academy to the Lyceum, a passage that temporarily stops, Socrates tells us, at "the little gate [πυλίς] that leads to the spring of Panops" (*Lysis* 203a). The word πυλίς is the diminutive form of πύλη, meaning "gate," "opening," or even "orifice."[5] Socrates pauses his passage at a gate—an opening, an orifice in the broadest sense—where he holds a brief conversation with Hippothales before proceeding on a few more steps to a recently built palestra, where the remainder of the dialogue takes place.

It is also important to note that Socrates's mention of the spring of Panops in the opening line serves to invoke the figure of Hermes, to whom that spring was sacred.[6] As numerous scholars have observed, Hermes plays a dominant role in the *Lysis*, marking the boundaries, in various ways, of what the text accomplishes philosophically.[7] (Indeed, the drama of the dialogue itself takes place during the Hermaea, the festival of Hermes—see *Lysis* 223b.) The very presence of the god in the dialogue serves to solidify the emphasis on passage and conveyance being remarked on here[8]—for Hermes was, among other things, messenger of the gods, as well as he who ferried the dead down to Hades, that dark place of no substance that sits enclosed within itself beneath the earth.[9] As messenger of the gods and chaperone to the dead, Hermes is associated with movement and passage across boundaries and borders, passage that carries or transports something from one place to another. To the extent that Hermes brings to mind these various associations, his subtle conjuring at the beginning of the *Lysis* serves to draw our attention further to the phenomenon of passage—of movement from one place to another—as well as the transgression across thresholds and boundaries that such passage always entails.

Of course, as the messenger to the gods, Hermes was closely associated with listening.[10] More generally, the god was associated with communication, with speech, with λόγος in the broadest sense. In various ancient accounts, Hermes is shown to have a special affinity with λόγος and is often depicted as having invented the alphabet. In Plato's *Cratylus*, Socrates goes so far as to claim playfully that Hermes invented speech itself, suggesting that the very word *Hermes* (Ἑρμῆς) means "he who contrived speech [εἴρειν ἐμήσατο]" (*Cratylus* 408b).[11] Perhaps the best evidence of Hermes's intimate connection to λόγος is the manner in which his very name serves as the root for the word ἑρμηνεία, "interpretation."[12]

Λόγος, listening, and interpretation are all conceptually related to the phenomenon of passage, for what is at stake in speaking to another is a certain passage from oneself, across an expanse, and over to the other—indeed, over *into* them, into their ears and ultimately their minds. Said most simply, speech is, as sounded thinking, the conveyance of meaning.[13] As such, speaking and listening are always a matter of transgressing boundaries, of crossing over into the mind of the other—indeed, very often against that other's will. To speak is to risk the passage of meaning; to listen is to hazard its reception. The invocation of Hermes at the liminal boundary of the dialogue—which is, strictly speaking, a monologue, a story told by Socrates directly to us—thus further underscores the phenomenon of passage already voiced in the first word of the text.

The textual emphasis on passage or conveyance continues. Indeed, the very first question of the text—a question posed by Hippothales to Socrates—has to do with passage (πόρος): "To where and from where do you make passage [ποῖ δὴ πορεύῃ καὶ πόθεν]" (*Lysis* 203b; my translation). In his reply, Socrates again draws attention to the phenomenon of passage, once more employing the verb πορεύω: "From the Academy . . . , I am passing [πορεύομαι] straight to the Lyceum." The repetition of the verb πορεύω, which occurs three times in ten lines, foreshadows and prefigures the basic matter of the dialogue—namely, the matter of the conveyance of meaning from one place to another that takes place in λόγος, or, more specifically, that takes place in the listening that operates in the wake of sounded λόγος. We will also see, as we continue to listen to the dialogue, that genuine listening itself entails an additional passage—specifically, the passage from ignorance of ignorance to knowledge of ignorance, a passage characteristic of Socrates's philosophical practice in general.

That the *Lysis* is expressly concerned with listening comes to light in the dramatic situation that follows. Upon learning of Socrates's trajectory toward the Lyceum, Hippothales suggests that he rather come straight to him and the group of young men currently involved in a conversation (*Lysis* 203b). Before accepting Hippothales's invitation, Socrates first asks for more details regarding where precisely he should be headed, to which Hippothales gives the following response: "'Here,' he said, showing me there, just opposite the wall, a sort of enclosure [περίβολος] and a door standing open. 'We pass our time there,' he went on; 'not only we ourselves, but others besides—a great many, and handsome'" (*Lysis* 203b). As Hippothales goes on to say, this enclosure with the open door is a recently constructed wrestling school (which, as such, bears a special relationship to Hermes);[14] however, the particular group of young men who frequent this open enclosure primarily engage not in wrestling but rather in discussions (λόγοις) (*Lysis* 204a). This enclosed space with the open door is thus a place where speeches are given a place to occur, where words are sounded, received, and housed, a kind of chamber in which λόγοι are given a place to resound. In other words, the beginning of the *Lysis*, in describing the place where the remainder of the dialogue is to occur, describes nothing other than the shape and function of the human ear.[15]

The notion that Socrates's description of the palestra is meant to bring the ear to mind is bolstered by the fact that the ears are expressly mentioned almost immediately upon his entering into the conversation with these young men. Before accepting Hippothales's invitation to join the discussion underway, Socrates asks about the identity of the handsome boy inside the enclosure (*Lysis* 204a). At this, Hippothales blushes and coyly refuses to divulge the young man's name.[16] In the face of Hippothales's reticence, another character, Ctesippus, chimes in: "Quite charming, the way you blush, Hippothales, and shrink from telling Socrates the name; yet, if [Socrates] spends even a little time with you, he will find you a regular torment, as he hears you repeat it again and again. He has deafened our ears [τὰ ὦτα], I can tell you, Socrates" (*Lysis* 204c–d; translation modified). Within this open enclosure of the palestra—an enclosure that, like the human ear, stands open at the end of a long passage—Hippothales has been cramming (ἐμπίπλημι) their ears full of a single word: the name of his beloved. In other words, in the open enclosure that itself bears a resemblance to the human ear, Hippothales has been repeating a single word over and over to such an extent as to clog the ears of those present, cramming them full with his constant refrain. The word in question—a word so important as to serve as the very title of this so-called Platonic dialogue—is Λύσις.

What does one hear with this word? That is, before we learn anything about the man himself—about his character, his parentage, his beauty, or his intellect—what is it that the name Λύσις names, this word that fills the cavity of the palestra, annoying the ears of those who hear it? The word λύσις means "loosening" or "releasing," even "discharging" or "letting go."[17] Above all, the word bespeaks the manner in which something that was previously bound or entangled is released or dissolved from such bondage. To see this word in use, one may look deep within the labyrinth of Plato's *Phaedo*, where Socrates, while speaking to Simmias's and Cebes's very

Pythagorean ears, suggests that death is nothing other than the releasement (λύσις) or liberation of the soul from the body (*Phaedo* 67e). Another, more revelatory example of the use of this word can be found in book 7 of Plato's *Republic*, where one finds a certain λύσις of those prisoners bound to the wall in an enclosure beneath the earth—an enclosure that, once they have been released, they leave behind, traveling the long and hard journey up a passage and into the lightened region above. As Socrates later makes clear, this releasement, this λύσις, makes possible a certain passage (πορείαν) away from ignorance and toward knowledge:

> "This," I said, "is the release [λύσις] then from the shackles and the turning away from the shadows toward the images which cast them, and the light, and also the ascent from the cavern to the sunlight and there the inability still to look directly at the living creatures and the plants and the light of the sun, but see the divine reflections in water and the shadows of real objects, but not the shadows of images cast by some other such light which is just as unreal as compared with the sun: all this activity in the skills which we have discussed has the ability to uplift the best part of the soul toward the contemplation of the best in things that are in the real world just as previously it directed the part of the body with the clearest perceptions toward what is clearest in the physical, visible sphere." (*Republic* 532c–d)

Here, then, releasement from bondage (λύσις) is the first step in a movement toward the truth, a movement to which Socrates, just before the above-quoted passage, gives the name διαλεκτική (*Republic* 532b), a word one might here translate simply as *conversation*—that is, the activity of speaking with one's mouth and listening with one's ears.[18]

The word, then, that Hippothales keeps repeating and repeating, deafening the ears of those around him, is *releasement*, a word that conjures to mind the loosening or shedding of shackles in such a way as to be freed *from* something and freed *for* something. As Gary Alan Scott has astutely observed, the word λύσις (understood as a freeing or releasing) marks the manner in which the young Lysis is liberated from his bondage such that he can pursue philosophical knowledge.[19] As I further suggest below, such liberation has everything to do with Lysis's ability (or inability) to listen—that is, it has everything to do with his ears and the space between them.

Ctesippus continues to pan Hippothales and his obsession with Lysis (with that man, that is, whose name means "releasement"), criticizing not just the substance of what is said but also the manner in which it is said: "The descriptions he gives us in conversation [καταλογάδην], though dreadful enough, are not so very bad: it is when he sets about inundating us with his poems and prose compositions. More dreadful than all, he actually sings about his favorite in a terrible voice, which we have the trial of hearing [ἀκούοντας]" (*Lysis* 204d; translation modified). Ctesippus, it seems, has great trouble listening, at least if it is Hippothales who is speaking. Not only is the substance of what Hippothales says intolerable to hear ("Lysis, Lysis, Lysis"), but the modes in which he says it (e.g., poems and song) are intolerable as well. One imagines that if Hippothales had some way of blocking or stuffing his ears so that they would not have to hear that word any longer—some way of closing the gates, so to speak—he would jump at the opportunity.

No doubt to the annoyance of those present, many of whom are sick of having their ears crammed full of such things, Socrates asks Hippothales for a performance in order to determine whether Hippothales "understands what a lover ought to say of his beloved to his face or to others" (*Lysis* 204e–205a). In other words, unlike the others present in the open enclosure, Socrates, owing perhaps to a certain irrepressible love of λόγοι,[20] is eager to receive such words—that is, he is eager to listen. When it comes to λόγοι, Socrates is all ears.

And yet, in asking Hippothales to give a performance, Socrates makes it clear that he does not want to hear poetry or song; rather, he wants to hear the thinking (διανοίας) behind these.[21] Socrates wants to grasp the substance behind the words, irrespective of the manner in which that substance is expressed. In other words, Socrates wants to hear what Hippothales is *thinking*; he wants Hippothales's thoughts to traverse the distance between them, transgress the boundaries of his own body, and take up residence—perhaps only temporarily—in his own mind.

However, as Socrates tells it (to us), Hippothales is unwilling to attempt this passage, deferring instead to another:[22] "'I expect this fellow [i.e., Ctesippus] will tell you,' he replied: 'for he has an accurate enough knowledge and recollection of them, if there is any truth in what he says of my having dinned them so constantly in his ears [ὑπ' ἐμοῦ ἀεὶ ἀκούων διατεθρύληται]'" (*Lysis* 205b). Thus, Socrates will not be given the chance to glean the thoughts behind Hippothales's words from Hippothales himself but rather only from one who has listened to Hippothales so closely (much to his own agony) as to be able to repeat the words faithfully—so faithfully, in fact, that he swears on the gods that his recitation will be exact (ἀκριβής; *Lysis* 205b). Here again one sees an emphasis on listening, specifically on the sort of listening that is required to allow one to recite the ideas, if not the words, of another.

Such emphasis on listening is immediately intensified, for, as comes to light through Ctesippus's recitation of Hippothales's thinking, the principal drawback of Hippothales's encomia of Lysis is that he has nothing personal or specific—that is, nothing of his own (ἴδιον)—to say to him. Rather, he "only writes and relates things that the whole city sings of," such as his family's wealth and military victories as well as various "old wives' tales [αἱ γραῖαι ᾄδουσι]" relating Lysis's tenuous connection to Heracles (*Lysis* 205c). Thus, the primary problem with Hippothales's praise of Lysis is that it is hearsay—that is, it is exactly the sort of idle chatter that everyone else says. Having no personal experience of his own with Lysis nor any unique or genuine insight about him to draw on, Hippothales just parrots what he has heard everyone else say about the young man. In other words, Hippothales simply listens to others, without exercising any thinking, any διάνοια, of his own—he is just a mouth and a set of ears with no mind, at least when it comes to praising Lysis.

Socrates chastens Hippothales for his habit of flattering his erotic conquests, arguing that one should not say such things—for such words bring about a kind of prideful high-mindedness (φρονήματος) and arrogance on the part of those who hear them (*Lysis* 206a). Rather, according to Socrates, one should use λόγοι to charm (κηλεῖν) one's beloved (*Lysis* 206b), reducing them to a state of perplexity. Indeed, as Socrates will soon demonstrate to Hippothales, the true purpose of λόγοι in such contexts is to abase and humiliate one's beloved, making them acutely aware of their ignorance (*Lysis* 210e). To this end, Socrates asks to be introduced to Lysis, in order to provide "an example of the sort of conversation [διαλέγεσθαι] you should hold with him, instead of those things that your friends say you speak and sing" (*Lysis* 206c). Hippothales goes on to say that it will not be a problem to engage Lysis in conversation, owing to the fact that "he is a lover of listening [φιλήκοος]" (*Lysis* 206c). As will come to light through the remainder of the *Lysis*, it is precisely owing to his love of listening that Lysis will exhibit also a love of wisdom (i.e., φιλοσοφία) and will bring about his releasement, his λύσις—if only for a brief moment.

After a lovely and vivid dramatic scene where Socrates enters the open enclosure of the palestra, Socrates begins his conversation with Lysis. As quickly comes to light through the conversation that follows, Lysis is suffering from a certain pitiable condition. As Lysis explains to Socrates, his parents hinder (διкωλούσι) him from any number of things (*Lysis* 208a), such as holding the reins in his father's chariot races or controlling the mule cart (*Lysis* 208b). Moreover, he is even overseen and controlled in various ways by both his schoolmasters and his tutors, all of whom are themselves slaves (δοῦλος). In short, Lysis is suffering from a certain bondage, a perennial lack of freedom that is preventing him from obtaining happiness. In light of this, one must note, as Scott has, a piquant irony to Lysis's name, that name that Hippothales won't stop repeating. Lysis, the man whose name means "releasement," is bound—indeed, he is less free than a slave.[23] As the conversation between them goes on to clarify, it is not owing to his young age (as Lysis first suggests) that he is so bound but rather to his lack of intelligence. It is because he does not know (ἐπίσταμαι) about the various things he wishes to do that those in charge of him will not let him do them (*Lysis* 209c). In light of Lysis's admission of this ignorance, Socrates says the following: "Now is it possible, Lysis, to have a high notion of yourself in matters of which you have as yet no notion? 'Why, how can I?' he said. Then if you are in need of a teacher, you have as yet no notion of things? 'True.' Nor can you have a great notion of yourself, if you are still notionless. 'Upon my word, Socrates,' he said, 'I do not see how I can'" (*Lysis* 210d). Lysis is thus quick to admit it: he is notionless; he is without thinking (μήπω φρονεῖ). Lysis's head is an empty container; it is devoid of ideas regarding the true nature of things. However, as is soon revealed, this is the very best thing about him.

Recalling that Socrates began this conversation in order to demonstrate how one ought to talk to a would-be friend/lover, one now sees that one is to use such an occasion to make that person aware of his or her own ignorance. Rather than amplifying and inflating that person's sense of self-worth (φρονήματος), as Hippothales is accustomed to doing, one should reveal and underscore their utter lack of φρονεῖν. Phrased otherwise, in conversation with a friend, one ought to bring that friend to a place where they see themselves as ignorant and as empty or impoverished with respect to wisdom. The true purpose of such conversation (διαλέγεσθαι) is to bring one to a place where one's mental vacuity becomes manifest.[24] Indeed, Socrates immediately admits (though only to us, the auditors listening to his account) what the true purpose of his previous discourse was: to humble and abase (ταπεινοῦντα καὶ συστέλλοντα) Lysis (*Lysis* 210e). In other words, Socrates admits to the reader to have been trying to get into Lysis's head, and in such a way as to reveal to Lysis that there is not much in there of consequence.

One sees such a maneuver on Socrates's part in many so-called Platonic dialogues. Indeed, one could justifiably characterize it as the Socratic maneuver par excellence: Socrates the gadfly attempting to bring an interlocutor into an acknowledgment of his own ignorance. One also finds, in other dialogues, various characters who resist Socrates's efforts, who stubbornly insist on their own positions (see *Meno*), who dig their feet into the baseless ground on which they stand (see *Euthyphro*), or who hurl invective at Socrates as payback for their humiliation (see the *Gorgias*). By contrast, one sees that Lysis, in listening so attentively, lets Socrates's λόγοι into his mind, almost eagerly agreeing with the conclusion that he is mindless (ἄφρων) and even swearing to the gods (μὰ Δία) as he does so (*Lysis* 210d). In fact, Lysis has so enjoyed listening to Socrates humble and abase him that, once Menexenus returns from participating in the rites of the Hermae, Lysis leans in and quietly asks Socrates if he might repeat everything he just said so that Menexenus may hear it (*Lysis* 211a). Lysis's love of listening is so strong as to extend even to those λόγοι that demonstrate his own ignorance.[25]

Instead of simply repeating the conversation as requested, now for the benefit of Menexenus, Socrates says the following: "You shall tell it to him yourself, Lysis: for you gave it your full attention [προσεῖχες τὸν νοῦν]" (*Lysis* 211a). Lysis has given Socrates his full attention—he has allowed the open enclosure of his ears to be flooded with Socrates's words. Additionally, and even more importantly, Lysis lent Socrates not just his ears but also his νοῦς, his mind. Precisely during that discourse whose intention was to demonstrate his lack of φρονεῖν, Lysis demonstrates his ability to focus his νοῦς on a λόγος in such a way as to consider it deeply. Indeed, Lysis paid such close attention that he claims to be able to recollect and recite Socrates's speech at a later time (*Lysis* 211a–b).

This dramatic moment, which does not seem terribly important on first blush, is in fact crucial for understanding the philosophical accomplishment of the *Lysis*, for it marks Lysis's keenness for philosophical inquiry (as will soon be observed by Socrates himself) and his openness to hearing the sort of truth that Socratic philosophy makes clear—namely, that one does not possess knowledge but rather has a head full of ignorance, a head therefore full of nothing, an empty head. Rather than putting up a defense or plugging his own ears to avoid hearing such things, Lysis listens with enviable alacrity about the manner in which his mind is, for all intents and purposes, empty and lacking in knowledge. Lysis is able and eager to follow the λόγος where it leads, even if it leads to the conclusion that he himself is not wise. In demonstrating his willingness to make such a passage and to allow Socrates's λόγοι to pass into his mind, Lysis exhibits his suitability for Socratic philosophy—indeed, he exhibits this philosophy itself.

Although Lysis promises that he will indeed recount Socrates's conversation at a later time, Lysis presently asks Socrates to "tell [Menexenus] something else for now, that I may hear it too [ἵνα καὶ ἐγὼ ἀκούω], until it is time to go home" (*Lysis* 211b). Lysis's love of listening thus proves to be so extreme as to incline him to abandon his desire to see Menexenus abased in the manner that he himself had been, wanting instead to hear Socrates say something more.[26] One sees here the erotic attachment that Lysis has now developed, not so much toward Socrates himself but rather toward the λόγοι to which Socrates gives voice. Lysis so loved hearing about how ignorant he is that he cannot control his desire to hear more.

During his conversation with Menexenus that follows, Socrates, in a highly eristic fashion, offers a subtle and convoluted argument regarding friendship.[27] Whatever deeper philosophical value this passage has, one recalls Socrates's stated reason for having such conversations in the first place: to abase and deflate the other by reducing him to a place of ἀπορία and to attempt to draw his attention to his own epistemological emptiness. Socrates manages at the very least to bring Menexenus to such a place of befuddlement (*Lysis* 213c), though without drawing express attention to his ignorance as he had done with Lysis.

Just after thoroughly confusing Menexenus with his discourse on friendship, Socrates asks Menexenus if there was not perhaps something wrong with the manner in which they had been conducting their inquiry. Before Menexenus has the opportunity to answer, however, Lysis—in the single most important passage in the entire text—jumps in: "'I think there has, Socrates,' said Lysis, and blushed as soon as he said it; for it struck me that the words escaped him unintentionally, through his closely applying his mind to our talk [προσέχειν τὸν νοῦν τοῖς λεγομένοις]—as he had noticeably done all the time he was listening [δῆλος δ' ἦν καὶ ὅτε ἠκροᾶτο οὕτως ἔχων]" (*Lysis* 213d). With Lysis's interruption of Socrates—an interruption that causes him extreme and visible distress—Lysis demonstrates that he has been actively listening the entire time, that he has been following every word, and that he has been assiduously making a space within himself for Socrates's λόγοι. Moreover, it is clear that he has been lending more than just his ears to the discourse; he has been "applying his mind," his νοῦς, to the discussion. As Socrates goes on to tell us, this attentive listening is decisive, for it indicates Lysis's fitness for philosophical inquiry. According to Socrates, it is because he is so fond of listening (φιλήκοος) that Lysis demonstrates his affinity toward philosophy (φιλοσοφία).

In light of Socrates's remark—a remark, to be sure, made only to the reader, since telling it to Lysis himself would perhaps count as counterproductive flattery—one is permitted to ask: What is it to listen? In what way is listening integral to philosophical inquiry? And what kind of listening does philosophy require? To listen is a matter of opening up to the other, of almost literally letting the other inside of oneself so as to give space to the meaning that the other conveys. More so than seeing, where one always sees the other outside of oneself, and more so even than touching, where one always encounters the liminal outside of the other, listening entails taking the other inside of oneself—indeed, taking the *inside* of the other into oneself, internalizing the thoughts that the other, in speaking, made external. To truly listen to someone is to give their thoughts residence, by way of the ears, inside one's head.[28]

To grant such residence, however—that is, to give space to the ideas of the other—one must have the space to give. In other words, to truly listen to another, one must have a cavity sufficiently empty to accommodate their ideas; one must have a capacious opening that can be filled. To provide such a space, one must rid oneself of one's own pretensions of knowledge, as well as one's mere opinions regarding the truth of things—for if one's head is full of such things, there is hardly sufficient space to entertain the notions of others. Simply put, to truly listen to the other, to allow their thinking safe passage across the border of one's ears so as to take up residence in one's head, one must know oneself to be ignorant—that is, one must know oneself to be empty. If this precondition is not met and if this emptiness is not maintained, there is nowhere within oneself for the ideas of the other to dwell.

Genuine listening thus proves not to be a case of taking on the λόγοι of another as though they were a possession, filling one's head with the ideas that they disseminate with their words, but rather principally a matter of coming to know oneself as not possessing wisdom, as being empty inside. Genuine listening is a matter of recognizing the extent to which one's mind is empty of wisdom, and in such a way as to allow the temporary residence of the ideas of another. To love to listen (φιλήκοος) is to embrace the emptiness inside oneself that allows the reception of the other; it is to make a habit out of emptying one's mind in such a way as to make room for the ideas of the other. To truly listen, one must make an open enclosure out of oneself—one must come to recognize one's own ignorance.

This, of course, is precisely what happens to Lysis during his conversation with Socrates. Far from coming to possess something that he did not possess before and that was given to him by Socrates, Lysis has something taken from him—namely, any pretentions to knowledge that he may have had. In opening himself to Socrates in such a way as to make space for his ideas—that is, in engaging in διαλεκτική with him—Lysis comes to realize that he himself is empty inside, that he is nothing other than an openness wherein a λόγος may resound. It is for this reason that Socrates claims that Lysis, in listening so attentively to the conversation and applying his νοῦς to it, is practicing philosophy—for Socratic philosophy is nothing other than a process of coming to know that one does not know what one thought one knew and thereby coming to know oneself as an empty site wherein a reception of λόγος may occur.

## 2. ". . . And Out the Other"

After Lysis's interruption, whereby he displays his philosophical aptitude, Socrates embarks on a long conversation with Lysis, and eventually Menexenus as well, about the nature of friendship. Though there are many important moments during this conversation, all of which are essential to a comprehensive understanding of the text, the purposes of the present inquiry require noting only one—namely, that Socrates and the two boys fail to define the nature of friendship adequately, ending instead in utter ἀπορία (*Lysis* 222e). In other words, Socrates, very much like Hermes, leads Lysis and Menexenus along a passage, taking them to a place of emptiness, of vacuity, where they find themselves in possession of no real substance.[29]

One might liken such a place of emptiness—such a site wherein substance is lacking—to Hades itself, that realm beneath the earth where only the pale shades of human beings sojourn, the very realm to which Hermes was charged with transporting the deceased.[30] Socrates himself conjures such an image to mind as he reports (to us) the following: "Having thus spoken, I had half a mind to stir up somebody else among the older people there; when, *like spirits* [ὥσπερ δαίμονες τινες], there came upon us the tutors of Menexenus and Lysis" (*Lysis* 223a; my translation and emphasis). These tutors drift in, as it were, like spirits, like shades, leading one to suspect that the open enclosure of the palestra is somehow akin to the enclosed caverns of Hades.

As Socrates goes on to tell us, these tutors "called out [to the boys] the order to return home" (*Lysis* 223a). Being quite late (ἤδη γὰρ ἦν ὀψέ)—that is, very likely being dark, opaque, and even more so within the boundaries of the open enclosure of the palestra—the time has come for the boys to leave behind their conversation and once more return to the safety of home. At this moment, Lysis—he who had been led by Socrates to a place where he could recognize and acknowledge his own emptiness, the very place of philosophy—is called back into servitude: he is taken back into custody, back into the bondage of his parents and his tutors. Given the dramatic invocation of darkened Hades, full of spirits, one might say that Lysis, having made the journey to a free place where he was finally liberated from his bondage to opinion and falsity, is now once more called back into the cave below. For a moment, however, Lysis was free. For a moment—and owing entirely to his ability to listen—Lysis lived up to his name.

Such an ending underscores why genuine listening, such as Lysis had exhibited earlier in the text, is rare. For the most part, the manner by which we listen to others is characterized either by unreflective echoing (as was evidenced by Ctesippus back at the beginning of the text) or by simple, mindless obedience (as Lysis and Menexenus evince as they wander off to meet their tutors).[31] It is only a unique person who is able to lend both their ears and their mind to what is said so as to house it within themselves in an active, reflective, critical way—and even for such a person, the opportunities for such listening are few and far between. For the most part, the exigencies of the world are such as to prevent such listening from occurring, for once one makes the ascent to such listening—which is an ascent to philosophy itself—one is nearly always compelled or obliged to descend back into the world below.

Similar to the beginning of the *Lysis*, the ending of the text orients us toward an act of listening. Just as the boys are being led away by the tutors, Socrates calls out to them, "Today, Lysis and Menexenus, we have made ourselves ridiculous—I, an old man, as well as you. For these others will go away and tell how we believe we are friends of one another—for I count myself in with you—but what a 'friend' is, we have not yet succeeded in discovering" (*Lysis* 223b). The message that Socrates sends here has no particular content—that is, it imparts no "information" about the topic at hand (i.e., the nature of friendship). Rather, this call serves to make clear the manner in which all of them, precisely as a result of the preceding discussion, are without content, are empty, and are ignorant of what they seek. In other words, the call of Socrates here serves as an exhortation to Lysis, in the face of the domineering demand of the tutors, to hold fast to the emptiness inside himself, to the open expanse of his mind. It is an exhortation to remain a philosopher, one who knows only that he knows nothing, who knows, therefore, of his essential emptiness. Such an exhortation toward philosophical openness, one suspects, is the very substance of friendship (φιλία) properly understood.

In the end, one is left imagining Lysis wandering off, being led back to the bondage of his parents and tutors, as Socrates's words make their way to the opening of his ears.

## Notes

1. See Christopher Planeaux, "Socrates as Unreliable Narrator? The Dramatic Setting of the *Lysis*," *Classical Philosophy* 96, no. 1 (2001): 60–68, for an argument that there was in fact nothing straight about Socrates's path.

2. See John von Heyking, *The Form of Politics: Aristotle and Plato on Friendship* (Montreal: McGill-Queen's University Press, 2016), 122. For an excellent meditation on the narrative form of the *Lysis*, see Anne-Marie Schultz, *Plato's Socrates as Narrator* (Lanham: Lexington Books, 2013), 18, 32–35.

3. See also James Rhodes, who marks the maieutic character of the text: "The 'pregnant' characters in the play and we ourselves need to be delivered of the virtue of friendly love." "Platonic *Philia* and Political Order," in *Friendship and Politics: Essays in Political Thought*, ed. John von Heyking (Notre Dame, IN: University of Notre Dame Press, 2008), 26.

4. See Heyking, *Form of Politics*, 123.

5. See *Timeus* 71c, where Timaeus refers to the "gates" of the liver.

6. See J. Haden, "Friendship in Plato's *Lysis*," *Review of Metaphysics* 37, no. 2 (1983): 346.

7. See Francisco Gonzalez, "How to Read a Platonic Dialogue: *Lysis* 203a–207d," in *Plato as Author: The Rhetoric of Philosophy*, ed. A. Michelinei (Leiden: Brill, 2003), 15–44; Haden, "Friendship in Plato's *Lysis*"; Heyking, *Form of Politics*, 98–130; Planeaux, "Socrates as Unreliable Narrator."

8. Haden ("Friendship in Plato's *Lysis*," 344) calls Hermes "the pervasive image which lingers over the *Lysis* rather like the smile of the Cheshire cat."

9. See Haden, "Friendship in Plato's *Lysis*," 345.

10. One sees this in the following account, as told by Maurizio Bettini:

> In the market-square of Pharae in Achaea stood the stone image of a bearded Hermes. Before it, an altar, also of stone, was adorned with bronze lamps held in place by lead stays. This statue had prophetic powers and according to Pausanias the ritual

prescribed for consulting the god was this: if some-one wished to ask something of Hermes, he was to come at evening, burn incense on the altar, fill the lamps with oil and light them. Leaving a coin on the altar on the right side of the statue, he was to whisper his question into the god's ears. He was then to quit the square, holding his hands over his ears. Once outside, he was to remove his hands from his ears, and whatever voice he heard in that instant he was to interpret prophetically. (*The Ears of Hermes: Communication, Images, and Identity in the Classical World*, trans. William Michael Short [Columbus: Ohio State University Press, 2011], 4)

11. Although one cannot simply take this etymology straightforwardly but must understand it within the complicated and comic texture of the *Cratylus*, it nonetheless points to the manner in which Plato himself drew a conceptual connection between Hermes and speech, even if only playfully. For more on this, see S. Montgomery Ewegen, *Plato's Cratylus: The Comedy of Language* (Bloomington: Indiana University Press, 2014).

12. See Karly Kerényi, *Hermes: Guide of Souls*, trans. L. Davis and R. Hemenway (Baltimore: Johns Hopkins University Press, 1986), 108.

13. There is also, of course, writing, which entails the conveyance of meaning without sound.

14. See Haden, "Friendship in Plato's *Lysis*," 344.

15. Haden ("Friendship in Plato's *Lysis*," 349) has already suggested that the description of the wrestling school is meant to conjure to mind either the anus or the vagina. Despite Gonzalez's objections to this ("Read a Platonic Dialogue," 38–39), such possibilities cannot be reasonably foreclosed, given the ithyphallic figure of Hermes as well as the highly erotic (in the fullest, Platonic sense of the word) nature of the conversation between Socrates and Lysis (see Schultz, *Plato's Socrates as Narrator*, 28–29). (One notes that Hippothales seduces Socrates into the palestra by promising the presence of "handsome" young men [*Lysis* 203b].) However, there are additional textual reasons that suggest that perhaps the description of the wrestling school is meant to suggest the human ear—that is, those gates (πύλας) on the side of the human head—though there is no reason to assume that the description is not meant to carry the weight of all three orifices. Indeed, given Plato's proclivity toward playfulness and perverse polyvalence, there is every reason to assume that it does.

16. On Hippothales's blushing, see Schultz, *Plato's Socrates as Narrator*, 19, 25.

17. For an excellent article on the importance of the word λύσις to the dialogue as a whole, see Gary Alan Scott, "Setting Free the Boys: Limits and Liberation in Plato's *Lysis*," *disClosure: A Journal of Social Theory* 4 (1995): 24–43.

18. For more on releasement (λύσις) in the context of Plato's *Republic*, see S. Montgomery Ewegen, *The Way of the Platonic Socrates* (Bloomington: Indiana University Press, 2020), 124.

19. Scott, "Setting Free the Boys," 25. This would not be the first time such a thing has happened in a so-called Platonic dialogue. For example, as is well known, the name of the character Meno foretells, in an essential respect, the nature of that man's character as it is presented in the dialogue that bears his name: his stubborn inability to budge from his position. One also sees such a thing in Plato's *Cratylus*, where the name of the character Hermogenes plays such an essential role in the structure and development of the text that one cannot understand the theory of language at play therein without grasping it. See Ewegen, *Plato's Cratylus*.

20. See *Phaedrus* 227c.

21. Andrea Nightingale claims that Socrates "is concerned with the ethical and pedagogical rather than the aesthetic quality of [Hippothales's] compositions" ("The Folly

of Praise: Plato's Critique of Encomiastic Discourse in the *Lysis* and *Symposium*," *Classical Quarterly* 43, no. 1 [1993]: 115).

22. See Schultz, *Plato's Socrates as Narrator*, 19.

23. See Scott, "Setting Free the Boys."

24. See Heyking, *Form of Politics*, 108: "Socrates's ironic questioning of Lysis is an attempt to bring him to perplexity, to neediness, because that is the opening of the soul to otherness and to love and friendship."

25. Rhodes ("Platonic *Philia*," 31) sees a much more sinister element to Lysis's character: "Lysis is not wise or just. He wants to enslave and use other human beings for his own advantage, profit, and pleasure." Yet such a view is surely challenged by Lysis's eagerness to admit his ignorance and his longing to continue to be led by Socrates.

26. By contrast, Menexenus gets up and leaves in the middle. Evidently, there are things he loves more than listening to λόγοι.

27. Menexenus himself is said to be quite accomplished at eristics (ἐριστικός; *Lysis* 211b), something he doubtlessly learned from his teacher Ctesippus, who is himself amenable to sophistics. See *Euthydemus* 300d; see also Ewegen, *Plato's Cratylus*, 22.

28. This, of course, could happen by way of writing as well; however, the emphasis in the *Lysis* is on audible λόγος.

29. Indeed, as if to mark the connection to Hermes, Socrates asks the boys "to perpend the whole of what has been said [τὰ εἰρημένα]" (*Lysis* 222e).

30. See Planeaux, "Socrates as Unreliable Narrator," 65. See also Heyking, *Form of Politics*, 105.

31. As Scott ("Setting Free the Boys," 33) observes, it appears as though the boys want to stay: Socrates claims that "*we* [i.e., presumably Socrates along with Lysis and Menexenus] . . . tried to drive the tutors off" (*Lysis* 223a). However, in the end, Lysis and Menexenus yielded (ἡττηθέντες) to the tutors.

# Bibliography

Bettini, Maurizio. *The Ears of Hermes: Communication, Images, and Identity in the Classical World*. Translated by William Michael Short. Columbus: Ohio State University Press, 2011.

Ewegen, S. Montgomery. *Plato's Cratylus: The Comedy of Language*. Bloomington: Indiana University Press, 2014.

———. *The Way of the Platonic Socrates*. Bloomington: Indiana University Press, 2020.

Gonzalez, Francisco. "How to Read a Platonic Dialogue: *Lysis* 203a–207d." In *Plato as Author: The Rhetoric of Philosophy*, edited by A. Michelinei, 15–44. Leiden: Brill, 2003.

Haden, J. "Friendship in Plato's *Lysis*." *Review of Metaphysics* 37, no. 2 (1983): 327–356.

Heyking, John von. *The Form of Politics: Aristotle and Plato on Friendship*. Montreal: McGill-Queen's University Press, 2016.

Kerényi, Karly. *Hermes: Guide of Souls*. Translated by L. Davis and R. Hemenway. Baltimore: Johns Hopkins University Press, 1986.

Nightingale, Andrea. "The Folly of Praise: Plato's Critique of Encomiastic Discourse in the *Lysis* and *Symposium*." *Classical Quarterly* 43, no. 1 (1993): 112–130.

Planeaux, Christopher. "Socrates as Unreliable Narrator? The Dramatic Setting of the *Lysis*." *Classical Philosophy* 96, no. 1 (2001): 60–68.

Plato. *Lysis, Symposium, Gorgias.* Translated by Walter Rangeley Maitland Lamb. Cambridge, MA: Harvard University Press, 1925.

Rhodes, James. "Platonic *Philia* and Political Order." In *Friendship and Politics: Essays in Political Thought*, edited by John von Heyking, 21–52. Notre Dame, IN: University of Notre Dame Press, 2008.

Schultz, Anne-Marie. *Plato's Socrates as Narrator.* Lanham: Lexington Books, 2013.

Scott, Gary Alan. "Setting Free the Boys: Limits and Liberation in Plato's *Lysis*." *disClosure: A Journal of Social Theory* 4 (1995): 24–43.

S. MONTGOMERY EWEGEN is Associate Professor of Philosophy at Trinity College in Hartford, Connecticut. He is author of *Plato's Cratylus: The Comedy of Language* (Indiana University Press, 2013) and *The Way of the Platonic Socrates* (Indiana University Press, 2020), as well as cotranslator (with Julia Goesser Assaiante) of Martin Heidegger's *Heraclitus*.

# 8

## SOUND AND THE SOUL IN PLATO

Ryan Drake, Fairfield University

### 1. Socrates on How to Party Properly

A proper party, we learn, is first and foremost a matter of listening. Let us heed the distinction that Socrates makes for his adversary Protagoras on this very point. There is, first, improper partying, carried out primarily by "common market-folk" (i.e., the rabble). Such people, he says, "because they are incapable of getting together with one another just by themselves over drinks with their own voices and their own speeches (φωνῆς καὶ τῶν λόγων), on account of their lack of education, these people run up the price of aulos-girls, pay a great deal for the foreign voice (ἀλλοτρίαν φωνὴν) of the aulos, and conduct their get-togethers with one another by listening to its voice" (*Protagoras* 347c–d).[1] Where we bear witness to a proper soirée elsewhere (at the home of Agathon, for example), a party that boasts people of note will send any aulos girls off from the start to entertain themselves or others, as Eryximachus was right to do (*Symposium* 176e).

For the more cultivated, then, the good and noble (καλοὶ κἀγαθοὶ) who have been well educated, "it's enough for them to get together by themselves without such trifling and childish things and with the sound of just their own voices (ἑαυτῶν φωνῆς), each of them speaking and listening in turn in an orderly fashion (λέγοντάς τε καὶ ἀκούοντας ἐν μέρει ἑαυτῶν κοσμίως), even if they drink a great deal of wine" (*Protagoras* 347d–e). Sober or tipsy, a good party is populated first and foremost with the sounds of speeches. This is to say that mere voice in such gatherings is to be elevated to the level of the human voice, to the level of logos. Aristotle goes on famously to highlight the difference between these two in the early passages of his *Politics* by noting that, while animals are possessed of mere φωνή, only humans possess logos (1253a).[2]

Yet, with a view to Socrates's words above, it is not enough to simply have people speaking to one another in order to pull off a successful party; the entire affair must be conducted in an orderly (κοσμίως) manner, where each has an opportunity to speak while the other or others listen. This may take the form of a round of successive speeches like that which forms the larger structure of the *Symposium*, or it may even be elevated to an event in which individuals undertake to test each other's hypotheses on the truth of a given matter in the mode of an elenctic exchange that allows individuals to alternate between speaking and listening with regard to a given point—a kind of giving and taking of logoi, as Socrates puts it (*Protagoras* 348).[3]

It should not surprise us, then, that in examining what it takes to have a proper party in Socrates's understanding, we are led very quickly into the heart of Plato's ethical project of psychic examination. And this is precisely because it is necessary to become aware of those activities that can both promote and inhibit the production of the logoi to which the attendants at a gathering are to listen. Such activities, I wish to claim, are again characterized in the dialogues principally in terms of the voice, and what is more, they span the distance between those voices coming from without and those that, as we discover through various accounts of psychological forces in the dialogues, originate from within one's own soul. In this paper, I attend to that manner of voice in Plato that constitutes a danger and an impediment to thought, and I argue that Plato uses the sound of the voice as a heuristic among others for understanding the dynamics of both psychic and political order.

## 2. Racket

Let us take up for a moment one prominent mode of voice in human life that both falls short of and inhibits the proper production and exchange of logoi. We can grasp it initially by turning back again to the *Symposium*, where, after a feast of speeches have been delivered by each speaker, including the late and very dramatic addition of Alcibiades, the party at Agathon's finally begins to unravel. According to Aristodemus's report, at just the moment when the guests were making room for Alcibiades to sit, "a great crowd of revelers . . . marched straight into the party and seated themselves;

the whole place was in an uproar (θορύβου) and, losing all order (οὐκέτι ἐν κόσμῳ οὐδενὶ), they were forced to drink a vast amount of wine" (223b).[4] What occasions the slide from structure into chaos in their gathering is primarily the auditory phenomenon of the θόρυβος, commonly translated as a kind of clamor or uproar.[5] It is a descendant of θρόος (a noise, as of many voices, or the murmuring of a crowd[6]) and is sometimes used in the form of a verb, θορυβέω, meaning primarily to make a racket (as of a crowd) and secondarily to confuse someone through noise.[7] As such, θόρυβος bears an intimate dual relation between the vocal sounds of a human collective, on the one hand, and disorder or disorientation in relation to sound, on the other. Thus, the racket produced, the increased volume, and the plurality of voices occupying the company at Agathon's home bring about the dissipation of their party's articulate composition and the collective project of understanding that accompanied it.

Consider Socrates's pleas to his fellow Athenians assembled at his trial in the *Apology*. There, Socrates is forced to contend with a recurrent clamor from those gathered and, in the case of his pleas, struggles to be heard above the voices of the jurymen during his defense speech. These altogether seem to compose a spontaneous array of murmurings among those present that nonetheless amount to a general buzz, which dampens Socrates's ability to express his thoughts: "And, men of Athens, I urgently beg and beseech you: if you hear me making my defense with the same words with which I have been accustomed to speak both in the marketplace at the bankers' tables, where many of you have heard me, and elsewhere, to not be surprised or to make a disturbance (θορυβεῖν) on this account" (17c–d).[8] What is remarkable about this term's appearance in the *Apology*, moreover, is the repetition of Socrates's requests, either in advance of anticipated clamor of the gathering or as a means of overcoming its eruption; he expresses the same request several more times throughout, in the presumably futile hope that his speeches will be grasped by all of those present (20e, 21a, 27b, 30c).[9]

This is not to say, however, that such human vocal racket is essentially either unintentional or without direction whatsoever. In the *Protagoras*, θόρυβος makes its first appearance when Socrates explains his doubt to Protagoras about whether virtue—the subject of the sophist's educational program—is in fact teachable, whereupon he refers to the typical practice of the collective members of the assembly for dealing with a person who attempts to offer his opinion on technical matters in which he has no recognized training: "They merely laugh him to scorn and shout him down (θορυβοῦσιν) until either the speaker gives it up, overtaken by the clamor (καταθορυβηθείς), or the police drag him off by order of the chair" (319c). Here *θόρυβος* and its cognates comprise a use of the human voice whose intended effect has less to do with the specific words employed than the collective force that it exercises on the one to whom it is directed. That is, it implies a generalized speech act whose power is more brutishly direct and intimidating precisely in its sonority more than anything else, not unlike the roar of a lion or the barking of a dog. The purpose of the co-ordinated clamor in this case is thus twofold: to drown out the speaker's voice and to produce in him the requisite fear sufficient to silence him further.

## 3. Hit Parade

In this initial glimpse of the phenomenon of the θόρυβος, we are invited to look deeper into what constitutes the "force" according to which speakers may be overtaken or shouted down, as well as how such force impairs logos in its production—that is to say, how the recipient is typically affected by the clamor in these cases, as Plato seems to understand it. While this investigation necessitates a fair amount of speculation, a concrete starting point can be gained by turning to the *Timaeus*, where we find that sound (φωνή) itself is characterized as a blow (πληγήν) "transmitted through the ears by the action of the air on the brain and the blood, and reaching the soul" (67b).[10] In aesthetic terms, the idea that we must be "struck" to become aware of sound to begin with is not an unusual one. It is this auditory contact that makes hearing possible. The sound of a waterfall, for example, or the wind through tree leaves produces to a lesser or greater extent the strikes on our perceptive faculties that make us aware of their action. This is also the basic account of sounding and hearing alike that Aristotle later adopts in his discussion of the senses in *On the Soul*.[11]

In the typical interaction that constitutes dialogue, then, where hearing is engaged primarily for the purpose of listening to what a speaker says, we can imagine that these aural blows are themselves lightly delivered; their purpose in the exchange of properly human voices is to be registered by the hearing faculty only insofar as they can convey the articulate thinking (διάνοια) that elevates mere voice to the level of logos. Thus, the striking of hearing engaged in the dialogical process is not the primary focus of the listener's attention; rather, it is logos itself with which the interlocutors are occupied. To this extent, human vocal utterances are properly fulfilled in their disappearance, in receding from explicit consciousness once they have been expressed in order to then "make room" for the work of one's noetic faculties in grasping the meaning of what has been said, what is expressed in and through the λεγόμενα. However, in cases where the force of such vocal strikes becomes intrusive for the hearer's attention, a proper grasp or evaluation of the λεγόμενα in question can be either impaired or extinguished altogether. These effects, we find, can have both material and psychic results, and such is frequently the case where we encounter θόρυβος in the dialogues.

Indeed, Plato's treatment in certain cases of the effect of the θόρυβος accords quite faithfully with the more basic account of the physics of hearing presented in the *Timaeus* above. Let us refer again to the *Protagoras*, a dialogue that, as we discover, is especially attuned to the voice. When the sophist's eristic salvo against Socrates with regard to questions of correctness in poetic education is met with "a clamorous approval from many of his listeners (πολλοῖς θόρυβον παρέσχε καὶ ἔπαινον τῶν ἀκουόντων)" (339d–e), Socrates reports of his own mental state: "At first I, just as if I had been struck (πληγείς) by a good boxer, I was made dizzy (ἐσκοτώθην) and woozy (ἰλιγγίασα) by what he'd said and by the uproar of the others (ἐπιθορυβησάντων)" (339e). The loud clamor, for which Socrates here appears surprisingly unprepared, is startling; through what we must imagine is likely a combination of enthusiastic cheering and clapping, it manifests itself as a forceful percussion that for the young philosopher results in a momentary *concussion*. And insofar as this blow with its excessive force is transmitted to the soul, as Timaeus puts it above, Socrates finds his thinking disoriented; as a consequence, he must turn to Prodicus for help as a stalling tactic to gain time to think properly about the poem in question (339e). This violent meeting of the physical and psychological, then, upends not only Socrates's poise but also the orderly and effective assemblage of his thoughts.

Yet the effect of the θόρυβος on the hearer does not reside entirely in what we might call the physicality of its volume or the suddenness of its manifestation. Rather, it is a contextualized phenomenon that we find reserved almost exclusively in Plato for tumult produced within the human sphere, whether of a plethora of humans or of forces within the human organism itself, in which something is perceived as at stake.[12] As Socrates relates in his encounter with Protagoras, his vertigo is occasioned not just by the loudness of the sophist's adorers but also by the sophist's own verbal challenge. He is thus thrown off by these influences working in tandem, by a logical challenge first presented to Socrates alongside the startling uproar of applause that signifies the metaphorical landing of a blow in what he is perceiving no longer as an examination but now as a somewhat dangerous battle—one in which each participant has something to lose.

## 4. Cataclysmics

Along similar lines, let us turn to a moment in the dialogues wherein a θόρυβος impacts a younger, more vulnerable soul than Socrates himself. In the *Republic*, Socrates depicts for Glaucon and Adeimantus the delicate nature of a soul's education in the face of the influences of sophistry—a sophistry that is diffused in the nature of the voice of a multitude in public gatherings. For, here, not only does such clamor profoundly impact the hearer's soul, but the collective human voices at play reveal themselves to possess something of a subhuman character. Socrates describes the conditions under which this happens: "When . . . many gathered together sit down in assemblies, courts, theaters, army camps, or any other common meeting of a multitude, and, with a great deal of uproar (θορύβῳ), blame some of the things said or done, and praise others, both in excess, shouting and clapping; and besides, the rocks and the very place surrounding them echo and redouble the uproar of blame and praise (θόρυβον . . . τοῦ ψόγου καὶ ἐπαίνου)" (492b–c).[13] Any young man, Socrates emphasizes, educated in the traditional manner of the city would be deeply affected by both what is said and the forceful uproar through which praise and blame are expressed, forceful to the point at which these locutions are intensified through their echoes.[14] The entire tumult would produce, he goes on, such a violent impact that no sort of private education could withstand it but rather would be "swept away (κατακλυσθεῖσαν) by such blame and praise, and go, borne by the flood, wherever it tends so that he will say the same things are noble and base as they do, practice what they practice, and be such as they are" (492c).[15] As the Greek denotes, the effect of the θόρυβος on the thinking and beliefs of a young man in such cases would be something of a cataclysm, an experience of being dashed by a great and forceful tidal wave. Following Socrates's image, then, this public uproar possesses a sort of momentum that carries off dianoetic resources and structures, washes away beliefs and desires, and yet leaves on the soul of the listener an imprint not merely of its own vocalized character but of its confused tendencies and values as well. It is as if the young listener's mimetic impulse is activated in the midst of the disorientation brought about through the clamor of the multitude. There is for the impressionable, it seems, an awakening desire to take part, to lose oneself in the racket of the multitude, with the consequence that one's own character, with which one is otherwise to resist the temptations of the many, is rendered more pliable and susceptible to disorder.[16]

## 5. Party Animals

The noisy group whose collective voices are so devastating for the orderly structures of an individual's soul operates, we find, much like a fierce beast (θρέμματος) that must be tamed if one is to live with and establish mastery over it (493a). The likeness that Socrates draws here between a multitude and a beast revolves around the governing characteristics that they share: the affects of anger and desire that, as will become clear below, are emblematic of the mortal portions of the soul. Yet what the master—here correlated with the sophist—attempts to study and manipulate in his project of rearing the beast are the various noises (φωνάς) that the creature utters under certain conditions, and correspondingly "what sorts of sounds uttered by another make it tame and angry" (493b). A multitude, it seems, cannot rise above its sentiments or put them in question; its behavior displays little in the way of thoughtfulness, and thus the character of its vocality does not attain to the level of logos. For, to borrow from Aristotle's *Politics* once more, while logos serves to disclose the advantageous and disadvantageous and hence the just and the unjust, mere voice, that possessed by beasts, can only indicate "what is painful and pleasant" (1253a).

A human multitude, then, does not seem able to operate at the level of the properly human but instead in its collective θόρυβος produces mere φῶνή. Its agency is a beastly one, and it can communicate and replicate only through the acoustic force of its vocal expressions of fear, anger, desire, excitement, confusion, and the like. To this extent, its clamor is more than a creaturely counterpart to logos; within the human sphere, it is the adversary of logos and of the very articulate thinking through which logos is manifest. Such considerations help underscore the verdict that Socrates levels repeatedly in the dialogues with regard to the human multitude—namely, that "it is impossible that a multitude be philosophic" (*Republic* 494a). Consider, as well, Socrates's pronouncement in the *Crito*, where he explains to his companion, "I only wish, Crito, the people (οἱ πολλοὶ) could accomplish the greatest evils, that they might be able to accomplish the greatest good things (τὰ μέγιστα ἀγαθά). Then all would be well. But now they can do neither of the two; for they are not able to make a man wise or foolish, but they do whatever occurs to them (ὅ τι ἂν τύχωσι)" (44d)[17].

Taking these assessments into account, the voice of the many through which the θόρυβος is expressed is a voice attuned only to what strikes the many—what haphazard (by τύχη, chance), unforeseen, or externally orchestrated influences act on it.[18] As such, the praise and blame, the dogma of the multitude, is a reactionary force in general, and political power appears predicated, as the sophists show us, on how well one can manipulate the many precisely by feeding its fears and desires and outrages back to it, alternately soothing or enflaming it.[19] Lacking any natural self-order of its own, a human multitude exists as a collective, then, to the extent that its constituents are moved by shared affections, having common fears and desires provoked largely from without. So, with regard to the sophist or orator who attempts to bring the multitude under his sway or to teach others how to do this, communication between the demagogue and the many is reduced to a crude sphere of valuation: "Knowing nothing in truth about which of these convictions and desires is noble, or base, or good, or evil, or just, or unjust, he applies all these names (ὀνομάζοι) following the great animal's opinions—calling what delights it good and what vexes it bad" (493b–c).

Given that the thorubontic utterances of a raucous multitude are so striking—and potentially cataclysmic for the educative structures of both thought and value developed within the psychology of the individual hearer—it is also evident that its discursive behavior is self-reinforcing. Jarring one's ears in this way thereby disorients the thinking of each of its participants. When the multitude is thus disoriented, the absence of any independent ruling agency among them, the absence of nonaffective compulsory principles sanctioned by mutual understanding, ensures that mere appearances (of what is praiseworthy, for example, and what is shameful) and their attendant feelings will compose the objects that direct one's mimetic tendencies. Thus, whereas humanity's imitative resources allow it to better bring natural forces—animate and inanimate—under its control and so rise above the other animal species, the discursive behavior of a human multitude seems to drive it in the opposite direction, leading it back to the animality it was to transcend. It is not surprising, then, when

Aristotle makes figurative use of θόρυβος to indicate the "mere noise" of the orators who, in addressing their speeches before a crowd to the affections of the listeners rather than to their intellect, "bewilder (καταπλήττουσι [a "striking-down"[20]]) the listeners" into sympathizing with the emotional speaker (*Rhetoric*, 3.7.4–5).[21] In this sense, the orator whom Aristotle criticizes speaks in the language of the multitude itself, using a voice contrived not to conjure thought but to extinguish it in the onrush of feeling.

## 6. Crowd Control

Thus far, we have been viewing the acoustic phenomenon of the θόρυβος first as a forceful, arresting manifestation of a human multitude and second as a point of radical equivocation, wherein the dividing line between humanity and animality proves difficult to secure. Attending to the vocal and to what is heard beyond the interchange of logoi that takes center stage in Plato reveals certain vulnerabilities and dangerous tendencies for those inciting the clamor and those within earshot alike. Such points of danger in Plato appear to revolve around the loss of thoughtfulness as well as the knowledge that often attends it; either articulate mental activity or the hard-won convictions of understanding dissipate, briefly or permanently, into the oblivion of forgetting occasioned by the racket of the multitude. And while Aristotle finds fault with those who pander to the affections of the many when orating, Plato indicates that when communicating directly with a multitude, engaging in political discourse in a way that addresses the uniquely human capacity of thoughtfulness on the part of one's listeners does not appear to be a fruitful endeavor.[22] If one then attempts to speak directly with the many, the kind of speech directed at thoughtfulness that has come to be known as reason is not to be hoped for.

Politics must then involve, at least in part, a relation between ruler and citizens carried out at the level of beasts or children: the multitude must be managed—its affects must be manipulated to some extent—and successful persuasion will aim at a collective rousing or soothing of passions. As an illustration of such political discourse, we can turn to the arrangement of which the Eleatic Stranger speaks in the *Statesman*, when he is led to provide an outline of what the best city governed by law would look like. And as if echoing Socrates, the Stranger begins his accounting of lawful regimes by noting that one who possesses the science of true statesmanship cannot transmit this knowledge to the collective, since "never could a multitude composed of any men whatsoever get hold of this sort of science and prove able to manage a city with intellect (μετὰ νοῦ)—instead, that one regime that's correct must be sought in the neighborhood of what's small and few, even one" (297b–c). As a consequence of the educative limitations of the multitude, the Stranger finds it necessary that there be rhetoricians employed to persuade them "by telling stories (μυθολογίας), but not by teaching" (304c–d). For the select few, then, there is reserved education through the properly human function of logos, while for the many, there is storytelling, which never dispenses with the element of pleasure in hearing, a pleasure that, analogous to the practice of music more broadly, has an enchanting, bewitching effect on the minds of the audience.[23]

## 7. Out of Your Head

Such is the recommended political approach to managing the noisy many, a many that Socrates and the Eleatic Stranger also refer to rather disparagingly on occasion as an ὄχλος (304d), a "mob."[24] Yet there is a corresponding locus of trouble associated with a multitude, albeit a multitude of a different order, along with the θόρυβος that attends it. While Timaeus, as we have seen, conceives hearing as the transmission of a sonic blow moving through the ears and reaching the soul, we might assume that the soul itself, left to its own noncorporeal devices, is a locus of silence. Yet to account for the fact that an individual very often can and does find herself in a condition of self-opposition or inner struggle, in Plato we find within the person a replication in miniature of the noisy, beastlike multitude and, alongside it, the internalization of political concerns touched on above. The accounts of clamor in the soul are several, none of which fully maps onto the others, nor is there unequivocal agreement between them on whence exactly such inner noise issues. Below, I offer brief assessments of three accounts of psychic noise and the disruption that each threatens thereby. Though we find that metaphors of sight run through each, we find them accompanied as well by the language of sound.

## 8. Shake It: *Cogitatus Interruptus* in the *Phaedo*

If we begin from Socrates's (and others') repeated notion that the multitude is essentially unable to ascend to the level of philosophy, what allows a philosopher to be such? It has to do, as Socrates explains on his deathbed, with precisely what he is on the brink of doing that day: separating oneself from one's body as far as possible. Correspondingly, the attainment of thoughtfulness (φρόνησις) that is the hallmark of the philosopher is predicated on the soul's capacity not just for release from the body but furthermore for its own pure, unalloyed self-unification. Socrates puts is thus: "And I suppose the soul reasons (λογίζεται) most beautifully when none of these things troubles her—neither hearing nor sight, nor pain nor pleasure—when instead, bidding farewell to the body, she comes to be herself all by herself as much as possible and when, doing everything she can to avoid communing with or even being in touch with the body, she strives for what is" (65c).[25] In Socrates's language, the proper activity of thought—through which one grasps being and thereby allows the soul to be most fully what it is—takes place only when freed from the senses and from the body more generally. And it seems here to be the case that psychic engagement of one's logos, including its employment of a strict order in reproducing the orderliness of truth, implies protecting one's soul from external influences, from stimuli that impinge on the body. And it is the body, Socrates continues, that "shakes the soul up (ταράττοντος) and doesn't let her attain truth and thoughtfulness when the body communes with her" (66a).

Yet the body, as Socrates goes on to say, proves to have a troublesome interior as well, and in the *Phaedo* he locates the disruptive acoustics contained within an individual in the body itself:

> For the body deprives us of leisure on thousands of occasions through the necessity for food. And what's more, when it comes down with certain diseases, these get in the way of our hunt for what is. And it fills us up with erotic loves and with desires and terrors and all manner of images and lots of nonsense, so that because of the body it becomes truly and genuinely impossible to be thoughtful about anything at all ever! . . . And the worst of it all is that if a bit of leisure does come along for us and we get away from the body and turn to investigating something, the body constantly turns up again and makes a clamor (θόρυβον) and agitation (ταραχήν) in our searchings and drives us crazy (ἐκπλήττει), so that because of it we're incapable of seeing the truth. (66c–d)

In Socrates's account, the body is responsible for producing such a racket that it shakes the soul and thus "strikes" (ἐκπλήσσω) it of its capacity for thinking. This agitation or shaking up implies a haphazard and violent movement of psyche that counteracts the movement of dianoia and that, moreover, can prove destructive of any noetic structures, any efforts of understanding, secured beforehand.[26] The body's affections, its pleasures, pains, fears, desires, anger, and so on, then, represent not just interruptions or deferrals of thinking but also potentially the erasure and oblivion of past thought that the individual must work to remember.

In addition, while the body may be a single object in this account, it becomes clear at the same time that it is an agent of multiplicity. It manifests itself to the soul through this plurality as a host of varying, chaotic drives and perception, much of which is summed up in the "nonsense" (φλυαρίας) to which Socrates refers—a term that may hearken us back to the noisy revelry overtaking Agathon's home that appears of such negligible import when compared with the elevated discourses on Eros that had been delivered just before. In this connection, the interval between the rowdy voices within and the orderly procession of logos is further highlighted in the *Phaedo* where Socrates, speaking of the soul's release from the body, characterizes the latter as subjecting the soul to "wandering and mindlessness and terrors and wild loves (ἀγρίων ἐρώτων) and other human evils" (81a). Set together, the image of what is both wild and human is perplexing, yet it also most suitably captures the strangeness of that slippage from what is properly human, the capacity for logos, to mere φώνη, mere voice, where seemingly otherwise logical individuals collect themselves and multiply their utterances, letting them intermingle in the production of a disturbing and beastly clamor.

This raises the question regarding the nature of this other clamor, the clamor confined to the individual. For it appears to be manifest on another acoustic order, distinct from the order of the Athenian multitude or of the cheering audience of speeches. Whereas sound originating from without can reach not only the soul but that part of the soul responsible for logical, reflective activity, the sonics that emerge from within the individual here appear to be just as piercing and destructive with regard to thought, even if our own inner experience reflects that they do not "sound" in the same way. This sort of clamor never travels through the ears and does not seem to make use of quantities of air through which the hearing faculty is "struck." Nonetheless, according to Socrates, there is a sonic striking, an ἔκπληξις, that takes place in the region of thought, a forceful impact that displaces ordered noetic activity. And in laying out this antagonism, Plato provides us an image of the human individual at odds with herself, a presumably silent soul whose entire characteristic activity and striving are ever subject to the racket of the body, with all of its mortal reactions to the world in which it is compelled to survive.

## 9. After Dark: Desires in *Republic* 4 and 9

The picture of the disrupted mind, overtaken by the din somewhere within us, is presented via a significantly different structure where Socrates most explicitly develops his analogy between city and soul—namely, in the *Republic*. For rather than cast the soul as a whole as somehow a vulnerable recipient of the violence of the body and its urges, these interior disruptions are now located much closer to the activity of thinking; they emerge from within the soul itself. This is, of course, a necessary result of Plato's attribution of manifold and divergent motions to the soul itself, portrayed in a much more complex light than in its primary identification with the activity of calculation. Within the *Republic*'s tripartite psychic structure of intellect, spirit, and appetites, the body as such is largely reduced in its toxic influence on the soul, and the lowest, most plentiful portion of the soul— the ἐπιθυμετικόν—now adopts the role of noetic spoiler.

Indeed, the three parts of the soul are, we recall, to map straightforwardly onto the famous division of classes in the city in speech. And in distinction to the portion that rules, which has a single stated function— namely, calculation (λογιστικὸν)—we find that the desiring part, which had previously been assigned to the body in the *Phaedo*, is the pluralized psychic class, "the part with which it loves, hungers, thirsts, and is excited by the other desires, the irrational (ἀλόγιστον) and desiring, companion of certain replenishments and pleasures" (439d). In effect, this manifold agency of the soul is here explicitly excluded from the realm of the human by way of its inability to operate at the level of logos and thus to achieve a certain coherence and sustainable order.

This disorderly character of the appetites necessitates a certain ordering of the soul so that the best portion of it, λογιστικὸν, can rule. For Socrates, this means that the spirited part of the soul, its "middle" part, must be called into action to impose the dictates of logos on the excited and unruly desires, harnessing them and directing them toward what is best for the human overall. For in absence of the rule of thought, the manifold desires will more generally incline toward their own collective, rather haphazard regime in the soul, overtaking all else so that its host of desires can be pursued for as long as possible. Thus, it must be stringently kept from "attempting to enslave and rule what is not appropriately ruled by its class and subverting everyone's entire life" (442a–b).

While the story of the political subversion of regimes that devolve from being ruled by the best to tyrannical rule is a lengthy and detailed account, the corresponding understanding of just how the calculating part of the soul can be unseated by the desiring part remains comparatively undeveloped. Yet where the *Republic* and *Phaedo* are of a piece on the interaction between desire and intellect is that they share an emphasis on psychic acoustics as the terrain on which disruption occurs. It is also where human and animal once more diverge. For as Socrates discusses the case of what he calls the "unnecessary desires" (571b), we find that he repeatedly emphasizes their inherent animality. He calls the lowest portion the "beastly and wild part" (571c), referring to the desires therein as "terrible, savage, and lawless" (572b), and even portrays the "crowd of intense desires" as "hatched in the nest" (573e) and as a "swarm of pleasures densely gathered" (574d). Such language and accompanying images remind us that collective action in the animal sphere very often manifests itself as a more striking configuration of apparent intent or purposefulness, almost as the orchestration of a sort of plan, than we find in the behavior of its individuals. Contrariwise, as we have observed, the clarity, consistency, and deliberateness that is possible for the human at the individual level appears to recede when conjoined with a spontaneously gathered multitude. On one side, animal life seems poised for moments of self-transcendence in the collective; on the other, human life exhibits subhuman behavior in the form of the crowd.[27]

Of course, in the performance of their strivings, the lowly, unnecessary desires emerging in the human soul are said to "cry out" (βοᾶν) when stirred (573e), especially under the influence of eros, which among those desires heeds no law or order but proceeds to "lead the man whom it controls, as though he were a city, to every kind of daring that will produce wherewithal for it and the noisy (θόρυβον) crowd around it" (575a). And in kindred fashion, it is the noisiness of the appetites that proves subversive of the properly ruling agency within the individual. For Socrates details what must happen within the soul to keep the appetites from wreaking havoc while the thoughtful part of the soul slumbers in the night. Not only must intelligence be fed before sleep with arguments, and spirit must be soothed to avoid its being roused to anger, but the desires must be attended to in measured nourishment so that they too will rest and "not produce a clamor (θόρυβον) for the best part by its joy or its pain, but rather leave the best part alone pure and by itself, to consider and to long for the perception of something it doesn't know" (571e–572a).

In the discourse of purity reminiscent of the *Phaedo,* Socrates recapitulates in these passages of the *Republic* an account of psychic disturbance that is carried out in the realm of sound, or at least of what comes to pass as sound within the soul. It is as if the disquiet unleashed by the animal and multiform aspect of our psychic life attacks what is capable of being most unified and does so precisely at the level of the discursive that resonates silently within us. And Socrates thus makes clear a predominant condition of knowledge. For he continues, "When a man has *silenced* (ἡσυχάσας) these two latter forms [spirit and appetite] and set the third—the one in which prudent thinking (φρονεῖν) comes to be—in motion, and only then takes his rest, you know that in such a state he most lays hold of the truth and at this time the sights that are hostile to law show up least in his dreams" (572a–b). While elsewhere, in his conversation with the young and promising Theaetetus, Plato has Socrates characterize thinking (διανοεῖσθαι) as conversing "not with someone else, nor yet aloud, but in silence with oneself (σιγῇ πρὸς αὑτόν)" (*Theaetetus* 190a)[28], in this passage of the *Republic* he implies that silence is essential not only for the activity of orderly thought but for best getting hold of the truth—that is, revealing the nature of things through thinking.

Yet the two senses of silence here between *Theaetetus* and *Republic* are not straightforwardly equivalent. For while both *Phaedo* and *Republic* portray a realm of inner acoustics, silent to the outside world, there remains the question of whether the expression of logos within the activity of thought that constitutes the soul's conversation with itself nonetheless implies its own kind of inner sound—a sound that might, as with the typical operation of conversing calmly with an associate, pass unnoticed while one is occupied with the noetic contents signified by such sounds. We are thus led to wonder here whether the activity of thought is itself a doubly silent affair, both in the outer and inner senses, or whether it does produce its own kind of voice, a voice that would itself be no match for the boisterous *thorubos* of the appetitive agency within us or from without.[29]

## 10. Noise Violations: Prisons and Phantasms in the *Timaeus*

Can thought itself, then, produce its own inner acoustics? And can it thereby combat the noisy influence of the clamor of affects within us, according to Plato? These questions take us, finally, to the architectonics of the human within the overall context of what scholars have referred to as "Plato's Cosmology"—namely, the expansive discourse on nature that the *Timaeus* comprises.[30] For after Timaeus introduced the two mortal portions of the soul in contrast to the immortal portion outlined prior and gives a sketch of the placement of each within the body, we come to learn just why it is that intellect, the most divine of the aspects of soul, is located in the head and so far from the appetitive aspect, which occupies "the parts midway between the midriff and the boundary at the navel" (70d–e).[31] The initial concern, as Timaeus puts it, is that the mortal portion might pollute (μιαίνειν) the divine through the former's own nature. The problem that such placement is instituted to solve is, once again, mainly an issue of noise.

To begin with, the appetitive part of the soul is again referred to as a collective, with its passions "both terrible and unavoidable" (69d) composing a "tribe (γένος) of desires" (70a) that must be forcibly contained by the other portion of mortal soul, spirit, under the direction of intellect. Indeed, the appetitive part must itself already be confined to its lowest region by force, imprisoned (κατέδησαν), "as if it were a wild beast (θρέμμα ἄγριον) which, because it had been tied to the rest, they were compelled to feed if the mortal kind was ever going to be at all" (70e). There is, then, a more overt concession than in our previous investigations of the soul that the divine portion must make to the mortal; for the latter must be nourished—its appetites must, at least in part and in some measure, be sated. But equally important, it seems, the appetitive "tribe" must be kept quiet. Timaeus continues, "In order, then, that this part, while grazing at its trough and settling as far away as possible from the counseling part, and offering the least possible clamor and roar (θόρυβον καὶ βοὴν), might let the most masterful part take counsel in peace concerning what's beneficial to all in common and to each privately—for these reasons, it was here that they gave it its post" (70e–71a). Thus, the reason that the human body is constructed the way that it is, with a distribution of parts of soul among sections of the body, along with buffers between the most and least exalted parts, is a result of the gods' concern about internal acoustics, about the violence that noise can do to thought. It is the clamor of the beastlike horde within us that threatens the capacity of divine intellect, that prevents it from doing its noetic work of counseling with reference to goodness in its various aspects. Given the considerable lengths to which the divine architects have gone in fashioning us, it seems as if they themselves recognize that in the battle between internal logos and animal- or horde-like clamor, it is the latter that will most certainly prevail if left unchecked.

## 11. Screen Saving

As with the ostensible overall purpose of the *Timaeus*, the analysis of the soul gives way to an explanation of how its components function together in order and harmony so as to have a rightful place in the order of the whole of nature. The project of producing this harmony appears unlikely if νοῦς is to work solely within its native territory of logos. Here, Plato has Timaeus state most starkly the limitations of the desiring part, acknowledging that it "would not understand *logos*, and that, even if it did have some share in the perception of reasons, it would have no natural instinct to pay heed to any of them but would be bewitched (ψυχαγωγήσοιτο) for the most part day and night by images and phantasms" (71a). While this notion is implicitly suggested in the *Phaedo* and *Republic*, in Timaeus's telling we are made to reckon with the fact that the lowest portion of the soul is not open to education in and through logos—that rational discourse is neither the proper nor the potentially effective means of guiding, much less reshaping, the appetites.

As readers of the *Republic*, we would thus expect Timaeus to turn to a rehearsal of the account of thumotic pressure, under the direction of intellect, on the desiring part in order to achieve psychic harmony. However, Timaeus instead makes it known that the intellect's administrating repertoire is not yet exhausted. For he suggests that thought (διάνοια) lends itself to different media and thereby manifests material capacities in concert with them. Given that the natural state of the mortal portion is to be under the spell of "images and phantasms"—presumably correlated with external perceptions as well as dream images—and therefore to exist in an ongoing state of distraction and suggestiveness, intellect avails itself of a special organ, the liver, to participate in this enchantment without itself being distracted. God fashioned the liver "dense and smooth and bright and sweet, yet containing bitterness, that the power of thoughts which proceed from the mind, moving in the liver as in a mirror which receives impressions and provides visible images (εἴδωλα), should frighten this part of the soul . . . [when] the mental power bears down upon it with stern threats" (71a–b). And conversely, "when a breath of mildness from the intellect paints on the liver appearances of the opposite kind, and calms down its bitterness . . . using upon the liver the sweetness inherent therein rectifies all its parts so as to make them straight and smooth and free, it causes the part of the soul planted round the liver to be cheerful and serene" (71c–d).[32]

Hence, the extralogical powers of mind here, rather than the forces of *thumos*, are marshaled to manipulate the desires and thereby either scare or soothe them into silent acquiescence.[33] With the aid of the liver, which acts as a screen on which the soul can behold emotionally laden visions, the intellect's imaginative products can be made visible and thus be made to communicate directly with the desiring portion. Thought, then, in its translation into images by way of the body, finds itself able to speak the language, as it were, of the appetites and thus to manage them remotely. If we recall that it is the clamor produced by the mortal portion that disrupts the intellect's activity of thinking, in Plato's conception, this is a struggle resolved by intellect not on the terrain of psychic acoustics but instead by a higher authority of psychic vision.[34]

## 12. Cleaning Up

A view of these several accounts of psychic noise, borne out of analogical portraits of political and social life for Plato, reflects the apparently evolving difficulty he faced in reckoning with humanity's animal dimension, as well as his attempt to keep the divine aspect of humanity, its noetic activity, as pure—or as purely conceived—as possible. Tracing the θόρυβος throughout his work (and the present essay is only a start) helps highlight the shifting loci of disturbance with which our intellect must contend. If we take, as I do, the *Timaeus* to be Plato's final account of psychic harmony and disharmony, then we find that the original source of noise and disruption in the *Phaedo*, the body, turns out to function instead as something of a supplement for both mortal and divine parts of the soul—a material medium of communication necessary for each aspect to carry out its proper activity. And in its reliance on the bodily organs, it becomes apparent that mental products of thought must possess their own hidden resources, as yet uninterrogated powers, for interacting with its material counterpart.[35]

Though there is room enough only to gesture toward further directions for investigation, we should not overlook the special status for Plato of the image as a means of managing the raucous sources of clamor. Whether in the form of mythological recitation, with its various iconic illustrations of gods, monsters, heroes, and men, for the purpose of collective administration, or in the form of internal visions cast so as to captivate our unruly and boisterous animal desires, it seems that Plato locates no more useful device for securing intellectual peacefulness than the cleverly crafted image. For such reasons, it must be evident that the activity of poets, and even that of aulos players, must still have a place in some of Plato's gatherings.[36]

# Notes

1. Trans. R. Bartlett (Ithaca, NY: Cornell University Press, 2004).

2. See also Aristotle's discussion of voice in *On the Soul* 2.8, wherein he separates voice from mere sound (ψόφος) by attributing the former only to ensouled beings. Hence, even cases in which the flute is said to have a voice, as in Socrates's account above, it is done only metaphorically.

3. A qualification is called for here, given that not every proper philosophical gathering will conform strictly to the model of an ongoing—and especially proportionate—giving and taking of logoi. Truth testing may also be pursued via extended diaeresis, as we find in the Statesman and Sophist, where mutual understanding, while still present, is tested through occasional agreement with others whose role in the exchange is greatly reduced as the basis of an account given.

4. Trans. W. R. M. Lamb (Cambridge, MA: Harvard University Press, 1925).

5. *A Greek-English Lexicon* (LSJ), s.v. "θόρυβος."

6. See, e.g., Xenophon, *Hellenica* 2.1; Sophocles, *Ajax* 142.

7. See Thucydides, *The History of the Peloponnesian War* 3.78.

8. Trans. H. N. Fowler (Cambridge, MA: Harvard University Press, 1914).

9. Note also that Isocrates uses θόρυβος in this sense—that of murmurings of a crowd—in *Antidosis* 15, 272. Each of these early points where Socrates attempts to calm the crowd in fact highlights Socrates's radical difference from his fellow Athenians and marks a point at which he asserts his independence—whether in terms of his customary way of speaking, his avowal of a special kind of wisdom, or his insistence on continuing his idiosyncratic service to the god even in the face of death—from them.

10. Trans. R. G. Bury (Cambridge, MA: Harvard University Press, 1929).

11. See especially 419b 9–18.

12. The term and its variants are used more broadly by other authors. Xenophon, for example, applies it to the psychology of horses in the sense of panic or alarm in *On the Art of Horsemanship* 9.11.

13. Trans. A. Bloom (New York: Basic Books, 1968).

14. I am indebted to one of the reviewers of this volume for inviting me to think more deeply about the connection between the echo here—as repetition of praise or blame that becomes anonymous and takes on its own momentum as it is thoughtlessly transmitted—and the force of rumor in Athens, particularly that rumor to which Socrates refers in the *Apology* spread by his "first accusers" (18a–19a). The power of certain forms of clamor in the dialogues does hold something in common with those defamatory rumors disseminated to the young about Socrates—namely, that both overwhelm the resistances of those to whom they are addressed. In one case, this is because of the startling and sustained force of clamor

that asserts itself more powerfully than the staying power of what one has been taught already, and in the other it is because the young have little in the way of resistance to begin with: their adoption of such rumors as truthful is simply a consequence of an undeveloped critical capacity and an orientation of trust toward those from whom these rumors come. Socrates highlights the anonymity of these "echoes" of blame when he remarks that he is unable to name any person in particular responsible for this rumor (18c–d).

15. This passage of a person's education or training being swept away by external influences has a precursor in Gorgias's Helen, wherein Gorgias uses the example of the citizen-soldier who, when he perceives the threatening appearance of an advancing enemy army, flees in terror: "For however strong the discipline of law and custom, it is driven out by fear resulting from sight, which when it comes causes one to disregard the good discerned by law and the advantage that comes from victory" (16). Such evidence suggests an understanding of one's quiet composure (and the training through which it is achieved) as ever subject to oblivion (*Encomium of Helen*, in *The Texts of Early Greek Philosophy*, pt. 2, trans. D. Graham [Cambridge: Cambridge University Press, 2010]).

16. The notion of a loss of self amid a group is further articulated more recently by Sigmund Freud in *Group Psychology and the Analysis of the Ego*, trans. J. Strachey (New York: W. W. Norton, 1959), wherein Freud describes the individual's experience similarly: "His liability to affect becomes extraordinarily intensified, while his intellectual ability is markedly reduced, both processes being evidently in the direction of an approximation to the other individuals in the group" (26).

17. Trans. H. N. Fowler (Cambridge, MA: Harvard University Press, 1904).

18. This is an observation proper not only to Socrates; it seems to be held in common with his sophistic rivals. See, for example, Protagoras's objection to Socrates's proposal that they consult the many on a particular point: "Why, Socrates, must we consider the opinion of the many, who say just what occurs to them?" (*Protagoras* 353a–b).

19. In the context primarily of sophistic speech, Harry Berger Jr. ("Facing Sophists: Socrates' Charismatic Bondage in *Protagoras*," *Representations* 5 [1984]: 66–91) sees the many as more or less unconsciously exercising their mode of control over public speakers to the extent that the latter are constrained to reflect the values of their audience. The sophist or orator "is dangerous chiefly as a prismatic focus, an embodiment of the institutional, cultural, social, and historical structures that have made him an effective power . . . his power to help or harm lies less within himself than beyond himself, in the atmosphere that calls him forth," (77).

20. LSJ s.v.

21. On a more humorous note, we find a kindred use of θόρυβος in Aristophanes's *Knights*, wherein a group of senators gather together to produce much ado and "noisy talk" about the state of anchovies.

22. The divergence between Plato and Aristotle with respect to the capacities of the multitude can be seen by turning to I-Kai Jeng's excellent contribution to this volume ("Observations on Listening in Aristotle's Practical Philosophy"). Jeng details Aristotle's vision for rhetoric's positive role in cultivating a multitude whose powers of hearing and understanding transcend the "slavish" level that Plato seems to believe characterizes a multitude. Perhaps most striking is the fact that Aristotle finds in rhetorical performance itself a means through which the multitude would be elevated to excellence.

23. George Walsh (*The Varieties of Enchantment: Early Greek Views of the Nature and Function of Poetry* [Chapel Hill: University of North Carolina Press, 1984]) points out that

in the context of the Homeric tradition, performed poetry, like music in general, transports the audience out of the ordinary and practical and thus "invites an impersonal and passive response from the audience; it calls upon nothing in the listener's own experience or knowledge, and it discourages active judgment and interpretation." Moreover, "the pleasure song gives seems by definition to consist in the listener's unconsciousness of himself and his present situation" (14). For more on the choice of storytelling in the *Statesman*, see my "Adrift on the Boundless Sea of Unlikeness: Sophistry and Law in Plato's *Statesman*," in *Plato's "Statesman": Dialectic, Myth and Politics*, ed. John Sallis (Albany: State University of New York Press, 2016), 251–268.

24. Aristophanes, for example, finds on occasion the apt pairing of an ὄχλος with its characteristic θόρυβος, as in *Lysistrata* 328.

25. Trans. E. Brann (Newburyport, MA: Focus Classical Library, 1998).

26. Aristotle employs similar terminology in the *Poetics* when speaking of the psychological effect on the viewer of moments of reversal and recognition as "striking" (ἐκπληκτικόν) (1454a), which implies, as I argue elsewhere, the destruction of a set of suppositions set up by the plot in the minds of the audience. That is to say, the audience is surprised because the connective order of events and their implications are struck down at a crucial moment, and the audience must reweave the events together to accommodate the transformational new discoveries with which they are presented.

27. An important exception to my characterization of a multitude as tending toward subhuman behavior is marked by Freud, and I take his point. While he concedes that in a group, individuals permit their cruder inclinations and instincts to come to the fore, groups are on occasion also, under the influence of suggestion, "capable of high achievements in the shape of abnegation, unselfishness, and devotion to an ideal" (*Group Psychology*, 15). However, we find little in the way of acknowledgment of this higher capacity of groups in Plato's own writing.

28. Trans. H. N. Fowler (Cambridge, MA: Harvard University Press, 1921).

29. According to Adriana Cavarero, it is clear that Plato implicitly works with an ideal of thought as utterly silent, as freed completely from the materiality and hence the conventionality and factically laden aspects of the voice, striving for pure, self-contained, and perfect signification (*For More Than One Voice: Toward a Philosophy of Vocal Expression*, trans. P. Kottman [Stanford: Stanford University Press, 2005]). In her study, however, Cavarero overlooks the relations between represented portions of the soul that, as I wish to maintain, complicate such a picture of Plato's stance regarding the internal voice.

30. See, for example, Francis Cornford's monumental study, *Plato's Cosmology: The Timaeus of Plato* (Indianapolis: Hackett, 1935), as well as Gabriela Roxana Carone's more recent work, *Plato's Cosmology and Its Ethical Dimensions* (Cambridge: Cambridge University Press, 2005).

31. Trans. Bury.

32. Note that in Plato a kindred idea of a sort of painting or writing within the soul is also to be found as part of the intellect's discourse with itself in its attempts to establish a true account of its perceptions at *Philebus* 38e–39c.

33. This is not to assert that in Timaeus's account, the spirited portion of soul has no role to play vis-à-vis the appetites; *thumos* appears here to function as a last resort when intellect fails in its efforts to make the lowest part of the soul obey its dictates. See 70a, in particular.

34. In attempting to grasp the translatability of inner logoi into inner images, a potential modern correlate may be found in Ferdinand de Saussure's pioneering work in linguistics,

wherein linguistic thought—Plato's silent dialogue of the soul with itself—is conceived in part as possessing already the status of an ἔιδωλον, albeit in the medium of sound (*l'image acoustique*). See *A Course in General Linguistics*, trans. R. Harris (Chicago: Open Court, 1983), 11ff. We may wonder whether Plato would have assented to such a characterization of thinking and whether it would have been of use to him to view the inner θόρυβος of the appetites in similar terms.

35.  Indeed, throughout these passages (69c ff) in the *Timaeus* on the construction of the body in relation to the soul's functioning, it appears that the heart, lungs, blood, and various "channels" (στενωπῶν, 70b) through which blood and air pass all have their respective roles to play in supporting the hegemony of the intellect.

36.  Thanks are due to Jill Gordon, Michael Shaw, and Holly Moore, who have given me generous feedback throughout multiple iterations of this paper and who have helped me find the proper words to express thoughts that would have otherwise certainly remained elusive.

# Bibliography

Aristophanes. *Knights*. Translated by J. Henderson. Cambridge, MA: Harvard University Press, 1998.

———. *Lysistrata*. Translated by A. H. Sommerstein. New York: Penguin, 2002.

Aristotle. *Art of Rhetoric*. Translated by J. H. Freese. Cambridge, MA: Harvard University Press, 1926.

———. *On Poetics*. Translated by S. Benardete and M. Davis. South Bend, IN: St. Augustine's, 2002.

———. *On the Soul*. Translated by W. S. Hett. Cambridge, MA: Harvard University Press, 1957.

———. *Politics*. Translated by H. Rackham. Cambridge, MA: Harvard University Press, 1932.

Berger, Harry, Jr. "Facing Sophists: Socrates' Charismatic Bondage in *Protagoras*." *Representations* 5 (1984): 66–91.

Carone, Gabriela Roxana. *Plato's Cosmology and Its Ethical Dimensions*. Cambridge: Cambridge University Press, 2005.

Cavarero, Adriana. *For More Than One Voice: Toward a Philosophy of Vocal Expression*. Translated by P. Kottman. Stanford: Stanford University Press, 2005.

Cornford, Francis Macdonald. *Plato's Cosmology: The Timaeus of Plato*. Indianapolis: Hackett, 1935.

Drake, Ryan. "Adrift on the Boundless Sea of Unlikeness: Sophistry and Law in Plato's *Statesman*." In *Plato's "Statesman": Dialectic, Myth, and Politics*, edited by John Sallis. Albany: State University of New York Press, 2016.

Freud, Sigmund. *Group Psychology and the Analysis of the Ego*. Translated by J. Strachey. New York: W. W. Norton, 1959.

Gorgias. *Encomium of Helen*. In *The Texts of Early Greek Philosophy*, part 2, translated by D. Graham. Cambridge: Cambridge University Press, 2010.

Isocrates. *Antidosis*. Translated by G. Norlin. Cambridge, MA: Harvard University Press, 1928.

Plato. *Apology*. Translated by H. N. Fowler. Cambridge, MA: Harvard University Press, 1914.

———. *Crito*. Translated by H. N. Fowler. Cambridge, MA: Harvard University Press, 1904.

———. *Phaedo*. Translated by E. Brann. Newburyport, MA: Focus Classical Library, 1998.

———. *Philebus*. Translated by H. N. Fowler. Cambridge, MA: Harvard University Press, 1925.

———. *Protagoras*. Translated by R. C. Bartlett. Ithaca, NY: Cornell University Press, 2004.

———. *Republic*. Translated by A. Bloom. New York: Basic Books, 1991.

———. *Statesman*. Translated by W. R. M. Lamb. Cambridge, MA: Harvard University Press, 1925.

———. *Symposium*. Translated by W. R. M. Lamb. Cambridge, MA: Harvard University Press, 1904.

———. *Theaetetus*. Translated by H. N. Fowler. Cambridge, MA: Harvard University Press, 1921.

———. *Timaeus*. Translated by R. G. Bury. Cambridge, MA: Harvard University Press, 1929.

Saussure, Ferdinand de. *A Course in General Linguistics*. Translated by R. Harris. Chicago: Open Court, 1983.

Sophocles. *Ajax*. Translated by H. Goldner and R. Pevear. Oxford: Oxford University Press, 1999.

Thucydides. *The History of the Peloponnesian War*. Translated by R. Warner. New York: Penguin, 1972.

Walsh, George. *The Varieties of Enchantment: Early Greek Views of the Nature and Function of Poetry*. Chapel Hill: University of North Carolina Press, 1984.

Xenophon. *Hellenica*. Translated by C. L. Brownson. Cambridge, MA: Harvard University Press, 1918.

———. *On the Art of Horsemanship*. In *Scripta Minora*, translated by E. C. Marchant. Cambridge, MA: Harvard University Press, 1925.

RYAN DRAKE is Associate Professor of Philosophy at Fairfield University, where he specializes in ancient philosophy, nineteenth- and twentieth-century European philosophy, and aesthetics. He has authored articles on Greek tragedy, sophistry, Plato, Aristotle, critical theory, and modern art. He is currently at work on a manuscript dealing with enchantment and agency in Platonic philosophy.

# PART III
# SOUND POLITICS

# 9

## LISTENING TO THE *SEVENTH LETTER*

Jill Gordon, Colby College

P LATO PLAINLY AND PARADOXICALLY CLAIMS IN THE *SEVENTH LETTER* that serious people avoid writing (344c)—including himself (341c–e)—because language or logos is weak and fails to get to truth (343a–c).[1] There is voluminous scholarship that narrowly attends to the *Letter*'s so-called digression, from which these passages about writing and logos come, and that scholarship is epistemically and ontologically motivated, aiming to say something about the relationship between language and truth.[2] The *Letter*, however, also explicitly directs us toward a different aspect of logos, which has been sorely neglected. Language, whether spoken or written in the Greek context, is something heard, and the *Letter* relies heavily and self-consciously on this aspect of logos. Its aural references shape its many themes, and we gain a deeper, more coherent understanding of the *Letter* in its entirety if we pay attention to its hearers and its being heard.

The *Letter* is, moreover, essentially a political document, and the epistemic work being done in it is integral to those politics.[3] Hearing is central to those politics as well, I argue. I begin in the first section with a generalized focus on the aural and receptive aspect of logos in the Greek cultural context, expanding the notion of logos beyond most philosophers' implied understanding of it as propositional expression or "saying." On the contrary, logos for the Greeks includes hearing and listening. In the second section, I demonstrate that the *Seventh Letter* explicitly thematizes hearing and listening and that it comprises an exhortation to listen. In the third section, I demonstrate the political significance of the exhortation to listen based on a unified reading of the *Letter* that conjoins the concerns of the so-called digression with the rest of its content and that helps situate the weakness or failure of logos as an aural phenomenon within the *Letter*'s distinctly political aims. That is to say, the "weakness of logos" referred to in the so-called digression is also a weakness of hearers and hearing. The politics of listening in the *Seventh Letter* and in a broadly construed "Platonic" context rely on certain forms of domination, no matter how philosophical, and I therefore consider what role domination plays in the *Letter* and in the dialogues more generally. In the final section, I speculate on what a more liberated politics of listening and hearing might look like and what role the Platonic writings might play as a propaedeutic to better listening.

## 1. The Other Side of Logos

Most of the scholarship on the *Seventh Letter*, especially work that focuses on the "digression" as either centrally or exclusively important, takes *logos* to mean expressed language, something said or written, propositions. But for everything said or asserted—even asked—there is an act of hearing or listening that completes the communicative action or is at least a necessary element in the communication event.[4] This side of logos is, I argue, equally worth investigating, though seemingly invisible to most contemporary readers of the *Letters*.

The Greek infinitive verb *legein* helps tell a deeper story of logos and hearing. We might begin here with Heraclitus's fragment B50: "Listening not to me but to the *Logos*, it is wise to agree that all is one."[5] This fragment opens up the possibility of a new—or rather, renewed—appreciation for hearing among the Greeks. We might meditate on each element of this fragment to think through the connection between logos and hearing: what it might mean to listen to the logos, to be a hearer, to be wise, to agree, and to hear that all is one. Martin Heidegger is one philosopher who takes up these tasks, and his work helps us to understand logos in this expanded way that includes hearing. "What λόγος is we gather from λέγειν," Heidegger claims at the beginning of his study of logos.[6] Very early meanings of *legein* include "to lay" and "to gather together and let lie before us." His account asks how and whether these meanings can be traced forward to its meaning of "to say" and "to talk" that we ascribe to its use in later periods. But the question, he says, cannot really be raised in this manner. There is nothing, he says, to show that *legein* "advanced from one meaning, 'to lay,' to another, 'to say.'" Instead, there is an event "whose immensity still lies concealed" (63), and this momentous event that we fail to notice is the utter coincidence of the "laying together" and the "saying." Hence *legein* is a laying that he calls a "gathering-together-before-us" of Being as it "comes to presence." And "to say" is likewise a gathering together before us of Being as it comes to presence. They are thus equiprimordial semantic phenomena, not distant etymological cousins. Consequently, this means that *legein* is not merely to put forward some words; it is a rich and complex expression of Being as it is put before us.

If this is the essence of *legein*, then the implications for hearing are equally profound, according to Heidegger. Hearing is not, he says, merely an "activation of the body's audio equipment," and accounts of the "physiology of the senses" do not capture its meaning (65). The hearing that is *legein* is a hearkening and a heeding to the Being put before us. In the phenomenon of hearing, "the addressed is itself that which lies before us, as gathered and laid before us. . . . We are all ears when our gathering devotes itself entirely to hearkening, the ears and the mere invasion of sounds being completely forgotten . . . We have heard when we *belong to* the matter addressed" (65–66; emphasis in original). He is describing a unity here of the hearer and the thing heard, a coming together, a type of community. In this complex community, there is a coming together of speech, hearing, and Being, all laid out in the presence of one another.

Within this community, according to Heraclitus's fragment, wisdom resides in another *legein*: an agreement that all is one. This coming together is proper hearing or *homolegein*, the Greek word for "agreement," and *homolegein* occurs "when the hearing of mortals has become proper hearing." When such hearing occurs as *homolegein*, wisdom comes to pass (68), and with wisdom, as described by Heraclitus, something fateful "'comes to pass insofar as One All,'" as Heidegger translates Heraclitus.[7] Proper human hearing is thus an attentiveness to the gathering into one, and it is a communal coming together of sorts, an agreement, *homolegein*. We can begin to see how this understanding of logos has a political valence and will be relevant to the *Seventh Letter*.

Picking up where Heidegger leaves off, Gemma Fiumara explores the listening or hearing side of logos among the Greeks, to which we are no longer attuned: "Even though the logical genius of the Greeks is the basic source of our culture it may still in some respects be alien to us."[8] Fiumara sees the current age, by contrast to that of the early Greeks, as one in which this logos of unity and hearkening is absent, and the logos of saying dominates. In our logocentric culture, she says, "it is logical for us to remain anchored to assertive discourse." In doing so, however, "we are confronted by a way of thinking that is associated with only half of the meaning of our *logos*" (7), a meaning bereft of listening. She sees in the present age a reductive practice of logos that can no longer be considered an instrument that promotes the growth of rationality but instead serves as a means of rational suppression (12). Our current discursive practices, especially those we think of as "rigorous," are "deeply rooted in the exclusion of listening, in a trend which brooks no argument, where everyone obeys without too much fuss," and Fiumara recommends instead a forceful silence that arises from "serious, unyielding attention" (11). Fiumara's silence echoes Heidegger's hearkening, both of them educing openness to and connection to the other.

Even a view of philosophy as a hermeneutic enterprise situated in questioning, such as that laid out by Hans-Georg Gadamer, suffers from this impoverished view of logos without listening, according to Fiumara. We can follow Gadamer up to a point, she says, but she remains skeptical about what he calls "the logic of the question." This very logic circumscribes the questioning activity. The question still posits a range and limitation of thought, even as it opens up discourse. The question, as expression, structures its response or its range of responses: "Although it is certainly true that the answers are the material from which the edifice is built, the structure of the edifice is determined by the type of questions that were asked—in the sense that the answer collaborates with the question and produces everything that is demanded of it, and *nothing else*" (35; emphasis in original.). In questioning, we adhere "to a position that allows for and enhances the 'dialectical' splendours of questioning while, at the same time, distancing us from the risks that would be created by the transforming experience of proper hearing" (38). Fiumara thus indicates that proper listening has the potential to transform the listener. We shall see that while Fiumara associates listening with a less dominating logos, and she associates an actively listening logos with the Greeks, especially the Platonic Socrates, there are still strains of domination both in the *Letters* and in the Platonic dialogues. This tension will open up questions about the conditions under which a more liberated politics of hearing might be possible, a kind of liberation of the senses, and I turn to that in the final section.

Fiumara's and Heidegger's work on hearing as a necessary and central part of logos and *legein* nevertheless opens up the *Seventh Letter* to a new reading—or a new hearing. And, it turns out, Plato already shows himself carefully attuned to hearing. We see in the *Seventh Letter* that a more robust understanding of *legein*, one that includes listening and hearing, is at work. And we need not remain within the letter's so-called digression and its express concern with logos to do that. In a manner consistent with Heidegger's and Fiumara's arguments that the activity of *legein* had for the Greeks a different resonance much more bound up with listening and hearing, the text of the *Seventh Letter* indeed thematizes and focuses on hearing throughout. Examining the *Letter* and its explicit thematization of hearing contributes to a richer understanding of the so-called digression's diagnosis of a weakness of logos and to a deeper consideration of the *Letter* as a whole. It also helps us join the letter's epistemic and political concerns.

## 2. Hearing (in) the Letter

The thematizing of hearing or listening, through *akouō* and its cognates, resides first, but not only, in the frequency of their appearances—at least twenty times in this brief text.[9] The thematizing takes place, first of all, through the fact that the two primary figures, Dion and Dionysius, are distinguished on the basis of their ability to listen and hear. Second, the *Letter* exhorts its addressees to hear what Plato has to say and cautions them not to listen to certain other things, most especially invidious rumors. In both its warnings not to listen and its call to listen, the *Letter* addresses all of its hearers to heed its counsel. Because listening becomes central to both the epistemic readiness for philosophy and political stability, the many instances of hearing or listening in the *Letter* link the *Letter*'s political and epistemic concerns.[10]

The opening of the *Letter* signals that it will tell a story "not unworthy of hearing" (οὐκ ἀπάξιον ἀκοῦσαι, 324b). The first matter that Plato wants the letter's addressees to hear about is the fate of his beloved friend Socrates under two political regimes: the short, brutal reign of the Thirty, when Socrates was ordered to participate in unjust executions, acts that, had he chosen to do them, would have sullied him as doing the bidding of the Tyrants; and the return of the democracy thereafter, during which time men of standing accused Socrates of impiety, and he was convicted and executed—by the very men whose friends he had refused to seek for execution (324c–325c). The events during these two regimes so forged the young man, Plato, that, although he first desired to enter political life in order to fix these situations (325b, 325e), he ultimately despaired of any regime being justly and incorruptly ruled unless rulers became truly philosophical. This is the view with which he first arrived in Sicily (326b, 326d), and in this frame of mind he began his instruction of Dion, then a young man of about twenty. Plato was in these early years "secretly, and all unwittingly, working for the future destruction of the tyranny" (327a), but what he is about to relate is "the beginning of everything" (πάντων ἀρχὴν, 326e).[11] So, in the prime of his life, a somewhat politically disillusioned but still hopeful Plato sets out on what turns out to be a fateful political journey; that journey then leads to two further journeys, and, at the time of the letter's writing, an unraveling political situation requires this importunate letter to the friends of the now-assassinated Dion. That assassination is presumably at the center of the heavy, portentous "everything." The stakes are thus dramatically high at this early juncture in Plato's letter, and at this juncture, hearing enters the letter robustly.

The *Letter* tells us that it is young Dion's keen listening that distinguishes him—from Dionysius, surely, as the narrative will reveal, but also from all other youths:[12] "For Dion was in all things quick to learn, especially in the matters upon which I talked with him. He listened (ὑπήκουσε) with such zeal and attentiveness as I have never encountered in any other young man" (327a–b). As a result of his listening to Plato during his first visit to Syracuse, Dion committed to live a virtuous life that was contrary to that lived by most, a way of life described as burdensome to the indulgent, hedonistic, profligate citizens of Syracuse (327b). More to the point, however, the *Letter* reveals that Dion's fervent listening is where Plato rests his political hopes, it is what Dion's assassination ultimately results from, and it is plausibly why Dionysius's tyranny will prevail if the letter's addressees— the friends of Dion—do not listen. The absolutely crucial role of hearing is thus established early in the *Seventh Letter*.

Plato's second trip to Syracuse comes at the urging of Dion, now around forty years of age, in order to teach his nephew, Dionysius, about the good life, virtue, and happiness, just at the time Dionysius ascends to rule Syracuse upon the death of his father (Dion's brother-in-law).[13] We see in these passages the importance of Plato's controlling what people hear, both about his own motives and about rumors concerning Dion's actions. There is an insistent defensiveness in his account:[14] "My own self-respect was foremost in my thoughts, for I shrank from thinking of myself as a mere theorist, unwilling to touch any practical task; and I realized also that by refusing I might be betraying Dion's hospitality and friendship at a time of no little real danger to himself" (328c–d).[15] Plato then goes on to imagine how he might be reproached if he does not go to Syracuse, conjuring up Dion's voice for his addressees to hear and reflecting on how he heard it in his own mind (328d–329a). "Oh, Plato," the imagined voice of Dion begins, "you are able to turn young men toward goodness and justice . . . You are always praising philosophy . . . And do you think you can now meet the charge of cowardice by pleading the length of the journey and its great difficulty?" (328e–329a). To such an entreaty, there is no other response. And "so, from motives as rational and just as is humanly possible" (329a–b), he sets off to teach the new tyrant of Syracuse.

Upon Plato's arrival in Syracuse to counsel Dionysius for the first time, the situation is roughly this: the city is full of strife, and slanderous stories are circulating about Dion's alleged plots against Dionysius (329b–c). Plato attempts to defend Dion against these rumors, but to no avail, and Dion is exiled from the city about three months after Plato's arrival. Fearing even more unrest, especially among the friends and comrades of Dion, Dionysius then receives them all back as allies, including Plato, whom he urges to stay on in Syracuse. Plato does so—"but everyone knows that the requests of tyrants have force behind them" (329d–e)—knowing, too, that Dionysius is hindering his departure behind the scenes. Dionysius and his people are spreading the rumor that he is fond of and devoted to Plato and philosophy, which is not true, though Plato observes that he did show some improvement after getting to know Plato's character and ways. The problem, however, was that Dionysius needed to hear Plato praise him more than he heard Plato praise Dion (ἑαυτὸν δὲ ἐπαινεῖν μᾶλλον ἢ Δίωνα ἐβούλετο με, 330a). Plato counsels him that he needs to be occupied with learning and listening (μανθάνων καὶ ἀκούων, 330b) to Plato's philosophical lessons, but Dionysius is nonetheless preoccupied with Dion and his followers and what they might do to undermine his rule. Despite Plato's hopes, Dionysius and his resistance to listening win the day, so Plato departs Syracuse without really making any headway in instructing Dionysius (330b).

What follows in the *Letter* is an interlude of sorts in which Plato tells us that before he relates details of the second voyage to Syracuse to remedy the rule of Dionysius, he wants to provide advice and counsel to the letter's addressees, the friends of Dion (330c). The counsel he gives to them mirrors in some respects the counsel he and Dion gave to Dionysius. It almost has the tone of gossip—or rather the tone of someone desperately wanting to dispel gossip and set the record straight. It is filled with further defensive explanations of motives, but most importantly, it is firmly situated in a concern with listening—who said what to whom, who listened attentively, who spread rumors and who listened to those rumors, who could safely say certain things, who would react badly to hearing certain things, and how one might deftly approach the rather sticky situation of Dionysius's invitation for the third and final visit, given all that.

Plato begins with an analogy: just as a doctor might advise a patient whose way of life was threatening his health to change that way of life, so must Plato advise Dionysius. If someone will not listen to such advice, however, there is no point in advising. It is the same if one is advising one's city: one should advise, but if the stakes are such that there will be violence, then he should be silent (ἡσυχίαν, 330c–331d). Plato and Dion advised Dionysius, and now Plato advises the friends of Dion, to cultivate political friendships with those who seek virtue and to do so with an aim toward consolidating power in Sicily more effectively by forming relationships built on trust. Dionysius is apparently not good at making friends and allies, at least not with the right people (331e–332c). Plato and Dion cannot, of course, "say it thus bluntly, for that would scarcely have been safe, but instead made veiled references to his weaknesses" (332d). Meanwhile there are also rumors spreading that Dion is again plotting against Dionysius (333a), just as the rumors had circulated earlier that he was working with Plato to distract him with philosophy during the first voyage while Dion plotted a coup behind his back (329c). Dionysius, unfortunately, listens to the rumors (τοῖς διαβάλλοθσιν [ὑπήκοθσεν], 333b–c).[16] Needless to say, these rumors also trouble the second visit for Plato to instruct Dionysius after the failed first visit. A second visit from Plato might quell the worries of rebellion and save Dion, but a visit might just as easily add fuel to them. It is clear to Plato that Dionysius wants and needs the public show of Plato's approval that another visit from him would convey (333d–e), and behind all of this, still, is Dionysius's extreme neediness to hear praise. It would be difficult to understand why, under these circumstances, Plato might return yet again to Syracuse some six years later, but he does so in response to an urgent message from Dion.

At the time Plato addresses this *Letter* to the friends of Dion, they already know that Dion was indeed executed, and Plato's efforts to save him and to improve rule in Syracuse were undermined by the slanderers and their power over their hearers. As a consequence of all that, the *Letter* states pointedly that a man, a keen listener who was persuaded by Plato's lessons, has died nobly, and another man, who did not listen and who was not persuaded by Plato's lessons, lives on ignobly (334d–e). This injustice reminds Plato of the stories of the fates of our souls in the afterlife, linking their fates to their condition and ways of life in this life; these are stories that a poor soul does not listen to (οὔτε ἀκούει) but that a good soul does hear (ἀκούσῃ, 335b). Again, the divergent moral and political fates of Dion and Dionysius hinge on listening, and the *Letter*'s addressees are likewise, through this narration, being called to listen to what they ought.

Taking a somewhat distant view of the *Letter* so far, it sounds like this: The voice of Plato the letter writer comes to the fore, urging its addressees, friends of Dion, to listen to its authority alone.[17] Dionysius did not listen to that voice but rather to rumor and slander, and he is a lost cause, both politically and personally. Dion listened to Plato and chose to live uprightly as a result, but his murderers listened to false rumors, which Plato's voice and presence could not dispel. You, addressees, must listen to that voice now, and you must see that the real problems here are not listening to what you should listen to and listening to what you should not.

All of the rationalization for his voyage to Syracuse and its express theme of listening set the stage for the so-called digression, where the theme of listening is again compellingly present. Not knowing whether the rumors of Dionysius's ardor for philosophy were true, Plato tells us that there is a test (πεῖραν, 340b) for that sort of thing—a clear and most infallible test (πεῖρα . . . ἡ σαφής τε καὶ ἀσφαλεστάτη, 341a)—which is not ignoble (οὐκ ἀγεννής, 340b) but which is appropriate to use with tyrants (ἀλλ'ὄντως τυράννοις πρέπον, 340b): show them how arduous the task will be, how many things need to be done, and see if they still desire to philosophize (340b–341a). Not only is this test appropriate for testing tyrants, it is especially good for testing those who are full of what R. G. Bury translates as "borrowed doctrines" and Glenn Morrow translates as "philosophical commonplaces": *parakousmatôn*, which is literally a compound of "a thing heard" joined with the prefix that then renders the term along the lines of "a thing misheard."[18] The aim of the test is to get the listener to hear correctly what is entailed in philosophy and how challenging it is and then to see if he is still interested. "You must show to such a man the whole of the philosophic undertaking, describing what its nature is, and how many difficulties must be surmounted, and how much labor is involved. For whoever hears (*akousas*) this described, if he is a true lover of wisdom and possesses the divine quality which makes him worthy of pursuing it, will think you have told him a marvelous journey which he must at once undertake with all his strength, or life is not worth living" (340c).[19] The test Plato describes is thus a kind of hearing test: are you the sort who mishears bits and pieces of facile thought and thinks he is doing philosophy, or are you someone who can, after hearing exactly how difficult it can be to engage in philosophy, still retain your zeal for the task? The "digression" is this hearing test.[20]

Plato drives this point home in the passage that most clearly situates the "digression" as a hearing test and establishes Dionysius's character as weak—or, we might say, deaf—in response to the call of philosophical inquiry. This is the passage that introduces the "digression." It introduces what Dionysius is unable to hear and what would enthuse a person more genuinely zealous for philosophy. It is worth quoting at length:

> It was thus that I spoke to Dionysius upon my arrival. Consequently I did not explain all of my philosophy to him, nor did he ask me to, for he claimed to have already a sufficient knowledge of many of the most important points from his casual conversations with others (*tôn allôn parakoas*). Later, I hear (*akouô*), he wrote a book about what he had heard (*peri hôn tote âkouse*), putting it forward as an outline of his own philosophy and not things he heard from me (*ouden tôn autôn hôn akouoi*). Whether this is true or not I do not know. I do know that others have written on this subject, but without knowing what they were about. And this much at least I can affirm with confidence about anyone who has written or proposes to write on this matter pretending to a mastery of the problems with which I am occupied: It matters not whether he claims to have learned what he knows from [having heard] me (*eit'emou akêkootes*) or someone else or to have discovered it for himself, any man who ventures to write upon such subjects can know nothing (*epaiein ouden*) about them, in my opinion. There is no book of mine that expounds them, nor will there ever be one; for this knowledge is not a matter that can be transmitted in writing like other sciences (*mathâmata*). It requires long-continued intercourse (*pollês sunousias*) between pupil and teacher in joint pursuit of the object they are seeking to apprehend; and then suddenly (*exaiphnês*), just as light flashes forth when a fire is kindled, this knowledge is born in the soul and henceforth nourishes itself. (341a–d)[21]

Hearing, this passage makes abundantly clear, is unequivocally the excellence most needed. It is needed in order to be taken under Plato's tutelage and ultimately to become a virtuous person; it is needed for the long-term communal interactions necessary for philosophy. It is, as well, the excellence that Dionysius lacks. Even the claim in this passage that those who do write know nothing comes from a root verb, *epaiô*, that literally means "give ear to." Given this bold, even repetitive, introduction to the "digression" that homes in on hearing, we are attuned to the impending test. We already know that Dionysius will not fare well in grasping the technical and complex ideas Plato next describes. We already know that he does not have ears for philosophy. We already know the political costs of his deaf ears.

Dionysius's inability to hear what Plato says to him thus sets the context for and introduces the "digression." The letter then proceeds to make a case against the act of writing and explains the kind of weakness (ἀσθενές) in logos.[22] Plato lays out five distinct components in his account of the weakness of logos. Briefly, each existing thing has a name (ὄνομα), a definition (λόγος), and an image (ἔιδωλον), and without an understanding of each of these three, we cannot have knowledge (ἐπιστήμη)—a fourth component—of the thing itself (αὐτὸ, 342a–b), the fifth. Knowledge (ἐπιστήμη) of things does not reside in the voice or in bodily shapes of things (οὐκ ἐν φωναῖς οὐδ' εν σωμάτων σχήματων, 342c).[23] Humans make do in our everyday lives with the first four instruments of knowledge; when it comes to things in themselves, however, there is a problem. Since any definition consists of names and verbs, and since they are not at all stable (μηδὲν ἱκανῶς βεβαίως εἶναι βέβαιον)[24] and are obscure (ἀσαφές, 343b), we are left with inaccuracy in trying to convey the being or essence (τὸ ὄντος) of a thing in this way (343c), in either a written or spoken form (343d). The soul endeavors to know the thing itself, which is fixed and stable (*bebaios*, 343b), unlike the logos that attempts to grasp it, as the *Letter* emphasizes.[25] Consequently, there is a fundamental fissure between logos and the thing itself. We fare adequately enough when using and testing the four instruments of knowledge (name, definition, image, and knowledge of these three), but not with knowledge of the real thing itself, and these therefore give the soul what it is not seeking and instead fill everyone with the utmost perplexity and confusion (*aporias te kai asapheias*, 343c). The weakness of logos is thus its failure to grasp being or essence and convey it to the soul, which is what the soul seeks.

When it comes to answering questions or making explanations about the thing itself, the *Letter* tells us,

> But when it is the fifth or real object about which we are compelled
> to answer questions or to make explanations, then anyone who likes
> and is proficient in refutation can carry the day and make a speaker
> or writer or respondent seem to most of his listeners (*tois pollois tôn
> akouontôn*) completely ignorant of the subject on which he is trying
> to speak or write. Those who are listening[26] sometimes do not realize
> that it is not the mind of the speaker or writer which is being refuted,
> but these instruments of knowledge, each one of which is by nature
> fundamentally defective. (343d–e)

Plato concludes his account of Dionysius's test by telling us (twice) that the
young tyrant heard these things from Plato only once (ἅπαξ μόνον, 345a;
ἀκούσας μόνον ἅπαξ, 345a–b) and never again afterward, and Plato specu-
lates on the various reasons that there was never a second or third hearing,
gesturing at Dionysius's having failed the test.

Despite Plato's claim in the opening pages of the *Letter* that he was still
of a mind that rulers must be philosophers (326a–b), later in the letter, he is
arguing that good laws, instead of good men, are needed for good politics
(337a–e), as Drew Hyland notes.[27] As a consequence of the consistent portrayal of Dionysius as not up to the rigors of philosophy and as a dull, un-
practiced listener, the *Letter* shows his unfitness for philosophy and for rule.
It is reasonable to infer that Plato's experience thus dissuaded him from the
possibility and hope for philosophical rule, rule by good men. Hyland cites
a crucial passage in the *Letter*: "This is the attitude a wise man should have
toward his native city. . . . Let him warn her, if he thinks her constitution is
corrupt and there is a prospect that his words *will be listened to* and not put
him in danger of his life; but he should never use violence upon his mother
city to bring about a change of government. If he can establish the perfect
state without the exile and slaughter of men, he will keep his peace and pray
for the welfare of himself and his city" (331c–d; emphasis mine).[28] We have
another indication here of the centrality of listening for good politics. Even
wise men who aim to better the city face obstacles, obstacles that are rooted
in being heard. We have, furthermore, an indication that the *Letter* itself is
being written under those conditions. The letter is composed in conscious
awareness of its unlistening audience and of the very real danger surrounding it.

It is explicitly clear here that the inadequate logoi are things heard. The
weakness of logos that concerns Plato in the "digression" then must include

a weakness that lies either in the literal sounds of things expressed, the perception of the agent speaking, or in the agent to whom the audible expression is addressed and their inability to hear. Listeners can be deceived and manipulated by a speaker or writer. Listeners hear persuasive and clever arguments and become convinced, even when these convictions lack truth, and listeners fail to abide by the counsel they hear. And thus the weakness of logos must include things heard and hearers. Stability and knowledge reside not in voice (342c) but elsewhere, beyond the logos.

We saw in the first section that logos must necessarily include listening for the Greeks, and here I have argued that Plato is thematizing hearing in the *Letter* as a necessary excellence before engaging in philosophy—and hence necessary before virtue and good rule. We can now see the digression in this new light, as both a continuous part of the discussion, generally speaking, and more specifically as a hearing test aimed at determining whether Dionysius has the fortitude to take on the study of philosophy and to rule. The weakness of logos, then, is richer. Yes, it is an onto-linguistic weakness in the manner many interpreters talk about it: language fails to capture Being, and what language conveys to the soul is not the Being it (the soul) seeks. But beyond that, we can now see the weakness of logos also as rooted in hearing and listening. If logos includes things heard, it now involves social relations of speaker and listener, thus bringing it into the political realm. If logos includes things heard, it will not be heard by all, even if it could be said to them. If logos includes things heard, its weakness lies, as well, in its power, whether or not it is a true logos. Untruths, half-truths, rumor, slander—all of these have a power that needs to be reckoned with in the city.

## 3. The Politics of Hearing and Listening

The political importance of the aural thus emerges from the digression as well as the *Letter* in its entirety.[29] Those political concerns are rooted in the *Letter*'s stated aims of bringing political stability through truth-telling and working against the slanderers and irrational stories that threaten to destabilize the political situation further. These political instabilities mirror the instability (*bebaios*) of logos, which is rooted, in part, in failures of hearing and listening. What cannot be overlooked, in addition, is the manner in which the letter commands the ears of its audience, forcefully directing them to listen to the author and not to listen to other sources—to take its authority as singular. The *Letter* thus distinctly aims to control what and from whom the audience hears and in this way bring stability to the logos. "Forget the rumors about Dion's plans. Don't listen to the slander about my motivations," it says to us. "Here is the one true account, and political stability depends on your hearing it as such." Hearing thus links the stability of logos to political stability. Likewise, the weakness of logos and the weakness of the polis are linked.

The *Letter*'s complicated function, then, is to exhort a listening audience to hear—but to hear what its author wants the audience to hear, and to hear what will bring stability to a city. The *Letter*'s compelling force to make its audience hear one thing but not another, its powerful, coercive, constraining direction to its addressees, however, seems to belie its implicit juxtaposition between tyranny and philosophy.[30]

Victoria Wohl argues powerfully that the letters' obsessive focus is the entanglement of tyrant and philosopher:

> All thirteen letters are written to or concerning tyrants. Why tyrants? Tyrants haunt the Platonic corpus . . . As both his inverse and his double, the tyrant is the philosopher's other . . . This tyrant-other thus represents a power that the philosopher both longs for (the autocracy to rule himself and others according to reason) and must reject (for he has his eyes on a greater kingdom) . . . The [Second] letter's alternation between hierarchy and equality speaks to the paradox of being the equal of a tyrant—a man who, by nature, has no equal—and indeed the *Epistles* as a body reproduce this dynamic by giving us a dialogue in the form of a monologue: there are two voices, but only one can be heard.[31]

The narrative of the *Seventh Letter* is certainly controlled by its author in this way, and not just on the level of being a literary artifact written from a single narrative voice. Its central aim is to control the narrative in the world beyond the letter: to tell the story of a particularly controversial chapter of Plato's life, to portray his actions in a certain light, to justify his actions and failures to act, to save a city from violence and upheaval, and, equally important, to exculpate philosophy from the failure of a tyrant while maintaining philosophy's dominance as the cure for tyranny. To whom shall we listen? Plato. To whom shall we not listen? Tyrants who think they know Plato's philosophy and slanderers who tell falsehoods of Plato's actions and of Dion's plots in Syracuse. The *Seventh Letter* is thus an exercise of political power that dictates modes of hearing.[32] In these preliminary ways, we can begin to see the politics of hearing in the *Seventh Letter*, though it is not unique among Platonic writings.

The politics of hearing in the *Apology* track the politics of hearing in the *Seventh Letter* closely, specifically in its opening pages where Socrates first distinguishes himself in mock modesty from his accusers, whom the jury has just heard and by whom they were no doubt impressed. What they have heard from his accusers was powerful but false, and what they will hear from him, while less rhetorically impressive, will be true. He then mentions the terrible slander that he will also have to address in his defense; the jury will hear his account of the source of slander and his disputation of these damaging rumors that are in part responsible for his indictment, conviction, and execution. Repeatedly using cognates of *akuô* in these brief opening passages, Socrates disparages what the jury should not listen to and urges them to give him the hearing of which he is worthy (17b, 17c [twice], 18e, 19d [three times], 20d). As in the *Seventh Letter*, the political stakes are high. The Athenians' reception of the slander that has plagued much of Socrates's adult life, combined with their failure to listen appropriately to Socrates's defense, results in the death of the wisest, most right-minded man Plato and his companions had ever known (*Phaedo* 118a). What and whom we are prepared to hear and not to hear are thus politically central themes not just in these two works but in Plato's personal life and struggles with the city. His dashed hopes in Athens, as in Syracuse, are rooted in the politics of hearing. His concern with hearing in the polis seems to have motivated significant parts of the Platonic corpus.

The *Republic*'s famous opening, in which Polemarchus threatens to compel Socrates to stay for an evening of conversation, is exemplary of a concern with the politics of hearing. When Socrates indicates that he is on his way home, Polemarchus points out that Socrates is outnumbered—a threat, albeit a friendly and jocular one—and he tells Socrates he had better prove himself against them or remain for conversation. Socrates then suggests that there is another alternative: Socrates could persuade them to let him go. Polemarchus then retorts, "What if we won't listen?" (ὡς τοίνυν μὴ ἀκουσομένων ὅθτω διανοεῖσθε, *Republic* 327c). Regardless of how one might want to interpret this passage or its overall relationship to themes in the *Republic* or other dialogues, it shows clearly that force and persuasion are two modes of power, possibly even difficult to distinguish at some point, and that at least the latter depends on a listening audience.[33]

We see also in the *Republic* that, in addition to the philosophers' being lovers of the forms and of truth (476b–480a), they are administrators who put in place and sustain a specifically ordered regime, and they do so, in part, through compelled hearing. They must propagate a myth that ensures that their hearers accept the identity ascribed to them by the state (414b–415c). The citizens hear the myths from a young age, and presumably they must be repeated generation after generation. The origin myth establishes a social ontology. In the *kallipolis*, all will function well in the city if they are persuaded by the fabricated story they hear of who they are and what they should attend to in the city. Beyond myth, however, further gifts of the Muses are also necessary in the *kallipolis*, and these too are necessarily things heard. While philosophy and gymnastics make guardians more fit and braver—enhancing their high spirits—philosophy and gymnastics alone are not enough for the city (*Republic* 411c). Such a high-spirited soul, a potential guardian raised only with these, has no love of knowledge, and since such a soul does not share in music (*tâs mousikâs*), it becomes "feeble, deaf, and blind" (411d). This type of soul becomes the misologist, never turning to persuasion anymore and instead resorting to violence and savagery (*bia kai agriotêti*, 411d). But if music is poured into a guardian soul like a funnel to his ears (*katachein tês psuchês dia tôn otôn ôsper dia chônês*, 411a), it first softens his spiritedness like iron is softened so that it can be forged to be useful (*chrêsimon*), presumably useful for the city. If the citizen listens to too much, however, he is bewitched (*kêlêi*), becoming too soft, and the spiritedness melts away (*ektemêi*, 411a–b). The formation of the guardians and their requisite psychological shaping is crucial to the city not just because of their role as protectors but because from their lot will also emerge the philosopher-rulers, the same rulers who will propagate the useful lie to the next generation and establish the city's music—music that will shape future guardians and rulers.

The aim of music in the *kallipolis* is therefore twofold. First, it is in the mythic useful lie, to be heard appropriately so as to prescribe an identity and to dictate to citizens their place and role in the city. Second, and most salient here, the aim of music is nothing less than the self-perpetuation of the city, which relies necessarily on what is heard and by whom; music is necessary to create the guardian class, and the guardian class in turn creates and recreates the city through music. To put it yet another way, the education of the guardians aims, through the appropriate hearing of music, to create certain kinds of citizens, the best of whom can in turn compel the actions of others through more storytelling and persuasion that must be heard, and if successful, they will not have to resort to violence. In this way, the city creates the very subjects it needs to reproduce itself, and the reproduction of the city relies on hearing. To do one's own thing (τὰ αὑτοῦ πράττειν) in the city is, in truth, then, to do what one has heard is the task appropriate to the identity one has heard is one's own. And for the rulers, to do one's own thing means to compel others to hear the appropriate myths and other music in order to sustain justice in the city, and to prevent them from hearing what might destroy justice in the city.

Nor are these coercive politics of hearing limited to the *Republic*. More broadly speaking, what we see play out dramatically across the corpus could be described as Socrates vying for the ears of Athens and exercising his dialectic powers over some of them in contestation with the sophists, the young men's parents, the conservative elements in Athens, or other sources of political power.[34] Dialectic on this reading is not the benign counterpart of tyrannical edict or even physical force but a rival political power aimed at compelling hearers to listen to it to the exclusion of others. This reading of Platonic dialectic sits happily alongside Wohl's observations about the entangled relationship between tyranny and philosophy in the *Letters* and across the corpus. Taking just one example, Socrates argues explicitly in *Crito* that we should consider some people's opinions and not others' when it comes to training the body and, a fortiori, training the soul (47a–48a), thus countering Crito's concerns about what others will think if he is not able to aid Socrates's escape. Socrates's argument implies that Crito is not listening to whom or what he should listen to. This position is reinforced in the latter portion of the dialogue, in which hearing is explicitly taken up. Socrates ventriloquizes the personified Laws whose words command, shame, coerce, and ultimately force Crito into submission: "Be well assured, my dear friend, Crito, that this is what I seem to hear (ἐγὼ δοκῶ ἀκούειν), as the frenzied dervishes of Cybele seem to hear (δοκοῦσιν ἀκούειν) the flutes, and the sound of these words re-echoes within me and prevents my hearing any other words (ποιεῖ μὴ δύνασθαι τῶν ἄλλων ἀκούειν). And be assured that, so far as I now believe, if you argue against these words you will speak in vain. Nevertheless, if you think you can accomplish anything, speak" (54d).[35] Crito's response is, "No, Socrates, I have nothing to say." What Socrates seems to hear, he then forces Crito to hear. And what he forces Crito to hear completely shuts off any further argument.[36]

We frequently hear interlocutors protest that they are being tricked, manipulated, bewitched, or otherwise coerced into saying things they would not otherwise.[37] It seems appropriate to construe passages such as these as Socrates's attempts to compel hearing, at the very least, but hearing aimed at behavior and belief of a certain kind. The power—and danger—of Socrates's dialectic is in the listening and being compelled by its power. Wohl's reading of the letters as both grounds of contestation and mutual dependence between tyrannical and philosophical power would therefore seem to hold more generally across the dialogues. As she argues, the tyrant is never quite erased but rather lingers on "in Plato's fantasies of power: the Basileus, the philosopher king—and Socrates. Socrates," she says, "is the dead tyrant resuscitated."[38]

It is important to tread carefully here with the terms *tyrant* and *tyrannical*. While Wohl is certainly intending these terms in their literal Greek political context, referring to ruling and actual rulers as she discusses the letters and Plato's role in Syracuse, I intend something in addition to that. When talking about the dialectic, as opposed to Plato's involvement in Syracuse's politics and his own political views, I mean to suggest that there is an element of asserting power over the interlocutors and compelling behavior that they would not otherwise engage in.[39] The heteronomous compulsion of the dialectic—which distinctly vies for power over other voices, demanding to be listened to—is, at least in this sense, tyrannical. Socratic dialectic is competing for the ears of young men who would rather listen to sophists, it harangues the social elite to stop listening to the many, and it cajoles everyone to stop up their ears when the poets begin telling traditional tales. In these ways, the tyranny of the dialectic is up against other compelling logoi.[40] The dialectic could be described as a benign compulsion, literally aimed at the good, but it is nonetheless compulsion contrary to the will of the interlocutors in many instances. While I do not address here the Socratic argument that it *is* the will of the interlocutors to do good and that Socrates is only helping them do as they will, I mean to describe a face-to-face meeting with Socrates phenomenologically. Many interlocutors certainly experience the encounter as being harangued, harassed, bullied, tricked, or otherwise forced into a certain position and exhorted to behave contrary to their habitual desires. So, I want to place the dynamics of Socratic dialectic alongside Wohl's political claims about Plato's entanglement with Syracusan politics and his wrestling, qua author, with the tension between tyranny and philosophy in the dialogues.

The dramatization of dialectic is a clear demonstration of Socratic practices that compel a hearing. That compulsion may be required in the charged atmosphere of the many logoi competing for the souls of the Athenians (or Syracusans). That is to say, in the polis where there exist many strong logoi competing for hearers, the speakers of those logoi engage in behaviors to compel an audience. The *Letter*, while neither dialectic nor Socratic, contains just this kind of politics of hearing.

The compulsion of listeners draws back the curtain on an expanded account of the "weakness of logos" that Plato frets about in the *Seventh Letter*. As indicated above, that weakness includes the fragility of audience: people listen to and act on false stories, we can be persuaded by fear or anger to believe, and the powerful and charismatic can talk us into acting against our interests. "Listen to me" can be heard in many registers, including, " . . . or else!" The politically subordinate are especially attuned to the ways in which they are commanded to hear something a certain way and to engage in actions that demonstrate that they have gotten the message. Moreover, those forced to listen are often prevented from being heard. Soldiers and various others, for example, are compelled to a silence that is as much about their status and lack of power as it is about the power and status of those for whom they serve as audience.[41] There is a veiled threat in such commands to hear or listen, and although that threat does not appear in the *Seventh Letter*, we might see vestiges of it in some dialogues. In their way, the dialogues strong-arm the interlocutors and us into practicing philosophy, and they attempt to shame us if our beliefs do not pass dialectic muster or we do not heed the call.[42]

Although the *Seventh Letter* is not structured around Socratic dialectic, we see in it this demand to be heard—that is, we see its politics of hearing. Wohl says, "But if Dionysius lords it over Plato, Plato is still leader and master (ἡγεμόνα . . . καὶ κύριον) over the secret knowledge of true being (345c2). We have already been told, moreover, that a man must have an affinity for the thing in order to know it (344a2-b1). This means that although Dionysius acts the tyrant in the surrounding narrative, it is Plato who really knows tyranny . . . Platonic logos becomes king-law and tyrant-god; the philosopher trumps the tyrant by apotheosising himself."[43] Because Dionysius hardly fits the role of a low-level soldier being silenced, his very status as tyrant whom Plato is trying to silence with this letter to Dion's friends is therefore more evidence of the tyrannical aims of the letter. With Dion's keen listening and Dionysius's poor listening as background, the *Letter* obsessively talks about its hearers and exhorts them to listen while simultaneously admonishing them for listening to anything but the *Letter*.[44]

The *Seventh Letter*, along with the entire Platonic corpus, thus raises the questions of whether a less tyrannical form of hearing is possible; if so, what it would look like; and whether we can imagine a less or nontyrannical logos being a part of a different politics of hearing.

## 4. A Liberated Politics of Hearing

As I have been arguing, the *Seventh Letter* has a politics of hearing in which its various audiences are compelled to listen to specific counsel and to pay no attention to rumor and false narrative, and this is the case whether that audience is the one addressed directly by the letter, as the friends of Dion are, or is depicted in the narration, as Dion and Dionysius are, or addressed indirectly, as any incidental reader of the letter would be. All of it serves the interests of Plato and philosophy in his attempts to clear his own name and preserve the reputation of philosophy as political salvific. The politics of hearing in the *Seventh Letter*, in other words, vie with the power of the tyrant to bend the ear of the listener. We saw, too, that the *kallipolis* creates citizens who hear and are suited to hear the origin stories telling them whom they must be and what they must do, and in this way the *kallipolis* reproduces the very city whose order the citizens represent. Even in Socratic dialectic, we saw evidence of coercive politics of hearing. We might imagine, then, generally speaking, that with a different politics of hearing, citizens would hear radically different things than they do now and would hear radically differently than how they do now. Different *poleis* would condition different ways of hearing, so we can productively politicize and historicize hearing.

Karl Marx historicizes our sensory experiences, much like Fiumara's and Heidegger's recovery of hearing from the ancient Greeks, and while I will not delve deeply into a Marxist interpretation of these texts and the social relations that condition them, I do want to think historically about the politics of hearing in the *Seventh Letter*, specifically about whether they gesture toward a future liberation of hearing from a moment of tyrannized hearing. The structure of our shared life, Marx says, provides the conditions for how we experience the world, and he imagines that under conditions of true freedom, humans would experience a complete emancipation of the senses. He articulates the manner in which our unemancipated, alienated senses functioned by contrast.[45] He saw humans' sensory relationship to the objective world in his own time as stultifying and an impoverishment of our humanity, and those conditions "made us . . . stupid and one-sided," he says.[46] Upon radical liberation from these political conditions, however, "seeing, hearing, smelling, tasting, feeling, thinking, perceiving, sensing, wishing, acting, loving—in short all the organs of [our] individuality" would be transformed.[47] As I have been arguing, the *Seventh Letter* is a domineering call to listen to its counsel to the exclusion of all other voices. From this starting point, we might think about what liberation from those conditions would look like. That is to say, we might consider how "the human ear," as Marx called it, might hear differently from what he calls "the crude ear," but in the Greek context.[48]

The "crude ear" might hear only a logos of expression—saying, commanding, declaring, even questioning—but would ignore a more genuinely human listening, as concerns Fiumara. She sees our contemporary, limited understanding of logos as having shrunk from a more robust and human conception of logos among the ancient Greeks. Her project is thus, in part, an excavation of the change in meaning of *logos* in an effort to recover an older understanding of it: "If we start out from this basic concern we can then perhaps go back into the cultural wire-netting and discover how the mechanism of 'saying without listening' has multiplied and spread, to finally constitute itself as a generalized form of domination and control."[49] Where Fiumara sees a more human form of listening present in the ancient Greeks that predates what she sees as a corruption of this earlier logos, Heidegger is explicit that the "gathering together before being" is not a meaning of *legein* prior to "saying" but that the two constitute a simultaneous founding of *logos*. I am positing, contrary to both Fiumara and Heidegger, a still-tyrannical logos and a still-alienated form of hearing in the Greek classical period and specifically in Platonic writings.

I want nonetheless to return to Fiumara's account of the "other side of *logos*" and to its political dimensions as a means of exploring the possibility of liberating the senses. Fiumara distinguishes between power and strength, a distinction that lies at the foundation of what she wants to say about listening. She associates power with dominant and dominating contemporary expressive discourse, and she associates strength with a kind of receptive silence in listening. Against the exertion of power through logical discourse that continues to emerge from professional philosophy, Fiumara introduces the alternative strength that lies behind listening. The distinction is not, however, an immaculate differentiation, and at best we must "stumble and grope"[50] for the difference between power and strength from within the epistemic confines of the current cultural logocentrism.[51] Eventually, Fiumara links the strength of listening to Socratic midwifery and birth, saying that a certain open disposition, a "readiness to understand," gives life to a "listening event," which is relational: "The message from the other will not attain its expressive potential except in the context of a relationship through which the listening interlocutor actually becomes a participant in the nascent thought of the person who is talking."[52] The emphasis here on relation evokes traces of Heidegger's gathering together. I note that beyond relationality, her emphasis is also on birth and natality. She seems to locate genuine logos, necessarily inclusive of listening, in bringing forth the new from and with another. Over against this we might observe the "habitual use of the power of eloquence—that precious capacity to use language incisively and productively," which does not have the strength needed for midwifery.[53] That facility with expressive logos might even collude with deep defensive structures in the interlocutor and, instead of birthing any ideas, halt his nascent thinking.[54] The eloquent, the persuasive, the articulate, and the concise are hence, for Fiumara, associated with power, and they may be a cover for simple hostility or belligerence, as *philo-sophia* falls further and further from its earlier *philia*.[55] Strength, on the other hand, is more complicated and less well articulated.

Strength, for Fiumara, lies perhaps in something opposite to power—a kind of weakness but also something categorically different: "The emerging idea is that of a 'weakness' that distinguishes and distances itself from power, that neither disguises nor annuls itself, that neither attacks nor flees; such 'weak' mode, then, appears to be grounded upon an extraordinary strength."[56] And here we return to the weakness of logos, which is also central to the *Seventh Letter*, but we must parse out the quotation marks that Fiumara puts around this weakness. The weakness in silence is only a perceived weakness, and it is perceived as weakness only within the assertive or exclusively expressive context of logos. That is to say, when Fiumara puts *weak* and *weakness* in quotation marks, she means to indicate that this is a kind of weakness only from the perspective of domination and power. Hence, we can understand the seeming paradox of strength emerging from and rooted in weakness—or rather, "weakness." Strength emerges from the act of listening, and listening to another in relation.

Living in relation or in philosophical community is the focus of Hyland's treatment of the *Seventh Letter*, and he notes that living the philosophical life entails living over a period of time together or dwelling in community, emphasizing the Greek terms *sunousias* and *suzēn*.[57] He cites this passage from the so-called digression: "There does not exist, nor will there ever be, any written work of mine on these things. For it cannot at all be put into words like other objects of learning, but only after a long period of dwelling together (*sunousias*) concerning the subject itself and living together (*suzēn*) with it, when suddenly like a light kindled by a leaping spark, it comes to be in the soul and at once becomes self-nourishing" (341c–d).[58] In this regard, Hyland's project shares a deep connection to that of Robert Metcalf.[59] Both aim to understand philosophy as a way of life, or in Metcalf's terms, a life-structuring practice, and both understand philosophy as necessarily taking place within a community. I see in their work a way to think about a liberated politics of listening.

Hyland recognizes the ambiguity of the passage in the *Letter* just cited, which seems to say on the surface that the dwelling together is between the thinker and the object of thought, but he makes a case that even this must happen dialogically and so, "in the spirit of the dialogues," we can imagine that "philosophy is something that must be *lived together.*"[60] Even so, he expresses concern about the disappearance of the subject here, if the unity is only between subjective thinker and object of thought, for this would also seem to diminish any need for human community in the practice of philosophy. And yet, we can return to Heidegger's rich sense of community that involved the saying, the hearing, and Being. We can perhaps relish the ambiguity between subjects gathering together in community and the addressee experiencing *homolegein* with Being. Heidegger's "All One" seems to capture both of these kinds of community.

Hyland's anxiety about community comes through, however, even as he considers Plato's portrayal of Socratic dialectic. He expresses concern over the "diminishing of the significance of subjectivities in the name of philosophy, in the very presence of one astonishingly dominant—not to say domineering—personality, that of the Platonic Socrates."[61] I think Hyland is right to be worried. As I have argued above, Socratic dialectic, even if carried out with others, has its tyrannical aspects, and it seems fair to wonder whether this type of togetherness is true community.

Metcalf's work aims to understand community in a way that opens up our thinking about this tension between philosophy and tyranny, though not in a way that ultimately solves the problem of dialectic's tyrannical aspects, as I have laid those out. Instead of seeing a tension between community and *agôn*, Metcalf argues for their inseparability. He even argues that the *agôn* plays a constitutive role in creating community. Metcalf says that "while for us the word *agôn* seems to point most directly to a scene or event of contestation, in Homer, the most profound meaning of *agôn*, then, is the gathering-together of mortals in the testing and exhibition of strength or excellence, through which the community as a whole is bound together."[62] He explains further about the etymology and history of the *agôn*:

> While the *agôn* can certainly generate hostility between individuals, we must not overlook the fact that it allows for a unity among the groups who gather together to witness or participate in the *agôn*—and here we note the original meaning of the *agôn* as "gathering," its more familiar meaning as "contest" being derivative from this. Indeed when we examine Homeric portrayals of the *agôn* . . . we find a rich linguistic context wherein the meaning of *agôn* is clarified by way of words from the same root—such as *agora*, "gathering place," and the imperative ἄγε, "Come, gather-together," which summons participants and spectators to the *agôn*.[63]

The *agôn* summons us, and it gathers us together, and for that gathering to happen we must hear the call. Metcalf's vision of Platonic philosophy then is essentially agonistic, "where the *agôn* is structured so as to draw the adversaries together in agreement, *homologia*, about the matters at issue, though that agreement is always open to future contestation."[64] Here again, we have a gathering together, as we saw in Heidegger's work on logos, where agreement, *homo-legein*, binds us with each other and with the Being we seek through logos. Metcalf and Hyland both share a slightly more benign vision of Socratic dialectic than mine, though Hyland does have some uneasiness about Socrates's domineering behavior. Metcalf, Hyland, Heidegger, and Fiumara collectively provide a vision of philosophy and Socratic dialectic as Plato constructed them, and while it shows glimpses of what a fully liberated politics of hearing would look like—a gathering together when we hear the call, to listen or hearken to Being and each other, to contend with each other in and through a shared life—I want to argue that listening, and dialectic, as they appear in the Platonic corpus are not fully liberated.

What we see in the *Letter* and in the dialogues more generally, I suggest, is a politics of hearing aimed at creating readers and citizens whose senses can be liberated—a propaedeutic, if you will, for a liberated politics of hearing. The propaedeutic is paradoxical, however: an audience that does not yet exist is called by an auditory it cannot yet hear properly, so as to bring about the hearing it needs to heed that call. It is not controversial to claim that the dialogues, ideally speaking at least, might turn the nonphilosopher toward philosophy, and we might look at specific writing techniques Plato employs in the dialogues that do just that. Through philosophy, Plato turns the nonphilosopher toward philosophy.[65] What I claim here is a cousin to that view: that Platonic writing aims to take a certain kind of hearer and hearing that are not yet liberated and prepare them for liberation, to prepare ears to hear a logos they have not yet heard. Indeed, there are other examples of philosophers who aim to bring into existence the very audience they think needed through writing techniques that attune audiences to more proper hearing.[66] Metcalf, Hyland, Heidegger, and Fiumara help us see how the Platonic writings might prepare their readers for a gathering together in human community in which hearing is liberated from tyranny. That is to say, the *Letter* and other Platonic works bend our ears toward liberation and call us to a true human community without any guarantees that we can or will hear the call.

As Wohl and Hyland agree, the Platonic corpus—letters and dialogues—is shaped by dominance and submission, and I argue that such measures are necessitated by the politics that condition the writings that comprise the Platonic corpus. In this sense, Platonic writings are tyrannical because there are tyrants.[67] Plato's writings are conditioned by the weakness of logos, which includes, as I have argued, weakness of hearing. The ears of listeners can be compelled by logoi that are false or harmful or misleading, and Plato is therefore vying for the ears of the audience to compel them in a direction toward no longer needing such compulsion. But despite Hyland's and Wohl's concerns about domination in the Platonic writings, Metcalf makes the case that the *agôn* creates the conditions for a certain kind of community, that the *agôn* creates a type of both *philia* and *koinônia* "compatible with friendship and productive of excellence." Metcalf goes on to distinguish philosophical practices from rhetorical practices that aim at the enslavement of their audiences and "relate to others within a complicated web of compulsion, domination, and submission."[68] I take issue with Metcalf here, seeing similarities between Socratic dialectic and rhetoric, at least insofar as they work through compulsion, domination, and submission. As I have argued, these strike me as exactly the means through which

Socrates often, though not always, works and the means through which the *Seventh Letter* certainly aims to compel a specific hearing. I do agree with Metcalf, however, that the Platonic writings do not aim at the enslavement of their audiences but at their liberation. We might think of the *agôn*, as Metcalf describes it, as aspirational in Platonic writing. In the *Seventh Letter*, Plato compels exclusive hearing in a tyrannical way so that its addressees and readers can enter into better listening, hearkening, silence, and receptiveness.

To create and foster community is one of the primary functions in ancient Greek letters, whether those of Plato or Epicurus or even Paul's letters to the various early communities of pagan converts to Christianity in the Greek-speaking world.[69] Certainly, there was an aim to forge a connection between the writer and the addressees. Extending beyond that, letters aim to expand the community by communicating a message that, it is hoped, will be shared by yet unknown addressees. Ancient letters cross geographical and temporal space to create and expand community, to join together a group of people through knowledge, belief, and practice. This is perhaps akin to Hyland's notion of our shared life. Plato's letters aim exactly at that, accompanied by an explicit anxiety over the weakness of logos that can plague a city.

The weakness of logos, however, is not purely political. It is ontological as well, and here we return to the digression and its integration into the *Letter* as a whole. The weakness of logos introduced in the digression is an ontological and a political weakness. First, in its attempts to capture Being or grasp the ungraspable, logos fails to wrestle into submission what cannot be subdued. Second, the weakness of logos is an equally intractable failure of humans to consistently hear the truth, instead often heeding the call of lies, rumor, deception, and demagoguery. This is an auditory failure built into the human condition.[70] The *Letter* exposes twin problems: neither can logos reach out toward Being in a unifying grasp, nor can humans hear the correct logos, the one needed for genuine community, true gathering together. This weakness of logos, however, does not stop Plato from wielding the logos for the purposes of human thriving, philosophy, and improvement. That is at the root of his politics. The *Letter*'s politics of hearing are situated in our human limitation yet also situated in our connection to others, our potential for listening and acting in concert with each other in the polis. This politically and ontologically integrated reading of the *Seventh Letter* thus implies an inherent weakness, central to the human condition, and perhaps not capable of being overcome in any political context. And yet, in the face of this weakness, there is a call to unite, to gather together.

The gathering together in community, then, must necessarily be a unity in the face of this weakness inherent in the human condition, having both the onto-linguistic and political resonances. The hearkening is to Being and to truth.[71] The *alêtheia* toward which logos reaches out Heidegger calls the "unconcealment," but this is a distinctly visual appreciation of *a-lêtheia*. The escaping notice of the Greek verb *lanthanô* at the root of this strange word for "truth" need not be tied to the sense of seeing. It could also be a cessation of the silencing of Being. We might think of *alêtheia* as, instead, the unmuted, the unmuffled, or the voice of Being and beings with whom we are gathered together.

The gathering together or community we have been discussing in light of the *Seventh Letter* is, I argue, merely and necessarily aspirational. The political conditions for its existence were not present in Plato's world, nor are they present in ours. The senses are not yet, and may never be, liberated in a fashion that permits hearkening, *homolegein* with being, gathering together, or true philosophical community. What I argue the *Seventh Letter* aims to do—as well as Socratic dialectic as depicted in the Platonic dialogues—is to condition our hearing toward discernment and listening, though doing so necessarily through coercive means. Those means are necessary because we are not yet in a liberated condition. Dialectic therefore has its tyrannical side in an effort to make us into proper listeners. The visions of logos in the works of Hyland, Metcalf, and Fiumara are visions of philosophy more akin to what I imagine might be possible after a radical revolution of the senses— or perhaps we could call them the sound of philosophy that is being created while Plato has our ears, telling of the conditions needed for a kind of action that is possible only after those conditions hold. This is the challenge Plato takes up: to call to us in a manner that we can hear, in order to tell us that we cannot hear properly and to direct us toward more liberated hearing. If we listen to the *Seventh Letter*, we just might hear that call.[72]

## Notes

1. The paper neither takes a position on nor depends on the authenticity of the *Seventh Letter* as a Platonic text, though I refer to its author throughout as "Plato."

2. See, for example, Ludwig Edelstein, *Plato's Seventh Letter* (Leiden: Brill, 1966); Francisco J. Gonzalez, "Nonpropositional Knowledge in Plato," *Apeiron* 31, no. 3 (1998): 235–284; Drew A.

Hyland, "Why Plato Wrote Dialogues," *Philosophy and Rhetoric* 1, no. 1, (1968): 38–50; Drew A. Hyland, *Plato on the Question of Beauty* (Bloomington: Indiana University Press, 2008); Glenn Morrow, *Studies in Plato's Epistles* (Urbana: University of Illinois Press, 1935).

3. What is called the "digression" can be found at 341c–345a. I have argued for the integrity and continuity of this dialogue's political concerns and its concerns about logos in "Knowledge/Power in the *Seventh Letter* or Why the Digression Is Not a Digression," in *Philosopher Kings and Tragic Heroes: Proceedings of the First Interdisciplinary Symposium on Hellenic Heritage of Southern Italy*, eds. Heather L. Reid and Davide Tanasi (Sioux City, IA: Parnassos, 2016).

4. And we know, too, that during this period most reading would have been done aloud, and reading silently to oneself would have been rare. I shall not distinguish here between hearing and listening, relying on cognates of ἀκούω for both English terms.

5. Οὐκ ἐμοῦ ἀλλὰ τοῦ Λόγου ἀκούσαντας / ὁμολογεῖν σοφόν ἐστιν Ἕν Πάντα. Modified translation of Richard McKirahan and Patricia Curd in Patricia Curd, ed., *A Pre-Socratics Reader*, 2nd ed. (Indianapolis: Hackett, 2011), 42. As the ensuing discussion shows, Heidegger's translation of the Heraclitus fragment differs most significantly with respect to the connection between "all" and "one" and with respect to *homologein*—what is in agreement with what and what the nature of that "agreement" is.

6. Martin Heidegger, *Early Greek Thinking: The Dawn of Western Philosophy*, trans. David Ferrell Krell and Frank Capuzzi (New York: Harper and Row, 1984), 60. Hereafter cited parenthetically.

7. In what follows, pp. 69–78, Heidegger addresses the verbs *eidenai* and *einai*, which some manuscript editors conjecturally supply, moving toward the common translation "All is One" or "One is All." Ultimately, Heidegger continues his work on the fragment by taking the elliptical (at least to our ears!) Ἕν Πάντα in its literal presentation.

8. Gemma Fiumara, *The Other Side of Language: A Philosophy of Listening* (New York: Routledge, 1995), 16. Hereafter cited parenthetically. See Jonathan Rée's review of her book in *Radical Philosophy* 58 (1991): 41–42. Despite some of Rée's criticisms of this book's limitations—some apt and others off the mark—I find the kernel of Fiumara's analysis salient: twentieth-century philosophy, and European and American culture more broadly speaking, operate with an impoverished conception of logos as expressive language, overlooking and diminishing "the other side" of logos: listening. Moreover, I find the political implications of Fiumara's thesis especially salient, even beyond the academy. She is attuned to the issues of domination and subordination that result from the derogation or omission of listening in our dialogical encounters (issues that Rée ironically reproduces in his sarcastic, condescending, and arrogant review, in my opinion), and I turn to these political implications in the final section of the paper.

9. 324 b, 327a, 330b, 333c, 335b (twice), 336c, 337e, 338e, 339a, 339e, 340c, 341b (four times), 341c, 344d, 345a, 349a.

10. Though I suggest this with some lightness, it would not be surprising if Plato were aware of the pun on Syracuse, *Sur-akousas*. It is certainly clear in other contexts that he intentionally puns and uses homophones to great effect. See Jill Gordon, *Turning toward Philosophy: Literary Device and Dramatic Structure in Plato's Dialogues* (University Park: Pennsylvania State University Press, 1999); Jill Gordon, *Plato's Erotic World: From Cosmic Origins to Human Death* (Cambridge: Cambridge University Press, 2012), 53–80.

11. Unless otherwise noted, translations come from Morrow, *Studies in Plato's Epistles*. Here only the first phrase comes from Morrow's translation; the second is my own.

12. I use "Dionysius" to refer to Dionysius II, the central historical figure in the *Seventh Letter*. Morrow (*Studies in Plato's Epistles*) has a useful review of Dionysius II's appearance in ancient sources.

13. There are three trips to Syracuse in all: first, when Dion is a young man and Plato tutors him, a time at which Dionysius is a child; second, when he tutors Dionysius, now a ruler, for the first time; and third, when he returns to tutor Dionysius a second time. Because the first trip to educate Dion plays such a small role in the narrative, the text is sometimes equivocal on which is the "second" trip, whether it is Plato's second voyage overall or the second trip to work with Dionysius the tyrant. I follow the text and sometimes refer to Plato's "second" trip as the second trip he took to educate Dionysius (but third overall). I believe it is clear in context which trip I am referencing.

14. Morrow notes that Plato was clearly responding to criticisms that had been made about his actions and motives and that those "criticisms rankle a little" (*Studies in Plato's Epistles*, 196n2.

15. The phrase that Morrow (*Studies in Plato's Epistles*) translates as "I shrank from thinking of myself as a mere theorist," Bury translates as "lest haply I should seem to myself to be utterly and absolutely nothing more than a mere voice": μὴ δόξαιμί ποτε ἐμαυτῶι παντάπασι λόγος μόνον ἀτεχνῶς. While both capture Plato's fear of failing to do in practice what he claims is good and right to do in words, I find Bury's gloss interesting. Bury's implication is that a mere voice is ineffectual, but logos that results in action or action consistent with one's logos is laudable. Since I want to read the *Seventh Letter* as a type of logos that commands a particular hearing followed by particular action—that is to say, the letter is a political logos—this would mean that it is a logos that is no "mere voice" but one that commands to be heard and heard in a certain way, even by oneself.

16. Additional text supplied by Bury.

17. In two places during the advice and counsel, which runs from approximately 331e to 337e, Plato explicitly invokes the listening relationship with his addressees. He urges them to hear (ἀκοῦσαι) what took place (333c), and he emphasizes that his addressees have now heard (ἀκηκόατε) of Dion's way of life and its worthiness of imitation (336c).

18. See the LSJ entry, which gives these definitions: "thing heard amiss, false notion," "false story or report," and "equivocation." Henry George Liddell and Robert Scott, *A Greek-English Lexicon*, s.v. "parakousmatôn," via the Perseus Digital Library, accessed December 29, 2021, http://www.perseus.tufts.edu/hopper/text?doc=Perseus%3Atext%3A1999.04.0057 %3Aentry%3Dpara%2Fkousma. A bit later in the *Letter*, those who only feign philosophic inclination are like sunburned bodies that are only tinged with skin-deep color (340d–e).

19. Slightly modified from Morrow's translation: ὁ γὰρ ἀκούσας, ἐὰν μὲν ὄντως ἦ φιλόσοφος οἰκεῖός τε καὶ ἄξιος τοῦ πράγματος θεῖος ὢν, ὁδόν τε ἡγεῖται θαθμαστὴν ἀκηκοέναι ξυντατέον τε εἶωαι νῦν καὶ οὐ βιωτὸν ἄλλως ποιοῦντι μετὰ τοῦτο δὴ ξυντείνας.

20. See Gordon, "Knowledge/Power," where I first argued that the digression is a test of Dionysius aimed at discerning whether he is suitable for philosophical engagement. There I emphasized Plato's distinction between those who can and those who cannot "follow," and I made connections to the digression (*planô*) as a wandering or a roaming. I argued, as well, that this wandering has continuity with what comes before and after. The so-called digression in *Theaetetus* is something beside the main point, a parergon. (Though, of course, the digression in *Theaetetus*, like that in the *Seventh Letter*, is also of a piece with the rest of that dialogue.)

21. Slightly modified and supplemented translation from Morrow, *Studies in Plato's Epistles*. Just an aside: Humorously, at least to my ear, Plato seems to complain that Dionysius

presented his philosophical ideas without crediting him ("Hey, those are *my* ideas!"), and, at the same time, he complains that Dionysius does not know anything about his ideas ("What are you talking about? I never said that!").

22. There are many, many detailed accounts of the digression, its structure and meaning. As just a tiny and perhaps idiosyncratic sample, see Giorgio Agamben and Julia Schiesari, "The Thing Itself," *Substance* 16, no. 2 (1987): 18–28; Gonzalez, "Nonpropositional Knowledge in Plato"; Andrew Hull, "The Mystery of the Seventh Platonic Epistle: An Analysis of the Philosophical Digression" (PhD diss., Emory College of Arts and Sciences, 2012); V. Bradley Lewis, "The Rhetoric of Philosophical Politics in Plato's 'Seventh Letter,'" *Philosophy and Rhetoric* 33, no. 1 (2000): 23–38; Eric W. Robinson, "The Sophists and Democracy beyond Athens," *Rhetorica* 25, no. 1 (2007): 109–122; Harold Tarrant, "Middle Platonism and the Seventh Epistle," *Phronesis* 28, no. 1 (1983): 75–103. What follows draws from Gordon, "Knowledge/Power."

23. It is interesting to note that Morrow translates οὐκ ἐν φωναῖς as "not in words" instead of "not in voice " or "not in sound" (*Studies in Plato's Epistles*, 207).

24. Note the cognate object, which Bury translates as "fixed with sufficient firmness."

25. Cognates of this term appear four times in just this portion of the Stephanus page at 343b. One could perhaps make the argument that the inherent instability in logos corresponds to an inherent instability in political power, as depicted in the *Seventh Letter* and in other Platonic texts.

26. The subject of a later clause in the passage, the listeners, is not actually repeated in the Greek. Morrow (*Studies in Plato's Epistles*) breaks up the long sentence that comprises this passage into two, and he begins the second sentence, "Those who are listening," thus repeating its subject from the clause in the first sentence, "his listeners."

27. Hyland, *Question of Beauty*, 101–103.

28. Cited in Hyland, *Question of Beauty*, 102, using a slightly different translation. I use Morrow's translation here. The phrase that I emphasize, "if . . . his words will be listened to," which appears in both Hyland and Morrow, could also be translated as "if . . . his words would not be in vain" (λέγειν . . . εἰ μέλλοι μήτε ματαίως ἐρεῖν). Hyland notes, with regard to the violence mentioned in the passage, the contrast with the *Republic* in which all those over the age of ten must be slaughtered in order for the *kallipolis* to come into existence.

29. See Gordon, "Knowledge/Power," where I make an argument for the continuity between the digression's epistemic focus and the *Letter*'s political concerns on yet other grounds.

30. It is worth laying out a complication with regard to audience. The structure of the *Seventh Letter* consists in Plato's giving counsel to four different audiences: to Dion; to his nephew, Dionysius II; to the addressees of this letter, the friends of Dion; and, finally, to the unknown readers of the *Seventh Letter* beyond the friends of Dion. These counsels do not appear sequentially, however, since at various times multiple audiences are hearing the counsel. It is productive to ask which of these counsels was heard, by whom, and whether it was heeded. Answers to those questions are relevant to what I argue here about the kind of political power exercised by the letter.

31. Victoria Wohl, "Plato avant le Lettre: Authenticity in Plato's Epistles," *Ramus* 27, no. 1 (1998): 66–67.

32. Despite the history of scholarship on "Platonism" that tells us that Plato eschews the bodily senses because of the burdens and obstacles they place on the soul and its desire for truth, there is evidence across the Platonic corpus of an awareness of the power of hearing,

or more properly, the power of making people listen. In the *Letter*, Plato is appealing to our sense of hearing, and he deploys that toward his own ends, hence finding our bodily and sensual faculties philosophically and politically useful and perhaps necessary. I provide a few other examples in the following discussion with respect to hearing, but there is vast evidence across the Platonic corpus of Plato's deep understanding of human sensory perception and imagination—and his willingness to appeal to them. See Gordon, *Turning toward Philosophy*.

33. A similar description of coerced hearing appears at *Philebus* 15e–16a just after Socrates tells the interlocutors that once boys discover "the one and the many in *logos*" (ἓν καὶ πολλὰ ὕπο λόγων, 15d4), they are so delighted that they want to set every argument in motion and engage everyone and anyone promiscuously, all humans who can hear (τῶν ἀκουόντων, 16a)—young, old, peer, father, mother, any human, animals, and even the barbarian.

34. Aristophanes's *Clouds*, despite its comic exterior, cloaks a serious fear of Socrates's dialectic power. This play shows repeatedly that dialectic power aims to assert itself as political power. If it is allowed to reign, sons will beat their fathers, literally and metaphorically. And as my discussion of the *Apology* above makes clear, the significant public audience who heard this play performed, or merely heard about it, had quite an effect not just on Socrates's fate but on the fate of Athens, as Plato describes it.

35. Trans. Harold North Fowler (Cambridge, MA: Harvard University Press, 1990).

36. Again, the text seems to emphasize what is heard and by whom through its concentrated repetition of cognates of *akouô*, occurring six times between 49e and 54d but nowhere else in this dialogue (Perseus Project Online cognate search, August 13, 2019). For a different interpretation of this passage in *Crito*, see Mitchell Miller, "The Arguments I Seem to Hear," *Phronesis* 41, no. 2 (1996): 121–137.

37. See, for example, *Meno* 79e–80a; *Republic* 340d, 341a–b. (Note, too, that at 344d Thrasymachus is described as having poured his speech over the ears of those gathered, but Socrates will counter with a different account of justice for the audience.)

38. Wohl, "Plato avant le Lettre," 83.

39. The reader, however, is another matter entirely, and as my conclusion here details, the relationship Plato may inculcate with the reader is distinct from what I am claiming about the relationship between Socrates and interlocutors in the dialectic. I treat Plato's relationship with the reader in depth in Gordon, *Turning toward Philosophy*.

40. Jesper Svenbro (*Phrasikleia*, trans. Janet Lloyd [Ithaca, NY: Cornell University Press, 1993]) likens the reader to the submissive *eromenos* and the writer to the *erastês*. When I speak of tyranny and compulsion, I don't intend that particular kind of domination and submission, though I don't necessarily see it as wildly inconsistent with the domination that Socrates asserts over his interlocutors in the dialectic, in which they must listen to Socratic argument. I am focused on a kind of political domination here in which the stability of our common life in the city is at stake. Where Svenbro is making an analogy, my view tends more toward a literal politics of hearing. For a treatment of eros in the dialogues, see Gordon, *Plato's Erotic World*.

41. Jeremy Bell, in this volume, lays out the evidence for the deployment of logos as a means to silence, and his account of the politics of silence in the classical period is a welcome companion here.

42. See Gordon, *Turning toward Philosophy*, regarding an array of inducements to philosophize embedded in the dialogues' literary devices and dramatic structure. On shame, in particular, see 22–28.

43. Wohl, "Plato avant le Lettre," 70.

44.  See Eric Havelock, *Preface to Plato* (Cambridge, MA: Belknap Press of Harvard University Press, 1982), who argues that "the speaking place of the prince who commands the speech which will resolve a quarrel and control a throng, is not Mycenaean but contemporary. It is a picture of the oral technique at the service of government in a non-literate community. And these habits of communication long survived in Greek culture. They are in fact essentially part of the secret of Greek culture and the Greek way of life down to the Periclean age" (121).

45.  Karl Marx, "Economic and Philosophic Manuscripts," in *Karl Marx: Selected Writings*, ed. Lawrence H. Simon (Indianapolis: Hackett, 1994), 74.

46.  Marx, 74.

47.  Marx, 73.

48.  Marx, 74. The crude ear, of course, is the ear of bourgeois private property ownership for Marx, and I do not want to ascribe this particular ideological form of hearing, or the economic base that gives rise to it, to the classical Greeks. As I have been arguing, however, the *Letter* and dialectic in other dialogues can be tyrannical, but other, perhaps more humane, politics of hearing are possible.

49.  Fiumara, *Other Side of Language*, 2.

50.  Fiumara, 62.

51.  Fiumara, 63.

52.  Fiumara, 144.

53.  Fiumara, 146.

54.  Fiumara, 145.

55.  Fiumara, 109.

56.  Fiumara, 62.

57.  Hyland, *Question of Beauty*, 104–114.

58.  Hyland, 103. Hyland's translation. For a deeper look at these Greek ideas of living together in community, see Sara Brill, *Aristotle on the Concept of Shared Life* (Oxford: Oxford University Press, 2020). Brill also discusses shared perception or *sunaeistheia*.

59.  Robert Metcalf, *Philosophy as Agôn: A Study of Plato's "Gorgias" and Related Texts* (Evanston, IL: Northwestern University Press, 2018).

60.  Hyland, *Question of Beauty*, 104; emphasis in original.

61.  Hyland, 105.

62.  Metcalf, *Philosophy as Agôn*, 13.

63.  Metcalf, 13.

64.  Metcalf, 7.

65.  The thesis of Gordon, *Turning toward Philosophy*.

66.  Heraclitus's riddling and paradoxical logoi attune us to hear the logos when we previously could not; see Decker in this volume. Zarathustra in Nietzsche's prologue to *Thus Spoke Zarathustra* claims, after speaking of the Übermensch to the crowd, that he is "not the mouth for these ears" (stanza 5) and later that he is "far from them" and "his sense did not speak unto their senses" (stanza 7). And then Zarathustra awakes from a long sleep, and when light dawns on him, he realizes that what he needs are companions (stanza 9). We might look at the Nietzschean project as the attempt to create, or at least search for, those companions. That is to say, Zarathustra is looking for ears to whom he can speak, and the work could be understood as a project to create those listeners, to bring them into existence through the writing itself.

67.  I owe this expression to Ryan Drake, personal conversation, July 17, 2019.

68.  Metcalf, *Philosophy as Agôn*, 142.

69. For deeper work on the epistolary tradition among the ancient Greeks, see Ruth Morello and A. D. Morrison, eds., *Ancient Letters: Classical and Late Antique Epistolography* (Oxford: Oxford University Press, 2007), especially their preface; John Muir, *Life and Letters in the Ancient Greek World* (New York: Routledge, 2008); Owen Hodkinson, Patricia A. Rosenmeyer, and Evelien Bracke, eds., *Epistolary Narratives in Ancient Greek Literature* (Boston: Brill, 2013).

70. Nor is it to be confused with the weakness that Fiumara designates by her scare quotes.

71. The openness and receptiveness of proper listening, of course, cannot be an openness to everything and anything. Hearkening cannot be promiscuous. Liberation of the senses is not license of the senses.

72. I owe a large debt to Ryan Drake and Holly Moore for constructive feedback, productive challenges, great conversations, and, of course, attentive listening during the writing of this chapter.

# Bibliography


Agamben, Giorgio, and Julia Schiesari. "The Thing Itself." *Substance* 16, no. 2 (1987): 18–28.

Brill, Sara. *Aristotle on the Concept of Shared Life.* Oxford: Oxford University Press, 2020.

Curd, Patricia, ed. *A Pre-Socratics Reader.* 2nd ed. Translated by Richard McKirihan and Patricia Curd. Indianapolis: Hackett, 2011.

Edelstein, Ludwig. *Plato's Seventh Letter.* Leiden: Brill, 1966.

Fiumara, Gemma. *The Other Side of Language: A Philosophy of Listening.* New York: Routledge, 1995.

Gonzalez, Francisco J. "Nonpropositional Knowledge in Plato." *Apeiron* 31, no. 3 (1998): 235–284.

Gordon, Jill. "Knowledge/Power in the *Seventh Letter* or Why the Digression is Not a Digression." In *Philosopher Kings and Tragic Heroes: Proceedings of the First Interdisciplinary Symposium on Hellenic Heritage of Southern Italy.* Edited by Heather L. Reid and Davide Tanasi. Sioux City, IA: Parnassos, 2016.

———. *Plato's Erotic World: From Cosmic Origins to Human Death.* Cambridge: Cambridge University Press, 2012.

———. *Turning toward Philosophy: Literary Device and Dramatic Structure in Plato's Dialogues.* University Park: Pennsylvania State University Press, 1999.

Havelock, Eric. *Preface to Plato.* Cambridge, MA: Belknap Press of Harvard University Press, 1982.

Heidegger, Martin. *Early Greek Thinking: The Dawn of Western Philosophy.* Translated by David Ferrell Krell and Frank Capuzzi. New York: Harper and Row, 1984.

Hodkinson, Owen, Patricia A. Rosenmeyer, and Evelien Bracke, eds. *Epistolary Narratives in Ancient Greek Literature.* Boston: Brill, 2013.

Hull, Andrew. "The Mystery of the Seventh Platonic Epistle: An Analysis of the Philosophical Digression." PhD diss., Emory College of Arts and Sciences, 2012.

Hyland, Drew A. *Plato on the Question of Beauty.* Bloomington: Indiana University Press, 2008.

———. "Why Plato Wrote Dialogues." *Philosophy and Rhetoric* 1, no. 1 (1968): 38–50.

Lewis, V. Bradley. "The Rhetoric of Philosophical Politics in Plato's 'Seventh Letter.'" *Philosophy and Rhetoric* 33, no. 1 (2000): 23–38.

Marx, Karl. "Economic and Philosophic Manuscripts." In *Karl Marx: Selected Writings*, edited by Lawrence H. Simon, 54–97. Indianapolis: Hackett, 1994.

Metcalf, Robert. *Philosophy as Agôn: A Study of Plato's "Gorgias" and Related Texts.* Evanston, IL: Northwestern University Press, 2018.

Miller, Mitchell. "The Arguments I Seem to Hear." *Phronesis* 41, no. 2 (1996): 121–137.

Morello, Ruth, and A. D. Morrison, eds. *Ancient Letters: Classical and Late Antique Epistolography.* Oxford: Oxford University Press, 2007.

Morrow, Glenn. *Studies in Plato's Epistles.* Urbana: University of Illinois Press, 1935.

Muir, John. *Life and Letters in the Ancient Greek World.* New York: Routledge, 2008.

Plato. *Crito.* Translated by Harold North Fowler. Cambridge, MA: Harvard University Press, 1990.

———. *Seventh Letter.* Translated by R. G. Bury. Cambridge, MA: Harvard University Press, 1989.

Rée, Jonathan. Review of *The Other Side of Language*, by Gemma Fiumara. *Radical Philosophy* 58 (1991): 41–42.

Robinson, Eric W. "The Sophists and Democracy beyond Athens." *Rhetorica* 25, no. 1 (2007): 109–122.

Svenbro, Jesper. *Phrasikleia.* Translated by Janet Lloyd. Ithaca, NY: Cornell University Press, 1988.

Tarrant, Harold. "Middle Platonism and the Seventh Epistle." *Phronesis* 28, no. 1 (1983): 75–103.

Wohl, Victoria. "Plato avant le Lettre: Authenticity in Plato's Epistles." *Ramus* 27, no. 1 (1998): 60–93.

JILL GORDON is Professor of Philosophy and Class of 1940/NEH Distinguished Professor of the Humanities at Colby College. She is author of *Turning toward Philosophy: Literary Device and Dramatic Structure in Plato's Dialogues* and *Plato's Erotic World: From Cosmic Origins to Human Death.*

# 10

## OBSERVATIONS ON LISTENING IN ARISTOTLE'S PRACTICAL PHILOSOPHY

I-Kai Jeng, National Taiwan University

ONE CAN DISTINGUISH SEVERAL MODES OF LISTENING BY their objects: listening to sounds, voice, music, or speech (λόγος). The latter two are more immediately relevant to Aristotle's practical philosophy. This paper focuses on the phenomenon of listening to speeches. Its purpose is to show that listening, as constitutive of λέγειν, reveals a neglected aspect in Aristotle's project. The arguments in this paper are animated by the idea that rhetoric, or the practice of public speaking, functions not merely as an instrument for realizing civic virtue but in and of itself manifests the political nature of human beings.

Below, I first argue that Aristotle conceives of rhetoric as a kind of "vicarious reasoning" on behalf of the audience and that its practice tends to promote truth. To highlight how unusual Aristotle's views are, I use the familiar charges against rhetoric in Plato's *Gorgias* as a foil. I then turn to *Politics* 3.11 and argue that, while rhetoric is the vehicle for producing a multitude worthy of holding some political power, this benefit is realized only when both the speakers and their audience making up this multitude are to some extent active listeners (I specify what this means there). The final section turns to two passages in the *Nicomachean Ethics* (hereafter *EN*) and explores an "ethics of listening" called for by the first two sections.

## 1. Rhetoric as the Ἀντίστροφος of Dialectic

Plato lends voice to the familiar idea that rhetoric is a distortive element in discourse (λέγειν). Discourse is about communicating one's thoughts or what is the case to another, and what we call "rhetoric" identifies the nonsubstantive aspects of communication—what is merely decorative, or worse, intentionally misleading. Someone has only a weak argument supporting a tax reduction proposal; with the help of rhetoric, she convinces more people than she would have without it. Rhetoric is an art of deception, of making unjust arguments just or better arguments worse.

While agreeing that rhetoric includes a dimension of distortion or deception, Aristotle nevertheless believes that something is missing in this characterization. While rhetoric can make weaker arguments stronger or stronger ones weaker, it is much more effective at making weak arguments even weaker and strong ones stronger. Differently stated, while the Platonic Gorgias argues that rhetoric is neutral to truth and falsehood, and the Platonic Socrates claims that it is partial to falsehood, Aristotle makes the less obvious claim that rhetoric is partial to truth. The more rhetoric is practiced, the more does truth come to light in public: "What is true and just by nature are more persuasive than their opposites" (*Rhetoric* 1355a21–22). The purpose of this section is to offer an interpretation and a defense of this claim.

According to Aristotle, rhetoric primarily studies arguments. What is usually referred to by the term *rhetoric*—how to organize a speech into prologue, narration, and epilogue; the classification of rhetorical figures; how to speak in different emotional registers—is, in Aristotle's view, secondary. The justification for this unusual conception of rhetoric is that good arguments are what truly persuade. Once equipped with a strong argument, the temperament of the orator or speaker, their choice of words, and so on fade in importance.

One would think that, since rhetoric is about persuasion and different people find different things persuasive, there is no reason to privilege arguments. Some are taken by impassioned oratory, while others prefer calm, straightforward reasoning. But Aristotle finds that, putting the differences between different kinds of audience aside, generally speaking they all prefer persuasion through proper arguments. A deductive argument sounds more impressive than arguing by examples, since the latter allows for exceptions, but the former is universal (*Rhetoric* 1356b23–25, 1394a9–10). But more importantly, "everyone has attempted to examine or submit an account [for examination], defend, and accuse" (1354a4–6). This is a remarkable statement. First, it says that rhetoric exists in the context of a common examination of some view or defense and accusation in law courts. Otherwise put, rhetoric shows up in the absence of knowledge; it is needed where there are problems that other arts cannot deal with (1356b37–1357a4). It happens whenever one needs to "examine, defend, or accuse." People examine what they do not yet understand well; they defend and accuse concerning matters that can be reasonably doubted. In such absence of knowledge, rhetoric is rather investigative than deceptive. It tests the pragmatic truths of what matters by common consent. Such tests of truth naturally center on arguments, which relate what we understand to what we do not yet comprehend.

Moreover, in other arts, only a small number of people have tried to make shoes or build boats, for example, before they develop those activities into an expertise. Not so with rhetoric, because *everyone* has tried to persuade—everyone has tried to be "rhetorical." The activities that can be artfully carried out by rhetoric are even nowadays done over and over by amateurs and experts alike. An important implication of this is that everyone has some experience with using arguments in speech. (Consider the following relevant fact: in an introductory logic course, many common argument forms do not require any explanation of why they are valid. Students recognize them as patterns they employ in their own speeches.) From Aristotle's point of view, this means that the audience, despite not being experts at public speaking, is nevertheless relatively qualified to assess public speeches, because their own everyday experience has equipped them with some competence in discovering the arguments therein.[1] In short, it is the pretechnical and everyday ground of rhetoric that justifies Aristotle's privileging of arguments.[2]

On this basis, Aristotle carves out the rhetorical mode of arguing and calls it ἐνθύμημα.[3] Briefly put, ἐνθυμήματα are action-oriented inferences employing reputable opinions as premises.[4] The inference patterns are not limited to purely deductive ones, because debates concern human action (whether to do something or not to do something), and whenever there is action, one must reason about probabilities. Therefore, inference patterns include probable reasoning (τὸ εἰκός), what Aristotle calls nonnecessary signs, and so on.[5] But, more importantly, at least one premise in a rhetorical argument is a reputable opinion, ἔνδοξον (*Rhetoric* 1357a7–13).[6]

The well-known definition of reputable opinions is "what seems the case to everyone, or to most people, or to the wise—to all of them, or to most, or to the most known and reputed (ἐνδόξοις)" (*Topics* 100b22–3). Reputable opinions are best understood by contrasting them with premises in scientific demonstrations. The latter are "true on account of themselves" (100b18–22)—that is, they are believed because they are true. Reputable opinions, on the other hand, *seem* true, or are thought to be true, because they are either widely believed or believed by those widely believed to be wise. In other words, they are not necessarily true. Furthermore, an opinion counts as reputable only in (this perhaps explains the ἐν- prefix) a certain group.[7] The same opinion might be reputable in one group but not in another. Scientific premises do not have such relative status, since they are true in themselves. In addition, while different groups might hold opposing reputable opinions, even within the same group, reputable opinions can disagree with one another. For example, those deemed wise by Athenians (such as Socrates and his friends) might hold an opinion about happiness that is different from the opinion held about happiness by most Athenian citizens.[8] This explains why it is possible to be persuasive on both sides of a given issue. Finally, despite the diversity and relativity just highlighted, this does not mean that any random opinion is or can be a reputable opinion. Opinions held by only a few who are obscure, opinions held by those reputed to be foolish or unwise, or idiosyncratic and mad opinions are excluded (*Rhetoric* 1356b35; *Topics* 104a9–13). There is, in other words, a relative specificity and stability to reputable opinions.

Aristotle can now respond to the Platonic charges against rhetoric, but, at the same time, he incurs a new one. Plato compares the rhetorician to a charlatan or a quack. The rhetorician does not know medicine, but, equipped with rhetoric, she can persuade the patient to take pills that have no curative power. The doctor, by contrast, knows what is good for the patient but fails to persuade the patient to do what needs to be done. In short, rhetoric makes it difficult for laymen to distinguish the spurious from genuine experts (*Gorgias* 459a–c).

In Aristotle's view, the comparison of rhetoric with medicine or other arts is not appropriate. If rhetoric is needed precisely where knowledge or expertise is lacking, then, strictly speaking, whenever there is rhetoric, there is no clear distinction between genuine and spurious experts. All speakers might be experts in speaking, but none of them truly knows the answer to the issue at hand. If two speakers are taking opposing sides in debating whether to raise taxes, for example, it is not the case that one is always the true expert and the other the rhetorical trickster. More accurately, neither of them is an expert or a deceiver; both are employing the gift of human speech to orient themselves when facing the unknown.

Not only does Plato misunderstand the character of the context of rhetoric, but he also assumes the wrong sort of elitist attitude toward the people (that is, the audience in democratic societies). Aristotle partly agrees that the people, as a collective, are not particularly bright and might be duped by clever speakers. But he also thinks that to characterize the people as helpless victims at the mercy of the orator's manipulations is simplistic and naive.[9] To repeat, since everyone has practiced rhetoric, the people have experience of it in a way they do not with respect to other arts. To that extent, as a whole they can be tolerably reliable judges of the substantive character of speeches.

The Platonic view, however, is yet not fully refuted. Plato also accuses rhetoric of flattery—that is, it appeals to what delights the audience, what is pleasant to them, without concern for what is good. The chef who aims to make food tasty without concern for its effects on health is "flattering" the diner and not benefiting him. The rhetorician is such a chef, who feeds the audience speeches that they want to hear but not necessarily what they should hear. What is worse, Aristotle's very conception of ἐνθύμημα appears unable to avoid this charge. Since it requires reputable opinions as premises, it appears to admit that the rhetorician is compelled to say what the audience would like or accept and therefore must say what flatters their understanding. The Aristotelian conception of rhetorical arguments therefore blurs the lines between persuasion and flattery (cf. *Gorgias* 513b8–c2).

In principle, food can be both healthy and delicious; perhaps likewise, arguments made from the ingredients of ἔνδοξα can both flatter and benefit the audience. This appears to be what Aristotle has in mind, and here I defend the claim that "what is true and just are by nature more persuasive than their opposites." There is a natural coincidence between truth and what is commonly believed to be true or proper. Aristotle means something like the following. In a law court, for example, when the defendant and the accuser are more or less equally competent in their rhetorical skills, the side defending what is true will persuade the jury of his or her case more often than not.

Aristotle's argument could be schematized as follows. Rhetorical arguments use reputable opinions as premises and commonly accepted argument patterns; reputable opinions resemble truths; the accepted argument patterns are for the most part truth-preserving; rhetorical arguments are persuasive; therefore, the persuasiveness and the truth of those arguments tend to go hand in hand. To be clear, this argument is, in Aristotle's own terms, only probable. Since reputable opinions can contradict each other, since the rhetorician argues for both sides, and since not all argument patterns in public speaking are deductive, there are clearly rhetorical arguments that persuade without being true. The nerve of this argument lies in the second premise—namely, the statement that "reputable opinions resemble truths."

To see why Aristotle would think so, I turn to *Metaphysics* 993b4–5. Although the context there concerns the inquiry into first philosophy or wisdom, it is relevant here because Aristotle characterizes the initial human condition with respect to truth. He says that truth is like "the proverbial door"—namely, a door so large that it is impossible to not hit upon at least a part of it. The image of truth as a large door highlights two ways in which our initial relation to truth is deficient. First, to hit upon only a part of truth means to fall short of comprehensiveness—a part of the door is not the whole door, and the rest of the door cannot be assumed to be like the part that one has hit upon. Moreover, one's epistemic status is defective as well, since one initially only "hits upon" it. This could be akin to knowing merely *that*, in contrast to knowing *why*. The person who sees that, for example, a certain star at night is visible and guesses from experience that there will be a storm the next day "hits upon" what is true. However, only the meteorologist no longer hits upon this but knows why—that is, possesses an account or an explanation. Note that, in possessing an account, the astronomer can relate the phenomena to one another. This ability means that the meteorologist has a larger share of the proverbial door of truth than the person merely hitting upon a part of it.

This twofold deficiency, however, is complemented by two positive features. Even in lacking a comprehensive grasp of the truth, one nevertheless captures a part of it, which is not nothing. Regardless of what the rest of the door is like, presumably, the unknown parts would not contradict what is now grasped. There is a place from which inquiry can begin. Moreover, even though, strictly speaking, only the meteorologist truly knows the relation between the star and the approaching bad weather, in a relaxed sense, the amateur who grasps also "knows" since what he believes "hits upon" how things are.

It is easy to see that our initial relation to truth is closely related to the status of reputable opinions, since reputable opinions arguably exist in that mode of "hitting upon a part of truth." The person who discerns the connection between a star and bad weather has already advanced beyond the ignorant person who sees no such connection. The former, with enough experience as guidance, is in a position to ask "why" questions, while the latter cannot even begin.

Reputable opinions are also like that. The reputable opinions about happiness (happiness consists in wealth, in having a number of good friends, in having virtuous children), for example, make up parts of the truth about happiness (*Rhetoric* 1360b18–20). Through generations, people act on such opinions and test them. Such tests might confirm and reinforce the opinions; they might also show their deficiencies, and these opinions would then be refined and undergo change. People then reach a belief that appears to work or continues to be confirmed or not disproved in other pragmatic contexts. For example, they might have come to believe that "the wise person is just" based on their experience of wise people in the past, and they choose rulers of their cities on the basis of this (*Rhetoric* 1357b11–13).

This account of how reputable opinions emerge implies that the very process transforming beliefs into reputable opinions itself partly involves rhetoric. Not only does the practice of rhetoric rely on reputable opinions, but reputable opinions themselves are the product of rhetorical activities.[10] In other words, ἔνδοξα are accepted by the majority as true without further examination, not because the majority is generally uncritical but because these opinions have been, however imperfectly, tested in the past.

This is a roughly virtuous circle. The practice of rhetoric as an art depends on the relative stability and soundness of the majority of reputable opinions. If people were fickle and their beliefs rarely true, then rhetoric would not promote what is true and just. Plato's accusation of rhetoric as flattery would then by and large be right—the harm caused by rhetoric would far outweigh its benefits. But this is not the case, according to Aristotle—the beliefs of people, as tested by time and arguments in the past, are generally stable and roughly true. In this way, their beliefs become reputable and can be used in future public debates. Reputable opinions are thus both the basis of rhetorical practice and the result of it.

Let me elaborate. From an Aristotelian point of view, the orator needs to start somewhere in making her argument intelligible to her audience. If she is skillful, she discerns the link between what her audience understands and what she intends to persuade them of. What her audience understands is ἔνδοξα. Insofar as the orator is not there to challenge and criticize what her audience accepts, and, crudely speaking, their beliefs are true or resemble truth anyway, she is reinforcing their beliefs. However, she is also generating new reputable opinions. The connection between the conclusion or judgment she urges her audience to accept and the audience's initial beliefs was not evident to the audience before she spoke. What the orator brought out was a new belief (the conclusion) that is implied by their old beliefs—something consistent or not incompatible with them. And if the same argument gets repeated and passed on generationally, presumably there comes a point at which the argument itself does not need to be repeated anymore. Its conclusion will itself become a part of the collection of reputable opinions.

Aristotle can therefore respond to the charge that rhetoric is flattery as follows. Plato characterizes rhetoric as one-way communication, which involves silencing the other (either one's opponent or one's audience). A rhetorical speech is only about whether it receives applause or disapproval. Aristotle, by contrast, sees rhetoric as a subdued mode of two-way communication. As he famously opens his *Rhetoric*, "Rhetoric is the ἀντίστροφος of dialectic" (1354a1). This statement has often been taken to mean that they are similar in some fundamental respects and yet different in some other ways.[11] The basic similarity, it is said, is that both rhetoric and dialectic concern arguments that argue from reputable opinions. But there is another dimension that goes unmentioned: despite the necessary compromises, rhetoric remains dialogical. To be clear, the compromises required indeed make public speaking resemble a monologue. Even worse, public speaking can degenerate into "debates" where people talk past each other instead of truly arguing. The size of one's audience makes genuine, dialectical back-and-forth between individuals impractical. And despite the previously noted disagreement with Plato, Aristotle still distrusts the people and repeatedly notes the unfortunate need to simplify complicated affairs.[12] And matters of common concern do not put one's audience in a state of mind that is impartial, since their interests are involved and the issues are often urgent.[13] Nevertheless, the silence on one side does not make oratory a monologue. The audience "converses" in a reduced fashion. The orator is not compelled to flatter simply because she has to begin with reputable opinions. The Aristotelian conception of rhetoric instead sees this necessary starting point structuring her speech as a tacit dialogue, where she speaks both from and to the audience's point of view.

The orator is not manipulating the audience. On the one hand, she is restricted by the interpersonal context: she can argue for good policies or practices only in the context of the reputable beliefs held by the audience. This does not make the orator a slave of the audience's demands; instead, it makes her responsive, in a comparable way to how the dialectician is responsive to the interlocutor's affirmations and denials. Rhetoric is not all-powerful, because it requires responsive and responsible speaking to achieve success. And the orator, far from manipulating her audience, is more precisely "thinking out loud on behalf of them." We have, in effect, a dialectical argument without pausing every sentence to confirm or verify that the interlocutor accepts or rejects something. The orator lends voice to the reputable opinions held by her audience; through skillfully spelling out their implications in a manner that is also largely intelligible,[14] she shows what the audience themselves would be committed to, should they reason as skillfully as she does. She leads them to guess or "hit upon" the other parts of truth (that proverbial door) by inferring on the basis of what seems true and indeed resembles truth. What is true is brought to light in a rhetorical argument no less than in a dialectical one, despite the fact that the former is about action and practice, and not about inquiry and discovery like the latter. Rhetoric, in other words, is a kind of "vicarious reasoning," where the speaker speaks for the listener.[15]

Aristotle sees the relation between the orator and the audience as less asymmetrical than is ordinarily assumed. On the surface, there is a division of labor, in which the orator is in charge of speaking, her skill consists in speaking well, and the audience listens. The audience needs guidance, and the orator provides it. Aristotle sees this picture as simplistic. On closer analysis, the audience is speaking as well—namely, through the orator. And likewise, the orator's status as an expert in speaking is evinced not merely by her speaking but by the prior work in listening—namely, listening to the beliefs, opinions, hopes, and fears of her audience. The excellent rhetorician, in promoting truth through persuasive arguments, must be an excellent listener.

Plato might be refuted, but the skeptical reader remains unconvinced. Plenty of examples, historical or contemporary, appear to refute Aristotle's optimism about rhetoric. Just to mention one, the debate on climate change seems to suggest that the quality of debate actually deteriorates and prevents the truth from becoming clear. To be sure, Aristotle's view does not mean that rhetoric always promotes truth. But an account of how rhetoric can fail is still required to justify his optimism.

The key to answering this question lies in his qualification: what is true and just are by nature more persuasive than their opposites. In other words, it is under healthy regimes, healthy political arrangements, and noncorrupt laws that rhetoric can be a reliable ally of truth (*Rhetoric* 1354a19–b26). The implication is, of course, that most political communities are not healthy enough to "hear each other better." But this answer is clearly inadequate. Aristotle needs to further specify what it means to be politically healthy, or even better, to also point out the way to recover from illness. The next section specifies these conditions.

## 2. *Politics* 3.11 and the Conditions for Rhetorical Listening

*Politics* 3.11 deepens Aristotle's conception of rhetoric as a truth-promoting dialogical process in two ways. First, it illustrates more concretely how Aristotle envisions the process and goal of debates. Second, it specifies the kind of healthy structure that would make such truth-promoting debates possible.

The main focus of this chapter of the *Politics* is whether and to what extent the multitude (τὸ πλῆθος) should partake in political office. The multitude is understood here to be people who collectively wield influence in a city not because of wealth or virtue but only because of their sheer number. Because of this, it is not surprising that this chapter has the aristocrat as the imaginary opponent—namely, those who think that poverty, vice, or ignorance disqualify someone from political participation.

Aristotle's overall position is clear: a certain sort of multitude (τι πλῆθος) as a whole can be better than virtuous, outstanding, or intelligent individuals, and when such a multitude comes to be, they can hold political offices that concern auditing public officials and judging law trials. Aristotle first considers three analogies that help specify what sort of multitude can have this character: the potluck analogy, the multitude as a single human writ large, and the beautiful painting analogy. Eventually, he sees problems with them and favors the fourth: the mixed food analogy. It is instructive to turn to the three rejected options first for two reasons: because it is helpful to know why Aristotle rejects them, and because already in that discussion, Aristotle tacitly advances a novel conception of debate. So I turn to them now.

The potluck analogy (1281a42–b3) argues that every person who is in charge of bringing a dish might be inferior to any expert chef; however, collectively, the feast itself as a whole might be a feast not inferior to what one excellent chef by herself can produce. A modern parallel to this might be the way sports teams can sometimes be built. Signing contracts with the most outstanding players does not necessarily produce the most outstanding team, and sometimes a team that has only average or only below-average players can work together to beat a team with great players.[16] This analogy emphasizes that the whole is more than the sum of its parts. The less virtuous individual can be more valuable as a part of the multitude than by herself.

The second and third images are similar to each other and can therefore be dealt with together (1281b4–10). In the former, the good multitude is described as a human being writ large: "When they are many, each has a part of virtue and prudence, and coming together, the multitude emerges like a single human being, having many feet and many hands and many perceptions— and similarly concerning characters and thought. This is why the many judge (κρίνουσιν) works of music and of poets better. For everyone [perceives] some part, and all observe all" (*Politics* 1281b5–9). In the painting analogy, each person has a part that is beautiful. The painter combines these parts into one portrait and creates an image of a human being that is more beautiful than the most beautiful human. These two analogies are different from the potluck one in two respects. While the potluck analogy envisions the possibility of combining two inferior dishes into a superior course, the two analogies here combine only what is excellent or beautiful into a whole. Aristotle does not speak of two plain features combining into a more beautiful face in the analogy of painting. The second difference is that both analogies highlight the fact that the multitude contains inferior or bad parts. Unlike a painting, one cannot allow only the virtuous aspects of an individual into the group. The individual comes with her virtues and shortcomings.

As commentators have noticed, these images are double-edged.[17] A potluck can easily be a disaster if people do not coordinate with one another concerning what dishes they are bringing. To have many feet and many hands invokes not an organic being with an integrity of its own but a monster—that is, a nonnatural combination of parts of different animals. And if to have a part of virtue means to be incompletely virtuous and therefore vicious in other ways, there must be some mechanism weeding out the harmful or vicious parts and letting only the beneficial, virtuous parts function in a multitude. The very analogies designed to show that the multitude as a whole can be wise remind the reader that it can also be unwise.

Before turning to the fourth and final analogy, note that the three analogies all remind one of the *Metaphysics* passage discussed in the last section. Both passages involve individuals in possession of a part of something (truth, virtue, something beneficial to the city). What the *Politics* passage makes clearer is that if each person is partly outstanding, then it is better and more desirable that the pursuit of truth or goodness become a collective enterprise. My having only courage, by itself, might benefit me and my country; but without being tempered by moderation, which I lack, my courage could become harmful. But by being in a crowd or a community, where there are moderate people, I might be able to check my courage from becoming reckless through their influence. In Aristotelian terms, although I am still not moderate, I become at least enkratic.

The above example suggests a novel conception of debate. Imagine a city of courageous people forming a pro-war party and moderate people forming an anti-war party. They debate, and one side wins; the other side loses. For Aristotle, this is not at all an accurate description of what happens. Debate is not simply a matter of making one's opinions prevail over others. Instead, it is meant to complement and enrich the view that allows for a more comprehensive judgment of the issue under consideration. All three images emphasize the goodness of diversity, and all portray members of the multitude coming together not as antagonizing parts but as balancing and harmonizing with one another. Indeed, in debates, one party's view prevails, and the ensuing policies by and large follow its vision instead of the other party's. Ideally, however, the process of the debate does not therefore become meaningless: the losing side always exerts some modifying and complementing influence on the winning side, much as a courageous person can be modified by other moderate fellow citizens. Such an influence is usually recognized as a compromise, something undesirable. From the Aristotelian point of view, it is not a compromise at all. Actually, it is a decision based on a more comprehensive view of what is true and good.[18] It is the result of fruitful debating. To return to the proverbial door simile, public debates ideally are less like rivalry than putting together pieces of a puzzle. The result of such debating is to provide access to a larger part of truth. So, not only does Aristotle have a novel view of public debates, but, for him, rhetoric exercises a pivotal role in producing a multitude superior to an outstanding individual.

Obviously, the kind of debating just described does not exclude the possibility of a systematic predominance of falsehoods or base opinions. Perhaps what prevails is not what is true or just on one side of the debate but what is vicious and selfish. The question tacitly raised by the second and third analogies returns—namely, what prevents the less desirable aspects of the multitude from exerting their influence and joining together.

A hint is suggested in the painting analogy: the need for an organizer. Here, the organizer is the painter. Without the painter, the parts of beauty would not come together in the way they do. The painter has three tasks: to discern which parts of which individuals are beautiful, to evaluate how to properly represent it on his canvas, and finally, to assemble them in his work accordingly. The multitude itself is not beautiful; only a proper selecting process by the painter produces the beauty. This leads to the fourth analogy and, in my view, to Aristotle's considered view of the kind of multitude required for making rhetoric beneficial.

According to Aristotle, the multitude should be "mixed with the best, . . . like impure nourishment, in being mixed with pure nourishment, makes the whole more useful than a tiny amount of [pure] nourishment" (*Politics* 1281b34–37). While the potluck analogy suggested that two inferior dishes can combine into a superior course, and the person writ large and painting analogies suggested that two good traits can combine into a virtue or beauty that is more complete, this last analogy recommends a mixture of superior and inferior parts. Three advancements are made here. First, the nourishment analogy confronts the inferior aspects of each individual by making those aspects constitutive of the multitude. Second, while in the painting analogy the organizer is not part of the multitude, here the organizer is a participant as "pure nourishment." Finally, the first three images were about combining things; here, Aristotle speaks of mixing them.

The mixture is desirable, because "each separately is incomplete (ἀτελής) with respect to judging (κρίνειν)" (*Politics* 1281b37). Why the inferior majority is incomplete in its capacity to judge is obvious. It is like "impure nourishment," since each person has only a part of virtue but vices in other respects. Those who lack justice would commit injustices if given power, and those who lack not justice but moderation would commit mistakes (*Politics* 1281b25–30). Only through the influence of the superior minority can they be checked or moderated, and even transformed and improved. As the views and attitudes of the virtuous people spread and scatter throughout the multitude (this is how I unpack the metaphor of "mixture"), the multitude as a whole are made to behave more reasonably or less irrationally than before. In other words, two heterogeneous elements are made to become alike through debating and arguing. In the first three images, each member of the multitude retains their differences from each other;

here, they become more alike. Of course, becoming alike does not mean the voice of the virtuous becoming swallowed by the loud and deficient many. Instead, it means that the virtuous people make them better without becoming corrupted.

But the quote above (1281b37) also implies that the outstanding minority, by itself, is also incomplete with respect to judging. What does this mean? Commentators do not appear to notice the strangeness of this claim. My interpretation of the Aristotelian conception of rhetoric, however, readily provides an explanation. To reiterate, rhetoric occurs wherever there is a lack of knowledge and an accompanying awareness of such a lack. Λόγος is what we resort to in order to overcome that lack to some extent. The virtuous few might have what is right and true on their side; however, without being tested and submitted to a collective examination, their judgment is not robust. And since rhetorical debates, as just explained, are meant to broaden one's relation toward truth, the few engaging in oratory, hoping to sway the crowd toward what is good, should submit their understanding and judgment to the test. Only the pure nourishment that maintains its potency when mixed with impure nourishment is genuine.

If this is correct, then Aristotle's characterization of the good multitude comes very close to expecting virtuous "opinion leaders" in a crowd, but not quite. This is because the usual view of the opinion leaders is that they are the active element in persuasion, while the crowd is passive. Rhetoric is again seen as a one-way affair. But if both of them are "incomplete with respect to judging," then both "opinion leaders" and the rest of the majority are equally active and passive. The virtuous few must listen, bring the challenges (whether base or vicious) into the open, and address and respond to them.

The virtuous few of such a multitude are thus both organizers and participants. They have an organizing function because, through their influence, they incorporate what is virtuous, good, or advantageous among the less virtuous majority. The base or corruptive thoughts are refuted and weeded out. In this sense, their listening activity is analogous to the painter's examination of which parts of real individuals can serve as paradigms for his painting. But they are also participants, as their viewpoint eventually constitutes only a part of that comprehensive view that is the genuine goal of debating. And they participate because their viewpoint, while virtuous and outstanding, is still incomplete, ἀτελής. Only when their views enable them to respond to seemingly opposing or alternative views do those views become complete. In this sense, listening comes from that innermost need to grasp the truth as comprehensively as one can.

The excellent multitude, then, is one that has virtuous leaders who are ready to listen. But there is more. In the rest of the chapter, Aristotle engages in a dialectical back-and-forth with the imagined aristocrat who insists on the rule of experts. The opponent argues that only a doctor is qualified to judge the work of another doctor; amateurs are either not qualified at all (*Politics* 1281b38–42) or qualified only to a much lesser extent than the expert (1282a7–12). Therefore, the multitude, which is a group of amateurs, should not be judges of other political officials.

Aristotle's response is that, first, the "educated" amateur can judge even though she cannot administer medicine, which belongs to the work of a doctor; second, as long as the crowd as a whole is "not excessively slavish" (μὴ λίαν ἀνδραποδῶδες, 1282a15), its judgment can be as good as or even better than that of a single expert; and finally, in some cases, the user of a product can judge the product even better than the maker of the product. For example, the household manager might judge the house better than the house builder. Here, what is particularly relevant to my purpose is the meaning of the phrase "not excessively slavish."

The term for judging, κρίνω, has occurred several times already in this chapter of the *Politics*, and this connects it with rhetoric: the multitude are given political offices related to judging (auditing of officials and being a jury member at law courts), and the public speaker should provide informed arguments for the audience to make a decision or judgment (*Rhetoric* 1354a26–31). There is a clear connection between judging and listening in Aristotle. To make someone judge in a certain way is to persuade (πείθω); to judge based on a consideration of speeches made by others is correspondingly a matter of being persuaded, of πείθομαι. One might distinguish at least three different levels of listening in the semantic range of πείθομαι. The first and simplest level is where one grasps the meaning of a statement and accepts or takes it for granted in an unreflective manner. When I hear someone ask me to do something (such as "hold the door") and I act accordingly, or when I read the news and accept quite unthinkingly what is reported as fact, I am listening in this sense, and this is where πείθομαι is often translated as "to obey, to yield to."

The next two levels of listening are more reflective and less passive. One could be somewhat doubtful of the statement, but nevertheless one accepts it on account of the character of the speaker. In other words, one is aware of reasons to think otherwise, but either the reasons are not strong enough, or it is not worth the time to doubt, given the credentials of the speaker—she has proved herself to be truthful and honest in the past—so one accepts the statement and judges or decides accordingly. This is the sense of πείθομαι that might be rendered as "trust" or "believe." The third level is a genuine agreement with what is spoken—less on account of the character of the speaker than on account of the substantive content of the speech—where the listener reaches a judgment by herself concerning the argument. This is πείθομαι, being persuaded, in its most rational sense.[19]

Aristotle's remark on slavishness can be parsed in terms of listening as πείθομαι. The multitude will clearly be at the mercy of whoever has the rhetorical art without the relevant expertise that is in question if they as a whole can only listen in a passive and elementary sense. Better if they learn to recognize the reliable speakers and to distinguish them from the unreliable ones. Even better still, the multitude would truly show its advantage over experts if, as a whole, it is capable of critical and reflective engagement with what is spoken. Only at this level would the partial insights add up to something larger than what an individual is capable of seeing.[20]

In sum, this reading of *Politics* 3.11 argues for two points. On the one hand, developing the notion that rhetoric is a subdued mode of dialogue, Aristotle implies that public debates are meant not to eliminate one view for the sake of another but to reach a more comprehensive view that recognizes the relative strengths and limitations of each position. It is a process of making the good parts more robust through "mixing" them with the bad ones. On the other hand, rhetoric can create such a multitude only when there are virtuous leaders equipped with rhetoric and the multitude as a whole is able to listen to public speeches in a more active, "less slavish" sense of πείθομαι. The natural conditions for promoting truth and justice through rhetoric are, simply put, the citizens' mature capacity to listen.

## 3. An "Ethics of Listening" in the *Nicomachean Ethics*

If it is good to grant some kind of multitude some political power, and such a multitude comes to be only through the practice of rhetoric adopted by a virtuous minority to mix its viewpoint with that of the multitude, and this rhetoric can be beneficial only when both the minority and the majority can exercise a more active capacity to listen, then the cultivation of the virtuous minority should involve a cultivation of a character of openness and responsiveness. That Aristotle is concerned with such cultivation is confirmed by two passages in the *Nicomachean Ethics*, which I turn to now.

The first passage is where Aristotle discusses the appropriate audience for ethical lectures. To the person who cannot easily comprehend the beginning points of ethical studies, Aristotle has the following to say: "Let him hear (ἀκουσάτω) the words of Hesiod: 'he who is intelligent in everything is the best of all, / and he who obeys (πίθηται) the person who speaks well is good too. / But he who neither is intelligent nor takes to heart (ἐν θυμῷ βάλληται) / in listening to another—now that's a useless man'" (*EN* 1095b7–13). This passage is usually read as a warning: this work is not accessible to everyone. Only those with the requisite experience in human affairs and brought up by the right and noble habits can grasp the principles of ethics and follow Aristotle's reasoning. Young people, who listen to their passions more than their reason, will not derive benefit from reading or listening to it. Aristotle's claim, understood on its surface, implies that those who need education the most—young people under the sway of their passions—will not benefit from his ethical works. Consequently, some commentators, on the basis of the claims made here, have argued that the *EN* is written primarily for legislators, who are in charge of the common education meant to nurture civic virtues. In other words, the *EN* itself does not provide the education needed for young people directly. Instead, it provides principles to the legislators-to-be, who are already virtuous but require guidance on how the principles of virtue work together in a city. They would then provide, on the basis of the *EN*, habituation and education tailored to the context of their cities and thereby produce virtuous citizens.[21]

I disagree. While cogent in many ways, this reading falls short of grasping certain peculiar features of the text. For example, near the end of the book, Aristotle raises the question concerning the suitability of young people for moral education through speech, in contrast to being educated through habituation. There, his answer differs from what he said at the beginning of the work. Now it is no longer good habituation and experience that determine the suitability of young people but their natures with respect to the noble (τὸ καλόν). Those who are naturally attracted to what is noble and beautiful can benefit from ethical discourse. Moreover, Aristotle repeatedly reminds the reader throughout that we are investigating ethical phenomena to act virtuously, not to make others virtuous or to understand what virtue is. Such remarks would appear hardly necessary for an experienced adult who values deeds over words and is potentially qualified to legislate. And finally, it would seem odd, if not totally absurd, that those who need ethical discourses the most would not benefit from them. The claim that the *EN* is written for potential legislators, all things considered, seems too narrow.

A careful consideration of the rhetorical effect of Aristotle's quotation of Hesiod suggests a more subtle and subversive reading concerning the intended readers of Aristotle's lectures. Note what Aristotle says beforehand. He mentions two groups of people who grasp and understand the beginning points of ethical inquiry. One group both understands that they are the beginning points and presumably can give an account of why we must begin where we do. The other only understands that they are the beginning points but does not know why. The first group would not learn anything new from the *EN*; they would merely find their earlier beliefs confirmed by Aristotle. The second group would learn the why of the cultivation of each virtue in studying *EN*. And there is a third group, unable to grasp even the *that* that begins inquiry. They do not recognize why ethics begins where it does. They question and challenge these starting points. Their interruption makes it difficult to proceed with the planned line of reasoning. To them, Aristotle provides Hesiod's advice.

But consider the effect of hearing Hesiod, from the audience's point of view. Hesiod calls those who lack their own understanding and are unable to follow those who do understand "useless." This is a harsh saying. A young person hearing or reading this might react in one of the following two ways. One is perhaps an indifferent shrug. The young person says to herself, "Perhaps I am not ready for this work. I shall come back to it when I am mature enough." Someone reacting this way would then effectively be obeying the person who speaks well—listening to Aristotle's warning and following those who know. Hesiod's advice is good for this person, and she "takes the advice to heart."[22] But the second possible reaction is more interesting: the listener feels provoked by Aristotle. Aristotle appeals to an ancient authority to silence challenges made by the impetuous youth concerning the beginning points of ethical inquiry. It is quite likely that the reaction will not be a tame submission to the advice.[23] Indeed, they might feel challenged to study and understand the work precisely because of this very warning. I cannot prove that this is an effect calculated by Aristotle. But it is quite plausible that this was intentional, given his own understanding of the general characteristics of youth—how they respond to arguments and their desire for superiority (*Rhetoric* 1389a10–13, a28–35). Aristotle appropriates that youthful passion for superiority, which usually causes the youth to be unable to listen to reason, and turns it upside down.

Otherwise put, I am suggesting that the intended audience of the *EN* is not restricted to potential legislators; it includes youth of a certain kind as well. Such young people are not inclined to submit to authority easily, and Aristotle provokes them to listen by challenging them to grasp his meaning. Aristotle is, in other words, looking for those who are "less slavish" in the sense defined before. It is such youths that carry the potential to become more active and reflective listeners—and perhaps lead the multitude responsively.

The second passage I examine discusses the virtues concerning sociability. The passion for superiority carries the risk of haughtiness and separation. While those who are provoked by the Hesiod quote to study the work have great potential for becoming *active* listeners, they usually are less fit for being *listeners*. Their natural passion for superiority, coupled with intellectual talents, would make them look down on the defective understandings of others. They tend to wish to not merely stand out from others but stand apart from them. Such a sense of separation or distance—a sense of being above others—is undesirable, since it is crucial that the virtuous and excellent ones be able to be a part of the multitude, to mix with them.[24] They need to recognize their own incompleteness in not having their views tested by the public. This is why what makes them active listeners also tends to hinder their ability to be responsive.

The passion for superiority, in other words, needs to be tamed or made gentle. The virtue of superiority is magnanimity. Magnanimity and the virtue concerned with honor (*EN* 4.3–4) are about superiority by comparison with others. And yet, book 4 concludes with shame, a character trait expressing self-awareness of one's inadequacy with respect to virtue. Magnanimity, the concern with honor, and shame all emerge from a sense of inequality, and one might say that the youthful passion for superiority moves between shame and magnanimity—what characterizes youth is their concern to avoid shameful behavior and to strive for noble deeds and characters. The four virtues discussed between magnanimity and shame—gentleness, friendliness, truthfulness, and wit (*EN* 4.5–8)—appear in this light as an attempt at disclosing characters that put interpersonal relations on a more equal footing. Here, I discuss the first three, which are all "nameless" virtues.

Ancient Greek society, it is well known, was agonic. This might have led to a glorification of the virtues that emphasize superiority. The nameless virtues, being based on equality, might not have been recognized as virtues in Aristotle's society. At the very least, their status as virtues is less evident than that of courage or justice, for example. By making something nameless named, Aristotle manages to make something heard and given a voice in his writings. In this way, he shows his own reflective stance toward Greek culture and his gentle critique and reform of it.[25]

Gentleness in Greece was not necessarily a virtue. Given the agonic character of Greek political life and its glorification of masculine over feminine traits, the gentle person might even be often mocked. Indeed, as Susan D. Collins notes, Aristotle mentions in passing that those who always try to take revenge are often honored and admired in the political realm, an indication that anger, the opposite of gentleness, is even counted as a positive emotion or disposition (*EN* 1126b1–2).[26] To call the mean between anger and excessive forgiveness "gentleness," then, is to promote the character traits that allow people to live together more peacefully. Those who are easily prone to anger "are worse for living together" (*EN* 1126a31). In this sense, it is not surprising that the discussion of gentleness is followed by what Aristotle himself calls "virtues that concern living together" or concern "the sharing in deeds and words" (1126b11–12).

One can be more precise concerning the intention of promoting gentleness. Anger is, in a way, resistant to reason. Being one of the most powerful motivators for action, anger makes it difficult to calm down the person inflicted by it.[27] This explains why, in the discussion of passions in the *Rhetoric*, Aristotle begins with anger: he begins with what is more action-oriented and less susceptible to rhetorical treatment. The angry person is somewhat deaf to reason and obeys only her passions. In marking gentleness as more opposed to the extreme of anger, Aristotle is in effect creating the conditions in the soul that are more amenable to reason. Similarly, in claiming that gentleness is more akin to excessive forgiveness, Aristotle is also urging that we engage in understanding the story from the other side before taking actions. The Greek word for forgiveness, after all, is συγγνώμη—"to share an understanding together."

This explains another interesting feature in the chapter on gentleness. If I am not mistaken, rarely does Aristotle discuss the "goodness" of vices as he does in this chapter. He mentions how even bad, vicious, or evil traits have their positive aspects. People who are prone to anger manifest it in different ways. Those who react immediately might strike back strongly, but their anger also dissipates quickly, and they forget about the slighting they suffered afterward. By contrast, those who bear a grudge might not cause serious injury to others, but they will always remember, and it becomes unpleasant over time. Aristotle seems to be practicing συγγνώμη in front of the reader. It is only when we discern goodness in the bad or base traits that "sharing an understanding together" becomes possible.

Learning to see oneself in another is further developed in the next virtue, friendliness. In my view, Aristotle's discussion reinforces the point that these nameless virtues are meant to counteract what he sees as harmful practices in Greek cities—namely, the agonic aspects that create faction. What is friendliness? It means treating nonfriends as friends, but without the emotions or dispositions that usually accompany friendship. Many people "live together" or associate for the sake of inflicting pain or giving pleasure without principle. The former are contrarians or misanthropes, the latter obsequious people. Since both are blamed, there must be a mean between them—the friendly person. We might say this person is sociable— she can be friendly without being a friend, pleasant without being slavish.

Aristotle provides an insightful description: the friendly person behaves the same way toward those she knows and those she does not know. But she does this without completely eradicating the difference between them, because the fitting ways to treat one's acquaintances and strangers do differ. In other words, the socially and politically relevant distinctions imply differentiated treatment of people. Friends and strangers, family members and friends, fellow citizens and foreigners, the respectable and the ordinary, and the rich and the poor demand differentiating responses. One should pay more attention to one's parents than to the parents of one's friends, or help the foreigners in need more than the well-to-do citizens. But more importantly, the friendly person does not absolutize these differences. A sameness in attitude underlies her differentiating responses. She remains her polite self regardless of whom she is dealing with. Her friendliness effectively treats the politically relevant distinctions as secondary—the humanity we all share transcends those differences.

Friendliness concerns pleasure and pain in living together. Truthfulness, the third and last nameless virtue, concerns telling truth or falsehoods in living together. At first sight, being truthful appears to be the opposite of being rhetorical. A truthful person says each thing as it is (αὐθέκαστος, literally "each-itself"); the rhetorical one, even if she does not lie, tactfully varies her speech according to the audience. Even more, it is not the virtue but the vices that are particularly obsessed with reputation. The boasting person, who overstates her worth, intends to appear as having features or possessions "deemed reputable" (τὰ ἔνδοξα); the ironic person, who understates her worth, particularly denies having whatever she has to be reputable. The truthful one, in other words, appears as someone who disregards τὰ ἔνδοξα, that crucial ingredient of rhetorical arguments, as merely resembling truth.

As Aristotle's discussion continues, however, it comes to light that, while boasting, truthfulness, and irony are conceptually different, in practice the latter two resemble each other. The reason is that the truthful person is also friendly and therefore intends to avoid unnecessary pain to others. And boastfulness is "burdensome." The truthful person therefore tends toward understatement of her worth. Accordingly, irony emerges as much less of a vice, since it is "graceful." There is a kindness that motivates irony, a kindness absent in boasting. The reader recalls that the magnanimous person is also ironic toward others, but in that case irony expressed only an indifference toward what others thought of oneself. Here, irony expresses a concern about how telling the truth might hurt others, especially when one's virtues and excellence might be cause for envy. Truthfulness, as a virtue, then, is not bluntness. It is tempered by or fused with a concern with how others might hear oneself. It is responsive to the element of τὰ ἔνδοξα in human interactions. Rhetorical sensitivity, then, is not a morally neutral skill; it also shapes and modifies the virtues worth cultivating. The three nameless virtues, on this reading, culminate in an image of the virtuous person who both listens and is listened to without becoming obsequious or compromising truth.

Let me summarize the observations of this paper. Aristotle's ethics partly intends to cultivate selected youths into outstanding citizens that can nevertheless relate to the less outstanding citizens in a responsive way. They are ready to become active listeners, capable of "mixing with" the multitude so that the latter deserves a share in political power. Rhetoric, when exercised in such a healthy multitude, transforms debates into a process of achieving a view of increasing comprehensiveness toward truth. And rhetoric is desirable because it meets the practical constraints of public speaking without losing the dialogical nature of λόγος.

## Notes

1. In *Politics* 8.6, 1340b20–26, Aristotle claims that those who have not learned to some extent how to play an instrument or sing cannot be adequate judges of music and enjoy them properly. If this is applicable to rhetoric (and there is a connection between rhetoric and

poetry; see *Rhetoric* 3.1), then the fact that everyone has tried to state their view in front of others qualifies them as adequate judges of public speeches as well.

2. The view that Aristotelian rhetoric privileges rational argument over sophistry or rhetorical tricks has been challenged in the past by scholars. See, for example, Jürgen Sprute, "Aristotle and the Legitimacy of Rhetoric," in *Aristotle's "Rhetoric": Philosophical Essays*, ed. David J. Furley and Alexander Nehamas (Princeton, NJ: Princeton University Press, 1994), 117–128; Robert Wardy, "Mighty Is the Truth and It Shall Prevail?," in *Essays on Aristotle's "Rhetoric,"* ed. David J. Furley and Alexander Nehamas (Princeton, NJ: Princeton University Press, 1996), 56–87. The overall evidence of the *Rhetoric*, however, supports the view of Larry Arnhart (*Aristotle on Political Reasoning: A Commentary on the "Rhetoric"* [DeKalb: Northern Illinois University Press, 1981])—namely, that Aristotle's main motivation is to make the practice of public speaking as reasonable as is practically possible.

3. Its anglicized form, *enthymeme*, often has the meaning of "truncated syllogism" (namely, a syllogism with an unstated, implicit premise); I avoid that term because it does not fully capture what Aristotle intended by ἐνθύμημα.

4. Arnhart (*Aristotle on Political Reasoning*, 24–26) provides a similar but briefer analysis. His view basically agrees with M. F. Burnyeat ("Enthymeme: Aristotle on the Logic of Persuasion," in *Aristotle's "Rhetoric": Philosophical Essays*, ed. David J. Furley and Alexander Nehamas [Princeton, NJ: Princeton University Press, 1994], 3–56) on these points I mentioned.

5. Probable arguments are defined as what happens for the most part but can turn out to be otherwise (*Rhetoric* 1357a34–36); nonnecessary signs are defined as those whose inferences are not deductively valid (1357b4–6). An example would be "Socrates was just and wise; that is a sign that the wise are just."

6. Not all premises are ἔνδοξα, though. Some are statements of facts. The requirement is that at least one premise belongs to ἔνδοξα.

7. Thomas W. Smith, *Revaluing Ethics: Aristotle's Dialectical Pedagogy* (Albany: State University of New York Press, 2001), 23.

8. The discussion of the ἔνδοξα on what happiness is occurs in *Rhetoric* 1.5. A number of opinions listed include the following: happiness is prosperity with virtue, or self-sufficiency, or secure enjoyment of pleasures, or health and the ability to protect one's possessions, or some combination of these (1360b14–17). Glenn W. Most ("The Uses of Endoxa: Philosophy and Rhetoric in the *Rhetoric*," in *Aristotle's "Rhetoric": Philosophical Essays*, ed. David J. Furley and Alexander Nehamas [Princeton, NJ: Princeton University Press, 1994], 167–190) insightfully remarks that the view of certain philosophers—namely, that happiness consists in a contemplative life—is not mentioned in the *Rhetoric*, because although it counts as one of the ἔνδοξα concerning happiness, it is not relevant to public discourse.

9. This is because, first, there are limits to what the orator can do to change the people's passions (see, for example, *Rhetoric* 1380b9–11); and second, people as a whole can be more sophisticated than one thinks, as section 2 of this chapter shows. Here, some passages from the *Rhetoric* should be considered: 1355a1–3 sees the people as capable of distinguishing relevant from irrelevant arguments in the assembly, and 1391a13–14, together with b4–6, implies that the people might be less foolish and moderate in their evaluation of their powers.

10. This point is elegantly elaborated by Arnhart, *Aristotle on Political Reasoning*, 193. My account here is a simplified version of his. Compare also Jeremy Waldron, "The Wisdom of

the Multitude: Some Reflections on Book 3, Chapter 11 of Aristotle's *Politics*," *Political Theory* 23, no. 4 (1995): 569–570.

11. Arnhart, *Aristotle on Political Reasoning*, 14.

12. Some examples: the topic of delivery is a vulgar matter, but since people are easily affected by it, we must study it (*Rhetoric* 1403b36–1404a7; note the reluctant tone); the study of emotions is important because people make decisions differently under different dispositions (1377b24–1378a5).

13. The fact that interests are involved is not necessarily bad. Aristotle thinks that the jury in a law court is more easily manipulated precisely because they are judging other people's cases and not their own (*Rhetoric* 1354b23–1355a3).

14. "Largely intelligible" is an important qualification. It means that even though an orator might be able to conduct a lengthy chain of reasoning in the form of a well-composed speech, she should limit her speech to simplified, shorter inferences. Since the best enthymemes are those that are slightly unexpected but not extremely difficult to follow (*Rhetoric* 1400b26–33), there is something like teaching in a limited sense (the audience learns something new about their beliefs).

15. Lloyd F. Bitzer ("Aristotle's Enthymeme Revisited," *Quarterly Journal of Speech* 45 [1959]: 399–408) makes an ingenious argument, based on an analysis of the differences between dialectical and demonstrative syllogisms in the *Analytics* and *Topics*, for precisely this point. This deserves quoting: "An orator or a dialectician can *plan* a rhetorical or dialectical argument while sitting at the desk in his study, but he cannot really *complete* it by himself, because some of the materials from which he builds arguments are absent. The missing materials . . . are the premises which the audience brings with it" (407; emphasis in original). Also, "owing to the skill of the speaker, *the audience itself helps construct the proofs by which it is persuaded*" (408; emphasis in original).

16. The potluck analogy plays an important role in Waldron, "Wisdom of the Multitude," who attempts to argue for an Aristotelian justification of the modern practice of affirmative action. While it is an illuminating reading of that passage, it will soon be seen below that this analogy is not Aristotle's final word on the matter.

17. Mary P. Nichols, *Citizens and Statesmen: A Study of Aristotle's "Politics"* (Lanham, MD: Rowman and Littlefield, 1992), 66–72; Thomas Pangle, *Aristotle's Teaching in the "Politics"* (Chicago: University of Chicago Press, 2013), 138–145. According to Pangle (296n66), because Aristotle adopts comic language in this chapter, the arguments should be read as ironic, and Aristotle is not serious about advocating for the wisdom of the multitude.

18. Eve Rabinoff's paper in this volume seems to me to have provided the theoretical underpinning of listening for such a possibility: it is in speaking and listening that one becomes capable of seeing a thing from another person's point of view. If listening involves listening to different points of view, and rhetoric is a two-way listening, then the novel conception of debate advanced by Aristotle is grounded in his understanding of listening to λόγοι.

19. Compare the two meanings of πείθω as distinguished by Socrates in the *Gorgias* 453d–454d.

20. Incidentally, the construction in Greek at *Politics* 1282a15, a future more vivid conditional, suggests that the prospect of a less slavish multitude is not unrealistic.

21. Richard Bodéüs (*The Political Dimension of Aristotle's "Ethics,"* trans. Jan Edward Garret [Albany: State University of New York Press, 1993]) provides, to my knowledge, the

strongest arguments and evidence for this reading of the *Nicomachean Ethics* and *Politics* as a single, unified project of practical philosophy.

22. I note in passing that the original in Hesiod's poem for "taking someone's advice to heart" is "ἐν θυμῷ βάλληται," which readily echoes Aristotle's term for rhetorical arguments, the ἐνθύμημα. To be persuaded, to use a colloquial expression, is a process of "letting the argument sink in."

23. For a literary illustration of such provocative rhetoric appealing to the youthful temperament, consider Nestor's speech designed to encourage the Achaean warriors to fight Hector in *Iliad* 7.123–161.

24. My emphasis is on the political undesirability of the inclination to separate oneself from others. Indeed, Aristotle's praise of the contemplative life—whether ironic or not—is in a sense a praise of separation.

25. This also illustrates how the virtuous circle discussed in section 1 can generate new practices or values—the *Nicomachean Ethics* is partly if not wholly rhetorically structured.

26. Susan D. Collins, *Aristotle and the Rediscovery of Citizenship* (Cambridge: Cambridge University Press, 2009), 148.

27. That anger is an effective motivator of action can be seen in Aristotle's comment on the causes of why tyrants are overthrown. While anger toward a tyrant and hatred of him both cause the tyrant's downfall, anger "is often more productive of action (πρακτικώτερον) than hatred, for angry people attack more vehemently, since that passion does not use calculation" (*Politics* 1312b26–29).

# Bibliography


Aristotle. *Aristotelis Ethica Nicomachia*. Edited by I. Bywater. Oxford: Oxford University Press, 1894.

———. *Aristotelis Politica*. Edited by W. D. Ross. Oxford: Oxford University Press, 1957.

Arnhart, Larry. *Aristotle on Political Reasoning: A Commentary on the "Rhetoric."* DeKalb: Northern Illinois University Press, 1981.

Bitzer, Lloyd F. "Aristotle's Enthymeme Revisited." *Quarterly Journal of Speech* 45 (1959): 399–408.

Bodéüs, Richard. *The Political Dimension of Aristotle's "Ethics."* Translated by Jan Edward Garret. Albany: State University of New York Press, 1993.

Burnyeat, M. F. "Enthymeme: Aristotle on the Logic of Persuasion." In *Aristotle's "Rhetoric": Philosophical Essays*, edited by David J. Furley and Alexander Nehamas, 3–56. Princeton, NJ: Princeton University Press, 1994.

Collins, Susan D. *Aristotle and the Rediscovery of Citizenship*. Cambridge: Cambridge University Press, 2009.

Most, Glenn W. "The Uses of Endoxa: Philosophy and Rhetoric in the *Rhetoric*." In *Aristotle's "Rhetoric": Philosophical Essays*, edited by David J. Furley and Alexander Nehamas, 167–190. Princeton, NJ: Princeton University Press, 1994.

Nichols, Mary P. *Citizens and Statesmen: A Study of Aristotle's "Politics."* Lanham, MD: Rowman and Littlefield, 1992.

Pangle, Thomas. *Aristotle's Teaching in the "Politics."* Chicago: University of Chicago Press, 2013.

Smith, Thomas W. *Revaluing Ethics: Aristotle's Dialectical Pedagogy.* Albany: State University of New York Press, 2001.
Sprute, Jürgen. "Aristotle and the Legitimacy of Rhetoric." In *Aristotle's "Rhetoric": Philosophical Essays,* edited by David J. Furley and Alexander Nehamas, 117–128. Princeton, NJ: Princeton University Press, 1994.
Waldron, Jeremy. "The Wisdom of the Multitude: Some Reflections on Book 3, Chapter 11 of Aristotle's *Politics.*" *Political Theory* 23, no. 4 (1995): 563–584.
Wardy, Robert. "Mighty Is the Truth and It Shall Prevail?" In *Essays on Aristotle's "Rhetoric,"* edited by David J. Furley and Alexander Nehamas, 56–87. Princeton, NJ: Princeton University Press, 1996.

I-KAI JENG is Assistant Professor of Philosophy at National Taiwan University. His research focuses on Plato's conceptualization of *philosophia* in relation to sophistic discourse on the one hand and political action on the other.

# 11

## MIS-AULOGY

### *Aristotle on the Politics of Sound*

Sara Brill, Fairfield University

I F THE IDEAL OF FRANK SPEECH DEMONSTRATES THE power of the voice, Echo's fate provides an uncanny reminder of voice's vulnerability. Whether we follow Ovid's version of her story, in which Echo is punished by Hera for her role in concealing Zeus's dalliances, or the depiction in the Homeric hymn to Pan, in which Echo is penalized for refusing Pan's advances, the central issue at stake for her character is the same as that for the *parrhēsiastes*—namely, the relationship between the speaker and what is said. The underlying tension implicit in frank speech is made explicit in Echo: the divergence between the voice as an organ of one's own meaning and the voice as an organ of the meaning of another.[1] Doomed to mimic the words of others, the formerly loquacious Echo loses the ability to put herself, her meaning, her intention, her desire, into words. Denied the ability to speak her own mind, torn from her own meaning, Echo is condemned to speak (or steal) the meaning of another. Her voice is a voice in name only, an uncanny fragment; errant and detached, it floats into the ear of the other with the promise of a presence that can only ever be denied because it is, in the end, only the shadow of another speaker. As such, her voice represents the anxiety-provoking possibility that voice will slide from bearer of meaning to parrot of meaning, and from there even to "mere" sound or noise. In Echo's fate, the "living" voice simply gives sound to the "dead" letter—a Platonic nightmare if ever there was one. To be sure, this should give us pause to wonder about any presumed collision of voice and presence. If, following Giorgio Agamben, the rhyme represents the divergence of sound and sense, the echo completes or intensifies their severance.[2] After all, the intimacy of voice is, in part, a function of its distance from the ear, of its passage between speaker and auditor, its play between internal and external. And indeed, the possibility of this sonorous wandering, this errancy of voice (i.e., this possibility of speaking as or for another), has salvific and playful as well as oppressive possibilities. Adriana Cavarero is surely right to point to the many pleasures that belong to it.[3]

My interest here is in tracing the political valence of the intimacy between voice and ear. The dual power and vulnerability of the voice is something of which the tyrant, for instance, is acutely aware; indeed, as Aristotle points out to us, its exploitation is a tool for the preservation of the tyranny. The tyrant's control of public space is assured by the manipulation of the entire human sensorium, a manipulation that plays in particular on the bond between speaker and listener. For instance, under tyranny, "leisured discussions are not allowed, or other meetings connected with leisure, but everything is done to make all as unknown to one another as possible, for understanding tends to create trust toward one another" (*Politics* 1313b3–6).[4] The tyrant promotes a form of listening that threatens frank speaking—in the attempt "to let nothing that is done or said by any of those he rules escape his notice," the tyrant employs spies (*kataskopous*), "for men speak less freely [*parrēsiazontai*] when they fear such persons, and if they do speak freely [*parrēsiazōntai*] they are less likely to escape notice" (1313b11–16).[5] Tyranny also encourages a form of speaking that interferes with the reception of true meaning: "Also [a feature of tyranny is] to slander them to one another, and set friends at odds with friends, the people with the notables, and the wealthy with themselves" (1313b16–18).[6] All of these incursions into the relationship between voice and ear serve the three essential presuppositions (*hupotheseis*) of tyranny: "That [citizens] not trust one another, that they not be capable, that they have modest thoughts" (1314a28–29).[7] That is, in order to assure the erosion of the political bond, the tyrant must manipulate what is said and what is heard, must pervert the reception of fearless speech—and the trust that is engendered by such speaking and listening—into the covert word of the fearful and the coerced ear of the spy.

And yet, if the manipulation of voice, sound, and hearing is an essential part of the tyrannical city, it is also, for Aristotle, an essential part of the best city.[8] Charged with the generation of citizens of a certain character, the statesman cannot but attend to what citizens say and hear: "Generally, then, the legislator should banish foul speech from the city more than anything else (for by speaking readily about some foul matter one comes closer to doing it), and particularly from among the young, so that they neither say nor hear anything of this sort" (1336b3–68).[9] It is this circuit between speaking, listening, and doing that makes the auditory realm an especially critical political sphere.

I am interested in what makes listening a privileged site of political manipulation and control. That hearing is privileged, even over seeing, is clear from Aristotle's contribution to the question of whether the young should be educated in music. They should be so educated because "it happens that no likeness of characters is present in other perceptible things . . . in tunes by themselves, however, there are imitations of characters" (1340a28–1340a39).[10] This connection between music and character is certainly not Aristotle's invention. It was a well-established trope by Aristotle's time, championed especially by the controversial figure Damon of Oa and represented in a body of pictorial as well as literary sources.[11] It is to this cultural background that Plato is, in part, responding when his Socrates entertains the expulsion of the poets from the city, and, to be sure, Aristotle engages this Platonic line of thinking in several texts.[12]

However, the scholarly tendency to read this passage from the *Politics* as a response to the question of the value of poetry overlooks the specificity of Aristotle's concern with music as such.[13] I follow Andrew Ford in insisting that the object of Aristotle's interest in this discussion of music education is *mousikē* more narrowly understood as harmony and tune themselves.[14] I argue that Aristotle turns to music in outlining the course of education in the best city because tune and harmony are especially good at conveying character, and their capacity to do so is related to the sense medium through which they operate. That is, my claim is that the educative value of listening to music, and the connection between music and character on which it is based, is grounded in the very structure of the perception of sound as Aristotle conceives it.[15]

This shift in perspective does not remove us from the realm of logos, however; rather, it requires us to read logos in another register, for what is received in the case of hearing tune and harmony is not logos in the form of speech but logos in the form of ratio.[16] For Aristotle, the reception of ratio is common to all sense perception. Nevertheless, hearing is unique in its ability to hold together both senses of logos—both speech and ratio—which collide in the case of listening to the human voice. Thus, while poetry as such is not the focus of Aristotle's comments at *Politics* 8.5, careful study of the privileging of tune and harmony does reveal the unique depth of experience that comes from listening to the sound of the human voice. That is, in the bond between voice and ear, we find anticipation of another bond, the political bond. The point of music is not only that the listener is powerfully affected by it but also that a community of listeners is similarly affected, and thus music serves as a means of promoting not only particular *pathē* but the sharing of *pathē*. Music thus offers a powerful tool for unification, and for this very reason, it reveals the depth of human vulnerability to its misuse. To make good on these claims, I begin by exploring in greater detail the relationship between music and character in the *Politics* (section 1), then turn to Aristotle's account of the nature of sound and hearing in *De anima* (section 2), and conclude by returning to the political manipulation of sound, voice, and hearing to highlight how Aristotle's account helps us understand a particularly human vulnerability (section 3).

## 1. Music and Character

Aristotle marks his contribution to the question of the value of musical education by taking issue with its traditional justification as a form of rest, wondering if this effect is perhaps accidental and whether the true nature of music might lie elsewhere, such that "one should not only share in the common pleasure that derives from it, of which all have a perception—for music involves a natural pleasure, hence the practice of it is agreeable to all ages and characters—but see whether in some way it contributes to the character of the soul" (1340a2–6).[17] And the question of whether music contributes to character and the soul "would be clear if we become of a certain quality in our characters on account of it" (1340a7).[18] The answer to this question is, for Aristotle, obvious: "But that we do become of a certain quality is evident through many things, and not least through the tunes of Olympus; for it is agreed that these make souls inspired [*enthousiastikas*] and inspiration is a passion of the character connected with the soul. Further, all who listen to imitations come to experience similar passions [*sumpatheis*], even apart from rhythms and tunes themselves" (1340a10–13).[19]

Aristotle's emphasis here is twofold: on what music makes—on its capacity as a maker (connected to its status as an imitation)—and on its global power, or its ability to make all who listen to it be in a similar state, to share passion. In what follows, Aristotle offers an account of why music should be studied on the basis of its privileged capacity to imitate character and thus for its unique ability not only to resemble character but also to shape the characters of those exposed to it. Indeed, what Aristotle emphasizes throughout, as we shall see, is less the grounds of the likeness between music and character than music's capacity to make one be of a certain character, to put its listeners, however briefly, into the condition of one with such a character. It is less music's capacity to be *made like* than music's capacity to *make* that is at stake here. As both patient and agent, the listener is affected and effects by merit of the curious generative power of music. In this section, I am interested in this power, and to better understand it I follow Aristotle's argument closely. That music has this power over all who hear it is something I explore further in sections 2 and 3.

Aristotle opens his exploration of the pedagogical value of music by drawing it together with what one must learn to do in order to be virtuous: "As music happens to be among the pleasurable things, and virtue is connected to correct enjoyment and affection and hatred, it is clear that one should learn and become habituated to nothing so much as correct judgment and enjoyment of suitable characters and beautiful actions" (1340a14–18).[20] Aristotle then immediately turns to strengthen this connection by identifying the relationship between music and character: "For in rhythms and tunes there are the greatest likenesses to the true nature of anger and gentleness, and further of courage and moderation and all the opposites of these and of the other things pertaining to character. This is clear from the facts: for we are changed in soul by listening to such things" (1340a18–23).[21] Thus, as with his earlier invocation of the music of Olympus, Aristotle argues for the likeness between music and character on the basis of the evident psychological transformation undergone by its listeners. Aristotle then makes explicit the connection between likeness and that of which it is a likeness in the context of things such as pain and enjoyment: "Habituation to feel pain and enjoyment in similar things is close to being in the same manner toward the true thing. For if someone enjoys viewing the image of something not for any reason other than its shape alone, then the very study of the thing the image of which he studies is necessarily pleasant" (1340a23–28).[22] The necessary transfer of pleasure between image and original does more than simply mark the ontological dependence of one on the other. This is about how we come to be properly disposed in and toward pleasure and pain, how we learn to feel pleasure and pain at the right things, an essential feature of successful ethical and political life in the ethics.

Aristotle's point here draws together affect and cognition in a particularly intimate way, one that reveals the profoundly important work of the polis in creating and fostering this transmittable (shared, habituate-able) orientation toward pleasure and pain. For it suggests that a shared emotional comportment is deeply akin to a shared intellectual comportment—that pain and enjoyment are truth disclosive (or at least truth orienting) in some way, so that sharing in them is close to sharing in truth. But it also suggests that truth has some bearing on what should be enjoyed and what pains. The importance of being similarly oriented toward pain and enjoyment is "ethical" and "political" in the deepest of senses, then—that is, in being so oriented, we approximate a shared orientation toward the truth. And while Aristotle is clear that virtue is not a feeling, he is equally clear that how we take up our capacities for pleasure and pain is decisive for our ethical lives and a sign of our character.[23] The suggestion here is that music can help us be pleased by and feel affection and hatred for the right things at the right time and in the right way by making us into the kind of people who do this. In this, music provides a kind of training in and habituation or orientation toward good character by directly shaping our souls, no matter how briefly.

Aristotle then turns to make explicit the privileged relationship music has with character, in a lengthy passage whose significance merits full citation:

> It happens that no likeness of characters [*homoiōma tois ēthesin*] is present in other perceptible things—in things touched or tasted, for example, while in visible things it is present only to a slight degree (for there are figures of this sort, though only to a small extent, and all participate in this sort of perception; and further, these things are not likenesses of characters [*homoiōmata tōn ēthōn*], but the figures and colors that exist of this sort are rather indications [*sēmeia*] of characters, and these only as manifested by the body when it is in the grip of the passions; but to the extent that there is a difference in connection with the study of these things as well, the young should not study the [paintings] of Pauson but those of Polygnotus or of any other painter or sculptor who is expert in character [*ēthikos*]). In tunes by themselves, however, there are imitations of character [*mimēmata tōn ēthōn*] (this is evident; the nature of the harmonies diverged at the outset, so that those listening are in a different state and not in the same condition in relation to each of them. In relation to some—for example, the so-called mixed Lydian—they are in a state more of grief and apprehension [*pros men enias odurtikōterōs kai sunestēkotōs*]; in

relation to others—for example, the relaxed harmonies—they are softer of mind [*pros de tas malakōterōs tēn dianoian*]; they are in a middling and settled state [*mesōs de kai kathestēkotōs*] in relation to one above all, this being what Dorian alone among the harmonies is held to make them; and Phrygian makes them inspired [*enthousiastikos*]. This is what those who have philosophized in connection with this sort of education argue, and rightly; they find proofs for their arguments in the facts themselves). (1340a28–1340b7)[24]

Aristotle's approach here is less that of offering a broad explanation of the relationship between music and character than that of marking a distinct aspect of the sense perception of hearing by demarcating its relation to the conditions of soul indicative of particular character types. That is, Aristotle takes the sensory field as the place in which to search for likenesses of character, displaying, as Andrew Barker describes it, a "scientist's eye for biological and physical subject matter."[25] The only sense that comes close to hearing's connection to character is sight; however, even sight provides not a likeness but a sign. The distinction Aristotle draws here between being a likeness of character and being a sign of character carries significant weight, and the suggestion seems to be that the sign can indicate but does not transmit character in the way that a likeness does. This capacity to transmit accounts for music's status as an imitation.[26] The transmission, in turn, marks a transformation in the listener, and this is clear because of the differential condition in which listeners to various songs find themselves. In short, to hear, more so even than to see, is to be transformed.

What is true of tunes is true of rhythms as well: "Things stand in the same manner with respect to rhythms. For some of them have a character that is more steadfast, some more prone to motion, and of these some have movements that are more vulgar and some more liberal" (1340b7–10).[27] Aristotle concludes by observing,

It is evident from these things that music has the capacity to make [*paraskeuazein*] the character of the soul be of a certain kind. If it has the capacity to do [*poiein*] this, it is clear that it must be administered and the young must be educated in it. The teaching of music is fitting to those of such an age, for because of their age the young do not readily submit to anything not sweetened, and music by nature is among the sweet things. And there seems to be a kinship [in the soul][28] with harmony and rhythm; hence many of the wise say either that the soul is a harmony or that it is like a harmony. (1340b10–19)[29]

It is worth marking the use of *poiein* here; once again, Aristotle's emphasis is on music's capacity to make the character of the soul of a certain sort. Because music has this curious feature—that, more than any other form of art, it conveys character—it must fall under the purview of the statesman charged with producing citizens whose character is of a certain kind. Because its conveying character is also shaping character, music emerges as having a strange sort of power: its ability to be affected as matched by its ability to affect. It translates character into movement and conducts this movement into the ear of another, where, once it enters, it cannot be put down, and this very intimacy is what requires legislative management.

It is here—in the politically motivated direction of listening—that we encounter the most explicit politics of listening in Aristotle. We can ask, what is it about character that makes it amenable to being placed in to or conveyed by sound? Is character like movement somehow? Aristotle suggests as much in the final sentence when he observes a philosophical tendency to associate soul and harmony (and we can certainly see grounds in his ethics for how character could be described under musical terms—its pitch, whether it is tightly or loosely wound, etc.). The thrust of Aristotle's point here, however, is not to motivate a study of the nature of soul but to motivate a legislative effort at its shaping. That is, Aristotle does not take up the question of how music is a likeness of character so much as he asserts the power of music to shape character—his repeated insistence that we attend to the matters themselves, to how things are, to direct experience of the power of music, enforces this sense. And if we follow his argument, music has this power because of a unique feature of the sense of hearing. We cannot fully understand Aristotle's conception of the political value of education in music, then, until we have a clearer sense of his understanding of the relationship between sound and ear. The ethical efficacy of music is in fact connected to the account of sound and hearing Aristotle offers in *De anima* and to the intimacy between sonorous collective and ear that he posits therein.

## 2. Sound and Hearing

In *De anima* 2.8, Aristotle presents the production of sound as a collaborative effort, occurring by way of the interaction between three objects: "Actual sound always comes to be from something, in relation to something, and in something; for it is a striking that makes it [*plēgē gar estin hē poiousa*]. Hence it is impossible for one thing alone to generate sound; for the thing striking and the thing struck are different [*heteron*], so that the sounding thing sounds against something, and striking does not happen without movement from place to place" (*De anima* 419b9–13).[30] Sound itself is the motion of air—Aristotle's acoustics is thus also an aerodynamics—and this qualification is important. Because of air's natural tendency to disperse, the production of sound requires something to counteract this tendency and hold the air together in one single moving mass: "The air itself is without sound, since it is easily dispersed, but whenever it is hindered from being dispersed, the motion of it is sound" (420a7–9).[31] This prevention can be accomplished by two kinds of objects: smooth and hollow. Smooth objects are capable of prohibiting the dispersal of air and concentrating or coalescing it into a single mass because "the surface of a smooth body is itself one" (420a1),[32] and because they are "uniform" [*homalon*], "the air jumps and shakes [*aphallesthai kai seiesthai*] as one mass" (420a25–26).[33] In their provision of a uniform surface against which air can bounce, smooth objects are akin to hollow objects, which produce sound "because they create many blows after the first one by a reverberating [*anaklasei*], since what is set in motion is unable to get out" (419b16–18).[34] This bouncing motion also proves essential to Aristotle's account of the echo: "An echo comes about when some air has become one mass because a vessel surrounds it and hinders its dispersal, and air is pushed back again [*palin . . . apōesthē*], like a ball" (419b25–27).[35]

The structural necessity of this bouncing, reverberating motion for the production of the single mass of moving air that is sound prohibits the reduction of the cause of sound to any single object—"Which of the two makes the sound, the thing that strikes or the thing that is struck? Or is it both in different ways?" (420a19–21)[36]—and requires Aristotle to parse carefully what is *kurios* in the case of sound and hearing. So he observes both that "sound is heard [*akouetai*] in air, and, though less so, in water, although air or water is not authoritative over sound, but there has to be a striking of solid bodies against one another and against the air; this happens when the air that is struck stands firm and does not move about" (419b18–22),[37] and that "it is rightly said that the void is authoritative for hearing [*akouein*], since what seems to be void is air, and this is what produces hearing, when it is set in motion as something that holds together and is one mass; but since air is apt to fly apart, it does not make itself heard if the thing that strikes it is not smooth" (419b33–420a1).[38] It also prompts him to posit the ubiquity of the echo: just as, in the case of seeing, light is always reflected, so also, in the case of hearing, sound is always bounced and "it is likely that an echo always occurs, but not distinctly" (419b27–28).[39]

The reception of sound occurs by way of a structural similarity between the ear and the sonorous collective of striking object, struck object, and air: "What is capable of producing sound, then, is what is capable of moving air that is one [*henos aeros*] continuously [*sunecheia*] all the way up to the ear, but there is air naturally present [*sumphuēs*] in the ear, and since that is also in the air, when the outside air is set in motion, the inside air is moved" (420a3–5).[40] Like the air outside the body, the air inside the body needs to be restricted in its tendency to disperse, and this preventative, coalescing work that is done by smooth things outside the body is accomplished by a morphological feature inside the body: "The air within the ears has been walled in [*egkatōkodomētai*] so as to be stopped from moving, so that there might be an accurate perception of every distinct sort of motion" (420a9–11).[41] And here too we encounter the ubiquity of the echo: "A sign of whether the ear is hearing or not is that there is always a murmuring [*ēchein*] in it, as in a horn, for the air that is in the ears is always moved with a certain motion that belongs to it, but sound is from an external source and not from its own motion" (420a15–18).[42]

There is a great deal of ambiguity here as to how the moving air is conveyed to the ear, and there is no scholarly consensus as to whether we are to think of this description as, for example, an early account of a wave theory of sound, or of the movement it describes as a motion of a block of air, or as an "extraordinary 'quasi-alteration,'" or as a simultaneous transmission/reception of motion.[43] What stands out in any case is that the symbiosis between inside and outside that Aristotle describes is a function of the ambient character of the air. The organ of hearing both is in air and has air in it. Hearing, then, emerges from this account as the translation of external motion into internal motion. In this it produces an intimacy between ear and sound that is predicated on the functional similarity between the uniformity of the smooth object struck and the walls of the ear, both of which allow the air to form a single moving mass, to bounce and reverberate against a surface. To be sure, Aristotle emphasizes the alterity of the sound to the hearing ear: while the air in the ear has its own motion, sound is from an external source. That is, the air in the ear does not become the source of the sound it is hearing. Rather, as with all sense perception, what is received in hearing is a ratio, a logos—in this case, the ratio of the moving air.[44] Instead of collapsing the distinction between internal and external, the act of hearing creates a bond between them, a circuit, that permits interaction without destruction. Indeed, the bond is such that the ear is most firmly what it is when it is hearing and the sonorous object (collective) most firmly itself when it is heard; each gives the other to itself.

For Aristotle, this character is true of all sense perception: all active perceiving activates both the organ of perception and the object of perception, most often through some medium.[45] Sound and hearing are distinct, if not entirely unique, in each of these three aspects. First, the organ of hearing, the ear, is particularly "open" to its medium, as is evident in attending to the differing morphology of eye and ear. While we can both see and hear underwater, Aristotle observes, this is true for the ear only so long as water does not enter into it, which it may do because there is an opening whose spiraling cannot always defend against the incursion of water.

Second, Aristotle goes out of his way to emphasize that the object of hearing is irreducibly dual. There is no single sonorous object—again, "it is impossible for one thing alone to generate sound" (419b9–13) because sound is the effect of an interaction between things. To be sure, Aristotle also casts seeing as requiring the interaction between color and light, and I suppose we could understand light as "striking" the visible thing, but not in the same way or sense—at least, this is not Aristotle's language for the interaction between light and color in *De anima* 2.7, where the emphasis is on light as the active mode of the transparent. The bond between sound and ear is anticipated by the bond that is created between what is striking and what is struck even as that sound stands at some distance from both its source and its destination—even if, as Eve Rabinoff puts it, sound is "untethered" from what strikes and what is struck.[46]

Third, the medium of sound, air, requires this dual and dynamic source because of its tendency toward diffusion, a tendency that must be checked if sound is to occur. Hence the need for both an external smooth object and the anatomical feature of the ear "wall" against which air bounces and is concentrated. And this bouncing, reverberating, echoing motion challenges any notion of an original sound that is then conveyed, in part or in toto, to something else. Indeed, the very ambiguity that generates the debate on how sound moves from object to ear is a function of what appears to be the very structure of sounding here—that is, its reverberation. To sound is simply to echo. The significance of this point is made more evident if we move from the production and reception of sound to the production and reception of voice.

"Voice," Aristotle tells us, "is some sort of sound that is capable of carrying meaning [*sēmantikos*]" (420b33–34).[47] As such, it requires both the physiological structures necessary for the production of sound—that is, air and smooth objects that strike against one another to hold the air together in a single moving mass of sound (in this case, the windpipe)—and also soul and imagination (420b). Presumably, soul and imagination are needed for the formulation of meaning, but the conveyance of meaning still requires material properties. It is these properties that create a likeness between the ensouled creature that has a voice and objects without soul that approximate a voice, which are, tellingly (for our purposes), objects such as musical instruments: "While nothing without a soul has a voice, such things as a flute or a lyre are said to have a voice by way of a likeness [*homoiotēta*], as is any other thing without a soul that has a scale of sounds with pitches and articulation [*melos kai dialekton*], and this is appropriate because the voice also has these" (420b6–9).[48] The sonorous element of the conveyance of meaning creates the conditions for the likeness between musical instrument and voice and also transfers the connection between sonorous collective and ear to the transmission of meaning. And while logos cannot be reduced to this sonorous element, in the context of ancient Greek thought, neither can it be entirely divorced from it; this is so whether we conceive of it as ratio, as speech, or even as argument or reason, which retain their connection to the sonorous even in their silence.[49] That is to say, with voice, the bond between ear and sound is also a bond between ear and meaning, and the intimacy unique to hearing is translated from one register of logos to another—from the reverberations of the ratio of moving air to the repetition and amplification of human speech.

This connection between sound and sense allows us to better see the importance of another feature of music from *Politics* 8.5—namely, its ability to unify, to produce similar passions in all its listeners. For while Aristotle theorizes a sharing of perception, a *sunaisthēsis*, with powerful political implications, and while this shared perception includes a shared viewing [*sunidein*, from *sunoraō*], a shared feeling [*sumpatheis*], and a shared living [*suzēn*], he has no need to theorize a *sunakouein* because by his account of hearing, the *su(n)-* is already implied.[50] That is, to hear is already to share in the movement that is sound, to resonate with it; hearing is a co-moving.

To be sure, this sonorous element brings with it the possibility of errancy, of a detachment of sound from meaning, of the fading of the voice from sense to nonsense. But I believe we can now see that the real threat lies elsewhere. Because of the penetration of sound, because of the depth of its effect, the human is particularly vulnerable to the misuse of sound to convey meaning. That is, not only can we be delighted by the conjunction of sound and sense; we can also be tyrannized by it. For if the capacity to share a common deed produces a particular kind of intimacy, and if the possession of speech and voice and a capacity to hear and be heard intensifies this intimacy, so too does it intensify the vulnerability that accompanies it: the tendency for humans to misrecognize themselves and one another, to fail to share a perception of what it just or unjust, to share an erroneous perception rather than the truth, to wound, to injure, to insult, to slander, to misspeak and mishear, to force to speak and force to hear, and thus to motivate a refusal to speak and a refusal to hear. The concern, then, is less with the errancy of sound than with its misuse. I explore the possibilities of this misuse below.[51]

## 3. Mis-aulogy

In her recent study on self-perception in the *Eudemian Ethics*, Mary Margaret McCabe asks a provocative question: "Why should we not be able to think of a rich perceptual life together, just as we might have a rich shared intellectual life? . . . Is it the mischief of skeptical arguments that prevent us from seeing Aristotle's point in *EE*—that we can have a genuinely shared life of the eye and the ear?"[52] The context of her question is the scholarly debate surrounding Aristotle's conception of the degree of intimacy attained between virtuous friends—such friends are "another self"—and the access to one's self one gains by this intimacy. Aristotle invites this reflection by his use of *sunaisthēsis*, a word that was to play a fateful role in the history of philosophy, being taken up by his commentators to indicate consciousness. But Daniel Heller-Roazen is right to insist that in Aristotle we hear its more literal meaning, a perceiving together, or shared perception, which is the effect of participation in a political community with a common task.[53] McCabe is asking, just as we might imagine a community of thinkers, could we not also imagine a community of seers and hearers?

McCabe's question is remarkable for both its familiarity and its strangeness. After all, it is just such a community that is envisioned in the community of pleasure and pain in Plato's *Republic*, a community in which citizens reach such a condition of unity as to say "my own" of the same things by means of the legislative supervision of all cultural construction and familial reproduction in order to produce a total cultural environment.[54] And it is instructive to consider what this supervision is guarding against: the sophistic environment in which mass praise or blame is collectively uttered with such force that "the rocks and the very place surrounding them echo and redouble the uproar of praise and blame" (*Republic* 492b). And while Aristotle is explicitly critical of this valorization of unity (e.g., *Politics* 2.2.1261a15–23), he too holds the synchronization and uniformity of desire as an end toward which legislators should aim (e.g., *Politics* 2.7.1266b30), as part of the larger job of politics to produce similarity out of the irreducible different components of the polis. Indeed, the regulation of the human sensorium is endemic to the political project as Aristotle constructs it insofar as the happiness of the largest number of people depends on feeling the right things in the right way at the right times. How could a collective pursue a common deed without a shared vision of that deed and the ability to come to agreement about how to attain it? That is, does political life not presuppose a shared and common world? And we must also inquire, just as importantly, into the damage to the political bond when world-building activities are disrupted. Here too we can see Aristotle tracing such possibilities through perception and through the diremption of *sunaisthēsis* to which pathological political communities give rise.

But if Aristotle gives us resources for observing the damaging effects of the dissolution of *sunaisthēsis*, we must also follow Susan Buck-Morss in tracing the damage wrought by its manipulation. After all, totalitarianism, fascism, and neoliberal globalization also attempt a "shared life of eye and ear." Buck-Morss's account of phantasmagoria—that is, various forms of intense sensory manipulation deployed for the sake of producing a narcotic effect, permitting a flight from the sensory shock of the industrialized world, a flight from perception to oblivion, or, in Buck-Morss's own terms, from aesthetics to anaesthetics—illuminates their use as a form of social control. Her masterful account of this control provides a powerful reminder of the deeply nefarious political ends that the exploitation of the human sensorium can serve.[55] The ease with which the created human environment can become toxic to its residents and can motivate a flight from perception is striking, as is the human ability to build worlds that are so contrary to human capacities, joys, and needs as to ultimately become unlivable; in such an environment, the impoverishment of the human sensorium, the dulling and even dismembering of the senses, appears as the only viable adaptive response, the only way to live through the unlivable.[56] We encounter in such a response not only a flight from the "burden" of politics, as Hannah Arendt saw, but also a flight from consciousness itself.[57]

Aristotle is not unaware of the nefarious manipulation of *sunaisthēsis*—his account of tyranny hinges on precisely such a manipulation—and of the failures of *sunaisthēsis* on its own to assure political well-being and stability. Aristotle attributes instability to oligarchies and democracies, for instance, precisely on the grounds that their shared sense of justice and injustice is erroneous (*Politics* 5.1, 1301a35). And it is precisely because he is sensitive to the capacity of shared perception to produce a unified body of experience—recall that part of the evidence of the connection between music and character lies in ability of the tunes of Olympus to affect all listeners with shared passions—that he insists the legislator cannot do without requiring education through music. What I hope to have drawn out here is that Aristotle helps us better understand the particular role hearing plays in political coercion and control, and he provides resources for accounting for the very specific human vulnerability to the exploitation of the intimacy between voice and ear.

Both Aristotle and Buck-Morss demonstrate that the human is an animal that can choose not to hear. The political stakes of such a refusal are particularly high, as was already evident in the ancient Greek world: "How could you persuade us," asks Polemarchus of Socrates, "if we will not listen?" (*Republic* 327c). But of course, Polemarchus's desire to listen is revealed by the very force with which he detains Socrates and Glaucon. Stopping up one's ears, denying oneself access to this aspect of reality, takes work and practice. One has to be motivated to do so—motivated, perhaps, by deafening sound, by the constant maddening buzz of a crowd or even a single insect, by the deadly seduction of a voice that lures you in only to destroy you (the Sirens), by the pernicious effects of false and politically motivated slander, or by efforts to force hearing, efforts that foster a hatred for human speech and reason that is also a hatred of sound and hearing, a misology that is also a mis-aulogy.

If we move from a negating impulse to remove sound and voice to a positing impulse to force listening to certain sounds and voices, we can imagine an aural environment that has become so toxic as to poison its listeners. This is precisely the environment engineered in the use of sound as a form of torture, a practice that galvanized activist, scholarly, and performer response in light of recent revelation of the use of the practice on detainees of US-operated detention centers across the globe.[58] The aim of sound torture, as with sleep deprivation and excessive light exposure, is to exploit human perceptual sensitivity and bodily limit, to create an unlivable environment to which the human body cannot adapt, an environment that attacks the terms of human embodiment themselves. Observers and victims of the practice alike describe its incursion on equilibrium and bodily integrity as unbearable.[59] And here too the efficacy of the practice is due partly to the specific anatomy of human hearing: the anxiety and tension that sound torture creates are functions of the fact that, as musician Lawrence English puts it, "we have no earlids."[60]

A less violent, although markedly coercive, deployment of forced listening is evident in the case of the auditory component of a wave of proposed antiabortion legislation that would either require a physician to play the rhythmic electrical activity of a cluster of cells that could eventually form a fetal cardiac system and that is detectable at around six weeks of pregnancy, or require the physician to give the pregnant woman the option of hearing this activity before abortion services are given.[61] In this scenario, fetal cardiac activity is presented as an unambiguous bearer of obvious meaning, correlate to the treatment of the ultrasound image as a first baby picture, as though these perceptions were not occurring in a context and power structure that shape their meaning, as though they were not simultaneously objects of perception and interpretation, as though they had only one correct response.[62] In this context, forced listening is also forced meaning reception; it forces a particular interpretation while treating that interpretation as naturally adhering to the sound—that is, it treats the sound as a voice. Like the use of sound torture, such legislation exploits the particular vulnerability, or openness, that accompanies the capacity for hearing; one cannot avert one's ears in the way one can avert one's gaze, and so the option to not listen simply masks the demand to listen. Or, as one scholar concludes, "Since the option to avert one's ears ought not to be taken seriously, it is clear that a law that forces a woman to listen disrespects autonomy."[63]

Pathological political formations normalize these kinds of extremes and create a tyranny of the senses, perhaps the natural end of a society of the spectacle. We must weigh our interpretation of Aristotle's optimistic claim that all humans by nature desire to know (*Metaphysics* 1.1, 980a) against the possibility of deforming, toxic environments that exploit this desire, and even the possibility that there resides in human nature some resistance to it. That is, we must measure this claim against the tragic rejections of sensory life, as with, for instance, Oedipus's self-blinding.[64] Unable to unsee what he has seen, to unhear what he has heard, to unknow what he knows, Oedipus rejects access to a world that holds only the promise of further suffering. But of course, this only condemns him to the memory of what he has seen and heard. Oedipus's fate suggests that avoidance of the risk of exploitation is not a viable form of resistance against encroachment on one's autonomy. To be sure, in his *Politics*, Aristotle displays an ambivalence toward personal autonomy—"One ought not even consider that a citizen belongs to himself, but rather that all belong to the city" (1337a27)—and certainly would not have conceded such autonomy to women. My point is simply that his conception of the nature of sound and hearing and his account of the connection between voice and ear provide a useful measure of the exploitation at work in such environments and suggest that effective resistance to sensory encroachment requires an ecological approach—that is, a focus on dismantling the framework that produces such environments in the first place.

## Notes

1. "The word parrhesia, then, refers to a type of relationship between the speaker and what he says. For in parrhesia, the speaker makes it manifestly clear and obvious that what he says is his own opinion . . . in parrhesia, the parrhesiastes acts on other people's minds by showing them as directly as possible what he actually believes." Michel Foucault, *Fearless Speech* (Cambridge, MA: Semiotext(e), 2001), 12. In response to a question about his use of the masculine pronoun, Foucault observed that in the ancient context the figure was primarily thought of as male. Judith Butler's Antigone might disagree, and in the conclusion, I return to the question of gender and voice.

2. Giorgio Agamben, *The End of the Poem: Studies in Poetics* (Stanford, CA: Stanford University Press, 1999).

3. Adriana Cavarero, *For More Than One Voice: Toward a Philosophy of Vocal Expression*, trans. Paul Kottman (Palo Alto, CA: Stanford University Press, 2005).

4. "καὶ μήτε σχολὰς μήτε ἄλλους συλλόγους ἐπιτρέπειν γίγνεσθαι σχολαστικούς, καὶ πάντα ποιεῖν ἐξ ὧν ὅτι μάλιστα
"ἀγνῶτες ἀλλήλοις ἔσονται πάντες (ἡ γὰρ γνῶσις πίστιν ποιεῖ μᾶλλον πρὸς ἀλλήλους)."
The Greek text is that of Ross for the OCT. Unless otherwise noted, all translations are my own.

5. "καὶ τὸ μὴ λανθάνειν πειρᾶσθαι ὅσα τυγχάνει τις λέγων ἢ πράττων τῶν ἀρχομένων, ἀλλ' εἶναι κατασκόπους, οἷον

"περὶ Συρακούσας αἱ ποταγωγίδες καλούμεναι, καὶ οὓς ὠτακουστὰς ἐξέπεμπεν Ἱέρων, ὅπου τις εἴη συνουσία καὶ σύλλογος (παρρησιάζονταί τε γὰρ ἧττον, φοβούμενοι τοὺς τοιούτους, κἂν παρρησιάζωνται, λανθάνουσιν ἧττον)."

6. "καὶ τὸ διαβάλλειν ἀλλήλοις καὶ συγκρούειν καὶ φίλους φίλοις καὶ τὸν δῆμον τοῖς γνωρίμοις καὶ τοὺς πλουσίους ἑαυτοῖς."

7. "τὰ μὲν ὅπως μὴ πιστεύωσιν ἀλλήλοις, τὰ δ' ὅπως μὴ δύνωνται, τὰ δ' ὅπως μικρὸν φρονῶσιν."

8. As Jill Gordon and Ryan Drake point out in their contributions to this volume, the manipulation of sound and hearing for aspirational political purposes was also a central feature of Platonic political theory and practice. In Plato's case as well, this sensory management draws the philosophical city into the orbit of the tyrannical; see also Victoria Wohl, "Plato avant le Lettre: Authenticity in Plato's Epistles," *Ramus* 27, no. 1 (1998): 60–93; Cavarero, *More Than One Voice*; Cinzia Arruzza, *A Wolf in the City: Tyranny and the Tyrant in Plato's Republic* (Oxford: Oxford University Press, 2018).

9. "ὅλως μὲν οὖν αἰσχρολογίαν ἐκ τῆς πόλεως, ὥσπερ ἄλλο τι, δεῖ τὸν νομοθέτην ἐξορίζειν (ἐκ τοῦ γὰρ εὐχερῶς λέγειν ὁτιοῦν τῶν αἰσχρῶν γίνεται καὶ τὸ ποιεῖν σύνεγγυς)."

10. "συμβέβηκε δὲ τῶν αἰσθητῶν ἐν μὲν τοῖς ἄλλοις μηδὲν ὑπάρχειν ὁμοίωμα τοῖς ἤθεσιν . . . ἐν δὲ τοῖς μέλεσιν αὐτοῖς ἔστι μιμήματα τῶν ἠθῶν."

11. On the pictorial sources, see Sheramy Bundrick, *Music and Image in Classical Athens* (Cambridge: Cambridge University Press, 2005); on Damon of Oa, see Robert W. Wallace, *Reconstructing Damon: Music, Wisdom Teaching, and Politics in Perikles' Athens* (Oxford: Oxford University Press, 2015).

12. In terms that often anticipate Aristotle's account of the power of music over the listener—for example, "Because rhythm and harmony most of all insinuate themselves into the inmost part of the soul and most vigorously lay hold of it in bringing grace with them; and they make a man graceful if he is correctly reared, if not, the opposite. Furthermore, it is sovereign because the man properly reared on rhythm and harmony would have the sharpest sense for what's been left out"(*Republic* 401d) and "When a man gives himself to music and lets the flute play and pour into his soul through his ears, as it were into a funnel" (*Republic* 411a).

13. For a recent example of this kind of argument, see Philipp Brüllmann, "Music Builds Character: Aristotle, *Politics* VIII 5, 1340a14–b5," *Apeiron* 46, no. 4 (2013): 345–373. It also suggests that the most informative place to go for further information on this line of thinking is Aristotle's ethics.

14. Andrew Ford, "Catharsis: The Power of Music in Aristotle's *Politics*," in *Music and the Muses: The Culture of Mousikē in the Classical Athenian City*, ed. Penelope Murray and Peter Wilson (Oxford: Oxford University Press, 2004), 309–336. If we want to understand the privileging of music in the *Politics*, then, we must look not only to what is said of character in the ethics but also to what is said of sound in *De anima*.

15. Of course, these need not and should not be mutually exclusive investigations. For a recent account of the role of perception in Aristotle's ethics, see Eve Rabinoff, *Perception in Aristotle's Ethics* (Evanston, IL: Northwestern University Press, 2018).

16. For an account of the significance of logos as speech to the *Politics*, see Jill Frank, "On *Logos* and Politics in Aristotle," in *Aristotle's Politics: A Critical Guide*, ed. Thornton Lockwood and Thanassis Samaras (Cambridge: Cambridge University Press, 2015), 9–26. For a recent comprehensive study of the senses of logos in Aristotle, see Ömër Aygun, *The Middle Included: Logos in Aristotle* (Evanston, IL: Northwestern University Press, 2017). While I agree that "speech" is the dominant sense of logos in the *Politics*, the use of logos as "ratio"

that permeates Aristotle's discussion of sense perception elsewhere in the corpus is invited by the particular context of inquiry in this section of the *Politics*.

17. "καὶ δεῖ μὴ μόνον τῆς κοινῆς ἡδονῆς μετέχειν ἀπ' αὐτῆς, ἧς ἔχουσι πάντες αἴσθησιν (ἔχει γὰρ ἡ μουσική τιν' ἡδονὴν φυσικήν, διὸ πάσαις ἡλικίαις καὶ πᾶσιν ἤθεσιν ἡ χρῆσις αὐτῆς ἐστι προσφιλής), ἀλλ' ὁρᾶν εἴ πῃ καὶ πρὸς τὸ ἦθος συντείνει καὶ πρὸς τὴν ψυχήν."

18. "τοῦτο δ' ἂν εἴη δῆλον, εἰ ποιοί τινες τὰ ἤθη γιγνόμεθα δι' αὐτῆς."

19. "ἀλλὰ μὴν ὅτι γιγνόμεθα ποιοί τινες, φανερὸν διὰ πολλῶν μὲν καὶ ἑτέρων, οὐχ ἥκιστα δὲ καὶ διὰ τῶν Ὀλύμ- "που μελῶν· ταῦτα γὰρ ὁμολογουμένως ποιεῖ τὰς ψυχὰς ἐνθουσιαστικάς, ὁ δ' ἐνθουσιασμὸς τοῦ περὶ τὴν ψυχὴν ἤθους πάθος ἐστίν. ἔτι δὲ ἀκροώμενοι τῶν μιμήσεων γίγνονται πάντες συμπαθεῖς, καὶ χωρὶς τῶν ῥυθμῶν καὶ τῶν μελῶν αὐτῶν." Although I continue to cite Ross's edition of the Greek text, I follow Ford ("Catharsis") in recommending Susmeihle's emendation to the text here.

20. "ἐπεὶ δὲ συμβέβηκεν εἶναι τὴν μουσικὴν τῶν ἡδέων, τὴν δ' ἀρετὴν περὶ τὸ χαίρειν ὀρθῶς καὶ φιλεῖν καὶ μισεῖν, δεῖ δηλονότι μανθάνειν καὶ συνεθίζεσθαι μηθὲν οὕτως ὡς τὸ κρίνειν ὀρθῶς καὶ τὸ χαίρειν τοῖς ἐπιεικέσιν ἤθεσι καὶ ταῖς καλαῖς πράξεσιν."
An emphasis on the pleasure of music returns at the end of this discussion, when Aristotle observes that its natural sweetness particularly recommends it to the young. Also, it is worth emphasizing the melding of thinking and feeling here that is brought about by the close proximity of judgment and enjoyment, of *to krinein* and *to chairein*, and already anticipated by the conjunction of learning and habituation, *manthanein* and *sunethezesthai*.

21. "ἔστι δὲ ὁμοιώματα μάλιστα παρὰ τὰς ἀληθινὰς φύσεις ἐν τοῖς ῥυθμοῖς καὶ τοῖς μέλεσιν ὀργῆς
"καὶ πραότητος, ἔτι δ' ἀνδρείας καὶ σωφροσύνης καὶ πάντων τῶν ἐναντίων τούτοις καὶ τῶν ἄλλων ἠθῶν (δῆλον δὲ ἐκ τῶν ἔργων· μεταβάλλομεν γὰρ τὴν ψυχὴν ἀκροώμενοι τοιούτων)."

22. "ὁ δ' ἐν τοῖς ὁμοίοις ἐθισμὸς τοῦ λυπεῖσθαι καὶ χαίρειν ἐγγύς ἐστι τῷ πρὸς τὴν ἀλήθειαν τὸν αὐτὸν ἔχειν τρόπον (οἶον εἴ τις χαίρει τὴν εἰκόνα τινὸς θεώμενος μὴ δι' ἄλλην αἰτίαν ἀλλὰ διὰ τὴν μορφὴν αὐτήν, ἀναγκαῖον τούτῳ καὶ αὐτοῦ ἐκείνου τὴν θεωρίαν, οὗ τὴν εἰκόνα θεωρεῖ,
"ἡδεῖαν εἶναι)."

23. See, e.g., *Nicomachean Ethics* 2.5. For this reason, I think Brüllmann ("Music Builds Character") overstates the relationship between virtues of character and emotions.

24. "συμβέβηκε δὲ τῶν αἰσθητῶν ἐν μὲν τοῖς ἄλλοις μηδὲν ὑπάρχειν ὁμοίωμα τοῖς ἤθεσιν, οἶον ἐν τοῖς ἁπτοῖς καὶ τοῖς γευστοῖς, ἀλλ' ἐν τοῖς ὁρατοῖς ἠρέμα (σχήματα γὰρ ἔστι τοιαῦτα, ἀλλ' ἐπὶ μικρόν, καὶ πάντες τῆς τοιαύτης αἰσθήσεως κοινωνοῦσιν· ἔτι δὲ οὐκ ἔστι ταῦτα ὁμοιώματα τῶν ἠθῶν, ἀλλὰ σημεῖα μᾶλλον τὰ γιγνόμενα σχήματα καὶ χρώματα τῶν ἠθῶν, καὶ ταῦτ' ἐστὶν ἐπίσημα ἐν τοῖς πάθεσιν· οὐ μὴν ἀλλ' ὅσον διαφέρει καὶ περὶ τὴν τούτων θεωρίαν, δεῖ μὴ τὰ Παύσωνος θεωρεῖν τοὺς νέους, ἀλλὰ τὰ Πολυγνώτου κἂν εἴ τις ἄλλος τῶν γραφέων ἢ τῶν ἀγαλματοποιῶν ἐστιν ἠθικός), ἐν δὲ τοῖς μέλεσιν αὐτοῖς ἔστι μιμήματα τῶν ἠθῶν (καὶ τοῦτ' ἐστὶ φανερόν· εὐθὺς γὰρ ἡ τῶν ἁρμονιῶν διέστηκε φύσις, ὥστε ἀκούοντας ἄλλως διατίθεσθαι καὶ μὴ τὸν αὐτὸν ἔχειν τρόπον πρὸς ἑκάστην αὐτῶν, ἀλλὰ πρὸς μὲν ἐνίας ὀδυρτικωτέρως καὶ συνεστηκότως μᾶλλον, οἷον πρὸς τὴν μιξολυδιστὶ καλουμένην, πρὸς δὲ τὰς μαλακωτέρως τὴν διάνοιαν, οἷον πρὸς τὰς ἀνειμένας, μέσως δὲ καὶ καθεστηκότως μάλιστα πρὸς ἑτέραν, οἷον δοκεῖ ποιεῖν ἡ δωριστὶ μόνη τῶν ἁρμονιῶν, ἐνθουσιαστικοὺς δ' ἡ φρυγιστί. ταῦτα γὰρ καλῶς λέγουσιν οἱ περὶ τὴν παιδείαν ταύτην πεφιλοσοφηκότες· λαμβάνουσι γὰρ τὰ μαρτύρια τῶν λόγων ἐξ αὐτῶν τῶν ἔργων)."

25. Andrew Barker, *Greek Musical Writings II: Harmonic and Acoustic Theory* (Cambridge: Cambridge University Press, 1989), 77–80, cited in Ford, "Catharsis," 315. For

Ford, "if Aristotle first approaches mousikē as a traditional social and educational practice, to understand its proper uses in the city he considers it as a natural phenomenon to be understood in scientific terms" and concludes that "the somewhat mysterious but undeniably potent resonance between sheer sounds and psyches will open a deep vein of reflection for the political scientist" (ibid.).

26. I take this notion of transmission to be implicit in ancient accounts of mimesis, especially those of both Plato and Aristotle. However else they may differ on the subject, Aristotle appears to be taking for granted Plato's Socrates's sense of the hold of mimesis—how could one stop someone from imitating what they find to be attractive or desirable? And here is where we must observe Aristotle's repeated point about the inherent sweetness of music (1340b17)—because music is naturally sweet, it will attract interest and desire, especially that of the young. And because it is so powerfully affecting, it will use that attracting to instill, inspire, and shape character. But this power cuts both ways, and just as it can mold souls into politically salutary conditions, so can it mold them into dangerous states.

27. "τὸν αὐτὸν δὲ τρόπον ἔχει καὶ τὰ περὶ τοὺς ῥυθμούς (οἱ μὲν γὰρ ἦθος ἔχουσι στασιμώτερον οἱ δὲ κινητικόν, καὶ τούτων οἱ μὲν φορτικωτέρας ἔχουσι τὰς κινήσεις οἱ δὲ ἐλευθεριωτέρας)."

28. Here I follow Ford ("Catharsis") contra Lord's assertion that the kinship is between the young and harmony and rhythm.

29. "ἐκ μὲν οὖν τούτων φανερὸν ὅτι δύναται ποιόν τι τὸ τῆς ψυχῆς ἦθος ἡ μουσικὴ παρασκευάζειν, εἰ δὲ τοῦτο δύναται ποιεῖν, δῆλον ὅτι προσακτέον καὶ παιδευτέον ἐν αὐτῇ τοὺς νέους. ἔστι δὲ ἁρμόττουσα πρὸς τὴν φύσιν τὴν τηλικαύτην ἡ διδασκαλία τῆς μουσικῆς· οἱ μὲν γὰρ νέοι διὰ τὴν ἡλικίαν ἀνήδυντον οὐθὲν ὑπομένουσιν ἑκόντες, ἡ δὲ μουσικὴ φύσει τῶν ἡδυσμάτων ἐστίν. καί τις ἔοικε συγγένεια ταῖς ἁρμονίαις καὶ τοῖς ῥυθμοῖς εἶναι· διὸ πολλοί φασι τῶν σοφῶν οἱ μὲν ἁρμονίαν εἶναι τὴν ψυχήν, οἱ δ' ἔχειν ἁρμονίαν."

30. "γίνεται δ' ὁ κατ' ἐνέργειαν ψόφος ἀεί τινος πρός τι καὶ ἔν τινι· πληγὴ γάρ ἐστιν ἡ ποι-οῦσα. διὸ καὶ ἀδύνατον ἑνὸς ὄντος γενέσθαι ψόφον· ἕτερον γὰρ τὸ τύπτον καὶ τὸ τυπτόμενον· ὥστε τὸ ψοφοῦν πρός τι
"ψοφεῖ· πληγὴ δ' οὐ γίνεται ἄνευ φορᾶς."

31. "αὐτὸς μὲν δὴ ἄψοφον ὁ ἀὴρ διὰ τὸ εὔθρυπτον· ὅταν δὲ κωλυθῇ θρύπτεσθαι, ἡ τούτου κίνησις ψόφος."

32. "ἓν γὰρ τὸ τοῦ λείου ἐπίπεδον."

33. "ὥστε τὸν ἀέρα ἀθροῦν ἀφάλλεσθαι καὶ σείεσθαι."

34. "τὰ δὲ κοῖλα τῇ ἀνακλάσει πολλὰς ποιεῖ πληγὰς μετὰ τὴν πρώτην, ἀδυνατοῦντος ἐξελθεῖν τοῦ κινηθέντος."

35. "ἠχὼ δὲ γίνεται ὅταν, ἀέρος ἑνὸς γενομένου διὰ τὸ ἀγγεῖον τὸ διορίσαν καὶ κωλῦσαν θρυφθῆναι, πάλιν ὁ ἀὴρ ἀπωσθῇ, ὥσπερ σφαῖρα."

36. "πότερον δὲ ψοφεῖ τὸ τυπτόμενον ἢ τὸ τύπτον; ἢ καὶ ἄμφω, τρόπον δ' ἕτερον."

37. "ἔτι ἀκούεται ἐν ἀέρι, κἂν ὕδατι, ἀλλ' ἧττον, οὐκ ἔστι δὲ ψόφου κύριος ὁ ἀὴρ οὐδὲ τὸ ὕδωρ, ἀλλὰ δεῖ στερεῶν πληγὴν γενέσθαι πρὸς ἄλληλα καὶ πρὸς τὸν ἀέρα. τοῦτο δὲ γίνεται ὅταν ὑπομένῃ πληγεὶς ὁ ἀὴρ καὶ μὴ δια-
"χυθῇ."

38. "τὸ δὲ κενὸν ὀρθῶς λέγεται κύριον τοῦ ἀκούειν. δοκεῖ γὰρ εἶναι κενὸν ὁ ἀήρ, οὗτος δ' ἐστὶν ὁ ποιῶν ἀκούειν, ὅταν κινηθῇ συνεχὴς καὶ εἷς. ἀλλὰ διὰ τὸ ψαθυρὸς εἶναι οὐ γεγωνεῖ, ἂν μὴ λεῖον ᾖ τὸ πληγέν."

39. "ἔοικε δ' ἀεὶ γίνεσθαι ἠχώ, ἀλλ' οὐ σαφής."

40. "ψοφητικὸν μὲν οὖν τὸ κινητικὸν ἑνὸς ἀέρος συνεχείᾳ μέχρις ἀκοῆς. ἀκοῇ δὲ συμφυὴς ἀήρ· διὰ δὲ τὸ ἐν ἀέρι εἶναι, κινουμένου τοῦ ἔξω ὁ εἴσω κινεῖται."

41. "ὁ δ' ἐν τοῖς ὠσὶν ἐγκατῳκοδόμηται πρὸς τὸ ἀκίνητος εἶναι, ὅπως ἀκριβῶς αἰσθάνηται πάσας τὰς διαφορὰς τῆς κινήσεως."

42. "ἀλλ' οὐ σημεῖον τοῦ ἀκούειν ἢ μὴ τὸ ἠχεῖν τὸ οὖς ὥσπερ τὸ κέρας· ἀεὶ γὰρ οἰκείαν τινὰ κίνησιν ὁ ἀὴρ κινεῖται ὁ ἐν τοῖς ὠσίν, ἀλλ' ὁ ψόφος ἀλλότριος καὶ οὐκ ἴδιος."

43. The cited ideas, in the order I have listed them, are from Mark A. Johnstone, "Aristotle on Sounds." *British Journal for the History of Philosophy* 29, no. 4 (2013): 631–648; A. Towy, "Aristotle and Alexander on Hearing and Instantaneous Change: A Dilemma in Aristotle's Account of Hearing," in *The Second Sense: Studies in Hearing and Musical Judgment from Antiquity to the Seventeenth Century*, ed. Charles Burnett, Michael Fend, and Penelope Gouk (London: Warburg Institute, 1991), 7–18; Miles Burnyeat, "How Much Happens When Aristotle Sees Red and Hears Middle C? Remarks on *De anima* 2.7–8," In *Essays on Aristotle's "De anima,"* ed. Martha Nussbaum and Amelie Rorty (Oxford: Oxford University Press, 1995), 421–434; Stephen Kidd, "Sound: An Aristotelian Perspective," in *Sound and the Ancient Senses*, ed. Shane Butler and Sarah Nooter (New York: Routledge, 2019), 79–91.

44. Kidd ("Sound") draws the necessary conclusion this holds for how sound is conveyed.

45. However, his account of touch famously complicates the presence of a medium.

46. Rabinoff, "Hearing, Touch, and Practical Intelligence in Aristotle's Philosophy," in this volume.

47. "σημαντικὸς γὰρ δή τις ψόφος ἐστὶν ἡ φωνή."

48. "τῶν γὰρ ἀψύχων οὐθὲν φωνεῖ, ἀλλὰ καθ' ὁμοιότητα λέγεται φωνεῖν, οἷον αὐλὸς καὶ λύρα καὶ ὅσα ἄλλα τῶν
"ἀψύχων ἀπότασιν ἔχει καὶ μέλος καὶ διάλεκτον. ἔοικε γάρ, ὅτι καὶ ἡ φωνὴ ταῦτ' ἔχει."

49. As with Plato's sense of thought as silent conversation with oneself, a point Gordon makes in her introduction to this volume and her chapter in it.

50. Both *sunakouo*, "to hear together," and *sunecheo*, "to ring with or echo to," were certainly available to him.

51. The sonorous wanderings of Echo, the "threat" of nonsense, would here provide a balm, a way of short-circuiting the effects of such misuse by diffusing its meaning.

52. Mary Margaret McCabe, "With Mirrors or Without? Self-Perception in *Eudemian Ethics* VII.12," in *The Eudemian Ethics on the Voluntary, Friendship, and Luck*, ed. Fiona Leigh (Boston: Brill, 2012), 72.

53. Daniel Heller-Roazen, *The Inner Touch: Archaeology of a Sensation*, New York: Zone Books, 2009), 81; see references in 310n1.

54. The pastoral terms Plato uses to illustrate this supervision are noteworthy: "And the incapable craftsman we mustn't permit to practice his craft among us, so that our guardians won't be reared on images of vice, as it were on bad grass, every day cropping and grazing on a great deal little by little from many places . . . Mustn't we rather look for those craftsmen whose good natural endowments make them able to track down the nature of what is fine and graceful, so that the young, dwelling as it were in a healthy place . . ." (*Republic* 401c–d).

55. Susan Buck-Morss, "Aesthetics and Anaesthetics: Walter Benjamin's Artwork Essay Reconsidered," *October* 62 (1992): 3–41.

56. For a development of the concept of unlivable life in the context of Aristotle's political theory, see Sara Brill, *Aristotle on the Concept of Shared Life* (Oxford: Oxford University Press, 2020).

57. Hannah Arendt, *The Human Condition* (Chicago: University of Chicago Press, 1958).

58. See, e.g., Suzanne Cusick and Brandon W. Joseph, "Across an Invisible Line: A Conversation about Music and Torture," *Grey Room* 42 (2011): 6–21; Morag Josephine

Grant, "Pathways to Music Torture," *Transposition: Musique et sciences sociales* 4 (2014), https://journals.openedition.org/transposition/494; Anna Papaeti, "On Music, Torture and Detention: Reflections on Issues of Research and Discipline," *Transposition: Musique et sciences sociales* 2 (2020), https://journals.openedition.org/transposition/5289.

59. For example, John Leach, "Psychological Factors in Exceptional, Extreme and Tortuous Environments," *Extreme Physiology and Medicine* 5 (2016): 7, https://extremephysiolmed.biomedcentral.com/articles/10.1186/s13728-016-0048-y.

60. Lawrence English, "The Sound of Fear," *Conversation*, October 6, 2016, https://theconversation.com/friday-essay-the-sound-of-fear-65230.

61. In this scenario, "just as doctors are required to show the images, with the pregnant woman having the option to avert her eyes, in at least one case, the law mandates that the doctor play an auditory recording of the fetal heartbeat, only allowing the pregnant woman to somehow avert her ears." James Rocha, "Forced to Listen to the Heart: Fetal Heartbeat Laws and Autonomous Abortions," *Southwest Philosophy Review* 30, no. 1 (2014): 188.

62. The authors of an early article on ultrasound technology are explicit in their assumption: early viewing of ultrasound images, they conclude, is likely to lead women "to experience a shock of recognition that the fetus belongs to them" (John C. Fletcher and Mark I. Evans, "Maternal Bonding in Early Fetal Ultrasound Examinations," *New England Journal of Medicine* 308 [1983]: 392–393). The manipulation of viewing here, the refusal to acknowledge the clinical context, the particular reproductive context of the woman, and indeed the erasure of the woman that is conducted by the image itself all resonate with the effects of forced listening. As Moira Weigel puts it, "The framing of the ultrasound image was notable for what it excluded: the woman. In order to make the fetus visible, it made her disappear" ("How Ultrasound Became Political," *Atlantic*, January 24, 2017, https://www.theatlantic.com/health/archive/2017/01/ultrasound-woman-pregnancy/514109/).

63. Rocha, "Forced to Listen," 188.

64. For an extended reading of the relevance of Oedipus to the ethical valence of perception, see Aygun, *Middle Included*.

# Bibliography

Agamben, Giorgio. *The End of the Poem: Studies in Poetics.* Stanford, CA: Stanford University Press, 1999.

Arendt, Hannah. *The Human Condition.* Chicago: University of Chicago Press, 1968.

Arruzza, Cinzia. *A Wolf in the City: Tyranny and the Tyrant in Plato's "Republic."* Oxford: Oxford University Press, 2018.

Aygun, Ömër. *The Middle Included: Logos in Aristotle.* Evanston, IL: Northwestern University Press, 2017.

Barker, Andrew. *Greek Musical Writings II: Harmonic and Acoustic Theory.* Cambridge: Cambridge University Press, 1989.

Brill, Sara. *Aristotle on the Concept of Shared Life.* Oxford: Oxford University Press, 2020.

Brüllmann, Philipp. "Music Builds Character: Aristotle, *Politics* VIII 5, 1340a14–b5." *Apeiron* 46, no. 4 (2013): 345–373.

Buck-Morss, Susan. "Aesthetics and Anaesthetics: Walter Benjamin's Artwork Essay Reconsidered." *October* 62 (1992): 3–41.

Bundrick, Sheramy. *Music and Image in Classical Athens.* Cambridge: Cambridge University Press, 2005.

Burnyeat, Miles. "How Much Happens When Aristotle Sees Red and Hears Middle C? Remarks on *De anima* 2.7–8." In *Essays on Aristotle's "De anima,"* edited by Martha Nussbaum and Amelie Rorty, 421–434. Oxford: Oxford University Press, 1995.

Cavarero, Adriana. *For More Than One Voice: Toward a Philosophy of Vocal Expression.* Translated by Paul Kottman. Palo Alto, CA: Stanford University Press, 2005.

Cusick, Suzanne and Brandon W. Joseph. "Across an Invisible Line: A Conversation about Music and Torture." *Grey Room* 42 (2011): 6–21.

English, Lawrence. "The Sound of Fear." *Conversation,* October 6, 2016. https:// theconversation.com/friday-essay-the-sound-of-fear-65230.

Fletcher, John C., and Mark I. Evans. "Maternal Bonding in Early Fetal Ultrasound Examinations." *New England Journal of Medicine* 308 (1983): 392–393.

Ford, Andrew. "Catharsis: The Power of Music in Aristotle's *Politics.*" In *Music and the Muses: The Culture of Mousikē in the Classical Athenian City,* edited by Penelope Murray and Peter Wilson, 309–336. Oxford: Oxford University Press, 2004.

Foucault, Michele. *Fearless Speech.* Cambridge, MA: Semiotext(e), 2001.

Frank, Jill. "On *Logos* and Politics in Aristotle." In *Aristotle's "Politics": A Critical Guide,* edited by Thornton Lockwood and Thanassis Samaras, 9–26. Cambridge: Cambridge University Press, 2015.

Grant, Morag Josephine. "Pathways to Music Torture." *Transposition: Musique et sciences sociales* 4 (2014). https://journals.openedition.org/transposition/494.

Heller-Roazen, Daniel. *The Inner Touch: Archaeology of a Sensation.* New York: Zone Books, 2009.

Johnstone Mark A. "Aristotle on Sounds." *British Journal for the History of Philosophy* 29, no. 4 (2013): 631–648.

Kidd, Stephen. "Sound: An Aristotelian Perspective." In *Sound and the Ancient Senses,* edited by Shane Butler and Sarah Nooter, 79–91. New York: Routledge, 2019.

Leach, John. "Psychological Factors in Exceptional, Extreme and Tortuous Environments." *Extreme Physiology and Medicine* 5 (2016): 7. https://extremephysiolmed .biomedcentral.com/articles/10.1186/s13728-016-0048-y.

McCabe, Mary Margaret. "With Mirrors or Without? Self-Perception in *Eudemian Ethics* VII.12." In *The Eudemian Ethics on the Voluntary, Friendship, and Luck,* edited by Fiona Leigh, 43–75. Boston: Brill, 2012.

Papaeti, Anna. "On Music, Torture and Detention: Reflections on Issues of Research and Discipline." *Transposition: Musique et sciences sociales* 2 (2020). https://journals .openedition.org/transposition/5289.

Rabinoff, Eve. *Perception in Aristotle's Ethics.* Evanston, IL: Northwestern University Press, 2018.

Rocha, James. "Forced to Listen to the Heart: Fetal Heartbeat Laws and Autonomous Abortions." *Southwest Philosophy Review* 30, no. 1 (2014): 187–194.

Towy, A. "Aristotle and Alexander on Hearing and Instantaneous Change: A Dilemma in Aristotle's Account of Hearing." In *The Second Sense: Studies in Hearing and Musical Judgment from Antiquity to the Seventeenth Century,* edited by Charles Burnett, Michael Fend, and Penelope Gouk, 7–18. London: Warburg Institute, 1991.

Wallace, Robert W. *Reconstructing Damon: Music, Wisdom Teaching, and Politics in Perikles' Athens*. Oxford: Oxford University Press, 2015.

Weigel, Moira. "How Ultrasound Became Political." *Atlantic*, January 24, 2017. https://www.theatlantic.com/health/archive/2017/01/ultrasound-woman-pregnancy/514109/.

Wohl, Victoria. "Plato avant le Lettre: Authenticity in Plato's Epistles." *Ramus* 27, no. 1 (1998): 60–93.

SARA BRILL is Professor of Philosophy at Fairfield University. She works on the psychology, politics, and ethics of Plato and Aristotle, as well as broader questions of embodiment, life, and power as points of intersection between ancient Greek philosophy and literature and contemporary critical theory. She is author of *Aristotle on the Concept of Shared Life, Plato on the Limits of Human Life* (Indiana University Press, 2013), coeditor (with Emanuela Bianchi and Brooke Holmes) of *Antiquities beyond Humanism*, and coeditor (with Catherine McKeen) of the forthcoming *Routledge Handbook on Women and Ancient Greek Philosophy*.

PART IV

*ALOGOS*, EMBODIMENT, AND
SILENCE

# 12

# THE SOUND OF PAIN IN SOPHOCLES'S *PHILOCTETES*

Rebecca Steiner Goldner, St. John's College, Annapolis

*P*HILOCTETES OPENS WITH DESCRIPTIVE SPEECH. IN PARTICULAR, Odysseus sets the scene for the audience as he controls our understanding of where we are and how we arrived there. The play opens as follows:

This is it; this Lemnos and its beach
down to the sea that quite surrounds it; desolate,
no one sets foot on it; there are no houses.
This is where I marooned him long ago,
the son of Poias, the Melian, his foot
diseased and eaten away with running ulcers.

Son of our greatest hero,
son of Achilles, Neoptolemus,
I tell you I had orders for what I did:
my masters, the princes, bade me do it.

We had no peace with him: at the holy festivals
we dared not touch the wine and meat; he screamed
and groaned so, and those terrible cries of his
brought ill luck on our celebrations; all
the camp was haunted by him.

Now is not time to talk to you of this,
now is no time for long speeches.
I am afraid that he may hear of my coming
and ruin all my plans to take him.[1]
(*Philoctetes*, lines 1–14)

By the end of this opening speech, Odysseus himself questions the role of such speeches and warns of what might be overheard if he continues. Thus, within the first twenty lines of the play, we are already both ensnared by words and warned about their power.

At a critical moment in Sophocles's *Philoctetes*, words fail. In spite of the absence of meaningful discourse, this moment is filled with sound and, importantly, sound made by a human being. As Philoctetes's pain becomes unbearable and he verges on passing out, he breaks from human language into inarticulate noises, interjecting into his discussion with Neoptolemus a series of short, plosive sounds that, while signifying nothing, means much.[2] Indeed, this episode and the communication between the two men that takes place here represent an important climax of the play, albeit one that is slowly revealed and expressed in dialogue later in the play. The claim of this paper is that it is not logos (that is, language or speech) but the reduction of the human voice to mere sound that demonstrates the importance of human community and the potential for the polis in this play.

*Philoctetes* raises questions regarding the meaning of speech and words in both explicit and implicit ways. These include the debate between Odysseus and Neoptolemus on lying and persuasion, Philoctetes's desire to hear spoken Greek, and Neoptolemus's prolonged silence in the latter part of the play. But sound is also a key part of Greek tragedy; in his *Poetics*, Aristotle calls poetry a form of imitation produced by a combination of rhythm, language, and harmony—all, of course, auditory phenomena. The audience's experience of the play is not reducible to comprehension of the words; the audible sounds of the words and other noises in the play are part of the overall spectacle. Choral episodes perhaps best typify the blurring of boundary between speech and sound with their reliance on meter and musicality. *Philoctetes* is an unusual play insofar as it offers the audience a different form of auditory experience, one that presumably would have evoked a different form of sympathy from that evoked by dialogue or expository. Like Neoptolemus, the audience hears Philoctetes but does not make literal sense of his sounding, and, also like Neoptolemus, the audience reacts to the sound of Philoctetes's pain in ways that could not have been elicited as a response to ordinary speech.

In what follows, I examine three episodes in the play to consider the interplay between speech and sound. First, I offer some consideration of speech and communication in the introduction to each of the major characters (Odysseus, Neoptolemus, and Philoctetes). Next, I examine the escalation and climax of Philoctetes's pain with an ear toward the devolution of speech into sound. Finally, I probe the significance of Neoptolemus's ensuing silence and the moral implications of his return to discourse. It has been suggested that "the *Philoctetes* is a case-study in the failure of communication," and insofar as we limit communication to logos, rational discourse, I would agree.[3] I want to suggest, however, that *Philoctetes* offers us a viable alternative to logos as the sole form of communication and grounds for political community and instead invites us to consider the possibility that sound alone might communicate meaning and even motivate human community and action.

## 1. Odysseus (Speech and Deceit)

Odysseus, of course, is a champion of logos, but we might also see in him a warning concerning the danger of words. Odysseus has no time or tolerance for the sound of suffering—words are what interest him. In the opening lines of *Philoctetes*, Odysseus attempts to justify his past action, explaining that while Philoctetes was in the camps, the Greeks could get no respite on account of the screaming, groaning, and terrible cries (δυσφημίαις, βοῶν, στενάζων) of Philoctetes (10–11). They could not sacrifice in peace because of the sounds of that man's pain and suffering—not the sight of him, nor the smell of the wound, but the sound. Odysseus, as the first speaker in the play, is tasked with introducing the audience to the setting and the mythical background of the play. His evocative language here, in particular his description of Lemnos, adds to the visual imagery the audience might be seeing onstage, but his words also demonstrate his belief that articulation lends credence to a phenomenon or experience.[4] That is, for Odysseus, saying something produces a kind of reality to which people can then respond. Odysseus's ability to explain his reasons for abandoning Philoctetes on Lemnos gives the decision moral weight, and he hopes that his words will overcome Neoptolemus's moral ambivalence about stealing the bow. Immediately, Odysseus juxtaposes the sound of Philoctetes's pain to his own rational discourse when, after a quick look to identify the cave in which Philoctetes dwells, Odysseus warns Neoptolemus that he may "hear some strange new thing, unlike anything heard before" (52). Odysseus's concern here proves well founded; ultimately, Neoptolemus will find himself having to choose between this strange new thing he hears and Odysseus's facility (perhaps even his flexibility) with words.

Neoptolemus hesitates at the idea of deceiving Philoctetes when Odysseus tells him he must "ensnare the soul of Philoctetes with your words" (54–55). Neoptolemus, the son of Achilles and a young man who hopes to be, like his father, a man of action, might inherently recognize the dangerous nature of words. After noting that he "hates to do those things that will cause bodily pain in being heard," Neoptolemus continues that he is "disposed to do nothing through evil craft, nor, as they say, was he who begat me" (86–89; my translation). Neoptolemus wants to act, not to lie. In the mouth of Odysseus, however, words are weapons capable of overcoming a man who cannot be taken by force—when Philoctetes later refers to someone "fearful and wise with respect to his tongue [γλώσσηι δὲ δεινοῦ σοφοῦ]," Neoptolemus erroneously assumes he must mean Odysseus (440), indicating that there is general acknowledgment among the Greeks of Odysseus's verbal prowess.[5] Persuasive and (presumably) honest words will fail to accomplish the task for which Odysseus and Neoptolemus have come to Lemnos, and therefore words must be used as a trick (δολός, 106). Neoptolemus is instructed to mix truth with lies, and the fact that words are signifiers allows for this particular kind of deception. The difference between honest and dishonest speech is not in the words, the material, but in the reality to which the words pertain and which they ostensibly signify. That reality—that is, the circumstances that brought Neoptolemus to Troy and precisely what he has been promised and awarded—remains unclear within the context of the play (assuming we discount any surrounding mythology). Odysseus urges Neoptolemus to tell Philoctetes that he was lured to join the Greek cause with the promise of his father's arms, arms subsequently awarded to Odysseus. Though we, as audience, know it to be untrue, Odysseus suggests a story wherein Neoptolemus is sailing home in anger at such treatment on the part of the Greeks. Odysseus's story appears to weave together elements of truth and falsity and to paint a picture of reality that will appeal to Philoctetes, one consistent with his own experience. In the story that Odysseus suggests to Neoptolemus, the audience, like Neoptolemus, might find a warning about trusting any version of reality that is offered only through expository.

## 2. Philoctetes and Neoptolemus (Sound and Silence)

Philoctetes is heard long before he speaks. The first acknowledgment of Philoctetes is as a noise-maker rather than a sense-maker; he makes sounds but not language. In contradiction to Odysseus, who immediately opens by storytelling, Philoctetes is first heard as a sound in the distance. "Hush," the chorus says, "hush, I hear a sound (κτύπος), that of a man oppressed by pain" (204). κτύπος is a nonvoiced sound—a crash, a din, like that of thunder or horses' hooves (LSJ).[6] The fact that the sound is that of pain indicates that it is vocalized pain, not merely the sound of him thrashing through the brush or moving things around. Only a few lines later do we get a reference to the sound as being that of a voice, φθογγά, and it is still merely a voice at this point, with no distinct words. As Philoctetes draws nearer, the chorus continues to narrow in on the nature of the sound they are hearing—a voice (αὐδά) and then, finally, the singing of a dirge (διάσημα θρηνεῖ) (205–208).[7] Odysseus toys with language when we first meet him, but Philoctetes cannot even voice language at first, only the sound of pain and finally a dirge.

While Odysseus strains his native tongue to accommodate his will, Philoctetes longs merely to hear Greek. We might note that his own ability to speak Greek does not satisfy this need. One does not hear oneself in the same way one hears others, and talking to oneself fails to satisfy the relational, communicative aspect of language. We learn later in the play (935) that Philoctetes has tried to communicate with the inanimate things around him simply to hear his own voice out loud. These attempts must prove unsatisfactory, as Philoctetes begs to hear the voices of the strangers he finds near his dwelling, apparently fearing that they will remain silent: "It is not reasonable," he tells them, "that I fail [to get words] from you or you from me" (230–231). The failure that Philoctetes fears here is precisely the failing with which he and Neoptolemus will confront each other later in the play: Philoctetes will fail to use words because of his pain, while Neoptolemus will choose silence over voicing his moral uncertainty.

These early soundings, Odysseus's language and Philoctetes's noise, along with Philoctetes's explicit concerns about voices and silence, introduce us not merely to the characters of the play but also to the questions of communication that are at stake. Words, thus far, can equivocate, mixing reality with deception. Sound, even when it is not yet clear, is unequivocal. Short of auditory hallucinations, the experience of hearing attests to the reality of something sounding. When you hear a bush rustling, even if someone is rustling the bush to make you think there is something there, the sound of the bush is real (even if the judgment about what is there is false). Words can be heard when the reality they point to is not real. Words are therefore more like judgments than sounds, and errors of signification or representation become a real possibility, especially if the speaker is not to be trusted.

It is not surprising, in light of this, that the most important choice of the play occurs in wordless noise and then silence. The decision about how to respond to a man alone and in pain is better made in the absence of logos, beyond its power to falsely persuade, to misjudge, and to make the weaker argument better. Since words can accurately describe reality or intentionally misconstrue it, language becomes problematic, as does knowledge or understanding that is based on words. In this play, only when logos is dismissed can moral clarity be attained.

Philoctetes, of course, does not intentionally lose his ability to speak. Rather, his pain interrupts the flow of his words and his discourse with Neoptolemus. His sentences and his very thinking are disrupted by the onset of his paroxysm. He does not use his pain in an instrumental way to sway Neoptolemus (in fact, his pain occurs before he is aware of Neoptolemus's deception). He tells Neoptolemus that his pain is "terrible and cannot be communicated in words [δεινόν γὰρ οὐδε ῥητόν]" (756; my translation). Philoctetes both acknowledges and struggles against this loss of language as the pain worsens and the expression of the pain—even the syllables in which he expresses it—grows longer and more disruptive to his meaningful speech.

Indeed, it is hard to think of a human being willing her own loss of logos. We tend to think that our ability to communicate lies in our capacity for logos, that herein lies our capacity to persuade others and to express what is most fully human. Elaine Scarry, in *The Body in Pain*, argues that "physical pain does not simply resist language but actively destroys it, bringing about an immediate reversion to a state anterior to language, to the sounds and cries a human being makes before language is learned."[8] That pain is resistant to language, however, does not render pain utterly incommunicable, as Hannah Arendt claims it does: "The experience of great bodily pain is at the same time the most private and least communicable of all."[9] Pain is, instead, both private and nonlinguistic yet also communicable, and the fact that we make sounds when in pain attests to a desire to communicate and make demands of others that is prelinguistic in its form. Such communication of pain through mere sound is meaningful but also, problematically, apolitical, at least according to Aristotle. In the *Politics*, Aristotle distinguishes voice (φωνὴ) from speech (λόγos) and demonstrates that humans are even more political than other animals because they have speech (1253a10–15). Mere communication is relational and therefore forms the foundation of a community; being together requires recognition and response at some primitive level. But without language, there can be no universalizing, no abstraction, nothing higher or more valuable than immediacy. The communication of pain relates and bears meaning from one person to another, but it does not create or build; it is stuck in the present and has no past or future.

The communication of pain though a human voice is notably disruptive to meaningful speech, so much so that we might desire to hear significance where there is rightfully none. In the passage below, we can see how Philoctetes's cries disrupt the dialogue he is having with Neoptolemus as his interjections become increasingly long and more robust. In line 732, we first hear a simple, staccato cry of pain from Philoctetes, simply a vowel punctuated by rough breathing (ἃ ἃ ἃ ἃ). The rough breathing seems necessary here for the separation of each alpha into its own syllable (here, adding an extrametrical line, as well). Discussion then continues until 739, when we hear those syllabic alphas again, forming their own line once again and breaking the iambic tetrameter. The next time Philoctetes interrupts speech with pain, the rough breathing alpha has been folded into a syllable completed with a consonant, first the tau (in line 743) and then a pi in later lines. So, at the end of line 745, we find παπαῖ continued directly into line 746, ἀπαππαπαῖ παπᾶ παπᾶ παπᾶ παπαῖ, and one more prolonged interruption at 754 consists entirely of strung together syllables, παππαπαππαπαῖ.

It may not be altogether insignificant that the noises of Philoctetes's pain border on words without fully becoming speech. It is tempting to hear the word *child* or *father* in his παππαπαππαπαῖ, but what we actually hear is nothing more than breathing—that is, plosives and breath.[10] The pi sound is a voiceless bilabial stop—the vocal cords are not employed at all until you add the vowel (oppose this to our B sound, which cannot be articulated without the vocal cords). The pi sound is merely breathing accentuated by the movement of the lips. As Philoctetes's pain gets worse, as the paroxysm heightens, his expression of pain becomes almost inseparable from his attempts to breathe—it is breathing given sound, and the sound is clearly indicative of struggle. One could imagine that such an extreme amount of pain might reduce someone only to labored, rasping breathing. The continuation of the vowel sound, which first interjected his pain into the dialogue, voices the breath and makes it something more. That it verges on significant sound but falls short seems appropriate here. Philoctetes is somewhere between *ktupos* and logos; he is a human entirely cut off from human discourse by his own pain, but he still makes voiced sound. His breath is articulated but lacks the ordinary expressiveness of human speech.[11]

It might be helpful to consider why we voice our pain. To move beyond the mere struggle to breathe might seem an unnecessary expenditure of energy when one is in excruciating pain. Yet the voicing of pain seems an attempt to represent to others a phenomenon that would otherwise remain largely private. That we make sound in pain is an attempt to articulate what is inarticulate, as John Russon puts it.[12] Research suggests that wincing in pain is an attempt to communicate danger.[13] Pain itself does not seem to require external expression. Living in a community, however, necessitates that we make public what could easily remain private, among which we might include our thoughts, our desires, and our pain. While language is the public appearance of thought (and can even include the cloaking or distortion of a thought), wincing, yelling, and sounding seem to be the public demonstrations of pain. Sounding our pain is an attempt to make a certain (bodily) reality apparent to others and, moreover, to demand a response from them, be it pity or help. Philoctetes's insignificant sounds ask something of Neoptolemus.

It seems that it takes some time for Neoptolemus to formulate a response to the sound of Philoctetes's pain. Throughout the play, we see Neoptolemus wrestle with meaningful speech, which can both present reality as it is or distort it. Neoptolemus first attempts—and fails—to position himself as a man of action rather than words when Odysseus engages his help. The son of Achilles desires to do something grand in scope and massive in consequences. But Neoptolemus is ultimately swayed by Odysseus's speech, and the first discussion he has with Philoctetes is the mixture of truth and lies that Odysseus has urged him to deploy. We know that, initially, Philoctetes feared that Neoptolemus would confront him only with silence, and we now arrive at a point in the play (after the theft of the bow) when this initial fear concerning what he would hear (or fail to hear) is brought to fruition. Neoptolemus remains onstage but silent for nearly one hundred lines of the play, even when Philoctetes enjoins him to respond: "Son of Achilles, your voice has no word for me? Will you go away in silence?" (1066–1067). Thus, while Philoctetes no longer hears his beloved Greek, he also does not hear deception or trickery from Neoptolemus. Neoptolemus has no words for him at all.

At this point in the play, we hear from Neoptolemus only when he issues a command to the chorus of sailors that they are to remain with Philoctetes. Neoptolemus finds himself on a middle ground now, too filled with pity for Philoctetes to utterly abandon him yet aware that he falls short, in this exercise of compassion toward Philoctetes, of Odysseus's demands of him. His refusal to speak, broken only by a compassionate command to his sailors, suggests his uncertainty about his actions. He has heard Odysseus—eloquent yet deceptive—urge dishonest behavior. He has heard Philoctetes's words devolve into nonsense, but the sound of his pain had an honesty and openness that could not be doubted and that urged pity.[14] Neoptolemus seemed to begin with an assumption that words were weak and action was bold. He longs for the large-scale, public sorts of actions that might imitate his father. The course of action he comes to through his silence is a far more moderate form of action, one aimed at a single individual rather than toward the Greeks as a whole. When he next comes onstage (1222), Neoptolemus is no longer in that liminal place in which he pleases no one, fails to speak, and takes no action. He has chosen a course of action, and he once again has words for both Odysseus and Philoctetes.[15]

Philoctetes, however, now knows better than to trust Neoptolemus's words: "Yet previously you made me suffer with your words, doing a bad deed with good words [ἐκ λόγων καλῶν κακῶς ἔπραξα]" (1268–1269; my translation). Philoctetes was taken in by Neoptolemus when he naively thought that words were a description of reality, but he now knows that bad actions can be articulated through good or beautiful words. When he first met Neoptolemus, he longed to hear Greek, calling it then ὦ φίλτατον φώνημα, "most beautiful of sounds" (235). Now, more cautious, he suggests that, of things spoken, they are only most beautiful if also true: ὦ φίλτατ'εἶπον, εἰ λέγεις ἐτήτυμα (1290). Words themselves have no moral value or beauty; their beauty comes only from their conformity to reality and actions. Neoptolemus, however, has seen a reality through the meaningless sounds of Philoctetes's pain. His silence is the space in which he weighed Odysseus's deceptive logos against Philoctetes's *alogos ktupos*. When he returns to the stage and to communication, Neoptolemus uses only honest words—words that reflect reality as he knows it.

## 3. The Sounds of Community

*Philoctetes* is often read as a play concerned with the lack of human society, with a man cut off from the polis and his community.[16] Philoctetes's reduction to nonhuman noise at various points in the play might be read as paradigmatic of his exceptional status as a savage in a wild place. This reading would also accord with Aristotle's claim that speech is particularly bound to the polis. But instead, we find a man who loses his speech, whose pain replaces his words, and who, as a result of those very things that should make him apolitical, calls forth from another an honest response and action. As Philoctetes lapses in and out of logos, he likewise hovers between isolation and society. He appears imprisoned in his own private world and body, yet, through the sound of his pain, he demonstrates his need to make himself seen—and heard—in the space of the public. Insofar as pain, for Arendt, belongs entirely to the private realm and is not communicable, she surmises that pain cannot be made manifest in speech and is therefore excluded from the political (that is, public) sphere. She writes, "In his two most famous definitions, Aristotle only formulated the current opinion of the *polis* about man and the political way of life, and according to this opinion, everybody outside the *polis*—slaves and barbarians—was *aneu logou*, deprived, of course, not of the faculty of speech, but of a way of life in which speech and only speech made sense and where the central concern of all citizens was to talk with each other" (27). It is true of Philoctetes that he is *aneu logou* in this way, a fact emphasized by his isolation and his desire to hear and speak Greek. It is also true, however, that this vision of the polis is challenged by Philoctetes's ability to create sound with some meaning. As Arendt says, the polis is the place where only speech made sense, but Philoctetes offers another possibility because his mere sounding communicates and requires response from others. Arendt remains bound to the incommunicability of pain, which, she says, "cannot assume an appearance at all" because she thinks that only speech and action "appear"—that is, exist in the shared world of humans and constitute its reality.[17] Philoctetes's life, according to Arendt, "has ceased to be a human life because it is no longer lived among men" (176). I submit, however, that in this play we find an alternative to the notion that only the political life, insofar as that life requires logos, is fully human. Philoctetes's pain remains *aneu logou*, but he nonetheless does communicate and make his pain public. His pain has an appearance and constitutes a reality to which those around him must respond, even if, before Neoptolemus, the response has consistently been the choice to abandon him, to exclude him from the public and common world of humans.

The sounds of his pain are not, then, utterly meaningless or entirely private, and their meaning is best demonstrated by the change we see in Neoptolemus. Initially, the play presented a juxtaposition between the community of the Greeks (and the deceptive words that come with them) and the isolation of pain. Philoctetes's wordless sounds have offered another alternative. Philoctetes has successfully communicated with Neoptolemus, who has responded with a new sense of what it means to act among and toward others. An animal in pain might well draw our pity, but Philoctetes's pain demands moral resolution and action. He must be either abandoned or aided. Previously, those who heard his pain chose abandonment; they could not hear his cries and remain near him. Neoptolemus, however, hears something else in those cries precisely because they are juxtaposed to the falsity of Odysseus's words. Odysseus's persuasive speech looked like a step toward action, and Odysseus assures Neoptolemus that if he does as ordered, he will win renown worthy of his father. However, if action depends on the recognition of the community, and the community or the polis depends on logos, what kind of action can result from deceptive words? More importantly, perhaps, what kind of polis would we have if action and activity depended on deception? What kind of virtue could such a community cultivate? Faced, on the one hand, with doing the kinds of deeds—lies— that "cause bodily pain [ἀλγῶ]" (86) and, on the other hand, with a man who cannot lie through his pain, Neoptolemus finds a virtue that directly and immediately connects him to another human being. Sound, that which is *ktupos* or *aneu logos*, proves the more apt guide for his action. Neoptolemus's action toward Philoctetes is both genuinely human and therefore a part of reality rather than a description of it. If Aristotle is correct that logos is the foundation of the polis, we should be wary of the potential of the polis to lead us away from the immediacy on which it is founded. The logos of the city, like that of Odysseus, might obscure rather than make explicit our desire for honest communication with one another.

A community founded on sound rather than speech seems, however, a rather bare and limited political community. Perhaps it is fitting, then, that there is a sense in which this play is morally unsatisfying in its resolution. Since Philoctetes refuses to help the Greeks and Neoptolemus cannot convince him otherwise, Neoptolemus simply agrees to take him back to Greece, though he is aware that such a choice will doom the Greek army to defeat. Once again, persuasive speech has failed, and this strange little community, founded on the sound of pain, threatens the Greek cause as a whole. Neoptolemus and Philoctetes briefly forge their own community against the Greeks, with Philoctetes vowing to use the bow of Heracles against any Greeks who might besiege Neoptolemus for his abandonment of them in Troy (1405). Heracles must intervene as a deus ex machina precisely because the ending is otherwise politically impoverished. The independent community forged by Neoptolemus and Philoctetes gets absorbed into the greater community, perhaps demonstrating what Aristotle would later say, that the "polis comes to be for the sake of life but continues for the sake of the good life" (*Politics* 1.2) The community between Odysseus and Neoptolemus was founded on logos, but a logos that lied and shifted reality. The relationship between Neoptolemus and Philoctetes is founded on honesty toward one another but lacks much more than that in the way of virtue and remains limited in scope. It is a community founded on a *ktupos* that has meaning and attests to a reality, a reality grounded in and inextricable from its immediacy.

## Notes

1. Translations are from David Grene, "Philoctetes," in *Sophocles II* (Chicago: University of Chicago Press, 2013), except where noted as my own. They are cited parenthetically by line number.

2. This essay owes a great debt to a sophomore language tutorial that I taught in the academic year 2016–2017 at St. John's College, in which we translated *Philoctetes* together. In particular, I am indebted to Mr. Rhys Davis, who repeatedly drew our attention to the sound of Philoctetes's pain and probed these sounds for their potential meaning.

3. Anthony J. Podlecki, "The Power of the Word in Sophocles' *Philoctetes*," *Greek, Roman and Byzantine Studies* 7, no. 3 (1966): 233.

4. Felix Budelman (*The Language of Sophocles: Communality, Communication and Involvement* [Cambridge: Cambridge University Press, 2000]) points out that from the opening lines of the play, the audience should be inclined to mistrust Odysseus, who introduces the setting of the play by claiming that Lemnos is a land untrodden by mortals. The audience would not have this association for Lemnos, which both in mythology and reality was not uninhabited, and Odysseus, as Budelman says, "interferes with the myth" in "conspicuous language" (98). In the line in question, Philoctetes is actually asking about Thersites, though he has previously referred to Odysseus's use of tongue for deceptive ends (407–409) and will do so later (see, for example, 633–634, where Philoctetes says he would rather listen to the snake that bit him than to Odysseus's words).

5. When the embassy comes to Achilles in *The Iliad*, he says to Odysseus, "I hate that man like the very Gates of Death / who says one thing but hides another in his heart" (9.378–379). Homer, *The Iliad*, trans. Robert Fagles (New York: Penguin Books, 1990).

6. Henry George Liddell and Robert Scott, *A Greek-English Lexicon*, s.v. "ktupos," via the Perseus Digital Library, accessed February 2, 2022, http://www.perseus.tufts.edu/hopper/text ?doc=Perseus%3Atext%3A1999.04.0057%3Aentry%3Dktu%2Fpos.

7. αὐδά, too, could (more rarely) be a sound, in which case we might see the chorus as wavering as to the nature of what they are hearing.

8. Elaine Scarry, *The Body in Pain: The Making and Unmaking of the World* (New York: Oxford University Press, 1985), 4.

9. Hannah Arendt, *The Human Condition* (Chicago: University of Chicago Press, 1998), 50–51.

10.  Seth Schein (ed., *Sophocles Philoctetes* [Cambridge: Cambridge University Press, 2013]) points out in his commentary that the lines "conspicuously reiterate(s) sounds suggesting 'παῖς' and 'πάππας'" (238). It is especially tempting to hear these words since Philoctetes himself calls Neoptolemus παῖ at lines 750 and 752. I take this to induce us to hear or make sense of his nonsense, with Sophocles pointing out to us our own desire that Philoctetes use words and express himself in logos even though the word παῖ could have no meaningful context in his cries of pain.

11.  Aeschylus used the same expression of pain in the Persians (1031), but only in the form παπαῖ. The development and expansion of the cry seems to belong to Sophocles.

12.  John Russon, "Haunted by History: Merleau-Ponty, Hegel and the Phenomenology of Pain," *Journal of Contemporary Thought* 37 (2013): 88. Russon argues that language itself is about articulating pain and that literary traditions are likewise articulations of vulnerability that invoke compassion as a fundamental human relation.

13.  Nathan H. Lents, "Why Do We Wince When We're in Pain?," *Psychology Today*, September 12, 2016, https://www.psychologytoday.com/us/blog/beastly-behavior/201609 /why-do-we-wince-when-were-in-pain.

14.  Scarry claims that because the pain of others cannot be confirmed in the same way as the certainty of our own pain, "to hear about pain is to have doubt" (*Body in Pain*, 13). Though perhaps cases might be thought of where expressions of pain such as those of Philoctetes could be faked or exaggerated, these would seem exceptional and require enormous deceptive and acting skills on the part of the expresser of such pain. That Philoctetes passes out from the pain seems to confirm the extent of his suffering. Rarely do we see people respond to the expression of extreme pain as if the pain is in doubt. A reply similar to my objection to Scarry is offered by Ludwig Wittgenstein in *Philosophical Investigations* (4th ed., trans. G. E. M. Anscombe, P. M. S. Hacker, and Joachim Schulte [West Sussex, UK: Blackwell, 2009]) in his discussion of pain and language (see especially 244–246): "In what sense are my sensations private?—Well, only I can know whether I am really in pain; another person can only surmise it.—In one way this is false, and in another nonsense. If we are using the word 'know' as it is normally used (and how else are we to use it?), then other people very often know if I'm in pain" (246).

15.  For an interpretation of the play as representing Neoptolemus's choice between Odysseus and Philoctetes, see Mary Whitlock Blundell's chapter on Philoctetes in *Helping Friends and Harming Enemies: A Study in Sophocles and Greek Ethics* (New York: Cambridge University Press, 1989).

16.  For more overtly political interpretations of the play, see, for example, Charles Segal, *Tragedy and Civilization: An Interpretation of Sophocles* (Cambridge, MA: Harvard University Press, 1981), especially chap. 10, "Philoctetes: Society, Language, Friendship"; Jonathan Badger, *Sophocles and the Politics of Tragedy, Cities and Transcendence* (New York: Routledge, 2013). Podlecki (n. 1) provides a more than adequate survey of this literature.

17.  Arendt, *Human Condition*, 51.

## Bibliography

Arendt, Hannah. *The Human Condition*. Chicago: University of Chicago Press, 1998.
Badger, Jonathan. *Sophocles and the Politics of Tragedy, Cities and Transcendence*. New York: Routledge, 2013.

Blundell, Mary Whitlock. *Helping Friends and Harming Enemies: A Study in Sophocles and Greek Ethics.* New York: Cambridge University Press, 1989.

Budelman, Felix. *The Language of Sophocles: Communality, Communication and Involvement.* Cambridge: Cambridge University Press, 2000.

Grene, David, trans. "Philoctetes." In *Sophocles II.* Chicago: University of Chicago Press, 2013.

Homer. *The Iliad.* Translated by Robert Fagles. New York: Penguin Books, 1990.

Lents, Nathan H. "Why Do We Wince When We're in Pain?" *Psychology Today*, September 12, 2016. https://www.psychologytoday.com/us/blog/beastly-behavior/201609/why-do-we-wince-when-were-in-pain.

Podlecki, Anthony J. "The Power of the Word in Sophocles' *Philoctetes.*" *Greek, Roman and Byzantine Studies* 7, no. 3 (1966): 233–250.

Russon, John. "Haunted by History: Merleau-Ponty, Hegel and the Phenomenology of Pain." *Journal of Contemporary Thought* 37 (2013): 81–94.

Scarry, Elaine. *The Body in Pain: The Making and Unmaking of the World.* New York: Oxford University Press, 1985.

Schein, Seth, ed. *Sophocles Philoctetes.* Cambridge: Cambridge University Press, 2013.

Segal, Charles. *Tragedy and Civilization: An Interpretation of Sophocles.* Cambridge, MA: Harvard University Press, 1981.

Wittgenstein, Ludwig. *Philosophical Investigations.* 4th ed. Translated by G. E. M. Anscombe, P. M. S. Hacker, and Joachim Schulte. West Sussex, UK: Blackwell, 2009.

REBECCA STEINER GOLDNER is a tutor at St. John's College in Annapolis, Maryland. She has previously published on the ancients and the sense of touch.

# 13

## SOCRATIC DEATH RATTLES

### *Pythagorean Hearing and Listening*
### *in Plato's* Phaedo

Kris McLain, Pennsylvania State University

Anne-Marie Schultz, Baylor University

PLATO'S *PHAEDO* PROVIDES US WITH AN INSPIRATIONAL ACCOUNT of Socrates's final hours. On the day that Socrates drinks the poison hemlock, he and his companions gather in Socrates's prison cell and participate in a long discussion about the nature of the soul and the fate of the soul after death. As many scholars have noted, the *Phaedo* contains numerous references to Pythagorean practice and doctrine.[1] Both the structure and the setting of the dialogue reinforce the Pythagorean auditory dimensions. Preliminarily, a simple example of these dimensions resides in the structure of the dialogue itself. Throughout the conversation, hearing and listening are established as philosophically important activities. In the construction of the dialogue, Phaedo, our dialogic narrator, retells the story of Socrates's death to a group of specifically Pythagorean auditors. Echecrates acts as the speaker for the group, and although he may appear to be the only attendee, J. M. Cooper claims that Phaedo is actually addressing a group of Pythagoreans "who settled there since their expulsion from Southern Italy."[2] The ancient Greek auditors can be assumed to be eager to hear the news and so represent active and invested listeners, especially as the Pythagoreans are renowned for their capacity to listen and thus to provide an eager and attentive audience. Echecrates tells Phaedo that no one has come to visit Phlius from Athens "for a long time" (57a), noting that this will be the first clear account they have had of Socrates's last moments. Furthermore, the internal conversation of the dialogue occurs between Socrates and two well-known contemporary Pythagoreans, Cebes and Simmias.[3] Plato chooses to present the Socratic death ode to Pythagoreans through conversations with other Pythagoreans (both those in the cell and those listening later). It is vital that the Pythagorean philosophical community and spiritual practices are structured around listening. In reading and hearing the dialogue through a Pythagorean lens, we must reassess the position of the women in the dialogue, especially Xanthippe and those of Socrates's household. While we are not arguing that Xanthippe was herself a Pythagorean, we do know that Pythagorean philosophical practice necessitated the participation and inclusion of women. In this inclusive spirit, we reassess Xanthippe's role in the dialogue.[4]

This paper unfolds in the following manner. First, we point out some important Pythagorean aspects of the narrative frame of the dialogue, particularly those that refer to practices of hearing and listening to establish that the likely audience of Phaedo's report is a group of Pythagorean *akousmatikoi*. We then discuss the role of women in Pythagorean philosophical communities. In sections 2 and 3, we reassess the interaction between Socrates and Xanthippe with an ear toward hearing how their spoken exchanges and important silences are modified by this interaction's presence in a dialogue that is narrated to a group of Pythagorean listeners. Finally, we consider the interplay between sound and silence in the moments surrounding Socrates's death.

## 1. Listening Along with the Pythagorean Auditors

Indications of the Pythagorean setting of the dialogue are scattered throughout the opening frame (57a–58e). The outer frame of the *Phaedo* is set in Phlius, a city in the Peloponnese where some of Pythagoras's students fled after the uprisings in Croton. The community was probably established after the second series of uprisings around 450 BCE. Kurt Von Fritz believes that this group is part of "the so-called last Pythagoreans."[5] Interestingly, it is also the home of Axiothea, one of the two women whom Diogenes mentions by name as having studied in Plato's Academy.[6]

Furthermore, nuances of the language in the opening exchange between Echecrates and Phaedo suggest that we should imagine that Echecrates and the other residents of Phlius were Pythagorean *akousmatikoi*, one of the two split branches of Pythagorean followers who adhered closely to the religious teachings (*akusma*) attributed to Pythagoras himself.[7] There is significant debate about when this split actually occurred. Leonid Zhmud argues that the split is an invention of a later tradition, because the first written description of the two groups of Pythagoreans is not found until Clement of Alexandria.[8] Carl Huffman notes that "Burkert and many others think that it occurred in the fifth century and is already found in the testimony of Aristotle."[9] Regardless of the type of Pythagorean group Phlius is, it is clear that Phaedo is visiting there and that the Pythagoreans there know him. By setting the dialogue in Phlius, a Pythagorean enclave that Echecrates is said to have founded, Plato casts the entire retelling of the dialogue in a Pythagorean context. The silence of Phaedo's audience evokes resonances of the Pythagorean five-year silent initiation period, during which disciples simply listened to the words of Pythagoras without asking questions of him directly.[10] Numerous references to hearing provide an obvious indication of the particular orientation of this Pythagorean audience. The first reference occurs when Echecrates asks Phaedo, "Were you present yourself or did you hear (ἤκουσας) about it from someone else?" (57a). A little later, Echecrates remarks, "I would like to hear (ἀκούσαιμι) the story" (57a). Phaedo picks up the echoes of this word: "It is always my greatest pleasure to be reminded of Socrates whether by speaking of him myself or by listening (ἀκούντα) to someone else" (58d). Echecrates encourages his narration by assuring Phaedo that "you will have hearers (ἀκουσομένους) who feel as you do" (58d).

There are several other references to speaking and hearing in the opening narrative frame that reinforce the Pythagorean dimension of the setting. Echecrates establishes himself and his colleagues as listeners dependent on the spoken reports of others. The listening is not a passive receiving of information; rather, it is an active and engaged process. For example, Echecrates mentions that no stranger has been able to relate anything clearly or describe anything exactly about the manner of Socrates's death (57b). When Phaedo asks if they heard about the trial, Echecrates affirms that "someone told them about this" (58a). Echecrates and Phaedo's initial exchange establishes Phaedo as the expert and Echecrates as an active listener—in other words, liable to ask questions and desire clarification. In fact, Echecrates asks a series of urgent questions about Socrates's death, querying what was said, what was done, and who was present or if he died alone (58c). After the flurry of questions, Echecrates insists that Phaedo "tell them as clearly as he can" (58d). Echecrates makes his request using the superlative adverb σαφέστατα.

Σαφέστατα is utilized to pinpoint an experience specifically related to an auditory event—a type of speaking that asks for precision for the sake of the listener identifying the desire for clear or distinct things to be heard and known.[11] In tandem with Echecrates's claim of being sympathetic "hearers," his use of σαφέστατα at this point affirms the importance of the role of listening and speaking in the enclave in Phlius. In the course of the opening narrative, Echecrates asks fourteen distinct questions of Phaedo (57a–59d). A. M. Bowery has argued that Plato's use of these *akouô* words calls to mind the primary means of education employed by the *akousmatikoi*—an education that focuses on the oral teachings of the master, on the things said and the things heard.[12]

The silent and unidentified group of auditors in Phlius, if they are Pythagoreans, are likely to have included women. The women would be the wives and daughters of the male Pythagorean auditors in Phlius. With the Pythagoreans, we should regard these women as philosophical participants in the conversation in their own right descending from a lineage of prominent Pythagorean female philosophers, including Theano (~580 BCE), Arignote (~550 BCE), Myia (~550 BCE), and Themistoclea (~600 BCE).[13] Sarah Pomeroy notes, "More Pythagorean woman are known by name than are women in any other Greek philosophical school. They were not 'muted' like their respectable Athenian contemporaries in old Greece."[14] In fact, according to Pomeroy, "they are the same as or equal to men, to be given the same education, to follow the same rules of conduct, and deserving of the same respect."[15] A late source, Hermippus (~206 BCE), writes that those who listened to Pythagoras after his legendary journey to the underworld were so "taken in by his words, they wept and moaned and were sure that he was some kind of divinity; so that they even entrusted their wives to him, thinking that they too would learn something from him. And they were called πυθαγορικαί."[16] Iamblichus also reports that Pythagoras addressed the wives of his followers at Croton.[17] Similarly, the *Speeches of Pythagoras*, which are generally thought to be from the late fifth or early fourth century, are addressed to both sexes and include specific instruction for both male and female behavior.[18] It is in this sense that we propose that Xanthippe's presence in a Pythagorean-oriented dialogue reported to a Pythagorean audience would be read more generously by that audience than modern readers typically acknowledge. While one could argue that Xanthippe's banishment from the jail cell during the last day of conversation would cast her in an unphilosophical light, we would point out that Xanthippe is present in the cell before the male philosophers arrive and that she returns at the end and is with Socrates "for a long time"(116b). Indeed, Socrates's male philosophical students are, in turn, excluded from their private conversation. It is plausible that she and Socrates practice philosophy together without his students present and so her "banishment" from their philosophical conversations does not mean that she is banished from all philosophical dialogue with Socrates. While we are not claiming that Socrates and Xanthippe were practicing Pythagoreans, the Pythagorean audience might have heard the report of their shared time together on Socrates's last day in philosophical terms that would resonate with their own Pythagorean context.

To explain further, Pythagorean tradition seems to require, both early on and throughout the later neo-Pythagorean tradition (if we keep writers such as Phintys in mind), that women, especially wives, were a significant part of the Pythagorean philosophical tradition.[19] Nowhere is this truer than the continuation and maintenance of the *akusmata*. Pomeroy explains, "Pythagoreans followed detailed, nonintuitive rules that encroached on private life, including regulations for diet, clothing, bedding, sexual intercourse, and childrearing; it would have been virtually impossible for a married man to adhere to Pythagoreanism if his wife did not."[20] To maintain the extensive rituals and practices, women were intimately important. The inclusion of women as supporters and potential practitioners of Pythagoreanism seems to be important in common household practices of eating, bathing, and maintaining relationships as well as in the maintenance of the relationship between the Pythagorean tradition and generation of children. Not only is the relationship of the husband and wife central due to the maintenance of *akusmata*, but as Pomeroy argues, "Pythagoras elevated the private sphere by comparing the governance of the *oikia* (household) and the *polis* (city-state) (Iambl. *VP* 183)."[21] In governing both the household and the state, Pythagoras argued that there must be friendship between the members of the household, especially the wife, children, and relatives.[22] Women did not necessarily play a subordinate role; they played a more equitable role. Furthermore, "Pythagorean doctrine was sympathetic to women; the proof that bears repeating is that Pythagoras required the same sexual monogamy of husbands that was mandatory for wives."[23] When talking about Aesara's natural law theory, Mary Ellen Waithe remarks, "In the Pythagorean view, women are not peripheral to social justice, they make it happen."[24] Simply put, the Pythagorean tradition is the high point for the appreciation of women in ancient Greek philosophy. If we emphasize this aspect of Pythagoreanism in the history of philosophy, we see that women had a prominent place in the very beginnings of philosophy. The relative equality of women in the Pythagorean tradition provides a helpful model of *harmonia* and reciprocity in philosophical discussion. This strong female tradition within Pythagoreanism both precedes and postdates the time Plato would have composed the *Phaedo*. This background shapes our reassessment of Xanthippe's appearances in the *Phaedo*. With this broader context in mind, Xanthippe becomes more philosophical.

## 2. Xanthippe as Sonorous

It is difficult to sort out our own culturally laden reading of the text from how Phaedo's account of Socrates's last day might have been heard by a group of Pythagoreans in Phlius.[25] Contemporary readers often view Socrates's interactions with Xanthippe in an unfavorable light on the basis of the presumed hierarchical and binary gender dynamics of both Athens and our contemporary moment.[26] In modern readings of the *Phaedo*, an apparently shocked Socrates responds to Xanthippe's outcry by banishing her from his last day of philosophical discourse when he asks Crito to have someone take her home (60a). Similarly, Socrates's final exhortation to his friends that they are not to break into tears and act like women raises additional concerns about Socrates's and Plato's views on women (117d). The negative attitudes toward Xanthippe begin early in the commentary tradition.[27] Our tendency to view her negatively is not simply our modern imposition on the text.[28] The continued view of Xanthippe as overwhelmingly negative should be reassessed through the nature of the dialogue as narrative, the actual events of the dialogue, and Xenophon's contemporaneous account of her.

The *Phaedo* is a reported dialogue. Like all of the reported dialogues, both those narrated by Socrates and those narrated by characters other than Socrates, the narrator provides additional information about the characters in the story. This narrative act has important pedagogical implications because it draws the audience more deeply into the story and causes them to reflect on the information that they are hearing. The *Phaedo* is told by a male narrator, with Pythagorean inclinations. He speaks to other Pythagoreans. We learn about Xanthippe's presence at Socrates's death because Phaedo chooses to include these details in his narrative recounting to Echecrates and the others. Phaedo does not list Xanthippe as present in his initial accounting of the local people and foreigners who were there; rather, he provides a space separate for her, as she is already in attendance at the prison (59b–c). Xanthippe appears as a figure in two key moments of the text: first, at the very beginning of Socrates's last day, and second, when Xanthippe returns with the women and children of the household. Their return is simultaneous with a critical shift in the demeanor of the philosophical participants: the moment when Socrates turns from mentally preparing for death to physically doing so. Phaedo (and Plato) uses the figure of Xanthippe in two critical shifts that are extreme auditory registers in the piece. In the beginning, she heralds the entrance of Socrates's friends with a sonorous cry. In her second appearance, she silently (to our ears) stands witness to Socrates's final death preparations. It is critical to keep in mind that Phaedo/Plato can make choices as to what he decides to relay about the other characters present. The action could begin already in the jail cell when Cebes and Simmias begin their questioning. Instead, Xanthippe is given a critical positioning: being present at the dawn of Socrates's death day.

Notably, Xanthippe's first appearance is of an unknown and unrecounted duration. Xanthippe is already in the jail cell with Socrates when our narrator arrives; Phaedo and his friends arrived quite early in the day but were required to wait on the discussion between Xanthippe and Socrates.[29] It is safe to assume that Xanthippe and the child have been there with Socrates for some time, even throughout the evening. At this point, Phaedo has just described the habitual practice that he and Socrates's other students make of going to the jail every day; it is possible that spending the night together was Xanthippe's and Socrates's habitual practice as well. Phaedo had mentioned previously that the prison "did not open early" (59d). On this particular day, Xanthippe has access to Socrates while the men of the philosophical circle do not. Arlene Saxonhouse notes, "It is Phaedo and his friends entering the prison who disrupt this communing—on what level we do not know—of husband and wife."[30] In fact, the guard seems to be safeguarding the space for Xanthippe and Socrates, as he knows that it is the day of Socrates's death. The jailor tells them "to wait and not go in until he told us" (60a). Taking up Saxonhouse's claim of disruption, we turn to look at the moment of entry by the cohort of men. Xanthippe's fame proceeds her in Phaedo's reiteration. Phaedo motions to Echecrates, stating, "We went in then and found Socrates . . . and Xanthippe—you know her (γιγνώσκεις)"(60a). While one might overlook the importance of Phaedo's assumption that Echecrates "knows her," to us it is quite suggestive. Xanthippe was known, at least in some general sense, by a member of a Pythagorean community far removed from Athens. Even though the text does not support a supposition that Xanthippe might have been engaged in Pythagorean practice, it is likely that listeners of Phlius, including the women, might read her in those terms. They might recognize a potential Pythagorean compatriot in Xanthippe or, at the very least, a potential philosophical partner to Socrates in the home. She is importantly well known. The significance of Xanthippe as wife to Socrates may not be readily apparent to Phaedo. He associated with Socrates from age eighteen to twenty. He would be unmarried at the dramatic date of the trial and the subsequent retelling of the events in Phlius.[31] He would not have had direct experience of how a wife might uphold and make possible philosophical practice, whereas the members of the community in Phlius would have this awareness.[32] Even if Phaedo does not recognize her full importance, he appreciates that Xanthippe is a significant part of the reiteration of Socrates's final day, at least enough to preserve her place in his retelling of the events to the members of the Pythagorean community in Phlius.

Phaedo's introduction of Xanthippe follows a list of the various attendees with many men from Athens as well as four foreigners from various city-states. Upon entry of this large group, (nine-plus Athenians and four foreigners [59b–c]), Phaedo recalls Xanthippe's response, providing his own clarificatory remarks: "Now when Xanthippe saw us, she cried out and said the kind of thing that women always do say, 'Oh Socrates, this is the last time now that your friends will speak to you and you to them'" (60a). Phaedo at this point has just finished characterizing his own complex emotional reaction to Socrates death (59a). He oddly notes that her outcry is "the kind of thing that women would say," giving a significantly gendered resonance to her remarks (60a); Xanthippe is cast into the role of "woman" by the entrance of the male citizens, especially the foreigners, when she cries out as representative of a public understanding of her gender.[33] Typically, this remark is read back through the end of the *Phaedo* when the men are critiqued for acting like women (117d). This interpretation paints Xanthippe as unable to control herself and Phaedo's remark as highlighting her essentialized female nature and thus extreme overreaction. Returning to our frame and Pythagorean listeners—ones who have not yet heard Socrates's condemnation of Apollodorus—we should not read Phaedo's remark as a dismissive one based on sexism but rather an acknowledgment of a type of gendered speaking overladen with cultural meaning. He is signaling to his audience a socially significant, if ultimately gendered, manner of speaking by Xanthippe. It is most likely the case that Xanthippe, for her part, is not making a foolish outcry that shows her particular care for Socrates or that she is overwhelmed by emotion.

Xanthippe's sonorous cry is centered by Plato to mark a strong tonal shift inside the jail cell and for the dialogue listeners. Xanthippe's private conversation with Socrates has been interrupted by Athenian socialites and wealthy foreigners—the private has become public. She is bound by social customs and laws of Athenian gendered identity that demand she perform the proper public response. Plato signals to the attentive reader how she should understand Socrates's last performance—as a public display of mourning, a position typically reserved for those with kinship ties to the soon-to-be-dead male.[34] In other words, Socrates and Xanthippe's private conversation shifts to the realm of the public rather than that of philosophical mysteries or private rituals. The conversation to be had is a type of public discourse and public philosophy that will be practiced by Cebes, Simmias, and Phaedo's Phlian auditors. Xanthippe's speaking before Socrates does interrupt a potential hierarchy of the social order, perhaps noting that her loss takes precedence over the tradition of philosophical conversation about to occur. Recall that Socrates, for our readers, is already a figure of public memory, and this literary reality emphasizes a movement away from Socrates's words and deeds and toward a collective experience of death.[35] As Rana Saadi Liebert puts it, Phaedo's recollection of these events contributes to "the means by which the community reconstitutes itself and reconceives the dead."[36] In other words, it is a (perhaps) controversial act of mourning in a philosophical practice that has a tendency to deny expressions of grief.

As a pivotal figure in the *Phaedo*, Xanthippe acts as a multifaceted amplifier for various and disparate Pythagorean and Athenian practices. First, Xanthippe, like Socrates's admirers, has followed him around for the large part of his public career, longer even than Phaedo himself, who has only recently come into Socrates's fold. Second, Xanthippe is linked with the Pythagorean context of the dialogue from the very beginning. Saxonhouse notes that "Xanthippe marks a transition in the dialogue, technically from an exterior framing that sets up the dialogue as a conversation between Phaedo and Echecrates to one that is narrated by Phaedo."[37] In this way, she marks the moment when Echecrates and the others start "listening to the account," as well as marking how one should listen to the account with the resonance of sadness from Xanthippe's cry. Saxonhouse also notes that Xanthippe "marks a transition from the world of the physical, the bodily transitory existence we all share, to the abstract language of the unseen soul whose immortality is the topic of conversation."[38] Her placement here emphasizes the audience's Pythagorean role as auditors. They are those who listen. They are now listening to the words of Socrates as reported by Phaedo, catching the carefully crafted social cues.

Xenophon's treatment of Xanthippe adds additional philosophical depth to our understanding of her. Xanthippe's place in these final moments of the *Phaedo* are tied to her role as Socrates's wife. In Xenophon's accounts, Xanthippe occupies a more active role in their marital relationship. Often, she ends up in the agora taking Socrates home from his philosophical dialogues.[39] In fact, Socrates notes that he has a wife who is not educated as a submissive Athenian wife but rather is "high-mettled." Socrates argues that this relationship is ideal for him because he becomes an expert in human behavior through association with his wife. The result is that he can "have no difficulty in [his] relations with all the rest of human kind."[40] According to Xenophon, Xanthippe helps Socrates learn to practice philosophy. Saxonhouse suggests that Xanthippe's main accomplishment was to be "known" in a world that did not acknowledge women by name: "Xanthippe, like Aspasia, was a personality in her own right, a force who by the mere fact of demanding attention from Socrates and thereby violating the expectations of the unseen/unheard women Pericles appears to praise is worthy of that attention."[41] With Xenophon, Socrates, Plato, our Pythagorean listeners, and Saxonhouse, we should acknowledge the significant context in which Xanthippe is placed as a philosophical companion for Socrates. Saxonhouse is correct to note that "Plato gives us no indication why Echecrates would know her," but even more important is her observation that "with Phaedo's side comment, Plato ensures that his readers attend to Xanthippe."[42] We too attend to Xanthippe as the harbinger of the movement from private to public (and vice versa, as we shall see) and as a significant philosophical partner in her own right.

We turn now to consider Xanthippe's sonorous phrase uttered at the intrusion of the masculine public force into the jail cell. Turning to her specific words, Phaedo reports, "Now when Xanthippe saw us, she 'cried out' [ἀνηυφήμησε] and said the kind of thing that women always do say, 'O Socrates, this is the last time now that your friends will speak to you or you to them'" (60a). One standard translation reads, "Xanthippe . . . cried out and said the kind of thing that women always do say (60a)."[43] Karen Stears provides an analysis of a similar turn of phrase in Plato's *Lysis* and notes that the "kind of thing" is potentially a socially significant act that women do to maintain intergenerational education and provide social touchstones.[44] What most translations fail to convey is that Xanthippe literally shouts in a manner that is reserved for "sorrowful occasions."[45] Plato's particular use of the third-person aorist indicative of ἀνευφημέω gives a singular completed aspect to Xanthippe's cry. She cries out in a manner that is sorrowful but singular. If we break down the verb, ἀνευ-φημέι, we hear the resonances of interwoven meaning. The prefix should be understood as ἀν: a negation of εὐφημέι holding resonances of the root verb φημί. The Greek verb φημί alone recalls either "an unprompted utterance by the gods" or "a report of good character." Xanthippe's cry could be understood as a divinely suggested utterance, which would begin and end the action of the *Phaedo* with an appeal to the gods. Alternatively, Xanthippe is uttering a "not good" omen. If we take the breakdown to be ἀν plus εὐφήμει, then she is negating what is typically "words of good omen." Both of these understandings shift her to a figure who is anticipating the death of Socrates for us as readers and reminding our attendants that this is the final day. Her voice resonates with the sorrow of the interlocutors of the jail cell and also the sorrow of those hearing the retelling in Phlius. She speaks within the tone of the dialogue and not inappropriately outside of it.

Xanthippe's outcry should be taken as setting a tone of sorrow; however, this sorrow is not improper or excessive. With Xanthippe cast in this light, the dramatic frame of the dialogue shows some resonances with the practices of postdeath lamentation. Plato masterfully evokes a sense of mourning while avoiding specific verbs and nouns typically associated with lament. He develops a pattern in the dialogue that foreshadows the ritual laments that we assume occurred after Socrates's demise. To hear the echoes, though, we must first recall the traditional components of a lament. Margaret Alexiou's historical work identifies the typical ritual funerary lament as beginning with an "introductory address, which frequently contained questions," after which "the mourner turned to reflect on what the dead was in his lifetime, and what he has come to now."[46] These rituals occur not long after death. While the central action of the *Phaedo* occurs before Socrates's death, Xanthippe's outcry combined with Echecrates's actions recalls the practices of Athenian lament. Our Socrates, while literarily both dead and not dead, is not participating in the highly particular ritual of funerary lament; however, he is being and will be lamented, and there is no more proper source for that lament than Xanthippe. Echecrates's fourteen questions begin the lament, including his opening question, "Were you with Socrates yourself, Phaedo, on the day when he drank the poison in prison?"[47] Xanthippe then reflects on the typical character of the near-dead Socrates, that of conversing with his peers, mirroring the pattern identified by Alexiou. If we take the resonances of φημί as a "report of good character," she gives a clear and concise report of Socratic character. To reiterate, Xanthippe points out that "this is the last time now that your friends will speak to you or you to them."[48] Xanthippe's characterization of Socrates directly follows Echecrates's questioning. Xanthippe's words are slightly too early for a still-living Socrates and should not be taken for an active practice of funeral lamentation. As Alexiou points out, it is bad luck to mourn for those who are not yet dead.[49] However, to our outside listeners and our author, Plato, Socrates is already dead. Xanthippe's tonal shift should resonate with our outside listeners and the readers. The listeners in Phlius are already mourning the dead Socrates. Xanthippe echoes that grief for the listeners. In other words, the dual temporality of listeners of the frame and those of the main action of the *Phaedo* place us between the two Socrateses—the living and the dead. We hear Xanthippe's words with an already-dead-to-Plato Socrates, even though he is alive to our interlocutors. While Plato may write Xanthippe as giving her sorrowful cry perhaps spontaneously, we should see it as a masterful storytelling tool that sets us up to cry for the dead Socrates as if we too are Greek listeners. Stears argues that it was most socially acceptable for women (and old men) to show emotional distress in the Greek context, as Plato also notes with Socrates's later critique of Apollodorus's outcry.[50] In other words, socially sanctioned shows of emotional distress reside with Xanthippe as female character, and her lamenting of Socrates socially would be "perceived . . . as fulfilling an emotionally necessary, even a satisfying, function for both the lamenter and the bereaved," even outside of the ritual funerary lamentation.[51]

Throughout the *Phaedo*, Socrates disrupts the traditional order of the death rituals, especially in reference to women's duties and the body. Recall that Socrates is reminded of Xanthippe's now-public position as the men enter the jail cell. He asks Crito to guide her away from the suddenly socially vulnerable position she is occupying. Phaedo recounts that "Socrates glanced at Crito and said, 'Crito, let somebody take her home.' And some of Crito's people took her away wailing and beating her breast" (60a). Xanthippe's wailing and beating of her breast as she leaves the now-public jail cell for the public outside of prison reinforces a lamenting sense combined with the socially acceptable emotional outcry.[52] Some translators overemphasize the emotional aspect of Xanthippe by translating her cry as "hysterical." Saxonhouse gives two significant readings of this passage. First, Xanthippe "sees what they see and puts into words what they themselves feel when they weep at the end of the dialogue."[53] Second, Saxonhouse calls attention to the fact that translations (such as Tredennick's) rendering the lines, "Some of Crito's servants led her away crying hysterically," place the feminine in a negative light. Saxonhouse throws into sharp relief the gendered manner in which Xanthippe is rendered. The use of the word *hysterical* establishes Xanthippe in the reader's sexist imaginary as excessively and modernly effeminate and overemotional. By leaving terms like *hysterical* aside, we can instead read Xanthippe's response as appropriate sorrow in the proper historical and cultural context of mourning the loss of her husband.

Xanthippe represents a measured and collected response to Socrates's death, albeit pre-dating his dramatic death by a few hours. The quiet sniffling of Phaedo and his companions as well as the later outburst by Apollodorus should not be compared with Xanthippe's. The comparison falls flat in light of Xanthippe's fame, which marks her as falling into a unique category of women rather than part of a nebulous stereotype of "all women." Returning to both our Pythagorean auditors and our contemporary readers, the culturally laden references to Xanthippe's (and Echecrates's) practices as echoing lamentation rituals could be apparent to those who practice such funerary rites as second nature. As we argued earlier, they would see her as a significant part of the social fabric and network being woven by Phaedo. Many of these resonances are lost on contemporary auditors whose mourning, lamenting, and funerary practices are significantly different from the Greek context. Keeping these temporal and cultural distances for the modern reader in mind, Xanthippe returns to the dialogue in another significant moment when Socrates's body is out of time with the traditional practices of funerary rites. Here Xanthippe is a silent participant in the group of "women who were sent away" to avoid their typical sonorous social function.


## 3. Xanthippe as Silence

Theorist Josine H. Blok argues that Aristophanes's *Lysistrata* focuses on "an Athenian housewife's intermittent balancing of speech against silence, of deference toward her husband against the need to act on behalf of her own responsibilities."[54] Reading Xanthippe as both sonorous and silent highlights the tension that Blok is identifying in Attic comedy. While we do not have access to Xanthippe's own psyche, we can posit through *Lysistrata* the balance that she is attempting to strike in the two positions that she holds in the dialogue. We now analyze Xanthippe's return to the jail cell and the accompanying silence in two registers: the silence of the women as speakers and the social silencing of women by Socrates.

After the conversation concerning the fate of the soul with Cebes and Simmias dwindles, Phaedo reports to Echecrates that "when he had bathed and his children had been brought to him—for he had two little sons and one big one—and the women of the family had come, he talked with them in Crito's presence and gave them such directions as he wished; then he told the women to go away, and he came to us. And it was now nearly sunset; for he had spent a long time within" (116b).[55] The women have returned to converse with Socrates for a long time. Their private conversation does not include the public—that is, the men who have come to speak with Socrates, as they do daily. The nature of the conversation is kept private by Plato as well, but as we argued earlier, the relevance of the household and their philosophical acumen is evident to our Pythagorean auditors. With them, we should hear this conversation as one that is philosophically significant, lengthy, and private. As both Echecrates and Phaedo note, Socrates had nearly an extra month to put his affairs in order. It would be hasty to assume that this long conversation is merely to figure out and solidify economic care for his family.[56] While it is speculation to posit a philosophical conversation in the lengthy discussion between Socrates and his family, if we are to assume that Socrates is a consistent character, his interests reside in making those around him philosophically better. Xenophon's earlier anecdote claiming that Socrates's prowess in philosophy stems from his interactions with Xanthippe suggests that this closed-door conversation with those of his household would assuredly include significant philosophical precepts. The presence of the women in conversation with Socrates for a long part of the day would resonate with Pythagorean auditors. The literal silence of the women to the face of the public present in the jail cell as well as the public reading the piece suggests a type of secretive philosophical dialogue that held enough significance to occupy the majority of Socrates's last day.

At the end of the Socratic meeting, the significance of women's silence in the dialogue shifts. Rather than private interlocutors, Socrates sends the women away so that they do not fulfill their public obligation of lamentation. We turn to the second formulation of silence: the social muting of women by Socrates. Socrates (and perhaps Plato) misunderstands the rami-fications of social power for Athenian women. In many dialogues, Socrates finds social consequences irrelevant to his decision-making process. Crito, who often attends to Socrates's bodily and economic needs, queries, "How shall we bury you?" (115c). Socrates laughs quietly (we must imagine hearing the laughter at this final moment, as we must imagine hearing the wailing and the lamenting of Apollodorus throughout the dialogue). Socrates re-bukes Crito and responds that they should bury him in whatever way they like and think most customary (116a). Just previous to this, though, Socrates interrupts the typical pattern of postdeath care, which may have sparked Crito's question. As the conversation dwindles, but before the women are called to return, Socrates states, "My fated day calls me now, as a tragic character might say, and it is about time for me to have my bath, for I think it better to have it before I drink the poison and save the women the trouble of washing the corpse" (115a). Socrates's words anticipate the burial rituals, but he deviates from the customary as the act of bathing the corpse usu-ally occurs postdeath. Bathing of the corpse was typically performed by women. Alexiou notes that "the body was washed, anointed and dressed by the women of the house."[57] The washing act traditionally occurred after death as a form of postdeath care but also as an important ritual of griev-ing. Socrates upsets the standard pattern of funeral rites by performing one while still alive, reinforcing Socrates's habit of breaking with social tradi-tion. Socrates makes the choice for the women that they not be included. Significantly, Socrates (and perhaps the readers too) forgets the messiness of death. The women will still have to wash the body as it goes through typi-cal postdeath biological reactions. This Socratic misstep attempts to "save the women the trouble," perhaps for other, more important engagements, but in the end, we should hear an echo of reality from Socrates's misunder-standing of death and women's rituals as saving no one the trouble. In the dialogue, the bath stands as a solid transition from the public conversa-tion with the Athenians and foreigners to the private conversation with the women and children of his household.

Along with Xanthippe's leaving at the beginning of the dialogue, the So-cratic character refuses typical public forms of mourning, while the writer, Plato, still sneaks moments of mourning into the dialogue. In this tension, contemporary readers can fault Socrates for not recognizing that his ac-tions silenced and displaced women in a space that was typically reserved for them. Socrates is consistent—he upsets Greek normative social rituals, traditions, and cues—but with a more modern lens, we should note that the power dynamics affecting women could have far-reaching consequences more significant than those that affected the wealthy landed aristocrats with whom Socrates typically conversed. It is at this moment of bathing, rather than Xanthippe's earlier exit, when we critique Socrates's expulsion and silencing of women. The act of bathing does not include a notable human sound register, but one should imagine the splashing of the water in the bath attended by the absence of women and its reverberation with the later required anointing and washing of the corpse that the women will do anyway.

## 4. "Good-Omened Silence"

The quiet of Socrates's jail cell—albeit filled with sniffles and tears—is again shattered by the "crying out" of a figure at the end of the *Phaedo*: Apollodorus. After Socrates takes the hemlock, Apollodorus yells out, unable to control himself. Phaedrus describes this as follows: "Apollodorus had not ceased from weeping before, and at this moment his noisy tears and anger made everybody present break down, except Socrates. 'What is this,' he said, 'you strange fellows. It is mainly for this reason that I sent the women away, to avoid such unseemliness, for I am told one should die in good omened silence" (117d–e). Apollodorus's loud cry (ἀναβρυχησάμενος), translated generously by Cooper as "noisy tears and anger" and less generously by Fowler as "wailed aloud," does not have a special meaning that resonates with sorrowful occasions.[58] Rather, the LSJ defines it as "wailing aloud" with no other context. It is a formless utterance of genuine sorrow that is not associated with typical funerary rites or lamentation. Unlike Xanthippe's cry, which is denoted as specifically reserved for sorrowful occasions, this wailing could occur in myriad events. Both Cooper and Fowler translate Xanthippe as "crying out." Cooper undertranslates the vocal magnitude of Apollodorus's shout, presenting a more masculine-toned perspective of "anger." This contemporary translation choice obfuscates or at the very least makes less transparent the culturally laden significance of the two distinct sonorous moments.

Turning to a typical reading of this section, readers understand Socrates's condemnation of Apollodorus as a direct reference to the exit of Xanthippe at the beginning of the dialogue.[59] Recall the correct order of events: (1) Xanthippe leaves; (2) Socrates converses with the men; (3) Socrates converses with the women of his household, Crito, and his sons; and (4) Socrates sends the women home. We see that the women in the household, not Xanthippe alone, are the ones sent away. Socrates's refutation of Apollodorus is twofold: first, the reminder that the sonorous mourning practice is demonstrated by women and not men;[60] and second, that good-omened silence should surround his death.

Returning to the Phlian Pythagorean listeners, resonances of Pythagorean practices echo throughout the *Phaedo*. Socrates's dying proverb, "He [Socrates] has heard (ἀκήκοα) that it is better to die in silence" (117e), evokes these practices.[61] The *akousmatikoi* remained silent before Pythagoras, but they were not surrounded by silence; rather, they were attentive to the words of Pythagoras. The room in which Socrates accepts death is similarly quiet and without words, except for the philosophical master Socrates's final words. They listen attentively. The backdrop of nonverbal, quiet weeping is acceptable to Socrates. When the officer of the Eleven leaves, he is weeping. Socrates lauds his form of genuine mourning: "A most agreeable man. And how genuinely he now weeps (γενναίως με ἀποδακρύω) for me" (116d).[62] The gentle hum of weeping is agreeable to Socrates as a form of good-omened quietness, a manner of care that comes upon the officer individually—a non-public, nonritual, and very personal form of grief.[63] This somber sound offers a marked contrast to Xanthippe's public show and the weeping that would be required by the sent-away women of the household. The *Phaedo* ends without a linguistical reflection by Echecrates and his colleagues, and so we must guess, given Pythagorean practices and resonances, that the practices of silence and listening after the women left were understood by Phaedo's listeners. *Akousmatikoi* practices embraced silence while still attending to bodily engagement and embodied existence in the words of their leader. The quiet of the jail cell maintains a type of quiet intimacy that still allows for emotion as well as the quiet of our Phlian auditors at the end of Phaedo's narration. Phaedo has the last word of the dialogue. We are called to imagine the silent listeners in Phlius holding the intimacy of the story in silent reverence.

Similar to Socrates's attendants, our contemporary readings need to be still in good-omened silence, listening to the resonances and intricacies of Platonic writing. We should always attend to the fact that our own weeping may accompany the text quietly in ways that deeply influence our understanding of the resonances of the piece in ancient and modern times. Through a reading that pairs Pythagorean practice with a more nuanced understanding of Xanthippe, we have argued that expansive Pythagorean gender practices provide a better understanding of Xanthippe's philosophical place in the *Phaedo*. In turn, Xanthippe represents both sonorous and silent moments heralding and anticipating significant philosophical moments in the *Phaedo*. The relationship between the type of utterances that she makes and how an audience of attentive listeners would have understood them paints Xanthippe in a more culturally critical light. In turn, we should look forward to further reassessments of Xanthippe as someone who has not been silenced and ostracized from the hallowed, echoing halls of philosophy. Instead, we should continue to listen for echoes and resonances of her words and deeds along with Socrates's own.

## Notes

1. See Phillip Horky, *Plato and Pythagoreanism* (Oxford: Oxford University Press, 2013).

2. J. M. Cooper, *Complete Works of Plato* (Indianapolis: Hackett, 1997), 49.

3. Cebes and Simmias are students of the famous Pythagorean Philolaus, as noted by Socrates at 61b.

4. See Arlene Saxonhouse, "Xanthippe: Shrew or Muse?," *Hypatia* 10 (2018): 2–16; R. Graves, "The Case for Xanthippe," *Kenyon Review* 22 (1960): 597–605.

5. Kurt Von Fritz, *Pythagorean Politics in Southern Italy* (Cambridge: Cambridge University Press, 1940). He notes that "they belong to the same generation as Archytas and since we find them living in continental Greece at the beginning of the fourth century, are either identical with the group which, according to Iamblichos, emigrated from Italy when Archytas was the only one to stay or must at least have been in close contact with this group" (28).

6. Diogenes mentions Axiothea of Phlius and Lastheneia of Mantinea in the list of "top Platonic students." It is plausible there were more women and these women were among the most important ones (Diogenes Laertius 3.46).

7. See Walter Burkert, *Lore and Science in Ancient Pythagoreanism* (Cambridge, MA: Harvard University Press, 1972), and Huffman, "Pythagoras," on the two branches of Pythagoreans. Burkert remarks, "The *mathematici*, followed in this by Eudoxus, did not attack the ritual observances taught by Pythagoras, but the *acusmatici* saw a defection from Pythagoras in the further development of scientific study. But neither tendency could endure except in altered form: . . . And since the 'mathematical' tradition in its Platonic metamorphosis, became completely dominant in the literary realm, the contention of the *mathematici* also won out, that the *acusmatici* were not genuine, but only imperfect, Pythagoreans" (*Lore and Science*, 205).

8. See Leonid Zhmud, *Pythagoras and the Early Pythagoreans* (Oxford: Oxford University Press, 2014), 93. For an alternative view, see M. Laura Gemelli Marciano, "The Pythagorean Way of Life and Pythagorean Ethics," in *A History of Pythagoreanism*, ed. Carl A. Huffman (Cambridge: Cambridge University Press, 2014), 131–148.

9. Huffman, *History of Pythagoreanism*, 7. Elsewhere, Schultz, writing as A. M. Bowery, argues that the constant use of the *akouô* language in the *Phaedo* should be taken as evidence that the split had occurred during Socrates's and Plato's lifetimes. See A. M. Bowery, "Recovering and Recollecting the Soul," in *Plato's Forms: Varieties of Interpretation*, ed. William Welton (Lanham, MD: Lexington Books, 2002), 111–136.

10. Huffman tells us that "Isocrates reports that even in the fourth century people 'marvel more at the silence of those who profess to be his pupils than at those who have the greatest

reputation for speaking.'" Isocrates, "Busiris," in *Isocrates*, vol. 3, sec. 28, tr. Larue van Hook (Cambridge, MA: Harvard University Press.) The ability to remain silent was seen as important training in self-control, and the later tradition reports that those who wanted to become Pythagoreans had to observe a five-year silence (Iamblichus, *On the Pythagorean Life*, 72). Carl Huffman, "Pythagoras," in *The Stanford Encyclopedia of Philosophy*, winter 2018 ed., ed. Edward N. Zalta, https://plato.stanford.edu/archives/win2018/entries /pythagoras/.

11.  See σαφής in the Lidell-Scott Jones: "clear, plain, distinct, of things heard, perceived, or known."

12.  Bowery, "Recovering and Recollecting"; Huffman, "Pythagoras." Burkert (*Lore and Science*) believes that the *acusma* themselves can be traced back to Pythagoras himself.

13.  See Gilles Ménage, *The History of Women Philosophers*, trans. Beatrice H. Zedler (Lanham, MD: University Press of America, 1985), 47–48, 51–53, 81–84; Sarah B. Pomeroy, *Pythagorean Women: Their History and Writings* (Baltimore: John Hopkins University Press, 2013).

14.  Pomeroy, *Pythagorean Women*, xvi.

15.  Pomeroy, xxi.

16.  Burkert notes that Pythagoras often spoke to groups of women, boys, politicians, and various other individuals one would not normally fit together (*Lore and Science*, 114). By contrast, Burkert posits that in the larger Greek culture, "the practices both of the *akusmata* and the people who participated in them seemed strange" (190).

17.  Pomeroy, *Pythagorean Women*, 11.

18.  Pomeroy, xxi.

19.  Phintys, who was originally regarded as a pre-Socratic philosopher but is now presumed to be post–350 BCE, highlights in her work the importance of women who are philosophically aware and active in the maintenance and thriving of the household and the state. For a translation of her work, see Mary Ellen Waithe, ed., *A History of Women Philosophers*, vol. 1, *600 BC–500 AD* (Dordetch: Martinus Nijhoff, 1987), 19–40.

20.  Pomeroy, *Pythagorean Women*, 11.

21.  Pomeroy, 25.

22.  Pomeroy, 25.

23.  Pomeroy, 12.

24.  Waithe, *History of Women Philosophers*, 25.

25.  This is made all the more difficult because what we know occurs within the context of a dialogue constructed by Plato. Christopher Celenza notes, "From Plato onward it becomes impossible to separate the Platonic from the Pythagorean." "Pythagoras and Pythagoreanism," in *The Classical Tradition*, ed. Anthony Grafton, Glenn W. Most, and Salvatore Settis (Cambridge, MA: Harvard University Press, 2010), 796.

26.  Saxonhouse, "Xanthippe," helpfully surveys both contemporary and historical presentations of Xanthippe.

27.  For examples of commentary about Xanthippe, see Xenophon, *Symposium* 2; Plutarch, *De cohibenda ira*; Diogenes Laertius, *Lives of Eminent Philosophers* 2.37. She is often regarded as a shrewish or nagging wife. The Socratic character usually responds to these accusations by instrumentalizing Xanthippe and claiming that her contrary attitudes make him a better man.

28.  Also see the entry on Xanthippe in *The Classical Tradition*. It lists several positive assessments of her throughout the centuries. Jan M. Ziolkowski, "Xanthippe," in *The Classical Tradition*, ed. Anthony Grafton, Glenn W. Most, and Salvatore Settis (Cambridge, MA: Harvard University Press, 2010), 996.

29. Saxonhouse, "Xanthippe," 8.

30. Saxonhouse, 8.

31. See Debra Nails, *The People of Plato: A Prosopography of Plato and Other Socratics* (Indianapolis: Hackett, 2002), 231.

32. Through the works of Xenophon, who popularizes an image of the fraught Xanthippe, it is possible to posit a more active wife role for Xanthippe even as she still participates in certain Athenian constraints. In Xenophon's *Symposium* (2.10), Socrates's interlocutor notes Xanthippe's nonstandard behavior. Additionally, Diogenes Laertius in his *Lives of Eminent Philosophers* (2.36) tells how Xanthippe must often physically and sometimes roughly retrieve her philosophically promiscuous husband from the agora.

33. See Josine Blok, "Toward a Choreography of Women's Speech in Classical Athens," in *Making Silence Speak: Women's Voices in Greek Literature and Society*, ed. André Lardinos and Laura McClure (Princeton, NJ: Princeton University Press, 2001), 95–116, for helpful distinctions of private, public, and semiprivate.

34. See Margaret Alexiou, *The Ritual Lament in Greek Tradition* (Lanham, MD: Rowman and Littlefield, 2002). Alexiou productively highlights a shift in Solon's time from aristocratic group mourning to a more private type of mourning that prioritizes the closest relatives. She argues that this may be related to mourning, signaling those who would inherit the estate of the deceased (15, 20–23). Historically, then, Xanthippe would be the proper publicly approved figure of mourning even if Socrates rejects mourning categorically.

35. For a stellar explanation of this collective experience of mourning in the *Phaedo*, see Rana Saadi Liebert, "Mourning Socrates: Plato's *Phaedo* and Tragic Philosophy," *Classical Philology* 115 (2020): 442–466.

36. Liebert, 442.

37. Saxonhouse, "Xanthippe," 8.

38. Saxonhouse, 8.

39. Xenophon, *Symposium*, trans. William Heinemann (Cambridge, MA: Harvard University Press, 1979), 2.10

40. Xenophon, *Symposium* 2.10. This form of story is reiterated in Diogenes Laertius, *Lives of the Eminent Philosophers* 2.37.

41. Saxonhouse, "Xanthippe," 12.

42. Saxonhouse, 8.

43. Cooper, *Complete Works of Plato*, 52.

44. Karen Stears, "Death Becomes Her," in *Lament: Studies in the Ancient Mediterranean and Beyond*, ed. Ann Suter (Oxford: Oxford University Press, 2008), 139–155.

45. *The Online Liddell-Scott-Jones Greek-English Lexicon*, s.v. "ἀνευφημέω," accessed December 17, 2021, http://stephanus.tlg.uci.edu/lsj/#eid=8881.

46. Alexiou, *Ritual Lament*, 165.

47. *Phaedo* 57a.

48. *Phaedo* 60a. Liebert argues, specific to the *Phaedo*, that "from the survivor's point of view, it is . . . the realization that communication and reciprocity with the deceased are no longer possible (at least in any meaningful sense), that makes death so difficult to bear" ("Mourning Socrates," 443). Liebert's poignant articulation of the loss that the community present in Socrates's jail cell suffers resonates with Xanthippe's explanation: "This is the last time your friends will talk to you and you to them" (*Phaedo* 60a).

49. Alexiou, *Ritual Lament*, 4. It should be reiterated that Plato specifically avoids the typical Greek words for lament, instead choosing words typically used for mourning and sorrow, even as he develops resonances of lamentation practices.

50. Stears, "Death Becomes Her," 147.

51. Gail Holts-Warhaft, *Dangerous Voices: Women's Laments and Greek Literature* (London: Routledge, 1992), 29.

52. Since there is no comment by Phaedo denoting that Xanthippe is acting in excess in this moment, we believe that the wailing and beating of her breast should be taken as a socially acceptable emotion for Xanthippe. It is not leaning into the type of excessive madness that is variously associated with funerary lament practices. See Holts-Warhaft (*Dangerous Voices*) and Alexiou (*Ritual Lament*) for more detail on those practices.

53. Saxonhouse, "Xanthippe," 9.

54. Blok, "Toward a Choreography," 95–96.

55. We use Fowler's 1966 translation here.

56. In fact, we see in Plato's *Crito* that Socrates seems to lack concern for his family affairs, trusting them to be carried out by his friends. If we presume the Socratic character to be consistent, then Socrates here should also be dismissive of the need for such conversations.

57. Alexiou, *Ritual Lament*, 5.

58. Cooper, *Complete Works of Plato*, 99.

59. See also Naomi Weiss, "Noise, Music, Speech: The Representation of Lament in Greek Tragedy," *American Journal of Philology* 138, no. 2 (2017): 243–266. A stronger reading here might be to reiterate Nicole Loraux's position, aptly described by Weiss: "The female lament stands directly opposed to male, civic discourse in classical Athens, a form of discourse represented by the *epitaphios logos*" (250). However, Weiss problematizes this strong dimorphic gendering of lament as absolute.

60. See Andrea Fishman, "Thrênoi to Moirológia: Female Voices of Solitude, Resistance, and Solidarity," *Oral Tradition* 23, no. 2 (2008): 267–295. Fishman argues that in Euripides's *Suppliants*, Adrastus's lamentation cry is reiterated by the all-female chorus. When the male Adrastus cries out, he simultaneously becomes "embarrassingly feminized" by his own admission. Fishman argues that Euripides imparts to Adrastus a portion of "feminine agency," which is culturally evoked most strongly in the practice of vocal lamentation. This relates to Apollodorus here as a figure who reiterates Xanthippe's call, echoing the lamentation that should accompany Socrates's death but that Socrates strangely rejects. However, this action does not impart a connection with Apollodorus like the call-and-response lamentation of the *Supplicants* but rather an admonishment by Socrates.

61. Burkert remarks, "Pythagorean Greeks went past ηρωα in silence, in order not to disturb the κρείττονες" (*Lore and Science*, 185).

62. While Cooper translates γενναίως as "genuinely," it may also be rendered as "nobly."

63. This is how we take the translation of *gennaios me apodakruei*—which can mean "lamenting loudly." But the genuine, noble, or true-to-oneself nature of this weeping denotes it as nonritualistic and not required by social decorum.

# Bibliography

Alexiou, Margaret. *The Ritual Lament in Greek Tradition*. Lanham, MD: Rowman and Littlefield, 2002.

Blok, Josine. "Toward a Choreography of Women's Speech in Classical Athens." In *Making Silence Speak: Women's Voices in Greek Literature and Society*, edited by André Lardinos and Laura McClure, 95–116. Princeton, NJ: Princeton University Press, 2001.

Bowery, A. M. *See* Schultz, A. M.

Burkert, Walter. *Lore and Science in Ancient Pythagoreanism*. Cambridge, MA: Harvard University Press, 1972.

Celenza, Christopher. "Pythagoras and Pythagoreanism." In *The Classical Tradition*, edited by Anthony Grafton, Glenn W. Most, and Salvatore Settis, 796–799. Cambridge, MA: Harvard University Press, 2010.

Cooper, J. M. *Complete Works of Plato*. Indianapolis: Hackett, 1997.

Fishman, Andrea. "Thrênoi to Moirológia: Female Voices of Solitude, Resistance, and Solidarity." *Oral Tradition* 23, no. 2 (2008): 267–295.

Gemelli Marciano, M. Laura. "The Pythagorean Way of Life and Pythagorean Ethics." In *A History of Pythagoreanism*, edited by Carl A. Huffman, 131–148. Cambridge: Cambridge University Press, 2014.

Graves, R. "The Case for Xanthippe." *Kenyon Review* 22 (1960): 597–605.

Holts-Warhaft, Gail. *Dangerous Voices: Women's Laments and Greek Literature*. London: Routledge, 1992.

Horky, Phillip. *Plato and Pythagoreanism*. Oxford: Oxford University Press, 2013.

Huffman, Carl. *A History of Pythagoreanism*. Cambridge: Cambridge University Press, 2014.

———. "Pythagoras." In *The Stanford Encyclopedia of Philosophy*, winter 2018 ed., edited by Edward N. Zalta. https://plato.stanford.edu/archives/win2018/entries/pythagoras/.

Iamblichus. *On the Pythagorean Way of Life*. Translated by John Dillon and Jackson Hershbell. Atlanta, GA: Scholars Press, 1991.

Isocrates. "Busiris." In *Isocrates*, vol. 3, sec. 28, translated by Larue van Hook. Cambridge, MA: Harvard University Press, 1945.

Liebert, Rana Saadi. "Mourning Socrates: Plato's *Phaedo* and Tragic Philosophy." *Classical Philology* 115 (2020): 442–466.

Ménage, Gilles. *The History of Women Philosophers*. Translated by Beatrice H. Zedler. Lanham, MD: University Press of America, 1985.

Nails, Debra. *The People of Plato: A Prosopography of Plato and Other Socratics*. Indianapolis: Hackett, 2002.

Plato. *Plato in Twelve Volumes*. Vol 1, translated by Harold North Fowler. Cambridge, MA: Harvard University Press, 1966.

Pomeroy, Sarah B. *Pythagorean Women: Their History and Writings*. Baltimore: John Hopkins University Press, 2013.

Saxonhouse, Arlene. "Xanthippe: Shrew or Muse?" *Hypatia* 10 (2018): 2–16.

Schultz, A. M. [publishing as A. M. Bowery]. "Recovering and Recollecting the Soul." In *Plato's Forms: Varieties of Interpretation*, edited by William Welton, 111–136. Lanham, MD: Lexington Books, 2002.

Stears, Karen. "Death Becomes Her." In *Lament: Studies in the Ancient Mediterranean and Beyond*, edited by Ann Suter, 139–155. Oxford: Oxford University Press, 2008.

Von Fritz, Kurt. *Pythagorean Politics in Southern Italy*. Cambridge: Cambridge University Press, 1940.

Waithe, Mary Ellen, ed. *A History of Women Philosophers*. Vol. 1, *600 BC–500 AD*. Dordetch: Martinus Nijhoff, 1987.

Weiss, Naomi. "Noise, Music, Speech: The Representation of Lament in Greek Tragedy." *American Journal of Philology* 138, no. 2 (2017): 243–266.

Xenophon. *Symposium*. Translated by William Heinemann. Cambridge, MA: Harvard University Press, 1979.

Zhmud, Leonid. *Pythagoras and the Early Pythagoreans*. Oxford: Oxford University Press, 2014.
Ziolkowski, Jan M. "Xanthippe." In *The Classical Tradition*, edited by Anthony Grafton, Glenn W. Most, and Salvatore Settis, 996–997. Cambridge, MA: Harvard University Press, 2010.

KRIS MCLAIN is a dual-title PhD candidate in Philosophy and Women's, Gender, and Sexuality Studies at the Pennsylvania State University. She is a graduate student consultant at the Schreyer Institute for Teaching Excellence. Her dissertation explores metaphors of gestation historically and thematically in order to produce contemporary epistemic methods.

ANNE-MARIE SCHULTZ is Professor and Undergraduate Program Director of Philosophy at Baylor University. She recently received the designation of Master Teacher. Anne-Marie is author of *Plato's Socrates as Narrator* and *Plato's Socrates on Socrates*.

# 14

# SOCRATES'S BODY AND THE VOICE OF PHILOSOPHY

James Barrett, Colby College

IN DISCUSSING THE HISTORY OF THE GREEK BODY, Jean-Pierre Vernant identifies a rupture between what he calls "the pre-Socratic body" and the body as reconfigured by Plato and others.[1] The former he calls a "sub-body," defined in opposition to the "super-body" of the gods,[2] whereas the body as reconfigured by Plato became nothing more than a tomb for the immortal soul. Vernant's telling use of the familiar term *pre-Socratic* reminds us that Plato produces his most powerful effects through the figure of Socrates.[3] And in the case of the body, Socrates's role is unlike what we find elsewhere: in addition to his arguments and characteristic engagement with his interlocutors, the very body of Socrates proves to be a signal achievement. Indeed, as I argue below, Plato's contribution to the history of the Greek body includes his creation of what might be called the "philosophical body," exemplified by the unique body of Socrates.[4]

In making such a claim, I take a cue from Adriana Cavarero's discussion of Socrates's voice and its central role in "the strange history of the devocalization of logos."[5] This strange history shows that from Heraclitus to Plato, for example, the acoustic is subordinated to the visual, which alone is the "guarantor of truth as presence" (42; see also 36–37).[6] In the dialogues of Plato, she argues, we witness the transformation of the bewitching, embodied logoi of Socrates into the metaphysical logos of Plato. Taking seriously Alcibiades's portrait of Socrates in Plato's *Symposium* as a silenic figure whose logoi Alcibiades equates with the aulos-playing of Marsyas,

Cavarero finds that Plato plays Apollo to Socrates's Marsyas: Plato "flays" Socrates and "devocalizes" his logoi by dispensing with his silenic exterior, as "the beautiful and divine inside" (the signified) displaces "the superficial outside . . . [or] acoustic signifier" (72). Such banishment of the Socratic voice means, according to Cavarero, that the "videocentric enchantment of metaphysics, the noetic flute playing of the *inside*, is an inheritance that Plato does not receive from Socrates" (74). In banishing Socrates's voice, that is, Plato also dispenses with his body.

Although Cavarero here identifies a central strand in the *Symposium* as well as in Plato's broader project, and although her case is persuasive, we do well to remember that any flaying of Socrates is far from complete. In other words, the *Symposium* itself preserves the most vivid and compelling representation of a silenic Socrates. Even if we agree that the Socratic voice is ultimately moved to one side by Platonic metaphysics, we must remember that the dialogues cling tenaciously to the voice—and body—of the unflayed Socrates, as Plato plays the part of a new Odysseus lashed to the mast, seemingly transfixed by the magic of Socrates's voice and body.

In Plato's dialogues, I suggest, we witness a struggle with the very potential and limits of devocalization, with the dream of wielding a disembodied voice—any flaying of Socrates, that is, must be seen as inseparable from his persistently silenic self. Indeed, I suggest that this emphatically and uniquely embodied Socrates is hardly a failure for Plato. Instead, he reaps great rewards from a silenic Socrates whose voice and body prove to be incomparable.

The question of Socrates's voice is of greater significance than it might at first appear, as can be seen in the fact that Alcibiades's characterization points in two directions at once: on the one hand, it points to overlooked aspects of the history of devocalization as discussed by Cavarero; on the other hand, it is an important witness to Plato's construction and definition of his model philosopher, revealing the value of Socrates's unique body in this project. In other words, in pursuing the significance of Alcibiades's characterization, I touch on one of Plato's broader aims—namely, his effort to define what philosophy is.[7] This is a large topic, of course, and beyond the scope of this essay, but it will be helpful to keep in mind that for my purposes the presentation of Socrates in the *Symposium* is definitional, not descriptive—the question I ask is not whether Alcibiades's depiction of Socrates is true or false but rather what it does. And I suggest that it does quite a lot. As I attempt to show, the Socrates conjured by Alcibiades proves to acquire a unique embodiment that endows his voice with a privileged status, reminding us that the voice is necessarily of the body. In what follows, then, as I attempt to decode Alcibiades's dense portrait, I try to show the linkage between Socrates's unique body and his uncanny voice, as I also highlight some key aspects of what (for Plato) defines a philosopher. In so doing, I consider what we can learn from other, earlier engagements with embodiment and vocalization, as I suggest how these illuminate what is entailed by Alcibiades's characterization.

## 1. The Muse

Devocalization, for Cavarero, produces the detached gaze of the philosopher (*theoria*), a gaze that enables "the contemplation of real, lasting, immobile things" (38). Such a philosophical gaze, furthermore, is predicated on a robust form of presence: "This presence refers to both the spatial dimension that is typical of the object that lies in front of the onlooker, and to the temporal dimension of a simultaneous 'now' that is eternalized by the contemplator" (38). Aside from the important distinction between the ephemeral events witnessed by the gods and the ideas "eternalized in the now of their presence" contemplated by the philosopher (39), this characterization applies equally well to the Muses.[8] The *Iliad* makes this clear:

> Tell me now, you Muses who have your homes on Olympos.
> For you, who are goddesses, are there, and you know all things,
> and we have heard only the rumour of it and know nothing.[9]

> (2.484–86; trans. Lattimore)

These famous lines underscore both the presence of the Muses and the eternity of their "now," qualities highlighted by comparison to those of mere mortals, who must rely on rumor because they (we) are not present and therefore know nothing. As Cavarero remarks, the Muse preserves the story "in a sort of eternal actuality" (97). She goes on to say that it is "the philosopher himself who will come to occupy the privileged place that the poet had reserved for the Muse" (98). Because devocalization denies the physicality of the voice (the inescapable bond between voice and body), the problem faced by the philosopher lies in the difference between the divine body of the Muses and the mortal body that the philosopher aims to elude, escape, or deny—Vernant's pre-Socratic body.

The Hesiodic Muses present in salient form the challenge faced by Cavarero's philosopher. They, after all, know things that are, things that will be, and things that were before.[10] And yet some of the first words we hear about them in the *Theogony* tell us that they dance lightly on their feet, their skin is soft, and their dances are beautiful and seductive.[11] In other words, the song and dance of the Muses are convincingly embodied, and yet these goddesses are able to tell both coarse and fine grain, both the beginnings of the cosmos and, for example, the unspoken thoughts of Prometheus as he tries to trick Zeus at Mekone (*Theogony* 535–552). Their embodiment and its specificity prove elusive, constituting no hindrance to their ability to sing about all things present, past, and future—and their song will, of course, be irrefutable.[12] This is possible because the divine body, as Vernant reminds us, is not subject to the constraints that define the pre-Socratic body, a body that "precisely positions every individual, assigning him (or her) one and only one location in space. A god's body escapes this limitation . . . The gods are here and there at the same time."[13]

## 2. The Tragic Messenger

The rather great distance separating the realm of divine embodiment with its attendant epistemic and discursive powers (as demonstrated by the Muse), on one hand, and the realm of human embodiment with its pro-found epistemic and discursive limitations, on the other, proves to be not an empty space but rather a site of vigorous experimentation. Tragedy in particular proves to be a productive workshop. Forgoing not only the Muse of epic but also its narrator, tragedy takes as a premise the collisions of various points of view onstage, the incommensurability of different kinds of speech, and the semantic ambiguity of its language. These various cleavages are all intensified by the genre's formal exclusion of an authoritative, organizing voice. As a result, tragedy is characterized by contestation not only for formal reasons following on the absence of a narrator: themes of conflict and dispute are also common in these dramas, which exploit the ambiguities and multiple meanings in the vocabularies they employ. We might even say that the formal condition of tragedy becomes a principle of its thematic construction.[14]

The multiplicity of voices onstage thus requires that the audience ne-gotiate competing claims to authority, as the juxtaposition of these differ-ing voices highlights the idiosyncrasies and limitations constraining each speaker. In performance, the partiality of each voice becomes even more salient for spectators than it is for readers, inasmuch as the physical enact-ment emphasizes the differing vocalizations. But even for readers, tragic language rehearses the inseparability of voice and body, the speaker and the spoken, and thereby underscores the limitations of all speech.

In this context, however, several voices stand out in seeming to escape these conditions: those of divinities, prophets, choruses, and messengers. The first two types, of course, claim divine privileges, while choruses have access to communal or traditional knowledge insofar as they typically re-count shared understandings of the past. The tragic messenger, however, operates on unique terrain: without special dispensation, this figure pro-duces a voice that has generally been heard as one emphatically not subject to the limitations mentioned above, one not characterized by partiality. In-deed, this lack of partiality and the discursive privilege it brings with it en-able the messenger to perform his typical function: incorporating offstage events into the drama. And so effective is the rhetoric of this figure that, even in the richly contestatory tragic context, until recently few saw any rhetoric at all.[15] Although such a naive view has relatively few adherents today, the messenger's success at avoiding scrutiny points to the powers of his rhetoric. I draw attention, in particular, to the fact that this figure is able to forge a voice that largely escapes the limits of embodiment, one that in some respects resembles that of the Muse. I offer an example from Aeschy-lus's *Persians*.[16]

After the devastating defeat of the Persian fleet at Salamis, a Persian mes-senger arrives in Susa with a report that confirms everyone's worst fears. His lengthy account of the defeat mimics the scale of the battle in creating "an overpowering vision of vast landscapes and events."[17] For example, the mes-senger describes the naval engagement in such a way that the vast scope of the battle and of his visual field are brought to the fore (*Persians* 412–420): "At first the flood of the Persian force put up a resistance; but when the mass of their ships was crowded together in a narrow strait, and they could not bring any assistance to one another, they struck each other with their bronze-mouthed beaks, and shattered all the rowing equipment; the Greek ships ju-diciously encircled them and made their strike, and ships' hulls were turned upside down, and it was no longer possible to glimpse the sea, which was brimming with wrecked ships and dead men"[18] (trans. Hall). The broad scope of the messenger's vision, however, is attended by description of surprising specificity, a specificity and narrowness of scope that suggests an entirely dif-ferent point of view. For example, he provides a vivid view of Matallos's death in fine detail (314–316): "Matallos from Chrysa died, the commander of ten thousand, and his thick, bushy, tawny beard changed colour as he dipped it into the dye of the purple sea"[19] (trans. Hall). As the adjectives accumulate, piled on without grammatical connection (πυρσὴν ζαπληθῆ δάσκιον), they reproduce the thickness of the beard they describe. The result is a stark contrast between the finely detailed close-up perspective here and that of the broad narrative sweep of the ships in battle. In this context, descriptions such as this one stand out as they point to the double perspective of the messenger: he sees in both broad strokes and fine detail. In positioning himself alternately at some distance from the scene and close up to it, he proves to be free from one of the key constraints of the pre-Socratic body. Freed from the limitations of place, the messenger speaks with a voice that may be understood to have acquired something of the Muse's privilege: no longer bound to a single location, the messenger proves to wield the power that comes from attenuating the connection of the voice with the body. (In fact, Aeschylus's text pointedly compares the messenger to the Muse.[20]) And this weak association between voice and body endows his narrative with an authority unavailable to the others onstage. For my purposes here, the unique position of the tragic messenger matters because it points the way to understanding the significance of Socrates's unique embodiment (according to Alcibiades, at least) and what this can tell us about the philosopher's voice.[21]

## 3. Socrates's Body

The day after a big party in honor of Agathon's victory in the tragic competition, a group of friends gathers at Agathon's house for another party, which becomes the scene of Plato's *Symposium*. Given all the drinking of the previous day, Eryximachus declares that a number of those present are incapable of "serious drinking" (τὸ ἐρρῶσθαι πίνειν, 176b) again.[22] Socrates, he says, is a special case because whether he drinks or not has no effect. All agree that, in place of a raucous party, they will offer speeches in praise of Eros. After several speeches, Socrates relates what the wise Diotima once told him about Eros, before a drunken Alcibiades enters and agrees to join the group by offering an encomium not of Eros but of Socrates.

It won't be easy to praise Socrates, Alcibiades says, given his oddities. As a way of navigating these difficulties, Alcibiades explains, he will offer an encomium of Socrates that proceeds by means of images (δι' εἰκόνων, 215a). The image he offers is that of the satyr: Socrates, he says, resembles most of all those familiar sculptures of Silenus. As a matter of fact, he says, Socrates resembles the satyr Marsyas, particularly with regard to his appearance.[23]

Alcibiades's use of the satyr to explain Socrates's unique charm captures well what has been appreciated by all: namely, that the (ironic) discrepancy between Socrates's exterior and interior—between his apparent ugliness and his professions of ignorance, on the one hand, and his inner beauty and wisdom, on the other—corresponds to that of the figurine with which Alcibiades begins his account (215a–b). Socrates's appearance, that is, turns out to be a visible sign of his ironic character.

Although I try to show that there is far more to the analogy than the familiar understanding envisions, the emphasis on the discontinuity between Socrates's exterior and his interior does in fact point the way to the analogy's broader implications. What is at stake in the conventional reading of Alcibiades's portrait of Socrates as satyr is the reliability of the exterior as a guide to the interior. Unlike what we find in the world of Homer, for example, the beautiful no longer necessarily coincides with the worthy. If the *Iliad* teaches that the ugly and complaining Thersites deserves a beating, Plato's *Symposium* teaches that in the realm of philosophy the heroic figure may in fact be ugly.[24]

But the famous ugliness of the heroic philosopher is no small oddity of Plato's text. Rather, it argues for a new scheme of values, as it suggests that the yardsticks that Plato's contemporaries rely on may no longer work. Philosophy, it seems, is changing the rules of the game. But as Alcibiades's claim that Socrates most of all resembles a satyr formulates a new aesthetic/moral paradigm, it also suggests that he can be neither evaluated nor understood in conventional terms. If the discontinuity between Socrates's less-than-beautiful exterior and quasi-divine interior problematizes reliance on the normative equation of exterior and interior, it also proposes Socrates as the unique exemplar of this new aesthetic/moral standard. Socrates himself, that is, no less than the radical form of evaluation on offer, is revolutionary—we have not seen his like before.[25]

The long history of reading Alcibiades's portrait as an expression of the discontinuity between Socrates's interior and exterior suggests two things. The first is that the status of Socrates as a figure incomprehensible by ordinary standards has been widely embraced up to the present day. The second, implied by the first, is that Alcibiades's portrait has long been considered a reliable guide to Socrates's unique charms. Given who the historical Alcibiades was, this second implication may be surprising, but it is clear that few have been troubled by the apparently inconvenient source of this persuasive portrait.[26] I suggest, in fact, that this portrait constitutes a far more potent and compelling guide to Plato's Socrates than has been appreciated. Or, put differently, the implications of the standard reading of the portrait have not been appreciated. By means of the satyr analogy, Alcibiades's portrait opens the way to seeing Socrates's uniqueness (or *atopia*) as one of his key features, one that reveals what remains unexplored in Cavarero's otherwise brilliant analysis.[27]

As Paul Zanker writes, the comparison of Socrates and satyr derives from his "squat figure with big belly, broad and flat face with bulging eyes, the large mouth with protruding lips, and the bald head."[28] Plato's *Theaetetus*, for example, supports this view, depicting another (younger) Socrates who is "not beautiful at all" but rather "snub-nosed with eyes that stick out" (143e) and who therefore resembles the Socrates we know so well.[29] So widely confirmed is this picture of the historical Socrates that critics typically read its appearance in Plato as a sign of Plato's realism. The ugly Socrates in Plato, that is, is nearly always seen as a sign of the historical Socrates. In short, Plato's Socrates is assumed to be ugly because the historical Socrates was ugly.[30]

But this realism obscures something of much greater consequence— it serves as a kind of mask for more important work done by the portrait. Socrates's ugliness, particularly as expressed in terms of his likeness to a satyr, transposes his philosophical distinction into the cultural realm and condenses into the vocabulary of myth key aspects of Plato's model philosopher. The work done by this image, that is, proves to be advantageous to Plato in his efforts to distinguish philosophy. And much of this work hinges on the philosopher's body, as the satyr might suggest.

As Cavarero reminds us (68–70), Socrates's peculiar embodiment is inseparable from his peculiarly embodied logoi. Indeed, Alcibiades makes clear that Socrates's logoi are the equivalent of Marsyas's aulos when he tells Socrates that the "only difference between you and Marsyas is that you need no instruments; you do exactly what he does, but with words alone" (215c).[31] Emphasizing the unique auditory experience of hearing Socrates's voice, Alcibiades sums up his experience this way: "So I refuse to listen to him; I stop my ears and tear myself away from him, for, like the Sirens, he could make me stay by his side till I die" (216a).[32] Socrates's voice, like and inseparable from his unique body, proves comprehensible, then, on the model of Marsyas's aulos or on the model of the Sirens' seductive and devastating song.[33] Indeed, the incomparability of the Sirens' song proves to be an apt parallel for Socrates's own incomparabilities, as Alcibiades's Odyssean "solution" suggests.

Such a silenic/Sirenic Socrates, however, does not arise ex nihilo in Alcibiades's speech—it is anticipated already by Diotima's account of Eros. Even though it has become something of a critical commonplace to see that Diotima's Eros bears a striking resemblance to Socrates,[34] the implications of the resemblance for our understanding of Socrates as satyr remain to be pursued. I suggest first that the rough equivalence of these two figures—Socrates and Eros—should make us think more seriously about Alcibiades's portrait. After all, the satyr is characterized by Eros, even if it is an Eros conventionally (and mythically) conceived. The intensity, energy, and ceaselessness of Socrates's philosophical pursuit—figured in this dialogue, at least, as erotic pursuit—find themselves concisely expressed in the ithyphallicism of the satyr, a figure always in pursuit of sexual fulfillment and never managing to achieve it. Socrates as satyr, then, evokes the erotic aspect of philosophy in the register of myth, but it does more than that: the in-between status of Diotima's Eros—between wisdom and ignorance, between mortality and immortality, between beauty and ugliness—finds an analogue in the satyr, an analogue that addresses the cultural and historical positioning of the Socrates of Plato's making.[35]

Like drama, its Dionysian sibling, the symposium is predicated on the participant's encounter with alterity. If successful, of course, this encounter may approximate less a beholding and more an experience of alterity, temporary though it may be. After all, the symposium's Dionysian elements include not only wine and painted drinking cups but also the aulos (see below) and song. Indeed, the ecstatic potential of Dionysian ritual suggests that in both contexts participants may, briefly at least, lose something of the distance entailed in this alterity and find fulfillment in that seductive, Nietzschean loss of individuation.[36] When the party is over, however, and sobriety returns, this distance reappears in even more certain terms than before. This encounter, that is, reassures and reaffirms by emphasizing the distance between the normative self and the represented other. In other words, the grotesque face at the bottom of the drinking cup, which may run the risk of shattering this distance by looking back at the enthusiastic symposiast and sharing his world, serves ultimately to reproduce the order that sustains the self of the ritual drinker. Similarly, the aulos, which calls the participant into a transgressive acoustic realm, ultimately falls silent. This temporary flirting with alterity teaches primarily the value of remaining faithful to the familiar and to one's certainties.[37]

When the participants in the symposium at Agathon's house decide to forgo serious drinking and music (176e), therefore, more than one familiar member of such parties goes missing. Along with wine and the flute girl, that is, familiar forms of alterity are displaced—Dionysus, along with his companions, is "exiled." Without wine, there is no need for those drinking cups elaborately decorated with provocative images drawn from the realms of fantasy and excess. Without the flute girl, the raucous acoustics of the aulos disappear. Along with wine and aulos, of course, also go the ithyphallic satyrs otherwise so much at home in the symposium and not infrequently depicted on sympotic crockery. And the complex scheme made possible by all of these elements—the ritual suspension of certainties—gives way to a novel form of symposium in which yet new ways of suspending certainties appear and even the notion of alterity is remade. For much of the dialogue, of course, alterity as an operative principle is in fact banished. The arrival of Alcibiades, however, changes all that.

Alcibiades—"very drunk and very loud . . . half-carried into the house by the flute-girl" (212d–e)—may well reintroduce (a familiar) Dionysus in some sense. But this return of the Dionysian carries an irony that only Plato could give it. For example, that such an Alcibiades speaks the remarkable praise of Socrates suggests that we can make some sense of this praise by considering it as a (familiar) Dionysian moment—the return of the satyr implies as much. And yet his speech proves to rewrite the form and function of alterity that passes under the name of Dionysus. The ithyphallic Socrates that emerges is thus prepared for by the banishment of wine and music at the party's outset, as the space made by this banishment opens the way for novel forms of alterity.[38]

One novelty here lies in the fact that Socrates, a mere mortal, displaces the quasi-divine figure who most compellingly embodies the sympotic Dionysus: the satyr.[39] Key, though, is the suggestion that Socrates, in his everyday activity, performs work comparable to that which—in the case of the satyr—is ritually circumscribed by the festival or sympotic context. The thoroughly mundane Socrates is the satyr at the symposium to the same degree that he is the satyr everywhere. The form of alterity that he embodies, unlike that of the model on which he is fashioned by Alcibiades, works its magic not for a designated period within prescribed boundaries but rather always and everywhere. Socrates as satyr carries out the work of this fantastic and ritually circumscribed figure, but in a very real and uncircumscribed manner. And rather than being an elaborate means of reaffirming certainties, this satyr offers stiff challenges to them.

But if Socrates's resemblance to the satyr produces such a novelty, the resemblance itself underscores most of all the *atopia* at the center of this encomium.[40] In summing up, Alcibiades (re)turns to this *atopia* and notes the impossibility of finding a (real) analogue for Socrates (221c–d):

> But as a whole, he is unique; he is like no one else in the past and no one in the present—this is by far the most amazing thing about him. . . . There is a parallel for everyone—everyone else, that is. But this man here is so bizarre, his ways and his ideas are so unusual, that, search as you might, you'll never find anyone else, alive or dead, who's remotely like him. The best you can do is not to compare him to anything human, but to liken him, as I do, to Silenus and the satyrs, and the same goes for his ideas and arguments.[41]

That Socrates's *atopia* should be understood on the model of the satyr provides a strong clue to the nature of his strangeness—at least as represented by Alcibiades here. But why should it be the satyr that makes Socrates comprehensible, and just how is it that the satyr "explains" Socrates?

As a shortcut to an answer, I turn to Euripides's *Cyclops*. This, our only complete satyr drama, offers a glimpse of what satyrs (can) do. And because this play reworks a familiar Homeric text, it offers an accessible example of the satyr's characteristic effects. Odysseus's encounter with the Cyclops Polyphemus in *Odyssey* 11 has been shown to put on display an oppositional structure anchored on one side by the monstrous beast Polyphemus and on the other by the crafty and "civilized" Odysseus.[42] Euripides's play rewrites this plot in large measure by adding a chorus of satyrs who now are the captives of Polyphemus. As David Konstan notes, the dyadic structure of the Odyssean account (Cyclops and human) becomes in the satyr drama a triadic structure: it is the satyr that is this tertium quid.[43] In short, the binaries that underpin the Homeric story no longer hold—key distinctions between the human and the bestial in *Odyssey* 11 become blurred with the addition of the satyrs. On the one hand, in Euripides's play, Odysseus and his companions are distinguished from both Cyclops and satyrs, who are called "beasts" (θηρὸς πανούργου, 442; θῆρες, 624). On the other hand, the third term in the mix produces identifications between human and Cyclops as well as between human and satyr.

Not only does this triangulation question "the boundary between man and beast," in Konstan's words[44]; more importantly for my purposes, it displays a figure who is entirely at home in none of the categories that lie behind this opposition, a figure who transgresses the boundaries that distinguish human, beast, and god. The hallmark of the satyr, in this drama and elsewhere, is precisely his elusive quality that makes it impossible to assimilate him to familiar schemes. Indeed, satyrs are endowed with this elusive quality from early on. They appear already in Hesiod as worthless and unfit for work (γένος οὐτιδανῶν Σατύρων καὶ ἀμηχανοεργῶν, fr. 123), and yet they are also perennial companions of the god Dionysus and the bearers of a wisdom that is more than human. The result is, in Richard Seaford's words, "an ambiguous creature, cruder than man and yet somehow wiser, combining mischief with wisdom and animality with divinity."[45] The value of this figure, then, lies in his status between and on the margins of familiar categories.[46] With one foot, so to speak, firmly in each of these otherwise separate domains, the satyr is in a sense nowhere. He is, in other words, a figure characterized by *atopia*. And it is this *atopia*, I suggest, that can help us understand the import of Alcibiades's speech.

The satyr, then, is a model of experimentation and transgression. François Lissarrague, for example, speaks of satyrs as "a means to explore human culture through a fun-house mirror."[47] He goes on to say that satyr drama, unlike tragedy, "does not seek to settle a controversy. . . . It plays in a different key, with the displacement, distortion, and reversal of what constitutes the world and culture of men."[48] The satyr, that is, disturbs familiar categories as he crosses the boundaries that sustain them, and he uses this freedom to offer novel perspectives on the rest of us. Incomprehensible by ordinary standards, this figure returns to us a recognizable, if disturbing, version of ourselves.[49]

And such an uncanny ability is precisely the one identified by Alcibiades, in fact, when he says that Socrates affected him so deeply that "my very own soul started protesting that my life was no better than the most miserable slave's." He goes on to speak of Socrates as "this Marsyas here at my side who makes me feel all the time . . . that my life isn't worth living" (215e–216a).[50] The impossibility of understanding Socrates in familiar terms is accompanied, as in the case of the satyr, by "displacement, distortion, and reversal"—under the influence of Socrates, Alcibiades sees his own life (as) distorted, reversed.[51] And it is this double effect—placing Socrates beyond the familiar schemes, on the one hand, and endowing him with the uncanny power to engender in his interlocutor a sense of displacement, distortion, and reversal, on the other—that is produced by Alcibiades's comparison of Socrates and satyr. For all the possible historicity behind Alcibiades's insistence that Socrates was "unique, strange, and bizarre," the philosophical implications of this characterization render that historicity nearly moot: Alcibiades's presentation of Socrates expresses in cultural and mythical terms the unique status claimed for Plato's philosopher. And as the comparison suggests, Socrates's cultural positioning has philosophical implications: his difference is transgressive and thus frees him from the constraints of the categories that fail to capture him. This freedom in turn bestows an epistemic privilege that manifests in part as the disarming view of those (still) trapped and the ability to produce a voice that is heard as the equivalent of the aulos or the song of the Sirens.[52] In Seth Benardete's formulation, "Socrates is always the other of the other."[53]

## 4. Thersites

If Alcibiades's portrait suggests how Socrates's *atopia* may serve Plato's interests in establishing philosophy as a distinct and privileged form of intellectual endeavor, this portrait finds complements elsewhere that can illuminate the workings of Plato's creation. Although, as I have suggested, the satyr constitutes a touchstone of sorts for understanding the effect of Alcibiades's portrait, others can complement it. In particular, marginal figures demonstrate the privileges and problems that attend the kind of difference that characterizes Plato's Socrates.[54]

Socrates's resemblance to the satyr is marked in the first instance on his body and in his logoi (*Symposium* 215b; see above), and in presenting a Socrates whose physical ugliness and remarkable speech form key parts of his identity, Alcibiades's portrait compounds the analogy to the satyr.[55] Alcibiades's attention to Socrates's bodily ugliness and the unique voice it produces, that is, mobilizes a history of the physically repulsive and socially marginal, as it situates the paradigmatic philosopher within this history, which reaches back to the Iliadic Thersites.[56] Plato's text, in other words, does not invent the notion of ugliness from whole cloth—Homer has already shown what it is and what it can do.

In making this (perhaps heterodox) claim, I am not the first. Arlene Saxonhouse has suggested that Socrates resembles this famously ugly Iliadic figure who in book 2 criticizes Agamemnon, only to be savagely beaten by Odysseus for doing so.[57] Embracing the equation of physical beauty with worth of various kinds, the *Iliad* demonstrates not only the limits of the ugly body but also the powers that derive from the marginality of such a body and the voice it produces. In short, Thersites is rebuked, beaten, and laughed at by all, but he has spoken truth to power, as we say. If he repeats the criticism of Agamemnon voiced earlier by Achilles, the difference between his humiliation and Achilles's proud refusal to fight derives in no small part from the differences measured by their bodies and the qualities of their speech.[58] Each of these figures, Thersites and Achilles, occupies a marginal position of sorts in the Greek army, and it is this position, I suggest, that makes possible—or, at a minimum, is indissociable from—the critiques they launch. In the dominant cultural matrix of the time, ugliness betokens a marginality that can prove to be the source of speech that is, as in the case of Thersites, "out of order."[59] As part of rewriting the facile equation of beauty and value, Plato's text mobilizes the history of figures like Thersites to suggest the marginality of the philosopher as well as the *sophia* made possible by this marginality—indeed, Plato's Socrates might also be said to produce speech that is "out of order."

When fully appreciated, however, the *atopia* that characterizes Socrates proves to be even more far-reaching than the model of Thersites might indicate. As Socrates's affinity with the satyr suggests a kind of elusiveness with respect to the categories of mental mapping, so does it endow him with a privileged view: his vantage point proves to be as elusive as he is. In short, his *atopia* is no metaphor. Socrates as satyr becomes a figure freed from the limitations of place, both in his behavior and in his logoi. If his highly marked body positions him as a marginal figure, this same marginality reveals itself as a kind of privilege: the Socrates of Alcibiades's portrait is literally an *atopos*, a figure who is "out of place": he and his ideas would seem to derive from nowhere (in particular).[60] In this sense, then, Socrates's *atopia* resembles that of the tragic messenger: both wield the uncanny power of seeming to speak from a place that is no place.

## 5. Aesop

Perhaps more than any other, the figure of Aesop offers a rich example of what the marginality of the position occupied by the likes of Thersites has to offer. If Thersites can indicate the general outlines of what Alcibiades's portrait makes possible for Plato's Socrates, Aesop can do even more in this regard. By the fifth century BCE, after all, Aesop had become a cultural resource, "available as a mask or alibi for critique, parody, or cunning resistance."[61] And the propriety of examining Socrates on the model of Aesop stems not only from the fact that in his last hours Plato's heroic figure spends time versifying stories (μῦθοι) of Aesop (*Phaedo* 61b). Leslie

Kurke argues that Plato's Socrates is in fact "shot through with elements drawn from an older, popular Aesop tradition—elements that borrow for Socrates himself and his distinctive *logoi* the edgy particularity and disruptive social energies of Aesop."[62] And if we are inclined to see the role of Aesop in Plato's construction of Socrates as providing a kind of ready-made template for illustrating what is mere biographical truth ("Socrates just happened to be like that"), Kurke warns that "such a naive and sentimental reading crucially effaces the ground of conflict on which Plato constructs the edifice of philosophy."[63] Especially in such an agonistic context, the value of representing Socrates in this way comes into focus.

The *Life of Aesop* presents Aesop as the consummate outsider: he is a barbarian (Phrygian); he is a slave, even a worthless slave; and his appearance marks the limits of ugliness.[64] This is how the *Life* begins:[65] "The fabulist Aesop, the great benefactor of mankind, was by chance a slave but by origin a Phrygian of Phrygia, of loathsome aspect, worthless as a servant, potbellied, misshapen of head, snub-nosed, swarthy, dwarfish, bandy-legged, short-armed, squint-eyed, liver-lipped—a portentous monstrosity. In addition to this he had a defect more serious than his unsightliness in being speechless, for he was dumb and could not talk" (1).[66] The final addition here—that Aesop was deprived of speech—performs two key tasks. First, it puts into doubt even his humanity, thereby suggesting his strangeness.[67] Second, it highlights the role of Aesop's newly acquired voice: his remarkable achievements derive from his remarkable speech. In these ways, then, Aesop serves as a model for understanding Socrates, but there is more. As the opening words of the *Life* make clear, Aesop's outward appearance provided no (obvious) clue to what lay inside. Indeed, if the discrepancy between Socrates's interior and exterior looms large in Alcibiades's portrait, the same "inconsistency" plays an even greater role in the case of Aesop. From his initial position of abjection and voicelessness, of course, Aesop moves to one of mastery through speech—the "worthless" slave becomes master of his master, the philosopher Xanthos.

Why was Aesop so ugly? Few, presumably, would suggest that the *Life*'s insistence on Aesop's extravagant ugliness constitutes nothing but an accurate historical record. After all, there is no more reason to believe in the historicity of Aesop than in the historicity of Homer.[68] The answer to this question reveals itself in the many examples of Aesop's wit and his mastery of Xanthos. A number of these small "victories" conform to a pattern that illustrates the characteristic talent of this most unusual slave. And this talent, I suggest, is the principal signified of Aesop's enigmatic appearance, as the emphasis placed on it by the *Life* implies.

Unhappy with Xanthos's "unnecessarily stern attitude," Aesop decides to "give this philosopher a lesson in how to give orders" (38). What follows is a lengthy sequence of tricks, most of which have a linguistic basis. For example, when Xanthos orders Aesop to get "the oil flask and the towels" (38) to take to the bath, the clever slave takes the flask but leaves the oil behind. Confounded by the absence of oil at the bath, Xanthos—the earnest philosopher—accepts Aesop's explanation: "Because you told me 'take the oil flask and the towels,' but you didn't mention oil" (38).

Not satisfied that Xanthos has learned his "lesson," however—indeed, there is no evidence that Xanthos learns much of anything—Aesop continues with his program to teach the learned philosopher. At the bath, Xanthos gives an order to his slave: "Aesop, go on home, and . . . cook us lentil [φακὸν ἕψησον]. Put it [αὐτὸν] in the pot, put some water in with it [μετ' αὐτοῦ], put it [αὐτὸν] on the cooking hearth" (39). Aesop went home and "put one lentil [ἕνα φακόν] in the pot, and cooked it" (39). The full impact arrives when Xanthos invites his friends from the bath to a meal at which the "lentil" is served. Rather than a dish of lentils, Aesop has cooked a single lentil. Again, the philosophical master can find no fault with Aesop, who merely followed instructions. Aesop even explains to Xanthos the difference between the grammatical categories of singular and plural: "Didn't you tell me to 'cook lentil' and not 'lentils'? The one is singular, and the other plural" (41).

The word for lentil, φακός, could be used in either singular or plural to refer to a dish of lentils—a soup, for example. Xanthos's use of the singular here would therefore be unremarkable were it not, of course, for Aesop's willful mishearing and unconventional construal, and it is this construal, I think, that holds the clue to Aesop's characteristic talent. While the jokes involved here operate on several levels, they all turn on the distinction between a literal and decontextualized word (φακός), on the one hand, and its conventional, contextualized meaning, on the other. We laugh not only because the slave has outwitted the master, not only because the once-mute Phrygian is cleverer than the philosopher, but also and most of all because the conventional meaning of φακός is shown to be somewhat fragile.

What does all of this have to do with Aesop's body and his famous ugliness? It is my contention that Aesop's characteristic talent and his bodily singularity function in tandem. Aesop's extravagant ugliness serves principally to mark him as unique and beyond the bounds of the familiar. His extraordinary appearance, that is, betokens his characteristic ability to confound his interlocutors—his ability, on view in the case of the lentil, to speak a language so freed from the conventional constraints of context that it evades even conventional meanings. In short, his enigmatic appearance—Croesus calls Aesop "this riddle, this monstrosity among men" (αἴνιγμα καὶ τέρας τῶν ἀνθρώπων, *Life* 98)—is an essential aspect, or token, of his identity. It is precisely Aesop's ugliness, abjection, and oddness—his physical distinction and the *atopia* associated with it—that make possible his signal linguistic successes. In these regards, then, Aesop provides a model for understanding (Plato's) Socrates, both in his appearance and in his logoi characterized by *atopia*.

# 6. The Aulos

After Aesop won his freedom and gained notoriety, the *Life of Aesop* explains, he sacrificed and built a shrine to the Muses, erecting in their midst a statue of Mnemosyne, not of Apollo. Thereupon Apollo became angry with Aesop, the *Life* continues, "as he had once been with Marsyas" (100). Aside from preparing for Aesop's end at Delphi, this passage suggests an affinity between Aesop and the satyr Marsyas, an affinity that we might well suspect even without this notice: not only is Marsyas also a Phrygian of beastly aspect, but the hybris of Aesop, the *Life* suggests, is comparable to that of the notorious satyr. Marsyas, of course, offended Apollo by challenging him to a musical contest pitting the satyr and his aulos against the god and his lyre. Given that Aesop and Marsyas appear to share more than physical repulsiveness, and given that Alcibiades calls Socrates an αὐλητής (aulos-player) while equating his logoi with the aulos-playing of Marsyas and charging him with hybris (215b), the *Life*'s evocation of Marsyas here invites us to consider the satyr and his aulos for what they can tell us about Aesop and about Socrates.[69]

Although the hybris of Marsyas is twofold—comprising both the randiness that characterizes all satyrs and the musical insult to Apollo—his transgression with the aulos signals the danger and power that lurk within this instrument. "The *aulos* was a danger," writes Peter Wilson: "it threatened self-control; it marred the aesthetics of the body; it introduced the allure of the alien."[70] The instrument, furthermore, disfigured the face of its player. Athena invents or discovers the aulos but discards the instrument as soon as she sees a reflection of herself playing it on account of the disfiguring facial contortions required.[71] No sooner does she discard the aulos, though, than Marsyas takes it up and adopts what becomes a characteristic prop of satyrs thenceforth.[72] The satyr is repulsive in part because he is a satyr and in part because he plays the aulos. When Alcibiades calls Socrates αὐλητής, then, he not only extends and compounds the association of Socrates and satyr; he also invokes the disfiguring consequences of playing the aulos and identifies Socrates's unique appearance as one befitting a satyr. Like all who play the aulos in Athens, Socrates as αὐλητής is "aligned implicitly on the side of the satyr."[73] And conversely, as one aligned with the satyr, it seems, Socrates is an αὐλητής. Indeed, if Alcibiades did not make this conjunction explicit, we might well imagine it ourselves.[74]

Athena's invention of the aulos arises from another, closely related myth—that of Perseus and the Gorgon Medusa—and the origin of the aulos in the Perseus story illuminates the role of Marsyas as well as the "alien" status of the instrument. Upon the decapitation of Medusa by Perseus, her sisters, the immortal Gorgons, shrieked and wailed in grief. And from this wailing, as Pindar reports, comes the art (τέχνη) of aulos-playing, which

> Pallas Athena once invented
> by weaving into music the fierce Gorgons' deathly dirge
> that she heard pouring forth from under the unapproachable
> snaky heads of the maidens in their grievous toil.[75]

(Pythian 12.7–10; trans. Race)

The aulos's alien aspect derives from a number of sources, but its origin as the musical instantiation of the "Gorgons' deathly dirge" is surely chief among these.[76] Although the Gorgon is known chiefly for its hideous face or mask, its sound, too, I suggest, "expresses and maintains the radical otherness, the alterity of the world of the dead, which no living person may approach."[77] This is a music that sounds the grief of death.[78]

Not only does the sound of the aulos recall and commemorate Medusa's gruesome face and decapitation; Pindar tells us that it also embraces "every voice":[79]

> But when she had rescued her beloved hero from
> those toils, the maiden composed a melody with every voice for *auloi*,
> so that she might imitate with instruments the echoing wail
> that was forced from the gnashing jaws of Euryale.

> The goddess invented it, but invented it for mortals
> to have, and she called it the tune of many heads.[80]

(Pythian 12.18–23; trans. Race, modified)

The instrument that makes possible "the tune of many heads" (κεφαλᾶν πολλᾶν) works its effects through its radical alterity as well as through a kind of epistemic interference. Like both Gorgon and satyr, the aulos through its multiplicity—it contains "every voice"—crosses boundaries and conjoins the incommensurable: "All the categories . . . overlap in confusion and interfere with one another."[81]

Although the comparison between Gorgon and satyr has its limits, it is important to note that in archaic and classical Greek art, the "disembodied frontal face" is the exclusive province of satyrs, Gorgons, and Dionysus.[82] The Dionysian pedigree of the satyr helps make sense of his affinities with the Gorgon. As Eric Csapo remarks, "Frontal faces can also distinguish all those who are possessed by the god—his apostles: drunkards, satyrs, menads, ecstatics, actors wearing masks, musicians, and especially pipers [aulos-players]. . . . The glare of the masked actor, like the Gorgon, casts a trance-like spell upon his audience, transporting them into different worlds and different identities."[83] If he who is aligned with the satyr is also an αὐλητής in some sense, and if the aulos recalls the Gorgons' "deathly dirge," it makes sense to find something of the Gorgon's effect in the Socrates of Alcibiades's portrait. Insofar as Socrates is an αὐλητής, that is, his is also an "alien" presence that "casts a trance-like spell upon his audience."

Of course, this is precisely what Alcibiades claims (215d–e), and it is what Plato's Meno identifies as Socrates's characteristic effect:

> Socrates, before I even met you I used to hear that you are always in a state of perplexity and that you bring others to the same state, and now I think you are bewitching and beguiling me, simply putting me under a spell, so that I am quite perplexed. Indeed, if a joke is in order, you seem, in appearance and in every other way, to be like the sting ray, for it too makes anyone who comes close and touches it feel numb, and now you seem to have had that kind of effect on me, for both my mind and my tongue are numb, and I have no answer to give you.[84]

(Meno 80a–b; trans. Grube, modified)

Like Alcibiades, Meno portrays Socrates as a kind of αὐλητής, sharing with Gorgon and satyr the ability to "take possession of another's wits."[85] But for my purposes here, what is most important is the role of alterity in producing these "bewitching and beguiling" effects. If Gorgon and satyr seem to inhabit vastly different realms, they nonetheless share a radical otherness, and it is otherness that produces these effects.[86] As Meno makes clear—much as Alcibiades does when he turns to the satyr to "explain" Socrates—the characteristic effect of Socrates is much like that of the stingray. So unusual is Socrates that his difference is comprehensible only in terms of radical alterity.[87]

And like these other "frontal faces," Socrates produces a kind of epistemic interference. Again, both Alcibiades and Meno point to the perplexity they feel in Socrates's presence, and such perplexity is the consequence of the confusion of categories and "disquieting mixture" that he embodies.[88] Like satyr and Gorgon, Socrates and his logoi refuse to conform to ordinary categories—their exceptionalisms are bewildering because they cannot be accommodated by familiar schemes. For the grotesque and monstrous figures of myth, we can say that it is precisely their "function" to transgress and to put into question the boundaries that sustain an ordered cosmos. For Plato's Socrates, a comparable exceptionalism has the effect of situating him beyond the realm of confusion that others feel, as it undermines our ability to "explain" him and his logoi according to what we know. The epistemic "interference" that others report is the corollary of his own epistemic privilege.[89]

## 7. The Alien Tongue

Plutarch reports that Alcibiades, having successfully refused to play the aulos, urged the Athenians to follow his lead and to emulate Apollo and Athena.[90] The goddess, after all, had discarded the instrument, and Apollo had flayed Marsyas, the paradigmatic αὐλητής.[91] Plutarch's Alcibiades explains the dangers of aulos-playing: becoming unrecognizable even to those whom one knows best and losing one's voice and intelligence (τήν τε φωνὴν καὶ τὸν λόγον). The first is dangerous because it makes it possible to be seen and heard as a slave, a barbarian, or perhaps a woman; and the second could put even one's humanity at risk.[92] In two registers, that is, Alcibiades's warning highlights the capacity of the aulos to compromise one's identity. The full range of what such an identity might encompass is broad, but it certainly includes Athenian citizenship, itself a complex category. A key part of such an identity, in any case, is a coherence such as is suggested in Alcibiades's warning: discrepancies between one's (true) identity and one's appearance constitute an incoherence, or inconsistency, arising in this case from the intrusion of an alien—servile, barbaric, feminine—element. That such a concern should find its way into this warning seems perhaps inevitable, given the "alien" status of the aulos, as discussed above.

But there is yet another kind of alterity at the heart of (the meanings attached to) the aulos, an alterity that explains both a key aspect of the instrument's symbolic force and why Plato's Socrates makes such a good αὐλητής. This becomes evident in Philostratus's biography of Critias.[93] In concluding this short biography, Philostratus makes a summary judgment that aims to refute those seeking Critias's rehabilitation: "No one who dies for a cause unjustly embraced, dies with honor [καλῶς]. This is why, I think, his skill and his ideas are so little respected by the Greeks." He continues by explaining, "For if our *logos* does not agree with our character, we will seem to speak with an alien tongue, just as *auloi* do"[94] (*Lives of the Sophists* 1.16). There is more at work here than meets the eye. The word for "tongue," γλῶττα, is also the equivalent of English "reed." The reed of the aulos, that is, allows it to "speak," but it is a tongue that belongs not to the aulos itself; it belongs, rather, to another (ἀλλοτρίᾳ). It is a removable tongue, and Philostratus presents this mobility as a lack of coherence. He might well have called on the testimony of Aeschines, who says of Demosthenes (*In Ctesiphonta* 229), "As with the *aulos*, if one were to remove his tongue there would be nothing left."[95] On the model of the aulos, the autonomy and mobility of Demosthenes's tongue are imagined to be so great that it becomes capable of displacing its "host." For Aeschines and Philostratus, the fundamental distinction between "self" and γλῶττα—between body and tongue—means that the aulos ventriloquizes: it speaks with an alien tongue.[96] This play on the physicality of the musical instrument trades on the familiar notion that the instrument is not only from elsewhere (Phrygia) but also "alien" to behavior appropriate for Athenian citizens. The aulos, then, embodies and exemplifies the danger it threatens: the incoherence that Plutarch's Alcibiades warns against is precisely what characterizes the aulos itself—at least in such (apparently normative) views of the instrument.[97]

The aulos in its manifold otherness—the inconcinnity between its body and tongue, its own alien status and sound, and its capacity to make its player "alien"—proves an apt emblem for Plato's Socrates. As I've tried to show, Alcibiades highlights Socrates's strangeness (*atopia*), the difference between his outside and inside, and his ability to make others "alien" (at least to themselves). And all of these qualities are succinctly expressed in the figure of Socrates as satyr and as αὐλητής. But another of Socrates's most characteristic qualities, in evidence in his very appearance, finds expression in his satyric, auletic form as well: his irony. Put differently, the consistency between the satyric Socrates of Alcibiades's portrait and the ironic Socrates we all know and love should remove any hesitation we may feel about taking Alcibiades's portrait seriously. Like the satyr, after all, Socrates wears a mask.[98]

## 8. Conclusion

Plato's devocalization of logos, then, rests on an emphatically embodied Socrates who nonetheless proves to wield an embodiment that sets him apart. In freeing logos from the voice, that is, Plato produces a portrait of his paradigmatic philosopher who may be said to share in both the old world and the new insofar as he, Socrates, straddles the divide between the constraints of the pre-Socratic body and the unfettered freedom of a truly disembodied, devocalized logos. Socrates's peculiar embodiment, in other words, can be neither wished away nor equated with other, more familiar forms of embodiment. Yes, the dialogues insist, Socrates is a special case. In particular, the *Symposium* tells us, his unique body—immune to the hardships of military service, hunger, winter, and excessive alcohol (*Symposium* 219e–220e)—and the *atopia* that it indicates make him assimilable only to the satyr. Unequivocally identified with and tethered to his silenic body, Plato's philosopher nonetheless finds in that very identification and tethering a distinctive freedom. Although, as Cavarero reminds us, Socrates and his logoi remain embodied, this embodiment is unlike what is available to others.

The atopic Socrates of the *Symposium* is, of course, familiar from the dialogues more generally. Several passages already mentioned suggest that Alcibiades's portrait has Plato's endorsement, so to speak: Meno's testimony that Socrates "bewitches" and "beguiles" him and that he resembles a stingray (*Meno* 80a–b); Callicles's objection that Socrates, if serious in what he says about wrongdoing, is turning the world upside down (*Gorgias* 481c); and the atopic status of the philosopher in the *Republic*'s cave allegory.[99] To these I add the recurring theme in the *Apology* that Socrates is not only unlike others but also at odds with them (21b–23b).[100] In spite of this continuity, however, Alcibiades's elaborate presentation of Socrates as satyr accomplishes what other (passing) references to Socrates's oddity don't: it condenses into myth and expresses in cultural terms the position claimed for Socrates throughout the dialogues. And because this characterization of Socrates as satyr works its magic by means of Socrates's body and his logoi, it highlights the privilege that this oddity enables. In particular, Socrates's unlocatable and incomparable body mean that his voice—his very much vocalized logoi—sounds rather like the voices of those who speak in incomparable ways: the Muse, the tragic messenger, Thersites, Aesop, the Sirens, and even the aulos itself. In the contentious skirmishes for cultural authority that took place in the fourth century BCE, the value of such a feat is not to be underestimated. This claim to distinction for the *atopic* philosopher must be ranked among the most important of Plato's interventions in this arena.

# Notes

1. Jean-Pierre Vernant, "Mortals and Immortals: The Body of the Divine," in *Mortals and Immortals: Collected Essays*, ed. Froma I. Zeitlin and Anne M. Wilson (Princeton, NJ: Princeton University Press, 1991), 28.

2. Vernant, 31. Vernant refers us to *Iliad* 6.146 (οἵη περ φύλλων γενεὴ τοίη δὲ καὶ ἀνδρῶν): human ephemerality is indistinguishable from its particular form of embodiment, which itself is a sign of its own mortality.

3. In this essay, I speak of Plato's Socrates rather than the historical figure or other versions such as Xenophon's, unless otherwise indicated.

4. The body of Socrates contributes to the rupture identified by Vernant, although the nature of this contribution is a concern neither of Vernant's nor of mine. Here I limit myself to an account of what makes Socrates's body and voice unique and what the significance of this uniqueness is.

5. Adriana Cavarero, *For More Than One Voice: Toward a Philosophy of Vocal Expression*, trans. Paul A. Kottman (Stanford: Stanford University Press, 2005), 40. Hereafter cited parenthetically in the text.

6. See Heraclitus D-K 101a: ὀφθαλμοὶ γὰρ τῶν ὤτων ἀκριβέστεροι μάρτυρες.

7. On this question, see, e.g., Andrea Wilson Nightingale, *Genres in Dialogue: Plato and the Construct of Philosophy* (Cambridge: Cambridge University Press, 1995); Noburu Notomi, *The Unity of Plato's Sophist: Between the Sophist and the Philosopher* (Cambridge: Cambridge University Press, 1999); Marina McCoy, *Plato on the Rhetoric of Philosophers and Sophists* (Cambridge: Cambridge University Press, 2008).

8. Cf. Cavarero, *More Than One Voice*, 95–98.

9. ἔσπετε νῦν μοι Μοῦσαι Ὀλύμπια δώματ' ἔχουσαι: / ὑμεῖς γὰρ θεαί ἐστε πάρεστέ τε ἴστέ τε πάντα, / ἡμεῖς δὲ κλέος οἶον ἀκούομεν οὐδέ τι ἴδμεν.

10. τά τ' ἐόντα τά τ' ἐσσόμενα πρό τ' ἐόντα (*Theogony* 38).

11. πόσσ' ἀπαλοῖσιν / ὀρχεῦνται . . . καί τε λοεσσάμεναι τέρενα χρόα . . . χοροὺς ἐνεποιήσαντο / καλούς, ἱμερόεντας, ἐπερρώσαντο δὲ ποσσίν (*Theogony* 3–8).

12. Marcel Detienne, *The Masters of Truth in Archaic Greece*, trans. Janet Lloyd (New York: Zone, 1996), 39–52. Although Hesiod's Muses say that they are able to speak many lies

like true things (ἴδμεν ψεύδεα πολλὰ λέγειν ἐτύμοισιν ὁμοῖα, *Theogony* 27), it is important to note that their doing so would compromise neither their epistemic privilege nor their discursive and vocal power.

13. Vernant, "Mortals and Immortals," 46. The voice of Hesiod's Muses also constitutes a paradigm of sweetness and enchantment (*Theogony* 39–40, 65–68), as does their gift of song to singers (*Theogony* 96–103). Their remarkable bodies produce a voice remarkable for its status and effects. See Pietro Pucci, *Hesiod and the Language of Poetry* (Baltimore: Johns Hopkins University Press, 1977), 27–33.

14. Such coincidence of theme and form may not be an accident. Indeed, Timothy Reiss argues that tragedy appears in periods of epistemic and discursive instability, claiming that tragedy is "a discursive type that performs a specific role within the totality of discourses . . . at certain moments of seemingly abrupt epistemic change" (*Tragedy and Truth* [New Haven, CT: Yale University Press, 1980], 2).

15. This changed with the publication of Irene J. F. de Jong, *Narrative in Drama: The Art of the Euripidean Messenger-Speech* (Leiden, Neth.: Brill, 1991).

16. There are many more such examples. For an extended treatment of the peculiar role of the messenger in tragedy and a much-expanded version of what appears in this section, see James Barrett, *Staged Narrative: Poetics and the Messenger in Greek Tragedy* (Berkeley: University of California Press, 2002).

17. C. J. Herington, *Aeschylus* (New Haven, CT: Yale University Press, 1986), 69.

18. τὰ πρῶτα μέν νυν ῥεῦμα Περσικοῦ στρατοῦ / ἀντεῖχεν· ὡς δὲ πλῆθος ἐν στενῷ νεῶν / ἤθροιστ᾽, ἀρωγὴ δ᾽ οὔτις ἀλλήλοις παρῆν, / αὐτοὶ δ᾽ ὑπ᾽ αὐτῶν ἐμβολαῖς χαλκοστόμοις / παίοντ᾽, ἔθραυον πάντα κωπήρη στόλον, / Ελληνικαί τε νῆες οὐκ ἀφρασμόνως / κύκλῳ πέριξ ἔθεινον, ὑπτιοῦτο δὲ / σκάφη νεῶν, θάλασσα δ᾽ οὐκέτ᾽ ἦν ἰδεῖν / ναυαγίων πλήθουσα καὶ φόνου βροτῶν.

19. Χρυσεὺς Μάταλλος μυριόνταρχος θανὼν / πυρσὴν ζαπληθῆ δάσκιον γενειάδα / ἔτεγγ᾽ ἀμείβων χρῶτα πορφυρᾷ βαφῇ.

20. See Barrett, *Staged Narrative*, 40–44.

21. The messenger, in fact, might well be called *atopos*. See below.

22. All translations of Plato come from John M. Cooper, ed., *Plato: Complete Works* (Indianapolis: Hackett, 1997).

23. φημὶ γὰρ δὴ ὁμοιότατον αὐτὸν εἶναι τοῖς σιληνοῖς. . . .καὶ φημὶ αὖ ἐοικέναι αὐτὸν τῷ σατύρῳ τῷ Μαρσύᾳ. ὅτι μὲν οὖν τό γε εἶδος ὅμοιος εἶ τούτοις, ὦ Σώκρατες, οὐδ᾽ αὐτὸς ἄν που ἀμφισβητήσαις (*Symposium* 215a–b). Note the force of the particle *γε*, indicating that this much, at least, Alcibiades considers beyond dispute. He is even more explicit later, referring to Socrates as "this Marsyas here" (τουτουὶ του Μαρσύου, 215e). See below.

24. See Paul Zanker, *The Mask of Socrates: The Image of the Intellectual in Antiquity* (Berkeley: University of California Press, 1995); Ruby Blondell, *The Play of Character in Plato's Dialogues* (Cambridge: Cambridge University Press, 2002), 73.

25. The discrepancy between Socrates's exterior and interior forms part of Plato's "flaying" of Socrates. As Alcibiades explains, even Socrates's logoi mimic this relation between inside and outside: "If you see them when they open," Socrates's logoi are "truly worthy of a god" (*Symposium* 222a; Cavarero, *More Than One Voice*, 71). Indeed, the common reading of the analogy Alcibiades draws between silenic statuettes and Socrates (and his logoi) seems to affirm Cavarero's key insight. The story does not end here, however, for Alcibiades goes on to explain that Socrates in fact resembles Marsyas, a "real" satyr, and in so doing makes clear that the philosopher's exterior, like that of his logoi, does much more than hide internal gems.

26. On the reliability of Alcibiades, see Elizabeth S. Belfiore, *Socrates' Daimonic Art* (Cambridge: Cambridge University Press, 2012), 187–196; Andrea Capra, *Plato's Four Muses: The Phaedrus and the Poetics of Philosophy* (Washington, DC: Center for Hellenic Studies, 2014), 97n21.

27. Socrates as *atopos* is a familiar figure in Plato, of course; see Pierre Hadot, *Philosophy as a Way of Life: Spiritual Exercises from Socrates to Foucault*, trans. Michael Chase, ed. Arnold Davidson (Malden, MA: Blackwell, 1995), 57 and below. This fundamental consistency between what Alcibiades says and what we find elsewhere in Plato can only urge us to take his speech seriously. For more on Socrates's *atopia* in Plato, see Blondell, *Play of Character*, 106, 73–74 with n. 102.

28. Zanker, *Mask of Socrates*, 34.

29. οὐκ ἔστι καλός, προσέοικε δὲ σοὶ τήν τε σιμότητα καὶ τὸ ἔξω τῶν ὀμμάτων. Concerning the boy, Theodorus adds that "these features are not quite so pronounced in him" (ἧττον δὲ ἢ σὺ ταῦτ' ἔχει). Trans. Levett and Burnyeat.

30. In addition to Aristophanes's *Clouds*, Xenophon encourages the view that Alcibiades's portrait is simply accurate. See his *Symposium* 4.19, for example, where he reports Socrates's resemblance to Silenoi.

31. σὺ δ' ἐκείνου τοσοῦτον μόνον διαφέρεις, ὅτι ἄνευ ὀργάνων ψιλοῖς λόγοις ταὐτὸν τοῦτο ποιεῖς.

32. βίᾳ οὖν ὥσπερ ἀπὸ τῶν Σειρήνων ἐπισχόμενος τὰ ὦτα οἴχομαι φεύγων.

33. As Pucci reminds us (*The Song of the Sirens* [Lanham: Rowman and Littlefield, 1998], 6–9), Homer's Sirens identify themselves in terms that characterize the Muses (*Odyssey* 12.184–191).

34. R. G. Bury, *The Symposium of Plato*, 2nd ed. (Cambridge: W. Heffer, 1932), lx–lxii; Catherine Osborne, *Eros Unveiled: Plato and the God of Love* (Oxford: Clarendon, 1994), 93–101; Belfiore, *Socrates' Daimonic Art*, 190–196. Hadot finds not similarity but identity: "The whole dialogue is constructed so as to make the reader guess the identity between the figures of Socrates and Eros" (*Philosophy*, 160), which identity he then documents. Cf. Jill Gordon, *Plato's Erotic World: From Cosmic Origins to Human Death* (Cambridge: Cambridge University Press, 2012), 64–65 with n. 21.

35. For a sustained discussion of philosophy as erotic pursuit in Plato, see Gordon, *Plato's Erotic World*.

36. Albert Henrichs, "'He Has a God in Him': Human and Divine in the Modern Perception of Dionysus," in *Masks of Dionysus*, ed. Thomas H. Carpenter Faraone and A. Christopher (Ithaca, NY: Cornell University Press, 1993), 31–36.

37. "What the men of Athens . . . seem to be searching for in the practice of communal wine-drinking . . . is the chance to become other," comment Françoise Frontisi-Ducroux and François Lissarrague ("From Ambiguity to Ambivalence: A Dionysiac Excursion through the 'Anakreontic' Vases," in *Before Sexuality: The Construction of Erotic Experience in the Ancient Greek World*, ed. David Halperin, John Winkler, and Froma I. Zeitlin [Princeton, NJ: Princeton University Press, 1990], 229). They go on to say that such drinking is part of a "regulated approach to otherness" bearing "a clearly defined ideological message" (232). See also François Lissarrague, "The Athenian Image of the Foreigner," in *The Athenian Image of the Foreigner*, ed. Thomas Harrison and Antonia Nevill (New York: Routledge, 2002), 108–111; Edith Hall, "Ithyphallic Males Behaving Badly: Or, Satyr Drama as Gendered Tragic Ending," in *Parchments of Gender: Deciphering the Bodies of Antiquity*, ed. Maria Wyke (Oxford: Oxford University Press, 1998), 13–37; Mark Griffith, "Satyrs, Citizens, and

Self-Representation," in *Satyr Drama: Tragedy at Play*, ed. George W. M. Harrison (Swansea: Classical Press of Wales, 2005), 172–186.

38. Nietzsche seems to have anticipated such a view in *The Birth of Tragedy*. Quoting from this text, James I. Porter asks, "Who would think to compare Socrates with Dionysus or with one of his votaries, say that 'fantastic and seemingly so offensive figure of the wise and rapturous satyr' who, we are told, 'is at the same time "the simple man" as opposed to the god'—that bearded, goatlike creature, that wholly 'made-up' being (*fingiertes Wesen*), in short, that mythic projection if not product of a self-imagining, loaded, like Silenus, with negative wisdom? And yet this is, I believe, just what *The Birth of Tragedy* requires us to do: to read in Socrates the image of Dionysus, and *vice versa*" ("The Invention of Dionysus and the Platonic Midwife: Nietzsche's *Birth of Tragedy*," *Journal of the History of Philosophy* 33 (1995): 485). Hadot sees in the *Symposium* "a conscious and deliberate ensemble of allusions to the Dionysiac nature of the figure of Socrates" (*Philosophy*, 169). See also *Phaedo* 69c–d, where Bacchants, those close attendants on Dionysus, are described by Socrates as "no other than those who have practiced philosophy in the right way" (οὐκ ἄλλοι ἢ οἱ πεφιλοσοφηκότες ὀρθῶς).

39. According to Aelian, Theopompus described Silenus as less notable than a god but superior to a human because he was ἀθάνατος (*Varia Historia* 3.18). On satyrs as "implicitly immortal," see Richard Seaford, *Euripides: Cyclops* (Oxford: Clarendon, 1984), 32; Pierre Voelke, *Un Théatre de la Marge: Aspects Figuratifs et Configurationnels du Drame Satyrique dans l'Athènes Classique* (Bari: Levante Editori, 2001), 84.

40. Alcibiades says that it will be difficult to give an accounting of Socrates's *atopia* (215a). Bury calls this *atopia* "the main theme" of Alcibiades's speech (*Symposium of Plato, ad* 215a). Blondell identifies many facets of Socrates's *atopia*, with an eye toward the effect of his peculiarity on those who would imitate him. She argues that this *atopia* renders Socrates "inimitable in his strangeness . . . in so far as he is incomprehensible to others" (*Play of Character*, 106).

41. ἀλλὰ τῶν μὲν ἄλλων ἐπιτηδευμάτων τάχ' ἄν τις καὶ περὶ ἄλλου τοιαῦτα εἴποι, τὸ δὲ μηδενὶ ἀνθρώπων ὅμοιον εἶναι, μήτε τῶν παλαιῶν μήτε τῶν νῦν ὄντων, τοῦτο ἄξιον παντὸς θαύματος. οἷος γὰρ Ἀχιλλεὺς ἐγένετο, ἀπεικάσειεν ἄν τις καὶ Βρασίδαν καὶ ἄλλους, καὶ οἷος αὖ Περικλῆς, καὶ Νέστορα καὶ Ἀντήνορα—εἰσὶ δὲ καὶ ἕτεροι—καὶ τοὺς ἄλλους κατὰ ταῦτ' ἄν τις ἀπεικάζοι· οἷος δὲ οὑτοσὶ γέγονε τὴν ἀτοπίαν ἄνθρωπος, καὶ αὐτὸς καὶ οἱ λόγοι αὐτοῦ, οὐδ' ἐγγὺς ἂν εὕροι τις ζητῶν, οὔτε τῶν νῦν οὔτε τῶν παλαιῶν, εἰ μὴ ἄρα εἰ οἷς ἐγὼ λέγω ἀπεικάζοι τις αὐτόν, ἀνθρώπων μὲν μηδενί, τοῖς δὲ σιληνοῖς καὶ σατύροις, αὐτὸν καὶ τοὺς λόγους. Trans. Nehamas and Woodruff.

42. See, for example, Pierre Vidal-Naquet, "Land and Sacrifice in the Odyssey: A Study of Religious and Mythical Meanings," in *Reading the Odyssey: Selected Interpretive Essays*, ed. Seth L. Schein (Princeton, NJ: Princeton University Press, 1996), 39–42.

43. David Konstan, "An Anthropology of Euripides' *Kyklops*," in *Nothing to Do with Dionysos? Athenian Drama in Its Social Context*, ed. John J. Winkler and Froma I. Zeitlin (Princeton, NJ: Princeton University Press, 1990), 208.

44. Konstan, 227.

45. Seaford, *Euripides*, 7.

46. Perhaps only coincidentally, dances representing satyrs and silenoi are said to "resist all attempts to label them" (οὔθ' ὅτι ποτὲ βούλεται ῥᾴδιον ἀφορίσασθαι, Plato, *Laws* 7.815c).

47. François Lissarrague, "Why Satyrs Are Good to Represent," in *Nothing to Do with Dionysos? Athenian Drama in Its Social Context*, ed. John J. Winkler and Froma I. Zeitlin (Princeton, NJ: Princeton University Press, 1990,) 235.

48. Lissarrague, 236.

49. Seaford notes that the unique position of satyrs who belong both "to the wild, and to the very point indeed at which culture is created out of nature . . . gives them a special perspective on mankind" (*Euripides*, 33).

50. ἠγανάκτει ὡς ἀνδραποδωδῶς διακειμένου, ἀλλ᾽ ὑπὸ τουτουῒ τοῦ Μαρσύου πολλάκις δὴ οὕτω διετέθην ὥστε μοι δόξαι μὴ βιωτὸν εἶναι ἔχοντι ὡς ἔχω. Socrates's effect on Alcibiades would appear to be a characteristic effect of his inasmuch as it is the same as what Apollodorus reports (173a). Note that the futility of human life was a teaching of Silenus, according to Aristotle (fr. 44 Rose, cited by L. Roller, "The Legend of Midas," *Classical Antiquity* 2 [1983]: 306). See Voelke, *Théâtre de la Marge*, 87.

51. Echoing Callicles at *Gorgias* 481c, Gerasimos Xenophon Santas calls Socrates "a Greek upside-down" (*Socrates: Philosophy in Plato's Early Dialogues* [London: Routledge and K. Paul, 1979], 7).

52. The epistemic privilege and disarming view resemble those in the allegory of the cave (*Republic* 7).

53. Seth Benardete, *Socrates and Plato: The Dialectics of Eros (Sokrates und Platon: Die Dialektik des Eros)* (Munich: Carl Friedrich von Siemens Stiftung, 1999), 85.

54. On satyrs as marginal figures, see J. Michael Padgett, "The Stable Hands of Dionysos: Satyrs and Donkeys as Symbols of Social Marginalization in Attic Vase Painting," in *Not the Classical Ideal: Athens and the Construction of the Other in Greek Art*, ed. Beth Cohen (Leiden, Neth.: Brill, 2000), 43–70.

55. The ugliness of Socrates's body is made clear by the contrast with the divine, golden, beautiful, and amazing statues inside (θεῖα καὶ χρυσᾶ . . . καὶ πάγκαλα καὶ θαυμαστά, 217a).

56. Thersites was "the ugliest man who came beneath Ilion. He was / bandy-legged and went lame of one foot, with shoulders / stooped and drawn together over his chest, and above this / his skull went up to a point with the wool grown sparsely upon it" (*Iliad* 2.216–19, trans. Lattimore).

57. See Arlene W. Saxonhouse, *Free Speech and Democracy in Ancient Athens* (Cambridge: Cambridge University Press, 2006), 112–126, on Socrates's lack of shame (αἰδώς) and his resemblance to Thersites on this count.

58. On the relationship between Thersites's rebuke of Agamemnon and Achilles's own critique of their commander, see Peter W. Rose, "Thersites and the Plural Voices of Homer," *Arethusa* 21 (1988): 19.

59. The narrator at *Iliad* 2.213 calls Thersites's speech "out of order" (ἔπεα ἄκοσμα). On account of the high ratio of correption and synizesis, Richard P. Martin says that "Thersites slurs his words" (*The Language of Heroes: Speech and Performance in the Iliad* [Ithaca, NY: Cornell University Press, 1989], 112); see 2.246. See Ralph M. Rosen, "The Death of Thersites and the Sympotic Performance of Iambic Mockery," *Pallas* 61 (2003): 121–136, on the *Iliad*'s "transparent effort to dehumanize Thersites" (134). On Thersites's marginality and the potency of his critique, see also Richard P. Martin, "Hesiod's Metanastic Poetics," *Ramus* 21 (1992): 20–21. Some might object that Thersites could hardly play a role in the construction of Socrates, since Socrates himself makes clear in *Apology* 28b–d that Achilles is his heroic analogue (see James Barrett, "Plato's Apology: Philosophy, Rhetoric, and the World of Myth," *Classical World* 95 [2001]: 3–30). My suggestion, however, is not that Socrates's ugliness recalls the Iliadic Thersites per se. Rather, I propose that the case of Thersites shows what ugliness and marginality can do. Thersites, that is, offers a model for thinking the power of an *atopos*.

60. Bury translates *atopos* as "out of the way" (*Symposium of Plato, ad* 215a).

61. Leslie Kurke, *Aesopic Conversations: Popular Tradition, Cultural Dialogue, and the Invention of Greek Prose* (Princeton, NJ: Princeton University Press, 2010), 12.

62. Kurke, 325.

63. Kurke, 325. On the parallels between Socrates and Aesop, see also T. Compton ("The Trial of the Satirist: Poetic Vitae (Aesop, Archilochus, Homer) as Background for Plato's *Apology*," *American Journal of Philology* 111 [1990]: 338–342), who finds in Aesop the paradigm to which Socrates is assimilated by Plato; Markus Schauer and Stefan Merkle ("Äsop und Sokrates," in *Der Äsop-Roman: Motivgeschichte und Erzählstruktur*, ed. Niklas Holzberg, Andreas Beschorner, and Stefan Merkle [Tübingen: Narr, 1992], 85–96), who dispute Compton's claim; Edward W. Clayton ("The Death of Socrates and the Life of Aesop," *Ancient Philosophy* 28, no. 2 [2008]: 311–328), who argues that Plato uses the strong resemblance of Socrates to Aesop to illustrate the philosopher's superiority; and Zanker, *Mask of Socrates*, 33–34. On Aesop and Socrates in Callimachus, see Benjamin Acosta-Hughes and Ruth Scodel, "Aesop Poeta: Aesop and the Fable in Callimachus' Iambi," in *Callimachus II*, ed. Annette Harder, R. F. Regtuit, and G. C. Wakker (Leuven: Peeters, 2004), 8, 16–19, who speak of Aesop as an "associative matrix" (1). To forestall any unnecessary qualms here, I do not argue that Plato's Socrates was produced consciously on the model of Aesop (or Thersites); rather, I suggest that these models can help us understand the range of meanings that Alcibiades's portrait of Socrates may carry. It should nonetheless be noted that there are numerous grounds on which one might well argue for closer ties between these two figures, as some mentioned above do. In addition to qualities mentioned elsewhere, both Socrates and Aesop were victims of an unjust charge of impiety, for which they were killed; and both were masters of a disarming indirection that operated in the realm of *sophia* (see Aristotle, *Rhetoric* 1393a23–1394a8).

64. Maximus Planudes says that Aesop surpassed Thersites in ugliness (B. E. Perry, *Aesopica: A Series of Texts Relating to Aesop or Ascribed to Him or Closely Connected with the Literary Tradition That Bears His Name* [Urbana: University of Illinois Press, 1952], 214–215); in Francis Barlow's 1687 version of this comparison, Thersites is "but an imperfect transcript of so stupendous a deformity" (*Aesop's Fables with His Life: In English, French and Latin* [London: Hills, 1687], 1). On Aesop and Thersites, see Gregory Nagy, *The Best of the Achaeans: Concepts of the Hero in Archaic Greek Poetry* (Baltimore: Johns Hopkins University Press, 1979), 280–281.

65. I use the abbreviation *Life* to refer to the *Vita Aesopi* G (Perry, *Aesopica*; Barlow, *Aesop's Fables*), unless indicated otherwise. Text from Perry, *Aesopica*; translations from Lloyd W. Daly, *Aesop without Morals* (Thomas Yoseloff: New York, 1961). References are to chapters.

66. ὁ πάντα βιωφελέστατος Αἴσωπος, ὁ λογοποιός, τῇ μὲν τύχῃ ἦν δοῦλος, τῷ δὲ γένει Φρὺξ τῆς Φρυγίας· κακοπινὴς τὸ ἰδέσθαι, εἰς ὑπηρεσίαν σαπρός, προγάστωρ,προκέφαλος, σιμός, σόρδος, μέλας, κολοβός, βλαισός, γαλιάγκων, στρεβλός, μυστάκων, προσημαῖνον ἁμάρτημα. πρὸς τούτοις ἐλάττωμα μεῖζον εἶχε τῆς ἀμορφίας τὴν ἀφωνίαν· ἦν δὲ καὶ νωδὸς καὶ οὐδὲν ἠδύνατο λαλεῖν.

67. Aristotle famously remarks that speech (λόγος) is a distinctively human capacity (*Politics* 1253a9–10). Aesop, of course, soon acquires speech and more, but the Samians remark when they see him, "Bring us an interpreter to interpret this portent [σημεῖον]. What a monstrosity [τέρας] he is to look at. Is he a frog, or a hedgehog, or a potbellied jar, or a captain of monkeys, or a moulded jug, or a cook's gear, or a dog in a basket?" (87). Croesus,

too, calls Aesop a τέρας; see below. See also Nagy, *Best of the Achaeans*, 315, with n. 6; Kurke, *Aesopic Conversations*, 163–166; François Lissarrague, "Aesop, between Man and Beast: Ancient Portraits and Illustrations," in *Not the Classical Ideal: Athens and the Construction of the Other in Greek Art*, ed. Beth Cohen (Leiden, Neth.: Brill, 2000), 136.

68.  Jeremy B. Lefkowitz poses the same question ("Ugliness and Value in the *Life of Aesop*," in *Kakos: Badness and Anti-value in Classical Antiquity*, ed. Ineke Sluiter and Ralph M. Rosen [Leiden, Neth.: Brill, 2008,] 61) and, using Aelius Theon's definition of μῦθος, offers a provocative answer: Aesop's body is itself a fable, "a kind of false λόγος concealing his true nature" (69). He accordingly calls Aesop's ugliness "heuristic" (76). On the opening of the *Life*, he remarks that this representation of Aesop "reads less like a description of an historical figure than a catalogue of types of badness" (59).

69.  Alcibiades's entrance in the *Symposium* underscores the role of the aulos, for he is led in by "the voice of the *aulos*." Peter Wilson, "The Aulos in Athens," in *Performance Culture and Athenian Democracy*, ed. Simon Goldhill and Robin Osborne (Cambridge: Cambridge University Press, 1999), 90.

70.  Wilson, 58.

71.  See the fragments from two fifth-century dithyrambic poets: Melanippides's *Marsyas* (Page, *Poetae Melici Graeci*, 758) and Telestes's *Argo* (Page, *Poetae Melici Graeci*, 805) with discussion in Wilson, "Aulos in Athens," 60–68; Richard P. Martin, "The Pipes Are Brawling: Conceptualizing Musical Performance in Athens," in *The Cultures within Ancient Greek Culture*, ed. Carol Dougherty and Leslie Kurke (Cambridge: Cambridge University Press, 2003), 160–165; cf. Aristotle, *Politics* 1341b3–6. Plutarch reports that the young Alcibiades refused to play the aulos because it was "ignoble and unworthy of a free man"; if a man plays the aulos, says Alcibiades, "even his friends and family can barely recognize his face" (*Alcibiades* 2.5–6). Aristotle (*Politics* 1341b1–8) adds that Athena's rejection of the instrument stemmed also from her recognition that it contributes nothing to intelligence (πρὸς τὴν διάνοιαν οὐθέν ἐστιν).

72.  Françoise Frontisi-Ducroux explains, "La déformation du visage explique aussi pourquoi c'est un satyre qui ramasse l'aulos et donne libre cours à ses dons musicaux: sur sa face bestiale le jeu de la flûte n'entraîne pas de déformation supplémentaire" ("Athéna et l'Invention de la flute," *Musica e Storia* 2 [1994]: 244). She goes on to speak of an "affinité naturelle" between satyr and aulos.

73.  Wilson, "Aulos in Athens," 62.

74.  At *Minos* 318b, Socrates calls the music of Marsyas "most divine" (θειότατα). Wilson speaks of Socrates's "auletic logos" ("Aulos in Athens," 91n115).

75.  Παλλὰς ἐφεῦρε θρασειᾶν Γοργόνων / οὔλιον θρῆνον διαπλέξαισ' Ἀθάνα· / τὸν παρθενίοις ὑπό τ' ἀπλάτοις ὀφίων κεφαλαῖς / ἄϊε λειβόμενον δυσπενθέϊ σὺν καμάτῳ.

76.  The otherness of the aulos shows up in many forms and in many places. Among the more intriguing is Diodorus's account of the contest between Apollo and Marsyas. The first round of the contest was won by the satyr: "Marsyas, striking up upon his pipes, amazed the ears of his hearers by their strange music [καταπλῆξαι τὰς ἀκοὰς τῷ ξενίζοντι]" (3.59, trans. Oldfather). The key verb here, ξενίζω, encodes both the strangeness and the otherness of the aulos. On the instrument's alien qualities, see Frontisi-Ducroux, "Athéna"; Wilson, "Aulos in Athens."

77.  Jean-Pierre Vernant, "Death in the Eyes: Gorgo, Figure of the Other," in *Mortals and Immortals: Collected Essays*, ed. Froma I. Zeitlin and Anne M. Wilson (Princeton, NJ: Princeton University Press, 1991), 121.

78.  Frontisi-Ducroux calls the aulos-player "Maître d'Epouvante, le musicien qui sait faire entendre les cris furieux des Gorgones endeuillées, et dont le visage se fait semblable à ces faces monstrueuses" (Frontisi-Ducroux, "Athéna," 253). Elsewhere, she sums it up this way: "L'aulos accompagne ou suscite le délire et la transe, arrachant l'individu à lui-même" (Françoise Frontisi-Ducroux, *Du masque au visage: Aspects de l'Identité en Grèce ancienne* [Paris: Flammarion, 1995], 97). Martin reads this passage somewhat differently, suggesting that Athena "is interweaving the female utterance [of the Gorgons] here with the more important sound, the voice of the man who in effect generated the Gorgons' wail" ("Pipes Are Brawling," 163). But he goes on to speak of the aulos as "inhuman, whether toad-like or goose like. . . . Piping is an auditory disturbance, hard to incorporate into the sphere of human speech, a croaking encroachment" (167). Martin cites Annie Bélis's interpretation of an Attic black-figure amphora depicting a goose intently focused on an aulos-player. She argues that the vase's painting is a joke drawing on the fact that aulos and goose shared a certain vocabulary (Bélis, "L'Aulète et le jeu de l'oie," *Bulletin de Correspondance Héllenique* 110 [1992]: 499–500). Bélis points to Athenaeus's report (14.657e) that, in a work of the comic poet Diphilus, the verb "to honk" was used of aulos-players (χηνίζειν δὲ εἴρηται ἐπὶ τῶν αὐλούντων). Bélis identifies the goose, furthermore, as "un animal particulièrement anti-musical" (499).

79.  Race's "every sound" obscures the fact that the word used here, πάμφωνος, is a compound of φωνή, which, especially in such a context, carries the meaning of "voice," as emphasized by Frontisi-Ducroux, "Athéna," 257.

80.  ἀλλ' ἐπεὶ ἐκ τούτων φίλον ἄνδρα πόνων / ἐρρύσατο, παρθένος αὐλῶν τεῦχε πάμφωνον μέλος, / ὄφρα τὸν Εὐρυάλας ἐκ καρπαλιμᾶν γενύων / χριμφθέντα σὺν ἔντεσι μιμήσαιτ' ἐρικλάγκταν γόον. / εὗρεν θεός· ἀλλά νιν εὑροῖσ' ἀνδράσι θνατοῖς ἔχειν, / ὠνόμασεν κεφαλᾶν πολλᾶν νόμον.

81.  Vernant ("Death in the Eyes," 137) writes here of the Gorgon's face (which he treats as a mask), but his comments apply with equal force to the sound imitated by the aulos. Frontisi-Ducroux explains that the tune is of many heads "parce qu'il répète celui qui s'élève des têtes multiples des Gorgones couronnées de serpents" ("Athéna," 258). In Plato (*Republic* 399d), the aulos is the "most many-stringed" instrument (πολυχορδότατον).

82.  Thomas H. Carpenter, *Dionysian Imagery in Fifth-Century Athens* (Oxford: Clarendon, 1997), 96, cited in Eric Csapo, "Riding the Phallus for Dionysus: Iconology, Ritual, and Gender-Role De/Construction," *Phoenix* (1997): 258n21. Cf. Frontisi-Ducroux, who remarks that "la frontalité de l'aulète constitue l'un des quelques cas de frontalité humaine, présentation utilisée également pour signifier la mort, le sommeil, l'ivresse, la folie, et autres situations comportant une rupture de communication, une sortie hors de l'espace iconique" ("Athéna," 245).

83.  Csapo, "Riding the Phallus," 257.

84.  ὦ Σώκρατες, ἤκουον μὲν ἔγωγε πρὶν καὶ συγγενέσθαι σοι ὅτι σὺ οὐδὲν ἄλλο ἢ αὐτός τε ἀπορεῖς καὶ τοὺς ἄλλους ποιεῖς ἀπορεῖν· καὶ νῦν, ὥς γέ μοι δοκεῖς, γοητεύεις με καὶ φαρμάττεις καὶ ἀτεχνῶς κατεπάδεις, ὥστε μεστὸν ἀπορίας γεγονέναι. καὶ δοκεῖς μοι παντελῶς, εἰ δεῖ τι καὶ σκῶψαι, ὁμοιότατος εἶναι τό τε εἶδος καὶ τἆλλα ταύτῃ τῇ πλατείᾳ νάρκῃ τῇ θαλαττίᾳ· καὶ γὰρ αὕτη τὸν ἀεὶ πλησιάζοντα καὶ ἀπτόμενον ναρκᾶν ποιεῖ, καὶ σὺ δοκεῖς μοι νῦν ἐμὲ τοιοῦτόν τι πεποιηκέναι· ἀληθῶς γὰρ ἔγωγε καὶ τὴν ψυχὴν καὶ τὸ στόμα ναρκῶ, καὶ οὐκ ἔχω ὅτι ἀποκρίνωμαί σοι.

85.  Csapo, "Riding the Phallus," 257.

86.  Commenting on the Gorgon, Vernant suggests the same: "The usual conventions and typical classifications are syncopated and intermixed. Masculine and feminine, young and

old, beautiful and ugly, human and animal . . . in short, all the categories in this face overlap in confusion and interfere with one another. . . . A disquieting mixture takes place, analogous to the one Dionysos achieves through joy and liberation" ("Death in the Eyes," 137).

87.  Here is how Alcibiades puts it: "The moment he starts to speak, I am beside myself: my heart starts leaping in my chest, the tears come streaming down my face, even the frenzied Corybantes seem sane compared to me" (215e). On Socrates's ability to charm and his status as magician or wizard (γόης/φαρμακεύς), see *Phaedo* 77e–78a; *Charmides* 155e; *Theaetetus* 149d, 157c; *Symposium* 203d; Jacques Derrida, "Plato's Pharmacy," in *Dissemination*, trans. and ed. Barbara Johnson (Chicago: University of Chicago Press, 1981), 117–119; Catherine H. Zuckert, "Who's a Philosopher? Who's a Sophist? The Stranger v. Socrates," *Review of Metaphysics* 54 (2000): 78–79.

88.  Vernant, "Death in the Eyes," 137.

89.  Some may object to my attempt to take seriously Alcibiades's characterization of Socrates as an αὐλητής, given that elsewhere Plato "himself" rejects the aulos (*Republic* 399d; *Laws* 700e). One might explain the discrepancy as Wilson does, for example, by positing that the author of *Republic* and *Laws* was an older Plato "less open to its [the aulos's] powers" (Wilson, "Aulos in Athens," 92). Others may problematize the reading of the "rejections" (see, e.g., David K. O'Connor, "Rewriting the Poets in Plato's Characters," in *The Cambridge Companion to Plato's Republic*, ed. G. R. F. Ferrari [Cambridge: Cambridge University Press, 2007], 55–89). How we read this passage of the *Republic* makes little difference to my argument, though—my claim is not that Plato endorses emulating the satyr or playing the aulos. My aim is more modest: I intend only to suggest that in certain key ways the Socrates of Alcibiades's portrait resembles the aulos-playing satyr and, further, that understanding the mythical figure—as well as the symbolic meanings of the aulos itself—enables us to make sense of Alcibiades's portrait as valuable testimony about Plato's model philosopher. In this limited sense, then, the meanings of the aulos and the satyr who plays it can tell us much about the philosopher of Plato's making.

90.  *Life of Alcibiades* 2.5. Plato, *Alcibiades* 106e, also mentions that Alcibiades refused to play the aulos, although without explaining why he did so.

91.  ἡ μὲν ἔρριψε τὸν αὐλόν, ὁ δὲ καὶ τὸν αὐλητὴν ἐξέδειρεν.

92.  See Frontisi-Ducroux, "Athéna," 246.

93.  Critias was a fifth-century Athenian tragic poet and notoriously ruthless member of the Thirty Tyrants.

94.  εἰ γὰρ μὴ ὁμολογήσει ὁ λόγος τῷ ἤθει, ἀλλοτρίᾳ τῇ γλώττῃ δόξομεν φθέγγεσθαι, ὥσπερ οἱ αὐλοί. Wilson provocatively suggests that Philostratus here may be quoting Critias himself ("Aulos in Athens," 86).

95.  τὴν γλῶτταν ὥσπερ τῶν αὐλῶν ἐάν τις ἀφέλῃ, τὸ λοιπὸν οὐδέν ἐστιν.

96.  Cf. Frontisi-Ducroux, "Athéna," 260–261.

97.  If we are to trust Plutarch, Athenians took to the view of Alcibiades: free men ceased playing the aulos, and the instrument fell into disrepute (*Alcibiades* 2.6). On this question, see also Martin ("Pipes Are Brawling"), who offers a helpful diachronic view of attitudes toward the aulos; cf. James McKinnon, "The Rejection of the Aulos in Classical Greece," in *Music and Civilization: Essays in Honor of Paul Henry Lang*, ed. Edmond Strainchamps and Maria Rika Maniates (New York: Norton, 1984), 201–214. Although he pushes back against the notion that the aulos is thoroughly explained as a Dionysian instrument, Martin does see the instrument as an apt symbol for Socrates ("Pipes Are Brawling," 174),

in part because the "controlling nature of the *aulos* accords with its power to bind the listener" (173).

98.  "Son visage, comme celui de la Gorgone, est un masque" (Frontisi-Ducroux on the satyr, "Athéna," 245). See also Charles Griswold, "Irony in the Platonic Dialogues," *Philosophy and Literature* 26 (2002): 94–95. Hadot sees Socrates's satyric self expressed largely through his irony, which functioned as a mask (*Philosophy*, 148–153). Michelle Gellrich studies Socrates's "magic" (γοητεία), finding that "doubleness is at the heart of Socrates' performances" ("Socratic Magic: Enchantment, Irony, and Persuasion in Plato's Dialogues," *Classical World* 87 [1994]: 306) and that "his enchantment moves hand in hand with his irony" (298).

99.  Andrea Wilson Nightingale, *Spectacles of Truth in Classical Greek Philosophy: Theoria in Its Cultural Context* (Cambridge: Cambridge University Press, 2004), 101–107.

100.  For other examples of Socrates's atopia, see Blondell, *Play of Character*, 73–74 with n. 102, 106.

# Bibliography

Acosta-Hughes, Benjamin, and Ruth Scodel. "Aesop Poeta: Aesop and the Fable in Callimachus' Iambi." In *Callimachus II*, edited by Annette Harder, R. F. Regtuit, and G. C. Wakker, 1–21. Leuven: Peeters, 2004.

Aeschylus. *Persians*. Translated and edited by Edith Hall. Warminster: Aris and Phillips, 1996.

Barlow, Francis. *Aesop's Fables with His Life: In English, French and Latin*. London: Hills, 1687.

Barrett, James. "Plato's *Apology*: Philosophy, Rhetoric, and the World of Myth." *Classical World* 95 (2001): 3–30.

———. *Staged Narrative: Poetics and the Messenger in Greek Tragedy*. Berkeley: University of California Press, 2002.

Belfiore, Elizabeth S. *Socrates' Daimonic Art*. Cambridge: Cambridge University Press, 2012.

Bélis, Annie. "L'Aulète et le jeu de l'oie." *Bulletin de Correspondance Hellénique* 110 (1992): 497–500.

Benardete, Seth. *Socrates and Plato: The Dialectics of Eros (Sokrates und Platon: Die Dialektik des Eros)*. München: Carl Friedrich von Siemens Stiftung, 1999.

Blondell, Ruby. *The Play of Character in Plato's Dialogues*. Cambridge: Cambridge University Press, 2002.

Bury, R. G. *The Symposium of Plato*. 2nd ed. Cambridge: W. Heffer, 1932.

Capra, Andrea. *Plato's Four Muses: The Phaedrus and the Poetics of Philosophy*. Washington, DC: Center for Hellenic Studies, 2014.

Carpenter, Thomas H. *Dionysian Imagery in Fifth-Century Athens*. Oxford: Clarendon, 1997.

Cavarero, Adriana. *For More Than One Voice: Toward a Philosophy of Vocal Expression*. Translated by Paul A. Kottman. Stanford: Stanford University Press, 2005.

Clayton, Edward W. "The Death of Socrates and the Life of Aesop." *Ancient Philosophy* 28, no. 2 (2008): 311–328.

Compton, T. "The Trial of the Satirist: Poetic Vitae (Aesop, Archilochus, Homer) as Background for Plato's *Apology*." *American Journal of Philology* 111 (1990): 330–347.

Cooper, John M., ed. *Plato: Complete Works*. Indianapolis: Hackett, 1997.

Csapo, Eric. "Riding the Phallus for Dionysus: Iconology, Ritual, and Gender-Role De/Construction." *Phoenix* 51 (1997): 253–295.

Daly, Lloyd W. *Aesop without Morals*. Thomas Yoseloff: New York, 1961.

de Jong, Irene J. F. *Narrative in Drama: The Art of the Euripidean Messenger-Speech*. Leiden, Neth.: Brill, 1991.

Derrida, Jacques. "Plato's Pharmacy." In *Dissemination*, translated and edited by Barbara Johnson, 61–171. Chicago: University of Chicago Press, 1981.

Detienne, Marcel. *The Masters of Truth in Archaic Greece*. Translated by Janet Lloyd. New York: Zone, 1996.

Frontisi-Ducroux, Françoise. "Athéna et l'Invention de la flûte." *Musica e Storia* 2 (1994): 239–267.

———. *Du masque au visage: Aspects de l'Identité en Grèce ancienne*. Paris: Flammarion, 1995.

Frontisi-Ducroux, Françoise, and François Lissarrague. "From Ambiguity to Ambivalence: A Dionysiac Excursion through the 'Anakreontic' Vases." In *Before Sexuality: The Construction of Erotic Experience in the Ancient Greek World*, edited by David Halperin, John Winkler, and Froma I. Zeitlin, 211–256. Princeton, NJ: Princeton University Press, 1990.

Gellrich, Michelle. "Socratic Magic: Enchantment, Irony, and Persuasion in Plato's Dialogues." *Classical World* 87 (1994): 275–307.

Gordon, Jill. *Plato's Erotic World: From Cosmic Origins to Human Death*. Cambridge: Cambridge University Press, 2012.

Griffith, Mark. "Satyrs, Citizens, and Self-Representation." In *Satyr Drama: Tragedy at Play*, edited by George W. M. Harrison, 161–199. Swansea: Classical Press of Wales, 2005.

Griswold, Charles. "Irony in the Platonic Dialogues." *Philosophy and Literature* 26 (2002): 84–106.

Hadot, Pierre. *Philosophy as a Way of Life: Spiritual Exercises from Socrates to Foucault*. Translated by Michael Chase. Edited by Arnold Davidson. Malden, MA: Blackwell, 1995.

Hall, Edith. "Ithyphallic Males Behaving Badly: Or, Satyr Drama as Gendered Tragic Ending." In *Parchments of Gender: Deciphering the Bodies of Antiquity*, edited by Maria Wyke, 13–37. Oxford: Oxford University Press, 1998.

Henrichs, Albert. "'He Has a God in Him': Human and Divine in the Modern Perception of Dionysus." In *Masks of Dionysus*, edited by Thomas H. Carpenter and Christopher A. Faraone, 13–43. Ithaca, NY: Cornell University Press, 1993.

Herington, C. J. *Aeschylus*. New Haven, CT: Yale University Press, 1986.

Konstan, David. "An Anthropology of Euripides' *Kyklops*." In *Nothing to Do with Dionysos? Athenian Drama in Its Social Context*, edited by John J. Winkler and Froma I. Zeitlin, 207–227. Princeton, NJ: Princeton University Press, 1990.

Kurke, Leslie. *Aesopic Conversations: Popular Tradition, Cultural Dialogue, and the Invention of Greek Prose*. Princeton, NJ: Princeton University Press, 2010.

Lattimore, Richmond. *The* Iliad *of Homer*. Chicago: University of Chicago Press, 1951.

Lefkowitz, Jeremy B. "Ugliness and Value in the *Life of Aesop*." In *Kakos: Badness and Anti-value in Classical Antiquity*, edited by Ineke Sluiter and Ralph M. Rosen, 59–81. Leiden, Neth.: Brill, 2008.

Lissarrague, François. "Aesop, between Man and Beast: Ancient Portraits and Illustrations." In *Not the Classical Ideal: Athens and the Construction of the Other in Greek Art*, edited by Beth Cohen, 132–149. Leiden, Neth.: Brill, 2000.

———. "The Athenian Image of the Foreigner." In *The Athenian Image of the Foreigner*, edited by Thomas Harrison and Antonia Nevill, 101–124. New York: Routledge, 2002.

———. "Why Satyrs Are Good to Represent." In *Nothing to Do with Dionysos? Athenian Drama in Its Social Context*, edited by John J. Winkler and Froma I. Zeitlin, 228–236. Princeton, NJ: Princeton University Press, 1990.

Martin, Richard P. "Hesiod's Metanastic Poetics." *Ramus* 21 (1992): 11–33.

———. *The Language of Heroes: Speech and Performance in the Iliad*. Ithaca, NY: Cornell University Press, 1989.

———. "The Pipes Are Brawling: Conceptualizing Musical Performance in Athens." In *The Cultures within Ancient Greek Culture*, edited by Carol Dougherty and Leslie Kurke, 153–180. Cambridge: Cambridge University Press, 2003.

McCoy, Marina. *Plato on the Rhetoric of Philosophers and Sophists*. Cambridge: Cambridge University Press, 2008.

McKinnon, James. "The Rejection of the Aulos in Classical Greece." In *Music and Civilization: Essays in Honor of Paul Henry Lang*, edited by Edmond Strainchamps and Maria Rika Maniates, 201–214. New York: Norton, 1984.

Nagy, Gregory. *The Best of the Achaeans: Concepts of the Hero in Archaic Greek Poetry*. Baltimore: Johns Hopkins University Press, 1979.

Nightingale, Andrea Wilson. *Genres in Dialogue: Plato and the Construct of Philosophy*. Cambridge: Cambridge University Press, 1995.

———. *Spectacles of Truth in Classical Greek Philosophy: Theoria in Its Cultural Context*. Cambridge: Cambridge University Press, 2004.

Notomi, Noburu. *The Unity of Plato's Sophist: Between the Sophist and the Philosopher*. Cambridge: Cambridge University Press, 1999.

O'Connor, David K. "Rewriting the Poets in Plato's Characters." In *The Cambridge Companion to Plato's Republic*, edited by G. R. F. Ferrari, 55–89. Cambridge: Cambridge University Press, 2007.

Osborne, Catherine. *Eros Unveiled: Plato and the God of Love*. Oxford: Clarendon, 1994.

Padgett, J. Michael. "The Stable Hands of Dionysos: Satyrs and Donkeys as Symbols of Social Marginalization in Attic Vase Painting." In *Not the Classical Ideal: Athens and the Construction of the Other in Greek Art*, edited by Beth Cohen, 43–70. Leiden, Neth.: Brill, 2000.

Perry, B. E. *Aesopica: A Series of Texts Relating to Aesop or Ascribed to Him or Closely Connected with the Literary Tradition That Bears His Name*. Urbana: University of Illinois Press, 1952.

Porter, James I. "The Invention of Dionysus and the Platonic Midwife: Nietzsche's *Birth of Tragedy*." *Journal of the History of Philosophy* 33 (1995): 467–497.

Pucci, Pietro. *Hesiod and the Language of Poetry*. Baltimore: Johns Hopkins University Press, 1977.

———. *The Song of the Sirens*. Lanham: Rowman and Littlefield, 1998.

Race, William H. *Pindar: Olympian Odes. Pythian Odes*. Cambridge: Harvard University Press, 1997.

Reiss, Timothy J. *Tragedy and Truth*. New Haven, CT: Yale University Press, 1980.

Roller, L. "The Legend of Midas." *Classical Antiquity* 2 (1983): 299–313.

Rose, Peter W. "Thersites and the Plural Voices of Homer." *Arethusa* 21 (1988): 5–25.

Rosen, Ralph M. "The Death of Thersites and the Sympotic Performance of Iambic Mockery." *Pallas* 61 (2003): 121–136.

Santas, Gerasimos Xenophon. *Socrates: Philosophy in Plato's Early Dialogues*. London: Routledge and K. Paul, 1979.

Saxonhouse, Arlene W. *Free Speech and Democracy in Ancient Athens*. Cambridge: Cambridge University Press, 2006.

Schauer, Markus, and Stefan Merkle. "Äsop und Sokrates." In *Der Äsop-Roman: Motivgeschichte und Erzählstruktur*, edited by Niklas Holzberg, Andreas Beschorner, and Stefan Merkle, 85–96. Tübingen, Ger.: Narr, 1992.

Seaford, Richard. *Euripides: Cyclops*. Oxford: Clarendon, 1984.

Vernant, Jean-Pierre. "Death in the Eyes: Gorgo, Figure of the Other." In *Mortals and Immortals: Collected Essays*, edited by Froma I. Zeitlin and Anne M. Wilson, 111–138. Princeton, NJ: Princeton University Press, 1991.

———. "Mortals and Immortals: The Body of the Divine." In *Mortals and Immortals: Collected Essays*, edited by Froma I. Zeitlin and Anne M. Wilson, 27–49. Princeton, NJ: Princeton University Press, 1991.

Vidal-Naquet, Pierre. "Land and Sacrifice in the Odyssey: A Study of Religious and Mythical Meanings." In *Reading the Odyssey: Selected Interpretive Essays*, edited by Seth L. Schein, 33–54. Princeton, NJ: Princeton University Press, 1996.

Voelke, Pierre. *Un Théatre de la Marge: Aspects Figuratifs et Configurationnels du Drame Satyrique dans l'Athènes Classique*. Bari: Levante Editori, 2001.

Wilson, Peter. "The Aulos in Athens." In *Performance Culture and Athenian Democracy*, edited by Simon Goldhill and Robin Osborne, 58–95. Cambridge: Cambridge University Press, 1999.

Zanker, Paul. *The Mask of Socrates: The Image of the Intellectual in Antiquity*. Berkeley: University of California Press, 1995.

Zuckert, Catherine H. "Who's a Philosopher? Who's a Sophist? The Stranger v. Socrates." *Review of Metaphysics* 54 (2000): 65–97.

JAMES BARRETT is Associate Professor of Classics at Colby College in Maine. He is author of *Staged Narrative: Poetics and the Messenger in Greek Tragedy* (California).

# 15

## WORKS OF SILENCE

Jeremy Bell, Emory University

Ｉɴ Euripides's *Orestes*, Menelaus declares to the play's namesake that "there are times when silence would be better than speech, and the reverse also" (638).[1] While the axiomatic simplicity of his assertion betrays little of the prudential considerations that bear on the determination of who ought to speak and when, Menelaus does nevertheless gesture toward one of the most significant and pervasive principles organizing the trope of silence in ancient Greek and Roman literature: the concern over context—that is, a concern over determining who should speak and who should be silent, as well as when one should speak or remain quiet. Because this determination cuts across the diverse and, at times, shifting topography of the social land-scape, and because, as Menelaus indicates, it is also subject to the demands of the moment, the rules determining who ought to speak and who ought to remain silent are both manifold and frequently difficult to discern. For instance, in his *Letter to Demonicus*, Isocrates offers the following counsel: "Always when you are about to say anything, first weigh it in your mind; for with many the tongue outruns the thought. Let there be but two occasions for speech—when the subject is one which you thoroughly know and when it is one on which you are compelled to speak. On these occasions alone is speech better than silence; on all others, it is better to be silent than to speak" (1.41).[2] This sober and oft-ignored piece of advice suggests that we might reasonably draw a distinction between the right of speech and the wisdom of silence that cuts along an axis of knowledge and truth on the one hand and ignorance and falsity on the other—we ought to speak when we know the truth of the matter at hand; otherwise, we should be silent. Elsewhere, however, the distinction is drawn along other lines, as when Pindar declares, "There is a saying among men: a noble deed when it is accomplished should not be buried silently in the ground; and divine song is suited to boasting" (*Nemean* 9.5);[3] or when, in his denunciation of Aeschines, Demosthenes, citing Sophocles, declares, "I will not keep silent when that curse comes to steal my citizens' security" (*On the False Embassy*, 19.247);[4] or when "Adeimantus the Corinthian attacked [Themistocles] again, advising that a man without a city should keep silent" (Herodotus, *Histories* 8.16).[5]

In the passages above, the right of speech is alternately justified by the demand to honor and memorialize noble deeds, the urgency of denouncing dangers to the polity, and the privileges associated with citizenship. Other authors and texts reveal a still further proliferation of the rules governing when one should speak or hold one's tongue. Yet underlying these rules, we find a more or less consistent qualitative assessment of silence throughout the literature of the Greek archaic and classical periods, which regularly code its value negatively: silence amounts to a failure to praise where praise is due, to denounce political misdeeds, to merit certain rights or privileges under the law, and so on.[6] Even Isocrates, who offers a more tempered perspective, ultimately finds the value of silence to be negative—it is advisable to the ignorant but not to the knowledgeable. These passages are representative of the dominant trend in Greek literature: logos is commended; silence is proscribed. The former is aligned with the divine, with praise, with memory, and with rights and expressions of power, and the latter with subordination, forgottenness, and oblivion.

In the Roman imperial era, however, authors such as Epictetus, Plutarch, and Diogenes Laertius reverse the normative polarity established by their Greek predecessors. Motivated by an increasing suspicion of logos, these authors leverage the connotative plasticity of the terms ἡ σιγή and ἡ σιωπή to rehabilitate the practice of silence. This is frequently, though not exclusively, done through the invocation of Socrates and various pre-Socratic thinkers and rulers to whom the Roman authors ascribe a positive relation to silence, as if the assignation of a negative value in the archaic and classical periods were nothing more than a brief interruption of its true significance. For instance, in a passage to which I return below, Diogenes Laertius reports that Bias of Priene once refused to define piety for an impious man: "When the other inquired the reason, 'I am silent,' he replied, 'because you are asking questions about what does not concern you'" (*Lives* 1.86).[7] In contrast to Isocrates's advice above, Bias is here silent not because he lacks knowledge but because his interlocutor does. Nor, moreover, is his silence coded as harmful, shameful, compelled, or in any other way abhorrent. On the contrary, it is freely self-imposed and serves as an emblem of his virtue. This, I argue, is representative of an extensive and conspicuous transformation of the concept of silence, which occurs between the Greek classical period and the Roman imperial era. In the latter, speech is increasingly seen as a temptation leading to both vice and the assimilation of one's character or identity to that of the common, nonreflective, nonphilosophical masses. Viewing language as an inheritance of and repository for cultural norms, values, and practices, which does not simply endow the speaker with the ability to express herself but also immerses her in those customs, a number of Roman authors in the first few centuries of the Common Era mobilize the practice of silence against this process of acculturation, thereby inverting the earlier value ascribed to these terms: if logos tempts us into vice, silence helps us attain virtue; if logos binds our souls to the common modes of life and behavior within the city, silence liberates us; if logos is quotidian, silence is divine. In this way, they recast the practice of silence as a means of caring for and transforming one's soul in order to live a good and virtuous life.

## 1. Speaking over Silence

Due to its qualitative ambivalence, the value of silence may be inflected either positively or negatively, depending on the context in which it is situated, enacted, or enforced. The concern that effects its negative inflection with the greatest consistency and intensity is the association that it bears with oblivion or forgottenness (ἡ λήθη). Plutarch, whose views on silence prove to be rather complex, offers an exceptionally pointed and succinct account of the bond between silence and oblivion.[8] In *De E apud Delphos*, he contrasts the "correspondingly antithetic" terms that constellate around the gods Apollo, who is "clear" and "bright," and Pluto, who is "unseen" and "dark," declaring that "with the one [i.e., Apollo] are associated the Muses and Memory [αἱ Μοῦσαι καὶ ἡ Μνημοσύνη], with the other Oblivion and Silence [ἡ Λήθη καὶ ἡ Σιωπή]" (394A).[9] Plutarch here affirms a fundamental opposition between silence and memory or memorialization—those who are not spoken of are not remembered. This has the effect of organizing the connotative meaning of "silence" (ἡ σιωπὴ and ἡ σιγὴ) around the denotative meaning of "oblivion" (ἡ λήθη). Those who fail to speak or act in meritorious ways likewise fail to be praised and spoken of; denied even the shadow of immortality provided by song and speech, they are thus concealed in darkness and lost to history. Pindar captures this insight in a typically pithy declaration: "Those who attempt nothing face silence and obscurity [τῶν ἀπειράτων γὰρ ἄγνωστοι σιωπαί]" (*Isthmian* 4.31).[10] Yet the negativity of silence also serves as the soil in which countless worlds of words and deeds germinate and from which they spring forth, for this negativity begets the positive desire to speak and act in meritorious ways that will encourage others to speak or sing about one's life, to remember it even in death, and, in this way, to bestow on it a share of immortality. As Marcel Detienne notes, "Oblivion, or silence, represents the rearing up of the power of death in the face of the power of life, Memory, the mother of the Muses. Behind praise and blame is the fundamental pair of antithetical powers, *Mnēmosunē* and *Lēthē*."[11]

Even the gods, whose immortality exists independently of the praise they receive, cherish acclaim and speeches celebrating their deeds. In his *Helen*, Isocrates asserts that "one could cite many instances of goddesses who succumbed to mortal beauty, and no one of these sought to keep the fact concealed as if it involved disgrace; on the contrary, they desired their adventures to be celebrated in song as glorious deeds rather than to be hushed in silence" (10.60).[12] What I would like to draw attention to is less Isocrates's praise of Helen, whose beauty is said to outstrip even those mortals to whom the goddesses would proudly succumb, than the assumptions underlying his argument: in addition to the belief that beauty is sufficiently noble that even the gods would proudly submit to it, Isocrates takes for granted the belief that the gods desire their noble deeds to be praised and celebrated. Far from impugning their fondness for praise, then, the rhetorical nature of this document underscores the strength of the belief in this fondness, as it is this belief on which the effectiveness of the argument depends. Hesiod provides a further, and still more authoritative, account of this fondness in the *Theogony*, where he tells us that Zeus fathered the Muses, "whose hearts are set on song" (55–61), after spending nine nights with Mnemosyne (Memory).[13] The implication is that the Muses perform the function of their maternal lineage through their songs—they sing in order to celebrate "what will be and what has been" (32–33). In this way, they preserve the history of the cosmos, for they "celebrate . . . first of all the revered race of the gods from the beginning, those whom Earth and wide Heaven begot, and the gods sprung of these, givers of good things. Then next, the goddesses sing of Zeus, the father of gods and men, as they begin and end their strain, how much he is the most excellent among the gods and supreme in power. And again, they chant the race of men and strong giants" (42–51). The effect of Zeus's desire to celebrate his deeds and chronicle the earliest origins of all things is to render these events accessible through logos—that is, through the Muses, who both preserve the past and make it present through the medium of sung speech. Moreover, not only do their songs "gladden the great spirit of their father Zeus" (36); they also imbue the poets with song and "pour sweet dew" on the tongues of kings, from whose "lips flow gracious words" (1–90). Into the former, they "breathed . . . a divine voice to celebrate things that shall be and things that were aforetime" (31–32), while to the latter they grant the power of persuasion: "And he, speaking surely, would soon make wise end even of a great quarrel; for therefore are there princes wise in heart, because when the people are being misguided in their assembly, they set right the matter again with ease, persuading them with gentle words" (85–87). To poets, then, they grant the power to preserve the memory of the new gods and the old, as well as of the races of mortals; to kings, they grant the power not to recall the past or future but to transform the present in accordance with their judgment by easily persuading others. Through the Muses, then, is forged something like a great chain of logos, which, by the power of Memory, makes the past and future of the cosmos present and which likewise endows mortals with immortal speech.

Above, we find the two primary modes in which logos is deployed against silence: through the praise or recollection of others, and by earning praise through effective speech, whereby one affects the souls of others or transforms reality by convincing others to organize their speech or deeds in accordance with one's own judgment. Plato, however, notes that, in an important respect, these two modes of deploying logos against silence are motivated by the same concern: heroes, poets, and politicians all act and speak in order to earn praise (*Symposium* 208c–209e).[14] This is to say that the poets are not inert or disinterested media through which the songs of the Muses pass—they praise so that they will in turn be praised, and they memorialize so that they will be memorialized. For Plato, then, Homer is no less subject to the desire to be praised and immortalized than are the figures populating his works. He sings so that his name will not be consumed by silence. Silvia Montiglio has likewise shown that the right of speech was an important feature of the praiseworthiness of the epic heroes themselves, whose "charisma . . . can indeed be assessed by their ability to impose silence upon others without ever suffering this humiliation themselves."[15] The right to assert themselves, to speak where others must remain silent, to address both their subordinates and their fellow captains, to command and offer counsel, to issue praise and blame, to distinguish themselves in word as well as deed—this is an expression of the worth, value, and dignity, in short, of the *timē* afforded to the Homeric heroes. Indeed, as Montiglio notes, this right is so central to their identity that they preserve it even in the realm of Hades, which, for instance, failed to silence Achilles.[16] It is not in deeds alone, then, that the heroes endeavor to be remembered: like the poets who sing of them, they too speak so that they will be spoken of. This, as Montiglio again perceives, is quite different from the behavior of the anonymous soldiers captained by the heroes, who are silent both in life and afterward: "Sitting in silence only befits those listeners who are not expected to speak in turn, above all an undifferentiated group, which either status or circumstances exclude from verbal participation. It is the multitude that sits down in silence to listen to the words of a single hero, the anonymous multitude that has no right to speak in the Homeric *agorē*."[17] Having failed to speak in life, these anonymous masses are not spoken of in death: "The anonymity of the dead leads to a hasty burial, with no celebration or lament. The warriors who cannot be recognized will be recognized no more. Thus the silence of the living foreshadows the dead men's lack of name and renown in the future."[18]

Intriguingly, Montiglio finds a similar dynamic at work in popular representations of the Athenian Assembly, where, again, a few speak and are spoken of, while the many remain silent and are lost to anonymity: "To remain silent is just the neutral demeanor of the common, anonymous man."[19] Theseus comments on this anonymizing silence and its opposite in *The Suppliants*: "Freedom's mark is also seen in this: 'Who has wholesome counsel to declare unto the state?' And he who chooses to do so gains renown, while he who has no wish remains silent. What greater equality can there be in a city?"[20] This is a fascinating interpretation of and justification for the egalitarian nature of democracy. Whereas an oligarchy or monarchy grants to the few or the one the right of statesmanship—and with it the right to speak before the entire polis and shape it in accordance with one's view of the best political order—the promise of democracy is that it will allocate these rights equally among all citizens.[21] Thus, Theseus here frames the triumph of Athenian ἰσονομία in terms of the equal access that it affords the citizenry to the pursuit of praise and reputation, championing the right to offer up sound counsel before the assembly less for the sake of the benefit that such counsel may provide the city than for the acclaim that it may earn the one who speaks. This is not to suggest that he discounts the value of such counsel, which is, after all, the basis on which praise may be earned. He does, however, establish a clear order of priority: the proffering of good political counsel is undertaken for the sake of individual reputation. Those, on the contrary, who choose the side of silence, those who keep their counsel to themselves and offer no aid to their fellow citizens, receive no renown in return. Immortality is earned by advancing the good of the polis.

Demosthenes, who is particularly vocal on this issue, never tires of reminding his audience that it is the mark of a vicious person and a failed statesman to remain silent when an unjust or unnecessarily dangerous course of action is proposed. Thus, in *On the False Embassy*, he declares,

> How then can you find an easy answer to the question, Who was the rogue? Consult your own recollections, and mark who denounced the transactions at the outset. For it is clear that, if the evil-doer could hold his peace, escape immediate detection, and never afterwards allow himself to be called to account, that was good enough for him; whereas the man with a good conscience bethought himself that it would be very hard if by keeping silent he should become a reputed accomplice in scandalous and wicked actions. Well then, it was I who denounced these men from the outset, and none of them denounced me. (19.33)

Or, again, in *On the Crown*: "That is the salient difference between the statesman and the charlatan, who are indeed in all respects unlike one another. The statesman declares his judgement before the event, and accepts responsibility to his followers, to fortune, to the chances of the hour, to every critic of his policy. The charlatan remains silent when he ought to speak, and then croaks over any untoward result" (18.189).[22] Demosthenes's strategy not only has the effect of condemning his opponents' silence[23] but also justifies his own loquaciousness, establishing it as one of the terms on which the question of good counsel is to be settled: the opposition's guidance cannot be trusted because they remain silent when they should speak and speak when they should remain silent, whereas Demosthenes speaks in the right way and at the right time.

Importantly, however, the identification of speech with virtue extends only to Demosthenes's fellow statesmen; the reverse holds for his audience, for whom silence is a virtue. In the *Exordia*, for instance, he declares, "It is your duty, men of Athens, to listen to every proposal made, since it is your prerogative to adopt whichever of them you choose. For it often happens that the same person is wrong on one point and right on another; and so by shouting him down when displeased you may perhaps deprive yourselves of many useful ideas, whereas by attending with decorum and in silence, you will act on every sound proposal" (4).[24] Or, again, "Now, if you shall think it right to refuse to listen, you will make a mistake; but if you will listen in silence and bear with me in this, one of two benefits will accrue to you: for either you will be persuaded if we seem to advocate something advantageous, or you will be more firmly convinced of the rightness of your own views" (44.2). And in a letter addressed to the council and assembly, he writes, "If you will but consent to listen in silence and have the patience to learn all that I have to say, I think that . . . I shall myself be found to be doing my duty by you with all goodwill and that I shall demonstrate clearly where your interests lie" (*Letters* 1.3).[25] Here and elsewhere, Demosthenes trades on the prima facie value of quietly and attentively listening to others in order to reinforce his own right to speak—if the good statesman is the one who speaks in the right way and at the right time, the ideal audience is the one that silently yields to the statesman's wise and timely counsel. In contrast to the virtuous orator, who possesses good judgment and who knows where their interests lie, the audience is naive and partial and lacks knowledge sufficient for good judgment. Consequently, it is to the benefit of the latter that they sit in silence and listen to the former, for it is through this that they become capable of deliberation and of determining where their true interests and advantage lie. The ideal auditor, then, like the ideal soldier, is an anonymous, silent figure, who listens but does not speak and who thereby creates a space of silence wherein the sonorous orations of the statesman may be heard.

## 2. Silencing Women

In the classical world, men speak and act so that they will be spoken of. By projecting their thoughts, beliefs, values, desires, and so on into the world through the media of speech and deed, men leave their mark, as it were, by shaping our external, common reality in accordance with their inner, private reality. Praised for their words and deeds, they are remembered for what they have said and what they have done. Thus, they earn immortality through outward demonstrations of their inner ethos: the persuasive orator, the just statesman, the sublime playwright and poet, the brave soldier—each is praised and remembered because they speak or act in ways that are understood to be not only honorable but consonant with or expressions of their character and their way of being. In this manner, their inner psychical life is, in a qualified sense, preserved even after they are gone. It is this type of memorialization that Diotima speaks of in the *Symposium*, when she addresses those who are pregnant not in their bodies but in their souls: "Everyone would rather have such children [i.e., words and deeds produced by the soul] than human ones, and would look up to Homer, Hesiod, and the other good poets with envy and admiration for the offspring they have left behind—offspring, which, because they are immortal themselves, provide their parents with immortal glory and remembrance" (Plato, *Symposium* 209c–d).[26]

While women are not perforce denied access to this type of memorialization, the infrequency with which such access is afforded underscores the fact that in classical Greek society, those who achieved this feat were the exception that proved the rule. There are, of course, many reasons for this, most of which exceed the scope of the present study; however, an analysis of the trope of silence does bring one rather important cause into focus: on the whole, women are praised not for what they have said but for what they have left unsaid. As Montiglio notes, "Feminine reputation paradoxically rests on silence: it is inversely correlated with the woman's *kleos*, whether it be around her virtue or her defects. Men's beautiful deeds, by contrast, require song to be revealed and preserved in all their brilliance."[27] Consider Sophocles's *Ajax*, where, in response to Tecmessa's inquiry, the play's namesake "answered briefly in a well-worn phrase: 'Woman, a woman's decency [κόσμον] is silence.'"[28] Or Aeschylus's *Seven against Thebes*, where Etiocles, speaking to a chorus composed of women, declares that "it is a man's part, the sacrifice and consultation of the gods, when the enemy assaults us; it is yours to be silent and stay within doors."[29] Or Aristophanes's *Lysistrata*, where the title character is shouted down by a magistrate, who declares, "If I should take orders from one who wears veils, may my neck straightaway be deservedly wrung."[30] The proper role of or natural order for women is that of silence. This, the ancient authors never tire of reminding their audience, is one of the foremost social virtues available to women, a virtue to which women are likewise made to attest, as Macaria does in Euripides's

*Heracleidae*: "I know that for a woman silence is best, and modest behavior, and staying quietly within doors."[31] The determination of the norms of proper behavior for men and women—speech and activity for the former; silence and discretion for the latter—establishes the terms on which praise and blame are earned: if men are praised for their words, women are praised for their silence, even if, in reality, such praise is little more than an absence of blame. Yet the distinction between these two modes of praise is not a horizontal one, as there is little parity between the horizons of possible approval and acclaim meted out to those who ought to speak and those who ought to be silent.

The identification of womanly "virtue" with silence not only promotes the exclusion of women from participation in institutions such as the assembly, courts, and theater but also binds their success relative to available social roles to a conspicuous social inefficacy: men are praised for speaking up, for acting, for leaving their mark on the world; women are praised for remaining quiet, for staying out of politics, religion, military affairs, and the arts, for keeping their thoughts, opinions, pleasures, pains, and desires to themselves. Aristophanes, of course, finds a good deal of humor in this, lampooning the notion that women might achieve political efficacy through speech in the *Thesmophoriazusae* and entertaining the possible success of a rather different model—one based on deeds, or the withholding thereof—in the *Lysistrata*. The humor of the former succeeds in its context precisely by imagining a world in which women seize the rights of men, donning not only their garb but also their norms and through this escaping their political irrelevance. His message is that the world in which women's speech becomes effective is nothing more than a joke; the sobering reality is that silence, exclusion, and social inefficacy are their proper lot. Yet he remains silent about the fact that this first-level exclusion leads to a second: praised not for what they say but for what they leave unsaid, women are barred from projecting their inner psychical lives onto the world in the meritorious and memorable ways afforded to men. Thus, the ideal of the silent, yielding woman works to ensure that the social effect of women in general approaches zero, and this, in turn, works to ensure that those who are talked about, celebrated, memorialized, and studied are predominantly men. If the virtue of a thing names the excellence of that thing—if, that is, virtue is the name given to the ideal form that a thing may take—then the virtue of women in ancient Greece was not that of self-assertion but that of self-annulment. This ideal is tragically underscored by the figure of

Cassandra, who dared to speak and who is remembered precisely because no one listened to her. That she gave voice to an occult and portentous truth was, practically speaking, beside the point—she modeled for the ancient world the futility and danger of women breaking their silence and forsaking their naturally allotted virtue. Her memorialization thus serves as a reminder that it is better to disappear into the anonymity of silence than to speak and suffer the fate of a Cassandra.

## 3. The Silence of Gods and Philosophers

In contrast to the political, rhetorical, religious, and poetic celebration of logos throughout the world of classical Greece, we find an increasing concern over the excess, abuse, and frivolousness of logos in the Roman imperial period, during which time we also note a corresponding increase in the commendation of silence, which is frequently championed as divine and as a necessary feature of the pursuit and maintenance of wisdom and the good life. In this later period, speech, even more than sexual intercourse, is seen as the greatest of pleasures and the most enticing of desires; as a result, it is increasingly aligned with excess, vice (especially, though not exclusively, immoderation), and vulgarity. Thus, in his ironically verbose treatise, *De garrulitate* (*On Talkativeness*), Plutarch recounts "that Anacharsis, when he had been entertained and feasted at Solon's house and lay down to sleep, was seen to have his left hand placed upon his private parts, but his right hand upon his mouth; for he believed, quite rightly, that the tongue needs the stronger restraint" (505a).[32] This scene captures features common to many of the cautionary anecdotes of the period: they are often set at banquets, they highlight similarities between the excesses of drink or sex and those of speech, and they portray a philosopher who, in either word or deed, sets themselves apart from the common citizenry by admonishing the behavior of their fellow attendees.

In the *Lives of Eminent Philosophers*, Diogenes Laertius reports the following of Menedemus: "And as he could not bear the extravagance of one man who used frequently to invite him to dinner, once when he was invited he did not say a single word, but admonished him of his extravagance in silence, by eating nothing but olives" (2.17). And of Zeno, he says, "One day at a banquet he was reclining in silence and was asked the reason: whereupon he bade his critic carry word to the king that there was one present who knew how to hold his tongue" (7.24). In both passages, we find philosophers taking up silence as a means of admonishing the excesses of their company. The difference between this silence and the silence imposed on women is worthy of note: Menedemus and Zeno are not compelled into or constrained by silence; it is something that they freely and strategically perform as a means of social or political critique and that allows them to voicelessly condemn the poor behavior of others and enact their own dis-identification from accepted social norms. This gestures to what is perhaps the most significant difference between the understanding of silence that I noted above and that of the Roman authors of the first few centuries of the Common Era: for the Greeks, silence was a largely passive state into which one was compelled by one's superiors or by social norms, values, and practices more generally; now, however, it has become active—it is a practice that one enters into freely and deploys as an exercise of power, which, as we shall see below, works not only to condemn the viciousness of others but also to assist in one's own acquisition of virtue.

If the value and appeal of silence grew during the Roman imperial period, this is, in large part, because speech became increasingly associated with vice, both ethical and intellectual. In another passage from *On Talkativeness*, Plutarch reports that "Bias kept silent at a drinking-bout and was taunted with stupidity by a chatterer, 'What fool,' said [Bias], 'in his cups can hold his tongue?'" (503f–504a). Plutarch's critique continues: "Thus silence is something profound and awesome and sober, but drunkenness is a babbler, for it is foolish and witless, and therefore loquacious also. And the philosophers even in their very definition of drunkenness say that it is intoxicated and foolish talking; thus drinking is not blamed if silence attends the drinking, but it is foolish talk which converts the influence of wine into drunkenness. While it is true that the drunken man talks foolishness in his cups, the chatterer talks foolishness on all occasions" (504a–b).[33] Silence is here equated with sobriety, and loquaciousness with intoxication. And this to such an extent that the latter, which names a state of the soul, supersedes in the order of causality the presence of physical intoxicants within the body—it is not wine that makes us drunk; it is foolish talk. Plutarch's point is clear: foolish, unnecessary, excessive talk is the greatest source of immoderation. Neither the ills of sex nor those of drinking rival the ills of excessive speech, because loquaciousness presents a uniquely alluring pleasure for the sort of social animals that we are. Yet Plutarch is keen to note that the danger of loquaciousness extends beyond individual ethical failure to intellectual failure and the erosion of our social bonds. Talkativeness, he argues, makes one stupid, because "looseness of the tongue becomes impotence of the ears"

(502b). As a result of this affliction, "the babbler's ears have no passage bored through to the soul, but only to the tongue" (504d). The garrulous internalize logos for the sole purpose of externalizing it; lessons that ought to be taken in, slowly digested, and thoroughly assimilated bypass their souls and are immediately expelled through the undulations of the tongue. Thus, the pursuit of knowledge and wisdom is forfeited for the sake of the fleeting pleasure of idle talk. Plutarch notes one final consequence of this: "Speech, which is the most pleasant and human of social ties, is made inhuman and unsocial by those who use it badly and wantonly" (504d). The abuse of logos threatens the raison d'être thereof—it undermines rather than reinforces our social bonds, and it breeds contempt and mistrust instead of unity.

While the attempt to bisect logos for the sake of drawing a qualitative distinction within it is far from novel, the suspicion and distrust of speech generated by this critique takes on greater proportions and a fresh urgency in the Roman authors of the first few centuries of the Common Era. The power of speech maintains important vestiges of its prestige, yet it is increasingly circumscribed by the threat of its abuse. This is seen most clearly in the figure of the silent philosopher, whose reticence gestures to the fact that the concern over the misuse of logos extends beyond a simple critique of garrulousness. By maintaining a conspicuous silence where all others speak, the philosopher presents her audience with a mode of being that is antithetical not merely to garrulity but to the common forms of life and behavior within the city. The implication of this is that the intoxicating, stultifying, and antisocial allure of logos permeates our everyday modes of existence—even the teetotaler may be drunk on the thrill of gossip, the professor rendered stupid by her fondness for allocution, and the philanthropist turned into a canker on society by her love of idle talk. Here we find a fascinating inversion of the privileging of logos pervasive among the earlier Greek authors: once a divine right, the freedom to speak is now seen as a base temptation. Against this, the philosopher, exercising moderation in relation to logos, speaks only when necessary and says only what is necessary to the occasion. As Diogenes reports of Solon, "Silence he called the seal of speech, and occasion the seal of silence" (*Lives* 1.2). There is therefore an important pragmatic character to the silence of the philosophers, for it is necessary to know when, in what situations, in relation to what persons, and about what topics one ought to speak or remain silent. Indeed, this pragmatic awareness becomes a central theme in the literature on philosophical silence.

Diogenes Laertius, for instance, reports that Bias of Priene was said to have remained silent when an impious man asked him what piety is; to this request, Bias replied, "I am silent . . . because you are asking questions about what does not concern you" (*Lives* 1.5). Bias's reticence here is made particularly interesting by the fact that the issue he refuses to speak about, piety, not only concerns all humans but is of greater concern to the impious than it is to the pious, insofar as the former are in greater need of proper training than are the latter. And yet, according to Diogenes's account, it was precisely the man's impiety that rendered him unfit to be spoken to about piety. The implication is that the vicious character of the man's soul, the character that places him in greatest need of an education in piety, is also what disqualifies him from such an education: Bias remains silent because he judges the man's soul to be so destitute with respect to piety that he has excepted himself from a concern that is ubiquitous among mortals and constitutive of the human condition. This silence, then, bespeaks a paradox: piety is a concern for all humans, yet it is not a concern for the impious.

Moreover, the fact that Bias does not simply assert that the man will not benefit from a discourse on piety but rather asserts that piety does not even concern him indicates that this judgment is made by reference to an onto-logical register as much as it is an ethical one. This is to say that Bias's reticence responds to more than the man's deviation from a normative standard of piety—it responds to an ontologically deficient state of the soul, in relation to which the issue of piety has been rendered indifferent. The man's soul is too far removed from virtue to be concerned therewith. This is particularly damning given that the virtue under consideration regulates the appropri-ate respect, responsibilities, and devotion due to the gods and, by extension, to one's fellow humans.[34] The broader implication is that the impious ex-ist beyond, or beneath, the possibility of human excellence and obligation, since their adiamorphic indifference to piety situates them outside of any possible proper relation to gods or mortals. Consequently, Bias remains si-lent when confronted by an impious man inquiring about piety, because he judges the man to be beyond the reach of a logos concerned with the divine.

The silence that Diogenes attributes to Bias recalls the silence that Plutarch attributes to the daemons in *De genio Socratis*. In a fascinating account of the role that they play in the human acquisition of virtue and divinity, Plutarch asserts that daemons do not speak to all equally but are confined by the god to remain silent before those whose souls lack sufficient virtue to hear them. As with Bias, the daemons' silence testifies to the exis-tence of souls that, due to an absence of virtue, are beyond the concern of a logos from or regarding the divine:

For daemons do not assist all indifferently, but as when men swim at sea, those standing on the shore merely view in silence the swimmers who are still far out distant from land, whereas they help with hand and voice alike such as have come near, and running along and wading in beside them bring them safely in, such too, my friends, is the way of daemons: as long as we are head over ears in the welter of worldly affairs and are changing body after body, like conveyances, they allow us to fight our way out and persevere unaided, as we endeavor by our own prowess to come through safe and reach a haven; but when in the course of countless births a soul has stoutly and resolutely sustained a long series of struggles, and as her cycle draws to a close, she approaches the upper world, bathed in sweat, in imminent peril and straining every nerve to reach the shore, God holds it no sin for her daemon to go to the rescue, but lets whoever will lend aid. One daemon is eager to deliver by his exhortations one soul, another another, and the soul on her part, having drawn close, can hear, and is thus saved; but if she pays no heed, she is forsaken by her daemon and comes to no happy end. (593f–594a)[35]

According to Plutarch's account, the divine logos is not addressed to all equally but is withheld from those who are not in a position to hear or benefit from it; this is to say that the divine logos is, in an important respect, characterized by the possibility of its suspension. Thus, just as Bias demonstrates that the wise should not speak to all indiscriminately about the divine, the daemons demonstrate that the divine does not speak to all indiscriminately about wisdom and the other virtues. The implication here is that the logos of the wise and the divine is, in part, distinguished from other modalities of logos by the fact that it articulates a knowledge of those to whom one ought to speak and those from whom one ought to withhold speech. The antithesis of this logos, therefore, is not reticence but loquaciousness. Talkativeness, garrulity, prater—these do not merely indicate the absence of good manners; they bespeak one's lack of wisdom and one's distance from the divine. They bespeak, that is, a logos that, by virtue of its excessiveness and lack of discernment, drowns out the silence of the gods.

The logos that Plutarch and Diogenes denounce in the passages above stands in sharp contrast to the ubiquity, continuity, and pervasiveness of logos championed in the political, rhetorical, religious, and poetic traditions of the Greeks, which condemn silence as death or oblivion. Thus, Plutarch declares that "men teach us to speak, but the gods teach us to be silent" (*Talkativeness* 505e). The polarity of silence has been inverted: no longer aligned with the fugaciousness of human mortality, it has metamorphosed into a characteristic of οἱ ἀθάνατοι, "the immortals," "the deathless ones." This also marks the increasing disassociation of logos from the divine. It is our fellow humans who teach us how to speak, and all too often they teach us to speak only of mortal things. Consequently, logos ceases to be an unalloyed right of the powerful to secure their immortality and becomes a pleasure and a temptation to speak of mortal affairs, the effect of which is to ensnare one's soul in the mortal realm and scatter it among the sundry concerns thereof. One purchases the shadow of immortality afforded by memorialization with the divinity of one's soul—an exchange of gold for bronze. Consequently, to cure our garrulous and impious abuse of logos, "we must apply our reasoning powers to the effects of the opposite behavior, always hearing and remembering and keeping close at hand the praises bestowed on reticence [τῆς ἐχεμυθίας], and the solemn, holy, and mysterious character of silence [καὶ τὸ σεμνὸν καὶ τὸ ἅγιον καὶ τὸ μυστηριῶδες τῆς σιωπῆς]" (*Talkativeness* 511d–e).

This is not to suggest that Plutarch's and Diogenes's accounts are identical; indeed, there is an important difference between the two: Diogenes's narrative contains no discussion of the possible progress of one possessed of a vicious soul, whereas Plutarch's account is concerned with precisely this. According to the latter, a soul that lacks virtue and that is therefore beyond the call of the divine may, through great effort and across many lives, transform itself in such a way and to such an extent that it becomes like enough to the divine that it is able to hear the daemonic logos. The implication is that the human soul is not inherently endowed with the right or power to hear the logos of the divine and thereby to fulfill the acquisition of virtue. To discern the exhortation of the gods, the soul must transform itself to become similar enough to them that their voice may make the least possible contact with the mortal realm. Thus, this transformation necessarily entails the liberation of the soul from the tumult of worldly affairs, which ensnare it in the cares and concerns of mortals.

This last insight is shared by Epictetus, for whom silence plays a central role in the development of a philosophical soul, as it is capable of effecting a self-transformation that serves to simultaneously critique and distance oneself from existing social norms and to thereby strip one of those inappropriate and distracting investments that obstruct one's access to the good life. In the *Enchiridion*, Epictetus offers the following advice:

Immediately prescribe some character and some form to yourself, which you shall observe both when you are alone and when you meet with men. And let silence be the general rule, or let only what is necessary be said, and in few words. And rarely and when the occasion calls we shall say something; but about none of the common subjects, not about gladiators, nor horse races, nor about athletes, nor about eating or drinking, which are the usual subjects; and especially not about men, as blaming them or praising them, or comparing them. If then you are able, bring over by your conversation the conversation of your associates to that which is proper; but if you should happen to be confined to the company of strangers, be silent.[36]

The aspiring philosopher strives to unify her character, to shape her life and identity in a manner that is both self-given and consistent. To achieve this, she must eschew modes and topics of conversation characteristic of everyday life—she must speak only about what is necessary, proper, and beneficial; she must speak succinctly; she must not speak to just anyone; when she does speak, it should be with the aim of conducting others toward a proper mode of discourse; and, above all, she must keep silent whenever and wherever possible. The implication here is that the philosophic life—the good life, the life that is most fully aligned with the divine—stands at odds with the normal forms of existence, behavior, and speech found in the city. The philosopher must give herself an identity that is consistent over time because the modalities of identity formation common in the city are neither self-given nor consistent nor good; and she must maintain a silent vigil over herself because the tendency to speak excessively and unnecessarily, to prate about athletic competitions and banquets, to reveal secrets,[37] to gossip about or flatter others—in short, the tendency to rehearse the common speech of the common people—plays a crucial role in replicating the common forms of life in the city.

The necessity of the philosopher's silence reflects the fact that logos does not merely serve to externalize one's internal psychical states; it also affects the very nature and content of those states. Even when one's conversations are not idle, gossipy, or salacious, the fact that they tend to traffic in the pleasures, comparisons, values, opinions, judgments, aspirations, and modes of understanding characteristic of the quotidian and nonphilosophical forms of human existence has the effect of miring one's soul in the tumult of everyday affairs and obstructing one's access to a life in accordance with the divine. Consequently, the attainment of the good life and the happy state of the soul requires, among other things, that one retreat from common discourse into silence. This is to say that silence is employed as a practice intended to recover one's soul from the various concerns and commitments among which it is scattered and to which it is bound through one's everyday commerce with others. It is part of a process of giving shape and unity to one's character, the positive pole of which consists in a movement toward virtue and the divine, while the negative pole consists in a movement away from the everyday modes of human life, which are occupied with the pleasure of discussing pleasurable things, such as athletic competitions, food and drink, and the relative merits or demerits of one's fellow humans. This process, then, amounts to an extensive and protracted act of self-cultivation, whereby one works on and transforms one's soul so that it accords with nature and the divine.

The practice of silence is no less important for those who have become philosophers; however, it does take on a new meaning and significance. At *Enchiridion* 46, Epictetus writes,

> On no occasion call yourself a philosopher, and do not speak much among the uninstructed about theorems: but do that which follows from them. For example, at a banquet do not say how a man ought to eat, but eat as you ought to eat. For remember that in this way Socrates also altogether avoided ostentation: persons used to come to him and ask to be recommended by him to philosophers, and he used to take them to philosophers: so easily did he submit to being overlooked. Accordingly, if any conversation should arise among uninstructed persons about any theorem, generally be silent; for there is great danger that you will immediately vomit up what you have not digested. And when a man shall say to you, that you know nothing, and you are not vexed, then be sure that you have begun the work (of philosophy). For even sheep do not vomit up their grass and show to the shepherds how much they have eaten; but when they have internally digested the pasture, they produce externally wool and milk. Do you also show not your theorems to the uninstructed, but show the acts which come from their digestion.

Articulating a concern that is shared by both Diogenes and Plutarch, Epictetus cautions against speaking about philosophical matters to the uninitiated. He offers three reasons for this. First, the desire to speak about one's theorems to those who have not been inducted into philosophy renders one vulnerable to pretentiousness and ostentation. Consequently, philosophy is stripped of its value and is made into a mere adornment or showpiece. Second, in the haste to show off one's philosophical insights, one risks externalizing them before they have fully developed; or, to put it in terms more in keeping with Epictetus's colorful description, one risks regurgitating one's ideas without ever fully digesting and assimilating them into one's being.[38] By carelessly hawking one's beliefs, one expels the pith and marrow of philosophy from one's system, thereby depriving it of the power to transform (or sustain the transformation of) one's soul. Finally, because philosophy is undertaken as a practice of self-cultivation, its truest flower blooms in deeds, not words—it's easy to speak about moderation and the other virtues, but it's difficult to act and live in accordance with them. Thus, the philosopher should be less concerned with announcing her beliefs to others than she is with living by them, for it is this transformation of her way of life that most clearly and robustly demonstrates her full comprehension of them.

Accordingly, the true mark of a philosopher is increasingly identified with silent deeds and behavior. In *Quaestiones Convivales*, Plutarch addresses the suggestion that philosophers should not be invited to banquets, since they will bring with them a seriousness and sober-mindedness that are poorly suited to the Bacchic festivity of the occasion. Framing his response in terms of a contest between sophistry and rhetoric on the one hand and philosophy on the other, Plutarch offers two reasons for the exclusion of the former and the inclusion of the latter. First, he asserts that "the nature of philosophy is different [from oratory]. It is the art of life [τέχνην περὶ βίου], and therefore it is not reasonably excluded from any amusement or from any pleasure that diverts the mind, but takes part in all, bringing to them the qualities of proportion and fitness" (613a–b). Unlike oratory, the practice of which is appropriate only to particular venues and occasions (court-rooms, political debates, etc.), philosophy, being an art of life, is appropriate to all venues and occasions. Thus, one fundamentally misunderstands the nature of philosophy if one limits its practice to the gymnasium or class-room, for, by allocating its pursuit and relevance to these isolated fora, one deprives philosophy of its pervasive and transformative character, creating yet a further condition in which a study that is meant to be internalized, digested, and assimilated into one's very being is, on the contrary, treated as a mere hobby or adornment. In other words, one deprives philosophy of its essence and purpose—that is, the transformation of one's soul and the rule over one's life. Moreover, Plutarch finds something of a paradox in the view that the seriousness of philosophy renders it inappropriate for events such as banquets, for philosophy is what propriety itself depends on: "Those . . . who throw philosophy out of entertainments do worse than those who take away a light. For the candle being removed, the temperate and sober guests will not become worse than they were before, being more concerned to reverence than to see one another. But if dullness and disregard to good learning wait upon the wine, Minerva's golden lamp itself could not make the entertainment pleasing and agreeable. For a company to sit silent and only cram themselves is, in good truth, swinish and almost impossible" (716d–e). Philosophy is, as it were, the life of the party, which would be ruined by excess and gluttony if not for the temperate and sobering influence of the lover of wisdom.

While Plutarch praises those who attempt to illuminate their fellow revelers through philosophical discourse, he recognizes that such speeches may be poorly received by those set on conviviality. As such, he offers a second defense for inviting philosophers to banquets. Unlike orators, whose craft relies wholly on logos and whose proclivity for speech may "cause the Graces to abandon the company" (613b), the philosopher is capable of wordlessly performing her training: "In just such a manner a philosopher too, when with drinking-companions who are unwilling to listen to his homilies, will change his role[.] For he knows that, while men practice oratory only when they talk, they practice philosophy when they are silent, when they jest, even, by Zeus, when they are the butt of jokes and when they make fun of others. Indeed, not only is it true that 'the worst injustice is to seem just when one is not,' as Plato says, but also the height of sagacity [φιλοσοφοῦντα] is to philosophize without seeming to do so" (613f–614a). The highest expression of one's love of wisdom is found not in the delivery of philosophical orations but in the subtle and at times silent performance of one's philosophical commitments. Moreover, this performance occurs in the context of everyday social behavior and is transformative thereof—if others joke, celebrate, eat, or drink, so too will the philosopher; however, she will do so in a way that exhibits virtue and brings each of these things to their greatest possible perfection, thereby demonstrating in behavior rather than speech both her own excellence and the excellence of such activities.

The trope of the silent, virtuous philosopher is not limited to banquets. According to Diogenes Laertius, Xenocrates "was singularly free from pride; more than once a day he would retire into himself, and he assigned, it is said, a whole hour to silence" (*Lives* 4.2). And in *Adversus colotem*, Plutarch reports that "Zeno, the disciple of Parmenides, having attempted to kill the tyrant Demylus, and failing in his design, maintained the doctrine of Parmenides, like pure and fine gold tried in the fire, that there is nothing which a magnanimous man ought to dread but dishonor[.] For, having with his own teeth bitten off his tongue, he spit it in the tyrant's face."[39] Yet no figure looms larger in this respect than Pythagoras, whose name becomes for the Romans something of a catchword for the identification of silence with virtue. In his *Deipnosophistae*, for example, Athenaeus declares that "Pythagorean philosophy . . . shows us everything in silence more intelligibly than others who undertake to teach the arts which require talking."[40] And Diogenes tells us that Pythagoras's disciples were required to take a vow of silence throughout the duration of their novitiate: "For five whole years they had to keep silence, merely listening to his discourses without seeing him, until they passed an examination, and thenceforward they were admitted to his house and allowed to see him" (*Lives* 8.1).[41] Pierre Hadot notes that this story is likely apocryphal;[42] however, this does not undercut its significance. On the contrary, the fact that this belief became common currency throughout the first few centuries CE despite its likely falsehood underscores the strength with which the association between the philosophers' silence and their virtue gripped the authors of the time. In *De curiositate*, for instance, Plutarch invokes the silence of the Pythagorean novitiate as an antidote for the dangers associated with "much learning," foremost of which is that "a necessary concomitant of inquisitiveness is to speak evil" (519c).[43] And in *Quaestiones convivales*, he reconstructs one of the culinary taboos of the Pythagoreans around the trope of silence, suggesting that they refused to eat "fish because they had so great a regard for silence, and they called fish ἔλλοπας ["dumb" or "scaly"], because they had their voice *shut up* [ἰλλομένην]; . . . and they thought silence to be divine, since the Gods without any voice reveal their meaning to the wise by their works" (728d–e). If, as he suggested in *De curiositate*, silence is an antidote to the evils of excessive speech, this is not simply because by remaining silent one negates the ills of such speech—that is, the value of silence is not determined in the negative.

Silence is praised and recommended because it is divine; this defines its positive value. It is against this backdrop that the excessiveness of speech is deemed wicked or harmful, for the performance of such speech is impious. It is also against this backdrop that Plutarch seeks to affirm the virtuous origins of Rome itself. In his *Life of Numa*, Plutarch, undeterred by the fact that Numa preceded Pythagoras by approximately two centuries, attributes the "wisdom and culture" of the former to his association with the latter:

"For he ascribed the greater part of his oracular teachings to the Muses, and he taught the Romans to pay especial honors to one Muse in particular, whom he called Tacita, that is, the silent, or speechless one; thereby perhaps handing on and honoring the Pythagorean precept of silence" (*Numa* 8.6).[44] By attributing the various laws and institutions introduced by Numa to his Pythagorean education, Plutarch boldly, if anachronistically, grounds the origins of Rome's greatness in the philosophy of Pythagoras, thereby enshrining silence as the centerpiece of Roman virtue.

## Notes

1. Euripides, *Orestes*, in *The Complete Greek Drama*, trans. E. P. Coleridge (New York: Random House, 1938).

2. Isocrates, *Letter to Demonicus*, in *Isocrates*, trans. George Norlin (Cambridge, MA: Harvard University Press, 1980).

3. Pindar, *Nemean 9*, in *The Odes of Pindar*, trans. Diane Arnson Svarlien (New Haven, CT: Yale University Press, 1991).

4. Demosthenes, *On the False Embassy*, in *Demosthenes*, trans. C. A. Vince, M. A. Vince, and J. H. Vince (Cambridge, MA: Harvard University Press, 1926).

5. Herodotus, *The Histories*, trans. A. D. Godley (Cambridge, MA: Harvard University Press, 1920).

6. There are exceptions to this, of course, such as Isocrates's praise of the Pythagoreans, who, he claims, exhibit greater virtue in silence than others do in speech (*Busiris* 11.29), Hippocrates's impassioned defense of the physician's oath of silence (*Jusjurandum* 1), or when, in the *Phaedrus*, Socrates declares that true logos is "the word which is written with intelligence in the mind of the learner, which is able to defend itself and knows to whom it should speak, and before whom to be silent" (Plato, *Phaedrus*, trans. H. N. Fowler [Cambridge, MA: Harvard University Press, 1999], 276a). As such, I do not intend to suggest that the Greeks were unequivocal either in their praise of logos or in their denunciation of silence; nor, going forward, do I intend to suggest that the Roman authors were univocal in their inversion of these earlier Greek values. Because it is not possible to examine every reference to silence in Greco-Roman literature, I focus on the dominant trends organizing the understanding of silence therein. Incomplete though this account must be, it nevertheless demonstrates that the concern over silence was far more prevalent among the Greeks of the archaic and classical periods than it was among the authors of the Roman imperial era, who frequently embrace and champion reticence.

7. Diogenes Laertius, *Lives of Eminent Philosophers*, trans. Robert Drew Hicks (Cambridge, MA: Harvard University Press, 1925).

8. I return to Plutarch's views on silence in the final sections of this essay.

9. Plutarch, *De E apud Delphos*, in *Moralia*, vol. 5, trans. Frank Cole Babbitt (Cambridge, MA: Harvard University Press, 2003).

10. Pindar, *Isthmian 4: For Melissus of Thebes, Pancratium*, in *The Odes of Pindar*, trans. Diane Arnson Svarlien (New Haven, CT: Yale University Press, 1991).

11. Marcel Detienne, *The Masters of Truth in Archaic Greece*, trans. Janet Lloyd (New York: Zone Books, 1999), 47–48.

12. Isocrates, *Helen*, in *Isocrates*, trans. George Norlin (Cambridge, MA: Harvard University Press, 1980).

13. Hesiod, *Theogony*, trans. Hugh G. Evelyn-White (Cambridge, MA: Harvard University Press, 1914).

14. It should be noted that Socrates appears to hold that the philosopher is an exception to this, for she desires truth and beauty rather than praise. Nevertheless, the dialectical and dialogical nature of Socratic philosophy binds its practice to logos.

15. Silvia Montiglio, *Silence in the Land of Logos* (Princeton, NJ: Princeton University Press, 2000), 55.

16. Montiglio, 81.

17. Montiglio, 52.

18. Montiglio, 81.

19. Montiglio, 119. It should be noted that this silence refers only to the failure to address the assembly in speech. By all accounts, the anonymous common citizens who attended the assembly would frequently show support for or disagreement with those who addressed the body through cheers or jeers. The resulting tumult, however, not only failed to distinguish them as individuals but also reinforced their anonymity by consigning the identity of each participant to the masses with whom they roared their approval or disapproval.

20. Euripides, *The Suppliants*, in *The Complete Greek Drama*, trans. E. P. Coleridge (New York: Random House, 1938), 440–442.

21. The extent to which this promise within any given democratic regime is not merely made but kept is, of course, a separate issue—one in regard to which Theseus appears to be naively sanguine.

22. Demosthenes, *On the Crown*, in *Demosthenes*, trans. C. A. Vince, M. A. Vince, and J. H. Vince (Cambridge, MA: Harvard University Press, 1926).

23. The primary target of this critique was, of course, Aeschines.

24. Demosthenes, *Exordia*, trans. N. W. De Witt and N. J. De Witt (Cambridge, MA: Harvard University Press, 1949).

25. Demosthenes, *Letters*, trans. N. W. De Witt and N. J. De Witt (Cambridge, MA: Harvard University Press, 1949).

26. Plato, *Symposium*, trans. Alexander Nehamas and Paul Woodruff (Indianapolis: Hackett, 1989).

27. Montiglio, *Silence*, 83.

28. Sophocles, *Ajax*, in *Sophocles II*, trans. David Grene and Richmond Lattimore (Chicago: University of Chicago Press, 1969), 292–293.

29. Aeschylus, *Seven against Thebes*, in *Aeschylus II*, trans. David Grene and Richmond Lattimore (Chicago: University of Chicago Press, 1991), 230–232.

30. Aristophanes, *Lysistrata*, trans. Jack Lindsay (London: Fanfolico, 1926), 525–527.

31. Euripides, *Heracleidae*, in *Euripides*, vol. 2, trans. David Kovacs (Cambridge, MA: Harvard University Press, 1995), 475.

32. Plutarch, *On Talkativeness*, in *Moralia*, vol. 6, trans. W. C. Helmbold (Cambridge, MA: Harvard University Press, 1962). Here and throughout this essay, I treat the accounts of classical and preclassical Greek figures provided by Roman authors such as Plutarch and Diogenes Laertius as works that more accurately record the beliefs and values of the times in which they were written than they do the events about which they were written. By this I

do not mean to suggest that these authors fictionalized their subjects, as the accounts they provide were likely as reliable as was their source material; however, the likely spuriousness of these sources and the impossibility of verifying them is well documented. In the face of this concession, it seems more prudent to see in these works a reflection of certain trends in value and belief prevalent in Roman society during the first few centuries CE than a faithful recording of history.

33. A similar point is made in *Quaestiones convivales*: "In which lines the poet [Simonides] in my mind shows the difference between being a little heated and downright drunk; for to sing, laugh, and dance may agree very well with those that have gone no farther than a merry cup; but to prattle, and speak what had been better left unsaid, argues a man to be quite gone" (Plutarch, *Quaestiones convivales*, in *Moralia*, vols. 8–9, trans. Herbert B. Hoffleit [Cambridge, MA: Harvard University Press, 1969], 645a).

34. Consider, for instance, the Zeusian obligation of hospitality, which rests on a pious devotion to the god but which is exercised in relation to mortals.

35. Plutarch, *De genio Socratis*, in *Moralia*, vol. 7, trans. Phillip H. De Lacy (Cambridge, MA: Harvard University Press, 1959).

36. Epictetus, *The Enchiridion*, trans. George Long (Mineola, NY: Dover, 2004), 33.

37. An important aspect of knowing when to speak and when to remain silent is the ability to keep secrets. Thus, Diogenes Laertius reports that when Chilon of Sparta was asked, "What is difficult?" he replied, "To keep a secret, to employ leisure well, to be able to bear an injury" (*Lives* 1.3).

38. Note the similarity between this claim and Plutarch's assertion that the ears of garrulous people bypass their souls and are connected directly to their tongues (*Talkativeness* 504d).

39. Plutarch, *Adversus coletem*, in *Moralia*, vol. 14, trans. Benedict Einarson and Philip H. De Lacy (Cambridge, MA: Harvard University Press, 1967), 1126d–e.

40. Athenaeus, *Deipnosophistae*, trans. S. Douglas Olson (Cambridge, MA: Harvard University Press, 2007), 1.36.

41. Iamblichus makes the same claim at *De vita Pythagorica* 72.

42. Pierre Hadot, *What Is Ancient Philosophy?*, trans. Michael Chase (Cambridge, MA: Harvard University Press, 2002), 156–157.

43. Plutarch, *De curiositate*, in *Moralia*, vol. 6, trans. W. C. Helmbold (Cambridge, MA: Harvard University Press, 1962).

44. Plutarch, *Lives*, vol. 1, trans. Bernadotte Perrin (Cambridge, MA: Harvard University Press, 1914).

# Bibliography


Aeschylus. *Seven against Thebes*. In *Aeschylus II*, translated by David Grene and Richmond Lattimore. Chicago: University of Chicago Press, 1991.

Aristophanes. *Lysistrata*. Translated by Jack Lindsay. London: Fanfolico, 1926.

Athenaeus. *Deipnosophistae*. Translated by S. Douglas Olson. Cambridge, MA: Harvard University Press, 2007.

Demosthenes. *Exordia*. Translated by N. W. De Witt and N. J. De Witt. Cambridge, MA: Harvard University Press, 1949.

———. *On the Crown*. In *Demosthenes*, translated by C. A. Vince, M. A. Vince, and J. H. Vince. Cambridge, MA: Harvard University Press, 1926.

———. *On the False Embassy*. In *Demosthenes*, translated by C. A. Vince, M. A. Vince, and J. H. Vince. Cambridge, MA: Harvard University Press, 1926.

———. *Letters*. Translated by N. W. De Witt and N. J. De Witt. Cambridge, MA: Harvard University Press, 1949.

Detienne, Marcel. *The Masters of Truth in Archaic Greece*. Translated by Janet Lloyd. New York: Zone Books, 1999.

Diogenes Laertius. *Lives of Eminent Philosophers*. Translated by Robert Drew Hicks. Cambridge, MA: Harvard University Press, 1925.

Epictetus. *The Enchiridion*. Translated by George Long. Mineola, NY: Dover, 2004.

Euripides. *Heracleidae*. In *Euripides*, vol. 2, translated by David Kovacs. Cambridge, MA: Harvard University Press, 1995.

———. *Orestes*. In *The Complete Greek Drama*, translated by E. P. Coleridge. New York: Random House, 1938.

———. *The Suppliants*. In *The Complete Greek Drama*, translated by E. P. Coleridge. New York: Random House, 1938.

Hadot, Pierre. *What Is Ancient Philosophy?* Translated by Michael Chase. Cambridge, MA: Harvard University Press, 2002.

Herodotus. *The Histories*. Translated by A. D. Godley. Cambridge, MA: Harvard University Press, 1920.

Hesiod. *Theogony*. Translated by Hugh G. Evelyn-White. Cambridge, MA: Harvard University Press, 1914.

Isocrates. *Helen*. In *Isocrates*, translated by George Norlin. Cambridge, MA: Harvard University Press, 1980.

———. *Letter to Demonicus*. In *Isocrates*, translated by George Norlin. Cambridge, MA: Harvard University Press, 1980.

Montiglio, Silvia. *Silence in the Land of Logos*. Princeton, NJ: Princeton University Press, 2000.

Pindar. *Isthmian 4: For Melissus of Thebes, Pancratium*. In *The Odes of Pindar*, translated by Diane Arnson Svarlien. New Haven, CT: Yale University Press, 1991.

———. *Nemean 9*. In *The Odes of Pindar*, translated by Diane Arnson Svarlien. New Haven, CT: Yale University Press, 1991.

Plato. *Phaedrus*. Translated by H. N. Fowler. Cambridge, MA: Harvard University Press, 1999.

———. *Symposium*. Translated by Alexander Nehamas and Paul Woodruff. Indianapolis: Hackett, 1989.

Plutarch. *Adversus coletem*. In *Moralia*, vol. 14, translated by Benedict Einarson and Philip H. De Lacy. Cambridge, MA: Harvard University Press, 1967.

———. *De curiositate*. In *Moralia*, vol. 6, translated by W. C. Helmbold. Cambridge, MA: Harvard University Press, 1962.

———. *De E apud Delphos*. In *Moralia*, vol. 5, translated by Frank Cole Babbitt. Cambridge, MA: Harvard University Press, 2003.

———. "De genio Socratis." In *Moralia*, vol. 7, translated by Phillip H. De Lacy. Cambridge, MA: Harvard University Press, 1959.

———. *Lives*. Vol. 1, translated by Bernadotte Perrin. Cambridge, MA: Harvard University Press, 1914.

———. *On Talkativeness*. In *Moralia*, vol. 6, translated by W. C. Helmbold. Cambridge, MA: Harvard University Press, 1962.

———. *Quaestiones convivales*. In *Moralia*, vols. 8–9, translated by Herbert B. Hoffleit. Cambridge, MA: Harvard University Press, 1969.

Sophocles. *Ajax*. In *Sophocles II*, translated by David Grene and Richmond Lattimore. Chicago: University of Chicago Press, 1969.

JEREMY BELL is Lecturer of Philosophy at Emory University. He is author of multiple articles and co-editor of *Plato's Animals: Gadflies, Horses, Swans, and Other Philosophical Beasts* (Indiana University Press, 2013).